SECRETS FROM THE
MASTERS

CONVERSATIONS WITH FORTY GREAT GUITAR PLAYERS

FROM THE PAGES OF
Guitar Player Magazine

EDITED

BY

DON MENN

GPI BOOKS
Miller Freeman Inc.
San Francisco, Cupertino, Atlanta, Boston, Chicago, New York, Brussels

TO THE SPEAKERS WHO SPOKE IT,
TO THE WRITERS WHO WROTE IT,
AND TO MY FAVORITE MUSICIANS —
GRETCHEN AND KIRSTEN

GPI BOOKS

Miller Freeman Inc., Book Division, 600 Harrison Street, San Francisco, CA 94107

©1992 by Miller Freeman Inc.

Library Of Congress Catalog Card Number: 92-60949

ISBN 0-87930-260-7

Designer: Christian Ledgerwood
Production Editor: Linda Jupiter

Cover photos: (left to right)
Jimi Hendrix by Jim Cummins
Jerry Garcia by Chuck Pulin
Stevie Ray Vaughan by Lisa Seifert
Keith Richards by Paul Natkin
Eric Clapton by Ken Settle

Printed in the United States of America

97 96   5 4 3 2

— CONTENTS —

— INTRODUCTION —

"Guitar playing, as currently understood, has more to do with sports than it does to do with music. It's an Olympic-challenge type of situation. The challenges are in the realm of speed, redundancy, choreography, and grooming."
— *Frank Zappa, 1992*

I'M HAUNTED BY THE FEAR THAT *GUITAR PLAYER* MAY HAVE CREATED THIS very situation. We, after all — the writers of this book — were the first to ever really scrutinize guitar players, their playing, and that six-string tool of their trade. Did all that intense focus create a gang of show-offs, rank lick-spewers, and grotesque clones of the latest-greatest-fastest-cutest-nudest guitar hero? Did our four-color glossies, careful histories, and minutely rendered schematics conjure a collectible market out of wood slabs and wires? (I remember my horror when I was told that the value of vintage instruments was at one time related to who was on *Guitar Player's* covers — which explained a lot of odd calls I used to get from, well, speculators, really, wanting to know who would be holding what on next month's issue.) Whenever I hear that someone of the caliber of the people in this book was dumped by a label, I despair about the time we live in. Record companies are deaf. Education is kaput. Sometimes thinking is, too. Funding for music programs in schools has evaporated, MTV has replaced variety in music with monotonous little movies of dancers and posers and mumblers and scowlers, and guitar playing seems to have become one endless strafing of the planet by 128th-note pull-offs from roller-coasting whammies.

This book is our contribution to your alternative education. We've tried to present to you the best *parts* of the best interviews *Guitar Player* has published to date. Jas Obrecht proposed the book, and together he and I tightened its focus. Out of a long list of great musicians (of course these forty weren't *the* only "masters"), Jas found the articles that seemed still to have the most nourishment. Then they got dumped on me. I took those 80-plus stories covering 40 musicians, scavenged the redeemable morsels, blended them together, chopped out anything that seemed too topical, too specific, no longer true, or simply irrelevant to someone, say, in a hundred years wandering into a library wondering how guitar playing best happens or even what it is. (I hope it will help *you* know.) It contains little about equipment unless such information is an intregal part of a larger question. Nor does it contain any person already included in Obrecht's excellent compilation, *Blues Guitar*. The edit job was really hard, because it meant cutting out two-thirds of some stories that already approached zero body fat. Even though I took the words right out of their mouths, I hope the authors and artists won't view me as some hack government censor blacking out history. Instead, my intention was to show the core by cutting away what hid it.

Besides the artists, the authors deserve continued recognition. I consider them "masters" as well, for they were and are the best at eliciting information the musicians often never knew they knew. I have never ceased to be amazed at and humbled by the skills of those I had the pleasure of working with all those years.

I hope *Secrets From The Masters* will encourage you to focus on *music* more than guitar gymnastics, and to stick with it, even if you have to sometimes earn your living painting signs (like Tal Farlow) or flying airplanes (like Steve Morse) or teaching beginners (like Joe Satriani) or transcibing music (like Steve Vai) or giving seminars (like Howard Roberts) or running a record company (like Chet Atkins) or beating the world over the head with cat gut (like Segovia) to validate the voice of the six-string. I hope *you* will help guitar playing survive as more than a single-string sprint event. Most of all, I hope it will remind you to remember the most important secret of all: Be yourself. You'll go far. Others will follow. And you can tell them your secret: To go *their* own way.

— Don Menn

— DUANE ALLMAN —

BY JAS OBRECHT – OCTOBER 1981 & AUGUST 1989

URING AN amazingly fertile five-year career, Duane Allman metamorphosed from a teenager struggling for a psychedelic sound to the foremost slide guitarist of the day. Twenty years later, the importance of his great works — the Allman Brothers Band's classics *At Fillmore East* and *Eat a Peach,* Derek & The Dominos' *Layla,* and a handful of studio R&B and rock tracks — remains undiminished. Duane mastered bottleneck guitar as no one had before, applying it to blues and taking it to a very melodic, free-form context. He brought the style new freedom and elegance, and for many he is still considered *the* source for blues/rock slide.

As the founding and spiritual father of the Allman Brothers Band — surely one of the best rock acts of the era — Duane became the figurehead of a musical style known as "the sound of the South." With the Allman Brothers, he carried a deep-felt love for his native music — especially that of black bluesmen — to a rock audience, just as British guitarists had a few years earlier. Having learned his blues-based playing firsthand in the South, he had a more authentic feel than many contemporaries who had learned only through records. With co-lead Dickey Betts, Allman also helped popularize the use of melodic twin-guitar harmony and counterpoint lines.

Fortunately, Duane's playing is documented on close to 40 albums, many of these studio projects done as lead guitarist for the Muscle Shoals rhythm section. As a sideman, Allman added a compelling, natural feel and distinctiveness to whatever he played on. (A good sampling of his studio work was released by Capricorn as *Duane Allman: An Anthology* and *An Anthology, Vol. II.*) According to Jerry Wexler, who as VP for Atlantic Records used Duane on many sessions, "He was a complete guitar player. He could give you whatever you needed. He could do everything — play rhythm, lead, blues, slide, bossanova with a jazz feeling, beautiful light acoustic — and on slide he got *the* touch. A lot of slide players sound sour. To get clear intonation with the right overtones — that's the mark of genius. Duane is one of the greatest guitar players I ever knew. He was one of the very few who could hold his own with the best of the black blues players, and there are very few — you can count them on the fingers of one hand if you've got three fingers missing."

Friends describe Duane as an inspiration, a proud, likable man whose presence immediately drew attention and whose artistry profoundly influenced those who worked with him. He was an original, as unafraid to take chances onstage as he was in other sides of his life. By all accounts, he lived for music and the pleasure his playing brought people.

Howard Duane Allman was born in Nashville, Tennessee, on November 20, 1946. His only sibling, Gregg, was born a year later. Their father was killed while they were young, and the boys were raised by their mother, Geraldine. They attended Castle

— 1 —

Heights Military School in Lebanon, Tennessee, where they briefly studied trumpet. Their mother moved the family to Daytona Beach, Florida, in 1957. Both brothers took up guitar, and eventually Duane quit high school to stay home and practice on his new Gibson Les Paul Junior, by then sure that playing would be his life.

He listened to Robert Johnson, Kenny Burrell, and Chuck Berry albums during the day, and at night switched on R&B radio stations for further inspiration. He was influenced by Jeff Beck's playing with the Yardbirds, and always had a special affinity for B.B. King, Eric Clapton, Miles Davis, and John Coltrane.

The Allman brothers' first gigs were at a local YMCA, covering Chuck Berry and Hank Ballard & The Midnighters tunes. Although it was uncommon at that time for white and black musicians in Florida to mix, Duane and Gregg then joined the House Rockers, the rhythm section for a black group called the Untils. Duane remembered, "We were a smokin' band! Boy, I mean, we would set fire to a building in a second. We were just up there blowing as funky as we pleased; 16 years old, $41 a week — big time. And all we wanted was to hear that damn music being stomped out. That's what I love, man, to hear that backbeat *popping*, that damn bass plonkin' down, man. Jesus God!"

In 1965, the brothers formed a band called the Allman Joys. They loaded up a station wagon and began touring the southern roadhouse and bar circuit. At best, things were stormy at first as they threatened to break up several times. Then the Joys began getting all the work they could handle — six shows a night, seven days a week — and discovered they loved the energy of the stage.

After appearing at Nashville's Briar Patch Club in 1966, the Allman Joys were recorded by Buddy Killen and songwriter John Loudermilk. A pulsing version of "Spoonful," complete with organ and reverb-heavy, psychedelic guitar licks, was released as a 45 and sold well regionally. Other tracks from the Nashville session were issued in 1973 by Dial Records as *Early Allman*. Still, they were searching for a sound, and there was little hint of a future guitar star in their midst. Duane was to progress a long way in the next five years.

The original Allman Joys fell apart in St. Louis in 1967, and Duane and Gregg formed a lineup with drummer Johnny Sandlin and keyboardist Paul Hornsby. At first they used the name Allman Joys, then Almanac. The group moved to LA in 1968 and

signed with Liberty Records, which renamed them Hour Glass. By Gregg's account, this was one of the low points of the brothers' careers. There were plenty of clubs in the city's burgeoning rock scene, but the label would seldom allow them to perform in public. The musicians had little income. At best, Hour Glass was miscast in image and material. Most of their smooth, superficial debut album consisted of over-produced pop-vocal tunes, complete with overpowering horns and backup singers. "A good damn band of misled cats was what it was," Duane told Tony Glover. "They'd send in a box of demos and say, 'Okay, pick out your next LP.' We tried to tell them that wasn't where we were at, but then they got tough: 'You gotta have an album, man. Don't buck the system — just pick it out!' So okay, we were game. We tried it — figured maybe we could squeeze an ounce or two of good out of this crap. We squeezed and squeezed, but we were squeezing rock. Those albums are very depressing for me to listen to — it's cats tryin' to get off on things that cannot be gotten off on."

On the band's second release, *Power of Love*, the horns were mercifully gone, and Pete Carr had replaced the original bassist. For the first time Duane began to step out with supple rhythm grooves and several interesting, fuzz-heavy solos. In April '68, Hour Glass drove to Fame Recording Studios in Muscle Shoals, Alabama, where, without interference from slick LA producers, they could lay down blues tracks. With Jimmy Johnson at the controls, Duane opened up as never before — fluid, raw-toned, and emotional. The unmistakable Allman touch had finally been captured on tape. The group took the demos to the West Coast manager, who said they were "terrible and useless."

Hour Glass returned to the South and drifted apart after a few engagements. Duane and Gregg jammed with various bands and worked as paid sidemen on an album their drummer friend Butch Trucks was cutting with 31st of February.

Gregg went back to LA in 1968 to fulfill contractual agreements with Liberty, and Duane started jamming in Jacksonville with bassist Berry Oakley, who was in a lineup with Dickey Betts called the Second Coming. He moved in with Oakley until Fame owner Rick Hall, remembering the Hour Glass dates, sent him a telegram inviting him to participate in Wilson Pickett's November '68 sessions. Allman came up, and suggested that Pickett sing "Hey Jude," which eventually became the LP's title track and sold a million singles. According to Wexler, Duane's contributions to the tune were a dazzling departure from the usual R&B sound.

The Muscle Shoals rhythm section loved Allman's authentic country funk and blues playing, and invited him to become their staff lead guitarist. Duane signed a contract with Hall and moved up to Muscle Shoals, then a conservative town of 4,000 where you couldn't even buy a beer. The new musician in town was a striking sight with his long red hair, tie-dye shirts, jeans, and red-white-and-blue tennis shoes. For Duane, the first months in Muscle Shoals brought well-needed peace. "I rented a cabin and lived alone on this lake," he later remembered. "There were these big windows looking out over the water. I just sat and played to myself and got used to living without a bunch of that jive Hollywood crap in my head. It's like I brought myself back to earth and came to life again, through that and the sessions with good R&B players."

In January '69, Duane joined singer Aretha Franklin in New York to record *This Girl's in Love with You*. He also appeared on the singer's *Soul '69* album and added a track to *Spirit in the Dark*. A month later he accompanied his friend King Curtis on the saxophonist's *Instant Groove* album. He played electric sitar for Curtis' "The Weight" and "Games People Play," which won a Grammy that year for best R&B instrumental. Both tunes are on the *Anthology* albums.

After a few months in Muscle Shoals, Allman was asked by Hall if he wanted to try recording as a front man. In February, Duane recorded several tracks but an album was never completed. Hall sold his contract to Atlantic VP Jerry Wexler, who in turn later sold it to Otis Redding's manager Phil Walden, who was assembling a roster for a new Atlantic specialty label called Capricorn.

Meanwhile, Duane was becoming increasingly disenchanted with studio life. During one of his occasional visits back to Jacksonville, Duane jammed with Betts, Oakley, Butch Trucks, and Jai Johanny Johanson, a drummer he met at Fame. Except for Gregg, these were all of the future members of the Allman Brothers Band. "We set up the equipment and whipped into a little jam," Duane remembered. "It lasted two-and-a-half hours. When we finally quit, nobody said a word, man. Everybody was speechless. Nobody'd ever done anything like that before — it really frightened the shit out of everybody. Right then I knew — I said, 'Man, here it is!' I told Rick I didn't want to do session work full-time anymore. I had found what I really wanted to do."

On March 26, 1969, Duane called Gregg back from California. After years of disappointments, one-night stands, and studios, the Allman Brothers Band was born. In spite of his prior reputation, Duane insisted that they were all to be equals. They pooled their money, moved in together, jammed, and occasionally went to nearby Rose Hill Cemetery to play acoustic guitar and write songs.

Duane did a few more part-time sessions in Muscle Shoals on *Boz Scaggs*, *The Dynamic Clarence Carter*, and Arthur Conley's *More Sweet Soul*, but in September '69 the Allman Brothers band traveled to New York City and cut *The Allman Brothers Band* in two weeks. The album signaled a new direction an American rock and roll with its massive guitar hooks, double leads, counterpoint and unison lines, and plenty of slide and innovative blues. The album sold only moderately well, but the band continued, playing over 500 dates over the next two years. Johnny Sandlin recalls that "Duane was very well known throughout the South as *the* guitar player. He influenced a lot of people into playing their own thing instead of just being copy R&B bands. If he met other guitar players that he thought were promising, he'd either loan or give 'em a guitar, anything he could do to help."

Other guest appearances followed, as well as the Allman Brothers' next LP, *Idlewild South*. Their reputation for high-powered live shows began drawing larger and larger audiences, as did their free concerts on days off. In July 1970, Duane began his three-album association with Delaney and Bonnie Bramlett, which resulted in *To Bonnie from Delaney*, *Motel Shot*, and *D&B Together*.

In the last 13 months of his life Duane recorded his most important work, including Derek & The Dominoes' *Layla*, the Allman Brothers' *At Fillmore East* and *Eat a Peach*, and other studio projects. *Layla* proved to be the meeting of two kindred minds and 20 amazing fingers. Duane and Eric pushed each other to new levels, concluding with Duane's bottleneck symphony of imitation bird sounds.

With *At Fillmore East* rapidly becoming a hit album and two years of touring behind them, the Allman Brothers Band decided in late October to take a few weeks' vacation. Duane journeyed to New York to visit his friend John Hammond, and then returned home to Macon, where, on October 29, 1971, he went to Berry Oakley's house to wish the bassist's wife a happy birthday. After leaving the house about 5:45 P.M., he swerved his motorcycle to avoid hitting a truck that had pulled out in front of him. The cycle skidded and turned, pinning him underneath. He died after three hours of emergency surgery at Macon Medical Center. Duane was 24. He was buried at Rose Hill Cemetery, where he had often gone to meditate and play acoustic guitar in the early days of the band.

Our interview was assembled from an early-'70s Capricorn promo release, *Duane Allman Dialogues*. It begins with Duane's conversation with announcer Ed Shane just after the release of *The Allman Brothers Band* in 1969. The second half is from Duane's on-air appearance at WPLO-FM following the recording of Derek & The Dominos' *Layla* in early 1971.

This is Ed Shane with Duane Allman of the Allman Brothers. A great new album.

Thank you. We worked pretty hard on it. We're real proud of it; we think it's pretty good, too.

What were you after going into the album?

Live sound, like we sound when we play.

Can you categorize any of it? Some of it sounds like British blues, a little bit of it gets into some Johnny Winter.

Well, everything influences. As you go along, you pick up stuff. You just can't help it. It's just like how you learn to talk. You hear your folks talking, and whatever you hear, that's how you talk. That's just how people are. So we've all been involved with music, I guess, since our late teens, and stuff just soaks into you. The British approach to the blues certainly was a lot fresher than anything that anybody had any access to back when I was younger, when we were doing the Beatles songs and stuff like that, and it was getting to be pretty tiring. There was all that other slop, like the Searchers — remember all that? So we just got sick of traveling around playing it in bars for so long. So finally we just said, "Well, this has been a lot of fun, but we're tired of it," so we all quit our respective groups. Berry was with the Romans. Gregg and I was with the Allman Joys.

You were working where?

All over, man! There's a garbage circuit of the South, man, that you work at and you make about $150 a week and eat pills and drink — it's a bad trip! It was killing us, so we just all quit about the same time. Berry was staying down in Jacksonville, and we got together and jammed a lot. And none of us were working then; it was just like we needed a reprieve from that set. I was doing some sessions in Muscle Shoals — well, I was in California before that, but we won't even talk about that. But it was essentially the same thing — I was tired of it, man, because it re-

ally gets old. So we were all getting together and jamming, and saying, "Well, before we start anything, let's just say to hell with it, man! Let's don't get that same shit started up." The more we jammed, it got a little bit better. I knew these people at Atlantic Records, and I talked to them about trying to get something for real, something that we could do that would just sound like us, instead of something that they would just try to get to sell. We're proud of this — it's probably the best thing that ever happened to any of us.

Compare this to working in studios.

Oh, man! Studios — that's a terrible thing! You just lay around and you get your money, man. All those studio cats that I know, like, one of them gets a color TV, see, and then the next day, man, they're all down to Sears or wherever — "Hey, man, I'd like to look at some color TVs," you know. And this one place I know, man, all these cats — five cats at one time — had Oldsmobile 442s. One of them traded on a Toronado, see, and so all of them traded on a Toronado. And now one of them's got a Toronado and a Corvette, and now they're all looking at new 'Vettes! It's sickening. They're just keeping up with the Joneses and not playing their music. Their stuff sounds like crap now. I was down there working with them for about a half a year, and I got sick of it, man. Any sessions I do now, I just go in there and do it and leave.

Do you feel restricted playing in a ballroom as opposed to, say, free concerts in the park?

Well, anytime you're getting paid for something, you feel like you're obligated to do so much. That's why playing the park's such a good thing, because people don't even expect you to be there. And if you're there to play, that's really groovy, and so playing in the park's really a nice thing. About the nicest way you can play is just for nothing, you know. And it's not really for nothing — it's for your own personal satisfaction and other people's, rather than for any kind of financial thing. That hangs a lot of people — a lot of bread, and you try too hard. Either you can do something, or you can try to do something. Whenever you're trying to do something, you ain't doing nothing.

Bread'll stop you, too. It'll keep you there to make more.

Oh, sure! Yeah. I quit doing sessions because of that. I was getting to like it too much.

Where do you think the Allman Brothers and music in general might be going? Is there a direction back to the roots?

Well, in a lot of ways there is. There's a lot of groups now where it's coming down to everybody's expending all this energy in various ways to get that same old feeling out of it that Little Richard can get in five minutes. And people are finally waking up to the fact that you can expend just as much energy and get just as much of a good feeling out of a simple thing as you can get out of something that's hard. A lot of people who would have you believe that they're intelligent musicians are playing bullshit. Music's become intellectualized and everything.

Man, music is fun! It's not supposed to be any heavy, deep, intense thing, especially not rock music. That's to set you free. Anybody that ever listened to Chuck Berry or any of them cats know that. It's hard to believe the amount of emphasis that's been put on rock music and all the money that's been made by people who really are full of shit. And it squashed out a lot of people that was really good folks, kept them from making bread. And it's pathetic! It's pitiful. Like nowadays you get maybe one good record and ten really crappy ones, and they all go right up the charts together, and it doesn't make any sense. Some people that don't know where rock and roll came from will really settle for a hell of a lot less. They settle for a cheap, cruddy imitation of something that was really intense back maybe 10 or 15 years ago, like something Bo Diddley was really laying down.

Do you like the idea that rock sometimes talks about the times?

Sure, man. Yeah! It's like a newspaper for people that can't read. Rock and roll will tell you right where everything's at. It's just something to move your feet, man, and move your heart and make you feel good inside — forget about all the bullshit that's going on for a while and fill up some of the dead space.

On the new album, what's your favorite, most satisfying cut?

I like everything on there, man. I feel like we got a bunch of stuff done. I like it all. I don't have any particular favorites. Some of it's older — we worked it out when we first got together, and then as we went along we became a little bit more proficient. You can tell by listening to it — the earlier stuff's not near as complex as the stuff later on. When we started, we had one drummer, two guitar players, and a bass. And then Gregg came back from California and we had an organ, and then we got Butch Trucks, and that was another drummer. We worked the Muddy Waters song out first ["Trouble No More"], and it's

not that particularly impressive — it's just a good, hard, funky thing. And then as it went along, Butchy came into the group, and he likes to play with time, and that's where the 11/4 and 7/4 stuff came from. It just kind of grew, and we're getting more into a straight-time thing now. The two things we've done since the album's been completed were in straight 4/4 time, and they were rock and roll types of things. It's more fun to play and requires less effort, and it's a nice thing.

[Ed. Note: At this point the 1971 WPLO-FM interview begins.]

No matter how good the records are, the Allman Brothers seem better in person.

Yeah, man, that's really our natural element. When bands start to play, they play live. We haven't got a lot of experience in making records. I do, a little bit, from doing sessions and stuff, but not like a polished session man or anything. You know, we get kind of frustrated doing the records, and I think, consequently, our next album will be for the most part a live recording, to get some of that natural fire on it. *[Ed. Note: True to Duane's words, the next Allman Brothers Band release was their 1971 live masterpiece, At Fillmore East.]*

Does it have something to do with the natural interplay with the audience?

Yeah, a lot. And then, of course, the spontaneity of the music. There's rough arrangements, rough layouts of the songs, and then the solos are entirely up to each member of the band. So some nights are really good, and some nights ain't too hot. But the naturalness of a spur-of-the-moment type of thing is what I consider the valuablest asset of our band. We play live, and making records, you can't just do it over and over and over if somebody makes a mistake. Plus, the pressure of the machines and stuff in the studio makes you kind of nervous.

How does it feel, in the case of "Dreams," to have somebody else do your music?

Oh, it's real flattering, man. You know, it's nice that someone would like something we did enough to re-record it and do it again.

We're talking here about the Buddy Miles version, of course. I'm surprised somebody like Johnny Taylor hasn't done "Please Call Home" [on Idlewild South].

I wanted Clarence Carter to do that song, but I don't guess he ever will. I sure would like to hear him do it, though.

Who else could do a good job? B.B. King could.

Yeah, he'd do an exceptional job. He can do anything! He could sing "Happy Birthday" and bring tears to your eyes, man. I'd like to hear Joe Cocker or Elton John do one of them — they've both got powerful voices, both very good. Moving right along now [*laughs*] . . . Eric Clapton, man — let's talk about him. He's a gas. He's a real fine cat, and I consider it a privilege and an honor to play on his Derek & The Dominos album. He's a true professional in his field.

He has some nice things to say about you in Rolling Stone.

Oh, yeah. Man, it just tickles me to death to hear him say anything about me, ever, man! He wrote the book, you know. Just *Contemporary White Blues Guitar, Volume 1*. But his style and his technique is what's really amazing — he's got a lot to say, too, but man, the way he says it just knocks me out. He does so well. "Layla" — the title tune from that album — real proud of that one, I am, for sure!

I went down there to listen to them cut, and Eric had heard my playing and stuff, and he just greeted me like an old partner or something. He says, "Yeah, man, get out your guitar, man! We got to play." So I was just going to play on one or two, and then as we kept on going, it kept developing. Incidentally, sides 1, 2, 3, and 4 — all the songs are right in the order they were cut from the first day through to "Layla," and then "Thorn Tree" was last on the album. I'm as proud of that as I am of any albums that I've ever been on, man — I'm as satisfied with my work on that as I could possibly be. I was glad to have the opportunity to work with people of that magnitude, with that much brilliance and talent. Eric is just a real fine cat, an awful nice dude. It's hard for me to talk about him because I admire him so much, you know. It's hard for me to put him in a street context, but he surely is a man of the street, a gypsy — just like everybody else these days.

You said before that you thought blues and jazz are the same thing.

Yeah, it really is, man. It's just that as human feelings become more complex, as the world gets a little bit more divided and intelligent, complexity is the only difference between blues and jazz. It's all the portrayal of the feelings and the soul in a medium other than words. You can either complain and say, "Oh man, I really feel bad," or you can put your sadness into a musical context and make it desirable. Nobody wants to hear anybody bellyache, but everybody wants to hear him play the blues. You can say the same things, but make it to where it's a little less offensive to your fellow man by playing it with music.

Develop your talent, and leave the world with something. Records are really gifts from people. To think that an artist would love you enough to share his music with anyone is a beautiful thing. That's fascinated me ever since I piled up my motorcycle. Miles Davis does the best job, to me, of portraying the innermost, subtlest, softest feelings in the human psyche. He does it beautifully. He's a fascinating talent, man, a marvelous, marvelous man and a great entertainer. And John Coltrane, probably one of the finest, most accomplished tenor players, took his music farther than anybody I believe I ever heard.

You mentioned "entertainer." It's all a matter of the communication, rather than a guy standing over here making other people feel differently.

It's sort of like a different means of communication, man. Sometimes you can have things to say, but you can find no words for them — and I'm sure everybody gets caught in that position — or there's a feeling inside you that there are no words to explain. You can say "heartbreak" or "jubilation," but you can also set it up in music to make people actually feel it without ever saying anything about it. That's the grace of music; that's the blessing. You know, there's a lot of different forms of communication, but that's one of the absolute purest ones, man. You can't hurt anybody with music. You can maybe offend somebody with songs and words, but you can't offend anybody with music — it's just all good. There's nothing at all that could ever be bad about music, about playing it. It's a wonderful thing, man. It's a grace.

— CHET ATKINS —

BY DON MENN – OCTOBER 1979

JON SIEVERT

CHET ATKINS HAS done more for the guitar than anyone can say. An entire picking approach bears his name. "Atkins-style" is his two-, three-, and four-finger development, inspired by the thumb- and one-finger style that his idol, Merle Travis, poured into an ear plastered to a radio speaker back in 1939. On "Chinatown, My Chinatown," cut around 1956, Chet pioneered the use of artificial harmonics, a little steeler's gimmick now used by guitarists of all styles. Though Les Paul set much of the recording world rolling with his technological acrobatics, Chet Atkins also made important breakthroughs for recorded electric guitar. He bent ears with seminal examples of tone modifications now considered commonplace: With engineers Bob Ferris and Ray Butts he came up with a reverb in 1955 on "Blue Ocean Echo" [*The Best of Chet Atkins*], a tremolo in 1956 on "Slinkey" [*Mr. Guitar*], and a wah-wah in 1959 on "Boo Stick Beat" [*Teensville*]. He even concocted a nifty, in-sync boom-boom with a bass octave doubler (the "invisible bass man," he called it) around this time, not to mention a fuzztone before anyone else (though he never could figure out where to use *that*).

"Mr. Guitar" is only part of Chet's name. "Nashville Sound" belongs on his I.D., too. He, more than any other single being, created it. In 1957, RCA vice-president Steve Sholes, who had signed Chet as an artist to the RCA Victor label in 1947, made Chet his administrative successor. Atkins became manager of RCA's Nashville office (his real impact went back even further, since he'd been working with Sholes on a freelance basis since 1951). In 1968, Chet became vice president in charge of country music (and any and everything).

Over more than four decades he has discovered, produced, and counseled dozens of the biggest country, rock, and pop artists, such as Don Gibson, Perry Como, Charley Pride, Waylon Jennings, Eddy Arnold, Jerry Reed, Lenny Breau, Bobby Bare, Skeeter Davis, Jim Ed Brown, Rosemary Clooney, Jessi Colter, Dottie West, Jimmy Dean, Jimmie Driftwood, Al Hirt, Homer and Jethro, Sonny James, Willie Nelson, Boots Randolph, Charlie Rich, Hank Snow, Porter Wagoner, and on and on. And Chet was the person who brought pianist Floyd Cramer to Nashville and suggested he learn to play with that "bent-note" piano tweak that became his and Nashville's favorite keyboard embellishment.

His force crossed over: In 1954, Chet, along with others, encouraged Sholes to sign the biggest star of rock and roll, Elvis Presley, and it was Chet who led the sessions on such hits as "Heartbreak Hotel" and "I Want You, I Need You, I Love You." He hired the sidemen Elvis kept throughout his career, and even played some rhythm guitar on those and other Presley staples. Throughout the late '50s Atkins played *lead* guitar on Everly Brothers hits such as "Bird Dog" and "Dream" (later Hank Garland worked with Chet, Phil, and Don on other sessions). He signed jazz vibist Gary Burton. He even got Paul McCartney to record "Walkin' in the Park," a song written by the ex-Beatle's father.

In an interview with John Wilson in *The New York Times,* April 7, 1974, Chet denied his importance in all this: "'The Nashville sound' is just a sales tag," he said. "I don't think there is such a thing. The studios in Nashville are like the studios anywhere else. If there is a Nashville sound, it's the musicians." Still, he was the one who hired those musicians, signed many of the pop stars that came to matter commercially, listened to what they played, and told them what worked and didn't work about their playing. In order to broaden country music's appeal and to just plain surprise the public, he even began adding horns and violins to country music — took it "uptown," something for which he has subsequently apologized because he believes the resulting crossover sound came close to crossing out a unique musical identity. Even so, it is always a pat on the back and not a gauntlet at the feet when people around Nashville say, "If Chet likes it, it'll sell."

Atkins the guitarist has appeared in everyone's talent and popularity polls for years and years — *Playboy's* to *Record World's.* He was among the first ascendants into *Guitar Player's* Gallery of the Greats in 1975. In fact, Chet was a prime reason for the creation of the Gallery: Unless he were so enthroned (and therefore snatched out of competition), poll ballot tallies showed year after year that no one else would ever have a chance to win Best Country Guitarist (Chet usually won Best Overall Guitarist, too).

Objects of tribute enrich his closets and walls: gobs of citations, reams of flattering and/or complimentary letters. He used to keep a guitar in every room of his house. A guitar company, Gretsch, has attached itself like a Siamese twin to his name and nicknames and has used his counsel in the design of at least three of its major instruments — the Country Gentleman (the title, originally, of an early Atkins hit recorded in a garage in 1951), the Super Chet, and the Super Axe. The Country Music Hall of Fame in Nashville has a bas-relief plaque and a display case with his memorabilia. If there's ever been a guitar player likely to have his face on a stamp, his name on a bridge, his foot in the bow of a boat drifting towards Valley Forge as father of his country and President of the Guitar — it's Chet Atkins.

But he is one whose wisdom has kept ahead of his success. He knows where he — as well as all this potential mammon — came from. Johnny Cash once rhapsodized about Chet: "The downtrodden flock to him because he remembers what it was like to be in a cornfield on a side of a hill in Luttrell, Tennessee."

Outside that town, June 20, 1924, on a 50-acre farm, Chester Burton Atkins began his life as a malnourished Appalachian waif. His name itself seemed like a stray: "There used to be some trucks that ran around," he explains, "the C.B. Atkins Moving Company," and my dad used to see those signs on them. I guess he liked the 'C.B. Atkins' part, so he just made up 'Chester Burton.' There was a senator from Nebraska by the name of Burton, and I think that's where he got that part of the name. I don't know where he got the Chester. I kind of always wished he would have forgotten that. But that's it; that's my name."

He grew up in a family rife with luthiers, musicians, and divorce (his mother remarried three times and his father five). Inspired by relatives, especially his brothers Lowell and Jim, Chet was playing ukulele when he was four or five. He picked his way through various pieces he'd heard on the family's windup gramophone and through a radio he and neighbors built when Chet was 11. Inspired by George Barnes, Les Paul, Charlie Christian, Carl Farr, and the few other guitarists on record and radio of the day, Chet, nonetheless, intentionally avoided imitating them. It cut him then and still cuts him deep to hear himself compared to anyone.

The day he cites as one of the most important of his whole life was one in his early years when he vowed to become a guitarist after seeing a blind street musician. He became single-minded in the pursuit of his goal. In 1929, his brother Jim left home, teaming up later with Les Paul in 1938 and keeping Chet informed about the world of music outside of the east Tennessee hills. In 1935, Chet moved to Columbus, Georgia, to live with his father. By then he spent most of his time with a guitar in hand, sometimes even practicing in the bathrooms at school to luxuriate in the natural echo of the stall. In 1942, Chet got his first real job as a professional musician. He was hired as a fiddler with Bill Carlisle and Archie Campbell on WNOX, Knoxville. In the same year, he made the important switch to full-time guitar playing. He held the position of staff guitarist at WNOX for four years before skipping out and over the waves of some rough radio jobs elsewhere, from which he was usually fired for being "too modern" or "not commercial enough."

Chet the guitarist had a brief fling at being Chet

the vocalist in 1946–47. His first significant instrumental recording was "Galloping Guitar" produced in Atlanta's Fox Theatre in 1949. That cut in and of itself reversed the vocal trend that had been developing at the Grand Ole Opry. That, anyway, is what some people would say. Chet shrugs off the claim in the previously cited interview with John Wilson: "You can only eat so much caviar, then you want something else. I filled a void as an instrumentalist. There were no others around."

His first LP, *Chet Atkins Plays Guitar*, came out in 1951. Since then he has recorded in the neighborhood of fourscore others on both electric and nylon-string guitars (he switched away from steel-string acoustics in the '50s when he discovered classic guitar strings did not tear up his nails). He records in enough styles to prove that no one need be entrapped by his or her background: Classical, jazz, country, pop, and theatrical standards are all part of his repertoire.

And over the past 20 years, there have been plenty of nights he could watch himself on any given season's favorite TV shows: Jimmy Dean and Perry Como, NET specials with the Boston Pops, and Mike Douglas and Johnny Carson if he could stay up late enough (after all, he did quit producing Elvis when Presley's superstardom began necessitating night recording sessions). Chet's live performances have ranged from solo spots to duos, to those at the Newport Jazz Festival, to others with symphony orchestras around the world. His restless pursuit of excellence is matched by a keen awareness of the underdog's scramble up and out of the ditch; for years he's doled out prizes and scholarships to unknown guitarists.

In spite of the superlatives, Chet winces at anyone's attempts to puff him up beyond the natural and perfectly fitting confines of his own history and flesh. He would not like being launched as a kind of guitarists' Goodyear blimp floating slowly but regularly around the country scaring kids with his size and hurting the necks of old-timers trying to glimpse him on an endless PR job on behalf of guitar. He accepts credit for only one thing, and then only when stated with the proper perspective and joint credit he knows is due and is always quick to extend: "Merle [Travis] and I taught this country to play fingerstyle guitar, and I want credit for that sometime." Tennessee Governor Winfield Dunn, at the 1972 dinner given by the National Conference of Christians and Jews, presented Atkins with its National Human Relations Award and saw him in a more glowing light: "Music is the art of the prophets, and it calms the agitations of the soul. No one uses it more effectively than does Chet Atkins. He is a prophet with honor in his own community."

Prophet or disciple, Chet Atkins is synonymous with guitar.

What percentage of a Chet Atkins show is acoustic?

It's half acoustic and half electric. It's weird — I feel comfortable with *both,* because I have played them for so many years. It takes me just a few seconds onstage to get acclimated to the difference in neck width.

What advantage does the electric guitar offer you?

You have the volume when you're in an auditorium or when you're playing with a group of musicians. Another advantage is the amount of sustain you're able to get. The electric also has an entirely different tone quality that one doesn't get with a nylon-string guitar. A major disadvantage with the electric — at least for me — is the lack of control when I'm playing solo, because sometimes if I don't set the amp exactly right it will be too loud. I play with both hands, naturally, so I can't usually stop in the middle of a tune to readjust the volume if it's too high. That's the big disadvantage; another is the wear and tear on my nails. I don't play more electric onstage because the steel strings chew up my nails. I play a lot of my solos on acoustic.

What are the major advantages and disadvantages of an acoustic instrument?

The lack of sustain is a definite disadvantage. You know, if you're trying to duplicate the sound of an electric — particularly on the treble strings — a nylon-string guitar doesn't sustain enough. Also, the nature of the instrument makes it difficult to amplify properly. When you get into an auditorium, a lot of the soundmen think that you've got to knock the people over with volume. They can turn it up too loud, and you then get feedback. I would rather have people strain a little to hear me than have a booming, loud sound that resonates and can feed back.

Do you classify yourself as a country artist?

Yeah, I guess so. And I don't like to play for country audiences. I never did like to work the *Grand Ole Opry* — though I worked it for years — because all the time you're playing there are kids running up and down the aisles, and they're hawking songbooks and popcorn out in the aisles, and everybody's standing behind you talking about going fishing next week. It's a very difficult show to work. And all the time I'm on, everybody else in the audience is looking up at the ceiling wondering when Roy Acuff is coming on. But the country fans are more devoted, and they stick with you. You can have one hit and play for the rest of your life. So it comes down to survival, and you survive more with those country folks.

Do you think that when country music first started to become more popular you played a part in changing the guitar from acoustic to electric?

I was accused of, and I've apologized for, moving country music too far uptown. But I did very little, compared to what has been done since I almost quit producing. When you're making records, you are trying to keep your job; you're trying to make money for the company you work for. You're compelled to try new things because you're trying to sell a record. The public wants to be surprised. You give them new effects or they won't buy. So you get into a slot where you move in a certain direction, and if they tend to buy that then you give them more of it. Because of this, the music moves in certain directions. I think it's natural, and it's determined by the disc jockeys, the record-buying public, and the musicians. Musicians have very little to do with it, though, because we put on records what we think will sell. If something does sell, then we make more of it. That's the reason country music moved uptown. Also, there are social reasons. Back when I first got into the business, there was a lot of bigotry and prejudice towards country music: Middle-class people were afraid to say they liked it because people would look down on them. They thought they were supposed to like folk music and jazz; they wouldn't admit they liked country. But country music in the past few years has become respected. Its songs have become more palatable to city audiences, and some of the musicians are now big stars. So it's socially accepted now to like country music. Rhythm and blues once had the same problem.

What would you like to see happen to the electric guitar?

I'd like to see it keep its standardizations. I don't want to see 7- and 8-string guitars. I would like to see the standard tuning kept, and I would also like to see the guitar become more respected as a solo instrument. There are some great electric soloists. Unfortunately, some of them have not had the popularity or the attention from the public that I think they should have: People like Johnny Smith, Joe Pass, George Van Eps, and Lenny Breau are some of the great electric players.

Do you feel that the guitar is limited compared to, say, the piano?

In a few ways. It would be nice to play a melody line up high and a bass line down low like you can on a piano. There are limitations in the playability, but not in the sound. I love the sound. I have never especially admired the sound that I get, and I keep trying to improve it. I never disliked it enough to give up and stop trying, though.

Does the electric guitar sound pretty to you?

Yes. I love the sound of it, although I don't like a lot of highs. Most of the time, I tend to use the two pickups combined together. Sometimes on a very raucous tune I use the pickup close to the bridge. I will also use it when I play a real foot-stomper. But most of the time I use the two pickups combined; very seldom do I use the pickup closest to the fingerboard by itself, because it's too bassy. I don't like it too trebly, either; I like a mixture and a pretty sound.

At what point does electric music become simply noise to you? Is it a function of volume, or too many highs?

It's both. I don't like a lot of screechy highs with a massive volume. The two of them together are really too much for me, especially in a club, because sometimes you can be sitting where the speaker hits you in the ear like a drill. It's very disconcerting. I have some earplugs that I carry in my pocket in case I run into situations like that.

Are there any rock and roll guitar players you like?

Yeah, I like some. There are some great ones around now. That style of guitar has come a long ways since Chuck Berry.

When did you find it sounding good enough for you to like?

I've always liked it, and there was a period in my life, back in the '40s, early '50s, when I wanted very much to play that style. I kept thinking, "How can I get a sound like a saxophone and make it sustained?" That was the opposite from the style I played, fingerstyle. I never tried to do it, but I loved it. Guitar has replaced saxophone on records almost completely. There's some great players around — too many to mention. I used to love that Allman boy [Duane]. My daughter used to hang around with those kids when they were in Nashville. And she took me out to hear him one night, and boy, he was playing some super stuff. When he was 17 or 18 years old, his coordination was so good between his right and his left hand. I've never heard any of that stuff on his records sound as good as when I heard him at a little club.

What about jazz or fusion players?

I don't listen to a hell of a lot. I like Earl Klugh. I

think he's super. And I like George Benson. And I like Jim Hall's playing. And Lenny [Breau], of course.

Would stage antics or costumes turn your ears off?

No. I think showmanship is great. That's probably where about 50% of their popularity comes from. It's the image they're selling, and that happens with a lot of musicians, so I'm not putting them down. That's show biz.

Did you ever hear Jimi Hendrix' music?

Yes. I bought a couple of his albums right before he died just to see what he was doing, and I liked him. I think he used effects very well. Stereophonically, he used them to very good advantage, and he was a pretty nice player. And he played with a lot of soul. I think I saw him on television a couple of times; I believe he smashed his guitar.

Do you have any feelings about guitar smashing?

It doesn't bother me. Some of them need smashing.

You once sent Guitar Player **a picture of you and Andrés Segovia with the caption, "With Segovia just before he learned I played electric — 1960." Were you serious?**

I was just kidding. I understand from various sources that Mr. Segovia detests electric guitar; that was my response to those rumors about him. He didn't say anything to me about electric. He was nice to me. I played electric for him once at a banquet in Nashville 20 years ago. He didn't throw things at me. We sat at a table together, and he was very nice to me.

He didn't grimace through the meal while you were playing electric?

I didn't look, because I was watching my hands, trying not to screw up. I do think the old man is grossly wrong in a lot of his assessments of music, the electric guitar, and some of its players. I mean, when he says things like, "The only music worth listening to is classical music," we all know it's just not true.

Have you seen Segovia perform?

Yes. Hank Garland and I went to see him once. Hank was an eager beaver, and he said, "Let's go backstage." So we went back, and Segovia was kind of grouchy, as usual, and I said, "Can I see your hand?" He stuck up his left hand, and I said, "No, I want to see your right hand." I looked at his nails, and Hank said, "I want to see your guitar." And Segovia said, "I've locked it up." But he had to get into his case to put something in it, so he unlocked it and let Hank see the guitar, but he wouldn't let him play it.

Do you amplify your acoustic guitar onstage with a microphone?

Yes. I've never been able to find a pickup that faithfully reproduced the acoustic guitar's sound. I've tried using a pickup a few times, but never with any consistency.

How do you solve the problem of feedback?

I stop and tell the soundman to turn the PA down.

Do you have a specific point where you place the mike in front of the soundhole?

I'd say about a foot away. I aim it right at the end of the fingerboard. If I want a thin sound I move the guitar to my right, which gives a greater proximity effect to the microphone. You see, most microphones have a proximity effect, which means the closer you get, the bassier the sound becomes. So I move the guitar around to get different sounds and tone colors.

Do you have any feedback problems with your electric?

No, I don't, because I don't play it loud. I can't play the electric fingerstyle at high volumes, because it will feed back, making it difficult to control the music. The only time I ever play it loud is when I'm doing single lines. Then I'll crank it up.

How do you control your tone and volume?

I do it at the amp, mostly. All my life I've turned the guitar's volume control to its loudest point and controlled the overall volume on the amp. With most guitar control circuits, as you attenuate the volume, you also attenuate your highs. So if you turn your volume up and down on the guitar, you're also changing your tone.

Do you make any changes in your sound during a performance?

I make tone control adjustments on the guitar. To start with, I usually shave off the highs just a little bit. I don't set my controls to any specific numbers, though. I just use my ear.

What do you look for in the sound of a pickup?

I just look for a *good* sound. A lot of guitarists — especially novices who aren't too knowledgeable about electronics — look for the hottest pickups they can find. I think that's a mistake. I believe that's the wrong way to go. You can overdrive the first stage of your amp in many ways without having a hotter pickup. You can use preamps and things like that. So, I just look for a good sound out of a pickup without worrying a lot about the voltage output.

Do you use onstage monitors at all?

Yes, I do. The drummer, the bass player — everyone needs them. Otherwise they hear what's bouncing back off the auditorium walls, which makes it very difficult to keep a steady beat. So I use monitors. With the classical guitar, though, I do not use them at all, unless I'm playing something with an orchestra. Then we turn the stage monitors on just a little, so that the conductor can hear me. Sometimes, if I don't do that, the conductor will often wear headphones to hear me. Stage monitors usually have very cheap speakers that are often resonant at certain frequencies. I'd rather hear myself than listen to monitors.

How many guitars do you own?

All together, I've had about 100 in my entire career. I'm ashamed to count, but I think I have about 25 right now.

Do you keep them around just because you haven't thrown them out or are they collector's items?

I have a big house and I have a room for the guitars, so I keep them. Gene MacLellan, the boy who wrote "Snowbird," gave me an 1845 Martin that I'm very fond of. A lady in a clothing store gave me a guitar with no name on it that I keep around. They're not good to play, but they're collector's guitars. Then I have a Martin that's about 50 years old, which I will hold on to. Most of my guitars are like that. I also have a Gretsch Country Gentleman 12-string that was shown on the cover of *Chet Atkins Picks on the Beatles*. I also have four great classical guitars; I play those from time to time. Then I have various electrics, and Martins, and a Gibson L-10 that I used years and years ago. Les Paul built it. The fingerboard goes up to a high *F*. My brother Jim traded Les out of it and gave it to me around 1942. I played it up until I got a D'Angelico in the late '40s. I got that beautiful guitar and sawed a hole into it to put in pickups, tone controls, and capacitors to get the right tone. I later removed them; right before John D'Angelico died, he put a new top on it; it was just a rhythm guitar. Then, I got my first Gretsch Country Gentleman in the early '50s. I also have three Del Vecchio resonator guitars from Brazil.

Do you still play a Ramirez?

I sold that to somebody. I don't like Ramirez; they're too hard to play. The action usually has to be very high to keep from getting buzzes. I've got a Fernandez guitar now that's the same scale as the Ramirez. It's not the make so much as just the nature of the guitar. It's very easy to play, and it has to do with the vibration of the string. You can get the action down low and you don't get buzzes, and the neck is shaped real nice. On some guitars, a string doesn't immediately vibrate up and down. It'll vibrate sideways a while before it starts up and down.

I'm not an acoustic engineer, but after years and years I figured out that's what it's got to be. The Ramirez I had was the loudest one I could find. And it was a great guitar, but it also had to have very high action. So I kept it for a while. I never did use it much onstage, and I had a guy sell it for me. He sold it to some airline pilot.

Have you ever tried a scalloped fingerboard like John McLaughlin's?

Yes. Nato Lima of Los Indios Tabajaras had a guitar like that quite a few years ago — I played that. The high frets that I put on my guitar give it a similar effect. You tend to get more vibrato on the higher frets.

How do you get your vibrato?

In various ways: by pressing down harder and then releasing, or pushing sideways. But also if you do it just like a violin vibrato with high frets, you tend to get more vibrato than you would with lower frets.

How do you bend strings?

I push up towards my chin. I never pull down, although Les Paul does. It surprised me the first time I saw him do that.

Which finger would you most often use to bend with?

I push mostly with the third finger, but I rehearse pushing with all of them. I practice vibrato with all the fingers of my left hand. Most guitarists tend to play vibrato with their third finger.

Do you ever use your thumbpick like a flatpick for soloing, or do you actually use a flatpick for single-line solos?

The only time I have used, and still use, the thumbpick to play single-line solos is when they are slow. If it gets to be a lot of fast notes, I use the thumb and finger, and if it's *very* fast, I use the thumb and two fingers. The only time I ever used a flatpick was with an orchestra, where I had to play rhythm a lot. Anytime when I wasn't playing a solo I was playing rhythm, and it tended to wear the nail off of my index finger. To get away from that problem I used the straight pick, and I found that I didn't wear out my nails playing rhythm like that.

Were you actually using your first fingernail as a pick before that?

Yes. When I played with a thumbpick I tended to hit the strings more with the nail of my finger. And I would grip the first finger at the knuckle with my thumb and second finger.

Did you use alternating, down-up picking strokes with that first finger?

No. With an orchestra I would play rhythm, just like I was using a straight pick: two downstrokes and then two upstrokes.

How do you approach a solo?

First I learn the melody, and then I learn the chords from sheet music or from a record. Then I try to use substitution chords here and there that will make the tune a little more interesting. For instance, in place of an *Fm*, I would use an *A♭*, or in place of a *C7*, I sometimes use a *Gdim* going to *F*.

Were there any specific books that you learned from?

The first of the classic guitar books that I ever had were by Pascual Roch. He had a book out in three volumes called *Modern Method for Guitar.* He was one of Francisco Tárrega's students. Ezra Carter, the Carter Sisters' father, gave me those three volumes around 1949 or 1950. I don't think they're still in print. The George M. Smith book *Modern Guitar Method* was a good one, and still is. I had that book early. I think I had the old Manoloff books, but they didn't have much in them that I didn't already know.

And how did Ezra happen to have those Roch books?

That old cock was into everything. He would have spells: If he wanted to repair radios, he'd take a course and learn how to repair a radio. He once decided he wanted to build roads for the people up in Poor Valley and East Tennessee or up in Virginia where he lived, so he bought a bulldozer and built roads. He was into all kinds of things. I don't know how he became interested in classical guitar; I never asked him. But he had those books, and he gave them to me. He didn't play, so maybe he thought his daughters would pick up the stuff. He was a wild old guy — a great person. I had an awful lot of respect for him and Maybelle, and for the girls.

Was music always an important part of your life?

Yes, from the very beginning. My brother Jim, when he was at home, played guitar; and then my dad did a little, too. And so I started. I was playing ukulele when I was four or five, and then I tried guitar — but first I was dragging it through the yard, tying a string to it and filling it up with dirt. After my mother was divorced from my dad, she married a guitarist by the name of Willie Strevel. She stayed at the old home place, and my dad moved to Georgia. I stayed with my mother till I was 11. My stepfather played guitar with a thumbpick and his fingers — he'd go out and cut a toothbrush handle off and make a thumbpick from it. We played a lot with a "case" knife, too. That's what we called a kitchen knife. Slide guitar is what that was, you know, but I gave that up when I was about eight years old.

What jobs did you have before playing music professionally?

I worked on a farm a lot, but I never got paid anything for it and I didn't take to that too well. You know, we had a lot of farm work — tobacco, peanuts. I never raised any cotton like Johnny Cash, but could have if my dad had known how to raise it. My dad was a fellow who loved to farm, but he didn't like to do it himself. He'd love to hire people or get his kids to do the work. He was really just a music teacher.

Did he have an instrument that he concentrated on?

He played piano, mostly, and fiddle. And he sang — he gave concerts singing classics like "Ave Maria." He was into that stuff where they roll the "r"s when they sing. My first memory of him was doing his vocal exercises. He hated hillbillies. He hated the simple folk music stuff; he thought it was ignorant and dumb. Of course I rebelled. I liked it. He didn't like guitar, either.

How many hours a day were you working chores as opposed to practicing?

I'd get up very early, feed the stock, get my breakfast, and go to school. A lot of times I'd keep a guitar over at school, or take it with me. I'd always practice at recess and lunch. I'd go to the men's room and practice because there was an echo. Nobody used echo, but to me it sounded beautiful. The boys that had money would be shooting dice, and I'd practice guitar. I would walk to school in the morning because the bus would come by my house and then go 25 miles further and pick up other kids, so it was about an hour or so ride. So I'd walk about four miles to school. In the afternoon he would go right by my house, so I would ride home. And I might practice a little, or work — whatever I had to do. And chop wood, if it was in the winter, for two fireplaces — my dad and his wife's room, and my room. Then I'd stay up till midnight and practice at night, and listen to the radio and get four or five hours' sleep. One morning I was setting the milk down. We had a cream separator; I had to do all that job. Well, I set the milk down and woke up on the floor. I'd learned all about masturbation about that time, and I was running off a batch every few hours, and I fainted, and the milk turned over all over me, and I fell. I turned over the kerosene can, and milk and kerosene were all over. So after that, my dad said, "You've got to start getting some sleep, kid; you can't stay up and pick that damn guitar till midnight." So he started making me go to bed at night. But I was run down. I had asthma, too. I was a pretty sickly kid.

What instrument were you first interested in?

I always wanted a fiddle. We always had a guitar around, and my dad would come in and bring us instruments after he left home. He'd say, "Yeah, kid, I'll bring you a fiddle some day," and I guess he thought I was too young. He'd bring mandolins and guitars. Finally our uncle Joe came in from Nebraska, and he heard I wanted a fiddle. So he brought me a fiddle on his next trip. It had been struck by lightning. It was lying by the side of the house or something over in a corner, and the lightning struck the side. The top was busted in 22 different pieces, and somebody had done a great job of putting it back together. He had a bow with it, but the bow didn't have any hair in it. So we went out, me and my brother Lowell, to old Bob, our old white horse. Lowell said, "Fatty" — I was fat then — "you hold his tail." I held it, and Lowell cut off a strand of hair and we glued it in that bow. Then we went up to a fiddle player and got some rosin from him. So two weeks later I worked a job. We played over at the school for a sick person, and I knew two tunes. I think they were "Redwing" and "Sally Ann" or something like that. I was so little — I was only eight or nine years old — that the fiddle wouldn't fit under my chin. My sister and a cousin were operating the curtain at the show, so they thought, "He's going to drop it!" And so they closed the curtain right in the middle of my tune.

Was that the end of the performance?

No. Also during that show we did a comedy routine. We did blackface comedy and stuff, but a guy was arresting another guy, and he pulls out a pistol and shoots. He didn't have any blanks — he had a real pistol. And he turned it and shot into the wall. It was about a .45, and it put out every light in that building. They were kerosene lights. Did you know a gun will do that? The concussion will. It put out every damn light in that building.

Was that your first fiddling job?

Yeah, I didn't get any money for it, but somebody did — some sick person we were playing for. Somebody was dying with TB. They had a lot of TB out there in east Tennessee, and my sister died with it when she was 26. Back then they didn't have any drugs for it. I remember when I was a kid, when somebody would get sick, why, we would get together and put on a show and turn the money over to the person who was sick. My first job was when they opened up a grocery store. Me and my brother played, and we got $3 and some watermelon.

When did you first get an electric guitar and amp?

When I was 15, Eleanor Roosevelt started something called the NYA, the National Youth Administration, to keep kids busy in the summertime. It was kind of like the WPA, only for kids. I was part of it, and we built a gymnasium at Mountain Hill School near where I lived, in Hamilton, Georgia. I saved enough money to buy an amp, but we didn't have electricity. You see, we lived out in the sticks. Well, I ordered an Amperite pickup for my guitar from Allied anyway. It was basically just a coil of wire and a magnet that you clamped to the back of the bridge. Then I got a PA system: I ordered the amp from one place, a case from another, and tubes from still another — just to save a dollar or so. I put it all together and was ready to go. There was electricity over at the Mountain Hill School, but it was direct current, DC. My amp was made for AC, so I couldn't use it; it would have blown my amp up.

How did you power it then?

My dad used to go to town on Saturday and teach, so I would go with him. I also took my guitar and amp down to the church there, 25 miles away in Columbus, where my dad was the choir director. I would plug in and play and afterwards take it all back home again and wish for electricity.

Did you ever get into any trouble with the pastor?

No, he loved it. Parson Jack Johnson, the Baptist preacher, was the person who first wanted to put me on radio. He had his own show — 30 minutes on WRBL on Saturday morning at 10 o'clock. He heard me play when he came out to the farm. He said, "You sing all right. I'm going to have you on my radio program." So I'd sing hymns, play guitar, and he'd preach for 30 minutes. That was around '38 or '39. I got my first fan letter there. Somebody wrote in. I think the first song I ever sang was "Where Is My Wandering Boy Tonight?" That's an oldie but goodie. I was about 14, I guess.

When did you begin to do studio work?

When I went to Nashville I started recording right off with Hank Williams and all the big names. I worked the studios till about 1957. I was on every record that Hank made until he died — from 1950 on. The last record I made with him was "I'll Never Get Out of This World Alive." And he died a few days later. He'd make a cut and then fall over in his chair, and one fellow would say, "He's so skinny his ass rattles like a sack of carpenter's tools when he walks." He was into morphine and stuff. He got a shot in Knoxville, and he had already taken some and didn't tell the doctor, and it put him to sleep.

Why did you leave studio work?

After I started A&R [artists and repertoire] working and producing other artists, I just couldn't keep doing session work. You know, I'd try to play, and then you go in and listen to the cut, and it's not what you thought — it's not the balance you thought you had at all, so I'd hire Grady Martin or someone. I played on other people's records — I played on all the Everly Brothers hits. I didn't realize they had so damn many hits. I heard a medley on TV the other night — "Dream," "Bird Dog," "Bye Bye Love." When I first got the job as A&R man, the first hit I had was recording "Oh Lonesome Me" by Don Gibson. He wrote "I Can't Stop Loving You" and "Oh Lonesome Me" in one day.

Did you play on Don Gibson's "Sea of Heartbreak"?

Yeah, me and Hank [Garland]. We got so Hank and I would play duets. But we don't deserve a lot of credit for those. They're great solos, but Don was the one who would come up with them. I'd say, "What do you want us to play?" Well, he'd hum some wild damn thing that we'd learn, and it'd be different than anything we would think of. If we played a chorus, we'd play some jazzy something, and Don, he'd hum something and say, "Play this." And we'd get something similar to it, and it would turn out to be great.

And that's how that style of solo originated?

Well, it wasn't my idea. See, all these things are accidents. Like the style I play is an accident, because I was so far out in the damn sticks I didn't know any better. There's a songwriter named Don Robertson from California — had a lot of hits. He used to send me demo tapes, and he played that Floyd Cramer style of piano. He tried to imitate a steel guitar on his piano, bending notes a whole-tone. Well, I remember we did one with Elvis, "I'm Counting on You," and I thought, "Why don't we do the piano that way?" But nobody could do it. So Don kept sending me demos with this style, beautiful, and he's a beautiful singer. And so we were recording "Please Help Me I'm Fallin'" with Hank Locklin [*Souvenirs of Music City, U.S.A.*], and I told Floyd, I said, "Now take this demo home and learn this style. I want it exactly like this." So he came back the next day, and he could do it, which amazed me. And so we put the record out. I've told this story before; Floyd doesn't mind. The

record was a smash vocal by Hank Locklin. I said to Floyd, "Write you an instrumental like that, and you'll have a hit." So he wrote "Last Date."

And he recorded it?

Yes. The arranger didn't show up at the session, but Anita Kerr was there. She's got perfect pitch. So we went in and helped produce it, and she grabbed a pencil and wrote out a part for the strings, and we did it, and it was a big hit. Floyd deserves a lot of the credit, though, because Don hadn't written any instrumentals like that, and Floyd took it and did something with it, and Don should have. I'm sure a lot of people wanted Don to, but he didn't want to be a star that much. So people had stumbled on that style, but nobody had really done it till Don Robertson did it. Put that in your *Keyboard* magazine.

Did you ever appear on any of Elvis Presley's records?

Yes. I played on "Heartbreak Hotel" and "I Want You, I Need You, I Love You" — things like that. I played rhythm and Scotty Moore played lead. Elvis came in and did some more sessions after those first ones, but I don't remember any of the tunes. I never played electric on those records. With Elvis I hired the band, and he wound up using those guys for years. I hired Floyd Cramer; he'd just moved to town. And I tried to hire the Speer Family as singers, and I couldn't get them, so I got the Jordanaires. They wound up working with Elvis for 10 or 15 years. You never realize when you do a little something what effect it'll have on people's lives. It just turned out he liked the guys, you know, and he used them when he would come back.

Do you ever sit and play just to relax?

Oh, that's all I do.

If you go on vacation, do you take your guitar?

Always. I always do. Sometimes I don't play, but I want it with me for some reason or other — it's a security thing, I guess. And if I'm bored I just pick up the guitar and improvise, and half a day will go by real quick, just because I enjoy it so much.

Is it true that you sometimes fall asleep with the guitar on your lap when you have bouts with insomnia?

I still do that, yeah.

Do you still suffer from insomnia?

I don't have any trouble going to sleep; I wake up too quick. That's always been my problem. I go to sleep in five minutes, any time after I've been up a few hours. But I wake up after about six hours. And I don't feel like playing then. Actually, I think I'm much more creative in the morning. I can write better and everything, because my mind's clear and all my inhibitions haven't surfaced.

Do you work everything out before you record?

No. I improvise a lot, and sometimes I stumble onto some nice things by just playin' in the studio with another musician. Perhaps he'll do something that will make me think of a little lick. I think I'm at my best when I play live in the studio. Overdubs will sometimes give you more technically exciting or interesting results, but in the studio the spontaneity far outweighs anything you might get by sitting around a machine and working it out.

When did you start using right-hand [artificial] harmonics?

I first used them on a song called "Chinatown, My Chinatown." For years I had worked with steel guitar players who used harmonics. That's just part of steel guitar playing. I worked with a steel player in Knoxville named Tommy Covey. He played a harmonic and a pure tone at the same time. He would pluck the harmonic and let the thumbpick go out and get a pure tone, which gave him an inverted harmony. So I tried to do that, and then one day I accidentally played those things separately. I thought, "My, my, what have I discovered here?" I developed it enough so that I could play a harmonic with my thumb and first finger of my right hand and then pluck a pure tone with the third finger on another string. Eventually, I could pull off the pure tone and then slur it. I could play arpeggios, too. Lenny Breau and Ted Greene have developed it to such a high degree. But I'm very proud of that innovation. It's very different, and I think it gives a beautiful, beautiful sound.

How would you play a chord like that?

Let's say we've got a D9 chord. The tones from that chord would be [ascending from the sixth string, fret 5] A, D, F#, C♭, E, and A. With the third finger of the right hand you'd pluck F#. Then you'd play the harmonic A [sixth string] with the thumb and first finger. Next, you'd play a pure-tone C with the third finger, followed by a D harmonic played with the thumb and first finger. On the second string you'd pluck E with the third finger. Finally, you'd play an F# harmonic with the thumb and first finger. You can do this just by barring anywhere on the guitar and make a nice arpeggio.

How did you get the sounds on "Boo Boo Stick Beat" [Now & Then]?

Boo boo sticks were mainly just mailing tubes of different lengths that you could slap on your thigh. They would make a certain tone, depending on how long they were. By cutting them to a certain length you could get them in tune with the band. I don't think they're around anymore. The wah-wah effect on that record was created by using a modified DeArmond volume pedal that I used back in the '50s. I put a tone control circuit in it instead of a volume circuit. So it was actually a tone pedal, like a wah-wah.

What effect did you employ on "Blue Ocean Echo" [Best of Chet Atkins]?

That was a tape recorder called a Magnacorder. I ran the machine at 7 1/2 inches per second, and I moved the playback head over a certain distance so that it would echo at the tempo I wanted. I was messing around with it and wrote the tune specifically for that effect — a very slow reverb. I liked it a lot.

Did you use this effect on "Snowbird" [Now & Then]?

Yes, but by the time I did "Snowbird" I had a variable oscillator controlling the speed of the machine's capstan. I could slow it down or speed it up whenever I wanted it to change the rate of echo repeats. Every time I would play a note, it would come out of the tape machine as triplets.

What kind of tremolo did you use on "Slinkey" [Now & Then]?

I had an engineer alter the tremolo on an old Fender amp so it would go *very slow,* and then I just made up a little tune. Just like "Blue Ocean Echo," I wrote the song to suit the effect. It was very hard to play the song, because it's difficult to stay in tempo with a mechanical device — especially when you don't hear a definite one, two, three, four.

You must have experimented with electronics a lot.

Yes, I have. Too much.

Why too much?

Because it took away from the guitar. I always resent anything that takes me away from my guitar — like if I go out and shoot a 79 on the golf course, I know I'm playing too damn much golf, because I'm not a 79 shooter. And if I'm down in my studio working on my console too long and spend too much time, I think, "Boy, I should be practicing."

You must enjoy playing around with various equipment.

Yes, I like touching the wires together and watching them spark. Back in the 1950s I built a guitar with low-impedance pickups. It had two outputs, so it was a stereo. I amplified three strings at one volume, or on one channel, and the other three strings at another level, or on another channel. I could run either of those string groups through effects separately

— for instance, the tremolo. I could have tremolo on the treble strings but not on the bass strings, or vice versa. I experimented with a lot of stuff like that.

Did you ever use that technique on records?

Yes, although I don't remember which ones; I never listen to my records that much. I also substituted tape reverb for the tremolo sometimes so that I could have tape reverb on, say, the bass strings and not on the treble strings. There are all kinds of nice effects for playing fingerstyle.

Do you use effects in the studio?

Actually, I seldom use them. I guess I'm gradually becoming more of a purist. I just want a pretty, natural sound. I don't want to clutter up recordings with a lot of effects, except perhaps in the background.

What kind of strings do you use?

I use the Gretsch Chet Atkins Country Style strings — the same type that come on the guitar.

What are the gauges?

From highest to lowest, they're .010, .012, .020 wound, .028, .038, and .048 or .050. I haven't really measured them, but I like them a lot. The wound strings I especially like because they have good magnetic qualities. They have a lot of steel. You know, back in the '40s, you couldn't buy string gauges at all; you bought what they gave you. I got around that by using a banjo fifth string for a first. And I'd use a guitar first for a second, and so on. Back in those days a guy told me, "You should put a 'peck' string on your guitar." And I said, "What's that?" and he said, "An octave third." I don't know why he called it that, but they used that in Nashville years later for nice rhythm sounds, tuning the third string up an octave.

How often do you change your strings?

I don't change them as often as I should — every two or three weeks. On tour, I'll put on new strings before I go on out, and I won't change them until I get back. I don't perspire a lot. I think if you perspire a lot then you should change them often because they get to sounding pretty funky.

Do you ever treat them in any way to get their brightness back?

Yeah, I take them and flip them against the fingerboard, pull them away from the fingerboard and let them fly back against the wood. That shakes some of the dirt out. It will liven up the strings considerably. I think Buddy Emmons showed me that. He's one of the sharpest guys I know when it comes to string instruments. He's always coming up with a new idea before everybody else.

Do you ever wipe or wash your strings?

I have. I've taken strings and washed them in detergent and let them dry. It's easier to change them, but I would do it again if they quit putting out these strings that I use. I would just save them and keep cleaning them.

What kind of pick do you use?

I like a heavy one. I used to play with a little, thin thumbpick. I used it for many years and one day Paul Yandell said to me, "I think you used to get a bigger sound and a better sound with a bigger pick." So, I started using a heavier pick again — I'm not sure who makes them. I seem to play with more confidence when I use a heavier pick. With a small pick, if I get too excited and play with too many dynamics, the pick is likely to slip off my finger; a big, strong pick is less likely to do so.

How do you protect your hands?

In the winter I have to be more careful because the nails on my right hand become brittle. If the weather gets very cold, I can snap a nail without any effort at all, just by closing the car door or closing the car's trunk. So, I wear a driving glove on my right hand anytime I anticipate getting in or out of a car. It's just a habit that I've gotten into. I don't do things that would be injurious to my hands. I don't have any tools that might cut a finger. I'd love to have those tools and be able to work with them, but [Kentucky guitar builder] Hascal Haile told me of instances where guys would be in there helping him and cut off a finger. So that scared me.

Do you use any particular kind of nail polish?

Anything clear. I don't want pink.

Do you use specific files or emery boards?

I use an emery board to take off a lot of excess, and then I use 600 sandpaper.

Do you take any precautions when handshaking?

I always try to jab my hand right into a person's hand. That way, they can't hurt you. Now, if they just get part of your fingers, they can hurt you. I've had my hands hurt that way — not seriously, but now I am careful. Some of these jokers on the road really have a strong handshake, and they can crush you.

What about in the shower or shampooing or shaving?

Right before a concert, I don't shower a lot. It softens up my calluses so much on my left hand, and it softens the nails on my right hand, say, if I shower 30 minutes before a concert. If I do have to shower, I have medical rubber gloves in my suitcase that I put on. Then I can take a shower without getting my hands wet.

Are there any soaps or cosmetics you avoid?

I don't use shaving cream in an aerosol can for a

couple of reasons. The main reason is that I believe if it softens your beard, it can soften your nails. And I've always had a problem with soft nails. Also, I'm somewhat of an ecologist. I hate to see all these aerosol cans that you use and then toss away. I use a brush and shaving soap.

How many shows do you do each year?

Well, I always tell my agent that I want to do 30, and it always amounts to 35 or 40. I do little things that come up, like TV shows and golf tournaments. Or I get up and play for my supper; you don't count those as shows, because you just play a couple tunes. But it's quite a heavy schedule. I just played for the American Medical Association convention in Chicago, and with the National Symphony, and I just played a concert for a small group in Elmira, New York. Now, I'll be playing at the Ohio State Fair with [saxophonist] Boots Randolph. Later I will play with the symphonies in Honolulu, Hawaii, and Wichita, Kansas. So it gets to be quite a few. I'll also be playing in England, Norway, Sweden, Germany, and France. Then I'll play at the Country Music Association's Country Awards Show. Things like that come up all the time.

You do get around.

I do get around, yes.

— JEFF BECK —

BY JAS OBRECHT — OCTOBER 1980 & NOVEMBER 1985

JON SIEVERT

J EFF BECK IS ONE OF the greatest guitarists to have emerged from rock and roll. Led Zeppelin's Jimmy Page said in *Guitar Player*, "When he's on, he's probably the best there is." Beginning with his first major recorded part — the unforgettable sitar-flavored hook that propelled the Yardbirds' "Heart Full of Soul" to the top of the charts in 1965 — Beck has remained constant to his self-proclaimed goal of expanding the electric guitar's boundaries. Over the years he has led blues-based rock bands (introducing singer Rod Stewart and present-day Rolling Stone Ron Wood to the world in the process), fronted a power trio, and carved some of the first inroads towards what is now known as jazz-rock fusion. He has never compromised or sold out, remaining a law unto himself. And although he has recorded several albums that are now considered by many to be classics — *Truth*, *Beck-Ola*, *Blow by Blow*, and *Wired*, to name a few — there is surprisingly little similarity among them. Not only has he successfully changed styles, but, rarer still, he has become an archetype guitarist for most styles he chooses.

Because of his sonic innovations and ability to arrange tunes to best showcase his talents, Beck has garnered little of the he-can't-play-the-way-he-used-to criticism that has plagued other '60s axemen. His style blends snatches of early Les Paul, the best elements of rock and blues guitar, slide, subtle Eastern influences, lines derived from keyboards, and bits of everything he's heard — all performed with an elasticity, craziness, and flash that's unique to him. A true showman, Jeff is capable of ear-splitting feedback followed by surprising subtlety, wild theatrics, and solos that begin seemingly off-balance and out-of-key before being woven together in intricate, beautifully constructed climaxes. While his styles may have evolved, the unmistakable Beck fire and ingenuity remain.

Jeff Beck was born in Surrey, England, on June 24, 1944. He attended private schools until he was 11 and then enrolled in Wimbledon Art School. As a child he practiced piano with his mother for a couple of hours a day. "My other training," he adds, "consisted of stretching rubber bands over tobacco cans and making horrible noises." Early Les Paul recordings and broadcasts from the Near East that came over the family radio fired his desire to become a musician. When the family budget couldn't be stretched to include the cost of an electric guitar, he pounded together his own out of pieces of wood, homemade frets, and a pickup swiped from a nearby music store. As he described in his December '73 *Guitar Player* cover story, "I used to deliberately carry my guitar around without a case so everyone could see what it looked like. I used to stick it on my back and ride a bicycle. I could see then that it wasn't a fly-by-night thing, because the expressions on people's faces when they saw this weird guitar was something. It was bright yellow with these wires and knobs on it; people just freaked out. I got my first gig at a fairgrounds somewhere and boogied around there with that, playing Eddie Cochran stuff, but nobody was into it."

At 18 Jeff dropped out of school and began earning nine dollars a night as a guitarist. By 1964 he was steadily gigging in a band called the Tridents. In December Eric Clapton quit the Yardbirds — a London-based band that was pioneering heavy metal music while translating high-energy blues into hard rock — during the recording of their single, "For Your Love." Keith Relf, lead singer for the group, offered the position of lead guitarist to Jimmy Page, who at that time was a busy session player. Page declined and recommended Beck in his stead.

Although his playing was heavily blues-based when he joined the Yardbirds, Jeff began to change when he toured America for the first time and saw that B.B. King and other bluesmen were beginning to get booked at the Fillmores and other rock-oriented venues. His task of bringing blues guitar to white audiences done, he delved into rock, vowing to "expand it, experiment with it, do new things to it." Beck came into his own as a guitarist, and by the time his 20-month stint with the band was up, he had come to epitomize the rising breed of psychedelic guitar heroes. A dandy in ruffled sleeves and jewelry, he blistered audiences with loud volume and a progressive style incorporating feedback, distortion, tasteful fuzz, power chords, Eastern motifs, slide parts, and theatrics such as soloing with the guitar held over his head or behind his back.

By the end of 1965 Beck had appeared on two albums released in the U.S., *For Your Love* and *Having a Rave Up*. In May '66 *The Yardbirds* was released in England, and a modified version was distributed in the U.S. as *Over Under Sideways Down*. To relieve building tensions within the band, Jimmy Page came in on bass in mid-1966 and then switched to guitar so he and Beck could both play lead. That fall the Yardbirds toured with the Rolling Stones, Beck reportedly suffered a breakdown, and after smashing his favorite guitar onstage he returned home to pursue a solo career. Unfortunately, of the Page-Beck Yardbirds collaborations, only "Happenings Ten Years Time Ago," "Psycho Daisies," and "Stroll On" remain. The guitarists also appeared together in the film *Blow Up*, playing double lead on "Stroll On."

By the summer of 1967 Beck was one of the first British rock superstars who owed his celebrity to instrumental prowess. He embarked on a brief solo career, churning out the singles before organizing the first Jeff Beck Group with Rod Stewart and Ronnie Wood. The three men continued as a unit for more than two years while various drummers — notably Aynsley Dunbar and Mickey Waller — came and went. Their first album, *Truth*, to this day remains one of Jeff's most critically acclaimed efforts. Other incarnations and groupings came and went, receiving accolades in the press for their high-powered sound and command of the blues, until his band with bassist Tim Bogert and drummer Carmine Appice failed when Jeff fractured his skull in a car crash.

In April 1971 Jeff was back in public view in reformed entities, solo spots, and occasional sideman appearances. He described his new musical direction as crossing ". . . the gap between white rock and Mahavishnu or jazz-rock. It bridges a lot of gaps. It's more digestible, the rhythms are easier to understand than Mahavishnu's. It's more on the fringe." *Blow by Blow* and *Wired* both were voted Best Guitar Albums in the *Guitar Player* readership polls.

Though Beck's main pastime is tinkering with automobiles, he still performs on carefully chosen occasions as both a soloist and a sideman. The following interview was conducted while he was in San Jose, California, to attend a hot rod show.

Given the broad scope of your early musical environment, why did you choose the guitar as your instrument?

I remember messing around on a violin and not wanting to use the bow. I couldn't stand the thought of bowing instead of touching the strings. There was a frustration because the bow was getting in the way. And when you're a kid, I suppose you just want to get at the strings and pull them. It was more fun, and I was more accurate pulling the string than bowing it. But at the same time, having said that, the bow sound was better than the noise you'd make with your finger.

Do you feel the guitar is an unlimited instrument?

For me it's definitely limited. It seems to be limited for a lot of other players, too, judging by what I've heard on radio rock shows. They all sound like they've reached about where they're going with it. No experimentation seems to be happening on general terms. Obviously, like backroom boys are doing their things, but it's not really getting on record, is it? The stock sound is still there — the Gibson Les Pauls cranked up and loud Fender Strats. You get a few nice pedal effects going on the records, but it's not really much to make you sit back and think, "Wow! What's that?" And if you do, nine times out of ten it's a synthesizer that's making the noise rather than the guitar.

How has your relationship with the guitar changed over the last couple of years?

Well, I just ignore what's going on around me, really. I have to because living where I live, I haven't got a hotline to anybody telling me what's going on. But I still think that poetically the guitar is as limited as you want to make it. Tonally it is limited. If you've got a good ear, you can tell what's been done to the guitar, what circuits it's going through. You can tell how much the pure note is being doctored up just by listening to a record.

Have you learned a lot since Blow by Blow?

I've learned a lot, and I haven't learned a lot. I've learned that people are ready for anything. But I've also learned that it's difficult to continue once you've got someone's attention. That album *Blow by Blow* was a major change in my life, really; but that was an accident. The album was sort of put together naturally. You couldn't force out another album like that, so it's difficult to make a follow-up simply because one tends to start thinking, "Well, if they liked that, they'd like this. Maybe I should do another one like that," and so and so. The tendency would be to choose the most popular number and enlarge on that, but I don't work like that. You know, like with the old Motown things, if they had a number one hit with a star, then the star would probably turn out three records very similar in approach. They'd play it safe and get an identity going, but that's exactly what I'm not into.

At the time you recorded Blow by Blow *had rock gotten too stale for you?*

I reckon you're right. That's probably what it was. It's still pretty stale. I mean, aren't you tired of all the big-sounding heavy metal and crashing around? It's just so *standard.*

Do you listen to other forms of music?

I only listen to things that catch my ear, and that's not very often. I like to use the influence but not get too heavily buried in it. It's too easy to get marched off somewhere by somebody; you get swept away by them, and before you know it, you're copying them. The way I've got it is not very productive — it's not like I'm turning out albums by the dozen, far from it — but when I do do one, at least it seems to be tugging more in my direction and where I want to be, where I should be, rather than if I was a hot property on the road all the time and turning out

more albums. I think it works out better this way because nobody wants to keep hearing the same name — Beck, Beck, Beck, or whoever it is. It's an instant death once you start turning out loads of great albums, because you're so near the pinnacle of your career and then you can only go down. It doesn't matter how big you get; it's just that once that point is reached, you can only go down. I don't like that side of it. I like to just turn out an album when I think I've got enough decent material. If people are around to buy it, then that's all I want.

Do you have to be in a certain state of consciousness to play your best?

Yeah. There's no doubt about that.

Do you know what that state is?

No, I don't [*laughs*]. Even after you've played something and everyone is really into it and then you're playing it back and the whole studio's buzzing, you still don't realize what it was that made you play like that. You're enjoying what's happening at that particular time when people are listening to it.

Are your emotions tied in with the way you play?

It's purely emotional. I can sort of switch on automatic and play, but it sounds terrible. I've got to be wound up. In the right mood.

Have there been times when you've played better in a room by yourself than you ever could on vinyl?

Yeah. I can play unbelievably in a room on my own. But then, I have to know the door's locked and no one is listening.

Why is that?

Because there's going to be mistakes and maybe horrible goofs and things, but it's good fun. It's great therapy, you know, to just lock yourself away. You don't have to play at ear-shattering volume, but just loud enough to get the spirit of the stage thing going on your own. That's when you start really finding some nice, interesting things.

Do you use the guitar much to play yourself in and out of moods?

Yeah, but if one gets down that much — really down — picking the guitar up won't really help much, because if you happen to play a phrase that you don't like, you're worse.

Are you very self-critical?

They tell me that. And I must be because things take a long time for me to get them out. It's because I think overindulgence in anything is wrong, whether it's practicing 50 hours a day or eating too much food. There's a balance with me, as there should be with everything and everybody. I've tried to keep it so that I don't lose my technique, such as it is, and I'm able to execute the ideas that come out.

How do you do that? By practicing a lot?

No. I don't think I want to practice too much because that depresses me. I get good speed, but then I start playing nonsense because I'm not thinking. A good layoff makes me think a lot. It helps me get both things together — the creativity and the speed.

Do hooks come to you when you don't have a guitar in your hands?

Yeah.

How do you remember them?

You don't, really. Something gets stored in the back of your mind, and then you hope that something might come out, maybe in a different form.

How have your views on soloing changed through the years?

Playing with Jan Hammer sort of knocked all the soloing out of me. I mean a three-week tour, taking exchange solos with a person like Jan can take you to your limit on soloing, so I've got no particular desire to play ten-minute solos. Those were never valid anyway, in my book — *never*. It was just a cheap way of building up a tension in the audience. I remember that in the days of Ten Years After and several other groups, really the people were clapping in a sense of relief of tension when you'd finish the solo — not because it was amazing or anything. That's what I saw. Maybe some nights there was a valid long solo. Once one group got away with it, a lot of other groups started following by doing ten-minute rubbish solos, and started to make people clap, and that's wrong because it's misleading the people. They don't know what's going on, and they can only hear so much.

In the framework of your music, what do you think a solo should do?

It should do something; it shouldn't just be there as a cosmetic. It should have some aim, take the tune somewhere. I'm not saying I can do it, but I *try* and take the tune somewhere. You know, you never get people saying anymore, "Ah, listen to this guitar solo! Wait till this part comes!" They talk over it. When the first few bars of the tune come over the speakers, they say, "Oh yeah, right." And they'll just party over it and talk over it. Like in the old days — '68 — you actually used to listen for things, like in Sly Stone's records there would be some noise or some little solo or even a triad or a jab on the keyboard, and you'd say, "Wow! Listen to this bit!" You would carry the whole thing out somewhere else. An album was just one piece of flat music going along.

You just don't pick up anywhere along the line.

You've used the guitar in dialogue throughout most of your career, even back in the first Jeff Beck Group when you traded solos with Rod Stewart's voice. Has this been an attempt to get out of the routine of having to do extended solos?

No, it just comes naturally. Sounds corny, but it's just sort of like putting icing on a cake or holding a conversation with somebody. Really, that's all you're doing. You're saying something through the guitar or whatever it is you're playing. I just try to say it as clearly as possible, because there's no prizes for speaking double-Dutch. Nobody can understand you. There's nothing worse than a boring sermon that you know already, or you don't know and aren't interested in. It's as simple as that, really.

What influence has Jan Hammer had on your playing?

He's just a master of melody. His chords are *his* chords — if anyone else plays those chords, you say, "Hey, those are Jan Hammer's chords!" I mean, they're obviously not his; nobody can say that they've invented a chord because they are already there. You discover them. But he plays in a certain way that is unmistakably him. To my ears — I don't expect anybody else to dial in on it so readily — his soloing is just so picturesque. Anyone who has got music must like him. He's never flash — flamboyant, I suppose, but never flash. Even on his wild solos he's still creative. He still finishes off all the notes in the right, and he never makes a mistake unless it's something like counting the number of bars where you're supposed to change — maybe he'll forget. When he knows the number — look out! We played "Freeway Jam" about 50 times on the road — I've got a lot of tapes of the tunes we used to play — and not once did he ever play the same solo or even in the same strain.

Does that make you play the same?

No. The fun time for me is listening to those tapes and hearing the way I was altering as he would alter, neither of us copying each other. Like if there was a flurry of runs that he would do, I would take over; and if I did a flurry of runs, he would take over and it would just melt into one. That's music to me.

Have there been other people with whom you've shared this kind of musical relationship?

Not really, no. Not on such an electric level. Rod and I used to bounce off each other because that was just a simple blues-based rock band. I had a little bit of it with Max Middleton on a very low key. What was good about Jan's thing was that whatever shortcomings it had, it still had energy and life in it. And it was only the primary stages of what could have been something really good, but it was redundant from the start because he had his band and wanted to make himself a star with that band without having me in it. But he helped me become interested in rock music again, and I helped him get to where he wanted to go. At least he was able to play big, huge arenas with me where he wouldn't have on his own. So I've done my bit there.

Is the music you play for pleasure the same as what you record?

No. Isn't it funny! I'd really like to do that, but it never seems to work out that way. There's a free feeling about the stuff I play for myself. Obviously there's some wrong notes and things, but the freedom in the unrecorded stuff is really what should go on record. But it's always overindulgence, self-indulgence.

Do you find it easier to work within the context of a group where each member contributes?

It usually works out better that way. But at the same time, when you're playing live in a small room, there are all of the live frequencies there, and this sometimes blocks from your mind the essence of the tune. You don't notice this until they have gone home and you're listening to the tune turned down low on a little tape machine. Then you really hear the essence of it and how strong or how weak it is. There may be some great playing on it and the whole thing may be tight, but the guts of the thing just may not come across. It's amazing when you reduce it down to a small speaker and find out how little there is. And yet when you were playing live it sounded amazing because the sound was whitewashing a bit.

How equipment-conscious are you?

I'm not really worried about it. It's amazing — I've still got basically the same top to the Marshall amp that I had with Rod Stewart. It's the same chassis, same valves. One or two things may have blown up, but it's basically the same thing. In fact, some of the valves — the tubes — have rusted into their sockets and you can't take them out!

Have you kept certain guitars over the years?

Yeah, the ones that haven't been stolen. I've hung on to every guitar; I never sell guitars, really. In fact, one time I remember Max Middleton saying, "You've only got one guitar, and you've lost that." I used to have just one Strat because all the others had been ripped off. I had other guitars at different times, but they were all stolen and I wound up with one guitar. Then I lost that somewhere and thought, "Wow, I'm supposed to be a guitarist, and I haven't

got an instrument." This was back in '72 or '73. And then all of a sudden I looked around my front room the other day, and I've got about 70 guitars.

Do you go for the older, pre-CBS Fenders?

They're obviously the ones you would go for. Any guitar that feels right and sounds good is okay by me.

Do you shop for these guitars?

Never. I love guitars, but it's funny — I would never take the trouble to make an effort and go out and look for one. Even if I knew it was down the street, I wouldn't unless like the concert was going to suffer because I didn't have a good guitar. Then I might go down and look. I'm not a guitar collector fanatic.

What do you look for in a guitar?

I've got *my* guitar. It's a '50s Strat. It's just terrible, but it looks at me and challenges me every day, and I challenge it back. It has the vibrato, and it's difficult to play. It goes out of tune and all that, but when you use it properly, it sings to you.

Have your Strats been modified?

No, but I do little things to them. I kept breaking first and second strings every single night. The string was chafing backwards and forwards inside the tremolo setup, where it comes out through the block. So I just took a piece of piping — plastic stripped off a piece of wire — and slid the outer casing down the string and put it behind the bridge so that the string was resting on plastic. I never break a string now unless I really, really wind it up.

How do you set your action?

It's pretty high. It has to be because if you have it too low on a Strat, it plunks like a banjo.

Do you still use Gibson Les Pauls?

Not really. You just wind up sounding like someone else with a Les Paul. I think I can sound more like me with a Strat.

Do you consistently use any particular brand of strings?

No. I just get a bulk of strings, like two gross, and run through them. But I'm not really that fussy about strings. I start off with a soft gauge — really thin ones — if I haven't been playing in a long time. Within a few days, though, when the tips of my fingers are conditioned, I'm back on the heavy ones.

Do you use any effects?

I've got a booster — a modified tiny yellow box that was made by Ibanez. This gives me the same sound on the guitar, but louder. I don't like to have the tone changed too much because, hey, the guitar sounds great clean! But you want it to sustain and sound the same with a little more volume to it. And I have a Tychobrahe Paraflanger. They only made a few, and I've got two of the only ones left. They're amazing.

How much do you think equipment really matters to you musically?

It doesn't really matter. Sometimes you might pick up someone else's guitar and play a lot more inspired on that because it's just nice. And yet, having just said that, if you play it long enough and go back on your own guitar, you might be inspired by that. It's change — variety — that keeps the thing from kicking over.

Do you play much acoustic guitar?

No. They're a pain in the ass! You wind up sounding like some folksinger. I mean, John McLaughlin can play it better than anybody I've ever heard, so I'll leave it up to him. I'll never be like that, so I just sit around and enjoy what he does on it.

Do you experiment much with guitar synthesizers?

No. I've got one and can make it sound like the world is going to come to an end, but they're too unreliable. I used this one I've got, a Roland GS/GR 500, when we were in Spain. The equipment was set up in a bullring which they turned into a concert arena, and the sun was 110 degrees at lunchtime. Nobody covered up the synthesizer, and it was beating down on the control board. And I'll tell you what — that night, when it cooled off, all sorts of things were happening inside it.

Do you think there is much of a future in guitar synthesizers?

Only if they can keep the technique of playing like a guitar. Now if you have to alter anything, a lot of guys will need a lot of time to re-adapt to it. I admire what they've done so far — it's incredible — but if anything interferes with your fluid sort of playing, then you're in trouble. Or, if anything goes wrong onstage with them, which does happen, then they should be ruled out.

Do you keep right on top of the latest developments in guitar equipment?

Not really. You know how it goes: You might think, "Wow, I'm the first one to use this!" Sooner or later, you'll find out that somebody had it before you. I've just recently got a Chapman Stick, but I didn't actually search for it. I saw this guy playing it in a club, and I just thought he invented it. I had no particular desire to get one, but I just happened to mention to my manager, "This guy plays this weird stick thing really well. Let's go and see him." He went tick-

tick-tick up there in his head and went and bought one for me. So it was nice. I've got to mess around with it and see if I can make any tunes.

Where do you think the guitar is headed in its evolution?

It's a bit desperate. Los Angeles makes me worried. I was there for two days, and every time I was at the hotel I'd flick through the FM radio stations, and it just sounded like the same guy's album on every station. It got to the point where if you tuned in to a really good disco record, you were better off because there was more energy and less depression.

Are there any guitarists you feel are saying a lot with their playing?

Well, I really would like to answer that, but I don't get around enough to know. I've heard Steve Morse, and I was very impressed.

Do you still listen to John McLaughlin?

Yeah, but I find that I still go back to the old Mahavishnu Orchestra with him — *The Inner Mounting Flame* and *Birds of Fire*. Usually it works out that way — people play their best when there's a fusion in talent for the first time and the freshness is all there.

What do you think about when you're playing onstage?

Getting through [*laughs*], remembering things.

Do you usually try to avoid playing something the same way twice?

Well, it will happen. If you don't feel very well and are really ill or something you might fall back into old habits, but shoot, you're only human. I've never analyzed my playing because I don't like people taping things that aren't for real. I like to know if we're recording live. And yet having said that, I'd rather hear myself record a live album and not know I've done it. I still get a bit shaky when I know things are being recorded.

Do you ever listen back to what you've recorded and find that you've done things that you didn't know you were capable of?

Oh, yeah. That's neat. It's one of the neatest things about playing in this game, really. You have to keep it to yourself, though. You can't say to somebody, "Hey, listen to that!" I mean, I can play a solo on a record, and I can't even play it afterwards. It doesn't always happen, but there are some solos I can't play. In just a few hours I could probably learn it parrot-fashion, but that's just completely what I'm *not* into. Leave that thing alone and do something else, although it might be funny to sit down one night and work out exactly where I'm at.

Let's discuss a few of your techniques. When you're bending a string, how many fingers do you use?

Oh, I don't even know. It depends on how tired you are. One might do, but you might use two depending on what context the bend is in. The bend might be a slow blues, in which case you want to get your whole fist around the neck. Or it might be something really quick, and then it'll be a one-finger job.

What kind of slide do you use?

Just a piece of chrome steel tubing, and I wear it on my middle finger.

Do you have any guitars set up especially for slide?

No. I like to use the same guitar for slide, and since I have a fairly high action, it usually lets me get through on the slide things I do. I hate changing guitars; it's such a hassle unbolting one and bolting another one on. And they're always out of tune, no matter how carefully they are tuned. I've played all my life in standard tuning, too, because it would be disastrous to start twiddling around with the pegs on a Fender that's got a tremolo arm to tune it up to a slide.

What kind of picks do you normally use?

I've got the most rubbishy flatpicks ever. They're just dreadful. I forget what they're called now. They're horrible gray ones. The edges are all rough. But that doesn't make any difference because I don't use picks any more unless my fingers hurt or I've broken a nail. Usually I use my bare fingers, all of them I can. Sometimes I use all five. But if there's a rhythm to be played, then I use a pick for strumming the sharp chords.

Do you follow any conscious picking formulas?

No. My fingers just do what they do, and I have to follow along behind them. You are asking me questions that I ought to be able to answer, but I can't. I don't realize what I'm doing all the time.

When you're trying to learn something, do you follow the philosophy that slow is fast? In other words, learn all the notes to a passage before building up the speed?

Yeah, that's a pretty good rule of thumb.

Do you think that certain chords or keys have certain inherent moods?

Oh, yeah. Just by changing one note in a chord, you can change the whole meaning of the piece of music.

How much do you know of the technical side of music?

Nothing.

Can you read music?

I know enough to make myself understood when I don't like something. I can't read.

Do you have any systematic exercises or methods of practice?

No, I just pick up a guitar, and if I annoy myself within ten minutes, I'll put it down. If I'm not annoying myself, I'll keep going. In the winter I play on and off all the day, because usually the front door is frozen shut, and I can't get out anyway! I live in a large country house. I can't play if there's somebody else in the room. It makes me self-conscious.

Do you ever record your practice sessions to get ideas for songs?

The Japanese gave me a little tape recorder, and I used to record every phrase that came up. It just didn't seem to do anything. I would tape it and never play it back.

What's the hardest part of your repertoire?

There's a tune called "Space Boogie" [*There and Back*] that's pretty hard. It calls for listening and counting bars. It will come naturally after a few nights on the road. That way it will have had a public airing, and I'll understand more of what's to happen. But it's got to be great — that number is a killer!

Over the years you have been credited with pioneering many aspects of the rock guitarist's art, such as the use of feedback and fuzz. You've also been credited with pushing the sideman forward into the limelight. Some have said, in fact, that you were the first rock guitar hero. How much of this do you think is true, and how do you view your contributions?

I don't know [*long pause*]. That's a hard one to answer. All I know is that when the Yardbirds first came to America, all I ever saw were guys in blazers and ties playing stock-strung Fender Jazzmasters [*laughs*]. I suppose I did bring that freedom into the electric guitar, but that's just generalizing. My being a crazy lunatic made people think, "Wow! They might not like the music, but there's a chance. Now I don't feel embarrassed about opening up and playing." And if I've done that, then that's my job in a nutshell. Done.

Do you ever listen to Yardbirds stuff?

No. I find that a little bit too much of a blast from the past. It might upset me or make me feel good according to which tune it is and who's around when I play it.

What are your favorite cuts from that era?

I liked some of the stuff we did with Sam Phillips, the old producer for Elvis Presley. "I'm a

Man" [*The Yardbirds' Great Hits*] sounded all right. There's a kind of excitement there. It's still pretty hot, even if you play it now.

A lot of new-wave bands seem to have traces of the Yardbirds in them.

Oh, yeah. They sound just like the Yardbirds, but without any depth. Maybe the Yardbirds didn't have the technique or the frilly bits that you can get now in recording, but they had some magic, some depth.

It's amazing that the three guitarists in the band — Eric Clapton, Jimmy Page, and yourself — have each had a lasting impact.

Well, maybe not me. I'll tell you what — the crunch question is, "Would I swap places with anybody else?" The answer to that is no. You know, at one time you think, "Wow, would I like to be Pete Townshend! Would I like to be so-and-so. Do they have a better job than I have?" No, I wouldn't swap places with anybody, not in the last six years.

You've worked hard to expand the boundaries of your instrument.

That's my job. That's really what I'm trying to do. I'm not trying it; I'm just doing it.

Do you ever see Clapton?

I've been seeing him recently, and I really take a whole different view on him now because I've managed to get myself into a position where I can enjoy his playing. He no longer has anything to do with my style — you know, at one time we were blues. And he was better. I think he can play blues better than I can because he studies and is loyal to it. I'm not loyal — I try to hot-rod it up a bit and change it. But when I heard him play at a gig near his house the other day, I was so knocked out. He was slithering around with a slide guitar and sounding great! It was such a gas to see kids that had never heard him play in the Yardbirds or with John Mayall, and to see him blasting away at them. That was a buzz!

Do you ever hear from Page?

No. I don't ring him, and he doesn't ring me.

What was the origin of "Beck's Bolero"?

Oh Christ! That tune . . . Well, me and Jim Page arranged a session with [Who drummer] Keith Moon in secret, just to see what would happen. But we had to have something to play in the studio because Keith only had a limited time — he could only give us like three hours before his roadies would start looking for him. So I went over to Jim's house a few days before the session, and he was strumming away on this 12-string Fender electric that had a really big sound. It was the sound of that Fender 12-string that really in-spired the melody. And I don't care what he says, I invented that melody, such as it is. I know I'm going to get screamed at because in some articles he says he invented it; he wrote it. I say I invented it. This is what it was: He hit these *Amaj7* chords and the *Em7* chords, and I just started playing over the top of it. We agreed that we would go in and get Moonie to play a bolero rhythm with it. That's where it came from, and in three or four takes it was down. John Paul Jones on bass. In fact, that group could have been a new Led Zeppelin.

When one listens to some of the Yardbird cuts, you can hear where Led Zeppelin got some of its inspiration from you.

Yeah, they did. There's no doubt. Remember: When something has been deliberately or directly lift-ed from you, you either take it as a compliment or your heart starts pumping and you figure out which way the guy's going to die — whether with a pair of scissors or a gun or what!

What do you think when you hear people taking your licks?

That depends on if it's a horrible noise or not. If somebody says, "Wow! That sounds like you!" and it's a horrible noise, then I can do without it. But as long as my record sales are not being impaired or I'm not directly being thrown off course, then it's a compliment.

Was the tune "Blues Deluxe" on* Truth *recorded live?

No, it wasn't. It was live in the studio, but it was an accurate representation of what we were playing at the time. That's why we decided to make it sound live. We just needed more ambience to it, and we thought, "If we do that, we might as well put some people in there as well." All the time Hollywood movies have been tricking people; I don't figure that one track on an album is any sin.

What was your relationship with Jimi Hendrix like?

It was a bit difficult. We could never enjoy a real close friendship because of what we did. He and I were both after the wild guitar playing. I liked Jimi best when we didn't talk guitars. Like we used to go out — sometimes he'd be at the Scene club in New York and it wasn't happening, and he'd say, "Hey, come on, let's go." Then we would go to the Brass Rail, and all the time when we'd walk in the restau-rant, everyone would sort of be bugging us. Well, Jimi mostly. They'd say, "Hey, Jim, what's happening, man?" And I'd just sit and listen to all that. I'm still really sad about his not being here, because I need somebody around that I can believe in. I don't believe in anybody else.

Did your auto accident hurt your ability to play?

I had two accidents. I suppose they did. I suppose they must have slowed me a bit — it does when you get your head beaten around on a piece of concrete. You wake up and you're glad to be alive, and you do see things a bit differently. I honestly can't say how much it affected my playing. I can't tell whether it was natural to change or whether the crashes changed it.

Did you achieve the car horn sounds on Live **with your Strat?**

Yeah. It's just between fourths and fifths, slightly discordant. You just get two nails of the right hand, and as soon as you've plucked a bit by the bridge, you block the strings off with the left hand so the sound doesn't gradually die away. You let it go just long enough, and then by bending them down, it sounds like the Doppler effect, which is what you experience when, say, a fire truck comes along and you hear the siren at a certain pitch. Then when it goes past you, if you're stationary, the noise will die down. It's an audio illusion. That's just a funny thing be-cause the song was called "Freeway Jam" — you know [*mimics carnival barker*], "Hey, folks, the bloke can make it sound like a car!"

Near the end of Live **you threw in a little signature lick from "Train Kept a-Rollin'" Do you usually do this onstage?**

No, we were just pissed off at Aerosmith. I mean, I was known for playing "Train Kept a-Rollin'" with the Yardbirds, and these people would come up to me — and they weren't kids — they were saying, "Hey, I like your angle on the Aerosmith tune!" The Rock and Roll Trio's 1950s version of that song with Paul Burlison on guitar is bitchin'. That song is hot!

When you look back over your whole career, which tunes are your favorite?

I like "Bolero."

Do you think you've peaked yet?

No, I don't think I've peaked because it's been so spasmodic. You know, it's hard for me to think of a peak in these short periods. If I'd been playing all the time, I could say, "Well, June '77 was great, and then July wasn't so hot." But I can't answer that, really. It really makes me think about my career, though, when you dig out these questions.

— CHUCK BERRY —

By Tom Wheeler — March 1988

PAUL NATKIN

CHUCK BERRY came motorvatin' over the hill in the summer of '55, his Gibson ES-350T blaring and clanging like Maybellene's roadhog Coupe deVille. It was one of the most compelling and enduring images in pop culture: the loose-jointed, duck-walking hipster with the low-slung guitar, the happening threads, the wicked gleam in his eye.

Exploring his guitar playing requires a glance at his broader artistry, since both involve a mixing of musical styles. Chuck Berry was there when it all happened, or rather, he helped *make* it happen. Discussions of the birth of rock always entail terms such as "amalgamation" and "hybrid." Elvis Presley is invariably, and rightly, cited as the white man who broke character, the hillbilly who was steeped in gospel and country and yet loved black music, sounded like a black man, and sang the blues — or at least a new kind of blues.

Chuck Berry was the flip side of the Presley coin, the black man who broke character, who was steeped in blues and swing and yet loved country and western, routinely performed "Jambalaya" before he was famous, and sounded like a white man to many who first heard his records. Indeed, his debut album's liner notes characterized his style as "rockabilly," a term otherwise applied almost exclusively to Buddy Holly, Carl Perkins, and other white men.

Presley and Berry: two giants — one white, one black — standing shoulder to shoulder, both rooted in their respective traditions and yet each with one foot firmly planted in the other's territory. While this tidy analogy is far too simplistic to explain rock's deep and tangled roots, it suggests Berry's profound impact as a crosser of lines, a breaker of barriers. Still, the analogy is incomplete; the point is not that Elvis, Chuck, and others played "white" or "black" music, but rather that together they forged a new sound that helped obliterate such distinctions altogether. Disc jockey Alan Freed called it "rock and roll," and the name stuck.

Even if his writing, singing, and stylistic alchemy had not already secured him a place on rock's Mount Rushmore, Chuck Berry would be celebrated today for his guitar playing alone. His style was innovative in both sound and technique, and its ringin'-a-bell tone, jolting syncopations, slippery bends, and whole new vocabulary of double-stops simply changed the way the instrument is played. He reeled off his intros and fills the same sassy way he strutted the stage, the same way he rapped his finger-poppin' teen sagas. The look, the deft wordplay, the hipshot Gibson — all were integrated into some sort of transcendent Brown-Eyed Handsome Man persona, as if a guitar lick could have a pencil-thin mustache, as if a solo could swivel its hips. Never has a guitar style had more attitude.

Assessing this instrumental voice comes down to a choice of superlatives: Is it the most influential electric guitar style in history, or "merely" one of them? It's likely the most instantly recognizable (the first three seconds of a Berry hit usually suffice), as well as the most copied: For every bar-band performance of "Walk – Don't Run," "Purple Haze," or "Eruption," there have surely been 10 or 20 or 50 of "Johnny B. Goode," rock's perennial good-time guitar burner (there are over 100 recorded versions alone).

Revered the world over, his guitar style has reverberated throughout rock music, most apparently in the early songs of the Beatles and the Rolling Stones and often in the work of the estimated 500 other artists who have recorded his material, but also in the records of countless others who've borrowed from him to varying degrees. It was no surprise when John Lennon said, "If you tried to give rock and roll another name, you might call it 'Chuck Berry.' "

Charles Edward Anderson Berry was born on October 18, 1926, in a cottage at 2520 Goode Avenue in St. Louis, Missouri. The Antioch Baptist Church rehearsed in the living room, and Berry's very first memories are of music. As a youngster he was swept away by the melodies and rhythms of boogie-woogie, blues, and swing, and he soon found many favorites among the artists featured on St. Louis' black radio station: Tampa Red, Lonnie Johnson, Muddy Waters, and later T-Bone Walker, Louis Jordan, and others.

At a concert arranged by Sumner High School's class of '41 — the kind of show that usually offered sedate snoozers — Chuck belted out Jay McShann's "Confessin' the Blues." "When I began laying out the love lyrics, the school auditorium exploded with applause," he recalls in *Chuck Berry: The Autobiography*. "I realized as I was performing that the audience will respond if you give them what they want . . . ."

He worked as a carpenter, studied cosmetology, and dabbled in photography. After he and some pals stole a car, Chuck spent over three years in a reformatory, where he participated in Golden Gloves boxing.

Chuck had been playing a little guitar at parties by the summer of '51, when he bought a used reel-to-reel recorder. He began taping himself singing and playing, and a year-and-a-half later he landed a gig with a trio at the Cosmopolitan Club in East St. Louis. In '55 he traveled north to Chicago, where at the Palladium Club on Wabash Avenue he met the man he calls "my godfather." Muddy Waters advised him, "Yeah, see Leonard Chess. Yeah, Chess Records over on 47th and Cottage."

Mr. Chess asked Berry if he had any tapes, and Chuck replied that he could return with them on his next visit, which was technically true — despite the fact that he hadn't recorded them yet.

Seventy-seven days later, "Maybellene" skidded into the Top 10, spraying gravel all over tunes by the McGuire Sisters, the Nutmegs, and Frank Sinatra. By mid-September, it was the #1 rhythm & blues song in America, dethroning Bill Haley's mighty "Rock Around the Clock." By the time it faded, "Thirty Days" was already a Top-10 R&B song, as well. Chuck Berry had arrived.

After numerous disappointments and ripoffs, Chuck studied management, business law, accounting, and typing, evolving into a shrewd, self-protective businessman. Today, Chuck Berry runs his own business affairs.

During the past few years he received a Grammy for Lifetime Achievement, was a charter inductee into the Rock 'N' Roll Hall of Fame, gained his long-overdue star on Hollywood's Walk of Fame, and received *Guitar Player*'s Editors Award for Lifetime Achievement and membership to the magazine's Gallery of the Greats.

Well received by fans and critics alike, *Chuck Berry: The Autobiography* covers his life and career, as well as life on the road during the birth pangs of rock. It's a riveting story of a man who not long ago celebrated an emotional, triumphant concert at the same St. Louis theater where decades before he had been refused admission because of the color of his skin.

That concert, a 60th-birthday tribute, is the centerpiece of *Chuck Berry: Hail! Hail! Rock 'N' Roll*, a must-see documentary offering interviews with Bo Diddley, Bruce Springsteen, Little Richard, Jerry Lee Lewis, and others, as well as the rip-it-up concert by Berry and his backup musicians, among them Keith Richards (who freely admits that he owes his career to Chuck Berry), Eric Clapton, Robert Cray, Linda Ronstadt, Julian Lennon, and Johnnie Johnson, Chuck's original piano player.

And yet despite the book, the documentary, and all the rest, Chuck Berry remains a veiled figure. As Keith Richards says in the film, "The more you find out about him, the less you know about him."

A few years ago, U.S. satellite Voyager I was blasted into deep space, past Jupiter and Saturn and on towards Neptune, four billion miles from St. Louis, Missouri. Onboard are recorded greetings to anyone who might encounter it. Among the messages representing planet Earth is a recording of "Johnny B. Goode," lending new meaning to the refrain "long live rock and roll." Maybe some day, countless millennia from now, across the universe, some unimaginable alien thing will be snapping its fingers (or whatever) and grooving on the ancient tale of the country boy who could play his guitar just like ringin' a bell.

Mystery surrounds the roots of your style. When developing it, did you first hear a melody and then locate it on the fingerboard, or did you think visually, moving through patterns?

I didn't know anything about style when I started. I mean, I knew what a style was, but I wasn't aware of having one myself. That sort of thinking was far too technical for me at that time. But putting a song together — now that did come in anticipation of a melody that I heard in my head, or it could be by jamming with someone, or hearing something someone else was doing and maybe thinking I might like it to go a little differently. But you say *my* style — see, I still do not recognize any style of my own.

In the film Hail! Hail! Rock 'N' Roll *you apply the phrase "nothing new under the sun" to your own playing.*

That's right. What I do is just a portion of all that I've heard before me — Carl Hogan with Louis Jordan and His Tympany Five [in the '40s and '50s], blues players like T-Bone Walker. Illinois Jacquet, too — big influence.

His guitar player?

No, Illinois himself! Tenor sax player. His choice of notes, his melodies, you'll hear it in my music if you know how to listen. Charlie Christian, too. "Solo Flight" [*Solo Flight*]! It's so great, man — it's a son of a bitch! I got the first 16 bars down, took me 30 years [*laughs*]!

Still, don't you recognize the Chuck Berry style when you hear someone else do it?

I know what you mean, but if someone can play everything I can play, and that's the way he plays, then maybe it's his style now. That's how I look at it.

But don't you hear more of Chuck Berry in Keith Richards than Carl Hogan in Chuck Berry? You downplay your accomplishments, but if you take away your influences, there's a lot of pure, concentrated Chuck left over.

Well, that's a good way to look at it. In between the various things I was doing with the Muddy Waters things and Illinois Jacquet and Carl Hogan — my leftovers in between — that's maybe where my own creation comes in [*holds two fingertips close together, suggesting a wee bit*], trying to link those things. But it's still just a portion of what I knew. No one can reproduce another person's mind exactly like him, and that difference in there is what's new, what

one would call my style. That's all I can say.

What was it in Carl Hogan's playing that attracted you?

Simplicity. He stuck to the I-IV-V, played mainly quarters and eighths, and played right *on* the beat.

Did you really borrow the "Johnny B. Goode" intro lick from him, as you've hinted?

I can't really say exactly, but he did something that influenced the way I do "Johnny," something similar.

Your fans might be surprised to learn that your early goal was to play big band music, backed up by horn sections.

But that's what I really wanted, I really did. Wanted to comp chords behind a big band and play swing tunes.

If you liked big band, why play rock and roll?

At the time I was in need of a house, and a wife, and looking forward to raising a family, and even my friend Ira Harris, who could really play, he couldn't find a job playing jazz, if you see what I mean.

If the money and opportunities had been the same in blues or big band, would you have played different music all these years?

Come on, man — don't make me answer that [*laughs*]! Maybe if the money was good, I'd've even had a few hairdressing salons, big chain of them.

What did you learn from your friend Ira Harris?

He was into jazz, and the way he could *manipulate* the sound [*scat-sings a jazzy, major-scale riff*], I knew I had to do that. He played a bit like Christian, and a lot of what he showed me is a part of what I do.

You studied Nick Manoloff's Guitar Book of Chords.

Yes, that book had it down so plain. Many of the fingerings I couldn't do at first, because I couldn't double up on the strings for those 6-string chords. But I struggled with it, then took music at Ludwig's Music in St. Louis, studying theory and harmony.

Many of your tunes share tempos, progressions, or keys. How do you keep them separate, give them distinct personalities?

My approach doesn't matter from a musical, theoretical way of looking at it. I'd like to remember just what I did back on the record, but it's not always that way, unless it's really distinct, like "Brown-Eyed Handsome Man." Hey, about these keys — did you catch what Keith was talking about [in the film]? Piano keys, and all that?

He observes that several of your classics are in E♭ or B♭, or other "unusual" keys for guitar.

I wonder if he knows what he's saying! Man, the

symphonies are in *B♭* or *E♭*! Those keys, they've been *around*! He said, well, rock guitar players play in *A*! Come *on*, baby! You can tell that Keith must be a modern rock player [*laughs*].

And you don't really have separate approaches to songs with similar structures?

No, in fact, sometimes I have to catch myself, and go back to the record to check on something. There may be a lawsuit coming up about someone using one of my guitar things on TV. My lawyer called and said, is this "Roll Over" or "Johnny"? I had to go play them and listen to them myself to see [*laughs*].

Do you visualize patterns now, when performing live, or watch the fingerboard when you play?

I'd have to say no. I'm watching the faces in the crowd, and that's very intriguing. I mean, I look once in a while to make sure I don't go *way* flat or *way* sharp, but around the same fret, no. I've got a fast eye, and it's just by feel now.

Have you noticed that people who approximate your sound often play a watered-down version — more pentatonic or bluesy, less moving around the fingerboard, less major-scale?

Give me an example.

In the 4-bar intro to "Johnny B. Goode," the last bar is:

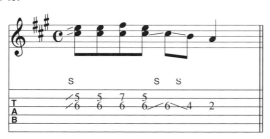

[*Slams the table, laughs*] Carl Hogan! Right there, that very figure! And this [*hums the head to "Solo Flight"*]! That's *it*, man! You're right, you've got to move around a bit to play that, and the Illinois Jacquet things, too.

Muddy Waters was your greatest career inspiration. Was he also a specific guitar influence?

Yes, I couldn't really get that inspiration without trying to actually play some of his things, and I still do, or try to, on my own blues. Definitely Muddy. His sound! That's what I played before "Maybellene" — before I turned pro, I guess you call it.

Were there other blues influences on your guitar playing?

Oh yes, Elmore James, T-Bone Walker; especially those two.

Do you see two distinct sides to your music, the rock and the blues?

Well, things like "Johnny B. Goode" and "Carol," those were for the mass market. "Wee Wee Hours" — that was for the *neighborhood*. But this isn't a black/white thing. That irks me. There's no such thing as black and white in music.

Roy Orbison had an impression of you as a black country singer. Was country music an influence?

Oh yes, I did it every night back in St. Louis before we recorded. It was called country, or hillbilly, or honky-tonk. We were doing "Mountain Dew," "Jambalaya."

This was your first band, with Johnnie Johnson on piano?

Yes. He had asked me to join his little group [Sir John's Trio] for a gig on December 31, 1952. We had Ebby Hardy on drums.

Who were your rivals around St. Louis at the time?

Ike Turner, over at the Manhattan Club. I'd have gone to see him more often, but we were always working the same hours. Me and Johnnie were at the Cosmopolitan Club, a big place that'd been changed over from a market, and we became quite popular, mainly with things by Nat King Cole and Muddy Waters.

How'd your hillbilly music go over?

That's a good question, with a very important answer. There's a great span in music, and variety I *cherish*. When you go to hear jazz, very often that's *all* you hear. Same thing with other types. But if you like *all* music, then variety adds to the performance. We'd do "Day-O" ["Banana Boat Song"] by Harry Belafonte, "Jamaica Farewell," then jump back with some Muddy, then some *sweet* Nat. No spirituals, though. I always say, when you sin, go ahead and sin. When you ask forgiveness [*laughs*], you know — keep it separate!

After hearing "Maybellene," Leonard Chess expressed surprise that country music could be written and sung by a black man. Did it seem like a country song to you?

Definitely. When I was growing up, the country people played fiddles and all that, but then there were these pianos, and these saxophones, and I liked it all — very much into it.

Is it possible to draw a line between '50s country and early rock and roll, or between '50s boogie and early rock and roll?

No, you can't draw *any* lines like that. You can't draw a line between science and religion, man! Even the edge of a razor blade is round if you get up close to it. It's like a shadow on the wall, no sharp edges. These people like Linda Ronstadt, coming out of rock and then doing country — you see what I mean? No lines.

At the end of Hail! Hail! you're playing a pedal steel. Is that "Blues for Hawaiians" or "Deep Feeling"?

I'm just improvising.

It sounds like the same instrument you used on those two cuts in the '50s.

No, it was rented for the movie. On the records I used a Gibson Electraharp. *Expensive?* It set me back five hundred *back then!* I'd seen someone playing blues on a steel guitar — took me *home,* Jack! And Elmore, too — he turned me on to that sound through his playing. And Muddy, with that slide [*mimics a slow, grinding blues turnaround and sings*]: "Mercy, mercy, baby!" Now *that's* blues! And do you know what? I wish there was just some way I could bring Muddy's blues to the white populace. I mean, not even all the black people know. Like I said, it's not a black and white thing. I've seen some of the white brothers: Yes, *sir!* Tonight we gonna play some Muddy! And they've got heart. Lord, they're close to him; they're right on his ass! And I look up, and I know Muddy looks down and just loves it so much!

Was Leonard Chess looking for something in particular? Did he guide you?

He just wanted to capture the sound I'd had on the tape I made at home on my little $79, 1/4", machine. He thought it was hilarious, in a way, and he knew how to market it as a product.

You did 36 takes of "Maybellene." Was that typical of those early sessions?

No, the next one was six takes. See, sessions were supposed to be six hours, and if you went overtime, you kicked it up to a higher rate, so they kept track, but we were just glad to be there. We also did "Thirty Days," "Wee Wee Hours," and "You Can't Catch Me." We had the trio — Johnnie on piano, and Ebby Hardy on drums. [*Ed. Note: Other sources name Jasper Thomas as the drummer on "Maybellene" and "Thirty Days" and Otis Spann as the pianist on "You Can't Catch Me"; according to Mr. Berry, Johnson and Hardy appeared on both tracks.*]

Whose idea was it to add Willie Dixon on acoustic bass for those first sessions?

Leonard Chess.

What did you think of the added bass sound?

Well, in the first place, I didn't see myself as hav-ing any authority to kick about it. I was glad for it to be there, anyway. It was a professional sound, a fuller sound.

But you didn't take a bass on the road.

No, me and Johnnie were so compatible, and the way I play, when I go down into the lower area of the guitar, I want it to sound real boomy already. I liked bass, and it would've sounded better, but it would've meant paying the extra air fare. I liked the way the piano could solo, and even the drums, but when you give a bass player a solo, he feels like he's got to do something *jazzy,* you know, and a bass doesn't really have an appetizing tone for take-off. It's a backup instrument.

What'd you think of electric bass when it came along?

Technology, I'm very much in favor of it. I was into the electric bass. It sounded good, but even if it didn't sound as good as the acoustic, it was so much more easy to carry, more practical.

Many of the early records have a great reverb sound, such as on the solo to "Sweet Little Rock and Roller."

On the first ones, like "Maybellene," we didn't have reverb, but later when I used Fender amps, I would just use the reverb right on the amp.

Did you have any control over the editing and mixing of the tapes?

Not one iota. They could cut 'em any way they wanted. And not always the right way, like sometimes they'd mess up an ending instead of fading it right.

Some of those early hits — "Reelin' and Rockin'" and "Sweet Little Rock and Roller," for example — have an unusual, sub-surface rhythm, not exactly straight 4/4 rock. There's a walking bass rather than straight eighths, and the drums sometimes lean toward swing or a shuffle. It's a hybrid of sorts, accenting 2 and 4. Was that conscious, or somewhat accidental?

It was both. See, Johnnie and I had such a thing together that we didn't have to talk about anything, just do it. But now, with these pick-up bands — like last night I had to go back to the bass player during the performance and holler at him about a few inches away from his face, to play what I wanted. Another time during the same show I had to talk to the drummer. Syncopation is a very important part of what I do, but you can't let everybody syncopate. Somebody has to be doing straight rhythm to give you something to syncopate against. Like this [*taps a straight 4/4 beat and sings the familiar bent-note figure from bars 5 through 8 of the "Johnny B. Goode" intro]*:

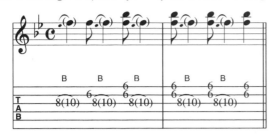

There's a characteristic rhythmic accent you do with staccato partial chords:

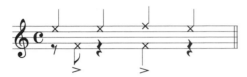

[*Hops up and laughs*] Harry James! "One O'Clock Jump," man! Listen to the trumpets! I keep telling 'em, it's big band, but they want to call it rock and roll!

In the film, when Keith Richards observes that some of your songs are in "piano" keys, he seems to be getting at Johnnie's influence on you. Did you sometimes adapt his piano style to guitar?

No, I don't know what he was talking about. First, Johnnie does not have a style; he has an *ability* to fill in over a progression, to play a solo. He and I discovered a harmony together, where I could be playing, then lay off for just two beats, and he'd pick it up, fill it out. I could just look back at him, and we had such a complete sense of each other that no other communication was necessary.

But how important was Johnnie to your style? Would you have played differently if you'd teamed up with another piano player?

No, I would have just had to play *more*, that's all.

Your early records have a unique overall atmosphere. Did you imagine a specific sound and experiment until you got it, or was it unpredictable?

Sometimes planned. Like when we were recording "Wee Wee Hours" [1955], it was inspired by Big Joe Turner. Then "Wee Hour Blues" [1965] was inspired by a particular *song* of Big Joe Turner's, "Wee Baby Blues," and when I recorded, I was trying to recreate the mood of that song.

In May '55 you were doing some carpentry and studying cosmetology; three months later your first record was #5 in the Hot 100 and #1 on the R&B chart. How did the almost literal overnight success change your life?

The only thing it changed was my determination to follow through as long as it could go. My lifestyle did not change one bit. I had been saving 80% of my income as a carpenter, and I saved 80% of my income as a musician.

Was fame what you had expected?

No, because I didn't expect it! I was making $21 a week at the Cosmo, and it went to $800 a week after "Maybellene." I didn't give a *shit* about the fame, and you can print that. Still don't. The only thing I cared about was being able to walk into a restaurant and get served, and that was something I should have had anyway, *without* all the fame. See, this was 1955, and all the [civil rights] marching and things were about to start. I liked the idea that I could buy something on credit and the salesman knew I could really pay for it. I could call a hotel, and they wouldn't automatically offer me the economy rooms after hearing how my voice sounded. *That* I admired.

In the late '50s you were on several whirlwind package tours. Did all the stars and musicians travel together?

Yes, on a couple of buses, or a couple of planes. We hit the Apollo Theatre in Harlem, the Howard in Washington, D.C., the Regal in Chicago, and we did Baltimore, across Canada, all around the South, Texas. We were out with LaVern Baker, the Platters, the Spaniels, the Orioles, the Cleftones.

Do you remember your first big white audience?

The Paramount in Brooklyn, shortly after "Maybellene" in '55. Damn near totally white, Tony Bennett on top of the bill.

What were your feelings upon going out on that stage?

Just that it wouldn't happen again. That was only our fifth engagement, and we really thought the whole thing would last for just a few months.

What did you think when your music was first reworked on a wide scale by the Beatles, the Stones, and others? Did you like the newer versions?

Did I like it? That doesn't come under my scrutiny. It struck me that my material was becoming marketable, a recognizable product, and if these guys could do such a good job as to get a hit, well, fantastic. I'm just glad it was my song.

After you left Chess for Mercury in 1967, your records had a different sound.

Yes, for the first time I didn't really have an A&R [artists & repertoire] man telling me how to play for a certain market, and also I now had a whole band. I hired Billy Peek's band as sidemen.

Mercury just wanted me to re-record my hits so they could have masters of their own, about 18 tunes.

Are they as good as the Chess originals?

Not as good, because I couldn't get them to play like Johnnie.

Do you remember your very first guitar?

I remember my first electric. I got it from Joe Sherman, who played *The Sacred Heart Club*, a religious program on WEW in St. Louis. He'd got a new one, so he let me have his old one for $30. I was making $10 a week, and he let me take it after I'd paid a $10 installment. I really started to play a lot after that — it looked so good, you know, and it was easier to play than the other ones I'd had.

A couple of the earliest pictures show you with an Epiphone noncutaway arch-top electric.

I never recorded with it. Those pictures were taken before "Maybellene." And I had a little matching Epiphone amp. It was just so beautiful, made out of maple — the whole thing was lovely wood — and on the front of it was a carved *E*, or maybe a treble clef sign.

Did you ever record with that amp?

No, when we went up to Chicago I had one of the little Fenders with the flat control panel carved out of the back, and the whole thing was covered with a leatherish, funkyish, tableclothish [*laughs*] material.

On those first Chess sessions, were you using the blonde Gibson ES-350T arch-top hollowbody you were so often pictured with?

Yes. I probably got that guitar at Ludwig's Music in St. Louis. It's at home now.

In Alan Freed's movie Rock, Rock, Rock, *you perform "You Can't Catch Me" with a little Gretsch Chet Atkins solidbody. Did you ever record with it, or was it just a prop?*

I didn't record with it; they might've just handed it to me for the movie taping. I did have a Gretsch for a while, but it was a big one, hollowbody. That was the only one I ever bought. And for a while I used a black Les Paul [a Custom, with single-coil pickups] at the Cosmopolitan Club.

The semi-hollow Gibson ES-355s you've been using for years have humbucking pickups, while your first 350 had single-coils.

Those two are really just about the same to me. One body's a bit thinner, the newer one. I haven't really paid that much attention to the sound. What made me get the Les Paul was the way it felt. It had these flat frets, and it was comfortable and seemed to never wear out, and it stayed in tune. My big Gretsch was heavy, so I like the hollowbody Gibsons. The lighter the better. Otherwise, doesn't matter. I don't notice the difference, unless it's got extra reach up the neck, like on a Fender. Range is important, getting up the neck. I've always liked a Fender, but I've never bought one because they don't do much in hollowbodies.

Your tone these days is noticeably different from the early records. Do you ever get the urge to get a big old hollowbody with single-coils and crank it up?

I'm telling you, there's no difference. It was all in the mixing board and the types of control knobs. They can make it sound different ways. I think they even pushed up the speed on my voice on the early Chess things [*sings, ascending*] to make my voice sound higher and higher so that I'd sound like the teenagers. I was 29 years old — I had two children!

On the cover of the autobiography you're holding one of Gibson's Lucille models, with no f-holes. Was that just handed to you for the photo?

No, that's mine; I use it.

Do you modify your guitars?

No.

Effects?

Tried a wah-wah once. Stubbed my toe on it [*laughs*]. Forget it.

You've written rock and roll songs about cars and teenagers, and you've written blues. Which songs mean the most to you, which style?

How can you love one child more than another? I love all my children, yet I love none of them. What I mean is, it's not this song, or that song. To me, the story of "Johnny B. Goode" is no more interesting than "Our Little Rendezvous," which is sweet, but no more sweeter than "Sweet Little Sixteen." So what counts is the response to a song from the audience, and it can come in one song or the other.

Do you play guitar when you're by yourself or just with a few friends?

Not a lot. There's my park, Berry Park, to manage. We've had dances out there, and we've renovated, and I've got real estate to take care of and all the touring. Too many irons in the fire.

When you tour, do you require promoters to furnish specific equipment, certain kinds of backup musicians, and so on?

Oh yes, these things are important. We'll send you a rider. [*Ed. Note: The rider to Berry's contract specifies that the promoter will provide "three (3) professional (AF of M) musicians, capable and familiar with Chuck Berry's music, to serve as a back-up group which must consist of only a 'show' drummer with drums, a pianist and a grand piano, an electric bass guitarist with a bass guitar . . ." and also "two (2) unaltered Fender Dual Showman Reverb amplifier sets."*]

What's left? What are your musical goals for the future?

To put some of the actual things you've been asking me and get it down on video, where young people and upcoming musicians, if they really want to, can see organized lessons about some of these questions and answers, and see about the execution of my music, my improvisations and innovations, if I can use that word — almost like Jane Fonda did with her dancing.

What did you think of "Johnny B. Goode" being sent into space aboard Voyager?

There are many, many records that I thought equaled it, and I don't object to it being chosen. Other than that, I guess I'm just a lucky guy.

Your fans never tire of hearing that song. Do you ever get tired of playing it?

No. Because of the former, because they never get tired of hearing it.

When you finally decided to write your autobiography, you specifically excluded any ghostwriters.

That's a fact. For one thing, I didn't want to pay anyone for something that might never have even been bound up. I thought it might just stay in the family, never really be published. But man, if I had any idea that this book would be so appreciated as it already has been just up till now, I would have taken another year on it.

You generally don't give interviews to magazines.

The last few years I've been doing some, but the reason why I didn't before is that I've found that if you don't give one, then they'll interview other people to get them to talk about you, and because you wouldn't talk to them, you get sort of a rasping article. Even when you do talk to them, it's juiced up and taken out of context. Way back years ago, [one magazine] had me saying "lawdy" [*winces*]. I don't say "lawdy"!

Does Hail! Hail! provide a reasonably accurate portrait of the real Chuck Berry?

I figure it like this: What does it matter what they think of me as a person? I've already had some idea of what they think of me as a product, as a music inspiration, so what they think of me as a person has nothing to do with my music. The person who would condemn someone for their personality, and infiltrate that condemnation into their product — well, it really doesn't matter.

Did you enjoy making the film?

I enjoyed the results. It was tiring, and there were some brand-new things about it that inspired me, and the part that I did was me, so that part of it was easy. The whole procedure brought out some parts of me that did not have to be in the film, although now I'm glad they were, because it shows more of the specific me. See, the truth in fact means a mighty lot to me. The actual, scientific value is the reality of a thing. Everything out there on that stage is real. The only thing I might change is if I'm tired, or maybe angry, I won't portrait that because in this business the people expect to be entertained. If I'm down, now *that* I can try and curb — the show must go on, and all that. I can fake down my hurt, but I won't fake up my status, so to speak. I don't think I'm too modest, but I will never be any bigger than I portrait myself.

— LARRY CARLTON —

BY DAN FORTE – MAY 1977 AND BY JAS OBRECHT – JUNE 1989

JON SIEVERT

PLAYED WITH GREAT heart and near-perfect technique, Larry Carlton's *On Solid Ground* celebrates life itself. It's the soul-searching music of a survivor, a man who's looked death in the face — on April 6, 1988, to be precise — and lived to tell the story. On that afternoon, Carlton had just come home to work on a recording. "I was standing at the west end of the room, talking to my secretary at the east end," he explained to *Jazztimes*. "Through the window near her desk I saw a German Shepherd dog run under the carport, with two black kids jogging after it. So I went to shut the door so the dog wouldn't come in the office. As I got to the door, one of the kids just raised his hand and fired a gun. He stood there and watched until I fell, and then he ran off. The amazing thing is that I actually had eye contact with him as I was falling." The .357-magnum slug struck Larry's neck, severing his carotid artery and causing his arm to go numb.

Paramedics rushed Carlton to a hospital where a thigh vein was grafted onto his carotid artery. Ten days later, he came home to begin physical therapy. "There were nights," he told *People,* "where my whole body would convulse and literally hurl me off the couch. The pain was so bad I'd break into tears. Sometimes it lasted all night.

"When I would try to pick up an acoustic guitar, my arm would shake and the instrument would fall. I couldn't push the strings down hard enough to get a tone. The first time I picked up an electric guitar and

bent a string, oh, Lord, did it hurt." Today, Larry reports that he's regained full playing skills, although his voice still sounds closer to Dirty Harry's than to the Larry Carlton of old.

The eight-month career standstill wrought by the stranger's bullet (the case is still unsolved) was preceded by an amazing string of successes that began back in the early '70s, when Larry became the man with the golden touch during Los Angeles' busiest studio era. Known as Mr. 335 (due to his preference for Gibson ES-335 guitars), Carlton was renowned for delivering the right part at the right time. His hits with Steely Dan, the Crusaders, Barbra Streisand, and others in more than 3,000 sessions served as a springboard for a solo career, which began with a self-titled debut album in 1978.

Carlton has released numerous solo albums and picked up the highest musical honors: "Most Valuable Guitar Player" (awarded several times by the Los Angeles Chapter of NARAS), Best New Jazz Guitarist (*Record World*), several Grammy nominations, and two Grammy Awards: 1981's Best Pop Instrumental Performance for "Hill Street Blues" (with Mike Post) and 1987's Best Pop Instrumental Performance for "Minute by Minute," from *Discovery*. His return "to the electric side" after various acoustic releases for MCA, *On Solid Ground,* was about six-tenths completed at the time of the shooting. A testament to Larry's resiliency, the LP's scrappiest instrumentals — covers of Derek & The

Dominos' "Layla" and Steely Dan's "Josie" (he played on the original) — were recorded after the injury.

Your new music is strikingly positive.

When you have to stare at reality, you get to make a choice: Is this going to be a real negative event in my life, or is it going to be a positive thing? And I choose to make it a positive thing. That's not to say that I don't daily live with the frustration of my voice. It's a drag, man, not to have full use of all your capacities, but it could have been so much worse.

You could have been a singer.

I could have been nothing. So I'm working on it.

Has your injury left you unable to play certain things?

No, thank God. I'm completely back as far as playing goes. The overdubbed guitar part in "The Philosopher" was the first thing I did after the shooting. For that performance, I ended up down here in the studio by myself, in pain, trying to make music. The guitar part in "On Solid Ground" was also overdubbed after the injury, and that's when I did "Josie" and finished "Layla," too.

Was the time spent as a studio musician — especially in the Steely Dan days — a good era in your life?

Oh sure, definitely. Those records — some of them are 12 or 13 years old, and they still hold up. They are just great songs. That time I spent in the studio sure has paid off for everybody. I was fortunate to be involved in making some timeless music with great pop writers of our day.

Do you have ways of psyching yourself to play at the outside edge of your ability?

That's a habit now. I think after playing so many years and always stretching, it doesn't feel good to me unless I'm going for it. Why make the music if it's not a personal involvement? So every time I play with the guys, it's like trying to hit a grand slam. Even if it's one note, it's that important.

Did you take guitar lessons as a kid?

Yes, I studied eight years with the same teacher, a local guy named Slim Edwards, in Torrance, California, where I grew up. I started when I was six-and-a-half.

Were you a good student?

Yeah, I played all the time. I practiced my lessons from the teacher an hour a day, and then I jammed all the rest of the time, learning licks off Elvis Presley records. And I was always in a rock or country band.

Did your teacher direct you towards jazz?

Not at all; he didn't play any jazz. He had a style that I don't even know the name of. He didn't even use a pick; it was kind of a flogging technique. He started me on the pick, probably for three or four years, and after that I spent two years just studying the fingerstyle technique, but not classical — it was different. I learned the bastardized version of "Malagueña" and "Tico Tico" — not the legit versions; these were arrangements the teacher had learned and changed. And I would learn them by ear, not with written music.

What was your first exposure to jazz?

Probably a Gerald Wilson big band album called *Moment of Truth* with Joe Pass on it. I heard Joe playing on that when I was in junior high, and it really turned me around.

Did that lead you to buy all kinds of jazz records?

Yes, a bunch. I got into [saxophonist] John Coltrane a lot, [guitarist] Johnny Smith — a lot of guitar albums. I used to listen to Barney Kessel, too.

Did you get interested in blues guitar at an early age?

When I was 16 I heard a B.B. King album that was made in the mid-'50s. I was at my grandmother's house, because my dad and all of his brothers were blues freaks when they were kids. That was the first blues record I heard, and that's the only blues album I owned for four or five years. I used to listen to that album before I'd go to my gig — my six-nighters, you know. I digested one concept from B.B.: He plays very little, but it means a lot. And I've always appreciated that in all instrumentalists. I was never really into flash, although I probably play flashier now than I ever have. It's something that I've grown into, and it's fun. The audience likes it, and it's another form of expression. But I would still say that my basic concept involves fewer notes than most people play.

Would you say that that's the most distinctive element of your style?

Yes, the taste I try to exercise in playing and also the sound I get out of the instrument. And the feeling is definitely a prerequisite for me. I can't play unless it means something. I surround myself with players that are in the same frame of mind and feeling. Of course, everybody plays with feeling. How can anyone say that John McLaughlin doesn't play with feeling just because he's not playing the blues? He's playing what *he* feels.

Who were some other guitar influences?

B.B. King and Wes Montgomery. I later took two lessons from Joe Pass — once when I was 16 and when I was 17.

Did you go to him to learn any specific techniques?

I just wanted to learn how to play jazz the way he did. The first time I went to him he showed me, basically, just some substitutions he uses while he's blowing; but harmonically I really wasn't ready for him. I'd thought I was, but when I got there he could see that I was at the very beginning stages harmonically. So I didn't go back to him for a year, because I realized that I had a lot of homework to do before I could understand what this guy was trying to tell me.

Did you study out of any method books?

It was mostly off records, by ear, and from playing all the time. I never studied out of any books — I didn't know that there were any at that time. By the time I was aware of any of those well-known books, I had already advanced to the stage where I knew everything that was in them.

Did you ever aim at developing an identifiable sound and style?

No, it just happened. It was there to be had. My playing has always been, and probably always will be, *sweet* sounding. Even when I play the blues, my choice of notes and the way I bend the strings sound sweeter than an "authentic" blues player. Robben Ford is almost the other extreme. I can't remember a time I've heard Robben really sound sweet; it always sounds sort of street-level, raunchy. He and I became very close, and I enjoyed his playing so much I knew I wanted to get farther into the blues — like Albert Collins. When I was about 16 Michael Allsup from Three Dog Night turned me on to Albert Collins' record of "Frosty." Oh, man! I loved it. But my blues playing used to sound more like country blues. So I would go downstairs at my house late at night and jam along with B.B. King or Albert Collins records and be aware that, "Oh, I played there and he didn't," or "I bent this way to the 7th, and listen, he bent to the 6th." There are certain technical points you can get down when you're trying to go for that sound.

Did you get interested in rock guitar in much the same way?

No, it took a hippie girlfriend — turned me on to Led Zeppelin. And the only solo of theirs that I can honestly say I ever liked was Jimmy Page's on "Whole Lotta Love" [*Led Zeppelin*], and then I read in *Guitar Player* that he'd worked it out before going into the studio. But that solo was a masterpiece.

Did you like Jimi Hendrix much?

No, my head wasn't anyplace near that when he was happening. Steve Lukather, the guitar player in Toto, brought all of his Hendrix albums over once when I was going to Japan. I taped them all and listened to about two of them on the plane, and I liked the effects, but it was a little too primitive for me. But I really liked the solos Eric Clapton played on the early Cream albums. What a sound, what a choice of notes.

Can reading charts stifle your imagination as a player?

It can be stifling only because you're playing licks all of the time — you're not stretching out, you have a three-minute tune.

Who were some of the first studio guitarists you met?

That all happened real quickly once I started doing dates; I met everybody within six months, you know. I know Louie Shelton was one of the first guys I met. He influenced me a lot.

In what ways?

Taste, mainly. Louie really opened my eyes in terms of recording. He was playing what I liked to hear, so I emulated a lot of things he was doing. He could take two or three notes, and they were so right you'd always hear them on the final record. Other guys would play all the way through, and you'd never hear them on the record. See, if the part's not right, the engineer or producer is going to mix the guitar way down low — or take it out. But with Louie they always mixed him very hot.

Is economy his main forte?

Yes, and also the sound he gets. He used to play a Byrdland through a Fender Princeton. On the backs of albums they used to call him Sweet Louie Shelton, because it was just the sweetest sound. In fact, other players used to call him the Miles Davis of the guitar — economy.

Is your style influenced a lot by musicians who play instruments other than guitar?

Not directly. It's more a gradual thing that came about just over the years that I've been playing. The one thing that I've always gotten into heavily, as I've said, is playing fewer notes. There's an album by John Coltrane called *Ballads*, and on the whole album all Coltrane does is play the melody, and it's beautiful. It's a great lesson for me in how to *phrase* a melody and make music out of it, rather than just making it sound like a melody. I put that album on every two or three months and just listen to John phrase the melody.

What sorts of changes did you see taking place in the studio scene while you were a part of it?

Well, when you go in to do a session, first off

there is always protocol in anything you do. So if I do a date and [Tommy] Tedesco is on it, I'm not going to sit down in chair number one. I mean, even if I can cut it, that is not the personable thing to do. You respect the guy. Tedesco has been around forever; he's great. Years ago when I was just getting started, I was a young guy. So if I walk in and ask the contractor who's on the date, and he says, "Tommy Tedesco, Dennis Budimir, and you," I'm going to sit down in chair number three. Out of protocol if nothing else, because I respect those gentlemen. And they respect me; if Tommy comes across a rock and roll solo he might say, "Hey, Larry, play this shit, will you? That's why you're here." You know what I mean? Our whole approach was brotherhood. We were all there for the same reason — do the job, make some money, and go home — and there was no ego.

Has that attitude changed?

It started changing in about 1974 or '75, so that the veteran — whether it be me or Tommy — would come to a date and one of the new players would already be set up with all his stuff at chair number one. Just the vibe was like a slap in the face. And then your ego says, "Well, what's this little fart doing?" So you take chair number two and let the guy do his thing — unless the leader says, "Hey, wait; Tommy, you were supposed to be playing that part." Or you might get to a record date and nothing's designated, and the producer says, "Larry, why don't you play some fills behind the vocal on this one," and "So-and-so, you play some rhythm parts." And then the guy on the rhythm chair still plays licks; he plays his rhythm, but when there's an opening he tries to fill all the holes, or most of them. It's just disrespect, and that's showing off. It's uncalled for in any business. Whether you can play better than the guy in that chair or not has nothing to do with it. It's protocol.

Some studio players have talked about a phase they experience after gaining a reputation, and it involves checking the charts and counting up the number of hits they appear on. Did you ever go through that?

Years ago I definitely did. I'd look at the Top 100 and tell my wife, "My God, I'm on 12 out of the Top 100 this week." But to beat that, Louie Shelton was once on six out of the Top 10. He played the solo on "Diamond Girl," by Seals & Crofts, for example. I always wanted to have the ultimate taste that I thought Louie had.

What sorts of technical questions do younger guitarists ask you most often?

Usually, they want to know about my approach to thinking chord upon chord, as opposed to linearly. That's a real difficult thing to explain, because a lot of times the notes come out the same, except I am thinking a different way. For example, if somebody is playing a *Cmaj7* chord, when I play a *D* note, I think of it out of a *G* triad — whereas another guitarist plays a *D* note against *Cmaj7* and thinks of it as the 9th of the C major scale.

Why is it easier to approach it from the G triad?

The G major chord, or triad, is *G, B,* and *D,* and it sits right on top of the C chord, which is *C, E,* and *G.* For the *Cmaj7* that the rhythm is playing, I'm looking at my solo as coming from a *Cmaj9* chord, and you get a *Cmaj9* — which is *C, E, G, B,* and *D* — by adding the *C* triad and the *G* triad. So I don't think of the *Cmaj7* in the rhythm as one chord; I think of it as a C chord and a G chord at the same time.

What's the result?

One result is that my interval relationships get wider, because I'm not thinking linearly. I'm leaving out connecting notes that other players might throw in all the time.

So what you're playing for the Cmaj7 *chord in the key of* C *might work just as well in the next song in the key of* G?

Exactly. It's not just in one location, this *G* triad on top of the *C* triad; it's all over the fingerboard. What I'm thinking of as part of the *Cmaj7* extension — the *Cmaj9* — is what other people would probably call just playing in the key of *G,* though a lot of times I'll end up on notes that'll tie in the key center. So thinking in terms of scale degrees is usually not my approach when I'm jamming. The notes I pick out are often out of some chord superimposed on the root chord, rather than notes out of that scale.

Do you often do the same sort of thing with a I-VI chord relationship, such as C *to* Am7?

No, that relationship doesn't strike my ear as good. Sometimes I might do it, but for, let's say, an *Am* rhythm pattern, more often than not I would think of maybe an *Em7* chord or a *G* chord, and resolve it to a *C* chord; I'd play all around that *Am.*

"Point It Up" on Larry Carlton *has some amazing playing on it. Isn't that a three-chord progression in a minor key?*

Yes, it goes *Gm* to *C,* then *Gm* to *Em9.* When I'm playing that fast, instead of thinking of the two triads I will tend to play more linearly, more scale-oriented. *But,* when it goes to the third chord, that *Em9,* more often than not I'll be thinking of a *D* triad in there someplace, which also leads back into the *G* chord very nicely.

Did you ever go through a stage of working off scales and licks?

Licks, yes — but not scales. Somehow, early on when I was into trying to understand the harmonic concept, it just intrigued me as soon as I was exposed to polytonality. It caught my interest to sit at the piano and spell out a *Dm* chord and just keep taking that extension up on the white keys, stacking thirds, and it comes out a *C* chord and a *G* chord — all the triads built on top of one another. So I started applying that to the guitar.

Do you find that thinking chord upon chord transposes into visual patterns that work conveniently?

Yes, it always does. Scales go from whole-step to half-step or whatever, while triads are spelled out very wide. That gives me those wider intervals I mentioned. Lots of people wonder, "Why do you play such strange notes?" I'm just picking them out. I have a lot of choices thinking of triads.

Does that method make for a wider range of possibilities when soloing?

I couldn't say more possibilities, but it definitely makes for a different sound. It wasn't until a couple of years ago that I even started thinking of ways to play off of scales. Scales are a good way to flash, and they're a good way to tie things together if you have to.

What sorts of things do you practice?

Real simple stuff, like major scales, just to limber up. Actually, though, I don't practice at all. After I started doing sessions in 1969, working all the time, there was just no time to practice.

Weren't there other disciplines you needed to learn, such as sightreading, when you first started doing studio work?

I never practiced sightreading. I've been reading all my life. Remember, we're talking about one individual who's been playing since he was six years old.

Could you describe your picking technique?

It's almost all up-and-down, except when I'm playing blues. Unless it's a gliss of some kind all my bebop is up-and-down, except I don't pick all the notes. That's the difference between my style and some other guys'. Al Di Meola picks almost every note; Lee Ritenour picks every note. I'll pick one note and do a lot of slurs and a lot more bends than most of those guys do. When I'm playing blues, I usually use a lot of upstrokes. The attack is different, the feel is different, the accents are all different.

Do you have ways of psyching yourself to play at the outside edge of your ability?

That's a habit now. I think after playing so many years and always stretching, it doesn't feel good to me unless I'm going for it. Why make the music if it's not a personal involvement? So every time I play with the guys, it's like trying to hit a grand slam. Even if it's one note, it's that important.

What attracted you to the 335?

I needed a guitar that I felt comfortable on, that I could play the way I liked to play — which was coming from a 175 approach but with a more contemporary sound. I needed something real versatile.

Which pickup do you play with most of the time?

About 90% of the time it's just the front pickup.

Other than your work with the Crusaders, what are good examples of your volume pedal technique?

I played on Joni Mitchell's *Court and Spark* album, and that has volume pedal on it. That was the first record she made with a rhythm section.

When you were doing sessions, did you have a whole array of gadgets?

Yes, I had the first Roland Chorus Ensemble in Los Angeles. Again, it was Dean Parks who told me they made a Roland sound in a box, as opposed to buying the Roland amp. Before that I had one of the first MXR compressors. I used an MXR phase shifter, and an Electro-Harmonix Small Stone phase shifter. Producers especially liked those things, because they wanted to hear new sounds. I had all that stuff, and went through them, and got hot on them, and then put them in the proper perspective.

Then is that tone and the sustain you get more a product of the guitar, your vibrato, or what?

Both. It's finding a special instrument set up the way I set my guitars up. The vibrato helps, but keeping the section high gives more sustain. So I decided years ago that I would give some technique to get it to respond the way I wanted it to. A lot of people think the action is too high; [session guitarist] Jay Graydon picks up my guitar and says, "Man, it sounds great, but I couldn't play this on one song."

And you always use brand-new strings?

Yes, I change them every set.

Would it really be noticeable if you changed them, say, every other set?

Yeah, they wouldn't stay in tune. I thrash the hell out of them for an hour and a half. They'll break during the next set if I don't change them. And I like for them to be perfectly in tune. When all that sweat gets on there, they won't stay at the right pitch.

Do you put the strings on the guitar any certain way?

As much bending as I do, they won't stay in tune

perfectly, but I can put strings on a guitar and do what I do to it and bend the heck out of them, and they're only going to slip less than a quarter-tone, which is just enough to where I have to keep touching them up during the set. I found that a minimum of three wraps is required at the top. If you go with just one or one-and-a-half wraps, it's not as secure. And when I put the string through the eye, I bring it back under and pull it up tight and wrap it at least three times. Then I go through the whole set of strings two or three times — tune them, take a rag, hold it at the 1st fret, really stretch them, tune them all back up, and do it again. I take all the stretch out of them, which does take a little bit of the brightness away — but they're in tune.

On Larry Carlton, *is the melody double-tracked on "Room 335"?*

Yes. Double-tracking works in instrumental music to strengthen the melody, especially when you do it with a guitar. It sounds bigger, and it also sets apart the theme for the solo — the solo is just one guitar. It creates a little more dynamics.

Was "Don't Give It Up" influenced by Jeff Beck's "Freeway Jam"?

Yes. Since it was my first solo album, I wanted to express myself in all the idioms that I enjoy playing in. So I sat down and put on "Freeway Jam" [Jeff Beck, *Blow by Blow*] and listened to it and said, OK, I'm going to do one for the people who like to hear Jeff Beck play that style. I'd like them to hear me play that style, and I wrote that tune.

Are there other cuts on **Larry Carlton** *with similar direct influences?*

"Room 335" is obviously a cop from "Peg" [by Steely Dan, *Aja*]. It's the same chord sequence, the opening.

Was the production of your whole album influenced by Steely Dan?

No, I'd have to say that it wasn't. On their records they cut their tracks spending four, five, or six days for one tune, and they would pick them apart. On ours, we played it until we got a performance and that was it — even with imperfections — because it felt so good.

Most of it was recorded live in the studio?

Yes, but I did overdub all of my solos. I wanted to have control and spend as much time as I wanted to on the sound of my guitar. So I did play live but with no leakage into the other tracks, with the intent to replace it later with an overdub.

How does the artistic satisfaction of doing a solo album compare to road work and live performing?

They're different in some ways and similar in others. In the studio, you get more than one shot at playing a solo. But when you're playing live, most of the time you really don't need more than one shot anyway, because the energy is so good. The audience is right there, feeding you energy. Again, you accept the imperfections, but it has something else that it offers: If you're a good performer live, that generates through your music to the audience, and the audience gives that energy back to you, and it makes you play differently than you would if you were just in the studio by yourself. With my guitar there's nothing that I produce in the studio that I can't do live, and that's the way I want it.

You really enjoy playing in front of an audience, don't you?

I love it; it's a lot of fun. We never know what's going to happen. I never know what I'm going to say, what the people are going to say. For an hour-and-a-half, it's just like party time.

Since the shooting, you've set up an organization called Helping Innocent People.

Because of what I've been through with the shooting and making it, forming HIP is my way of giving back a lot of what's been given to me. I have a lot of success, and I happen to have lived through a tragic thing, but a lot of folks don't have the facilities, the insurance, the bank account, to get them through eight months out of work and a major disaster in their life. So this is my way of just helping those folks who love music — and even if they don't like music.

Before we go, there's something I'd like to say to other guitarists. There's really no road in my mind for competitiveness and pettiness between musicians. It's so important that we just want the best for each other. There are guitar players who play wonderfully and entirely different from the way I play, and it doesn't mean they're better or I'm better. None of that matters. The idea is that there are guys out there trying to make great music from their hearts, and we just need to support each other.

– ERIC CLAPTON –

BY DAN FORTE – AUGUST 1976 & JULY 1985

LEGEND AND mystery have surrounded Eric Clapton. Like Robert Johnson, he is one of a handful of guitar virtuosos for whom the term genius is inarguable. But in his formative days, playing with England's Yardbirds in the early '60s, Eric "Slowhand" Clapton was impressive and flashy, but he was still struggling — first to break through the sped-up rock interpretations of the blues that the Yardbirds specialized in, second to tap into his own soul. Legend has it that when Clapton left the Yardbirds in 1965, he locked himself in a room with nothing but his guitar. That may be a bit romanticized, but he did leave for the seclusion of a friend's house in the country, with the aim of clearing his head and concentrating on the blues. A month later he joined John Mayall's Bluesbreakers. With Mayall's purist blues stance as his vehicle, Clapton immediately rose above the standard of his British R&B contemporaries and most of his American counterparts, as well. He remained true to the idiom's ground rules and spirit while pushing the form to its outer limits and occasionally beyond. Most of all he was able to express the full range of his emotions through his guitar as few players ever have.

Had the time been 1935 instead of 1965, some people would have no doubt assumed that Clapton, too, had sold his soul to the devil. As it was, his worshippers declared him a god.

In his 25 years — chronicled in the six-LP boxed retrospective, aptly titled *Crossroads* — Eric Clapton has had numerous personal and musical upheavals and abrupt changes in direction, often marked by radical changes in appearance. Much of his career — from the Yardbirds to Mayall to Cream to Blind Faith to Derek & The Dominos to solo projects — has also been punctuated by personal crises, including bouts with heroin and alcohol, a spiritual rebirth, and a sometimes agonizing personal life most recently shattered by the tragic deaths of his friend Stevie Ray Vaughan and several members of his crew in a helicopter crash, and especially by the death of his four-year-old son in a accidental fall from a window.

Throughout, Clapton's reclusive nature has only added to his mystique. But in the late '80s, Clapton became more visible and outgoing than ever before. His rendition of his classic "Layla" was one of the Live Aid concert's most stirring highlights. He lent his name to a new model of Fender Stratocaster; appeared in magazine and TV ads for Guild acoustics and Michelob beer; made videos (for "After Midnight," "Forever Man," and "It's In the Way That You Use It," from the movie *The Color of Money*); served as house guitarist for the star-studded Prince's Trust concerts; jammed onstage with Buddy Guy, Robert Cray, Roomful of Blues, and others; recruited Dire Straits' Mark Knopfler and singer/drummer Phil Collins for his own tours; and got into soundtrack work — beginning with his award-winning score for the 1985

British TV series *Edge of Darkness* and continuing with such films as *Lethal Weapon* and *Rush*.

But the most obvious change in attitude has been in his onstage demeanor. Though Clapton concerts have always been virtually devoid of theatrics, his 1987 shows were a far cry from the stoic, motionless Eric of old. Instead, he roamed the stage with the aid of a wireless transmitter and hammed it up with bassist Nathan East and keyboardist Greg Phillinganes — occasionally even mounting the drum riser or sprinting across the stage. The guitarist who always seemed oblivious to anything but the licks streaming out of his amp was now playing *to* the audience and obviously enjoying it.

Clapton attributes his new positive outlook to the fact that in 1985 he turned 40, and whatever demons or burdens he once endured were lifted, if not removed. And though critics have repeatedly tried to count him and the notion of guitar heroes out, he now commands perhaps his biggest audience ever. His 1986 *August* was one of the biggest-selling of his 13 solo LPs, and *Crossroads* hit #1 on the *Billboard* compact disc chart in only its second week on the charts, an unprecedented feat for a four-CD retrospective. (Meanwhile, the LP version of *Crossroads* entered *Billboard*'s Hot 100 at #80, and jumped 44 places to #36 in its second week.) In 1987 Eric Clapton won the BBI Lifetime Achievement Award (England's equivalent of America's Grammy). More recently his *Unplugged* album revealed once again his affinity for the simple but powerful relationship of a single performer holding an acoustic guitar. In 1992 he completed what amounted to nearly two years of touring with a guest appearance for the CBS' 25th Anniversary tribute to Bob Dylan.

[August 1976]

Do you still ever practice, sit down and run scales?

I never have done that, but I do sort of play around quite a lot. I can't play just to silence, though; I have to be prompted into it by listening to something or hearing something on the radio.

Do you think you're still improving?

I think I'm improving all the time, in my own particular fashion. The chances are that I'm probably slipping behind the times in my tastes or my direction. But when it comes down to my personal approach and playing the guitar, I'm still teaming and kind of progressing — I'm pretty sure of that. You always know when you come to a dead end; then you have to make up your mind about what you're going

to do. I haven't felt that too many times yet.

When you get into a new style, like reggae, do you have to alter your technique much?

I don't have to adapt much for anything like that. It's not difficult to play that way. What I always find the most difficult is keeping up my technique of just playing lead in any situation. What I would find hardest of all would be to be featured in a jazz composition of some kind and have to play a solo lead over strange chords. But things like reggae and just popular songs of any kind are always pretty simple.

Have you ever gotten into jazz?

Well, the one thing that hung me up straight away was that technique they have of double-picking, up and down. I use both downstrokes and upstrokes, but I've never been able to do that fast thing. Any of those guys seem to be able to do that.

What about jazz chording?

Well that's another situation. Watch any of those guys, like George Benson or someone. The amount of fret positions they can get out of, say, three or four chords — you know, I just don't know about that stuff [*laughs*].

Being self-taught, where did your chord background come from?

I just listened to records and tried to figure out which strings they were hitting at the same time.

Instead of barre chords, you seem to play down at the nut a lot.

Those were the chords I learned. I also think when you're using light strings, you tend to become a bit insecure about going up the neck too far with big, full chords. Because what will sound right at the bottom of the neck with light strings, by the time you've taken out twelve frets it could be out of tune.

When did you get into slide?

I always used to play slide on the acoustic guitar, and that was never employed on stage, and consequently it never got on record either. I think what really got me interested in it as an electric approach was seeing Duane [Allman] take it to another place. There were very few people playing electric slide that were doing anything new; it was just the Elmore James licks, and everyone knows those. No one was opening it up until Duane showed up and played it a completely different way. That sort of made me think about taking it up.

Are there any similarities between your electric slide technique and Duane's?

No, not a great amount, because I approach it more like George Harrison. Duane would play strictly blues lines; they were always innovative, but they were always in the blues vein. I'm somewhere in between him and George, who invents melodic lines often on the scales.

What do you use for a slide?

A glass tube about the width of the neck of the guitar, so I can get all the strings covered. It's a thick one [an Isis medium].

Do you have any special guitar setup for slide?

Yes, a Gibson ES-335. But it hasn't got a high nut; I just raise it at the bridge. I don't play it down at the bottom much; I usually keep it up near the top [high] frets. I use the same strings as I do normally on the other guitars; Ernie Ball Super Slinky — .009, .011, .016, .024, .032, .042.

[Ed Note: *Eric's road manager at that time, Willy Spears, says that the last lime the strings were changed on this guitar was mid-1974. Normally, Clapton's strings are changed only when they break, except for the high three which Spears sometimes changes when he feels they're going dead .Willy says, "He won't even let me buff them."*]

Do you play slide in standard tuning or open chords?

I use open G [D, G, D, G, B, D] most of the time, for acoustic and electric. I prefer G, because you get more of a country sound; it's more melodic.

Do you ever use open tunings when not playing slide?

Yes, on "Tell the Truth"; that's tuned in open E [E, B, E, G#, B, E]. But I wasn't playing slide; I was just making chords in open tuning. if you tried to transpose them onto a straight guitar, it would be very difficult. It's like a barre *A* on the 5th fret. I'm holding down the fifth and third strings in a — sort of *E7* shape — holding it on and taking it off. That comes directly from Keith Richards. Some of the Stones' things — like "Street Fighting Man" [*Beggars Banquet*] where he's got all these great guitar sounds — he just tunes it to an open chord and invents fingerings.

Did it get tiring playing in bands, like Cream, where you had to solo constantly?

Absolutely; it really did. Sometimes you just end up playing every lick you know before the end of the set, and then you're fucked, you know, because you're just repeating yourself over and over again. I've really become more devoted to the song itself and the presentation of the actual music. I think jamming, unless it's got a goal at the end of it, is pretty much a waste of time. It's just like exercising or something. If you're jamming, and something comes out of it, and you make something that you can stand

hearing again and has a form and turns people on, okay. I think musicians, as they grow older, usually become interested in doing something more lasting. It's a very youthful thing to go around and jam with everyone who's known — kind of like sowing wild oats. Then you've just got to settle down and make everything count and make sure that it's worthy of being heard again, not just a throwaway.

What causes you to switch guitars over the years?

It's a fad, I think. Like, at The Concert for Bangladesh I was playing a Gibson Byrdland. If you remember, Chuck Berry had a lot of publicity photographs taken with a Byrdland, and that looked like a very delicious guitar. I couldn't get hold of an old one with the black pickups, so I got one with humbuckers instead.

What other guitars do you own?

Let's just say I have a selection of Gibsons and Fenders and a few Martins. The Stratocaster is my basic stage guitar. I've also got a Switchmaster, the old Carl Perkins type, and a lot of good old acoustics — *f*-holes and flat tops — and an old mandolin-guitar. I've got a woodbody Dobro with a Martin-type neck. I also have a 12-string made by a guitar maker in England called Zemaitis It's reputed to be the biggest 12-string in the world. It's about the same dimensions as a mariachi bass. He really did a beautiful job.

Do you plan on presenting any more older bluesmen, like the records you did with Howlin' Wolf [The London Howlin' Wolf Sessions]?

Those kinds of things are usually on the spur of the moment, like within a week's notice. There's no one I can think of right now that I would go out of my way to do. With Wolf, on "Red Rooster," he was very, very vehement about it being done *right*. Because he considered us to be English and foreigners, and therefore we wouldn't have heard the song, right? So he just got his guitar out and said, "This is how it goes." It's not on the album, unfortunately, but he played it all the way through once on his own with us just sitting there listening. He was playing slide Dobro, and it was just bloody *amazing!* And he said, "Okay, you try it." So we all tried playing it like him, but it didn't really sound right, so I said, "Well, why don't you do it with us?" And that's the bit that got on the record.

Do you think those sessions, mixing a blues stalwart with several rock greats, come off well?

That one came off. But I am actually biased against those things. My ego told me to listen to the one I did with Howlin' Wolf, and I liked that — because I like the Wolf anyway, whatever he did. He never could go wrong, because you could put him in with, oh, Buddy Rich or someone, and he'd still dominate the show. The other reason I did that session was that for a long time I'd really wanted to meet his guitarist, Hubert Sumlin, because he did some things that freaked me out when I was picking up the guitar — that stuff on "Goin' Down Slow," just the weirdest playing. He's truly amazing!

[July 1985]

In the studio, when you take three passes at a solo section, how similar is one take to the next?

They would all be identical in every way, except that the high points would be in different places. If I was to spend a day in the studio recording the same solo for the same song, each one would have its high points. It would be up to *me* or the producer to say, "We can either have a solo of all high points, or we can leave one as it is," depending on what you want. I mean, I would prefer to be able to go in and play the solo and just leave it, but you never do that in the studio. As much as everyone wants to leave it alone, they all want to actually make something of it. "It's great, but wouldn't it be that much greater?" And they're right — for the finished product. You can't do that in a live situation, so why not do it in the studio? It's just taking creativity that one step further.

Before going in to overdub a solo, do you ever plot in advance what you're going to play?

Yes, and it never fails to come off as miserable. If I start, I'll compose the whole solo, and it will turn into a symphony. It's that whole Leonard Bernstein thing: If we start with a little motif and play it three times, and the third time we introduce a coda, and that coda becomes . . . . Suddenly, you've got a symphony on your hands, which everyone can spot straight away as being boring. And I'm not recognized for that; people don't like me to do that.

Cream's live version of "Crossroads" [Wheels of Fire] is often cited as one of the best live cuts — and live guitar solos — ever recorded. Was that edited from a longer jam?

I can't remember. I haven't heard that in so long, and I really don't like it, actually. I think there's something wrong with it. I wouldn't be at all surprised if we weren't lost at that point in the song, because that used to happen a lot. I'd forget where the 1 was, and I'd be playing the 1 on the 4, or the 1 on the 2 — *that* used to happen a lot. Somehow or another, it would make this crazy new hybrid thing —

which I never liked, because it's not what it was supposed to be. What I'm saying is, if I hear the solo and think, "God, I'm on the 2 and I should be on the 1," then I can never really enjoy it. And I *think* that's what happened with "Crossroads." It is interesting, and everyone can pat themselves on the back that we all got out of it at the same time. But it rankles me a little bit.

Do you think your guitar playing is distinctly British?

Not at all. I think all of the members of my band, myself included, are American, musically. I can see it much better in some ways than Americans can because I'm over there in England, looking at it from a distance. I have a lot of in-bred stuff that I heard as a kid, which I wouldn't have heard in America. English folk music is very much kind of in the back of my head, subconsciously. So, I suppose that comes out every now and then in terms of meter and length.

Obviously, your early playing was largely defined by how aggressive and forceful it was, but did you have that killer instinct, also?

Absolutely. And it's still there. I just don't get into a jamming situation very much these days. But if I do, yeah, it *has* to be there. What else are you going to do? You can't just sort of walk off. But there is a way of approaching it. There would always be a loudmouth in these situations — just like in samurai films. If you ever saw *The Seven Samurai*, the best swordsman of all gets into a situation where he *doesn't* want to fight, but he's up against this real bull of a man who's saying *he's* the best. The samurai finally says, "No, I won, but if you insist, you can *say* that you won." That's what I do: I let the loudmouth, or the villain, mouth off, get it all out of the way, and then I just come in very quietly like B.B., I would imagine. Just one note or something that will shut *everyone* up — if you can find it [*laughs*]. It doesn't always work.

In the Movie Moscow on the Hudson, ***Robin Williams plays a Russian saxophonist who gets blown off the stage by his idol of the sax. Did you ever have an experience like that?***

I think I've had that several times, and every time it's been healthy, as well as very heartbreaking. When it's done to you by someone who you really hero-worship, the first thing you feel is real betrayal. The bottom line of all these relationships should be a *colleague* feeling, and if that is taken away, you really feel like your father has just kicked *you* out or insulted you. That's very painful. At the same time, it teaches you to grow up very quickly and become self-reliant.

It must also feel weird to jam with your idols and smoke **them.**

Oh, yeah. That's also been possible. There have been times I've played with, for instance, B.B. or Freddie — Freddie and I did a lot of tours together — where the main contingent in the audience was my followers, who hadn't *heard* of Freddie King. So it would be possible for me to win in that situation just by being me — even if what I played wasn't better. You have to be aware of that, and not allow it to happen.

Did any of the ARMS shows get into all-out shootouts between you, Jeff Beck, and Jimmy Page?

It was very much there between me and Jeff, and I think it was also there between Jeff and Jimmy. But because I'm not familiar with Jimmy's playing — never worked with him — we had no time to develop a rapport. So, as a three-part thing, it couldn't happen. I also think Jimmy was pretty much under pressure as it was, and to have thrown him more of that would have been unfair. He was very nervous about going out there. He needed to be supported, and not attacked from every angle. He was very frail.

Beck seemed to be the most blatant gunslinger.

I think he is. And at that time, and for many months after that, I began to think of Jeff as probably being the finest guitar player that I'd ever seen. And I've been around. I still think that way, if I really sit down and mull it over. Carlos Santana, of course, is very high on my list; for pure spirituality and emotion, that man is number one. But there's something cool and mean about Becky that beats everyone else. I have to hand it to him in that respect.

You've become a model for a whole generation of blues and rock guitarists. You must hear a lot of your own style in other work of other guitar players.

I do, and the funny part is, the parts that I recognize as being directly taken from my playing are the parts about my playing that I don't like. Funny enough, what I like about my playing are still the parts that I copied. Like, if I'm building a solo, I'll start with a line that I know is definitely a Freddie King line, and then I'll — I'm not saying this happens consciously [*laughs*] — go on to a B.B. King line. I'll do something to join them up. So that'll be me — that part. And those are the parts that I recognize when I hear something on the radio — "That sounds like me." Of course, it's not my favorite bit. My favorite bit is still the B.B. or Freddie lines.

When you say you were copying various blues guys, you were still adding quite a bit of your own. For instance, your version of "Hideaway" [Blues- breakers] *differs quite a bit from Freddie King's original.*

Exactly. I was copying feel, I think, by that time, or atmosphere.

That's a hard concept for a lot of players to grasp.

I started working on what the guy would *live* like. I would picture what kind of car he drove, what it would smell like inside. Me and Jeff [Beck] had this ideal of one day owning a black Cadillac or a black Stingray that smelled of sex inside and had tinted windows and a great sound system. That's how I visualized these players living. That's what feel is all about. If I wanted to emulate somebody, I would try to picture what they would live like and try to live that way. You develop this kind of image.

So even if your image isn't completely accurate . . .

It helps you get to *somewhere* — which is another thing altogether.

Do you continually go back to the same sources when you need inspiration? Can you always get inspired by hearing Freddie King or Robert Johnson?

Or Otis Rush, Buddy Guy, yeah. And it's not so much technique that I listen for; it's content, really, and the feeling and the tone.

Is that what set Robert Johnson apart from the rest of the Delta bluesmen?

Yes, absolutely. It was so intense. It was difficult for me to take it when I first heard the album [*King of the Delta Blues Singers*]. A friend and I were both blues fanatics, and he was always a little bit ahead of me in discovering things. We went through Blind Blake and Blind Willie Johnson — working our way backwards, to the root of it — and he finally came up with Robert Johnson. He played it for me, and I couldn't take it. I thought it was really nonmusical, very raw. Then I went back to it, later, and got into it. First hearing it, it was just too much anguish to take on.

Do you think the faster-is-better trend of younger players misses the point that you see as the purpose of guitar soloing?

Well, it's not the way I would approach it, but it's hard to form a judgement on it when you don't know what it will turn into in the end. It may be that they're developing a whole new frame of reference. See, what may happen from that is a kind of rebellion in 5 or 10 years' time that may take it back to where we recognize it. Or it may just become brand new. I would hate to say, though, that they're all missing the point.

Did you ever slow down records to learn solos?

Not slow them down. Well, early on, I did that with Duane Eddy's records — like "Cannonball."

All of the guitarists who've played in your band have differed enormously. Is there a common prerequisite you look for?

With players, again, technique isn't as important as personality and feel. I can hang out with a guitar player for a very short time and either get a feeling from being with that person or not. I may get a feeling from being with that *player*, but I may not want to hang out with him. He may be dynamite — very aggressive and very to-the-front — to the point where I think, "I can't handle this more than twice a week." Every night would just be too much, too demanding. Constantly having to prove yourself is not very relaxing; it frays your nerves. I always end up with people in my band who I can really get on with as people, and that is what they play like, as well.

Playing with someone as extroverted as Jack Bruce must have pushed you night after night.

Night after night, to the point where it was really a question of just a battle, a war. I don't think he did it deliberately; it's just the way he is as a musician and as a guy. I mean, he has to clear a space around him, and you can't get very close a lot of the time.

In the video of the ARMS show in London, you switched to your Explorer when you did the slow blues Do you still see the Gibson as your blues guitar?

In some respects, yeah. When I get up there on-stage, I often go through a great deal of indecision, even while I'm playing. If I've got the black Stratocaster on and I'm in the middle of a blues, I'm kind of going, "Aw, I wish I had the Les Paul." Then again, if I were playing the Les Paul, the sound would be great, but I'd be going, "Man, I wish I had the Stratocaster neck." I'm always caught in the middle of those two guitars. I've always liked the Freddie King/B.B. King rich tone; at the same time, I like the manic Buddy Guy/Otis Rush Strat tone. You can get somewhere in the middle, and that's usually what I end up doing, trying to find a happy medium. But it's bloody anguish.

Is there any consistent setup that you try to have all your guitars conform to?

Yes, all of them need to be about 1/8" in the action, and I like it to be constant all the way down. I can't stand it if the nut is low, and the action gets higher as you go up the neck. I always take the wang bar off and have five springs, and just tighten the whole thing right up. I like frets to be generally somewhere between a Strat and a Les Paul. Les Pauls' are

too thick, and Fenders' are sometimes too thin. The Fender Elite is very nice because it's a blend. The neck on Blackie, the Strat I play all the time, is probably my favorite shape. It's almost triangular on the back — V-shaped — with a slightly curved fingerboard, as opposed to the flat one. That, to me, is the best.

The story goes that between the time you left the Yardbirds and when you joined John Mayall, you locked yourself in a room in the country with nothing but your guitar. Is that true?

Mmm, yeah, that's true, but they're missing something there. I actually stayed with a friend whose ideas had always interested me — Ben Palmer. His approach and philosophy of music — and life, too — were such that I regarded him as a bit of a guru. Through the Yardbirds, I was starting to feel very lost and alone. I was being made to feel I was a freak, and I started wondering if I *was* a freak. They all wanted the simple things of success and the charts, and what was wrong with that? "What's the matter with you? Why don't you want this?" And I began to think that I was really crazy. So I went off to see Ben Palmer, and it was just like, "Oh, yeah. Of course you've done the right thing." He immediately made me feel human again.

So the improvement in your playing was more a function of clearing your head than just woodshedding.

Clearing my head and playing the guitar as well. He made me feel normal again, and I wanted *us* to form a band together, but he was off the music scene [*Ed. Note: Palmer later played piano on the Eric Clapton & The Powerhouse sessions, and became Cream's roadie.*] He didn't want to get involved again. So I just hung out for about three or four weeks with him and we played together, and I got strong again, really. Strong in my ideas and my feelings and my self-confidence in what I was doing.

Once you eventually did achieve enormous success, with all its attendant problems, did you long to be just a sideman again?

Yeah. I'm still not absolutely sure about this but it feels to me like you can only really do exactly what you want when there is no pressure to be what you've become popular for. When you play a concert, there's so much pressure on you to do old things, new things, what the audience wants; and when you become successful, you've got to bow to that to a certain extent. That cuts off a lot of your creative energy; it's quite limiting.

When you first got interested in blues, what was the scene like in London?

Alexis Korner and Cyril Davies were already going before I played guitar — or while I was doodling. I'd go see them, and the Stones were forming — it was very stimulating. There was something about seeing a band play live what you'd only heard on records — it was fantastic. The first guitar player I ever heard in England bend notes was called Bernie Watson. He was in the original Cyril Davies band. Their hit was "Country Line Special." The story on Bernie Watson was that he was a classical guitar player who liked to do this for fun. He was the original one who sat down with his back to the audience. Never stood up. And he was the first one I saw play a twin-cutaway Gibson semi-acoustic. He was really a bit of a cult hero. He was a very mysterious man. I never spoke to him.

Were there any seminal inspirational records you heard in your formative years?

Both of the Robert Johnson albums [*King of the Delta Blues Singers,* Volumes 1 and 2] actually cover *all* of my desires musically. Every angle of expression and every emotion is expressed on both of those albums. Then *Ray Charles Live at Newport* album [reissued on *Ray Charles — Live*], B.B. King's *Live at the Regal, The Best of Muddy Waters,* the Howlin' Wolf album with the rocking chair on the cover — hasn't got a title [*Howlin' Wolf*], Jimmy Reed's album *Rockin' with Reed, One Dozen Berries* by Chuck Berry, the Freddie King album with "I Love the Woman," *Freddie King Sings* . Those were the formative ones.

When you need to be inspired, do you still turn to old records?

I can get stimulated by new things, too, but to retap the root of what I'm doing it for and what started me off, then I would need to go back to an old record. The first thing I'd think of then would be something like the Blind Willie Johnson album where the interview is on one side and then him playing "Nobody's Fault But Mine" [*Blind Willie Johnson — His Story*]. That's probably the finest slide guitar playing you'll *ever* hear. And to think that he did it with a pen-knife, as well [*sighs*].

Of course, if I come up to date, Stevie Wonder or Carlos [Santana] are always great. We had a funny confrontation. When Carlos was Devadip and I was *heavily* into the booze, we met up in Chicago, and he said that he would like to get me interested in his guru [Sri Chinmoy]. He took me to his room, and he had this whole assembly for the prayer — a little shrine and candles and incense. I said, "Well, I can go for all this — if you'll do my trip with me, which is

we'll drink a bottle of tequila together." He agreed. So I went in and meditated, and I thoroughly enjoyed it — because of the way Carlos presented it as truly spiritual, not a cloak or an act. I got a lot from it. And I almost felt funny about having to then take him the other way. But he went for it. We sat and listened to Little Walter and a bunch of blues records and drank tequila all night got smashed and very silly. To this day, I've heard reports that he enjoyed that part of it more than he did the meditation [*laughs*]. The spiritual thing never overcame him or converted him into anything other than what he already was — a very sweet, beautiful man.

On the first Yardbirds album released in America, For Your Love, *which cuts did you play on, and which featured Jeff Beck?*

I'll have to think. I'm on "Sweet Music," which was produced by Manfred Mann, "Got to Hurry," "I Ain't Got You," the middle of "For Your Love," "I Wish You Would," "A Certain Girl," and "Good Morning Little Schoolgirl." I'm not sure about "I'm Not Talking" or "My Girl Sloopy." That's Jeff on "Putty" and also playing slide on "I Ain't Done Wrong."

On "I Feel Free" [Fresh Cream] are you playing in the same key as the rest of the band? I don't mean that to sound critical...

[*Laughs.*] No, I know what you're saying. I think I was inspired by Jack's kind of dadaist way of thinking. That was a really weird song to do. But he wanted to have a double standard going; he wanted the band to sound straight but with a kind of weird twist to it. So he wanted to make a pop single that was just not quite what it seemed to be. When I got to my solo, I thought, 'Well, I'll play a solo that sounds a little off the wall, as well.' So I chose the lines to be sort of third harmony.

Your image now is pretty laid-back. But even the existence of Cream would suggest a much cockier side.

The cockier side is still there — and always has been — under a disguise. It's just that if you put yourself up for trouble all the time, it's easy to see what your moves are — if you've got a potential enemy, where he can hit you. My whole thing has been to be aggressive with my playing underneath a disguise of being laidback. So when it comes, they're not expecting it.

How did the slow coda at the end of "Layla" [Layla and Other Assorted Love Songs] come about?

Jim Gordon wrote that and had been secretly going back into the studio and recording his own album, without any of us knowing it. And they were all love songs composed on the piano. And we caught him playing this one day and said, "Come on, man. Can we have that?" So he was happy to give us that part. And we made the two pieces into one song. That's Duane [Allman] on slide on the ending.

Is he playing the high melody in the head fretted or on slide?

Both. Well, he played in standard tuning, so he could do both whenever he felt like it. He could start a line fretting it and end it on slide. I can't play slide in standard tuning; I'd really like to be able to. I use open *A* — like open *G* a step up [*E, A, E, A, C#, E*].

When you perform "Layla" onstage, you sometimes play the high part and sometimes play the low part. Who did which on the record?

Well, Duane and I played all of it together. We found that whenever we were going to do an overdub, neither of us would do it alone. We'd either do it in unison or in harmony. So we did all of it together.

All artists aspire to really make a statement, a masterpiece. Having done that with "Layla," what sort of pressure does that create?

Within, a great deal. But that's pressure mainly caused by fans or managers or record producers. It's always so subtle, you begin to wonder if it is just you who's making it that way. The greatest things you do are always done by mistake, accidentally. I had no idea what "Layla" was going to be. It was just a ditty. When you get near to the end of it, that's when your enthusiasm starts building, and you know you've got something really powerful. When I started to do that, it didn't feel like anything special to me. If you try to write something that's already got all of that, it's impossible. You just try to write something that's pleasing, and then try to get it to that.

Your fans' image of you as a guitar hero has often almost eclipsed their perception of what made you a guitar hero — your talent. Did that ever cause an identity crisis?

Yes. Quite a lot. I fall for the same thing. What they base that on is very much a kind of *wild* west, gunslinger image. And that appeals to me, as well. The crisis comes when I find that I'm *not* the fastest — or that, in fact, that isn't the important part. When the crisis comes, you have to sit down and think about it seriously — if your music is suffering because of how potent your image is.

How do you focus back on the essence?

You just have to stop, really. It's like doing anything over and over again. It becomes meaningless; it's just repetition — until you deliberately make

yourself stop because you're fed up and it's making you depressed. You go away from it, have a breather, and come back. I find that if I ban myself from playing the guitar for about a week — that's the longest I think I could ever do it — when I pick it up again, I have an idea. You've gone to the guitar because you've got an idea — a line or a riff — but you don't do that; you do something completely different that you had no idea you were going to do. Something inside you that is uncontrolled wishes to express itself, and that's where you begin — you look at that. Then, of course, the minute you start to polish it and hone it and take a look at it too much, it's gone again. I need to stop and let the thing express itself without controlling it. It's all that outside influence and self-conscious approach to your playing that actually ends up destroying it.

Do you often surprise yourself with something you've played?

Yeah. It usually is when you've made a mistake or you're not concentrating, or when you're just having too much fun. You try something, or you just go to the wrong fret, and you suddenly are doing something that you didn't want to do, but you like it. Then, you try to repeat it, and you get back into that polishing syndrome again, and it will become boring. It's usually when you're making mistakes that you find out there are other places to go that you hadn't planned out.

A lot of guitarists talk about this sort of zone they get into on their best nights when the guitar almost seems to be playing itself. When does that take place?

For me, it comes from outside as much as inside. I'm very, very influenced by the band. If everyone is playing really well, you can't help being inspired by that, and that drives you on, and suddenly you get to this point where you know that everyone, including you, is having a great time — and you're at the front of it, having the greatest time of all. You get to what seems like a peak. But suddenly you start thinking about what a great time you're having, and then it's gone. Or what I always do, without fail, is hit a bum note. I'll really be out there flying — I think, "God, I'm flying!" — then [*hums a sour note*], and it's all over. [*Laughs*] Everyone in the band just goes, "Aw, man!" You look around, and they're all smiling. But if you can get to that, you can get back up there within the space of a few minutes.

Did those nights happen more often when you were a certain age or with a certain band.?

I think with Mayall's band, it was always very

easy. With all the bands I've been with, I've found that time and place where you could just fly. Blind Faith was so short-lived, we didn't ever really groove. When we were rehearsing and hanging out before we ever toured, we did a lot of great stuff.

What's your objective when soloing?

It's almost like a samurai, again, in the pacing. I really want to hit everybody, but it's got a lot to do with timing and space. The objective, really, is to make everyone feel like they've just been struck by a bolt of lightning. And that's very difficult to do [*laughs*], time after time. It's the whole thing of construction and pacing and maybe making them wait — which I don't do enough; I really would like to perfect that. Make them all wait for the first note of the solo, and then hit exactly the right note so they're all satisfied. You only do that every now and then — I do, anyway. I see guitar players who seem to know exactly what they're doing and set it all right. For myself, one night a week I may get *all* of them like that, and then the rest of the nights I may get one solo exactly right. It all depends on how you start the solo — if you start it wrong, you've really got no chance.

Are there physical or technical things that you used to be able to do at, say, 22 that you find harder now?

No, because I was never involved in pyrotechnics or gymnastics. I'm very lucky in that way. I never set myself too high a goal. It was always tone and feeling, for me. Now, sometimes I can find it difficult to reach that because you can get jaded a lot easier as you get older. A lot of the fire is gone, so you have to stop and take a breather — even when you're on-stage, you can do it.

What, if anything, would you like guitarists to have learned from you?

I think exactly that: the economy. There's a certain construction that's based upon the feeling controlling the technique. I think that has to be the case — not the other way around. If you really want to do something tricky, just do that once — don't keep repeating it. It has to be an expression of feeling.

At what point did you feel that you'd graduated from being a disciple of the American blues greats to being a peer?

I've never really felt that. It's almost like a generation gap. Those guys are my heroes, and they'll never stop being my heroes. They'll always be ahead of me, because they were to begin with, and you can't change that. Ill never overtake them.

Your stage shows have always been completely devoid of theatrics yet you've openly admired people like Jimi Hendrix and Pete Townshend, who are just the opposite.

I think that was very shrewd on my part to choose a role that I could be fulfilling at the age of 60 [*laughs*]. I was reading where Sting said that he was going into films because he didn't want to be like Mick Jagger, cavorting around the stage at 40. Well, I've never done that, so I don't have to worry. I can do what I've been doing all my life.

– RY COODER –

BY STEVE FISHELL – MARCH 1980

JON SIEVERT

WHILE THE rest of the record industry has raced in the fast lane towards mega-platinum nirvana, Ry Cooder has been following his instincts along an alternate route — a detour through the heart of America's musical heritage — and quietly building what others rarely approach: His own idiom.

Cooder's deceivingly simple method is to unearth forgotten tunes from the folk-blues tradition and breathe new life into them with dazzling guitar skills, a bluesy, barrelhouse voice, and imaginative arrangements and production. Drawing from diverse composers such as Huddie Ledbetter, Bobby Womack, Burt Bacharach, and Jelly Roll Morton, he culls themes from the past that remain relevant and poignant — faith and inspiration, humiliation and humor, social injustice and marital infidelity — and filters them through his encyclopedic knowledge of regional ethnic musical styles. Although he remains true to the spirit of each writer, the results are always vibrant and, most of all, fun.

For years Ry Cooder has been revered among professional musicians as both a consummate fingerpicker and a legendary slide player; in 1970 *Rolling Stone* called him "the finest, most precise bottleneck player alive today." Favoring a Fender Stratocaster, he helped spawn a generation of slide guitarists in the late '60s and early '70s with searing performances on such tracks as the Rolling Stones' "Sister Morphine"

[*Sticky Fingers*], Randy Newman's "Let's Burn Down the Cornfield" [*12 Songs*], Little Feat's medley of "Forty-Four Blues" and "How Many More Years" [*Little Feat*], the soundtrack of the Mick Jagger film *Performance,* and the Stones' *Jamming with Edward,* a ragtag LP of jam outtakes.

Born in 1947 in Santa Monica, California, Ryland Cooder began banging on a Silvertone tenor guitar at age three. Seven years later his father gave him a Martin 6-string OO-18, and he became a rabid student of fingerpicking, learning first the country style of Merle Travis. While most guitarists his age were twanging along with Duane Eddy or copping the latest surf licks, Ry explored the almost lost art of country blues guitar. Inspired by Bahamian folk guitarist Joseph Spence and the bottleneck magic of Blind Willie Johnson, he brought home armloads of records and memorized the licks of every bluesman who caught his ear.

Shunning Little League and later high school sock hops, Ry practically lived at the now-defunct Ash Grove, LA's once thriving folk and blues club. He ravenously absorbed the stylings of any fingerpicker who would venture into town, and heard many of his favorites including Reverend Gary Davis [Davis gave Cooder a couple of lessons], Jesse Fuller, Sleepy John Estes, Doc Watson, Skip James, and Mississippi John Hurt.

Through Joseph Spence's influence, Ry became fascinated with the open tunings that he uses today almost exclusively. He mastered the open-finger style of Arthur "Blind" Blake, and his experiments with tunings continue to this day.

With a growing reputation as a player par excellence, Cooder became one of producer Terry Melcher's favorite choices for LA record dates. He could have settled into a long and comfortable career as a session specialist, but instead he assembled material for the first of many solo albums, which found Cooder immersed in numerous ethnic traditions: Hawaiian slack-key, Tex-Mex, gospel, early American jazz, late '50s R&B.

An unassuming and private man, Ry generally loathes the road, preferring the sanctuary of his family and a quiet recording studio to airport coffee shops and endless soundchecks. Occasionally he will venture out when a choice opportunity arises. Live Cooder is a rare, unforgettable experience. He bops and weaves subconsciously to the music, throwing out exaggerated grimaces and pop-eyed muggings, all the while blanketing the crowd with his virtuosity and infectious humor.

No one should second-guess Ry Cooder — each ongoing project eludes prediction — but fortunately for listeners he will likely continue his unique experiments with old and new sounds and expand his private idiom for years to come.

Was there a reason for your musical seclusion during your younger years?

I didn't know anybody who liked to play what I liked. I was trying to learn certain things and get myself together on my instrument. In retrospect, I see that you do better when you work with people — you progress faster. David Lindley and I have been doing some things together, but up until this time I seemed to do my best work alone.

How would you describe your own guitar playing?

The style that I've been working on for the last ten years has come to be kind of a Joseph Spence/slack-key/Mexican/gospel style — it's nothing more than that [laughs].

How did you come to use open tunings exclusively?

I started playing in tunings for rhythm, not for bottleneck. I was trying to get a fatter sound so many years ago, and I've been working on it ever since because it sounded like good gospel. That was the thing that made the church stuff come together. I don't like standard tuning in church music. I know Pops Staples does, and I like his sound. It's fat.

What tunings do you use most often?

For rhythm, I often use G tuning, spelled from bottom to top: D, G, D, G, B, D. I end up using the capo for different keys, different vibrations. For slide, I use D tuning, which is spelled from bottom to top: D, A, D, F#, A, D. One main reason I use tunings is that it's easier to work out arrangements for the records that way. You get a better idea how the whole thing might sound. Some of my best ideas have just been accidents or peculiarities of one tuning or another.

What's an example?

The overall sound of "The Tattler" [*Paradise and Lunch*] is strictly on account of playing D position in G tuning. You just can't get those passing chords in standard; you can't get the bass notes. It's confusing to keep all the tunings straight, but I've settled on four or five that I practice a lot. Also, certain guitars sound good in one tuning or another, and that helps to simplify it — if my Strat is always in D or G, then I know what I'm doing when I pick it up.

When fingerpicking, do you use your nails or your fingertips?

It's basically the nail and finger at the same time. That's something that Gabby [Pahinui] does all the time. It's a combination that's really nice. When you have good amplification, this technique means something. You can really snap it with the nails, then modify that sound with the softness of the fingertips. I never bothered with a flatpick. It just didn't come naturally to me.

Do you use a strong attack?

I play pretty hard, but I can play light if I want to. To do what I do, you've got to be strong or you'll get tired. If I have a gig and haven't played for a while, I'll get a terrible pain in my lower right arm.

Do you move your right hand to different positions for various tones?

You have to every once in a while, but the thing I have to maintain is string tension. If I lose string tension, I can't play. So I'm pretty much going to be around near the bridge where the strings are tight. I'm squeezing and playing really hard, and those strings have to be there.

What technical advice can you give to younger players?

If you play a new thing every day, which I like to do, then you're going towards something that'll serve you later on. If you learn one new thing, one new passing chord or note combination, then someday there will come a song that all of those things will relate to.

What kind of bottleneck do you use for slide guitar?

It's some kind of wine bottle; I don't know what it is. An auto glass shop ground it so that it would have a bevel and wouldn't cut me. It's a good one because it's straight and fairly heavy — you've got to have some weight.

Did you experiment with different pickups, searching for the right tone?

If you figure that a solidbody is nothing but wood with wires in it, you can contour it to fit your tastes. All the years that I spent playing Strats — trying different string combinations and pickups to get a certain sound — I never quite got there. I like their sound, but not always. It's always been so elusive. Once in a while they'll sound good — the current is good that day, the weather is warm enough — I don't know. Guitars are such temperamental things. They're so primitive.

Why do you prefer an arch-top over a flat-top?

Arch-tops have a lot more string tension than flat-tops, which I dig. I don't bend strings hardly at all, so I love lots of tension.

How do you define a good guitar sound?

I can't say exactly what it is. There's a warm quality that I like, a kind of vibrant, bell-like thing. I like a hard punch initially that has a softer hum to it as it fades.

How do you set the tone and volume controls on your guitar?

Everything's always all the way up. That's the only way that it will pull all of the sound out. The higher those things are, the more current will flow through and the better they operate.

What approach do you use for structuring your solos?

I know certain things that I like to hear. I like slide solos to sound like a vocal part. Find a melody and make it say something. It's speaking to you; it's not just notes. With slide you have the chance to get a real vocal quality to come out. Also, you should build — start a thing and go somewhere, make a little statement. That's what those jazz guys are always talking about. [Tenor saxophonist] Lester Young told a little story when he played. You also want to insert a certain attitude — is it up, is it down, is it happy, is it sad? Those are qualities that you can get in there with slide. Hopefully, you just play, you just know these things instinctively, like driving a car. That's when you're on it. If everyone had to think about what they do they wouldn't play anything — they'd end up with too many variables. The first actual work I did in music was accompanying singers, and I still tend to think of my playing primarily as an accompaniment. If for some reason I have to take a solo, I try to play off the vocal and maintain the feeling of the words and melody.

What are some examples?

My idea for "I Think It's Going to Work Out Fine" [*Bop Till You Drop*] was to change it from tough Ike & Tina Turner into a more peaceful, atmospheric ballad, so when I played the slide part I tried to imagine how the words, which are really nice, would sound with that feeling, like as if Gabby were to sing it. What a great idea! Sometimes I get fantasies about weird combinations of music and people that can really illuminate a song idea. How about Sleepy John Estes singing "Mustang Sally," or a Tex-Mex version of "Goodnight Irene"? You never know unless you try. Maybe it's a good idea, and maybe you'll get into trouble. For me that's the most fun thing about making records, the reason I wanted to make records in the first place.

Once you've found a song, what method do you use to arrange it?

I sit here like I've been doing forever and ever, just playing the song until I like the way it sounds on the guitar, making that part as rich as I possibly can. I'll come up with a bass part that corresponds to that, and maybe something else I'm doing can be formulated into a vocal part. Maybe I'm playing a drum beat here somewhere. In other words, I orchestrate my guitar part. I get it in a key that sounds good, and that sets it all up. Bobby King helps with ideas for harmony vocals, and if the studio musicians can get behind it, that's all there is to it. If my part doesn't sound right, I'll change it.

What's your formula for arranging background vocals?

I try to get them to come to the foreground, as is the case with the best gospel music, much of which is a cappella. I try to get those rhythmic elements into the song as if they were another instrument. I guess that's my major accomplishment — learning how to work with that form. I've been very lucky to be with people who could help me and show me these things.

How did you adjust to the change from sideman to leader?

It wasn't hard, just a matter of experience. You have to play on the stage. That's the only way to learn. I never did it when I was young, never seriously. You have to know how to deal with people, how to help them and let them help you as well. It's an interaction, and that comes from experience, I guess. I always find that when you're playing with other people, just listen and you'll know.

Were you a little nervous about jumping in with the guys from The Gabby Pahinui Band?

It's all a matter of attitude. If you adopt the right musical attitude — what's the groove here, what's the dominant aura — then I think a good musician can integrate into any situation if he just concentrates. But you have to be open and sensitive and ask yourself, "What is the scene here? Do I feel comfortable?" If you build up this awareness, you'll be a better guitarist. For years I tried to get the notes right. I wanted to play notes. But Gabby doesn't bother with that — he's way past the notes. It's the approach, the whole attitude. You just let yourself come out. Gabby will say, "If it comes from your heart, I can feel it." That's a very typically Hawaiian thing to say, and that's something that he does better than anyone else I've ever known. That's the key to it — getting the musician's expression of feeling across. The players who can do that are the great players. People have always enjoyed the spectacle of someone raging through a thing and playing a million notes, and as a piece of theater it can be good, but we know that music is really something more than that.

— DUANE EDDY —

BY DAN FORTE — JUNE 1984

IT'S BEEN 25 YEARS since his first hit and 20 since his last, and no one seems more surprised at the hero's reception he's receiving tonight than the man himself, bowing at center stage with his signature Duane Eddy model Guild arch-top at his side. It's been a good five minutes since he cut off the final chord of "Rebel Rouser," his 1958 smash instrumental, but the crowd is still on its feet cheering. Eddy looks a bit stunned. The audience continues to applaud, and the guitarist's own band joins in from the wings. Roughly translated, the ovation is their way of saying, "Welcome back."

To many in the crowd, Duane Eddy represents their first exposure to rock and roll guitar; for some, he may even be their inspiration for taking up the instrument. For others, he is the man behind the name they've seen in so many rock-star interviews, the man who inspired guitarists from the Ventures to Ritchie Blackmore. One thing is certain: Those who came expecting a nostalgic stroll down memory lane experienced instead some of the most vital, potent, timeless rock and roll *ever* performed.

Until last year, Duane Eddy had performed in public only a handful of times in the past 15 years. There was the odd rock and roll revival, a brief tour of England, some cameos at overseas military bases. But even while he was out of the limelight, his legend endured. The band that assembled to bring him out of retirement in 1983 is a good indication of the es-

teem in which he is held by fellow musicians. Pianist Don Randi, just off the road with Frank Sinatra, put the group together and organized the first shows at his club in Studio City, California, the Baked Potato. Making a rare appearance outside the studio drum booth was Hal Blaine, without doubt the most recorded drummer in history. On saxophone was Steve Douglas, who over the years has graced recordings by Bob Dylan, the Beach Boys, the Lettermen, and nearly every Phil Spector-produced group, as well as Duane's early hits, such as "Yep," "Peter Gunn," and "Forty Miles of Bad Road." To play slide and rhythm guitar behind Eddy, Ry Cooder put his solo career on a back burner, and even brought along his bassist, John Garneche.

Why would the cream of the LA session scene, each a heavyweight in his own right, go on the road to play second fiddle to an "unsigned artist" for a fraction of what they could earn per hour in a comfortable studio? Simple: As Greg Shaw wrote in the liner notes to *The Vintage Years*, one of Duane's many greatest-hits anthologies, "Duane Eddy, more than anyone else, deserves credit for discovering the potential of the electric guitar in rock and roll."

Of course, there were innovative guitarists playing rock and roll before Duane Eddy, but in Shaw's words, "It remained for Eddy to bring out the instrument's latent tonal possibilities, not to mention its commercial potential as a solo voice." Duane put the guitar out front and used it like a good singer used his voice. The melodies were simple but memorable; the beat was usually relaxed and loping, but the energy was undeniable. And that "twangy guitar" tone was unmistakable.

To say that Duane Eddy inspired a generation of rock guitarists is by no means an exaggeration; in fact, it may be an understatement. His influence touched more than just lead players and spread across several generations. As Who bassist John Entwistle once said, "Me first influence, and me last, was probably Duane Eddy." During the early '60s, amidst the teen-idol assembly-line pop of singers such as Frankie Avalon and Bobby Vee, instrumental rock was the closest thing to rock's primal roots that was left, and Duane Eddy was king of the hill. Between his first recording in 1958, "Movin' 'N' Groovin'," and his last major hit, 1963's "Boss Guitar," Eddy hit the charts more times than any rock instrumentalist before or since. "Rebel Rouser," "Ramrod," "Cannonball," "The Lonely One," "Detour," "Forty Miles of Bad Road," "Some Kinda Earthquake," "Shazam," "Because They're Young," "Kommotion," "(Dance with the) Guitar Man" — not even the Ventures, his nearest competitors, could match their mentor's track record. "I've always tried to give him credit in interviews I've done," says Ventures guitarist/bassist Bob Bogle. "We've never done a show with him, but I sure would like to someday. He's about the only act whom I'd have no qualms about opening for."

Like the Ventures' records, Eddy's music was direct and uncomplicated. One of the reasons they spawned a multitude of instrumental garage bands was that they were easy to copy. "I could probably play that," reasoned aspiring pickers, and with a little practice, they could do just that. Also, Eddy (like the Ventures) had the ability to bend ever so slightly to make his distinctive style accommodate whatever fashion was hot at the time — resulting in LPs such as *Twistin' 'N' Twangin', Have Twangy Guitar — Will Travel, Surfing with Duane Eddy, Twang a Country Song, The Roaring Twangies, Duane A-Go Go,* and even *Duane Does Bob Dylan,* in which Eddy took the poet's protest songs, removed the lyrics, and twanged out their melodies, as always on the bass strings.

But far more important than the idioms he experimented with was the way he made them sound. He could take a symphony or a shuffle, a waltz or a march, and make it sound like Duane Eddy. His trademark twangy guitar tone — a combination of the amp's tremolo, his Gretsch hollowbody, heavy re-

verb, bass-string melodies, and the guitar's vibrato bar — was obviously the most important ingredient to any Duane Eddy record. As John Entwistle recalled in the November '75 *Guitar Player,* "When I was playing at home, I used to stick tremolo on the amp and play Duane Eddy numbers on the bass. He was about the greatest influence on me; that's part of the reason why I use a trebly sound, as well."

Eddy's use of effects was anything but gimmicky. The tremolo fattened the tone of his hollowbody Gretsch, and he manipulated the wang bar as if it were part of his hand. He could dip down for exaggerated bends, as on "Movin' 'N' Groovin'," or subtly shake the bar for B.B. King-like "finger vibrato," as on "3:30 Blues." For the hook of "Boss Guitar," he played a left-hand bend over and over, 18 times.

In 1964, a combination of factors squeezed Eddy and many of his contemporaries off the charts. There was, of course, the British Invasion of the Beatles, the Rolling Stones, the Animals, and dozens of other English bands playing American-inspired roots rock. There was also the Beach Boys and a host of surf and hot-rod vocal groups. Add to this the girl-group fad and the rise of Motown. As Greg Shaw points out, these four trends alone accounted for 37 of 1964's 50 top hits. The Beatles and the Beach Boys became the role models for the next generation of garage bands. Ironically, Eddy was one of George Harrison's early influences, and the Beach Boys used the opening riff of "Movin' 'N' Groovin'" as the starting point of "Surfin' U.S.A."

Duane changed labels a couple of times before eventually moving to Lake Tahoe, Nevada, to pursue other interests. In the '70s he tried a couple of comebacks — scoring a European hit with "Play Me Like You Play Your Guitar" in 1975, and recording a beautiful version of "You Are My Sunshine" in '77 with the help of guest vocalists Waylon Jennings and Willie Nelson. He also produced Phil Everly's first solo album, as well as Jennings' tribute to Buddy Holly and the Crickets on *I've Always Been Crazy.*

Oddly enough, many of the punk and new wave groups reverted to Duane Eddy, Dick Dale, and the Ventures for their twangy, reverb-laden guitar sounds, and today Eddy's sound is as contemporary as the B-52s' is old-fashioned. The sold-out crowds that turned out for the then 46-year-old's 1983 gigs were an unlikely mix of middle-aged rockers and leather-skirted punks, with a who's who of guitar notables and pop celebrities — including Lee Ritenour, Lindsey Buckingham, Tom Petty, James Burton, Emmylou Harris, Dean Parks, Ron Wood, Larry

Carlton, and Rick Springfield — standing in line for tickets. When Cooder couldn't make a December date at the Baked Potato, Albert Lee filled in on second guitar. On a tour of ARMS benefits (for Action Research into Multiple Sclerosis), co-headliners Jeff Beck and Eric Clapton drove directly from the Los Angeles airport to the tiny Studio City club and sat in the second row.

"These shows have proved one thing I've believed for a long time," states Eddy, "and that's that there is an audience for this kind of music. Everywhere we've played, the reception has just been incredible. People have been telling me for years, 'If you go to Europe or Japan, you'll knock 'em dead,' but I think there's an audience for instrumental rock and roll right here in the States."

What made you return to active performing after such a long hiatus?

I ran into Don Randi in LA, and he said, "You ought to come play at the Baked Potato." I went, "Sure, fine." So he asked, "Who would you like to have for a band?" I named some guys, never thinking he'd really do it. But he called back a few days later and said, "Well, I've got Steve Douglas, Hal Blaine, and Ry Cooder, and I'll play keyboards." That really turned my head around. These guys all basically got together to get me started working again — that was the motive. And they don't go out and do this for just anybody. Of course, they didn't make any money playing the Baked Potato — it *cost* them money [*laughs*]. They haven't worked that cheap since they first started.

Randi, Blaine, and Douglas had all played on your early records, but how did you meet Ry Cooder?

I was making some demos in LA in 1982, because I decided I wanted to get back into recording. I got Jim Horn on sax and Spooner Oldham on keyboards, and Herb Pedersen played banjo on one cut. I even got the Rivingtons — who used to be called the Sharps — to do the yelling in the background, like they had on the original hits. Jim Keltner played drums, and Cooder came to the session with him — brought his guitar. We just started jamming, and wrote a couple of things. Ry's fantastic. I love him as a player and as a person. He's the most interesting person I've met in years. He's got such a different approach, and when he describes things — music or guitars — it makes it magical. Technically, I think he knows more about my sound than I do.

Did his input change the group's sound much?

Oh yeah. The old things are still the same because of Steve and I, but Ry makes them all new. It was funny — Ry was working on a movie soundtrack at the time, and wanted it to sound like what he thought I'd be playing if I were active today. So he called [Eddy's original pianist and rhythm guitarist] Al Casey and asked him how I got my sound, and he wrote a few tunes. Then he called Steve to play sax on the project, and Steve ended up going on tour with him. While working on these demo sessions, I was sitting in a restaurant with my wife, Deed, and I heard this song on the Muzak. I said, "That's the type of thing I wish I could write" — a real up-tempo, locomotive beat. The next day, I walked into the studio, met Ry, and he played this song right in the same groove as what I'd heard the night before. It was kind of spooky. We were both working toward the same idea before we ever met.

During your years off the road, did you play the guitar much?

Not a lot. I noodled around and played along with records or the TV to keep my chops up. But if I'm going to make a record, I feel the important thing is to play with some authority — not sound wimpy or try to get in everything that I know. When you're playing an instrumental, it's got to start somewhere and end somewhere, and it's got to say something.

Has your approach to soloing changed much?

No. Though what I do has been put down as being simple and even dumb, I don't agree. I'll continue on with my style. It's a process and a choice and a direction that I choose to take. I'll change things around it. I like to keep an open mind, but I'm not going to start playing hot licks and work up a lot of complicated stuff just to dazzle everybody and prove that I can do it.

Would you be open to a producer recording you in different settings than on the old hits?

Yes. That's what I want to do with my career. I'd like to do some things with different guitar players — some more electronic-type stuff with Larry Carlton, some rock and roll with James Burton and Albert Lee, and some things with Ry. I'd also like to work with David Lindley, maybe Lindsey Buckingham — a lot of people. I want to have different guys add their styles, because that really gets me going and inspires me. That really became apparent when I started working with Ry, and later with Albert Lee. He's another one of my favorite guitarists; he's unbelievable.

When the British Invasion hit, and a lot of the rock and rollers from the '50s were put on the back burner in terms of sales and airplay, why didn't you

make the shift to country music like Jerry Lee Lewis and a few other early rockers did?

To switch to country, I thought, would be kind of — not selling out, but . . . I don't know. I was a rock and roll player. I love country. I did a country album [*Twang a Country Song*] with Buddy Emmons on pedal steel, the Jordanaires on background vocals, and Floyd Cramer and Pig Robbins on piano. That's where my roots are; that's where everybody's roots are in rock and roll. I always maintained that Hank Williams started rock and roll. Ever listen to "Move It on Over" and some of those things? Then play "Rock Around the Clock" by Bill Haley — it's practically the same track.

Growing up in Arizona and playing country music and later instrumental rock, did you feel any sort of kinship with the rockabilly singers from Memphis and the Deep South with whom you were sharing chart positions?

Sure. Well, people called me rockabilly, too. I probably felt closer to them after getting to know them and realizing that we grew up with a lot of the same influences, musically and socially. The only difference was that in Memphis they had blues stations, which we did not have in Tucson.

Yet you had a very bluesy style.

I actually learned that when I got out on the road in 1958. It fit right in. It's all ethnic, including country music.

Having played country, what was your initial reaction when you heard people such as Elvis Presley and Carl Perkins?

Well, it was like what we had been doing. We had a drummer, which a lot of country bands didn't have in those days. Our piano player was a lot like Jerry Lee Lewis; he played the same type of church music and was uninhibited like Jerry. This was around 1953, before we'd heard of Jerry Lee. We listened to boogie-woogie or whatever they called it in those days, mixed it in with country, and added drums. I remember when Elvis' first Sun singles came out, and the DJs called it "race music" [an early term for black music].

But you didn't play like any of the rock and roll guitarists who preceded you — such as Scotty Moore, Carl Perkins, or Paul Burlison.

When we got down to doing instrumentals, "Raunchy" by Bill Justis came out and was a big hit in '57. So Al Casey and I sat down and worked out "Movin' 'N' Groovin'" and "Up and Down," which were the first two sides I cut. We tried "Ramrod" before that, but we didn't do anything with it. We took

"Movin' 'N' Groovin'" to LA and overdubbed Plas Johnson on sax. We cut all the early tracks in Phoenix and overdubbed the sax in LA, because we had three tracks to work with. But we had stereo — in fact, I think I was one of the first rock and roll people to use stereo. I talked to Elvis later, and he hated stereo. He liked mono, because everything was right up front. Most producers I know from those days prefer mono.

What gave you the idea to play the melodies on the low strings so often?

It recorded better, for one thing. Also, I wanted to do something different. Everybody had already done [*plays a string of Chuck Berry double-stops*].

A lot of people would be shocked to hear what you just played — "He can play above the 5th fret?"

Sometimes it's harder to do the simple things than it is to do the tricky stuff.

How did you get that distinctive echo sound on your original recordings?

The studio didn't have an echo chamber, so they bought an empty water tank and put a speaker in one end and a mike in the other. There was no room inside the studio for this big 500-gallon iron tank, so they set it outside, and we used to have to chase the birds off of it sometimes. We also had to stop recording if a siren went by or a plane flew over, because it picked up everything.

What kind of amplifier did you use?

I used a reworked Magnatone on "Rebel Rouser," and then I had one custom-built with a new tremolo circuit and everything. I compared it to everything that came around, and nothing could match it. A guy in Phoenix named Tom Howard McCormick made it — called them Howard amps. Now, I'm using the new Fender solid-state Showman. Paul Rivera at Fender really made a great new line of amps for them. It gets a sound pretty similar to what I used to have; it's got good bright midrange.

What are the structural differences between your Guild Duane Eddy model and the Gretsch Chet Atkins you recorded with?

The Guild is pretty similar, but it has two-tone controls — the Gretsch just has one tone and the two volumes. Both have master volumes, and both have DeArmond pickups. The bridge on the Chet Atkins has a wood base; the Guild is all gold-plated. Mike McGuire of Valley Arts Guitars in Studio City [California] redid the Guild completely, with 36 coats of hand-rubbed lacquer. He didn't change any of the wiring; in fact, he said the wiring was very modern. He was amazed at how contemporary it is. Since

Mike refinished it, it sounds deeper and crisper, and it sustains better. It made it come alive a little more. I can tell because I've lived with it for 20-some years. Mike also fixed up my black Danelectro, which I used on "Because They're Young" and some other records.

Having such enormous success at an early age, did you know enough about the business end of music?

I didn't. To me, it was all a happy, fun time, and I really didn't pay much attention to the business. I had more money than I'd ever seen in my life, and I figured it would last forever. I've learned a lot about the business in years since. I still get royalties from RCA. I didn't know it at the time, but I signed away my royalties to Jamie Records for all the early records — I thought I was signing something saying that I wouldn't audit them. I still get some of the writer's royalties, but no artist's royalties.

Why did you move geographically away from the industry, to Lake Tahoe?

I realized I didn't have to live in LA. I like LA, but there are some things I just don't like about living there. And Tahoe is an easy commute. If I do get lonesome for people and friends in the business — which I often do — there's always somebody in town. I went and sat in with Glen Campbell last year. I just played guitar, and he gave me a few solos. Took my Dan-o and played "Wichita Lineman." Then we did "Forty Miles" and "Rebel Rouser," and he played the sax parts on guitar — the whole damn solo, note for note [*laughs*].

Are there any new guitarists whom you especially enjoy listening to?

I'd have to say Eddie Van Halen, Steve Lukather, Lee Ritenour, Larry Carlton, of course, and Dean Parks. Also, Steve Morse knocked me out at the NAMM show last January. He impressed the hell out of me.

What's your reaction when you hear someone play Duane Eddy licks?

I'm honored and flattered, really. It's like they're saying, "Hey, I'm your friend. I like what you're doing, and I want to do it this way." Like Dave Edmunds' album called *Twangin'* — I think that's great. I'll tell you, during some of the lean years, when I've not gone out and recorded or played big shows, to hear people like him doing that has kept me going. It makes you feel like you did something worthwhile after all. I never get tired of hearing it, whether it's guys playing a couple of my licks or saying in an interview that they were influenced by me. That's worth more than the money would have been. It's influenced a great many people, professionals and amateurs of all styles — because no matter what they went on to play, a lot of them picked up a guitar in the first place after hearing one of my records. For example, surf music was just like watching a son grow up. Those groups were just branching out and going in a slightly different direction from what I was doing. And studio players tell me they used to get scores with instructions to "Play Duane Eddy." I saw Tommy Tedesco at Valley Arts about a year ago, and he said, "I just want to know one thing: Anyone ever ask you to play like me?"

– THE EDGE –

BY TOM NOLAN & JAS OBRECHT – JUNE 1985

JON SIEVERT

"WHAT DO I find challenging?" poses The Edge. "Tearing up the rule book and saying, 'Okay, given that this is my instrument, what can I do with it that no one else has done before?'"

In an almost classical sense, U2's guitarist has turned limitations to his advantage, using simple techniques and abundant imagination to produce one of the freshest styles in years. He displays little evidence of formal training, theoretical sophistication, or extraordinary dexterity, yet he has etched an instantly familiar style and sound of his own. It's perfectly suited for U2's intense, uplifting music. And while Edge strives to stay original, others now imitate him: Witness ads in British and American music journals for "Guitarist, U2 style."

Despite U2's streamlined instrumentation — Adam Clayton plays bass, Larry Mullen Jr. drums, and The Edge doubles on guitars and keyboards — the band fills a huge amount of space beneath Bono Hewson's passionate vocals. The Edge commonly uses partial chords, harmonics, and echo repeats to create sparse yet harmonically rich textures. Rather than concentrate on fast or flashy solos, he tends to create atmospheric backdrops using drone strings, slide, E-Bow, feedback, or other effects.

Dave "The Edge" Evans was born on August 8, 1961. "I've never lived anywhere but Dublin," he says. "Although I have Welsh blood — both of my parents are Welsh — in every other way I'm Irish." As a child, Dave took enough piano lessons to learn that he didn't appreciate musical regimentation. He got his hands on a guitar for the first time at 13, when his older brother Dick brought home a battered acoustic from a yard sale. He didn't begin to apply himself in earnest, though, until four pals from a multi-denominational school in Dublin's Ballymun district decided to form a band.

"Larry had some drums and decided that he wanted to form a garage group," the guitarist recounts. "I thought it would be good to play a few covers and do what we wanted — purely for the satisfaction of playing, rather than anything else. We were pretty disillusioned with a lot of the music that was coming out in the mid '70s. There seemed to be a lot of ground that had already been covered. So, there was a meeting between the people who wanted to be in a group. We sorted out who was good material pretty quickly, and it really boiled down to the four of us. None of us had equipment at that stage, but we didn't think that mattered. It was then that I bought an electric guitar. Once we had bought our own instruments, it was just a question of learning how to play them." From the beginning, Bono and Edge opted to keep the nicknames they acquired as kids knocking around the streets together. ("'The Edge,'" Evans recounts, "was a good-humored jibe that was originally supposed to be a caricature of my appearance.")

Inspired by the individualistic sounds of the Patti Smith Group and Tom Verlaine with Television, U2 decided early on to avoid well-trod musical paths. "Their music was so new and different," Edge explains, "it made us excited and enthusiastic. As a would-be guitar player, I was struck by the fact that all these bands had a really well-defined sound that was like no one else's. So when we first started putting material together, trying out a few chords and what have you, that was always in my mind: 'We have to find out what *we* have to offer, what we can do that's different.'"

The first signals of what U2 could do differently were heard on their 1980 debut album, Island Records' *Boy,* which drew critical praise for its originality. U2's first song on American airwaves, "I Will Follow," introduced The Edge's dramatic rhythm/lead guitar style.

After intermittent touring of the U.S. and Britain, U2 recorded *October* and played 217 shows in 11 countries.

The opening military drum march of 1983's *War* announced the maturing of U2. The album reached #1 on the English charts, sold over a million copies worldwide, and set the stage for U2's triumphant breakthrough tour of America. Shows in Boston and West Germany were recorded for *Under a Blood Red Sky.* Released in November, it went gold and remained in the charts for nearly a year. At the end of 1983, U2 was named Band of the Year by the *Rolling Stone* Critics Poll.

U2 toned down its aggressive side in favor of a more abstract, impressionistic approach for *The Unforgettable Fire,* which went straight into *Billboard*'s Top 15. Another indication of success: The March 14, 1985, *Rolling Stone* proclaimed U2 "Band of the '80s."

Unlike many acts that flee to large cosmopolitan areas at the first scent of success, U2's members still live in their hometown. "For us," Edge says, "Ireland is like a shelter from the storm. It's a place to escape, a refuge. It's also been one of the main reasons why the uniqueness of this group has never been compromised or diluted. Within a very short period of time, most of the groups that move to London start losing that individuality that sets them apart. The groups that succeed are the ones that stay where they are, where they've always been."

Did you go through a period of editing your playing? Were you ever one for long solos?

No. From the beginning, our music was very trim. The solos that I took were very short. And unlike what most guitar players were doing at that stage, they were quite melodic. I used to use a lot of harmonized strings, even in my solos — like droning, say, the E string against something I was doing on the B string. [*Ed. Note: "I Will Follow" is a prime example.*] It had an interesting sound, 12-stringish sometimes. I didn't use a distorted tone; it was very clean. And our music really needed more than just one-string solos of the blues variety. That sort of thing didn't work, and it also didn't interest me very much, because it was being done so well by other people.

Can you play conventional styles?

I could play in any style, but not to a very high standard. The most important thing with this group is that with everything we do, we try to maintain a certain originality, a certain challenge. Therefore, there's a high level of rejection for lines and songs. Nothing with this band comes without a lot of work. But it would be no contest to put me against a fast player like Gary Moore or any of those guys; I could not even begin to do anything like that. At a very early stage of my playing, I just decided that for me that was totally irrelevant. It may have thrilled listeners, but as far as I was concerned, that was something that had been done before and there was no need to repeat it. So instead, I put my energy into songwriting and approaching the instrument in a totally fresh way.

How do you develop a style like yours, which has little relation to blues or jazz? It just. . .

Sort of exists [*laughs*]. I think it's that I've never really had any guitar heroes. All of the guitarists that I've liked have been total anti-hero stuff. I think of Neil Young — that guy gets so much feeling into his playing, but he's stumbling around a few notes. It means so much, but it's so simple and basic. Tom Verlaine was never an incredible virtuoso, yet he revolutionized guitar playing, as far as I was concerned. He suddenly said, "Look, you can do something different. You don't have to do the same thing. This is nothing like anything you've heard before." There are bands to whom that is not an issue; it's not important for them to do anything new. But if you want to do something new, there is no reason why you shouldn't be able to. For us at our early stage, it was an important lesson. We've never as a group put up with anything that lacked that vitality, that originality. We've always dumped it if we felt it smacks of an era gone by or that it isn't musically relevant.

You've done well at turning your limitations into advantages.

That is true of the band generally, and I hope that we can continue in that vein. I'm almost scared to do some really serious practice because of what it might do. Whenever I start working on a song, I immediately try to forget everything, to empty my hands and head of anything that may be hanging over from another song or album. I try to approach it like, "This is the first time I've ever played a guitar. What am I going to do?" That's one way of getting straight through the conscious mind into the subconscious layer where the true creative spirit lies. I very rarely practice, but I think I might, just as an experiment, do some serious rehearsal by myself and see what happens.

Do you imagine parts before finding them on the instrument?

Not actual melodies; they definitely tend to be a product of playing. My parts come generally out of exploration; they come from improvisation and accident. My strength is seeing them when they come out and capitalizing on them. I have quite a good ear for music, so when I hear something that interests me, I normally stop to develop it and bring it to a conclusion. So, the original idea very rarely comes before I've actually started playing, but ideas for new sounds and new approaches to the guitar do come before I start. I very rarely follow conventional paths in any aspect of my playing or writing. In fact, that's probably one of the most important things about why I play like I do. For instance, if I feel I'm getting into some sort of rut, I do something really radical, like change the tuning of the guitar.

Your playing took on new dimensions in The Unforgettable Fire.

Yes. See, I was experimenting a lot with damping my guitar strings, using felt or gaffer's tape over the strings near the bridge to give zero sustain. Using echo, I found some remarkable effects. The intro to "Wire" is a case in point: Having damped the strings with gaffer's tape and using a bottleneck and an echo setting, I got this incredible sound. It sounded quite Eastern, but really bizarre.

Do you understand what you're doing in musical terms?

No, we're self-taught. We learned by bouncing a lot of ideas internally around the group. You know, we haven't come from Berklee, and we're not developing some new theory in music. None of us can read music. It's all instinctive. You can know all the jargon, all there is to know about music, and still be impotent when it comes to actually creating something new. We are lucky enough to have developed a

style that is natural. We never have to theorize about it or debate it. It's funny. I was talking to a very talented drummer in Sweden, an Irish guy who is well into knowledge of theory and polyrhythms. I was sort of wistfully saying that I'd love to be able to read music and do all that, and he said, "Edge, if I ever saw you with sheet music in front of you, I'd break your leg." He was saying that it would not work well with my talent, and he is probably right.

Does playing guitar come easily for you, or do you have to work hard at it?

I battle with it. I don't necessarily enjoy it so much as I see it as a struggle and a fight. Because I very rarely rehearse, at first I'm at odds with the guitar. It doesn't feel natural, but this means that my mind is open to new ideas. I haven't formed ruts down the fingerboard by playing the same things. It's still very much unexplored territory. Maybe that's why I don't feel that attached to my instruments. It's almost like I'm going to dominate them in some sort of way. I don't feel like they're part of me; they stand between me and something new.

How do you view the role of the guitar in U2?

To all intents and purposes, my guitar is the main influence in denoting a song's mood. I'm very aware of the tapestry of sound that it can produce. I like simple lines, simple guitar pieces that work with simple bass and drums. But oftentimes we work with many layers, as well. It's a combination of simplicity and complexity.

What's your method of recording guitar?

We've done all of our albums — in part, at least — at Windmill Lane Studios in Dublin. It's an excellent studio, but we've never found ourselves comfortable in the designated studio area. In fact, instinctively we've found ourselves drawn to the hallway and reception area, which is all stone. There's this 30-foot–high high staircase which spirals up to the top floor, and we basically put all the guitar amps out there with some close mikes and some Crown PZMs stuck to the ceiling and floors to get some of the top end. There were also some microphones at the very top of the staircase. Armed with that array of microphones, we found the sound that made sense to us. In the dead environment of the main studio room, the sound never had room to breathe. It was like playing inside a vacuum flask. The splashes of sound I could get out in the main hallway were just perfect for what I wanted to do.

How do you lay down backing tracks?

For the three studio records before *The Unforgettable Fire*, we'd been working on a layered approach because the structures of the songs in some cases were not fixed. We'd record drums to keep, and the bass would be recorded, as well. We'd try to get as much isolation as possible and do just guide guitars. At the end of the day, if you needed to lose everything but the drums, that was possible. Then we'd take over the best-sounding part of the studio and do each instrument in turn. But for *The Unforgettable Fire*, we wanted to get a certain feeling that you miss with that sort of layering. It's intangible, perhaps, but when you play together, you lean toward one another musically. In purely feel-based music, I'm sure that would be far more evident than it would be with our stuff. But the vibrancy of what we did live sort of outshone what we had done on record. That's why we wanted to make *The Unforgettable Fire* as live as we could. So we rented some mobile equipment and went to an old castle north of Dublin to record all of our basic tracks. Most of the album has live takes. In fact, some of the songs had no structure to them until we started playing; we actually improvised them as we were working. "Bad" is an example.

The instrumental "4th of July" is unusual.

Unbeknownst to myself and Adam — we were playing away inside, just working on a little improvisation — Brian Eno was next door recording what we were doing through a series of treatments that he had set up for the vocals of the previous song. He thought it was so nice that he didn't bother even putting it onto multi-track. He put it straight onto 1/4", and that was it, the final product. We just snipped out a three-minute section that we thought was the best and stuck it on the front of side two.

Could you detail what's going on in that track?

I don't remember all the details. I was a little tired of playing normal finger stuff, so I used a bottleneck. I was probably working with an echo in triplets with what Adam was playing, and he was in a very unusual time signature — something like 13/8. Adam finds 4/4 not only boring, but extremely difficult to maintain. He moves in these natural rhythms that to everyone else seem totally weird and experimental. Playing against that time signature, I started working with the bottleneck and some harmonics. I may have detuned one of the strings, but it's a kind of instinctive thing. Immediately when Adam started playing his line, I knew there was something there that we could work with. Everything went on in that split second. It's a mixture of serendipity and intuition.

What was your approach on "Pride"?

Well, I wanted something very percussive, because the whole rhythm of that song hinged on the guitar's 16-to-the-bar beat. It just made it skip along in a certain way. So, that was the main consideration for that piece. We started with a bass guitar chord sequence with some drum lines to it. Once we had the chord sequence and that guitar line . . .

What is the chord sequence?

[Laughs.] Adam's in charge of chord sequences, because I haven't played a proper chord in years. It's B to E to A to F#. It's quite a traditional sequence in a funny way, but it just works well against what Edge is playing.

You don't seem to play standard guitar chords very often.

No. I don't play proper guitar *[laughs]*. For a start, I avoid the major third like the plague. I like the ambiguity between the major and the minor chords, so I tread a very fine line sometimes between the two. I tend to isolate the chords down to two or three notes and then octaves of the notes. Like for an E chord, I play just B's and E's, including my big E string. With "Pride," for example, it's really just a couple of strings. The critical thing is the echo. I'm playing sixteenth-notes, and the echo device supplies the triplet, so it's a very fast thing.

Early in your career, you used an Electro-Harmonix Memory Man Deluxe for the echo effects. Is that still part of your setup?

That's been put out to pasture at this stage. It was getting so old and battered that our stage manager was having to dismantle it every night to try to get it to work. It was on a life-support system, the poor thing, by the time we stopped using it. Now I've got two Korg SDD-3000 digital echoes. They have the same sort of features as the Electro-Harmonix, but with a digital clarity. At first, I couldn't get used to digital because it is so clean. There were all these frequencies that I hadn't heard for years coming out of my amplifier. And the definition of the repeats was so clear that it was off-putting. What was an atmospheric thing from the old analog suddenly became a very scientific, precise repeat. I never find myself using the far reaches of the Korg's echo potential; I tend to stay within the mid-area, between the parameters of about 50 and 400 milliseconds. I began using the Korg at the start of the *War* tour.

Do you ever add effects during the mix?

No, I really hate this engineer job — you know, "We'll fix it in the mix. We'll put that echo back on later." I don't use the echo as an effect that is put on top of an already constructed guitar piece; it's actually an integral part of the guitar figure itself. I always record with my echoes; they go straight to tape with the guitar. Very rarely would I let an engineer have a clean guitar sound. The treatment is as much a part of the sound as the playing or the guitar tone itself. For me, when you're being creative in the studio or writing, the most important thing is being inspired by your equipment.

Do you prefer playing in the studio to the stage?

They are very different disciplines. I enjoy the challenge in the studio of working at new things. You've got to be fresh and creative and on form. On a stage, it's a question of reproducing something you have already done, or in fact, developing it, because it's often very hard to reproduce something perfectly accurately. But I equally enjoy the challenge of playing onstage. Live can become a little bit of a treadmill unless you're very careful to avoid it. For that reason, I find recording more fulfilling generally, but because you meet such great audiences being in this band, touring is such a thrill. I've never understood bands who say that touring is boring or stagnating. There's absolutely no reason it should be that way.

During a recent concert you played guitar and piano at the same time.

Yes. Obviously, there's a limit to what you can do on the guitar with one hand. I generally hit a chord and leave it to sustain while I do something with my left hand on the piano. And sometimes I just alternate between the two instruments, playing a verse on piano and going to the guitar for the chorus. I do that on "New Year's Day," and I used to do it for "I Fall Down" and "The Unforgettable Fire."

Why do you play bass onstage during "40"?

As that song was recorded in the studio, I played the bass. It seemed like a more interesting approach to make Adam learn the guitar than to make him learn my bass parts, and it's worked out very well. He's come up with his own approach to the guitar parts that I did in the studio. I think it's an interesting visual thing to see us changing instruments.

You seem to change guitars a lot. Is this due to different tunings?

It's really because each song suggests to me a different guitar sound. The strange tunings that I have are for the lap steel and the Fender Telecaster. The Tele has a very odd one that I made up: *F, A, D, D, G, D*. As I was putting down some guitars on "The Unforgettable Fire," I was having a little bit of difficulty coming out with something I was pleased with. So I decided as a radical change of approach to just tune the guitar up to the notes that seemed right. It

was pure chance, but it does sound a beautiful chord in relation to the song. I play "Unforgettable Fire" onstage with the Tele and an E-Bow. I used E-Bow for another few tracks that didn't make the album. It's an interesting device, but it tends to make everything sound the same. So whether or not you get a nice, pleasant effect or that same whiny sound is really down to how you treat your sound after the guitar. [Ed. Note: *The E-Bow is a small handheld electromagnetic bowing device for guitar.*]

What kind of lap steel do you use?

I bought an old Epiphone, dating from 1945, in Nashville around 1982. I used that on the *War* album, and I use it live for "Surrender" [*Under a Blood Red Sky*]. It's a great old thing, tuned in a very unusual way. When I first got it, I researched the tunings a little bit and found them all to be extremely uninteresting for me — I mean, they were country tunings. So I made up my own. I put the strings in couples an octave apart. The first and fourth strings are the same notes, the second and the fifth are the same, and the third and the sixth. So there's basically three notes making a minor chord with a ninth or a seventh. On standard guitar, I play slide in regular tuning, using a piece of chrome on the middle finger. A lot of good slide players use the training finger to stop any resonance in the strings behind the bottleneck. I don't do that. I control some of the problem with my picking hand, but I like the rest of the effect it gives, the sort of strange ambiance.

What kind of tremolo unit does your black Strat have?

It's a standard Fender tremolo. Sometimes I shake it. On the Explorer, which doesn't have a wham bar, I shake the neck. [Ed. Note: *This is not a recommended technique, since it could bend the neck or cause it to snap off.*] This is not to get a very exaggerated effect, but just to give it that natural modulation. If you have an echo on, a slight shift will give quite a nice sweeping feel.

Is the Gibson Explorer your favorite guitar?

I go through phases. I really like the Fender Telecaster at the moment. Sometimes you pick up an instrument and find that it has a natural balance and feel, and the Tele is one of those guitars. It's not a very old one — I think it's a 1970 or something — but it has that great quality that a good instrument should always have, which is that it inspires you. You pick it up, and you just know that you're going to do something good with it. The Explorer is like that, too, but I find I'm moving away from its sound as time goes on. It's great if you want a sound that is aggressive and yet not a cliché. It has a very individual quality, yet at the same time it has stock Gibson humbucking pickups, which give you that pleasant overdrive — not that awful heavy metal whine that so many new guitars have, which I think is so cheap. I also prefer wide fingerboards, and the Explorer's is really wide. I've bought a few guitars that I haven't really gotten into yet. I have an old Gretsch White Falcon that I've used a little bit in the studio. I've never felt confident enough to bring it out live, because it's such a different instrument than the rest of the things I play. It demands a different approach to amplification, and things like feedback become more of a problem.

Has it appeared on any recordings?

Yeah, I used it on *The Unforgettable Fire* sessions for "Indian Summer Sky" and stuff like that, as well as on a couple of songs that we didn't put on the record. It's a very versatile guitar with a really nice selection of sounds. It has the advantage of split pickups between the top and bottom strings, so you can change the overall emphasis of chords by tuning down, say, the bass or treble strings.

Is your Washburn Festival amplified acoustic guitar modified?

Yes. It's a compromise guitar, really. It doesn't sound like an acoustic, but I'm using it as one, which isn't exactly perfect. I like the feel of the guitar, but I was always let down by the sound. So I decided that the best way around it was to put in a Lawrence pickup over the soundhole, and now it is a very unique instrument. Apart from its shortcomings as a replacement for an acoustic — which I think are obvious — it is very, very interesting. I've used that an awful lot on the recording sessions. It can get that nice, sort of Rolling Stones clean sound and things that you can't even describe — beautiful, subtle tones. And it always sounds very warm.

Have you tried guitar synthesizers?

I've dabbled, and I've really not been inspired or impressed particularly. They make the guitar sound like synthesizers, which is totally ludicrous as far as I'm concerned. They have versatility in neither sound nor use. There are only certain playing techniques that are picked up well by the guitar synths. In the future, maybe. I'm interested in the new Roland with MIDI; I could get some good sounds that way. But to make a guitar sound like a synthetic trumpet or flute really doesn't interest me much. A police whistle, you know — what's the point? Guitars sound perfectly fine as they are. The last thing I want to do is make them sound like cheap synthesizers.

How do you go about choosing guitars?

I've never really been into the jargon. As a band, we've never really been into gear or guitars and stuff. A lot of my guitars are off the shelf. They're not vintage or anything. That's something that may change — maybe it's due to my inexperience — but at the moment, I've never found any vintage guitars that I really felt were worth the money. So, I've been happy to stick with the production ones. Obviously, it's down to personal taste. My stuff is not worthless by any means, but certainly not irreplaceable. But there is one thing I'm thinking about doing. It isn't actually my idea, so I don't know if I should explain it fully. But it's a guitar that plays itself [*laughs*]. You just depress the string, pluck it once, and get infinite sustain. I haven't actually perfected it or finalized the physics involved, but the principle should work. I can't wait to try that.

Could you describe your right-hand picking technique?

The only interesting thing about my picking technique is that I strike the string with the grip part of the plectrum rather than the pointed end. These are West German picks that have dimples to aid your grip, and I use the dimples to hit the strings. It gives a certain rasping top end that I've always liked. That's a really tough piece of plastic, and I use very tough strings as well: Superwound Selectras, gauged from .010 or .011 to .054. When I first started playing, I was lent this Les Paul copy that had the most awful flimsy sort of strings — .007 to .032. It was like playing with rubber bands. You had to stand perfectly still, or else you'd go wildly out of tune. I found that the heavier strings give a much better sound.

Do you ever bend strings?

Since I use quite heavy strings, I don't bend as much as modern guitar players. In fact, I do it quite rarely. I do add a lot of vibrato with my finger, especially in any sort of lead section where I'm playing a high melody.

When you're just strumming for a percussive effect, do you ever catch your finger on the strings?

Yeah, I do that all the time, especially on the nail. The nail eventually goes flat and breaks, and I get a very sore blood blister. It's all that flailing wrist on things like "The Electric Co." During a tour, those nails get very thin.

What's your approach to playing harmonics?

I don't play them in any unusual way. For me, harmonics are approaching the most pure sound available to a guitarist. There's no frets involved, so the tone of the harmonic is . . . I mean, I love it. It's one of the nicest sounds you can take from a guitar. I've taken it a step further with various different tunings and treatments. There are some sounds from a guitar which don't work with echoes or reverb or chorus. Big, fat chords sound like a mess; they just don't work. There's something about the purity of the signal from a harmonic that becomes such a big sound when it's treated well — very bell-like in many ways. They are very inspiring. I remember Steve Howe used to play harmonics when he was with Yes. I was interested by that sound because it was very delicate. They seemed like natural components for the sound of the group when I was putting together lines for our songs.

What would you advise young players trying to break out of stock playing patterns?

One of the best ways of developing an individual style is to start writing songs. It was actually in the development of songwriting that my playing style came. I would credit the other members of the band as having quite an influence, because there was a lot of chemistry. Being with other musicians is a very healthy thing.

Do you do any playing outside of U2?

Occasionally. I did a project with [bassist] Jah Wobble called *Snake Charmer*; that was interesting. It also had some German musicians, ex-Can members Holger Czukay [on French horn, guitar, piano, and Dictaphone] and [drummer] Jackie Leibezeit. I'm interested in meeting guys who come from different backgrounds. It's very stimulating. I'm not so interested in the conventional jamming of other people's material in clubs and the like. That seems to be a form of relaxation for a lot of guitar players.

What are your goals? Is there anything you hope to accomplish?

As a band, we have a kind of image of what the perfect album is. We're always striving towards that. Innovation and originality are important, but we're not interested in the idea of a cult music form for the chosen few. We're interested in music that has the power to touch everyone. We're always getting closer to it, but we probably will never attain that standard. In fact, it's not really important that we do. It's the trying that's important. It's almost an impossible standard to attain. It's like all your favorite groups rolled into one, with none of their faults. If we ever did make the album, we'd probably stop.

Have other artists achieved the perfect musical statement?

In moments, but those moments aren't really consistent. "Strawberry Fields Forever" [The Beatles' *Magical Mystery Tour*] might be a peak, or [Bruce Springsteen's] *Born to Run*. There are other tracks which have great power to communicate and stimulate.

What would you list among the essential Edge tracks?

It's funny, *Unforgettable Fire* was an experiment in staying clear of the guitar for the most part. I did an awful lot more keyboards and general atmospheric work on the guitar rather than taking it to the forefront. The tracks that display my playing the best are "Pride" and "Wire." "Wire" is interesting because of the new techniques being used. The intro has quite an unusual guitar sound that a lot of people think is keyboard. It's actually guitar with damped strings, echo, and bottleneck. That was a thrill for me because it was such a great sound. "Pride" was transformed when the guitar line came. Again, it's another use of echo from the digital delay, and it's very rhythmic. Those two are the strongest "Edge as Edge is" guitar playing.

Does it bother you to see advertisements for guitarists who play like The Edge?

No, not really. I think they've missed the point, actually. If there's anything that's good about my playing, it's because I'm me, I'm different. If somebody is trying to sound like me, then they really haven't understood me very well. I'm more interested in what Joe Blokes down the road in this garage band is doing than, say, what the new Jeff Beck album is like. Not that I don't respect Jeff Beck, who's an incredible musician. But I think we've seen what he can do, and there's a lot of guitar players out there that we haven't heard. A certain amount of that is because they are too busy trying to be Jeff Beck or whatever. If you do what a lot of players do — pick up a guitar and start playing lead blitzes, copying Eddie Van Halen or whoever else — you set off on a path which for me is a cul-de-sac. It's far more interesting to empty your head of anything anyone else has done and just start feeling sounds and making musical figures you can call your own. What I'm trying to say through my guitar is that everybody is different and can sound different. There's no reason on earth why guitar players should copy one another and end up sounding the same.

– TAL FARLOW –

BY ARNIE BERLE – JULY 1980

JON SIEVERT

EVEN THOUGH HE'S totally self-taught, can't read music, and spent less than ten years in the forefront of the jazz scene, Tal Farlow revolutionized the role of his instrument. In the words of fellow jazz great Howard Roberts, "Tal represents an epic milestone in improvising on the electric guitar. He set a pace for what became a style that now permeates the entire field of electric guitar playing." Tal came to New York to make his name in the mid-'40s, and within a few years almost every jazz guitarist in the nation felt his presence. The late Wes Montgomery, a jazz guitar giant in his own right, described it perfectly: "Tal came on the scene, poppin' and burnin'." Tal's influence burns on to this day, and such rock and fusion guitarists as John McLaughlin, Alvin Lee, and Steve Howe attribute much of their early interest in the guitar to Tal's recordings.

Talmadge Holt Farlow was born on June 7, 1921, in Greensboro, North Carolina. Like many of the men in town, Tal's father found great comfort away from his work in the cotton mills and textile factories by making music on the guitar, mandolin, or violin. Music ran in the Farlow family, and Tal's mother and sister were both pianists. At the age of nine Tal took up the mandolin. Although he listened to the so-called hillbilly music indigenous to the area, he never attempted to play it. Instead he kept his ear to the family radio, listening for the popular big band music of the day. By the mid-'30s Tal had picked up the guitar and was able to teach himself many of the songs he heard over the airwaves.

By the time the Second World War started, Tal had decided to turn his attention to developing a career as a commercial artist, a sign painter. During the war Greensboro became the location of an Air Force base, and here Tal came into contact with other players, notably pianist Jimmy Lyons. Farlow began gigging with local groups, entertaining in clubs and at USO functions. In 1944 he had his first break when he came to New York with a trio led by pianist Dardanelle. While appearing at the prestigious Copa Lounge with the trio, Tal came to know many of the leading bebop jazzers of the day. Tal's solos on "Zing, Went the Strings of My Heart," "Move," and "I Can't Believe That You're in Love with Me" [both on *Red Norvo Trio*] are rated among the most provocative jazz solos of the era. Norvo's penchant for playing sometimes-swing, sometimes-bebop lines at a lightning-fast tempo led Tal to become one of the fastest — if not the fastest — guitarists of the day. His amazing technique became the standard for other players, and his harmonic concepts had matured to the point where other guitarists wondered how he did it all. Due to his unusually long reach, Tal could play chord formations that enabled him to add color tones others couldn't reproduce. He also played thumb-style guitar well before Wes Montgomery ever recorded.

In 1958, Tal all but hung up his instrument to

– 67 –

move to the peaceful atmosphere of the small resort town of Sea Bright, New Jersey. "The music business — the backstage parts, the nonmusical parts — is terrible," he said. "It's just a crummy way to make a living. And it seemed that jazz was becoming too self-limiting; you had to be an expert to tell if what you were hearing was good or bad." In Sea Bright Tal divided his time between his boat, teaching private lessons, working a few clubs now and then, and plying his trade of sign painting.

Tal has come out of semiretirement a few times since 1958, but not many. In 1967 he came to New York for a seven-week engagement to open a new club, the Frammis. In 1969 he appeared at the Newport Jazz Festival and toured the U.S. with the Newport All-Stars. He also recorded *The Return of Tal Farlow* (since reissued as *Guitar Player*) for the Prestige label. In 1970 and '73 he returned to the Newport festival, and in 1976 he recorded for Xanadu Records. A year later he joined the roster of Concord Records artists and released *A Sign of the Times. Tal Farlow '78* followed, featuring two original Farlow compositions. Most recently Tal has been involved in helping the Public Broadcasting System assemble a film documentary on his life.

What were you playing in those early days?

Well, I used to listen a lot to fellows who sort of used a chord style. I thought that was real nice, and so I did a little of that. I used this style on the popular tunes that I heard on the radio, but then what really hit me was hearing Charlie Christian. He really turned me around. I heard him on a radio program in 1939 when he was with the Benny Goodman group. His sound, his choice of notes — he had such a horn-like quality that was so nice. Of course he was influenced by Lester Young. Then I got all the Charlie Christian records I could, and I started learning his solos. They weren't too easy, but they weren't too technically involved.

Are you completely self-taught?

I'll tell you what happened. When I was really young we didn't have much of anything, but my father did have a mandolin that he used to tune like a ukulele because it was very popular then to play ukulele. So he tuned this mandolin like the uke except that the fourth string was tuned down an octave, giving it the same intervals as the top four strings of the guitar. When I was about nine years old I started teaching myself how to play chords on this mandolin. I had a good ear, so I had no trouble. Then later on when I got to playing the guitar I played the same

chords, but now I had two more strings down in the bass, so I had to match those with the chords I was playing. Besides these two extra strings I also had this big thumb, so I wound up using the thumb on the sixth and fifth strings.

How did you learn the names of the chords so you could play tunes from books or song sheets?

We didn't have any song sheets, so I learned all my tunes by ear from hearing them on the radio. I would search around on the fingerboard for the chords that matched what I'd heard. It turned out that I wasn't always playing the same chords as the performer.

What were some of your influences besides listening to Charlie Christian?

I used to listen to all those broadcasts of the big bands coming over the radio from the big hotels or nightclubs. I enjoyed that and got to learn a lot of the latest tunes that way.

If you didn't know the chords you were forming and couldn't read music, how did you manage to play with bands in the early days of your career?

Since I listened to the radio so much, I knew all of the popular tunes of the day. So when I played with those local bands, I already knew most of the tunes. If the band had arrangements, I would just play the rhythm. If I didn't know the tune, then I would use my ear to match up with what I heard the band doing.

Were you always correct in what you played?

Yeah. They were never too adventurous, and most of what they did was easy to hear. There are many similarities in tunes, and when you know one you just about know a whole lot of other ones.

What was your first professional musical experience?

It was during the War. There was a little band that came through town from Philadelphia, and they needed a bassist because theirs had been drafted. I had just bought my first electric guitar from the money I had made painting signs for a music store in town. These guys asked me if I would play with them. So by adjusting the tone controls on the amplifier, I managed to do bass lines with the band on my guitar. After a while I also got to play solos. Then when the band left Greensboro to go back to Philadelphia, I went to Philly, too. Philadelphia was a big cocktail trio town, and I did what I've done several times in my life: I sort of alternated between the sign painting business and the music business. After all, I was limited musically and couldn't always cut everything that had to be done. I never could get too serious about my music. I never could feel that it was a real business. It was just something to do besides painting.

How did you get to New York?

Well, I was working with this girl piano player, Dardanelle, who had a trio — bass, piano, and guitar. I joined her in Baltimore, and then we worked in Philadelphia. Then she got booked into the Copa Lounge, the lounge of the famous New York nightclub, the Copacabana, which featured all the biggest entertainers in the country. We worked opposite the Nat King Cole Trio, and I met [guitarist] Oscar Moore, who was with Nat. There was also the Phil Moore Four, which had Chuck Wayne. Chuck was the first guitarist I heard who was into the new modern music, and he showed me some things. This was the time when that bebop was starting to get big. I used to go over to 52nd Street, which had all those great jazz clubs, and began listening to guys like [tenor saxophonist] Ben Webster and [pianist] Art Tatum. Then a bass player by the name of Paul Edinfield told me about this alto sax player, Charlie Parker; I had always preferred the sound of a tenor sax because of my admiration of Lester Young, Coleman Hawkins, and Don Byas. I went to hear Parker, and afterwards I made sure I went back every night to listen to him. I'd get there real early, get my beer, sit down somewhere out of the way, and just try to absorb everything about him I could.

Did you try to do some of Parker's saxophone parts on your guitar?

Yes, I did. I also tried to figure out what Parker's piano player, Al Haig, was doing harmonically. I'd try to get those chords on the guitar — like he'd be playing a 7th chord with the ♭5 in the bass. I must say that I didn't think that Parker tried to show off too much with that modern stuff. I think Dizzy Gillespie was much further out than Parker. Dizzy used to hold on to those flatted 5ths; he knew his music very well. Dizzy even played piano on some of the early Parker record dates. But Parker used to play a lot on the upper parts of the chords. Sometimes he'd start a phrase two beats late and run it into the next chord. Even if it didn't fit that chord, the phrase was so nice it didn't matter. Everything he did was so logical that it really did make sense and didn't offend you. Another thing I remember about Parker was that on the last chorus of a tune he'd end on the 4th of the chord — like a suspension — and he'd walk off the bandstand while still holding that 4th. He'd walk off into the kitchen, and then when he came back he would start with the same thing, the 4th, and then resolve it.

Do you think that Parker was very knowledgeable about the theoretical side of music?

He was very knowledgeable, but he was also a very intuitive player. As I said, Dizzy was the guy who really knew his music.

Did you ever get to talk to Parker?

Later on, after I had worked with Dardanelle's trio for six months at the Copa, I joined the Marjorie Hyams Trio. Marjorie played vibes. We were working opposite Parker at a club on 52nd Street called the Three Deuces. Whenever Parker came on, the rest of the clubs on the street would empty out and everybody came to the Deuces to hear Bird. Hearing him close like that every night was great, and I kept trying to play his things on the guitar. I got to talk to him a number of times, and we used to see each other at Charlie's, which was a favorite musicians' hangout on Seventh Avenue. He was always very friendly.

How did you come to work with Red Norvo?

I replaced Mundell Lowe. I knew Mundell real well. We both came to New York at the same time, he from Mississippi and me from Philly. Mundell got a job with Red's trio at a place called Bop City, over on Broadway and 49th Street. When Mundell left to go on the road with [singer] Frankie Laine, he recommended me to Red. It's funny, because I also replaced Mundell when he left Margie Hyams' group to go on the road with some singer. He was always going on the road with somebody, and I'd replace him. At the time I went with Margie Hyams I was working in Goldsmith's department store painting signs because I couldn't take any steady gigs since I had to wait six months in order to get my union card. Mundell recommended me, and I managed to get special permission from the union to take the job. Another job I had at that time was in Southampton with a leader named Marshall Grant. I learned a lot of show tunes on that job, which was good because later on a lot of jazz musicians began playing what they called obscure show tunes. When I got my union card and could work in New York, I joined Red Norvo and he decided to take the trio out to California. We went out there and then went to Hawaii for two months and then back to California. It was with this group that Red got a bass player who we heard about — he was delivering mail, but we heard he was real good, so Red got him. It was Charlie Mingus.

How was your relationship with Red?

I had heard Red when he was with Woody Herman's band, and he had some special arrangements of tunes like "I Surrender Dear" and "The Man I Love." Red would start the tunes slow, like a ballad, and then in the second chorus he would double the tempo. I had never really had to play that fast before, and I had some trouble making the tempos, both comping and soloing. We used to do a lot of things in unison, and then I had to play jazz and comp for Red at that tempo. This was rough, since I never had to do it before. But we rehearsed a lot, and of course I was finally able to make it.

What was it like working with Artie Shaw?

Artie is a tremendous musician. He's got ears, and everything had to be perfect. We had my man Hank Jones on the piano, and he was the foundation of the group. I had a good personal relationship with Artie. I had just come from playing with Red, where I played all these fast tempos. With Artie, when he kicked off a dance tempo, it seemed like either it wasn't slow enough or fast enough. It was an awkward thing for me. But I don't think I ever met a more professional guy than Artie Shaw.

At that time Shaw led a rather glamorous lifestyle. How was he with the musicians in the band?

He was one of the guys, but of course there were times he traveled by himself in his little Mercedes-Benz — there weren't too many of those around in those days. I remember one incident where I thought Artie might walk off the bandstand like he did in '38 when he walked off and flew to Mexico. We were opening one night at the Embers in New York. The place was packed with celebrities, and there were all kinds of TV and news cameras. It was a very big night. The band boy who had set up all the instruments happened to put Artie's clarinet on a peg near my amplifier. Just before Artie was to walk onstage I went to switch on my amp and accidentally knocked the clarinet off its peg, and it fell against the base of the microphone. I just picked it up and placed it back on the peg.

Now Artie comes on the stand and asks Hank to sound an *A* so he can tune up. Meantime the audience is applauding at Artie's entrance, and he starts to tune up his clarinet. All you hear coming from the instrument is "phh, phh" — no sound, just terrible noise. I thought Artie would explode or walk off the stand and go off to Mexico. He was quiet for a moment, and then he reached into the piano where he had another clarinet and went on as if nothing happened. Later during the break he asked me what happened, and I explained it to him and he said he wasn't mad. He never got mad at the musicians, but if a fan or anybody else touched the instruments he would get real mad at them. He told me that what had happened was like a nightmare come true for him. It seems he had a recurring nightmare that one day he would get up to play in a large concert hall and as he started, one of the keys on the clarinet would fall off. He was terrified that this would come true.

Why have you never tried to learn how to read on the guitar? Wouldn't it have made things easier for you?

I did try several times, but it was so slow in coming that when I got the pattern of the thing I was reading I would go back to relying on my ear. I guess I got into it too late. But I will tell you this: I think it's important for a youngster to learn to read early on before he finds it easier to use his ear. Nobody knows more than I about the importance of being a good reader.

Have you ever lost work because you couldn't read?

Yes, and I've been embarrassed like crazy about it. Sometimes I'd go with a band and they would tell me all I had to do was play rhythm. Then all of a sudden the leader would bring in some arrangements where I had to play some lines. I remember once when a 22-piece orchestra had to stop and wait while I tried to learn a part. I couldn't get it and had to turn it over to somebody else — that's very embarrassing.

And you've never studied theory or harmony?

No. I just learned by listening to records. It's better than live performances because there things go by too fast. With records you can do it over and over again until you get it down.

Do you have perfect pitch?

No, but I have very good relative pitch. My sister has perfect pitch. We discovered it one day when the radio was on, and a youngster who had perfect pitch had to identify some tones. Before she could call off the notes my sister called out their names perfectly. We all couldn't believe it, and she said to us, "What's the matter? Can't everybody do that?"

Do you work off the changes of another chord player, or go in your own direction and hope that the chord player can hear where you're going and follow?

If the chord player — say on piano or vibes — doesn't get too fancy and keeps his changes simple, then I'll try to add to it and not clash with him. But if he does some substitute changes, then I'll try to follow him.

But if you're the soloist, shouldn't you have the option of going where you want rather than having the accompanist dictate it?

There are a lot of musicians who don't like being

dictated to by another chord instrument. They would rather play with just a bass. But I get a little uneasy if I don't have a chord instrument backing me up. I feel someone should always be supplying the harmony. I hear the harmony in my head and have definite ideas that I want to express. I can relax more, though, if there is a piano or vibe going along with me.

Does it bother you when someone plays chord substitutions that you don't expect?

No. As a matter of fact, I kind of like to be surprised every once in a while, especially on a tune that's real well known. It sort of adds a little something to it. If you hear something different the first time around, you're going to remember it the second time.

You have a very large hand and can play chord formations many people can't reach. What happens when you write out forms that students can't reach?

Oftentimes they can't, so I leave out a note and simplify it. Another place where I have trouble with a student is where I can grab two strings with the end of one finger, and the student will have to use two fingers to play the same thing. This would take a finger away from one of the other notes. I also use my thumb for notes on the fifth and sixth strings. A lot of students can't do this — at least on the fifth string. There used to be a big thing about not using the thumb, almost like an unwritten law. It wasn't the "correct" thing to do. But now guys are beginning to use it.

When you're comping, do you always play roots in the bass form?

No, especially if I'm working with a bassist and there is no need for me to worry about that. Then I go out of my way not to play roots in the bass. If I'm not working with a bass player, then I think the ear almost calls for the bass notes. Then again, there are times when a tune sounds better without the tonic in the bass. Sometimes I might even just play two notes of the chord — like the 3rd and the 7th — and this by itself will sound so full you don't need anything else. It also doesn't get too muddy that way.

Do you ever sit down and just work out changes to tunes?

On some songs I work out changes that I like to use. Another thing I like to do is tune the *A* string down an octave. Of course you have to use the heavier *E* string to do that. What it gives you is the root of the *A* chord below the alternate bass note *E* rather than above it, and it gives you a nice fat sound. I hit that with my thumb, and I do the chords above it. It's good to use when you don't have a bass player with

you. I use it on tunes like "Little Girl Blue" or "Autumn in New York."

Do you ever practice or work out runs for different chords?

I do practice, but I don't work out runs, although I'm sure I have some favorite runs that I just can't help but fall into. Everybody has them. This is especially true when you're playing at a real fast tempo and can't always be creative. I'm sure I fall into runs I've done many times before, but each time I play something I try to make it come off just a little differently than the last time. Even just a different feeling will change the run.

Can you describe the process that goes through your mind when you're improvising?

Well, there are several things I might be thinking of. You can start with the melody and rework a phrase from the first part of it. You can take something out of another song and alter it a bit. It's hard to say what the process is. It just occurs to you while you're playing, but you must be sure that what you're doing fits the chords.

Do you ever think of different scales?

I have to know what something sounds like for me to play it if it isn't one of my pet phrases. I've always liked intervals — playing chord tones up and down the fingerboard — although I use a lot of scale-like runs in my playing.

Is there anything that you really practice?

No, but I do play a lot. I'll work out some tune I like or work on a chord progression.

You've spoken in the past about playing in a "box" or around a chord form. Could you elaborate on this?

Yes. I just mean that if there's a II-V progression, for example, I would put my hand in the position of the I chord where the II-V chords would progress and play around that position.

So if you have a Dm7-G7 progression, you place your hand in the Cmaj chord position and play around the notes of that chord form or scale, and this will cover the notes of the Dm7 and G7?

Yes, that's right. I think this helps a lot when that one position or box covers more than one chord. You have to hear where the chords are going to and move towards that chord. Then you're in a position where all the intervals of those chords will be found.

Let's say for a tune like "Satin Doll" you're in the key of C, and the first two measures are Dm7-G7, and then it goes to Em7-A7 for two measures. Would you start in the position for the C chord or C scale for the first two measures, and then move into

position for the D chord for the next two measures?

Yes. You would be in position for the C chord, even though you're not playing the C chord. You use just the C position as a basis for where to find the notes of the Dm7 and G7 chords. There is a logical relationship to C. Then what you do for the next two measures is to move up two frets into the D position for the notes in the Em7 and A7. It's been a tradition in jazz to almost make a certain amount of musical rhyming, where you play a phrase and then repeat it with just a little variation in another key, sort of like a sequence.

How about when someone substitutes a D♭7 chord for the G7 going to C? What would you play for the D♭7?

I'd just slip up to the D♭ position for the D♭7 chord. There is something else you can do, and that is play an A♭m7 in front of the D♭7 and run a phrase against that and spell out those chords. Now remember, this goes by pretty fast because you're dividing the time in half. A lot of my pet phrases sort of attempt to spell that out. It's the sound I'm trying to convey.

Do you also think in terms of rhythm patterns when you're improvising?

I do play a lot of eighth-notes. When you don't have any drums in a group, the tendency is to supply the time or an eighth-note feeling, so I play those real long phrases based on eighth-notes. I once told somebody that I was afraid to stop because the rhythm would stop. Most of the groups I worked with aside from Artie Shaw's didn't have any drums.

When you're comping for soloists, do you think of any kind of melody line behind them?

Sometimes if you're playing a phrase in chords the top notes will form a melodic line, but basically when you're comping for a soloist you should try to stay out of his way and yet confirm what he's playing by filling out the harmony. I don't like to get too busy

against another person unless it's lyrical and not much is happening, like maybe he's playing a lot of pretty intervals or flowing things, so a sort of busy background wouldn't be offensive. What really bothers me a lot is when you have a piano and guitar comping at the same time, and both are going in different directions. When I was with Artie Shaw we had both piano and guitar, but we didn't comp at the same time. When either of us comped the other would lay out. Of course this was all worked out: Artie never left too much to chance.

Do you have any hobbies outside of music?

Well, I like to tinker around with electronics. I like working around the house.

Do you still paint signs?

Oh, yeah. I paint all the signs over at the club I'm working at now.

But how many signs can you paint for one club?

A whole lot if they're all about me [*laughs*]. Sometimes I might letter a boat or truck for someone in town. I don't do it as much as I once did.

Do you listen to much music?

Yes. I like some classical music, like Ravel — he pleases my ear. His music has a lot of harmonic meat to it. I like a lot of piano music. I enjoy Hank Jones. I like Keith Jarrett; he plays a lot of Ravel-like harmonies. I don't listen to a whole lot of guitar players; they make me feel uncomfortable. There are so many good players around today.

Of the younger guitarists, whom do you like?

Well, I hear a lot of them when I put the radio on. I like John McLaughlin a lot. He's very much influenced by [saxophonist] John Coltrane. He certainly has a lot of technique, and he can play some nice chord melodies.

If you could do it all over again, would you do things differently?

Yeah. I'd learn how to read.

— JERRY GARCIA —

BY JON SIEVERT — OCTOBER 1978 & JULY 1988

WHEN JERRY Garcia collapsed into a d i a b e t i c coma in 1986, Grateful Dead fans — a.k.a. Deadheads — the world over held their collective breath. Not only were they concerned for the well-being of their beloved hero, but for the loss of an entire lifestyle, as well. For more than 25 years, Garcia's graceful single-line modal improvisations and thin, quavery vocals have been the voice of the Grateful Dead; if there were any single member whose loss would certainly spell the end of this unique American institution, surely it was he.

But Garcia and the Dead not only survived, they have thrived. Within a year and a half after his return to action, the Dead produced its first Top-10 single ("Touch of Grey"), a platinum LP (*In the Dark*), and a #1 hour-long music video (*So Far*). Outside the Dead, Jerry also took his own electric band and a new acoustic band to Broadway, selling out 17 shows in record-setting time at New York's Lunt-Fontanne Theatre.

All of this has brought the band a certain sort of, well, *respectability* among the establishment media. There have been cover stories in *USA Today* and *Rolling Stone* (which virtually snubbed — even disdained — the band for more than 10 years), *Forbes* examined their unusual path to success, and *People* magazine picked Garcia as one of its most intriguing personalities of 1987. Grateful Dead videos are even aired on MTV.

This newfound attention and success has had little effect on the way the band has always gone about its business, however. Long ago, the Grateful Dead created its own universe, which, as Garcia says, has its own parameters and goals. Where conventional music-business wisdom dictates that touring is a money-losing proposition embarked on only to support record sales, the Dead has literally survived on ticket sales. Until "Touch of Grey," the band never had anything near a Top-40 single, although two albums produced in 1970 — *Workingman's Dead* and *American Beauty* — have sold steadily enough over the years to be certified platinum (one million units sold). Nevertheless, for years the band has played about 100 concerts annually, selling out coliseums and stadiums with virtually no advertising beyond the Grateful Dead Hotline — an array of answering machines that provide tour and ticket information around the clock. And where most bands actively prohibit and police taping of concerts by fans, the Dead actually provide a special section for tapers at all of their performances, which last up to three hours.

Jerry Garcia and the Grateful Dead have become cultural institutions, though they never planned it that way. Other bands have achieved a similar status, but for different reasons; unlike the major rock attractions who are idolized from afar, the Dead are seen up close, enjoyed, and respected. They were patriarchs of San Francisco's psychedelic colony of the

the 1960s, city fathers in a community of crazies. As perceived by the general press, Garcia and company were *the* hippie band, playing music for getting stoned, seeing God, dancing, singing along, blowing bubbles, mellowing out, or whatever — good-time music without rock-star pretensions. But the Grateful Dead were more than that, and they have produced an extensive catalog of music that transcends the experiences of late-60s San Francisco.

Nearly three decades ago, instead of seeking the isolation of celebrity or big-bucks show biz, they gave free concerts. Their go-with-the-flow approach to live performing involved half-hour tuneups, long breaks between songs, marathon concerts, an eventual 23 tons of privately owned equipment and a lesser amount of drugs. These sometimes impromptu events were promoted by word of mouth or by flower children with rainbow clothes and pinwheel eyes, passing out handbills, perhaps balloons, and sometimes LSD, which was legal until August 1966. Concert posters with kaleidoscopic, highly stylized artwork were tacked up in head shops and on telephone poles. The Dead often comprised the house band for the multimedia, multi-drug extravaganzas organized to a large degree by novelist Ken Kesey and his pals, the Merry Pranksters, and documented in Tom Wolfe's book, *The Electric Kool-Aid Acid Test.*

Though the band's music was a virtual soundtrack for the Haight-Ashbury psychedelic experience, it was not what became known as acid rock. As Garcia pointed out, the music itself was always more important than the general public's conceptions (or misconceptions) of the counterculture. Like his various bands, Jerry Garcia — as a solo artist, Dead member, occasional session player, and bandleader — has evidenced an extraordinary range of influences. He has also forged for himself something of a reputation as a "playing junkie," turning up in bars — guitar in hand — in the middle of Dead tours that feature five- or six-hour sets. Ever since Jerry took up pedal steel, he has had some sort of steady recording/performing situation outside of the Grateful Dead. First came the country-rock New Riders of the Purple Sage, and then the outside jazz work with guitarist Howard Wales, a fruitful relationship with jazz organist/keyboardist Merl Saunders, a return to his 5-string banjo roots as he teamed up with some of the finest bluegrass musicians alive in Old and In the Way, and finally his quartet, the Jerry Garcia Band.

Garcia was born August 1, 1942, in San Francisco. His father was a Spanish immigrant and a working jazz musician who played clarinet and saxophone. His mother was a nurse. Jerry was introduced to music early; there were instruments all around the house, and the family often sang. His father died young, and his mother remarried and moved to the Palo Alto area south of San Francisco. Because there was a piano in the house, Jerry took a few "aborted" lessons. On his fifteenth birthday his mother gave him an accordion, which he promptly took to a pawnshop and traded for his first electric guitar, a Danelectro.

Not knowing anyone who could give him lessons, or even how to tune the guitar, Jerry adjusted it to an open tuning that "sort of sounded right to me." Soon he was emulating the licks of his first idol, Chuck Berry. Following another move and a transfer to a new high school, Garcia dropped out and joined the Army at age 17.

The Army hitch lasted about nine months, until Jerry and the Army came to an agreement that service life was not for him. The experience was not entirely a waste, because Jerry developed an interest in the acoustic guitar and began to work on rock-oriented tunes. After leaving the Army he returned to Palo Alto and soon struck up a friendship with another recently discharged G.I., Robert Hunter, later the Dead's nonperforming lyricist. Hunter also played a little guitar, so he and Garcia teamed up for their first professional gigs. It wasn't long before Jerry developed an attachment to the 5-string banjo, and for three years he practically abandoned the guitar in favor of its round-body cousin. A series of acoustic string bands followed, including the Hart Valley Drifters, which was a bluegrass band that featured Hunter on bass, David Nelson (later of the New Riders) on guitar, and a mandolin player named Ken Frankel. That group won the amateur Blue Grass Championship at the 1963 Monterey Folk Festival.

In the meantime, various musical elements were beginning to fall into place around Palo Alto. One was the establishment of Mother McCree's Uptown Jug Champions, which featured Garcia on acoustic guitar and banjo, Bob Weir, Bob Matthews (an engineer who later helped to form the Alembic Company and is still part of the Dead family), the late Ron McKernan (also known as Pigpen), and John Dawson (later of the New Riders). In late 1964, the jug band went electric at Pigpen's suggestion, and the die was cast when the group was renamed the Warlocks. Bill Kreutzmann became the drummer, and Phil Lesh took over on bass shortly thereafter. It wasn't long before they decided that they needed a new name and chose the Grateful Dead after spotting the term on a page randomly selected from a dictionary.

According to Garcia, the Grateful Dead has always considered the audience an integral part of the band, recognizing that one could not exist without the other. This kind of loyalty and identification has created a subgenre of Deadheads that literally follow the band around the country to all its shows. Other manifestations of this devoted loyalty include a well-written fan magazine, *The Golden Road*, and a periodically updated computer database called *Dead Base*, which includes a complete history of Grateful Dead set lists starting with 1965. In addition, David Gans, author of an excellent "oral and visual portrait" of the Dead, *Playing in the Band*, hosts a nationally syndicated radio program called the *Deadhead Hour*. There's even been a book *about* Deadheads, *Grateful Dead: The Official Book of the Dead Heads*.

Internally, little has changed and much has changed over the intervening years. Except for the addition of keyboardist Brent Mydland in 1979, the band's lineup remains intact: Garcia, rhythm guitarist Bob Weir, bassist Phil Lesh, and drummer/percussionists Mickey Hart and Bill Kreutzmann. Never a particularly prolific recording band, the Dead only managed to produce one studio LP [1980's disappointing *Go to Heaven*] between 1979 and 1987's *In the Dark*, though several aborted attempts were made. Conventional wisdom among the Deadhead network focused on various band members' personal problems, including drug dependency, as primary contributing factors. By the end of '84, members of the band and the Dead family had become so concerned about Jerry's downward-spiraling health that they confronted him and asked him to get help. In January 1985, Garcia was busted for drug possession in San Francisco's Golden Gate Park. He managed to beat the rap and, by most accounts, little changed.

On July 10, 1986, Jerry's body made the decision for him. Two days after the end of a short tour on which the Dead shared the bill with Bob Dylan, Garcia dropped into a diabetic coma. "The symptoms were all there," he recalls, "but I didn't recognize them. I was thirsty all the time, which meant I was dehydrated. When the doctors took a blood sample in the hospital, it was thick as mud." When he came out of the coma, he began an extended period of rehabilitation, learning to walk, talk, and play guitar again. "The neuro pathways were still there, but I had to learn to reconnect everything," he says. Gradually, things came back together, though he admits that it is still an ongoing process. Indeed, it was

a jolt to hear this well-read, extremely articulate man occasionally groping for words. "That's part of the fallout — I have to hunt for words. I used to have instant access."

Three months after his collapse, Garcia was ready to take his first tentative steps back into the performing arena, making a guest appearance on Halloween with Weir's band, Bobby and the Midnites. On December 15, 1986, the Dead was reunited, opening with "Touch of Grey" as the crowd emotionally sang along on its prophetic chorus: "I will get by. I will survive." With hard drugs and bad health behind him, Garcia revitalized the Grateful Dead upon his return.

In January 1987, the band rented the Marin Veterans Auditorium in their hometown of San Rafael, California, and in two weeks smoothly laid down the basic tracks for *In the Dark*. Jerry Garcia became again a very busy man. In addition to the hectic Grateful Dead touring schedule, which included a midsummer 1987 stadium tour backing up Bob Dylan, Garcia's long-running electric band stayed active, and he formed the new acoustic group. His onstage demeanor changed dramatically from moody and withdrawn to active and joyous, which was reflected in his guitar playing. He truly seemed to have found *new* life with the Dead. Alto saxophone legend Ornette Coleman invited Jerry to join him in the studio for work on his album *Virgin Beauty*. In the midst of all this, much of his important out-of-print early solo and ensemble work with artists outside of the Grateful Dead began to reappear on compact disc. In the summer of 1992, Garcia fell ill again — this time due to a more general lapse in health, by no means as threatening as his collapse six years before. He withdrew from the public eye to convalesce and to prepare for a resurrection of what Jerry calls "the longest running experiment in rock and roll" which did, in fact, occur in time for a live performance at Halloween.

[October 1978]

Previously you've said that you seem to go through cyclic learning stages. What causes that to happen?

I think it's something that happens to every guitar player as he keeps on playing through the years. You're struggling to learn a whole body of material, and you finally learn it and can play it expertly, and then you get bored. It becomes a *now what?* situation. You're struggling to obtain ground and you reach a plateau, and then your boredom finally drives you to develop to new levels. I think that's a healthy and normal thing. I seem to go through it about once every year and a half or two years pretty regularly. That's pretty much how my metabolism seems to work. I think of myself really as a guitar student as much as a player or performer, because there's so much being developed and so much that's already been done that I'll never learn it all.

What kind of things do you do during these stages?

First I go out and buy all the new guitar method books that have come out since the last time and read through them and try out ideas and exercises. I find it really helpful to see somebody else's handle on it, because it's possible they can show me new ways of looking at the instrument or music that I hadn't considered before. The state of guitar education today is incredible compared to just 15 years ago. You can learn an astounding amount from just reading books that are available today. I'm working very hard now. I'm working hard on things that I haven't worked hard on before. I have certain exercises that I do, but it's more like working out little bits and pieces of unfinished ideas. A lot of it is just free playing, exploring for places where all of a sudden something is vague or awkward — like suddenly finding yourself in a position that's odd in relation to the key you're playing in. Or, for example, you're doing a run that's going down scale intervals, and you're on like the top E string, and you're ending one part of the passage on your first finger and then jumping a position and starting the next part with your little finger and moving down. That's a difficult thing to do on the guitar.

How do you learn to master that kind of passage?

I'll just keep going over it until it's smooth, and then it starts to turn up in other places. Anything you work at technically always turns out to have unexpected rewards. You realize later, not only is this convenient for me to make a very full, long run, but it also gets me conveniently from position A to B to C. You start to really see interconnections.

How is your picture of the fingerboard developing?

The complete pattern of the fingerboard is becoming more apparent. I'm forcing it into shape in my own psyche, in my own way of seeing and feeling. I spend seven or eight hours a day with it. I'm trying to rebuild myself; I feel like it's time for me to do that in my playing. I don't know whether it will amount to anything, but in six months I'll know. I'm sort of in a two-year plan right now — the first phase of the next level.

When you're not going through these intense learning periods, how much time do you usually spend with a guitar?

It depends on the schedule. When I'm on the road it's a lot more, but when I'm home I'd say I spend no less than an average of two hours a day at the absolute worst. That's like really screwing around. I think four hours is more normal for me. On the road it goes up to about six, including the show. I lose my edge in a day if I don't stay on top of it constantly. Anything more than two days and it's like being a cripple. And the more you play, the more you notice it if you miss a day. But then there's also the thing that if you're away from the guitar for two or three days sometimes you can come back with something else. Now that's not one of those things you can depend on, but sometimes it does happen just in the flow. You come back and you have a little more of something. I don't know what — confidence, new ideas, or something.

What do you see as your major limitation?

A lack of an early musical education. I've been able to compensate for it some, but having an early education means that a lot of things become reflexive, automatic. Now, sometimes that can perpetuate bad habits on a technical level, but in terms of things like sight-reading and the like, I wish I had started earlier. I'm not unhappy with my progress, but that's the one thing. As it is, I'm glad to have been able to develop an intuitive approach to music, and I can see that there could be disadvantages to having a completely schooled approach. Sometimes that blocks out the intuition; there are people with great technique who have nothing to say.

How did your early process of music education work?

My first orientation was learning from my ear. So I learned mostly from records — Freddie King, B.B. King extensively — and, you know, everybody else. That was my first exposure, mostly because the [San Francisco] Bay Area didn't have that many guitar players back when I started playing, and there really wasn't a lot of local information, or at least I wasn't able to uncover it. For me, I would describe my own learning process as wasting a lot of time. I did it the hardest way possible, or it seems that way now. I had to spend a lot of time unlearning things — bad habits and so forth. I think I went through as many of these unlearning cycles as I could. It was around 1972 or '73 when I finally unlearned all the things that had hung me up to that point.

Like what, specifically?

Oh, like playing out of preference to certain positions. Like tending to think along certain positions because they were more available to my hand, rather than for musical reasons. It became a serious problem for me to correct onstage. I think that's an easy trap to fall into — doing things that are merely easiest for you and are within your immediate grasp with the excitement of playing onstage. And other things I would describe as rhythmic and idea habits in addition to technical habits — having a more or less limited kind of vocabulary and tending to depend on my ability to exploit it rather than developing a greater vocabulary. I've been through a lot of things like, for example, deciding never to play anything shorter than a half-note during a solo for a year in order to cut down the busyness. I get tired of busy stuff, and I decide that I want to exploit the single-note capability and the tone of the guitar, so for a period I play really slow leads regardless of the rhythmic path. After a while I get tired of doing that and start working on developing speed.

How do you keep track of the changes in your style?

For me the most useful thing is recording the show. That's something that a lot of musicians do. They just take one of those little cassette machines and put it right in front of their speaker or monitor. Pretty soon you realize that you've been playing nothing but eighth-note runs, for example. Using that with feedback from others can help you get through your boredom and enthusiasm cycles.

Do you use all the controls available to you on the guitar?

Yeah, whatever's there. If there were five more things I would use them, just because for me the guitar isn't really as important to me as music is. I love the guitar and I'm trying to become a guitar player, but it's the music that counts, so the more variety I can gain, the better off I am. There are times when I wish I were a combination of a French horn and an oboe. Anything that will give me more possibilities, I'm a nut for. The other side of that is that there has to be no hassle; the guitar should be predictable and repeatable. Usually I have a general category of tone that I'm involved in for any particular tune, and I just work off that. I think most of the changes I get in terms of dynamics and tone are a result of touch rather than fooling with the knobs, although I do fool with the knobs.

Could you discuss your approach to fingering?

I think it has something to do with my early 5-string banjo playing. Most guitar players I've noticed seem to use a kind of flat fingering. I've somehow trained myself to come straight down on top of the string. I play mostly on the tips of my fingers, so the high action doesn't get in my way at all. I'm not pulling other strings along with it and so forth.

Do you use the little finger on your left hand much?

Yes, early on I was lucky enough to have someone point out the usefulness of that finger. As a result it is one of my stronger fingers, and I prefer to use it even more than my ring finger. That's always made me different from most rock guitarists that I know — even the really good ones. I think in rock and roll a lot of guitar players favor something that lets them use the ring finger for greater articulation and vibrato effects. For me, I've got to be able to do it with every finger. I find it ridiculous to have to close all my ideas on my ring finger just so I can get a vibrato. That eliminates a lot of possibilities automatically.

How do you achieve your vibrato?

Well, I have about four or five different families of vibrato. Some of them are unsupported; that is to say, nothing is touching the guitar but my finger on the string. Other methods are supported, and I just move the finger for the sound. Sometimes I also use wrist motion, and other times I'll move my whole arm. I also use horizontal and lateral motion for different sound and speed. Each has its own separate sound, and it depends on what I'm going after and which finger I'm leading with. For example, if you're playing the blues, it's generally appropriate to use a slow vibrato. Generally speaking, I tend to be style-conscious in terms of wanting a song to sound like the world it comes from.

Do you play many notes by hammering-on and pulling-off?

Generally I like to pick every note, but I do tend to pull-off, say, a real fast triplet on things that are closing up — intervals that are heading up the scale. I do it almost without thinking about it. I almost never pull off just one note. I seldom hammer-on, because it seems to have a certain inexactitude for me. I think that was a decision I made while playing the banjo. My preference is for the well-spoken tone, and I think coming straight down on the strings with the knuckles makes it. So my little groups of pull-offs are really well-articulated; it's something I worked on a lot.

How do you approach right-hand technique?

Generally I use a Fender extra heavy flatpick which I sometimes palm when using my fingers. The way I hold the pick is a bit strange, I guess. I don't hold it in the standard way but more like you hold a pencil. I think Howard Roberts describes it as the scalpel technique. The motion is basically generated from the thumb and first finger rather than say, the wrist or elbow. But I use all different kinds of motion, depending on whether I am doing single-string stuff or chords.

Do you find your middle-finger injury causing any problems?

Not at all. My brother cut it off with an axe when I was four years old, so I've been without it for a long time. Actually, it might have even helped me because of the independence I've developed. Normally your first two fingers and your last two fingers tend to work as units. I used the first and ring fingers to develop my three-finger banjo style, so I have total independence in the fingers. Also, I can tuck the pick between the first finger and the stub and easily switch to fingerpicking.

Could you discuss your distinctive approach to accenting?

Again, a certain amount of it is related to banjo playing, where you have problem-solving continually going on. There are three fingers moving more or less constantly, and you have to change the melodic weight from any one finger to any other finger. What that really involves is rhythmic changes. So for me it's always been interesting to have little surprises like, for instance, accenting all the *off*-beats for a bar. There's also the constant playing in odd times with the Grateful Dead that contributes to that. For instance, if the band is playing in 7/4 time, I might play in 4/4. When you do that sort of thing, you begin to notice certain ways in which the two rhythms synchronize over a long period of time. Thinking in these long lengths, you automatically start to develop rhythmic ideas that have a way of interconnecting. If you're in the right kind of rhythmic context, then you have the option of being able to continually re-evaluate your position in time. For me it then becomes a thing of syncopations based on other syncopations. For example, I like to start an idea when the music is in flow on a sixteenth-note triplet off of four. So that's like intensely syncopated on its own, and if I start my phrase there, it's like constructing one sentence off of another one before the first sentence is completed. That sort of linguistic analogy is something I'm very attracted to.

Going back to the early days, why did you switch from electric to acoustic at first?

Well, economics were involved; I could get work as an acoustic player. And also, in terms of accomplishment, I wasn't very good when I stopped playing electric. I didn't really start to develop an understanding — more than just a feel for the music — until I got into acoustic. It gave me that chance to be more reflective about it.

How significant did playing electric prove to be?

For me it was like finding my musical identity. That's what it really boils down to, just because everything I was looking for led to it. Something about the rhythmic quality of fingerpicking and banjo was getting at something I wanted to develop further, but the rigidity of the banjo stopped me. Going electric meant really being able to satisfy that rhythmic complexity, and then it became the desire to have the ability to sing, to be spontaneous and not to be locked into one form of music. When we were doing the jug band — Weir, Pigpen, and I — our inventory included some Jimmy Reed tunes and Muddy Waters things that really cried out for electric treatment. The transition was very easy when the time came.

What are some of the things you've gained playing with people like Merl Saunders?

When I was playing with Merl we did a lot of instrumental material — standards and jazz tunes and things like that. That required a whole lot of quick education for me, and Merl was responsible for that. He really helped me improve myself on a level of harmonic understanding. Playing with him required a whole different style from three-chord rock and roll or even ten-chord rock and roll; it was a whole different thing. But what I was able to bring into that situation was the ability to use odd-length runs in conventional formats. I was able to use ideas that were rhythmically uneven because of working in odd time signatures so much with the Dead. Because Merl did not work in odd times, my relationship with his rhythms made it possible for me to create ideas that were, for example, seven bars long against something that was fundamentally a 4/4 feel.

How about your work with Howard Wales?

With Howard we never had tunes; Howard would just play through tremendously extended changes. That developed my ear to an amazing point because I had nothing to go on. I didn't even know what key we were in. Here were all these extended chords coming out, and I really had to be able to hear a correspondence somewhere. Merl helped me improve my analytical ability and to understand more about how substitution chords work in standard musical forms. Howard was a great in-between there, because his playing was so outside and totally unpredictable. Also, playing with Merl gave me a real feeling of freshness that carried over to later work with the Dead. So for me, it's very healthy to work with other people. I like doing sessions when I can, but my favorite stuff is really my own band and the Dead. Those are the two most complete experiences for me.

How did Old and In the Way happen to come about?

That band was like scratching an itch I'd had for a long time. I got very much into playing 5-string banjo early on but was frustrated insofar as never really having a *good* band to play with. Bluegrass is band music and I've always loved that aspect. In fact, that's what I like best — band music rather than solo music. Playing with Old and In the Way was like playing in the bluegrass band I'd always wanted to play in. It was a great band and I was flattered to be in such fast company. I was only sorry that my banjo chops were never what they had been when I was playing continually, though they were smoothing out toward the end.

What is your relationship with the pedal steel guitar these days?

I haven't played it much for quite a while, though I played it pretty steadily for about four years. I really got into it, but it kind of became an either/or situation: I found it very hard to play half the night with a pedal steel and a bar in my left hand and then switch to straight overhand guitar. The difference between a solid finger configuation and a moving arm, wrist, and fingers was too great. It was painful to the muscles. It got to where I couldn't play either of them very well, and I realized it just wouldn't work. I don't consider myself a pedal steel player, and I'm always embarrassed to see that I've placed in the *Guitar Player* poll.

Could you talk about your process of composition?

I usually compose on the piano; the melody usually comes first, then the accompaniment. Most often I'll record it on a cassette, though there are certain things that I feel must be written out, or I'll definitely lose them. I can play things on a piano and have no idea what they really are unless I analyze them. I don't play piano that well, but it's possible to come up with a six-note chord that could be anything when I hear it on a tape. So sometimes I find it helpful to keep track of how I arrive at an idea, though I do find that if the idea has enough weight it sticks with me, and I rediscover it again later. I'm a lazy writer, not at all diligent.

How do you and Robert Hunter work together on songs?

It works just about every way. Sometimes I have a melody that must have a certain kind of phrasing, and it becomes a matter of discipline for him. I get down to very specific terms in telling him what musical qualities a lyric must have — at this point I want a vowel, at this point a percussive sound. Then other times he gives me a sheaf of lyrics, and I'll go through them and find ones that appeal to me or whatever and start to work on them. Then sometimes when we're working together to polish things up, a whole new idea will emerge, and we'll go with that. We trust each other. He trusts my ability as an editor; and I edit extensively — sometimes it drives him nuts — but we work together pretty well. It's been a long working relationship.

Once you have a tune together, how do you communicate with other members of the band for the recording process?

Well, I make a demo with the vocal and the changes and any arrangement ideas I feel are part of the essential construction of the tune. Then the Grateful Dead get together and everybody offers their interpretation; sometimes it's better than I would have conceived it, and sometimes it's not what I want. So we talk about it and try to find some way to make it work musically. One of the things I've learned is that the Dead's contributions to my compositions are invaluable. Same with the stuff I do with my band. John Kahn's contributions there are really important and necessary. By preference I'm a band player.

Do you consciously consider musical factors such as counterpoint and harmony between your guitar and voice?

In a way. More in performance than in conceptualization. Like I'll be performing a tune and realize, Oh — there's a hole here. My guitar and my voice are almost interchangeable. I'm in my best state when I really know the song and can sing it well, and I know the chords perfectly and where I am on the guitar at all times. It's a thing of feeling very continuous between the person who's the guitar player and the person who is the singer. It's a very neat feeling, almost magical.

What process do you go through for building solos?

The way I start is to learn the literal melody of the tune if there is one. Then I construct solos as though that were happening, and I'm either playing with it or against it. That's a pretty loose description, obviously, because there are a lot of other factors involved. Later on I start to see other kinds of connections, but one of my first processes is to learn the literal melody in any position. I am very attracted to melody. A song with a beautiful melody can just knock me off my feet, but the greatest changes on earth don't mean anything to me if they don't have a great melody tying them together in some sense.

It seems that you really enjoy playing rhythm in the Garcia band, which has no other guitarist.

Oh sure, and I'd do it more with the Dead except that Weir is such a great rhythm player. We all feel he's just the finest rhythm guitarist on wheels right now. He's like my left hand. We have a long, serious conversation going on musically, and the whole thing is of a complementary nature. We have fun, and we've designed our playing to work against and with each other. His playing, in a way, really puts my playing in the only kind of meaningful context it could enjoy. That's a hard idea to communicate, but any serious analysis of the Dead's music would make it apparent that things are designed really appropriately. There are some passages, some kinds of ideas that would really throw me if I had to create a harmonic bridge between all the things going on rhythmically with two drums and Phil's innovative bass style. Weir's ability to solve that kind of problem is extraordinary. He also has a beautiful grasp of altering chords and adding color. Harmonically, I take a lot of my solo cues from Bob. He's got very large hands; he's able to voice chords that most people can't reach, and he can pull them off right in the flow of playing. And now he's taken up playing slide leads quite a bit, and that's neat, too, because that's another context for me to play against.

Have you noticed any particular logic to the way the Dead has progressed through the years?

No, and that's one of the things that I constantly find interesting about the band. Each one develops in a different way and with a different sense of his own development. All of a sudden there's somebody with a whole bunch of ideas that you haven't stumbled on and might never have. That's the fun part of playing with other people and exposing yourself to different musicians. You find all these possible ways to grow. The Grateful Dead has never developed as a *group*. I mean, we've developed as a group in a certain kind of large sense, but everybody's individual development has that thing of being surprising, interesting, and entertaining. That's one of the things that keeps the Dead interesting to be involved in.

Could you say a few words about any merits or disadvantages of playing stoned?

There's a thing about playing stoned without having pressure on you to play competently. If you have the space in your life where you can be high and play and not be in a critical situation, you can learn a lot of interesting things about yourself and your relation to the instrument and music. We were lucky enough to have an uncritical situation, so it wasn't like a test of how stoned we could be and still be competent — we weren't concerned with being competent. We were more concerned with being high at the time. The biggest single problem from a practical point of view is that obviously your perception of time gets all weird. Now, that *can* be interesting, but from a practical standpoint I try to avoid extremes of any sort, because you have the fundamental problems of playing in tune and playing with everybody else. People have to pay a lot of money to see us, so it becomes a matter of professionalism. You don't want to deliver somebody a clunker just because you're too high. I don't, anyway.

Do you have a practice schedule?

I have about half a dozen things that I regularly do. They are mostly involved with standard scale intervals working out of different positions. I do a lot of two-octave chord arpeggios and a couple of other things, but they are all designed fundamentally to develop the ability to move from any position to any other position, from any note to any other note on the guitar. Most of them stress alternate picking. One good thing is to take a scale or exercise from any competent guitar book or from *Guitar Player* or even something you already know and play it through, starting on a downstroke. You alternate-pick the whole pattern. Then repeat it, but start on an upstroke to get an understanding of where the rhythmic bias falls. Practicing that way will give you a consistent flow to your playing no matter what you want to do; how you draw things out of it is your own business.

Do you practice dynamic variations?

Yes, I'll turn my guitar all the way up with a practice amp and start doing arpeggios, playing very quietly at the beginning and then getting gradually louder as a function of touch. That makes it so you have a smoothness from your loudest, hardest picking to your softest picking while keeping the same position. Many guitarists change the way they hold their hands when changing dynamics. As a result they end up with a light-touch group of licks — the very fast stuff — but they can't develop any power. For me the thing is continually making those conversions back and forth from quiet to loud picking. It was something that hung me up for quite a while. The dynamics of a solo are something I think about a lot.

Do you have any suggestions concerning ear training?

Listen to a lot of music. I like to amuse myself by trying to figure out intervals whenever I listen to something. I realize I've gone through all kinds of processes learning how to do that, and they wouldn't necessarily apply to someone who is in the initial process of learning; it seems to be a cumulative thing. One very important exercise is to familiarize yourself with the sound of different kinds of chords. Listen and decide if it's major or minor. Is it the I chord? The II chord? Is it part of the dominant chain of chords? Does it have a raised or flatted 5th? A raised 9th? Everybody's ear is different, so each person has a different approach. My inclination is to hear the logic of the melody. Somebody else has a better ear for hearing the progression.

Have you ever done any teaching?

Yeah, I taught for a while before I could really play well — in Palo Alto. I learned a lot by doing that, and I still run into my old students occasionally, and some of them turned out to be quite good. Teaching gives you a lot of opportunities to observe how people learn, and that's very good feedback. You have to become more analytical to transmit it to someone.

How did you approach the teaching process?

I really stressed teaching my students how to hear and how to learn things off of records, because that was the way I knew best. I remember that one of those guitar instruction books — I can't remember who wrote it — said that people basically learn by one of three approaches or a combination: Some people learn best by having something explained to them conceptually; some learn best by seeing somebody play — seeing fingers on fingerboards; and some learn best by hearing. I know some guys who can't learn if you try to show them something but can pick it right up if they can hear it. It's helpful to know which kind of learner you are, and once you've gotten into learning from one source — be it books, records, or a teacher — you can become aware of the other ways of learning. For example, if you have a teacher, it might be helpful to develop your ear on the side if your teacher wasn't turning you on to that sort of thing. If you're listening to a lot of stuff, it might be helpful to look at books. It's all interesting to me. You can find out virtually anything these days about the guitar. Also, I've had a lot of luck with clarinet and piano books.

If you were going to teach someone to play guitar, what approach would you take?

I'd have to start with what they liked. That's the way I used to teach. I'd find out what kind of music they wanted to play. That has to be there. If there is nothing that they want to play, then they don't want to learn how to play the guitar. It's that simple. I would make every effort to get as close to what they wanted as quickly as possible in order to scratch that itch, because you want to accomplish something. If you're just doing the guitar, it doesn't make any sense. But if you can accomplish something like, "I heard this in my head, and now I can do it with my hands," then you've made that leap of faith that it's possible to play the guitar. Once somebody gets that going, they can learn.

Do you read music?

Sort of. As I mentioned earlier I'm a very poor sight-reader. I need a little time with something. I can read enough to figure out a lead line or chord chart if it's put in front of me. I've more or less taught myself to read as I go along, and I find it necessary. Reading notes has been mostly a matter of access. What good is a book of Django Reinhardt solos if you can't read them? Being able to read means there's more material out there I can pick up. It's certainly not something I'm called on to use a lot, but there are times when I find it necessary to sketch out an idea to somebody who has a legitimate background — a string player or whatever.

What kind of music do you listen to?

Just about everything, really. I buy lots of records, and I trade tapes. I also have a lot of friends turning me on to things, so I'm continually exposed to new music. And not only modern American music or guitar playing, but I listen to keyboard players a lot. I go through little fevers, like one time I suddenly got excited about orchestration and started listening to all of the Duke Ellington that I could find. I went through a period — actually I'm still going through it — of listening to as much [jazz keyboard legend] Art Tatum as I can find. So much great music has already happened that catching up is a hell of a job. And there's so much new stuff coming out all the time that's so impressive.

What do you like that's new?

It's really hard to draw a line on what's considered new. I really like Al Di Meola, George Benson, and Pat Martino. Pat's really one of my favorites; rhythmically he's really fine. There's a young flamenco player named Paco de Lucia who knocks me out. He has a beautiful flow to his music that's really rare to guitarists. And every once in a while I hear something on the radio, and I can't believe it and have no idea who it is I'm hearing.

What do you have to say about the state of guitar playing in general?

There are more good guitar players alive today than have ever existed. I welcome it. It's been a long time getting here, the legitimizing of the electric guitar. Everybody has something to say. I really feel that you can't avoid finding your voice if you keep playing. You have the voice, whether you recognize it or not. I remember reading the Oscar Peterson interview in *Keyboard* magazine, where he talks about seeing Art Tatum play. Tatum told him he knew a guy down in New Orleans who could only play one chorus of the blues in *C*, and that Tatum would give anything to play that chorus the way that other guy could.

Are there any disadvantages to music from the particular perspective of the guitarist?

For me, I think the only danger is being too much in love with guitar playing. The music is the most important thing, and the guitar is only the instrument. Any musician can gain something by analyzing his or her role in the context of whatever music they're playing. A guitar player who can back up tastefully, who can find something interesting to say behind a vocal, and who knows what music is all about is someone who is doing the whole job. I see the guitar as one of the leading voices in the evolution of ensemble music. For me, playing in my band — it's like a four-piece band, essentially — is like playing in the new string quartet. It's the new conversational music where the instruments speak to each other, and you have that kind of tightness and dynamic happening — the stuff of string quartets.

[July 1988]

What do you hang onto harmonically when you're working in chromatic modes with someone like Ornette Coleman or during the Dead's "space" segment?

It depends on what I hear. If somebody's playing something that supports me that has fundamentally, say, a *D* minor seventh tonality, then I have lots of different places to go. If a guy is hanging in there rocking between two chords like *Dm7* and *Em7* — he's doing that whole-step back and forth — then I can play in *C* major or *E♭* major or *E* major seventh. I take my cue from what I'm hearing, and then it's a question of appropriateness. I'm always leaning on the edge of, "Does this work?" If it doesn't, I change it. Part of it is just my own taste. I like the sound of some things that are dissonant and strange, and some I don't. I don't really know why, but as I develop them, they provide little pieces of furniture for me to

say, "Okay, I know that I can use this broken mode where the first part is a Lydian mode going up, and the second part is a double diminished scale that continues up a half-step higher." There are things that work sort of mechanically and sound good up to a point. But then you have to change it at some point or else it doesn't really sound good, because it's not purely double diminished. For instance, when you get to a certain point, you have three half-steps in a row. It's that kind of stuff. If I had enough time to sit around with it and analyze it, I could probably explain to you what it is that makes me think I'm doing okay. But really I'm going on, "Does it sound like it's working?"

How important is access to the fingerboard in that equation?

Very important. You have to have enough access to the fingerboard that you're not hung up about where you are. In other words, "What key am I in? What scale interval am I at?" You need to be able to let that go past you. I'm just getting into being able to get a good sound, regardless of the structure's mathematics. So much of the guitar is patterns. But if you look at it right, patterns start to melt into each other; pretty soon you can hit anything from anywhere. The quality of consciousness that you put into the note also has a lot to do with it. You can play any note in any context, and if you play that sucker like you mean it, it's going to sound good — almost. The note that comes after it, and when it comes, and how smoothly you play it, and how much expression — individuality you can give the note — that also has a lot to do with it. Like, choosing to give a note a really rich vibrato or a real dry attack. Or having a slow opening and a long sustain. The personality of the note has as much to do with its appropriateness as the setting does. I'm finding that out more and more. If you're two octaves above whatever instrument is playing the chords, you can play almost any note and it will work as an extended part of the chord. If you're in the same octave, then it will work because it darkens or brightens the chord — like an interior voice. It's like playing two hands in the same octave on the piano; it really clangs. If you spread it out more, it sounds prettier, though the darkness is sometimes real interesting. The rhythm is the final part of the equation. The way you release notes, their value, and the holes that you leave have a lot to do with the strength or the power of your playing. When the band is pulsing along, punching eighth-notes — where you can think of any note as *the one* — I like to do things like play a figure that's maybe seven beats long starting, say, on the end of beat four. You create this incredible tension, and the next thing you play is going to either increase the tension or you're going to find yourself back on a new *one*. It's like some kind of hypothetical jigsaw puzzle where all the pieces are white and all the same.

Do you feel that the space segment has gotten more successful over the years?

Well, it's gotten a little narrower lately, but I think it's going to expand out again pretty quick. The drummers have been adapting to a largely electronic setting over the last year, because they've replaced most of their stuff with electronics, and they're now getting used to it. Bob and I have been basically working together. Bob plays the setting, and I play over the top of it. That's pretty much the way it works. But I think we're going to start changing our space segment because we're capable of doing so much more now. And as we find ourselves more involved in the MIDI world, I think it's probably just going to get weirder and weirder — more orchestral.

Have you gone through periods when you've been in danger of falling into a structure?

Structure is not a problem with the space stuff. It doesn't even come close to having a structure. But there is a form. That is to say it's Bob and I with Phil. But in terms of actually falling into something that we could repeat, even if we wanted to, we're a long way from being anywhere near that.

As your grasp of technique becomes greater, how do you avoid the danger of technique taking over feeling? Does that ever become a problem?

Yes, it does. But in the long run it stops being a problem. The point is to keep looking. What happens with me classically is that I go through spurts of, "Wow, here's a whole bunch of stuff to learn," and start really poking away at my technique. Pretty soon I'm dominated by technique, which really is another way of saying, "Now I'm playing all habits." I'm doing these things because I practiced them so much. My fingers do them, and I'm not even there. Finally, I get bored with my playing and I make myself change somehow. But it has to come up to the wall because my musical me is delighted with being able to execute stuff that's difficult. That part of it is very satisfying. It's kind of like classical music. You're satisfied to be able to rip off that scherzo [*laughs*]. You want to be able to do that, but you want to be able to absorb the technique and let the musicality be the thing that comes forth. For me, the only way to do it is to over-amp at every level. I'll just bump into that technical wall, overamp on it, and then bounce off of it.

Sometimes it takes six months; sometimes more or less. And then I get bored with it and say, "Now I've got to do something really weird." I'll start busting myself. I decide I'm not going to play any figure with more than three notes next to each other. I start creating little problems. And those are just as weird because then you're avoiding stuff. The whole thing is kind of artificial in a way, but eventually everything normals out. That's why I like to keep playing. I'm involved in this series of ongoing problem solving and I haven't gotten to that place where I'm playing the way I want to yet. I've got to keep playing to get there. It's a dynamic problem.

What are the most important elements for getting a good tone?

It depends on what your concept of "good" tone is. First of all, it's important to have a concept of good tone — no matter what it is. And then the rest of it is just finding it. My concept of good tone is a clear, unambiguous sound on each note. For me, that means relatively high frets, relatively heavy strings, and a thick pick, so that your touch is coming from the hand and not from the pick. And that's as basic as it gets. The rest of it has to do with pickups and speakers. I go for a slightly higher action because I like a clear note. But if you set the action too high, you're out of tune. Intonation is real important to me now — more than it used to be. I'm much more conscious now when I pull or bend a string.

You get a very wide range of tones and colors. Do you have ways of organizing them?

I have basically *the* clean sound and *the* fuzzed-out sound. Those are my two basic colors. The rest of it has to do with the way I have my knobs set and my effects. My guitar's treble cuts are not normal. They have capacitors in them so that when I roll the volume back, the tone stays the same. I have a unity-gain amplifier in my guitars, and that's the only reason I have it — so I can change volume without changing the tone. The capacitors also serve as resonance boosters, so when I roll the knob all the way back, I get kind of a hollow horn-like quality with plenty of cut left to play a solo. It's doesn't really filter the way a wah-wah pedal does — it's not that narrow. It's more of a resonance boost. It does cut the top some, but it also does this other thing to the midrange. So I only choose the pots and capacitor combination that produces that kind of effect, so that gives me an all-the-way-on, all-the-way-off on each pickup, which provides six basic tone voices. Then, when I put those through the fuzz, it invents a new high end because of the way the fuzz hears low-end or midrange resonance. You no longer have the bright, screaming high end where you can pick out harmonics, although the fuzz adds a high end that brings out the fullness of the interior sound. Sometimes when I play a blues chorus or something where I use the distorted sound, I change the tone by whipping the tone knob all the way down. Most of the time the tone knob is totally useless, but in this case it really does change the tone. I also have a 5-position Stratocaster-type pickup selector so I can use the half positions, in- and out-of-phase, and with the humbucking and single-coil switch on each pickup. So right there, that's like 12 discrete possible voices that are all pretty different. And the whole thing with guitar and effects is getting something where you can hear the difference. That gives me a lot of vocabulary of basically different tones. And that's just the electronics. The rest of it is touch. I mostly work off the middle pickup in the single-coil setting and I can get almost any sound I want out of that. And touch is so individualized. It's something every guitar player has to find for himself.

Do you modify your effects setup frequently?

Not very frequently, but every two years or so Steve Parish and I go out to the music stores to see if there's anything new in the world of guitar stuff. There never is. It's all modifications of the same. I'm still waiting for someone to come with up a MIDI guitar system that I like, which will happen sometime in the next few years. It's one of those things I try periodically and say, "Well, not yet." I've got some stuff in my setup that I've had a very long time. But I do go out to try stuff, and if there's anything even remotely interesting, I buy it and stick it in my effects rack and see what happens.

How much do your speakers matter?

They're like your strings. You have to change them pretty regularly, or you start to get a real "wet"

sound. They're also the most weather-sensitive of anything. If you're playing in a humid climate, all of a sudden that cardboard turns to papier-mâché. Then you have something real soggy-sounding coming out. Speakers notice all those changes in pressure that are a function of altitude and changes in humidity — they're the most sensitive. That's what is finally producing the sound that everybody hears when you're playing an electric guitar. So they're like your strings. You have to be real careful with them. You have to listen to them carefully to notice whether they're dying out on you. And I can fry a speaker in no time flat. I can kill 'em. I have a lot of speakers onstage, and I try not to run them too loud because I hate blowing them.

Do you play both acoustic and electric at home?

Yes. To me, they're separate instruments. There's a certain amount of crossover, because when I play the acoustic I don't use a capo, for example. And I play in any key off the fingerboard. To me, it's what comes out. It doesn't matter how I get there. If it comes out and sounds right, then that's what I want. If I spend enough time working on the acoustic guitar, then my touch gets good enough that I can get it out the way I want it to sound. My sense of how I want it to sound is something that has evolved only very recently. It's just not the same instrument as an electric, and once you admit it, you save yourself a world of hurt.

It must be great to still be in love with what you do after nearly 25 years.

There's nothing like it. We've just been incredibly lucky, because personally and professionally we enjoy each other's company. But more than that, we still have that ability to baffle each other, which I think is really the key. I don't know where you come up with other people who are like this. It's just a rare thing.

— BILLY GIBBONS —

BY JAS OBRECHT — FEBRUARY 1981, AUGUST 1984, & MARCH 1986

PAUL NATKIN

ZZ TOP HAS enjoyed many a success during the past 15 years. Flip on MTV or practically any other rock video program, and chances are you'll soon sight the three baggy-suited mysterious trio materializing on and evaporating off the screen as they loan their customized '34 Ford coupe, cool guitars, and spectacular women to the cause of true lust or ultimate cool. A green three-fingered paw slithers from beneath the foil in "TV Dinners" to change a spaceman's channel back to ZZ, and the message is clear: Even an alien intruder digs the thick chords, pointed solos, and relentless boogie of America's foremost blues-rock trio.

Video has become pop music's reigning art form of the '80s, and ZZ Top is among the first bands to cash in on a grand scale. A few statistics: *Eliminator* peaked in the *Billboard* charts at #9. The album has sold over 3,200,000 copies and remains among Warner Bros.' top sellers. And, thanks to the videos of "Gimme All Your Lovin'," "Sharp Dressed Man," "TV Dinners," and "Legs," ZZ Top has clearly gone beyond their roots to capture a whole new audience.

The Texas trio's first fans were two-fisted drinkers around their hometown of Houston. "La Grange," from their third album *Tres Hombres*, spread their name coast-to-coast in 1973, and within a year "the little ole band from Texas" headlined for 80,000 fans at Austin's Texas Memorial Stadium. Then came 1975's *Fandango*, with its smoldering

"Blue Jean Blues" and two-minute hit "Tush." The album sold over a million copies and established a longevity record for an American band by staying in the charts for 83 weeks.

By 1975, *Newsweek* reported, ZZ Top had become one of the biggest acts in the country: "It has outdrawn Elvis Presley in Nashville, broken Led Zeppelin's attendance record for New Orleans, and reportedly sold more records last summer than the Rolling Stones at the height of their celebrated national tour." ZZ's Worldwide Texas Tour the following year was right out of Barnum & Bailey, resplendent with an onstage menagerie of bison, longhorn cattle, and rattlesnakes. Netting $11.5 million, it went down in rock history as one of the highest-grossing road shows. When the dust settled, guitarist Billy Gibbons, bassist Dusty Hill, and drummer Frank Beard parted as friends and went their separate ways for more than two years, while manager Bill Ham took on lengthy legal wrangling to switch the band's label. In late '78, ZZ Top signed with Warner Bros., reunited, and issued *Deguello*. "Thank You" and "Cheap Sunglasses" hit big, with "I'm Bad, I'm Nationwide" following in the wake. In 1981, the band released *El Loco* and, dressed in greasy mechanic's overalls, hit the stage again.

With the advent of MTV, the band had a shot at the top unlike any they had experienced before, and they were savvy enough to aim true. The trio boogied its way into homes across America with hit after hit from 1983's *Eliminator*: "Gimme All Your Lovin'," "Sharp Dressed Man," "TV Dinners," and "Legs." They became video superstars as toddlers to grand-folk stood transfixed by images of the bearded, baggy, mysterious trio and their customized coupe. The album spent more than a year in the Top 20; its sales now exceed 10 million copies worldwide.

On *Afterburner*, the distinctive, distorted guitar tone that fueled *Eliminator* hits slithers back into "Sleeping Bag," "Planet of Women," and "Dipping Low (In the Lap of Luxury)." Most tracks bristle with Gibbons' crunchy rhythms, sparkling solos, and trademark side-of-the-pick harmonics. A change of pace for ZZ, "Rough Boy" highlights chorus after chorus of emotional soloing. Billy's singing voice—once likened to a zipper being forced open—is stronger than ever.

Gibbons accepts his success with grace and appreciation. One of his most endearing qualities is the wry Texas wit that seeps through ZZ's music and sprinkles his conversation. His knowledge of the guitar and its lore is considerable, and he is a well-respected member of the guitar community. For years he's collected instruments rated from the highly desirable to the wildly improbable. His avid musical interests range from obscure blues to the latest news. Here, then, are excerpts from three of his interviews for *Guitar Player*.

[February 1981]

When you were beginning to learn, did you lean more towards imitation or innovation?

At the time I guess it was innovation. I was not really taking any lessons, just had to sit back on that porch and make up what I could.

What did you feel was most important to learn?

Well, I don't think that there was anything that seemed most important to learn. It's just what felt right, and that was all that wild music I kept hearing on that late-night radio, the same old stuff you hear in all these interviews, I guess — B.B. King, Jimmy Reed, Howlin' Wolf, T-Bone Walker.

Did you learn chords and leads at the same time?

Yeah, pretty much so. It all kind of fell into place about the same time.

Did other guitarists teach you things?

Oh, there's been a lot of exchange down the line. I think that it's probably the same exchange that most players experience when they're just getting started and going out and checking it out.

Who were some of your favorite soloists?

T-Bone Walker is an all-time favorite. Wayne Bennett with [blues singer] Bobby Bland is just a tremendous player. I still listen to "Stormy Monday Blues" that he did for Duke Records back in about '62 and still get a charge out of it.

Did you ever learn to read music?

What's the phrase — "Not enough . . . ." No, I'm not gonna say it! I'm strictly by ear. I can do charts, but it's mostly get up there and turn it up to Patent Applied For or Patent Pending and go for it!

What open tuning was "Mexican Blackbird" done with?

I think it was open G. I've used maybe 50 different tunings throughout our recording history, some unusual and some pretty standard, but that cut happened easiest with an open G.

What are some of the more unusual tunings you've used?

We got into a situation where two strings broke on a Strat. That must have been on the cut "El Diablo" on *Tejas*. Well, as you know, one string and you're stretching the issue, but when two go out, brother, you'd better go back and restring! At this time, the B and the G broke. It threw the other four strings into some strange Martian mode that I've yet to figure out. It's very interesting how many times you'll stumble on a tuning by accident, especially like with that Strat — completely uncalled-for and completely right there. It's just on you and you have to make the most of it. Usually I just get in there and fool around until something happens that sounds right.

Are there tunings that are particularly good for experimentation?

I have come up with a couple that might interest your readers aside from the standard E, D, A, and G tunings. In one you drop the biggie string down to D, you use the regular A, D, G, and B, and then drop the treble E to D. That puts a partial D chord on the bottom, and a G chord on the top three, which is kind of nice. And then there's the Cheater's 12: This requires a string change. You use a little first string in place of the big E and tune it in unison to your little E. Then you use a second string for the fifth, and tune it to an A. You use another second for your usual fourth string, tuned to a high D. So you've got standard tuning, but strange octaves — kind of a fake 12-string. It does produce a pleasant sound. I used the first open tuning on a lot of the slide cuts we do. I used the 12-string type tuning on a rhythm track of "Esther Be the One" on *Deguello*.

How do you set the action on your guitars?

I've been told that I play the action too high, and I've been told that I use too heavy of a string [*laughs*]. I've got the Billy G-strings [*laughs*]; they're pretty heavy. The gauges, starting on the bottom end, go from .011 and we work our way up to .052. I enjoy playing them.

Let's discuss a few of your techniques. Do you use the little finger of your left hand often?

Yes, constantly. Couldn't do without it.

Do you ever tap on the frets with your right-hand fingers?

Oh, sure! Listen to "Beer Drinkers and Hell Raisers" [*Tres Hombres*] and you'll hear it.

How many fingers do you use to bend notes?

Oh, it's just a wad of them!

When you use vibrato, is it more from the wrist or fingers?

Wrist. You get a little more control from the wrist.

What kind of pick do you use?

I use a quarter. I play with a 25¢ piece.

You're kidding.

I've been using a 25¢ piece for a long, long time. That's when I can get 'em [*laughs*]! It gives a real nice, rich tone. If you're not careful, it'll take a toll on the guitar strings. But it's beefy and chewy. I use that, and fingers.

Do you follow any conscious picking formulas?

Not really. [Bluesman] Albert Collins is a great finger technician, as is a good friend of mine, [Fabulous Thunderbirds guitarist] Jimmy Vaughan.

Do you anchor your right hand to any part of the guitar?

The heel of my hand is always right there glued to the bridge.

Do you do anything special to protect your hands?

No. Stay off the motorcycle!

In the context of your music, what do you think a solo should do?

I like to hit the right note. Even when you're stretching it all over the neck, it's important to know where you're going with it. You can definitely make someone wiggle in their seat a little bit if you know where you're heading with it and end up there.

Do you normally build your solos off of the chords and their inversions?

Yes. I don't think that it's unfounded in today's styles of playing to use discordant melodies and harmonies if the feel is right. With the vast array of tones available, it would be impossible to prescribe any particular right and wrong. I think music has arrived at a point where if it feels right and the tone is blending, then anything goes. And of course you can follow a chord structure, and you can follow a scale — a different mode structure — and come up with a delightful and correct piece. However, I think today it's a game of getting out there and getting after it, and if it feels right, you'll know.

Is there a difference between what you play for the public and what you play for yourself?

Not too much. We like the Norteña stuff — that border music — baja sexto and accordion. A little country and western pops up backstage every now and then.

When you're learning something, do you follow the rule of slow is fast?

Yeah. If you're really looking for something in particular, it helps to take your time.

Do you find that you're always learning?

Constantly. Without a doubt.

Do you visualize fingerboard patterns or hear phrases in your imagination before you hit them?

No, they just come out instantly. It's more spontaneous. We do tend to pay a lot of attention to tone. Even with music like ZZ Top, I think that obscene tones are quite acceptable.

Can you play everything you imagine?

No, that's still a glowing possibility.

Do you try new passages onstage, or do you tend to stick with structures you're familiar with?

Every night is something new. We really don't have too much set up. I think that it just goes fairly easily.

Do you have ways of psyching yourself onstage?

Yeah. We just take a moment to get into it. You know, just looking each other in the eye and making sure it's going to get low-down.

Could you describe the extent of your guitar collection?

We'll leave it kind of open-ended. They're in a big pile. I think there's probably close to 150, 200 maybe.

Do you keep your guitars unmodified?

Pretty much so. The majority of my collection is completely stock, just like it was right off the shelf. There's a corner that we've saved for some of the more exotic tortures that have been performed on a few instruments, but those are pretty much for laughs. We do get around to using most of these instruments, and it's pretty amazing. You know, American ingenuity doesn't stop with a paint job — I could show you some things. I've got a guitar that was made out of parts off a Model T!

How's it sound?

Oh, it's pretty rustic [*laughs*]. Primitivo!

Do you have any preference in fingerboard wood?

That rosewood's got a really nice texture, more open-grained than some of the harder woods such as maple or ebony. I feel I get more tone coloration out of rosewood.

How much do certain guitars or equipment matter musically?

Not much. They're tools that are a means to an end. I think ultimately it's what's inside you that brings it out. I'm sure everybody has found themselves in unfamiliar surroundings, suddenly banging away on an unfamiliar instrument, and yet the heart and soul and the art makes its statement.

There are instruments, though, that seem to teach you something.

Yes, without a doubt. Certain instruments lend themselves to either technical dexterity or the execution of some sophisticated passage.

Are there current players you admire?

Quite a few. The state of the art is definitely improving to the point where it is becoming unbounded for freshness and something new. Earlier I mentioned that some of my closest friends are the ones that I really admire. Jimmy Vaughan is a tremendous player. When we get the chance here in Texas, we always come back and see Doug Sahm, Van Wilks, and Eric Johnson. This tight little group constitutes a real friendly bunch, but they're still some of my favorites.

Over the years you've demonstrated increasing traces of humor in your blues.

Well, we're having more fun, and I don't think that it's wise to take anything we do so seriously that we can't just lay back and groove with it.

What do you want to accomplish in the future?

Oh, I think that's right around the corner — it's always tomorrow, always the next day. But if we can just keep getting low-down, keep getting funky and playing them blues, we'll always have a smile on our faces. I'd like to just keep spankin' the plank.

How would you like to be remembered when all is said and done?

Ha ha! That low-down dude from Texas!

[August 1984]

After all the years of recording and touring, why was Eliminator *the album that put ZZ over the top?*

Good timing — attention to tempo, musically. Once you get through your basic tracks with good time, everybody can breathe a lot easier and it takes a lot of pressure off any difficult technical passages that may come up — as long as it's got that beat.

Certainly, pretty girls wouldn't have anything to do with it [*laughs*].

How much have the videos contributed?

A great deal. I think that it's a great format. Even though it's in its youthful stages, it's a lot of fun to get into. Certainly, it's having an effect on records.

Was any of the Eliminator *material recorded with video in mind?*

Actually, no. The video was an invited afterthought.

Did you have much control over the videos?

Pretty much. An exchange went down between [ZZ Top manager] Bill Ham's Lone Wolf Video Production Service and the director, Tim Newman. Frank and Dusty and I and the entire production cast were actually on the set, blocking out the scenes and saying, "Do you want to do this? Well, how about a little of that?" So it was a real enjoyable kind of venture.

How did the trio get such a full sound on the LP? Was there much double-tracking?

Yeah, there was a lot of doubling of rhythm tracks. Basically, we turned the amps up to 10 and went for it [*laughs*].

Did you mix it for car radio speakers?

Yeah, as a matter of fact, we had that in mind. It makes a difference in the mixing process. If it sounds good to you in the car, what more do you want? Well, actually, there's a big debate going on right now. With the advent of improvement of sound quality—like the compact disc—we are heading for a situation where playback equipment will more than likely reproduce the exact sound you are hearing in a studio setting, be it in your car or in your home. I think people are becoming so discerning as to sound quality that the demand is, "Hey, let's get this to sound as much like the studio as possible." And that's becoming available just through newer technologies in playback equipment.

What was your order of laying down tracks?

Oh, standard — rhythm, bass, drums. Then we did singing and lead guitar. We did a couple of synth tracks, but it was pretty much straight ahead.

Almost all of your guitar parts on the album are textures and moods. You pretty much avoid the lead guitar syndrome throughout Eliminator.

Yeah. We didn't really extend it to the point of the obvious. I think it's there, but the concentration was on a little more technique, perhaps, instead of just extension: Rather, most of the tracks were done in two takes. Again, I'll refer to tempo — that's becoming a key factor in most modern music. If you can get a good-feelin' approach — just about all of your tracks with a good tempo — then everything can fall into place. You get that groove going, and it's just automatic.

Do you have to make compensations for playing any of the* Eliminator *material onstage?

Yeah. Bring in a tank of helium!

What are your plans for the future?

Currently we're working up variations on Laurie Anderson hair-dos. She is so fine!

[March 1986]

On* Afterburner, *there seems to be less experimenting with guitar tones. Have you found the tone?

Well, I tell you, Tom Scholz has found a tone! We got in the studio and tried a number of things. One of the greatest breakthroughs for us was Tom's Rockman [made by Scholz Research & Development], which I used. It had been modified to eliminate the echo and chorus functions, to play just straight distortion. When we combined that direct signal with a number of other traditional setups — amplifiers in the studio — we got a sound that I was really pleased with. The sessions for the new album were a little different; we built a thing that was nicknamed the "Amp Cabin." This was a pile of Fenders and Marshalls that were stacked up on top of each other and then supported to provide a roof and four walls, and we just stuck a big microphone in the middle of it and turned them all up as loud as we could get them. That's true. It was a true test of microphone technology — it was being bombarded from all sides. But it got that grinding tone, and that's what we were after.

Many players claim that recording at subtler volumes produces the "biggest" parts.

It hasn't been our route. Different recording techniques produce different results. Ours is go for the guts. I've tried not to go below turning the knobs under "patent applied for."

Has locking-tremolo technology had any impact on your playing?

Yeah, it's made me stay in tune! You know, I tend to lean towards the Hendrix school, when it was just balls to the wall, smash it to the face of the instrument, and who cares — just do a little string-bending and you're back in pitch. But now it's even more fun because you can just turn steel to rubber, and it still pops back right on the calendar.

How has modern recording technology affected the way ZZ Top records?

Recently, there have been some remarkable changes in the way people make records. A lot of new studios are making the larger space the control room and the smaller space the performing room. What we're finding is most guitar work, as far as lead and solo improvising would have it, is being performed right there next to the tape console behind the board, where you can actually come in, sit down beside a giant set of playback speakers, and feel so much a part of what has happened on the tape so far. That's where we managed to take leaps in the way we make records. We can go out as a group, look at one another, and play as a band instead of being locked up in isolation booths. There was a time when it was thought the best way to make records was to hide everybody in private booths, and you would communicate by way of headphones. This was great for isolation, but it did nothing for that camaraderie and that spontaneous moment where you can look at someone right in the eye, give a nod of the head, and say, "Let's make a left turn here." It was a great bonus to get back to doing that. The *Afterburner* sessions were done at Ardent Recording in Memphis. Joe Hardy, our engineer, was also present during a lot of the '60s Stax sessions.

Could you give guitarists a tip for playing side-of-the-pick harmonics?

If you're not using a quarter or a peso, use a regulation triangular pick. The small edge, which is designated as the picking side, should be turned away from the instrument. So you are actually picking with the fatter side, the shoulder. It gives you a wider grip and offers that meat connection: When the pick slides off, the edge of the thumb can graze that twine and make it whine.

What effects are best for enhancing harmonics?

Harmonics are the upper registers, and chorusing always enhances the higher end. So, it's not a bad idea to try a little chorusing when attempting to harmonic-out in the stratosphere there. Harmonics have really come into their own with the advent of great amplification, whereas years before a lot of the tonal qualities of harmonic playing would have been lost due to low-fi reproduction. It's basically been a phenomenon of the last decade where you can lean on harmonics as a definitive tonal signature.

When multi-tracking, are you concerned about how you're going to do it onstage, or is that something you worry about later?

It's a concern as you're cutting and as you're playing. Dusty and I have managed to be able to trade off a few signature passages in a live performance that may subliminally hint that we've actually pulled off the sound of two tracks when doing it with one instrument. And that works a lot of the time, if you're keyed into what you can do. But now it's foolish to ignore what technology has brought forth. I certainly think that it's a bona fide plus to investigate the possibilities of triggering a sequencer or doing so many things that have just not been available to entertain an audience with before. And as compositions go, I think that we've pretty much walked the safe side by executing those things we would feel comfortable doing live.

Who creates ZZ 's keyboard synthesizer parts?

Dusty and I have worked them out. In fact, when Dusty called for sessions back as far as last March, he and I had worked up some guitar and keyboard accompaniments that were going to be reserved for rhythm tracks only. And as far as the thrust of our involvement at that level, that's where it wound up. We haven't really thrust any soloing efforts on synth yet.

Who actually plays the keyboard?

Well, I played most of them on side one [of *Afterburner*]. Dusty filled in on side two. In fact, he did "Velcro Fly" and has managed to doff his bass for a couple of performance pieces in a live setting, during which you can see him executing his faultless fingerwork [*laughs*] — sausage fingerwork, I should say! He wouldn't like to hear me say that, but it's true.

Does Dusty play all the bass on the album?

I did a few tracks. I promised not to tell!

Are there disadvantages to hi-teching it up?

A few weeks ago, we did some shows in Canada. First night, a record low fell on the city and for a brief second knocked out the power. In doing so, the entire memory bank of everything that had been sequenced was lost! It was kind of wink, grin, turn it up to 10 [*laughs*]. There are some moments when it can be tricky, but it's either that or break a guitar string. It all revolves around a little bit of luck.

How do the live versions of the new songs match up to the recorded ones? Do you pretty much stick to the script?

Of course, in a live situation you are afforded the luxury of improvising. If you're following sequencing, your improvisations must only stray within the skeleton, which is not too tough. Then again, there's a way around that if you care to pursue that. There's even ways to script improvisation. It's a farfetched concept, but when served up on a silver platter, it says, "Hey, if you care to spend the time to work this out, it's yours."

Do you use any preprogrammed synthesizers or drum machines in concert?

I'm adapting some Fairlight [keyboard synthesizer] technology triggering off of Frank's drum kit, but it programs voices to complement either some rhythm or maybe some of the low-end stuff with Dusty. It's a little bit tricky, but what the heck — we've always given it a try. Our attempts at synthesizing and whatnot always sounds like a guitar stuck in a garbage can [*laughs*], so it works for me!

Do you foresee the day when the straight guitar-amp combination will be obsolete, as far as you're concerned?

No, I really don't. When all is said and done, I go back to the house and plug into a 4x10 Bassman and just turn it up.

What's your all-time favorite setup?

Pearly Gates and a Fender — give me a piggyback Bassman in blonde! [*Ed. Note: "Pearly Gates" is Billy's nickname for the classic sunburst 1959 Gibson Les Paul Standard used during ZZ Top's pre-Eliminator days.*]

What would you most like to improve about your playing?

What I'm striving for is to pick up speed. It's like rock and roll was built for the fast! What really sends me these days is listening to different kinds of applications, but yet done with an eloquence that defies speed. You know, everybody says, "You can't do that — it's going to be too difficult to execute at that speed," but I tend to disagree. I think that with a little perseverance, one can learn to endure those hours of practice and do it with great speed.

Do you practice?

Listen, I'll testify here. In the past, I recounted the words of Bill Wyman. He said, "I'm in the Rolling Stones; I don't have to practice." But we do; we turn in a couple hours a day if we can. I think it's important.

Do you play every day?

Oh, yeah. I travel with a guitar, and if there's one around, I pick it up and bash on it.

What do you play by yourself? Is it material other than what you're known for?

Yeah. We do that back-porch blues stuff that you'll find on a couple of the back ZZs, but it's kind of wishing we could be back in the days when it was party time and somebody would pass around an electric and say, "Turn it up and do something." What we wind up doing is probably three hours of blues before the show, and then that kind of gets us wound up in gear to do two hours of high carburetion!

– DAVID GILMOUR –

BY TOM MULHERN – NOVEMBER 1984

STEPPING OUT FROM the security of one of the world's best known bands to record and tour as a solo artist may seem to hold little peril. Yet David Gilmour's work apart from Pink Floyd is not without risk. In these changing times of rock's domination by video, past glories may mean little to a new generation of rock aficionados, and nothing is guaranteed to the individual striking out on his own. The 45-year-old English guitarist released his first solo album, *David Gilmour*, in 1978, predating the rock video boom, and to his good fortune, each of his solo efforts have been embraced enthusiastically by listeners.

Although volatile and unpredictable, the record sales charts do give a fair indication of how a band's doing in the long run. Few albums reach the top; few remain on the charts for very long. *Dark Side of the Moon* remained in the top 200 *continuously* for nearly two decades, attesting to Pink Floyd's tremendous staying power. Such sales are even more remarkable since, in the ensuing decade, after its release in 1973, the band produced another string of successful albums (including their 1979 hit *The Wall* with its accompanying movie) all of which climbed the charts and then slid off even as *Dark Side* clung unbudging from the most-wanted list.

The group always changed its sound and progressed slowly but surely. However, with the turning point of *Dark Side* in 1973, their first #1 album in the U.S. and an audio fanatic's headphone pleasure cruise, David Gilmour, bassist Roger Waters, drummer Nick Mason, and keyboardist Richard Wright demonstrated just how much they had matured, individually and as a whole. *The Wall* marked a dramatic upheaval in Gilmour's approach to guitar, as evidenced on solos in songs such as "Another Brick in the Wall, Part II," and "Comfortably Numb." The lead sound was cleaner and more defined, distinct and separate from his rhythm work. His lines had become far more piercing, less a part of a grand orchestration.

Gilmour's own *About Face*, while exhibiting traces of Floyd music, is a stylistic quantum leap from his 1978 release, revealing his expanded scope both as guitarist and songwriter. From a creator of spacey, floating, phase-shifted and echo-enhanced textures in the '70s has emerged the David Gilmour of a sharper, harder-edged sound. Below, he discusses the differences between his solo outings, his metamorphosis within Pink Floyd, the merits and drawbacks of self-producing an album, and the ever-changing electronic complement that helps him create one of the most distinctive sounds in rock guitar.

On "Until We Sleep" there's a dive-bombing tremolo effect on the guitar toward the end. Do you find that such radical string bending puts the guitar out of tune?

No, I push 'em as far as I can push 'em sometimes [*laughs*]. It depends on the string, too. The *G* seems to be the one you can push the farthest. I can sometimes push them up about three tones or so.

Years ago, you occasionally used a slide in your right hand while fretting notes and chords.

It was not really playing the slide guitar — it was more like making spaceship noises. But I usually hold the slide in my left hand. I mean, I don't really use bottleneck slides, and I usually work on some sort of a lap instrument if I'm going to play that style. I don't believe there's slide on *About Face,* though.

On "No Way," did you use any muting techniques with the slide?

A bit. I use the edge of my right hand to keep the other strings from ringing randomly. I also dampen the strings behind the bar with the back of my left hand. It's all done in a lap sort of fashion, not in an upright position.

Do you use a pick on acoustic guitar?

On that number, I did. But it depends on whether I'm strumming or picking. If I want to pick individual notes, I'll just use my fingers.

On the second half of "Murder," there's a really massive guitar sound. It's almost a trademark of yours. How do you get it?

I try different things every time, because the old tricks never seem to work quite right whenever you try them again [*laughs*]. It's just a lot of fiddling around with a bunch of things until it sounds right. And I usually wind up fiddling around with fuzz boxes and guitars and DDLs.

Do you record with your amp in a large room to get the ambience?

I've found that if you use a big amp, it only works in big rooms. And little amps only work in little rooms. I've got Fender amps, tiny little things, that sound *enormous* sometimes if you get them in the right place. But most of the stuff that sounds like that comes from fairly large amplifiers in fairly large rooms.

Do you ever just plug in direct to the mixing console?

Not very often, but it has happened once in a while. The solo on "Another Brick in the Wall, Part II" [*The Wall*] was done straight into the board. After it was recorded, the signal was then put through an amplifier. So we added a little bit of amplifier sound to it afterwards.

Have you ever considered using, say, a Les Paul or an ES-335 in addition to the Strat and the Tele?

I can't really get on with them that well. I don't really feel comfortable with them. I don't know why, though. I've just always been with Fenders, and I just

haven't managed to make the change. I've got a hybrid guitar that's sort of like a Strat with a tremolo and a humbucking pickup. I find that less and less do I play guitars without tremolos.

Do you find that the tremolo unit tends to make you put your vibrato emphasis mainly into your right hand?

I use both fairly indiscriminately. I mean, I can be in the middle of a solo and do one note's vibrato with my finger, and then the next one with the tremolo bar. It's a different sort of sound. I don't *plan* to use both; I just play it without thinking.

As a rule, do you leave all the springs in the unit?

It depends. Sometimes I have three, sometimes four. Then I adjust the tremolo up until it feels right with my gauge of strings and everything else. I don't find that I have too much trouble with it going out of tune, either. There are a lot of little things to make it go better, but it's never been too severe a problem for me. The white Stratocaster that I use during most of my set is brand new, just out of the box a few months ago, and nothing has been altered on it, apart from screwdriver adjustments you can do for yourself. It's absolutely stock.

Toward the end of "You Know I'm Right," there's a strong rippling effect. Did you use a tremolo or an electronic vibrato?

Any vibrato was just done with the vibrato bar.

Have you tried any electronic vibrato pedals?

Well, I used a vibrato pedal on "Until We Sleep," for a sort of guitar *noise.* I have the vibrato running in time to the drums on that track.

For the really staccato, evenly picked Strat on the song, do you use any special setting or picking technique?

No, most of the time I'm just on the treble pickup.

Do you play closer to the bridge for more brightness?

You know, I don't know. I never looked. I try not to analyze what I'm doing on the guitar too much. I just try to play so that it comes out with some sort of melody and meaning to me. It's very hard to describe.

It's more instinctive, then.

I hope so. I try to leave the instincts open at all times.

For the squealing sounds, do you bring your pick in closer to your fingers?

I sort of deaden a note with the thumb after I pick it. It's like pick and then thumb skin to get those harmonics.

In other places you're right on the edge of feedback.

Well, I *like* to be. If I want to get feedback, I just go into the studio and stay close to the amp. I control it with great difficulty. I like it to be at that point where it's all running away from you and you're only just about in control. In fact, I sometimes like it when I'm not sure whether I'm in control or the guitar and the amplifier are.

Do you prefer any one pickup over the others for getting feedback?

I use the treble pickup virtually all the time.

When you do the solos live, do you extend them or cut loose more?

Oh, yes. Some of them go on interminably long [*laughs*]. Well, not too long, I hope. For a lot of the songs, in the studio you have to cut them down, chop bits out, just to get them on the record.

Do you have a preference for studio or live work?

They seem to have little to do with each other, really. I think they're just different media. In the studio, I can be, for instance, ten vocalists, five or six guitar players, and all sorts of things when I'm aiming for perfection. I can add all sorts of things that aren't necessarily *important*. Onstage, the moment is the important thing, the moment that is here and gone. Making horrible mistakes onstage doesn't matter. The moment is gone as soon as it's gone. On a record, you can get really wild doing a solo. Anytime I get wild doing a guitar solo, I usually drop a few clangers. That's quite normal. I don't mind that. You restrict yourself if you play for safety margins, if you only play what you know you're going to get away with. In the studio, I like to do a number of solos that aren't playing it safe, and then make up one good one out of all the wild bits that do work. I often make up a composite track from three or four solos, and make certain that I don't have any mistakes in there, because who wants to listen to mistakes for the next 20 years?

Once the mix is done, and the album comes out, do you go back and learn the solos for onstage performance?

I get influenced by the solo. Sometimes I've heard it so many times or been so close to it that I actually play solos note-for-note, but not very often. The solo in "Blue Light," for example, is very short and very specific, and I tend to play that same solo. But on things like the end of "Murder" or the end of "Until We Sleep," I don't play what's on the record at all.

On "Let's Get Metaphysical," there's a beautiful guitar part with an orchestra. Did you record the guitar first and add the orchestra, or vice versa?

I wrote out the chord structure and made a demo with a guitar line on it, and I also recorded various melody lines that had come into my head. And Michael Kamen, in arranging, used some of my melody lines and some of the guitar lines and incorporated them into the string parts. We had a click track, and the strings were recorded first. We then did the guitar promptly afterwards.

When you're playing in the studio, do you put the echo on right away, or do you add it later?

I use a DDL on it — a little bit — most of the time, because I find that it stops the fuzz box from sounding like a fuzz box. It smooths off the unpleasant, raw frequencies that you get from the fuzz box. Then you get a nice sort of sound; that's what the Boogie does as well. That means that I get the sustain on the high notes of the Fender, which are usually hard to get on Fenders. Then I get it to smooth out a little bit.

Having used many electronic effects since the '60s, have you found that the changes in technology have made it easier to find certain sounds?

I don't know. I've never found it that difficult to get sounds. They've always been there. They just change. I can't tell sometimes if the old ways worked better or worse. I sometimes try to set up things that I did 15 years ago, and I can't get them to work. That's probably because I've forgotten how I used to *make* them work. These things are always very fine adjustments of many, many knobs, very minor tweaking in all sorts of directions until things are just right. It's purely esthetics that govern it, your personal ears at that moment. For example, in the studio, I can go in and get a guitar and an amplifier to sound perfect — to me. And then the next day, I just turn the mains on, and don't touch anything else at all, and it sounds completely different. And you hate it. You wind up going for a different guitar, different *everything*.

So, it may be nothing more than an aural illusion.

Yes, it could quite easily be, but I don't really know.

Do you find that being able to quickly change echo times and other parameters on newer devices makes your work easier?

Yes. I change my echo settings fairly often in concert. I have two units, and I have different echo settings on both. There are times when I have both running at the same time for certain effects. I usually try, in solos, to set the DDLs to have some rhythmic time signature in common with the tune. Because the notes all intertwine, it doesn't matter anyway, but I find that I usually set them on a triplet. It's a sort of melodic delay to use. That may be just my fantasy; I don't know. That's another one of the personal esthetic judgments that you use in trying to get something to sound nice to yourself.

Do you use the amplifiers' reverb as well?

No. I turn it off.

Have you tried out any guitar synthesizers?

I tried out one of the new Rolands before this tour, and it was too complicated to come to grips with and think that I'd be able to take it on the road with me this time. But I'm considering getting one.

Pink Floyd was always known for being heavily electronics-oriented, and it would seem that a guitar synthesizer would have fit in fairly easily. Was there any reason for not employing it?

I've never thought of us as being particularly ahead of technology, myself. I know lots of people do, but I don't think of us as being that way. I can adapt to things, and I'm not bad at learning things; I can get them together eventually. But that's not what I'm really aiming for — the use of technology. I mean, I'll take anything that comes if it's easy and it works. And I certainly don't see why I might not get into something like that. It's all about getting sounds and textures and stuff, whatever way you can find them. Some of the things we did with the early Pink Floyd material, which sounds incredibly electronic, was just Italian Farfisa organs through delays. We never even had synthesizers for the first four or five years that I was with the band. And the heyday of our most electronic-sounding music was before synthesizers had really been invented. We started using synthesizers — proper ones — on *Dark Side of the Moon.* We may have used a synthesizer on *Obscured by Clouds,* the soundtrack that came out between *Meddle* and *Dark Side.* That was an EMS Synthi.

Do you work mostly on your own?

On my latest solo album, I started off on my own, producing for a couple of months, and got all the basic tracks done. I got Ezrin in then. I was getting too tired, because you waste a lot of time if you do it yourself. You can waste hours doing something that could have been fixed if you had someone with the right ear and the right attitude in the control room at that moment, who stopped you after 10 minutes and said, "Listen to this, I think we're on the wrong approach." Sometimes being out in the studio playing it, you can't see that the approach is wrong until you go back into the control room and hear it. Ezrin had a lot of good ideas for *The Wall* and *About Face,* but nobody's perfect. He had some bad ideas, too. We all do. But it's very useful to get someone who's more or less neutral in there.

On "There's No Way Out of Here," there's a harmonica-like sound at the beginning. It's hard to get a handle on what the instrument really is.

Good. That was the intention [*laughs*]. It's a fuzztone-distorted guitar double-tracked with a harmonica. I can't remember what kind of fuzztone I used on it, though.

— JIM HALL —

BY JIM FERGUSON & ARNIE BERLE — MAY 1983

WHILE MOST jazz guitarists are bebop influenced and therefore somewhat alike stylistically, Jim Hall has managed to develop an approach rivaling that of Django Reinhardt, Charlie Christian, and Wes Montgomery in individuality. Inspired by tenor saxmen Lester Young, Coleman Hawkins, and Ben Webster, Hall's horn-like solos are either passionately lyrical or abstract and angular, but never predictable. Yet he's known equally well for the notes he *doesn't* play — his work is unusually sparse. And Hall's playing always reflects thoughtfulness and growth on over 100 LPs as either leader or sideman.

Much of Hall's repertoire consists of jazz standards such as "Angel Eyes," "I Can't Get Started," and "I Hear a Rhapsody," but he also plays his own compositions, including ballads, jazz waltzes, and calypso numbers. Regardless of the material, his approach is far more modern than that of most of his contemporaries, whose sound is rooted in the '40s and '50s. In fact, his progressiveness virtually makes him the elder statesman of younger players he's directly influenced: John McLaughlin, Larry Coryell, John Scofield, and Pat Metheny.

His solo work on ballads is often described as sounding composed, with every note having significance. Phrases are open, using sustain and silence to good effect, and quick bursts of notes are often added as melodic decoration. On uptempo work Hall can be extremely exciting, and his lines frequently utilize wide intervals. Occasionally venturing outside a tune's changes, he always resolves a phrase with taste.

Jim Hall's initiation to the jazz world was at the age of 13 (he was born on December 4, 1930) when he began playing in neighborhood bars in his hometown of Cleveland, Ohio. After deciding to make music his life's work, he subsequently graduated from the Cleveland Institute of Music with a bachelor of music degree. In 1955, halfway through his first semester of working towards a master's degree, Jim quit school and moved to Los Angeles, intent on establishing himself as a guitarist. Once in LA, Hall began studying with the great classical guitarist Vicente Gómez, while simultaneously making contacts with jazz musicians. His big break came when he replaced Howard Roberts in drummer Chico Hamilton's quintet, which typified the cool, laid-back sound of mid-'50s West Coast jazz. After a leave of absence to tour South America with vocalist Ella Fitzgerald, Hall briefly rejoined Giuffre before teaming with a small group led by tenor sax legend Ben Webster in 1959. During this same period, Hall made his first musical contact with pianist Bill Evans, and recorded the intimate *Undercover*.

Relocating to New York in 1960, Hall worked first in a duo with alto saxophonist Lee Konitz, and then joined a group fronted by Sonny Rollins. In a 1975 issue of the *New Yorker*, Hall made this comment about his solos: "I like them to have a quality that Sonny Rollins has — of turning and turning a tune until eventually you show all of its possible sides." Following the year-and-a-half stay with Rollins, Hall joined a very popular group led by Art Farmer. However, Jim's personal life wasn't going as smoothly as his music made things seem. With drinking getting gradually out of control, in 1965 he temporarily retired, sought help from Alcoholics Anonymous, and married.

Wisely avoiding the alcohol-oriented atmosphere of clubs, Hall found a place in the band on the *Merv Griffin Show*, then reunited with Evans.

The '70s found Jim in a variety of settings: with free-jazz saxophonist Ornette Coleman. Duos with bassist Red Mitchell and Ron Carter, on the concept album *Concierto,* featuring Carter, Desmond, trumpeter Chet Baker, and pianist Roland Hanna.

Combining with the Toronto-based rhythm section of bassist/pianist Don Thompson and drummer Terry Clarke, Hall recorded the classic *Jim Hall Live* in 1975. After recording *Commitment* with Art Farmer in 1976, Hall again teamed with Clarke and Thompson to cut the excellent *Jazz Impressions of Japan,* featuring all original material.

In addition to being a sideman on two jazz-oriented albums featuring classical violin virtuoso Itzhak Perlman, in 1981 he signed with Concord Jazz Records and produced the exceptional *Circle* with Thompson and Clarke, and *First Edition* with pianist George Shearing. Without a doubt, Hall's unending musical quest guarantees much pleasure for his listeners. And his often profound thoughts on how music is mobile, the hazards of bebop, and his special techniques, do much to contradict his sentiment: "I don't have any answers, only questions."

Why do you mainly use standards as a basis for improvisation?

I think it's because I grew up with them, and they're well constructed. A tune like "Body and Soul" — which I'm still trying to learn my way through — has a clear shape that you can work with and relate different harmonic and melodic ideas to. If you removed all of the limiting factors from music, it would sort of be like tennis without the net, court, and ball — just two guys standing in a field with rackets. For that reason, standards are good to know, even if you go beyond them. So much music today sounds amorphous — lacking in shape. I hate to say things like that because it makes you sound like an old cat.

Do you think it's possible to ignore the melody while improvising on a tune?

Yes, but I get bored with performers who do that. Many guys' solos sound the same. They play on the chord changes rather than improvise on the tune itself. I think it's more fun to improvise on the whole song — the melody gives you just all that much more to play off of. Also, I try to get the melody as correct as I can; a lot of times a melody will not be played accurately. George Shearing and I recently recorded "Street of Dreams" on our LP *First Edition,* and I had to call my good friend [pianist/arranger] Bill Finegan to find out what the actual melody was. Lyrics can act as a source of ideas for improvising, too.

How has your playing changed over the years?

I was listening to an old album of Gershwin tunes I did with [trumpeter] Ruby Braff called *Girl Crazy.* My playing seemed fairly emotional, but it didn't really get inside of the tunes. It was as if I built a frame for a house and then stopped. Now I have a better facility for going through chord changes and making melodic connections. Also, I think that my harmonic sense has evolved — at least in terms of the guitar — and I feel more adventuresome.

How hard do you try to be original when you solo?

Eventually you're going to run into the situation where you automatically play something you know or have heard someone else do. And sometimes it's fun to do that — play a cliché — and maybe make something out of it — but I try to keep the solo sounding like it was just invented. When I'm practicing I try to find a different way of ending a phrase. Players should force themselves to hear something and then play it, rather than just do whatever comes under the fingers.

Where did you get such a strong sense of interplay?

I learned from Jimmy Giuffre — who has a compositional approach to performing jazz — that you can use the whole group and not have it just be, say, a horn backed up by a rhythm section. Ideally a group should be in an evolving state like a mobile, with each player acting and reacting as the music takes shape.

How much of your approach to jazz improvisation is truly spontaneous?

I try to make my playing as fresh as possible by not relying on set patterns. When I practice, I often tie off some of the strings with rubber bands to force myself to look at the fingerboard differently. For instance, I might practice on the G and D strings only, or even the G and A strings. You can't help playing some familiar patterns, however.

What is improvisation?

Well, I don't think there's one answer, although I like to think of it as instant composition. It's the fun part of playing — a way of reflecting the melody of a tune and sharing it with somebody else. I'm sure that most of the terrific classical composers were good improvisers. But I think a lot of people find classical music safer than jazz because it's under control — you know what to expect. I think that those composers were much more daring and improvisational than their music indicates. People who go to classical concerts would probably run out of the room if the actual composers were there.

What classical influences have you had?

After high school I went to the Institute of Music in Cleveland, Ohio. I wrote some 12-tone piano pieces and composed a string quartet. I listen to all sorts of music from Gregorian chant to [composer] Witold Lutoslawski. One of my best friends is Don Erb, the contemporary avant-garde composer. He wrote a trio for guitar, violin, and cello that I recorded. I love to listen to just about anything by Bach. Also, I studied classical guitar with Vicente Gomez, but no longer play because my nails are constantly splitting apart.

Do you use classical ideas in your jazz playing?

I don't, say, take classical melodic phrases and use them in a jazz tune, but I do use compositional devices for developing melodies. Maybe some of my chord voicings come from [composer] Igor Stravinsky.

Did you get a lot out of studying with Gómez?

Definitely. Keep in mind that was 1955 and there was only a handful of guys playing classical guitar. He had a real feel for teaching, and made me listen carefully to what I was doing. He also worked with me on phrasing and emphasizing different parts. Gómez eventually asked me to teach for him — he had a small studio with a few teachers — and that was a big day because I finally realized I could make a living as a musician. Shortly after that, I went on the road with Chico Hamilton.

You once used the term free-form in reference to some recordings you did with Jimmy Giuffre. What did you mean?

Somebody would play a motif, and the rest of the band would try to react like composers. For example, Bob Brookmeyer might have done an imitation of what Jimmy played — it didn't have to be in one particular key — and I might try and complement it with a little phrase or note cluster. It was free in the sense that the form was allowed to take shape as we played.

You played with Ornette Coleman. What do you think of his free jazz type of playing?

Most of what I heard was with [trumpeter] Don Cherry, [bassist] Charlie Hayden, and [drummer] Eddie Blackwell — that was a great group. Ornette's playing had all the good elements of music: time, humor, pathos, and a lot of technique. It was very unpredictable. I've heard people say that he was into free jazz because he couldn't play in a 32-bar framework, but that's not true. I don't care if he can't play "God Bless America." I still enjoy his music.

Why are you thought of as an introspective and intellectual player?

Well, I guess I sound more reflective because I try to develop a solo compositionally. Also, I don't really play fast — speed has never come easy for me. Funny — I won a jazz critics' poll this year, and Emily Remler said I probably got the award for playing the fewest notes. Seriously, though, I think that figuring out a hundred ways to play "I Got Rhythm" fast is more intellectual than what I do.

Who are some of the younger players you like?

Emily is great. She sounds like she's more involved with playing music than playing the guitar. And there's a guy named Ralph Piltch, a Canadian who plays fingerstyle. I like Pat Metheny's stuff, and I was really impressed with a record by Michael Hedges [*Breakfast in the Field*].

Although you've had the same influences as Tal Farlow, Joe Pass, and Herb Ellis, your playing is quite different from theirs. How do you account for that?

Little by little I pared down my playing to suit my own personality. Tal especially has fantastic technique and harmonic sense — we used to play together a lot. Through lots and lots of playing it dawned on me that I'd never be able to do what he does. Of course, a lot of my style has to do with the things I've listened to. Aside from classical music, jazz horn, and piano players had a big effect on me. Bill Evans, Art Farmer, and Sonny Rollins were very influential — I don't find guitar players as interesting. It's a combination of my influences and training, as well as the way I physically approach the guitar.

Do you ever copy solos?

I remember a couple of Charlie Christian and Charlie Parker ones. I mostly tried to get a player's feel. For instance, on "Body and Soul" I try to play what I imagine Coleman Hawkins might do, because I associate him so strongly with that tune.

Were you ever into playing bebop?

Yeah, when I was a kid it was sort of in. Charlie Parker was hard to avoid — I saw him once with [trumpeter] Miles Davis, [drummer] Max Roach, [pianist] Duke Jordan, and [bassist] Tommy Potter. But I was also exposed to Lester Young and Coleman Hawkins, so I didn't completely fall under the bebop influence. I knew a lot of the tunes and hot licks, and have been trying to get them out of my playing ever since. They were good for then, but I bore easily and like to look for something different. I don't mean to knock bebop, but playing through chord changes one certain way can be a trap. Imitation can get carried too far. That's why you hear so many young sax players who sound like John Coltrane. I'm sure that he didn't mean for that to happen.

What are some other traps players get themselves into?

Many guys, including some well-known artists, play solos that are too long. They could have gotten it all said in 32 or 64 bars. The reputations of some of the greatest jazzmen were built on eight-bar solos.

Lester Young was a succinct player. What was it about his music that you liked?

I remember he played "After You've Gone" on an old Jazz at the Philharmonic album [*Bird and Pres: The '46 Concert*], and he was marvelous. Lester's playing sounds better to me now than when I first heard it. I took it for granted when I was a kid. You can't expect a guy who's 21 to be interested in older music. Lester played with so much grace and delicacy, but he had a stomping quality, too. And he always made things sound so easy.

Who are some of the best bass players you've worked with?

That's hard to say, because I've played with so many good ones. I've never heard anyone play like Red Mitchell. His solos sound like something Bill Harris might do on trombone. And Harvie Swartz, who works with [singer] Sheila Jordan, is great. He hasn't done anything to make him notorious yet, but he's a beautiful soloist. Ron Carter is a fantastic listener; every note he uses has a special meaning. Don Thompson, of course, is an incredible musician in every sense of the word. He plays great time and remarkable solos. I've only played with Ray Brown a little bit; he's the epitome of the walking bassist. I was honored to do a tune with Oscar Pettiford once. Other great bassist I've associated with include Carson Smith, Ralph Peña, Percy Heath, Bob Cranshaw, Milt Hinton, George Duvivier, Jay Leonhart, Michael Moore, Jack Six, Art Davis, Brooks Caperton, Mark Johnson, Eddie Gomez, and Steve Swallow.

Did you have any reservations about playing with Itzhak Perlman?

Although it was really fun, I almost didn't do the first record because it seemed like it was a gimmick. I had similar reservations about doing my *Concierto* album. Perlman's playing sounded spontaneous, although he was reading most of the time. We did this kind of Greek piece of [drummer] Shelley Manne's that sounded sort of like Bartók. Itzhak improvised on that one, but for some reason it didn't get used on the record.

In one of Sonny Rollins' groups you were the only white player. Did that create any problems?

A lot of times I was the only white musician in a band, but usually I felt privileged to be there. Occasionally there would be the kind of social side effects you might expect. For instance, when checking into a hotel, I was often mistaken for Sonny's manager.

What was collaborating with George Shearing on your LP First Edition *like?*

Great; his ear is incredible. The sound he gets out of the piano is unique and gorgeous, especially on ballads. His playing reminds me of classical music.

When backing up a soloist, would you rather lead or follow?

It depends on who I'm playing with. Art Farmer liked to hear a chord first. In other words, I'd play a chord, and Art would follow. On the other hand, Sonny Rollins would get irritated if you tried to lead him. After a while you develop a sense of what a player wants.

How much freedom do you usually have when playing accompaniment?

Sometimes I can do whatever I want, while at other times I have to play it relatively safe. [Saxophonist] Zoot Sims is very adventuresome. He'll often start a tune without calling the key or tempo. He's got a quick ear, so he picks up on what I'm doing right away. When I worked with Paul Desmond, Ron Carter and I would kind of fall into our own turnarounds. Paul didn't particularly like that — he wanted the chords to be a little more predictable. I've heard that [trumpeter] Dizzy Gillespie likes to hear only the basic chord. When I play with Bob Brookmeyer, we don't ever discuss a tune's changes. He likes it if I take chances. It's something that varies from player to player.

Has anyone ever asked you to play one particular set of changes on a tune?

Sure. Some tunes have problem spots, and different players prefer different changes. "Round Midnight" is one of those kinds of tunes; I don't think I've ever gotten through it right. You have to remain flexible.

Does being a jazz musician have much effect on your personal life?

Yes; it does seem difficult at times. The traveling is hard. And I thought that drinking had something to do with being a musician, but when I decided to quit and went to AA meetings, I found the guys there felt the same thing about their jobs. There can be a lot of stress involved. For instance, not too long ago I did a bunch of one-nighters. The contract said I was supposed to get paid before going on, although I don't always expect that. Sometimes I had to sit and wait for the money to be counted after I had played. That can make things tough, especially if I have to catch a plane at eight the next morning.

Are you very self-critical?

I am, but I do feel good about my playing. The instrument keeps me humble. Sometimes I pick it up and it seems to say, "No, you can't play today." I keep at it anyway, though.

Traditionally, clubs have been where jazz is performed. Do you have any favorites?

I like the Village Vanguard in New York. It's a funky little place, but so much good music's been played there. There's no place to go during intermission, so everyone — including the owner, Max Gordon — congregates in the kitchen. Blues Alley in Washington, D.C., is great, too; they have a good sound system. And McCabe's Guitar Shop in Santa Monica, California, and The Great American Music Hall in San Francisco are nice. Many clubs aren't nearly as good. I've been to hear friends of mine at places that were so noisy I actually got angry. The owners seem more interested in selling drinks than in presenting the music well.

Why don't you use an acoustic instrument more?

Well, it's really hard to use an acoustic in person because of the hassle involved with traveling with it. Also, there are problems connected with amplification. I do like playing acoustics, though.

There's an old Chico Hamilton album that shows you holding a Les Paul.

Do you know how I got that? We were playing in a club that had this semi-circular bar in front of the bandstand for customers to put their drinks on, and it made my Gibson L-5 sound really tubby. Because I didn't have enough experience to realize that the problem was with the club's acoustics, I got the Les Paul. It felt awfully cold, so about six months later I traded it for the ES-175.

How did your ability to read develop?

It just kind of happened. I started out reading when I was ten, and then I went through music school, where I had to do a lot of my homework on the guitar because I didn't have a piano. When I did the *Merv Griffin Show*, my reading picked up. I don't actually work on it, and I don't read nearly as well as a good studio clarinet player. Being able to take music off a piece of paper is important because that's how musical information is communicated; however, it isn't everything. Once Merv made this big thing out of the fact that Erroll Garner couldn't read music — like he was an idiot savant or something. That made me angry, because Garner was studying every time he sat down at the piano.

What do you do to warm up before you perform?

Sometimes traveling makes me so tired I actually feel crazy. Slow practice usually helps if I have time to be alone with the guitar. If I have to go right out, listening really hard to the other players often gets me through.

How did you get the idea to do that raga-esque part to "Bermuda Bye Bye" on Commitment***?***

I was going to stop the tune, but it felt like nothing had happened so I just started doing that. A student of mine who fooled around with different tunings showed me how to play those kinds of chords. The pedal bass gives them a modal sound:

[*Ed. Note: Numbers indicate left-hand fingering.*]

How did you come to write "Careful?"

I got fascinated with the diminished scale, and wrote a 16-bar blues with it in 1958 when working with Giuffre. George Shearing wanted to include it on *First Edition* — he had heard it somewhere. I recorded it with [vibraphonist] Gary Burton, too. It was probably influenced by Thelonious Monk.

Are there any techniques that you're working on these days?

Yeah, lots of things. I've been trying to expand my picking technique because it finally dawned on me that fiddle players and cellists have more than one way of bowing. I want to keep my way of playing legato in the left hand — using hammers and pulls-while trying to work on using alternate picking and holding the wrist like Larry Coryell and John

McLaughlin. I know that it seems kind of late to be doing this. Sometimes I work on chord voicings by listening to Bill Evans and trying to get his feel. I also work on playing solo — it would be sort of a challenge for me to do an album like that one day. And I've been experimenting with using my right-hand fingers *and* a pick.

Could you give an example of your left-hand legato technique?

Here's an example in B♭. It uses the notes from F to B♭ and is played all on the D string.

[*Ed. Note: Circled numbers indicate the strings on which notes are to be played.*]

Phrasing like that is a result of Jimmy Giuffre wanting me to get a slurring sound so I wouldn't interrupt the flow of the lines he'd write.

Do you ever think of scales when you play?

Sometimes. If I get stuck I might run through a scale and try to find something that works. In general, I try to make myself ignorant, and go only by sound and feeling. When things are going right, it feels like the music is happening because you finally got out of the way.

You often use fast arpeggios as a kind of decoration. Could you show how you finger a typical one?

I use this one a lot. It's a *Gm7* with a 9th added:

Sometimes I'll get a double-stop by playing the D and F together and hammering up to the F and A with my little finger. I think that I got that from listening to Bill Evans — it's supposed to sound like a piano.

Do you have a method for finding new chord voicings?

Sometimes with two voices I'll take just two voic-

es and either take them through a tune like "Body and Soul" or play them against a pedal tone [sustained note] like open *A*, for instance. You can get some interesting things if you try and make the notes go in different directions. George Shearing played a beautiful intro to "Emily" on *First Editions* that harmonized the chromatic scale in the upper voice:

Were there any books you especially benefitted from?

I worked quite a bit with *The George Van Eps Guitar Method* — the one about the harmonized triad. I'm still using voicings I discovered through some of the book's exercises:

What advice do you have for students of jazz guitar?

Don't just listen to guitar players. But if you have to listen to one, study the way Freddie Green plays rhythm with Count Basie's band. If you pruned the tree of jazz, Freddie Green would be the only person left. In the long run, I think it's more important to look at paintings than to listen to the way somebody plays bebop lines.

— GEORGE HARRISON —

BY DAN FORTE — NOVEMBER 1987

WITH ALL that's been written about the Beatles and their indelible stamp on music, fashion, and pop culture, they are individually still criminally underrated as *musicians*. Not only did they inspire a generation to plug in guitars and harmonize, but they also influenced *how* guitar players played, how bassists played, how drummers drummed, and how singers sang. And while each later took turns reinforcing the obvious — that something magical and greater-than-the-sum happened when they played as a band — their separate instrumental contributions can't be overemphasized.

Easily the most overlooked was George Harrison. Continuing (and distilling) the tradition of his melodic rockabilly idols Carl Perkins, Scotty Moore, and James Burton, the youngest Beatle was just coming into his own when Clapton and Beck ushered in the age of the Guitar Hero. George's forte was not extended improvised jamming; he was (and is), however, a supreme melodicist, a sensitive ballad player, a strong rhythm man, a fine acoustic guitarist, and one of electric slide's most distinctive stylists. And to this day, *no* one's been able to match his range of crystalline tones and textures.

The Beatles' music didn't lend itself to guitar heroics, and vice versa. The antithesis of the guitarist as gunslinger, Harrison was a *parts* player and a chameleon. From the very beginning, his egoless role (and tone) changed, depending on what the song called

for. Just try playing a different 12-string break to "A Hard Day's Night," and you'll see that Harrison's compact, worked-out guitar solos were as essential to the group's sound and success as Ringo's unique drumming or their multi-part vocal harmonies.

And if the song called for a Chet Atkins-ish country break (as on "I'm a Loser") — or a twangy, Duane Eddy-tinged bass line ("It Won't Be Long") or even some pseudo-bossanova on gut-string ("Till There Was You") — the group looked no farther than their own lead guitarist, and George never failed to deliver. George may downplay his 6-string abilities, pointing out that he's not the kind of player "who could just pop in on anybody's session and come up with the goods," but he did exactly that during his decade with the Beatles. He was everything anyone could hope for in a studio player and then some.

George Harrison was born on February 25, 1943, in Liverpool, England, the port out of which his father, a merchant seaman, was based. At 13 George bought his first acoustic guitar. He hated school, but at least one fortuitous event took place there: He met Paul McCartney. The subsequent history of the Beatles has been reported innumerable times. Here is the brief version:

With drummer Pete Best and bassist Stu Sutcliff (Paul then played guitar), the group began playing Liverpool's Cavern Club in 1960, the same year they made their first trip to Hamburg, Germany, where they played eight or more hours per night. Six months later they made their recording debut, backing singer Tony Sheridan. During the next year, Paul became full-time bassist, Brian Epstein became the group's manager, and the Beatles were auditioned and turned down by Decca Records (in favor of Brian Poole & The Tremeloes). After a few more months in Hamburg, the quartet auditioned for producer George Martin, at whose urging Best was replaced by Ringo Starr.

Their first single, "Love Me Do" backed with "P.S. I Love You," was recorded in September '62, followed by the release of "Please Please Me" a few months later. By the end of 1963 the Beatles had released their first two albums and given a Royal Command Performance, and their reputation was just beginning to spread to America. At the end of March '64 they had simultaneously secured *Billboard*'s singles chart's top five: "Can't Buy Me Love," "Twist & Shout," "She Loves You," "I Want to Hold Your Hand," and "Please Please Me," respectively, along with seven more titles in the Hot 100. By the end of 1966 the Beatles had released seven albums in England, starred in the feature-length movies *A Hard Day's Night* and *Help!*, and played their last live show (San Francisco's Candlestick Park, August 29, 1966). George had also begun studying with sitar master Ravi Shankar in India.

The 1967 concept-album masterpiece *Sgt. Pepper's Lonely Hearts Club Band* and British TV film *Magical Mystery Tour* took the experimental nature of *Revolver* several steps further. The following year saw the formation of Apple Corps and Harrison's first solo project, the film score to *Wonderwall*, which he produced in Bombay with a cast of Indian musicians and himself (playing guitar under the name Eddie Clayton). For *The Beatles,* the double "White Album" released in November '68, George enlisted Eric Clapton to play the solo on his composition "While My Guitar Gently Weeps." The following January the Beatles began work on the filming and recording of *Let It Be*, although it was not released until May 1970. During the interim, George released his experiments with synthesist Bernie Krause as *Electronic Sound*, and the band recorded *Abbey Road*. George also shared guitar chores with Clapton on Delaney & Bonnie's U.K. tour. By the end of 1970 the only place the Beatles got together was in court; their musical working relationship was ended.

While he may have toiled in the shadow of Lennon and McCartney for most of his life as a Beatle, Harrison quickly dispelled any notion that he was dependent on them with 1970's *All Things Must Pass,* a triumphant three-record boxed set co-produced by Phil Spector. In 1971, Harrison brought together Bob Dylan, Leon Russell, Eric Clapton, Ringo Starr, Billy Preston, Ravi Shankar, and others for the Concert for Bangladesh at New York's Madison Square Garden, the first rock concert staged to benefit famine victims.

Living in the Material World, from 1973, contained the hit "Give Me Love." In the fall of '74 Harrison formed a band encompassing fusion saxophonist Tom Scott's L.A. Express, Billy Preston, Ravi Shankar, and an orchestra of Indian musicians to tour America. Between then and his two-night appearance at the Prince's Trust concert in London in 1987, the only official onstage appearance Harrison made was in 1977, when he joined Paul Simon on *Saturday Night Live* to play acoustic versions of Beatles and Simon & Garfunkel songs. The program received the highest ratings in the show's history.

While he has released several more solo efforts, his energies have turned more towards filmmaking — producing, among others, Monty Python's *Life of Brian* and *Time Bandits*. His most recent gig has been with The Travelling Wilburys.

Do you still practice the sitar?

I do, yeah. I've got a nice sitar in my guitar room, and I pick it up occasionally. I'm still fascinated — it's such a great-sounding instrument. I mean, I'm no way very expert at it. The same with a guitar. You have to really play and practice if you're going to be any good, and I don't do that. Even with the sitar, I didn't touch it for years, but just over the last two years I got it out and all tuned up again. I really enjoy it.

During the five years between Gone Troppo *and* Cloud Nine, *did you play the guitar much?*

I tend to just use the guitar to write tunes on. And then — because I've got a studio in my house — to make demos. Like through those five years I never really stopped writing.

Clapton has mentioned you as an influence, and there was that period where you both sounded very similar. "Something" [Abbey Road] is not all that far removed from, say, "Wonderful Tonight" [Slowhand].

Yeah, I love Eric. I love the touch he has on his guitar. When he comes over to play on my songs, he doesn't bring an amplifier or a guitar; he says, "Oh, you've got a good Strat." He knows I've got one because he gave it to me [laughs]. He plugs in, and just his vibrato and everything . . . he makes that guitar sound like Eric. That's the beauty of all the different players that there are. There are players who are better than each other, or not as good, but everybody's got their own thing. It's like a 12-bar blues. You can't do a 12-bar the same way twice, so they say. There's things that Eric can do where it would take me all night to get it right — he can knock it off in one take. Because he plays all the time. But then again, when we're listening to some of my slide bits, he'll look at me, and I know he likes it. And that, for me, if Eric gives me the thumbs up on a slide solo, it means more than half the population.

It seems odd that the one real guitar-solo vehicle you wrote with the Beatles, "While My Guitar Gently Weeps," was the only Beatles song where you had Eric Clapton play the solo. From a producer's point of view, that's a perfect move, but as an artist with an ego, didn't you want your own stamp on that solo?

No, my ego would rather have Eric play on it. I'll tell you, I worked on that song with John, Paul, and Ringo one day, and they were not interested in it at all. And I knew inside of me that it was a nice song. The next day I was with Eric, and I was going into the session, and I said, "We're going to do this song. Come on and play on it." He said, "Oh, no. I can't do that. Nobody ever plays on the Beatles records." I said, "Look, it's my song, and I want you to play on it." So Eric came in, and the other guys were as good as gold — because he was there. Also, it left me free to just play the rhythm and do the vocal. So Eric played that, and I thought it was really good. Then we listened to it back, and he said, "Ah, there's a problem, though; it's not Beatley enough" — so we put it through the ADT [automatic double-tracker], to wobble it a bit.

Were many of the guitar solos cut live?

Yeah. In those days we only had, like, 4-tracks. On that album, the *White Album*, I think we had an 8-track by then, so some things were overdubbed, or we had our own tracks. I would say the drums would probably all be on one track, bass on another, the acoustic on another, piano on another, Eric on another, and the vocal on another, and then whatever else. But when we laid that track down, I sang it with the acoustic guitar with Paul on piano, and Eric and Ringo — that's how we laid the track down. Later, Paul overdubbed the bass on it.

That's the album people always point to as being the first sign of the Beatles separating — with

the different songs really exhibiting more of the individual composer's style, rather than the band's. But it still has an organic, band feel — with various members trading instruments.

Yeah, yeah. We still all helped each other out as much as we could.

Speaking of collaborations, on Cream's "Badge" [Goodbye] did you write the words and Clapton the music? Who played the guitar through the Leslie on the bridge?

That's where Eric enters. On the record Eric doesn't play guitar up until that bridge. He sat through it with his guitar in the Leslie [rotating speaker], and I think Felix somebody [Pappalardi] was the piano player. So there was Felix, Jack Bruce, [drummer] Ginger Baker, and me — I played the rhythm chops — and we played the song right up to the bridge, at which point Eric came in on the guitar with the Leslie. And then he overdubbed the solo later. Let me see — I wrote most of the words, Eric had the bridge, definitely, and he had the first couple of chord changes. He called me up and said, "Look, we're doing this last album, and we've each got to have our song by Monday." I finished the verses off, and he had the middle bit already, and I think I wrote most of the words to the whole song — although he was there, and we bounced off of each other. The story's getting a bit tired now, but I was writing the words down, and when we came to the middle bit I wrote "Bridge." And from where he was sitting, opposite me, he looked and said, "What's that — Badge?" So he called it "Badge" because it made him laugh.

It sounds as much like a Beatles song as a Cream song.

Yeah, well, that's because he did it with me instead of with Jack. Like, I wanted Eric on "Guitar Gently Weeps" for a bit of moral support and to make the others behave, and I think it was the same reason he asked me to play on that session with them.

In the Beatles, you always seemed to play solos as mini compositions and use different sounds and techniques according to whatever the song called for. That attitude tends to get overlooked a lot with so much importance placed on pyrotechnics.

Yeah, worked-out solos. I think that was largely because, like on the early records, we went straight onto mono or stereo. Then we got a 4-track. But a lot of those takes, we had to do everything at the same time, or as much as possible. So we'd say, "These guitars are gonna come in on the second chorus playing these parts, at which time the piano will come in, too, on top." And we'd have to get the individual sound of each instrument, and then the balance of those to each other, because they were all going to be locked together on one track. Then we had to do the performance, where everybody got their bit right. I think it was maybe to do with that, where we'd worked out parts. Listening to some of the CDs, there are some really good things, like "And Your Bird Can Sing," where I think it was Paul and me, playing in harmony — quite a complicated little line that goes right through the middle eight. We had to work those out, you know. In the early days, the solos were made up on the spot, or we'd been playing them onstage a lot.

What do you think of the Beatles on compact disc?

I'm not so keen on the *sound* on the CDs; I think I prefer the old mixes, the old versions. I think CDs are good on all this new stuff, but I don't know about the old stuff put on them.

But those early sounds, I hated them. I remember midway through the '60s there'd be all these American groups we'd bump into, and they'd say, "Hey, man, how did you get that sound?" And I realized somewhere down the line, I was playing these Gretsch guitars through these Vox amps, and in retrospect they sounded so *puny*. It was before we had the unwound third string, that syndrome, and because it was always done in a rush and you didn't have a chance to do a second take, we just hadn't developed sounds on our side of the water. I mean, listening to James Burton playing them solos on the Rick Nelson records, and then we'd come up with this stuff — it was so feeble. I got so fed up with that, and that was the time that Eric gave me that Les Paul guitar. And that gets back to the story of "Guitar Gently Weeps": It was my guitar that was gently weeping — he just happened to be playing it.

The White Album *was a definite departure in terms of guitar sounds — with more volume and fuzz. Was that a product of the times and the themes of those songs?*

It was partly that, and the type of bands that were around. We started out like this little group in mono; we just played a couple of takes, and that was it. And the engineers who worked on *Abbey Road* had been doing Peter Sellers records or skiffle. Nobody had had any experience like in America. America was always ahead, and we always looked to America for the sounds and the groovy players. We felt just like a lucky little group — we knew we had

something good to offer, but we were quite modest. The situation we were in was this old equipment, but we were happy with it in those days; we were just happy to be in the studio. And as things developed, we probably got a 4-track when America was all getting their 8-tracks, going to 16. Then we got an 8-track when they were all into 24. We were always that far behind, but this is the thing that puts me against a lot of the music now. Everybody's got 48 channels and MIDI'd and MAXI'd and 89,000 pedals on their guitars and everything — and yet, it's still not as good as "That's All Right, Mama" by Elvis Presley or "Blue Suede Shoes" by Carl Perkins, or Chuck Berry or Little Richard, Buddy Holly, Eddie Cochran, the old Everlys. You can go through all that stuff — they had greater sounds. So when the pedal syndrome came along, I couldn't be bothered with that. I got into the thing of thinking, "Now, if I can just get my guitar in tune and get it so that I can play *jing-jinga-jing* and a few little licks and it sounds nice, that'll do me." I ain't doing acrobatics with all these things.

Also, we used to do things like on that Carl Perkins program where he talks about hearing Les Paul and learning to *play* like that [not knowing that Les Paul used tape echo and overdubs]. Well, we used to do that, in a way. Like the slap echo that was on the old Sun records, Carl's and Elvis' — we used to *sing* like that, *sing* the tape echo, or try to play it. We thought, "Well, that must be the drummer drumming with the sticks on the bass strings" [*imitates a slap bass line*]. We were naive; we didn't have a clue. Even on *Abbey Road* we used to have to invent ways of keeping it interesting or making new sounds. We'd think, "Well, let's be Fleetwood Mac today," and we'd put a lot of reverb on and pretend to be Fleetwood Mac.

There's a volume pedal effect you got on songs such as "Yes It Is" and "Wait" and "I Need You." Were you using a volume pedal back then?

I think I tried to. There was a guy in Liverpool who used to go to school with Paul and I, and he was in a band called the Remo Four and played with Billy J. Kramer. And he got all that stuff and could play all those Chet Atkins ones where you can play both tunes at the same time — like "Colonel Bogey." He had a volume pedal, and I think we tried that, but I could never coordinate it. So some of those, what we'd do is, I played the part, and John would kneel down in front of me and turn my guitar's volume control.

That's like "Peggy Sue" by Buddy Holly. He had

a guy kneeling down to switch his Strat to the rear pickup for the guitar solo.

Yeah, that's great stuff, isn't it? That's still one of the greatest guitar solos of all time.

At some point, after the Beatles, you switched your solo playing almost exclusively to slide.

Right. In the '60s, I forget exactly which years, there was a period where I really got into Indian music. I started playing the sitar and hanging out with Ravi Shankar, and I took some lessons for a couple of years. Then after that period, I thought, "Well, really, I'm a pop person. I'm neglecting the guitar and what I'm supposed to do." I knew I was not going to be a brilliant sitar player, because I'd already met a thousand of them in India, and Ravi thought *one* of them was going to make it as a really top-class player. I still play the sitar now for my own amusement, and I enjoy it, but I thought I'd better get back on the guitar. By that time there were all these people like 10 years old playing brilliantly. I just thought, "God, I'm so out of touch. I don't even know how to get a half-decent sound." The result of that was I thought, "Oh, I'll see what happens here with this slide." And it sort of sounded funkier than what I could with my fingers at this time. It developed from that, without me realizing it. Then people would come up and say, "Would you play slide on my record?" I'm thinking, "Really? Are you sure?" Then, I don't know, I started hearing people sort of imitating me doing slide — which is very flattering. But, again, like I was saying about the sound — "How did you get that sound?" — I didn't think it was that good.

Do you think that Indian music and the sitar influenced your approach to slide?

Definitely.

Because you can get all those quarter-tones.

Yeah. See, I never really learned any music until I sat down with Ravi Shankar with the sitar. He said to me, "Do you know how to read music?" Oh, no, here we go again. Because I felt like there were really much better musicians who deserved to be sitting with this guy who's such a master of the instrument. I started getting panicky. I said, "No, I don't know how to read music." He said, "Oh, good — because it's only going to influence you." Then I did learn how to notate in what they call the *sofa* system, which is like the Hindustani classical way of notating. It was the first time I had any discipline — doing all these exercises. They show you how to bend the string. I talk briefly about it in *I Me Mine*. What they call hammering on with the guitar, there's exercises

for that, and bending. Because on a sitar, from the first string, you've got a good two inches of fret, and you're pulling it down. It's like Albert King playing left-handed, and he can pull that *E* string right across the neck.

It's amazing how that sounds different from a right-handed player pushing the string from the opposite direction.

It's because you've got more strength in your hand, I think, to pull it that way than you have to push. So that was the first time I actually learned a bit of discipline — doing all these little things in conjunction with what you do with your right hand, the stroke. If you strike the string down, it's called *da*, and if you hit it up, it's called *ra*. I'd be trying to practice one of these complicated exercises, thinking I'd just be getting it, and Ravi would say, "No, no. *Ra. Ra.*" I'm hitting it one way instead of the other — you know, "Does that matter at this stage?" We don't have that sort of frame of reference in guitar.

Then with slide what I could do is actually hit the string with one stroke and *[hums a scale]* — do a whole little wobbly bit. And because of the Indian stuff, it made me think a bit more about the stroke side to it, and I realized there's so many different ways of playing, say, a three-note passage. You can strike it and go down with one stroke; you can strike it each time; there's a million permutations of that one thing. The Indian music also gave me a greater sense of rhythm and of syncopation. I mean, after that I wrote all these weird tunes with funny beats and 3/4 bars, 5/4 bars. Not exactly commercial, but it got inside me to a degree that it had to come out somewhere.

When I did that tour in '74 with all the Indian musicians, I had Robben Ford on guitar. I think he's brilliant, because not only is he a great blues player and rock player, but he really got into playing all the Indian stuff, too.

The sound of the Beatles was influenced a lot by the changes in instruments — a lot of which were simply because some company gave you guys new guitars. Did Rickenbacker give you a 12-string?

Yeah, I got number two. This friend of mine in England who takes care of guitars, Alan Rogan, just found out that the Rickenbacker 12-string of mine is the second one they made. The first one they gave to some woman, and the second one is the one I got. I got another one from them with the rounded cutaways, but I'm glad to say that the one that went missing — I got a lot of stuff stolen or lost — wasn't that original one. That guitar is really good. I love the sound of it and the brilliant way where the machine heads fit so that even when you're drunk you can still know what string you're tuning.

On "If I Needed Someone," is that the Rick 12-string capoed up?

If it's not in *D*, it must be. It was written in *D* nut position [capoed at the 5th fret]. The opening to "A Hard Day's Night" is also that Rickenbacker 12-string. And in fact on the new album, "Fish on the Sand" is the Ricky 12-string.

What's your main guitar for slide?

I'm so dumb, really. It takes me years to figure things out. But through Ry [Cooder] — I really like his slide — I realized that you jack the bridge up a bit and you put thicker-gauge strings on it, so it doesn't clatter around. So I have my psychedelic Strat set up like that now.

What were the band politics in the instances where one of the other Beatles would play lead guitar? Didn't Paul play the lead on "Taxman," for instance?

Well, with certain things like that, in those days, for me to be allowed to do my one song on the album, it was like, "Great. I don't care who plays what. This is my big chance." So in Paul's way of saying, "I'll help you out; I'll play this bit," I wasn't going to argue with that. There's a number of songs that Paul played lead on, or John did, but people just think because it said "lead guitar" it was all me. Paul played slide actually on "Drive My Car" — that wasn't me. But likewise, I played bass on some tunes, and we all did various things. And to go track by track, like I think John did at some point — "I did this and I did that" — we all contributed a lot to it, and it doesn't matter to me. Like I said, if there's something where Eric can do it, and it's going to make my song sound better, it doesn't matter to my guitar player's ego. Same with Paul; I was pleased to have him play that bit on "Taxman." If you notice, he did like a little Indian bit on it for me. And John played a brilliant solo on "Honey Pie" from the *White Album;* sounded like Django Reinhardt or something. It was one of them where you just close your eyes and happen to hit all the right notes — sounded like a little jazz solo.

Most of the articles and interviews on the Beatles spend more time on the Beatlemania and seldom discuss the four of you as musicians — for instance, what first attracted you to taking up the guitar?

Exactly, right. My earliest recollection is that my dad used to go away to sea in the merchant navy, and sometime when I was a little boy he brought a wind-up gramophone that he bought in New York, and he had all these records. The old 78s with the *big* needles. And he had Jimmie Rodgers. Not the guy who sang "Honeycomb," but the old Jimmie Rodgers. And I just loved that — just the sound of those old acoustic guitars recorded really roughly. I don't know, something just appealed to me. I'll tell you who was really big in England was a guy from Jacksonville, Florida — Slim Whitman. And he did all these tunes like "Rose Marie," and he was on the radio and had a lot of hit records in England.

I heard there was a guy, when I was about 12 or 13, who went to the junior school I went to, and he was selling this guitar. I just went and bought it off him. Cost me three pounds, 10 shillings. This was when it was $2.50 for a pound, so it was about $10. Just a little cheap acoustic guitar, but I didn't really know what to do with it. I noticed where the neck fitted on the box it had a big bolt through it, holding it on. I thought, "Oh, that's interesting." I unscrewed it, and the neck fell off [*laughs*]. And I was so embarrassed, I couldn't get it back together, so I hid it in the cupboard for a while. Later my brother fixed it.

Then there was this big skiffle craze happening for a while in England — which was Lonnie Donegan. He set all them kids on the road. Everybody was in a skiffle group. Some gave up, but the ones who didn't give up became all those bands out of the early '60s. Lonnie was into, like, Lonnie Johnson and Lead Belly — those kind of tunes. But he did it in this sort of very accessible way for kids. Because all you needed was an acoustic guitar, a washboard with thimbles for percussion, and a tea chest — you know, a box that they used to ship tea in from India — and you just put a broom handle on it and a bit of string, and you had a bass. We all just got started on that. You only needed two chords: [*hums*] jing-jinga-jing, jing-jinga-jing, [*hums lower*] jing-jinga-jing, jing-jinga-jing [*laughs*]. And I think that is basically where I've always been at. I'm just a skiffler, you know. Now I do "posh skiffle." That's all it is. That's why I've always been embarrassed at the idea of being in *Guitar Player* magazine. It's just posh skiffle.

Once you got electrified, who were your main influences?

Once we got going it was like "Heartbreak Hotel," hearing that early Elvis stuff, Carl Perkins — I don't recall which order they came in — the Everlys, Eddie Cochran. You know, I've always wanted one of them orange Gretsches with a big "G" stamped on it. I finally got one — my wife got me the one I used on the Carl Perkins program for Christmas a couple of years ago — except it didn't have the "G" on it. I mean, I just loved that stuff. And the first time I ever saw a photograph of Buddy Holly with that Strat — I'm sure it was the same for millions of kids — but, you know, you *cream* yourself, your pants, looking at this. Wow! When I was in school, I was always bad in school — I didn't like it — and I'd always just sit in the back. But I've got some of my books still, from when I was about 13. And there's just drawings of guitars and different-style scratchplates — always trying to draw Fender Stratocasters.

Was "Cry for a Shadow," the instrumental you wrote with John, written in reference to the Shadows?

We always used to have a little joke on the Shadows. Because in England, [singer] Cliff Richard and the Shadows were the biggest thing; they were like the English version of the Ventures. And it was a time when — we were lucky because we didn't get into it — everybody had matching ties and handkerchiefs and suits, and all the lead guitar players had glasses so they looked like Buddy Holly, and they all did these funny walks while they were playing. Well, we went to Hamburg and got straight into the leather gear. And we were doing all the Chuck Berry and Little Richard and that kind of stuff — and just foaming at the mouth because they used to feed us these uppers to keep us going, because they made us work eight or ten hours a night. So we used to always joke about the Shadows, and actually in Hamburg we had to play so long, we actually used to play "Apache" or whatever was their hit. But John and I were just bullshitting one day, and he had this new little Rickenbacker with a funny kind of wobble bar on it. And he started that off, and I just came in, and we made it up right on the spot. Then we started playing it a couple of nights, and it got on a record somehow [*The Beatles Featuring Tony Sheridan — In the Beginning* (circa 1960)]. But it was really a joke, so we called it "Cry for a Shadow."

But you don't consider yourself to have been influenced by the Shadows' Hank Marvin, as was the case with most English guitarists of that period?

Naw, no. Although Hank is a good player — I would certainly not put him down — and I did enjoy the little echo things they had and the sound of the Fenders, which they started out on. But, to me, "Walk — Don't Run," the Ventures — I just always preferred the American stuff to the English. So I wasn't influenced by him at all. I'm more influenced

by Buddy Holly. I mean, right till this day I could play you the "Peggy Sue" solo any time, or "Think It Over" or "It's So Easy." I knew all them tunes, and Eddie Cochran stuff. Right before Eddie Cochran got killed, I was lucky enough to see him when he came to play the Liverpool Empire, and he was hot — I'll tell ya. He started the show with "What'd I Say" and "Milkcow Blues." He had his unwound third string and his Bigsby going — he was real cool.

Why did you end up with a Gretsch instead of a Strat, considering Buddy Holly's influence?

What happened was, my first guitar was this little cheap acoustic I mentioned, and then I got what they call a cello-style, *f*-hole, single-cutaway called a Hofner — which is like the German version of a Gibson. Then I got a pickup and stuck it on that, and then I swapped that for a guitar called a Club 40, which is a little Hofner that looked like a solid guitar but was actually hollow inside with no soundholes. Then this guitar came along called a Futurama. It was a dog to play; it had the worst action. They tried to copy a Fender Strat. It had a great sound, though, and a real good way of switching in the three pickups and all the combinations. But when we got to Hamburg, there was this Fender Strat, which was the first real Strat I'd ever seen in person, other than a photo. I was going to buy it the next day, and there was this other band called Rory Storm & The Hurricanes — which Ringo was with. And the guitar player ran out and got his money, and he got it. The next day when I got up there, it had gone, and he was up there playing it [*smiles, strumming air guitar*]. I thought, "Aw, shit!"

Then we started making a bit of money, because I saved up 75 pounds, and I saw an ad in the paper in Liverpool, and there was a guy selling his guitar. I bought it; it was a Gretsch Duo Jet — which is now on my new album cover. It was a sailor who bought it in America and brought it back. It was like my first real American guitar, and I'll tell you, it was second-hand, but I polished that thing; I was so proud to own that. That was the reason I think when we went to the States to play the *Ed Sullivan Show*, Gretsch gave me a Gretsch that I used on the show. I didn't realize at the time — because if I had, I'd have 20 Gretsches right now, with square ones, round ones, fur ones, and all them like Bo Diddley — but I read somewhere that after the Beatles appeared on the *Ed Sullivan Show* that Gretsch sold 20,000 guitars a week or something like that. I mean, we would have had shares in Fender, Vox, Gretsch, and everything, but we didn't know — we were stupid.

Nevertheless, they gave me a couple of Gretsches, which was very nice of them, and I wish they were still in business — the original company — because I've got some great ideas for what they should do. I mean, all these companies — I suppose it's the same as motor cars. They're so into making little wedgie turbos, but what about all them with the big wings? They could still put on all those high-tech switches and pickups, possibly, but you can't beat that Strat and those old pickups they had on it — I don't care what you say. The same with some of those designs of those older guitars. I mean, that book *American Guitars* is fantastic. I just look at that, and certain ones, like that D'Angelico with the real art-deco scratchplate. I'm still a kid when it comes to guitars. Anyway, Gretsch gave me those guitars, and I was pleased to have them, but I never really got the one I wanted, which was the orange — well, it's called the Chet Atkins, but to me it's the "Eddie Cochran" model.

In the past few years, when you were concentrating more on filmmaking, did you see yourself primarily as a guitarist still, as a songwriter, a filmmaker, or what?

I don't really see myself as a songwriter or a gui-tarist or a singer or a lyricist or even a film producer. All of those are me, in a way — just like I like gardening, digging holes and sticking trees in. But I'm not *really* a gardener, just like I'm not really a guitarist — but I am. If I plant 500 coconut trees, I'm sort of a gardener, aren't I? And if I play on records and stuff, then I'm a guitarist. But not in the sense like, say, B.B. King or Eric Clapton, who play constantly and keep their chops together and are really fluid. You have to play all that time to keep good, and in that respect . . . you know, I'm not trying to put myself down, but the reality is I'm *okay*. I mean, I've sat with people who are just learning the guitar and showed them some chords and a few things — and I realized I do know quite a lot about guitar; I've absorbed quite a lot over the years. But I've never really felt like I was a proper guitar player. You see all these guys with their chops together, with charts showing how they did it. In the sense of being a guitarist who works and plays, and who could just pop in on anybody's session and come up with the goods, I'm not that kind of player. I'm just a jungle musician, really.

— Michael Hedges —

By Dan Forte – February 1985

JON SIEVERT

INTERVIEWS WITH Michael Hedges often resemble Abbott & Costello routines. Example:
Interviewer: Who's playing bass on that song?
Hedges: That's me.
Interviewer: Oh, you overdubbed it?
Hedges: No, it was all done live.
Interviewer: You play guitar and bass simultaneously?
Hedges: No, I just play guitar.
Interviewer: Then who's playing bass?
Hedges: That's me.
Interviewer: And who's your percussionist?

Seeing Hedges perform live as a solo act helps clear up some, but not all, of the confusion one often encounters when listening to his "solo" recordings. You can see that all the sounds are indeed coming from one man and his acoustic guitar, but *how* he accomplishes his musical sleight of hand — combining a rhythmic ostinato chord structure in the treble register with bass slides and melodies, high harmonics, and explosive percussive taps and slaps — is another question. (Hedges likes to tell a story about a listener's response to hearing him on record: "He said, 'That's a nice band.' I was so pleased he thought that.")

To transpose the sounds he hears in his head onto an acoustic 6-string, Michael employs full-chord hammer-ons and pull-offs (sometimes using both hands), artificial harmonics, two-handed tapping techniques, and utterly unorthodox tunings. He has earned high praise from guitar greats such as Jim Hall and Larry Coryell, who stated: "I heard Michael Hedges' record, and I fell down. Couldn't believe it. It's not unlike what Ralph Towner did — something that was jazz, yet wasn't jazz. Traditional jazz phraseology was not being played. It wasn't the jazz heroes reworked."

Will Ackerman signed Michael to Windham Hill in 1980 after hearing him perform at a theater in Palo Alto, California. Hedges, a native Oklahoman (born New Year's Eve, 1953), had moved to California to study at Stanford's Center for Computer Research and Musical Acoustics under John Chowning, having earned a degree in composition from Peabody Conservatory in Baltimore. *Breakfast in the Field,* the LP Coryell mentioned, was released in '81, and immediately distinguished Hedges as probably the most unusual, certainly the most kinetic, performer on the Windham Hill roster. Songs such as "The Happy Couple" revealed a lyricism in keeping with labelmates Ackerman and Alex de Grassi, while "Silent Anticipations" sounded like a rock and roll version of Leo Kottke.

His follow-up, 1984's *Aerial Boundaries,* is a landmark acoustic guitar effort.

Could you explain the techniques you use in Aerial Boundaries?

Well, the whole technique is in the way that the performer thinks about the instrument. It was mental conditioning that led me to it. It started on "Rickover's Dream," which has a lot of the same effects — it sort of grew into *Aerial Boundaries*. The left hand provides sort of the ostinato hammer-on/pull-off, so the right hand has to do melodies or something. It's Chapman Stick technique — hammering on, pulling off, sliding — just like Van Halen, only applied to acoustic guitar. And it's different compositionally, of course; my licks don't sound like Van Halen's, but it's a lot of the same techniques. Usually instead of hammering on one string like Eddie does, I hammer on two or three bass strings with a barre, not with the fingertip. That seems pretty limited — slapping and pulling off. Well, I wanted to work it out to where these parts would be different, distinct, and then they would start working together as a unit, so the musical *ideas* would go from one hand to another. On regular fingerpicking guitar, I'm used to the right hand always making the attack and the left doing the fingering — traditional guitar technique. But why not get two different music makers going, and try to interweave them? Two different attackers. I learned all this stuff from Willis Ramsey. He's a progressive country singer; he wrote a song called "Spider John" that Jimmy Buffett recorded. His hammer-ons and pull-offs are so rhythmically correct and integral to his style, it made me realize I had a whole other way to pluck the instrument. Also, listening to John Martyn, Martin Carthy, and Leo Kottke.

Usually, when people use tapping technique, it doesn't get as true an acoustic tone as you manage to get. Sometimes you sound like an acoustic bass.

I'm trying to get as much sound out of that instrument as I can. That's my drive — to play the heck out of the thing.

Why do you sometimes reach over the neck with your left hand to hammer on chords?

Sometimes it's so I won't interfere with something else I'm doing. Sometimes it makes the treble strings ring more clearly.

What are your open tunings based on?

They're based on the harmonic structure of the piece and the type of voicing I want to provide most of the chords with.

Are they of such a nature that those pieces could not be played in standard tuning?

Correct. Why else would I go to all that trouble between songs to retune the guitar?

What is the tuning on, say, "Hot Type"?

It's almost the same as on "The Happy Couple." Low to high: *E*, down a fourth; the *A* string up a major second to *B*; the *D* string is up a major second to *E*; the *G* string is down to *F#*; the *B* string is down

a whole-step to *A*; and the high *E* is down to *D*. So it's *A B E F# A D*.

When you work in such an unorthodox tuning, are you thinking of that particular piece by rote, or are you able to improvise in that new environment?

Only if I know that tuning real well. Pierre Bensusan's philosophy is to find your favorite tuning and stick with it. That's great for him — I commend him for it — but I can't do that, because my compositions won't allow me to stick with it. On "Hot Type," I wanted that low string to be as low as possible without distorting, just to get a real animated feel. Tunings sometimes evolve. I'll say, "Oh, I can do this and this . . . but I can't do that, that, that, and that." So I try to reduce the number of *that's* until I have to compromise the least to get what I want — and that's the tuning.

Do you arrive at a tuning that fits a composition in your head, or do you take the Will Ackerman approach and find a tuning that suggests, or helps compose, the song itself?

It's both, really. Sometimes I'll find maybe one chord that I really like that's easy to play in a particular tuning, and maybe a composition will evolve from that. For some pieces, if I want them to sound more like a dulcimer, I'll tune two strings to the same pitch.

When you retune in various open tunings, can you immediately revisualize the fingerboard?

Only to the extent that the composition would lead me to, only in places in performance where I would want to go. It doesn't really lead me to much harmonic reorganization; it leads me to *rhythmic* reorganization. If I forgot where I was in the middle of something, to a certain extent I could pick up, to some extent I couldn't.

Studying theory at Peabody and playing acoustic guitar in open tunings seem to represent two different schools of thought.

Well, I went to the school of modern twentieth century composition. I listened to Kottke and Carthy and Martyn, but my head was headed more towards Stravinsky, Varése, Webern, and a lot of experimental composers like Morton Feldman. I wanted to take the guitar and just use it differently. I never went through a phase of going to college and playing Leo Kottke or John Fahey fingerpicking solos; it never interested me. I never had any ambition to sound like anybody — except Pat Metheny [*laughs*], and that came later.

Were your first musical influences folk?

I started playing Peter, Paul & Mary songs on a Goya nylon-string. Then I got a Fender Mustang and started playing Beatles. Next I got a Gibson Les Paul and played Led Zeppelin and Grand Funk Railroad in high school. But also in high school, I got interested in jazz and wanted to be in the school stage band. In order to be in the stage band, one also had to be in the marching band and concert band, so I started flute. I formed a jazz band and studied jazz guitar. I was also in a blues band in college. I sold the Les Paul because it was too heavy for me, and I recently bought a '63 Mustang, just like my old one. Someone recently gave me a Dean guitar, so I'm going to "rock my baby," like it says in all those sexist ads [*laughs*]. I try to work on electric about a third of the time. I'm also spending about a third of my time on harp guitar. I got a Dyer made in the '20s or earlier by Maurer in Chicago. Mine has five harp strings, but there's room for six. Right now, the harp strings are tuned *G B♭, D C A* and *D*, low to high. I'm working out bass lines to do with the right hand on the harp strings while I'm tapping with the left hand on the guitar strings. But Stanley Jordan has us all beat. That guy has unscrewed my head and put it on differently. I saw him up close at a coffeehouse. He's amazing. He's got to be the most fluent exponent of that stick-like technique. His technique and mine are radically different in that mine is not as precise a touch technique; mine is relatively high action with medium- to heavy-gauge strings — .013, .017, .026, .034, .044, .056. So I have to slap the thing.

Have any influences from your jazz studies stayed with you?

Well, I'm still into jazz and have been ever since I first heard Stan Kenton's band. Pat Martino's the biggest influence. He knows the fingerboard so well! Mike Marshall has opened my head up in terms of rhythm guitar playing. A good rhythm guitar — you can't beat it. Also Tony Rice, with his wonderful, clean flatpicking.

What type of music do you listen to?

Right now, I'm listening to a lot of Baroque music, Renaissance music, the recorder player Frans Bruggen, modern twentieth century music — I just got a record by Ligeti, who composed a lot of the music in *2001*. I listen to John Martyn, [bassist] Eberhard Weber, Genesis, [synthesist/trumpeter] Mark Isham, Cyndi Lauper, the Time, Prince — everything I can get my hands on that's good. Todd Rundgren is one of my idols as a songwriter, and I love John Scofield's guitar playing with Miles Davis.

Do you have many traditional folk influences?

Yes. As far as the British Isles, I don't know how much the Bothy Band has tampered with traditional, but they're a great influence, along with Planxty, Martin Carthy, DeDanaan, and the Chieftains. In mideastern music, the *dumbak* drum accompanying belly dancers at the Casbah restaurant in San Francisco influenced "Aerial Boundaries." So I went out and got a dumbak and really started listening to drummers, rock or otherwise, because I realized that rhythm was my weakest point.

– JIMI HENDRIX –

BY DON MENN & JOHN BURKS – SEPTEMBER 1975

HIS HANDS WERE what made him look so tall. They could have been stitched onto someone a foot taller. But James Marshall Hendrix, who only stood 5'11", made good use of what he had and what he heard.

What he heard to begin with were the sounds of the 40's and 50's blaring out of radios, phonographs, and televisions in his hometown of Seattle, Washington. He was acquainted as well with the sounds of other eras preserved in his father's extensive record collection, which contained primarily blues and R&B artists. The sounds from those around him must have stayed in his ears, too — his father slapping the spoons on his thighs and palms, his aunt playing keyboard with authority at the Dunlap Baptist Church (where Jimi's funeral was later to be held).

Jimi's dad, James Allen Hendrix, a landscape gardener, traded in his sax for an acoustic guitar to replace the broom his 12-year-old boy strummed, and Jimi began to train himself. He'd watch other guitarists and see them playing things which he'd pick up and try himself, usually left-handed but sometimes right-handed. Though he never learned to read music, he was always jamming, and logged much practice time gigging in a half-dozen rock-oriented groups in Seattle. They played the local clubs or traveled 120 miles north to Vancouver to work dances for 50 cents an hour and all the Cokes and hamburgers they could consume. Mr. Hendrix still

has a mental image of his elder son (Jimi's brother, Leon, was five years younger) flopped on the sofa, playing along with records, radio, and television, and that's where Jimi probably got that *Peter Gunn* theme he plays on the *War Heroes* album.

Jimi's parents were originally from Vancouver, and he spent much time there in elementary school and visiting his grandmother when gigging around British Columbia in the days after he'd entered Garfield High School back in Seattle. But, however highly he was later to be thought of, in Seattle a lot of people didn't consider Jimi that extraordinary a guitar player. Not then, anyway.

In 1959, when he was 17, Jimi convinced his father to sign the military enlistment papers (he wasn't 18 yet, and needed parental approval), and off he went with the 101st Airborne Division. This 26-month excursion into paratrooping ended on his 26th jump, which wracked his back and foot, and brought him an early discharge. But he'd kept up with his music. Earlier in boot camp he had written his father, begging him to send a guitar, because Jimi thought he was going crazy. With the instrument, he jammed with anyone — including Billy Cox, who would later play bass with Jimi in the Band of Gypsys.

Between 1963 and 1964 Jimi toured the South, "the chitlin circuit" as it was called, with a wide variety of acts. He landed in New York in 1964. His prominence as a sideman grew, and by the time he joined King Curtis in 1965 he had worked with Ike and Tina Turner, Little Richard, Joey Dee, Jackie Wilson, James Brown, Wilson Pickett, B.B. King, the Isley Brothers, and Curtis Knight and the Squires.

Chuck Rainey, who played bass with King Curtis while Jimi and Cornell Dupree shared lead guitar roles, recalls that Hendrix was an exceptional musician, just happy to be included. "If he was hired as the third guitar player," Rainey says, "he was happy; he never had a bad thing to say about anything." He also remembers that Jimi had perfect pitch, was ambidextrous, and had enough finesse with jazz numbers to lead him to conclude that Jimi had some knowledge of the Billy Butler and Charlie Christian eras. For anyone who doubted it, Jimi could and did play jazz solos, as opposed to strictly rock and rhythm and blues.

Jimi formed his own New York group in 1965. He called it the Blue Flames and himself Jimmy James. By mid-1966 they were gigging in pop music's backyard — Greenwich Village. Accepting a position as lead guitarist for John Hammond Jr., this Jimmy James character began to make a name for himself among an even more elite crowd that included Bob Dylan, the Beatles, and the Animals.

This led to a fortuitous visit from Bryan "Chas" Chandler, formerly the bass player with the Animals, who decided that his and this wild guitar player's futures should be zipped together. After arranging for passports, Chas presented Jimmy James with a ticket, some money, and a promise of meeting Eric Clapton — whom the young guitarist was just hearing about and gaining some interest in. After the arrival in England, Mr. Hendrix received a call from his son saying that he was going to be made into a star. He had also redeemed his original surname, but changed the spelling of his first. Now he was *Jimi* Hendrix.

In London, Chas snatched up Mitch Mitchell (a drummer) and Noel Redding (a lead guitarist who was handed a bass), and the Jimi Hendrix Experience was born. An immediate success in Europe at smaller and then larger clubs, the group signed a contract with Track Records, who released "Hey Joe" and "Purple Haze," which became instant hits. Though then considered to be the hottest act in Europe, the Experience was an underground rumor on Jimi's side of the ocean.

However, the group did not remain obscure for long in the United States. On the recommendation of Paul McCartney, the planners of the Monterey Pop Festival (June 16–18, 1967) booked the Experience. At the last show on Sunday, Jimi Hendrix flabber-

gasted those attending, and America got its first glimpse of what he could do with an electric guitar and lighter fluid. But guitar players were stunned less by his theatrics than by Jimi's unusual approach to music, and his fluent control over and use of distortion, which had previously been a game of chance or a factor to be eliminated from (not added to) one's sound system.

The second glimpse for America was from the wrong eye. The Experience was put on tour with the Monkees in early 1967, and the idea was not a bright one. The Monkees' young fans were not prepared for Jimi's wild sensuality and roaring music. After less than a half-dozen performances, management fabricated a story that the Daughters of the American Revolution had had the Experience banned, so the group pulled out of the tour.

Hendrix returned to England, where his popularity had remained high, and positive response from his records in America coupled with word of his performances in Europe helped erase the memory of the Monkees fiasco. Jimi played to standing-room-only crowds in tours of the United States in 1968 and 1969.

Hendrix became a guitarists' guitarist, jamming constantly with the top musicians in the pop field in famous after-hours meetings that included luminaries such as Johnny Winter, John McLaughlin, Stephen Stills, and artists from other realms, such as reed virtuoso Roland Kirk. The members of the Experience began to drift apart in late 1968. Jimi was showing signs of desiring to work with other musicians, most notably the Band of Gypsys, which included Buddy Miles on drums and Billy Cox on bass. Their performance at the Fillmore East in New York was recorded and portions were remixed in their only album, though the group never did tour together.

Talk of reforming the Experience and going on tour in the spring of 1970 came to nothing. Jimi apparently went through a period of intense re-evaluation of his music and artistic goals. In the spring and summer he toured with Mitch Mitchell and Billy Cox, and in August of 1970 he played at England's Isle of Wight Festival after staying awake all night with Eric Barrett for the opening of his own recording studio, Electric Lady Studios in New York. There he gave a bad performance which has been regarded often as indicative of depression or a general decline in his abilities, as opposed to being a to-be-expected slip-up resulting from sleep deprivation, jet lag, and the 2:00 A.M. slot.

On September 18, 1970, James Marshall Hendrix was pronounced dead on arrival at St. Mary Abbots Hospital in Kensington, England. Professor Donald Teare, the pathologist, explained the cause of death had been "inhalation of vomit due to barbiturate intoxication." Though there were not enough drugs in Jimi's body to have caused his death, speculation arose as to whether he had attempted suicide. This has been discounted by nearly every person who knew Jimi, many who recall that he was in fact rather enjoying life and the prospect of entering a new, highly creative phase of his career. It should be noted that the sleeping pills he took were not his own, and were in fact a German brand which are normally broken into quarters before ingesting. Jimi probably had no idea of the dose he was taking to catch a little sleep in the early morning hours of that day. From all appearances, his death was a tragic and avoidable mistake.

Gerry Stickells, his road manager, had Jimi's body flown home for the funeral, attended by such notables as Johnny Winter and Miles Davis as well as many of the musicians with whom he had performed. His burial took place on October 1, 1970, at Greenwood Cemetery in Seattle.

What would Jimi have done had he lived? All is speculation, but he expressed many dreams to those around him; some may have been pipe dreams, some may or may not have been brought to reality. Eric Barrett says he sensed "that a whole new trip was coming down." Jimi would call him, and they'd sit up all night discussing ideas. Hendrix had wanted to buy a Big Top, hire his own security guards, and set up three- and four-day concerts on the outskirts of towns; guards would have been there to keep order and things running smoothly, as opposed to turning a concert into a drug bust. Jimi died the week before he was to have completed preliminary meetings with master jazz arranger Gil Evans to do some recording. (*The Gil Evans Orchestra Plays the Music of Jimi Hendrix* contains selections that Evans presented in his all-Hendrix concert at Carnegie Hall as a part of the New York Jazz Repertory Company's 1974 programs.)

Jimi himself spoke of a desire to take a year or so off to study music more systematically to learn to write and read [music]. In one interview he expressed an interest in mixed media, in exploring the healing power of sound and color used in coordination. He told Roy Hollingworth, in an interview published the day before his death, that "In older civilizations they didn't have diseases as we know them. It would be incredible if you could produce music so perfect that it would filter through you like rays and ultimately

cure." As to his musical horizons, he told the same interviewer, "I dig Strauss and Wagner. Those cats were good, and I think they are going to form the background of my music. Above it will be blues — I still got plenty of blues — and then there will be Western Sky music and sweet opium music, and these will be mixed together to form one." Jimi also wanted to complete the work he'd begun on the *Cry of Love* album, as well as put together a big band with brass instruments and competent musicians for whom he could conduct and write.

Alan Douglas mentions innumerable plans of Jimi's to expand into filmmaking and book writing. Douglas also suggests that Hendrix was considering doing a fantasy biography about "Black Gold" (a character that was basically Jimi) done in 10 tunes linked together into a total story much like "Tommy," the Who's rock opera. Douglas and Hendrix conceived of developing this theme in an animated film (perhaps this is what Jimi alludes to as "cartoon material" in the interview below), on a record, and in an illustrated book. Unfortunately, the cassette on which Jimi had sketched out the original rough was among the items stolen from his apartment immediately following his death.

Regardless of the wealth of ideas that seem to have tumbled through his fertile mind, Jimi Hendrix, though untimely silenced, left a legacy of musical creativity that was richly satisfying in every way. His death was a tragedy, but his life was not.

On February 4, 1970, a day so cold and snowy that all the cabs in New York were occupied, John Burks (then managing editor of *Rolling Stone*), shivering in his California clothes, trudged and skidded through frozen slush to a chic midtown apartment to conduct what proved to be one of Jimi Hendrix' last major interviews. In attendance were Jimi, Noel Redding, Mitch Mitchell, various management personnel, and Baron Wolman, well-known photographer/journalist for *Rolling Stone, Rags*, etc.). The meeting had been initiated by Hendrix' management primarily to trumpet the reunification of the original Jimi Hendrix Experience, which turned out to be a short-lived regrouping that ran concurrently with the Band of Gypsys.

Burks and Wolman remember sensing an anxiety on the part of the interviewees. "Though the setup was like you do for a fan magazine writer," John recalls, "they knew they could not manipulate the interview for their own publicity purposes because they were dealing with *Rolling Stone*. Moreover, that particular time jag contained memories of a disturbingly dull concert in January at a peace rally at Madison Square Garden, at which an uninspired Jimi had simply stopped playing. Nevertheless, it is difficult to make a case for a depressed Hendrix, for if Madison Square had been a bummer, he also had the memory of a concert with the Band of Gypsys that rock promoter Bill Graham described as the finest he'd ever heard at Fillmore East. Whatever the initial mood, cognac, a warm fire in the fireplace, and a relaxed pace of questioning loosened things up."

Obviously, it did not occur to John [Burks] that the Hendrix portions of this interview with the Experience would be used 22 years later in this book. In fact, the tape itself — a hissy jumble of voices interrupting voices, captured by a wobbly recorder — was so discouraging in quality that Burks snatched from it what phrases he could for a quick article and stashed it away in a box where it rested untranscribed, unpublished, but fortunately not erased. When he learned of the first Jimi Hendrix special issue (*Guitar Player*, September 1975), John dug the cassette out, and we present here the discernible portions. This interview provides a last intriguing glimpse of a guitar genius.

Are you still living with a lot of musicians at your house?

No, I just try to have some time by myself so I can really write some things. I want to do more writing.

What kind of writing?

I don't know. Mostly just cartoon material. Make up this one cat who's funny, who goes through all these strange scenes. I can't talk about it now. You could put it to music, I guess. Just like you can put blues into music.

Are you talking about long, extended pieces or just songs?

Well, I want to get into what you'd probably call "pieces," yeah, pieces, behind each other to make movements, or whatever you call it. I've been writing some of those. But, like, I was into writing cartoons mostly.

If the cartoon is in your head, do you have the music, too?

Yeah, in the head, right. You listen to it, and you get such funny flashbacks. The music will be going along with the story, just like "Foxy Lady." Something like that. The music and the words go together.

When you put together a song, does it just come to you, or is it a process where you sit down with your guitar or at a piano, starting from 10 in the morning?

The music I might hear, I can't get on the guitar. It's a thing of just laying around daydreaming or something. You're hearing all this music, and you just can't get it on the guitar. As a matter of fact, if you pick up your guitar and just try to play, it spoils the whole thing. I can't play the guitar that well to get all this music together, so I just lay around. I wish I could have learned how to write for instruments. I'm going to get into that next, I guess.

So for something like "Foxy Lady," you first hear the music and then arrive at the words for the song?

It all depends. On "Foxy Lady," we just started playing, actually, and set up a microphone, and I had these words [*laughs*]. With "Voodoo Chile (Slight Return)," somebody was filming when we started doing that. We did that about three times because they wanted to film us in the studio, to make us [*imitates a pompous voice*] "Make it look like you're recording, boys" — one of them scenes, you know, so, "Okay, let's play this in *E*; now a-one-and-a-two-and-a-three," and then we went into "Voodoo Chile."

When I hear Mitch churning away and you really blowing on top and the bass gets really free, the whole approach almost sounds like avant-garde jazz.

Well, that's because that's where it's coming from — the drumming.

Do you dig any avant-garde jazz players?

Yeah, when we went to Sweden and heard some of those cats we'd never heard before. These cats were actually in little country clubs and little caves blowing some sounds that, you know, you barely imagine. Guys from Sweden, Copenhagen, Amsterdam, or Stockholm. Every once in a while they start going like a wave. They get into each other every once in a while within their personalities, and the party last night, or the hangover [*laughs*], and the evil starts pulling them away again. You can hear it start to go away. Then it starts getting together again. It's like a wave, I guess, coming in and out.

For your own musical kicks, where's the best place to play?

I like after-hours jams at a small place like a club. Then you get another feeling. You get off in another way with all those people there. You get another feeling, and you mix it in with something else that you get. It's not the spotlights, just the people.

How are those two experiences different, this thing you get from the audiences?

I get more of a dreamy thing from the audience

— it's more of a thing that you go up into. You get into such a pitch sometimes that you go up into another thing. You don't forget about the audience, but you forget about all the paranoia, that thing where you're saying, "Oh gosh, I'm onstage — what am I going to do now?" Then you go into this other thing, and it turns out to be almost like a play in certain ways.

You don't kick in many amps anymore or light guitars on fire.

Maybe I was just noticing the guitar for a change. Maybe.

Was that a conscious decision?

Oh, I don't know. It's like it's the end of a beginning. I figure that Madison Square Garden was like the end of a big, long fairy tale, which is great. It's the best thing I could possibly have come up with. The band was out of sight, as far as I'm concerned.

But what happened to you?

It was just something where the head changes, just going through changes. I really couldn't tell, to tell the truth. I was very tired. You know, sometimes there's a lot of things that add up in your head about this and that. And they hit you at a very peculiar time, which happened to be at that peace rally, and here I am fighting the biggest war I've ever fought in my life — inside, you know? And, like, that wasn't the place to do it, so I just unmasked appearances.

How much part do you play in the production of your albums? For example, did you produce your first [Are You Experienced]?

No, it was Chas Chandler and Eddie Kramer who mostly worked on that stuff. Eddie was the engineer, and Chas as producer mainly kept things together.

The last record [Electric Ladyland] listed you as producer. Did you do the whole thing?

No, well, like, Eddie Kramer and myself. All I did was just be there and make sure the right songs were there, and the *sound* was there. We wanted a particular sound. It got lost in the cutting room, because we went on tour right before we finished. I heard it, and I think the sound of it is very cloudy.

You did "All Along the Watchtower" on the last one. Is there anything else that you'd like to record by Bob Dylan?

Oh yeah. I like that one that goes, "Please help me in my weakness" ["Drifter's Escape"]. That was groovy. I'd like to do that. I like his *Blonde on Blonde* and *Highway 61 Revisited*. His country stuff is nice too, at certain times. It's quieter, you know.

Your recording of "Watchtower" really turned me on to that song when Dylan didn't.

Well, that's reflections like the mirror. [*Laughs.*] Remember that "roomful of mirrors"? That's a song, a recording that we're trying to do, but I don't think we'll ever finish that. I hope not. It's about trying to get out of this roomful of mirrors.

Why can't you finish it?

[*Imitates prissy voice*] Well, you see, I'm going through this health kick, you see. I'm heavy on wheat germ, but, you know what I mean [*laughs*] — I don't know why [*takes a pencil and writes something*].

You're not what I'd call a country guitar player.

Thank you.

You consider that a compliment?

It would be if I was a country guitar player. That would be another step.

Are you listening to bands like that doing country, like the Flying Burrito Brothers?

Who's the guitar player for the Burrito Brothers? That guy plays. I dig him. He's really marvelous with a guitar. That's what makes me listen to that, is the music.

It's sweet. It's got that thing to it.

[*In a deep drawl*] "Hello walls." [*Laughs*]. You hear that one, "Hello Walls"? "Hillbilly Heaven."

Remember Bob Wills and the Texas Playboys?

[*Laughs.*] I dig them. The Grand Ole Opry used to come on, and I used to watch that. They used to have some pretty heavy cats, heavy guitar players.

Which musicians do you go out of your way to hear?

Nina Simone and Mountain. I dig them.

What about a group like the McCoys?

[*Sings intro to "Hang on Sloopy," which featured Rick Derringer on guitar.*] Yeah, that guitar player's great.

Do you dig parodies like the Masked Marauders or the English radio program, The Goon Show?

I never heard it [Masked Marauders]. I heard about it. The Fugs, they're good. I've heard they don't have it [*The Goon Show*] over here. They're masterpieces. Those are classics. They're the funniest things I've ever heard, besides Pinky Lee. Remember Pinky Lee? They were like a classic of a whole lot of Pinky Lees together, and just flip them out together.

You a Pinky Lee fan?

Used to be. I used to wear white socks.

Were you really rehearsing with Band of Gypsys 12 to 18 hours a day?

Yeah, we used to go and jam, actually. We'd say "rehearsing" just to make it sound, you know, official. We were just getting off; that's all. Not really 18 hours — say about 12 or 14 maybe. [*Laughs.*] The longest we [the Experience] ever played together is going onstage. We played about two-and-a-half hours, almost three hours one time. We made sounds. People make sounds when they clap. So we make sounds back. I like electric sounds, feedback and so forth, static.

Are you going to do a single as well as an LP?

We might have one from the other thing coming out soon. I don't know about the Experience, though. All these record companies, they want singles. But you don't just sit there and say, "Let's make a track, let's make a single or something." We're not going to do that. We don't do that.

Creedence Clearwater Revival does that until they have enough for a record, like in the old days.

Well, that's the old days. I consider us more musicians. More in the minds of musicians, you know?

But singles can make some bread, can't they?

Well, that's why they do them. But they take it after. You'll have a whole planned-out LP, and all of a sudden, they'll make, for instance, "Crosstown Traffic" a single, and that's coming out of nowhere, out of a whole other set. See, that LP was in certain ways of thinking; the sides we played on in order for certain reasons. And then it's almost like a sin for them to take out something in the middle of all that and make that a single, and represent us at that particular time because they think they can make more money. They always take out the wrong ones.

How often will you space these concerts with the Experience so that you won't feel hemmed in?

As often as we three agree to it. I'd like for it to be permanent.

Have you given any thought to touring with the Experience as the basic unit, but bringing along other people? Or would that be too confusing?

No, it shouldn't be. Maybe I'm the evil one, right [*laughs*]. But there isn't any reason for it to be like that. I even want the name to be Experience, anyway, and still be this mishmash mooshmash between Madame Flip-flop and Her Harmonite Social Workers.

It's a nice name.

It's a nice game. No, like, about putting other groups on the tour, like our friends — I don't know about that right now; not at a stage like this, because we're in the process of getting our own thing together, as far as a three-piece group. But eventually, we have time on the side to play with friends. That's why I'll probably be jamming with Buddy [Miles] and Billy [Cox]; probably be recording, too, on the side, and they'll be doing the same.

Do you ever think in terms of going out with a dozen people?

I like Stevie Winwood; he's one of those dozen people. But things don't have to be official all the time. Things don't have to be formal for jams and stuff. But I haven't had a chance to get in contact with him.

Ever think about getting other guitar players into your trip?

Oh, yeah. Well, I heard Duane Eddy came into town this morning [*laughs*]. He was groovy.

Have you jammed with Larry Coryell and Sonny Sharrock and people like that?

Larry and I had, like, swift jams down at the Scene. Every once in a while we would finally get a chance to get together. But I haven't had a chance to really play with him — not lately, anyway. I sort of miss that.

Do you listen to them?

I like Larry Coryell, yeah.

Better than others?

Oh, not better. Who's this other guy? I think I've heard some of his things.

He's all over the guitar. Sometimes it sounds like it's not too orderly.

Sounds like someone we know, huh [*laughs*]?

Have you played with people like [saxophonist] Roland Kirk?

Oh, yeah. I had a jam with him at Ronnie Scott's in London, and I really got off. It was great. It was really great. I was so scared! It's really funny. I mean *Roland* [*laughs*]. That cat gets all those sounds. I might just hit one note, and it might be interfering, but, like, we got along great, I thought. He told me I should have turned it up or something.

He seems like a cat you might record particularly well with. I hear these bands like Blood, Sweat, and Tears and their horns, and CTA [Chicago Transit Authority, later known as Chicago], though I haven't heard them in person.

Oh yeah, CTA. In person, listen, that's when you should hear them. That's the only time. They just started recording, but in person. The next chance you get, you should check them out.

Do you listen to the Band?

It's there. They got their own thing together that takes you a certain place. Takes you where they want to go [*laughs*], you know. Where they want to. They play their things onstage exactly how they play it on record.

Have movie people tried to lure you into films by saying you'd be a hell of a gunslinger or an astronaut?

Astronaut! [*Laughs.*] Fly in space! We have one called "Captain Coconut." No, well, you know. I'm trying to get the guitar together, really.

Do you find American audiences more violent than those of other countries?

In New York, it's more of a violent climate. It's very violent, actually. They don't know it, really. But Texas is really fine. I don't know why. Maybe it's the weather, and the feeling of it. I dig the South a little more than playing in the North. It's more of a pressure playing in the Midwest, like Cleveland or Chicago. It's like being in a pressure cooker waiting for the top to blow off. The people there are groovy, but it's just the atmosphere or something, you know? But the South is great. New Orleans is great. Arizona is great. Arizona's fantastic. Utah.

How did they treat you in Utah?

[*Laughs.*] Well, once we're offstage, it's another world, but, like, the people are great. But when we played at the gigs, they were really listening; they were really tuned in some kind of way or another. I think it was the air.

Your tastes seem broader than the typical rock and roll fan or listener.

This is all I can play when I'm playing. I'd like to get something together, like with Handel, and Bach, and Muddy Waters, flamenco type of thing [*laughs*]. If I can get that *sound*. If I could get *that* sound, I'd be happy.

— ALLAN HOLDSWORTH—

BY TOM MULHERN — DECEMBER 1980 & 1982
AND BY MATT RESNICOFF — MARCH 1990

JON SIEVERT

BOUNCING FROM one band to another, album by album, was once the rule rather than the exception for Allan Holdsworth. Moments of brilliance left in his wake on LPs by jazz and progressive rock artists including Tony Williams Lifetime, Gong, U.K., Jean-Luc Ponty, Soft Machine, and Bruford created for Holdsworth a reputation almost exclusively as a soloist. His presence on some of the recordings was by and large similar to that of a saxophonist: Sitting out and waiting until it was time to fill a certain number of bars with a flurry of creativity. Holdsworth's chordal abilities were rarely showcased, and because strict limits often governed his approach, he grew tired of his role as a mercenary soloist.

Allan's renown was fairly limited as well: With the exception of Ponty and U.K., few of the musical amalgams in which he participated ever received much attention in the U.S. Despite virtual invisibility in the pop music world at large, Allan, through his unique sound and strongly independent approach, became a touchstone for many guitarists. Among lead players, "Allan Holdsworth" was elevated to a buzzword — if you wanted to perk your ears up, he was the one to listen to.

Regarding his sheer individuality, one might conceivably categorize Allan Holdsworth with the likes of Chuck Berry, Eric Clapton, Jimi Hendrix, or John McLaughlin. Although no artist is utterly without influences, these guitarists infused their work with so much originality that they created whole new styles. While Holdsworth has certainly not yet achieved the worldwide commercial success of the others, his musical voice is so unique that it may be best defined in terms of itself: More than just a gifted artist popular among his fellow musicians, he originated what has become the Allan Holdsworth school.

Neither a rock guitar wildman nor a limelight-seeking stage strutter, Holdsworth is instead an intense devotee of the guitar. His lead style is immediately striking as fast, fluid, vibrant, and deadly accurate. Upon closer examination, enigmatic melodies with large intervallic leaps and rhythmic syncopations and ambiguity emerge. Hand tremolo plays a strong part in his style as well, lending a shimmer to passages to add depth and immediacy to even seemingly inconsequential passing tones, rather than acting as a tool for creating half-octave bends and squealing feedback.

As a soloist, this English guitarist, born August 6, 1948, is certainly unique. However, as his abilities to play lead became better and better known and exploited, he found himself trapped into a one-dimensional mode; his chordal and melodic talents were lying fallow. This musician, who has drawn praise from Eddie Van Halen, Steve Morse, and many other well-known exponents of the electric guitar, felt that he had more to offer than just flashy embellishment to other people's songs. And in order to vent his ideas, he decided to form his own band.

In 1980, Allan teamed with bassist Paul Carmichael and drummer/pianist Gary Husband to form a trio in London known as False Alarm. Expanded later to include vocalist Paul Williams (formerly of Juicy Lucy and Tempest, a band in which he and Holdsworth had worked together in 1973), the group became known as I.O.U. Over the last decade a handful of other preeminent musicians have shared duties under the "I.O.U." label. Holdsworth originally described the music as having "some elements of jazz and rock, but we try not to be overly tricky."

Given the freedom to pursue his chordal, melodic, and soloing abilities with the new band, he developed material he had written over the previous years and, with I.O.U., began performing in England. According to Allan, though, the climate wasn't quite right for the type of music that the band was performing. Punk and new wave were the rage, making I.O.U.'s music less desirable to the general public. Holdsworth and company recorded in early 1981, and found their music met with less than enthusiastic response from record companies.

By 1982, the band decided to try their luck in the United States, and released their LP, *I.O.U.*, independently. It showcased for the first time the side of Allan Holdsworth's guitar playing that had only been hinted at on previous works: Complex, densely voiced chord melodies including unusual harmonic arrangements that sounded as if they came from neither guitar nor keyboard. Ambient, shimmering, and at times ghostly chordal swells rather than harsh rhythm chopping guided the songs.

As self-effacing as he is unconventional, Allan Holdsworth doesn't believe he has tapped his full potential as a guitarist, nor does he feel there will come a time when he has. Constantly changing and updating his equipment, in recent years he has become largely associated with his SynthAxe virtuosity. But whatever the instrument in his hands, he is a perfectionist who loves to experiment, and finds music the most rewarding pursuit he can imagine.

[December 1980]
What induced you to pick up the guitar?

When I was 16, my father bought an acoustic from an uncle of mine who played in various clubs — he paid about ten shillings for it. The guitar was always sitting around, so I started messing with it and gradually made progress, though I still wasn't that serious. Being very stubborn, I never took lessons. It's sort of my nature not to ask for information — even if I'm dying to find something out. I like to discover things. And even if I were screaming inside to ask, I just can't bring myself to do it. My father tried to help me, but I refused. That was a stupid thing to have done, since there was so much knowledge he could have given me. You know, I could have learned things three or four times faster from him than I did on my own.

How did you come to the realization that you wanted to pursue the guitar seriously?

Well, I used to sneak into a pub a few miles from where I lived with my brother-in-law — I wasn't old enough to drink legally yet. We watched the local bands. I really liked a lot of the guitarists — I just became more and more interested in it. I joined some bands that did note-for-note renderings of pop records. In each song, there were two guitar solos. One was supposed to be an impersonation of the one on the record, and the other was something of my own. And my solos were always so disgusting!

Why didn't you quit doing that?

I did. I realized that instead of learning, I was just calculating — copying something without any insight into what was going on in the mind of the guy who first played those parts. So I decided *that* wasn't the thing to do. I stopped copying, and for quite a long time afterwards I couldn't play solos that I felt were anywhere near as good as those I heard. I was trying to get something that was good in its essence — musically equal, but not the same.

Do you prefer to play your solos live — on the basic tracks — or do you generally overdub them?

I had never played a completely overdubbed solo until I recorded with [drummer] Bill Bruford a few years later. It's so weird, so sterile. You know, you feel like you're *outside*. But when you do solos live, there's a sort of spirit that's so difficult to get in overdub situations. When a band plays together, everybody interacts. And that feels much better to me. If you make mistakes, they don't feel so goofy as when you overdub and foul it up. I try to listen to everything and cue off of everyone in the band.

Were any of the parts written out for you?

I couldn't have read them if they were. I don't read music. I just listened to what they wanted, and played. It's hard sometimes, because I can get a mental block. It would be a great advantage to read because when you've got something difficult to remember — even if it's only two or three bars — you can look at it and jog your memory. And sometimes I get so worried about remembering something that I *don't* remember it. The biggest problem, though, is that I can't write anything down when composing a piece.

Do you use any chord symbols or other notation?

I can write down chords so that *I* can understand them, but nobody else can. So it's a really slow job for me to show anyone a tune. Everybody just has to be patient with me. It's awful, really — no excuse.

Tell us about your solo album, Velvet Darkness.

That was the biggest mistake of my life. As far as I'm concerned, it was just one big rip-off. We didn't have a chance to adequately rehearse the music, and we were given only nine hours in the studio. It was just like, "Get with it!" We were sort of rehearsing a song and the producer came out yelling, "Next!" They had recorded a trial run — not a song intended for final release. We didn't even get a chance to rectify any bad parts. If I were a stronger person, I probably would have packed my guitar and left right then. There were other things that were wrong, as well. For example, many of the songs don't even have endings — we hadn't gotten that far yet. So on the record, they just sort of peter out.

What did you do about these problems?

There wasn't anything I could do. I went back to England, and I never got so much as a cassette copy of the tracks. About a year later I received this album at my door. It was terrible. And now I suffer every time anybody mentions that album. I just die! It's so bad. In fact, afterwards I really wanted to stop playing — just give it up.

Did things become better with U.K.?

Not much. The rehearsals had almost nothing to do with what ultimately went on the records. We just played bits and pieces of songs, and they would shake them up and record them. Then we had to try to reproduce those parts live. And I just don't feel at home doing that. I'd rather play something first, and then record it. Now, I'm not against overdubbing — it's great. It's nice to embellish things, but I think that the important things should go down on the tracks so that when you play the songs onstage, nine times out of ten they'll sound *better.* With U.K., particularly, we had millions of overdubs, and then we had to decide who could play what parts live because one guy doesn't have four hands, and so on. Again it comes back to the magical quality of interplay between band members.

How did U.K. form?

Bill said he had an idea of working with [keyboardist] Eddie Jobson and [bassist] John Walton. He asked me if I would like to go to a rehearsal and play. I agreed, and it looked promising. But the closer we came to recording, the more sterile the music sounded. Just before I left the band, I used to daydream an awful lot while we were playing onstage; you know, thinking about a nice pint of beer or something. I was easily distracted. And because I couldn't associate all those bits — they didn't form any kind of cohesive picture in my mind — I wouldn't know if it was tune three or tune six or what.

Didn't you feel that your declining interest would be detrimental to the group?

Well, some musicians are very efficient in that they can wade through things and not get upset. Unfortunately, I can't do that. And as soon as something like that starts to affect me, I lose all heart. And once I've lost the heart of it, I don't even try anymore. It's wrong; it's a bad thing. But because I just couldn't fight it, I left. I started complaining a lot, and as a result, on Bill's *One of a Kind* I was able to play quite a few of the solos live. I really liked the solo at the end of "In Five G."

Did you try to duplicate your album solos onstage?

No. I just try to be spontaneous. I mean, that was one of the silly things that U.K. wanted me to do: They wanted me to play the same solos. I said, "Sorry, no can do." Once a solo is done, try something else. In fact I really get worried if my live solos sound like the ones on the records.

When you aren't employing the vibrato on your Strat, do you keep holding on to it?

No. I just let the thing hang, and I go for it when I need it. I also tend to rest my hand on the bridge, but that's more easily accomplished on my SG.

A prominent part of your style has been your use of vibrato.

Yeah, but you'd be surprised. Obviously, on "In the Dead of Night" I used the mechanical vibrato, but on many other songs I do it with my fingers. The effect I most like to create using vibrato is a slur between notes, like a pedal steel guitar. And I love the sound of pedal steel. Slurring like that can give the instrument a very vocal sound. But I'm always terrified of putting the guitar out of tune. Luckily, I've gotten to where I can feel when I'm going to do some harm to the tuning, so I avoid pushing down too hard.

Do you prefer a low action on your guitars?

Not on the Fender. I've found that I can get a good action on the Gibson, but if I set the action too close on my Strat, all the rattles show up. Maybe this is because of the bridge setup, or the very crisp, clean sound that is inherent in the Fender. In general, I prefer ebony fingerboards, too, because they help to make the overall feel of the guitar much better.

Do you ever play in nonstandard tunings?

Oddly enough, I've only experimented with them on the acoustic, because I think of them mainly as a novelty. I used one tuning — it's been so long that I couldn't begin to guess what it was — on "Gone Sailing" [from Soft Machine's *Bundles.*]

Do you ever fingerpick?

I use a flatpick for just about all of my soloing, but for chords I use a type of fingerpicking in which I grab all the strings at once. I can't perform gymnastics with my right hand like most people who fingerpick. So I strike all the strings at once, much like a pianist would do when playing a chord. I always use the flesh of my fingers, too — never the nails, because that feels uncomfortable.

Do you ever employ feedback in your playing?

Not in the sense of standing in front of the amplifier. I always like to get away from the amp. I just like the guitar to have a lot of natural sustain.

When you solo, do you organize runs in terms of scales, or chords, or whether you're high or low on the neck?

I try to just play naturally. I don't analyze what I'm playing — I follow my instincts. I suppose some people are very conscious of what they're doing: "Oh no! I played a high note; now I've got to play a low one." I try to hear something that makes sense — something that sounds reasonable — and play it.

Having been through many ups and downs in your career, are there any shortcuts or tips that you could suggest to aspiring guitarists?

I don't think so, because I don't know if there really is an easy way. I think that it means more to learn something on your own. The lesson is more valuable, because rather than just following someone else's path without much insight, you can understand how you did things. Really search yourself out. Go for the *essence* of things, and don't really worry about what others are up to. Try to look at it like, "This is a certain standard, so I should try to be *more* than that," but without going the same way. You can get to the point you want to reach by following many different paths. I know it sounds ambiguous, but like most people I guess it's not always easy to explain exactly what I'm thinking. The things that I'd like to do, I've barely started.

[December 1982]

Do you think that your playing is constantly progressing?

I hope so. I mean, I *think* so, because it seems to me that I've learned a lot in the last two or three years. It seems to be escalating at the moment. But I don't know. I could be vastly wrong and actually be playing a lot of rubbish now. I'm trying, though.

Do you listen to your old material on records to gauge your progress?

Oh, no! That's why I'm pretty confident about my progress, because when I listen to my old stuff, I just die. I can't believe it. It sounds like a caveman or a baby — just so primitive and so long ago and unbearable.

That must be a good sign.

I guess so. It's just that you know so much more about yourself. I just hate to hear them because I cringe. I just can't listen; I have to leave.

Do you ever fall into slumps and lose interest?

I fall into slumps, and I'm sure everybody falls into slumps where the creativity just can't seem to start and no matter how hard you try you just seem to fall back on things that you've already learned — as opposed to trying to improvise or whatever. Keep going. You have to persist, and out of the sheer frustration of what you've been doing or you haven't been doing you just come out the other side. Of course, when you come out the other side, you find that there's an even bigger hill to climb than the last one. And that's always the way. I'm really glad, though.

Do you ever tape your rehearsals to give you an indication of what you're doing right or wrong?

Oh, yeah. I listen to them a lot. It's very helpful, but it usually makes me depressed — only about myself, though. Who could be depressed listening to those other guys? So, I get a little depressed. And that's good, because it makes you say, "Oh, God, I've got to do something about *that.*" And off you go again.

Do you think that you might be too self-critical?

I don't think so. Maybe I am. *Maybe.* But I don't think so. But that's the way I am, and I can't do anything about it.

How do you use your tremolo?

Sometimes I use my fingers, and other times I sort of use the palm of my hand. Mostly I use my little finger.

How about left hand-finger vibrato and bends?

Well, I don't think I bend notes anymore. I used to, but I don't think I still do it. If I want a vibrato, I use a classical vibrato technique along the length of the string like a violin. The top two strings and higher up the neck, I change to a classical vibrato, and lower down the neck I go more from side to side. I physically pull the string. Up high I apply more tension and sort of squeeze the string.

Where did your wide hand stretches come from?

Basically, if you know you want to play over a certain chord or a certain scale, most of the time guitarists play the scale so that the notes are played consecutively. I wanted to avoid that by playing intervals that were spaced further apart. They're the same scales and chords, it's just that I wanted them to be juggled around more. I'm just juggling, really.

Do you ever find that your hands just won't stretch that way sometimes?

They usually stretch okay. I think my stretch has gotten a little worse as I've gotten a little older. I keep notes of the things I used to play, and sometimes I have trouble with them.

Will you take, say, an F# chord, and experiment with various ways to spread it out?

Yeah. I'll just experiment with different voicings. What I usually do is just try to find the kind of voicings of particular chords that I like. Turn them around. I don't like the sound of conventional guitar voicings. I love listening to jazz guitar; I listened to it a lot when I was younger, because my father introduced me to it. But I very quickly tired of the sound of the chord voicings. Whereas with a piano player I hear much more chordal inventiveness, not in terms of shuffling around with the chords, but with the inventiveness of voicings. I just decided that if I was going to get some chord things together that I might as well play some other voicings, instead of the kind of Jazz Book One or Jazz Book Two or Jazz Book Ten types of chords. I just searched for different voicings.

Do you think that different voicings evoke certain types of moods?

Oh, yeah. Sometimes you can use a simple chord and come up with a nice voicing. It's all important, because it's music.

Do you use two hands to fret very often? On "Shallow Seas," for instance, you use a right-hand finger to hit a bass note.

I use it very rarely: Mostly for chords. I can do it much more than I do it, but I just don't like to do it because it's almost become such a fashionable thing. And there's still a lot of things I can't do using what I've got already. I still want to work a lot on that before I decide I've had enough of my left hand.

Do you ever locate chords on certain groups of strings to change their mood or impact?

I wouldn't favor any particular one over any other, unless it was called for in a specific piece. Then I would. I just try to look for interesting ways to play around some simple things and make them sound

like they're not. Or the other way around: Make something simple seem much more involved.

Do you approach the use of the tremolo bar differently for solos and chords?

I guess so. Obviously, I try to get that steel guitar-like sound when I'm playing chords. It sounds more like floating between chords.

Do you have to be careful while bending chords not to clash with the bass?

No. I never bend chords that extremely. I just use it to sound like a slur, so it doesn't really upset your ears.

How do you relate your solos to the chord changes? Do you consciously try to cover those chords?

Yeah. I break it down to find out what the chord structure is, what scales I can use, if I can superimpose things over the top such as triad on triad. I generally experiment with it. There's no set way. I don't go about each tune thinking, "This is what I have to do." For me to be able to play it I have to be able to see it in my mind's eye. I can't play off a piece of paper. If I do, I've had it.

Have you ever tried recording a rhythm part on a cassette and working out a solo to the playback?

I have done that, but I usually don't. I usually just study the chords and make a few notes for myself.

Do you think the register that a solo is played in has an important bearing on it?

No. The solo itself has an important bearing on it. I don't say it has to be slow and low. I don't think being one way makes it any more of one thing than another. I don't make *any* rules about it. If it's a solo that starts out low, I'll think about the notes in that area, but I don't divide the neck up. It's all one.

Do you use hammer-ons or do you try to pick every note?

I use a mixture with a lot of hammer-ons. I don't use conventional pull-offs, though. I never pull my finger sideways, because I find that when you pull the strings off, you get a kind of *meowing* sound as you deflect it sideways. And I detest that sound. In the past I have practiced quite hard not to play like that. I don't think my fingers come off sideways at all. They just drop on and off directly over the top like I'm tapping the strings.

As you play faster, do you find that you are less conscious of your actual technique?

I don't consciously make any transition between playing slower and faster. Sure, you might be likely to make more mistakes as you start waffling around, but you try not to. Because if you continually do that, you obviously can't play that way anyway. Each has its own set of problems.

When you use a volume pedal to swell each chord in a series, does it seem cumbersome?

Not particularly. Using a volume pedal with echo is not the greatest way to get that effect, but at the moment that's the way I do it.

Some guitarists wrap their right-hand little finger around their volume knob to swell notes and chords.

I couldn't do that effectively because of some of the chords that I want to play; there would then be too much going on elsewhere. And I don't like the volume control so near to my little finger. I've displaced the volume control on each of my guitars further south than it would be on a normal Strat. On a normal Strat, you can turn the volume control with your little finger, but that used to get in the way of my wrist. So I moved it further away. I find it easier to do that and switching on the floor than with my hands, so I can concentrate more on my playing.

Do you ever mute your strings with your right hand?

No. I don't like the sound. Al Di Meola's done it to death. It's not something that particularly grabs me by the ear or anywhere else, although it's pretty easy to do. It's just not a very attractive sound to me.

When you fingerpick, what do you do with your pick?

I just tuck it in and hold it with my first finger, and then use the thumb and the other three fingers. I play most chords that way. I can strike all the notes at the same time, because I don't like that "droing" — the strum sound across the strings.

On some of your songs, particularly "Out from Under," you play the melody while holding chord forms. Is this for organization or an audible effect?

It depends on whether I want it to sound like a chord or not. Usually when I do that, I want the notes to ring into each other — hit more than one note at a time.

How do you execute artificial harmonics?

I just hold the pick and lightly touch the string with my middle [right-hand] finger, but I don't use them very often.

Do you find the technique to be awkward?

It's not awkward, but I've heard some people do it so good that it almost makes it not worth doing for me. Some people do it amazingly well. For me to play it as well as some of the people, it would probably take me as long as I've got left.

What do you think is good or bad about the current state of the guitar?

I don't think anything's wrong with it.

Do you think that the guitar is taking a back seat to vocals in music?

Oh, no. Everybody in the world plays a guitar. That's why there are so many good guitar players. Everywhere you go, *someone* plays the guitar.

Do you intentionally avoid playing common rock licks or blues licks?

In a word, yes. I occasionally use them if I'm in a particularly jovial mood. Sometimes I'll be caught doing it just for fun. Usually I try to avoid them; I try to avoid everything. I'm still looking, basically.

When you're just sitting around at home, do you fall into them just for entertainment?

No. I just keep looking for something else.

Do you think to a large extent playing guitar should be more of a science than an emotional outlet?

Oh, no! It's got to be emotional. That's the only reason I'm a musician — because I love music. If I had wanted to get into science, I would have been a mathematician. It's got to make you laugh or cry, or both. If I wasn't moved by it, I can think of a lot of things that I could have spent the last four years doing rather than this.

— WORTHY QUOTES —
BY MATT RESNICOFF – MARCH 1990

Another Kind of Passion: When the new kid on the block plays more notes, then everybody says, "Oh, it's not happening." But then, five years later, when they figure out that guy wasn't playing very many notes at all, because the new guy's playing twice as many notes, they accept the other guy, and they say of the new guy, "Oh, but he doesn't play with any feeling." I don't really pay any attention to it. I don't think music has anything whatsoever to do with how many notes anybody plays. I've tried in the past to make something have some sort of passion to it with less notes, but at times I like it fiery — that's passionate in another way. But I *do* think that some guys don't play with any feeling at all. Another thing that's so funny about some of the really hairy metal monsters I hear, is that it's as though they just took a [ProCo] Rat distortion and D.I.'d it into a console, but because they're playing a lot of notes, you don't hear the sound, and then when they sit on a note for a minute you go, "Oh, yuk!" It's terrible! It's just the gnarliest thing I ever heard.

The Precious Past: As time goes on, things move forward in some direction, but backward in others. It's like the quality of an automobile; they can make a car go faster, but it's not made like it used to be. People say that all the time. There are some really deep, really incredible high-quality things you can get from the past. For example, a saxophone player coming up now might not have heard anything further back than Michael Brecker, who's absolutely incredible. But when you go back and hear some of the *older* guys, then you realize — well, *I* did — that all these guys who came up afterwards and tried to sound like them never really did sound like them at all. There was something missing. When I go back and listen to a Charlie Parker recording, he sounds *unbelievable*; it's so fresh. You have to wade through the poor sound quality of the recordings, but boy, it was happening! Cannonball Adderley and Coltrane, man, those guys were unbelievable. Some of those Miles Davis albums both of them were on — wow, that was something. As things move forward, something else moves back. It's inevitable, because that's the nature of things. It's really great for people to go back and have a look, because otherwise they're really going to miss something. Things get lost that should never have gotten lost.

Winds of Change: I find that people — and particularly guitar players — tend to create barriers. It's kind of like the stories you hear about somebody like Adolphe Sax [who invented the saxophone in 1846] — man, I almost *cried* when I read the story about that guy! I mean, he invented a musical instrument and was *punished* for it; he and his family were given a hard time, just for his invention. Like the electric guitar, the saxophone for a long time wasn't even considered a musical instrument by classical people, or people with closed minds who weren't willing to accept that something can come along and do something different. And there he was, a persecuted guy who invented a really great instrument; there's nothing that sounds like a saxophone — *nothing*. It indi-

cates the amount of time it takes for people to accept something.

Of Pain . . . : I know what I'm trying to do, what I've done, what I haven't done, and what I can't do. It's too big to think that anything was worth anything. I can get on with it and just hope that one day I could elevate my playing to such a high level that it was undeniable that something was happening, but at the same time, no one knew really what it was. Then I guess I'd either be in heaven or in hell. That'll never happen, but you just keep chasing that dream. That's all you can do, really. It gets harder as you get older, because after a while you realize that every being has its own end, and when someone else is coming up in a different time, they're going to hear things completely different. I don't expect to get anything really happening.

On this tour we just did in London, there were a couple of nights that I felt that I played *so* bad that I couldn't believe it. I mean, some of it I might have psyched myself into, and got depressed because just being back in England reminded me of all the years I spent struggling there, that nothing-keeps-happening syndrome. But there was one night in Manchester when I was so disgusted with my playing that after the gig, I just left. I couldn't talk to anybody. I've been getting better. I've tried to hide it. I used to come offstage and say, "Oh, that was the worst. I played so bad." Then I thought, well, these people are trying to say that they liked it, and telling them it was horrible is kind of making a mockery of *them,* and I didn't want to do that, so I keep my mouth shut, even if I felt that way. But this gig was *so* bad that I split. I *couldn't* stay there, man, I could *not* have talked to anybody, and I got a letter from a guy saying that he was really pissed off that I left, that I didn't talk to him and be a nice guy like the other guys in the band. He said he understood the feeling, but he *couldn't* have, because if he had, he'd have left, as well. That was the worst one for a few years. I mean, I haven't actually felt that bad for a long time, so if that guy reads this, I'm sorry; that's the way it is, and if it happened again, I'd do the same thing.

. . . and Pleasure: The joy in music is the *music.* I do actually get great joy from it, and great joy from playing. I love music with such a big passion, it's overriding. I can't say how big it is, but it's *big.* I love trying to play, I love learning about music, and it always seems that every year, I learn more in that year than I did in the previous 20, so I'm happy in that respect. Sometimes I play something in the garage or to myself and feel pretty good about it. Everybody does, and then when they get out onstage, it all falls apart. But I enjoy it before I go on. I look *forward* to it. So I want to go out and do it, but I always fail. Like that night in Manchester — I'll walk away from it, and the next day I'll go, "I want to be better *so* much because of that;" because that was so bad, I have to struggle with myself and go. I can't let that feeling take hold of me. I've got to beat it. I've got to figure why this happens to me and just keep pushing.

"Man, You're the Greatest": It's *embarrassing.* What do you say? I'm just trying to do what I do, and it's marvelous that somebody else likes it. It's really, really flattering, but I feel like I want to run away. It makes me *cringe.* I don't know what to do, other than just stand there and say "Thank you very much." But at the same time I'm saying "Thank you very much," I almost hear that as me *agreeing* with them, and I *hate* that. I don't want to agree with them. In one way it's great because somebody likes what you're trying to do, and that's a really wonderful thing, that the music touches people — that's what music's for. It touches me, and it's the greatest thing, but I'm still embarrassed when people say things like that to me.

Does it happen a lot?
[*Pause.*] A little bit.

What It Is: It's okay that there are a lot of guitar players in my audience; I expect that if I played bass, I'd want to go see Jimmy, or if I played drums, I'd want to see Gary. That's healthy. But I'd just love it if there were more people at our gigs who weren't involved in music. Unfortunately, that's not going to happen, because the music doesn't *get* to them. It's only the people who are involved in it that find out about it, because they're in a different kind of circle. And that's one of the things that really disappoints me, especially as I've gotten older, because now I realize that I'm *never* going to reach anybody. We're never really going to find out who would have liked it or who would have hated it, because they're never gonna hear it to *know.* But what can you do? We live at a time when this is happening, and it's not just happening to me; it's happening to millions of struggling musicians. We're getting more and more into this kind of monopolies thing; this record company buys out this record company, and then you realize that if Sony had bought CBS before, for example, they could have killed vinyl immediately, because they owned all the technology for the DAT machine, and then the DAT machine and the CD would have been out. It's all money. That's what it *is.* It's the same in everything: The little guy is struggling to make it without the big bucks to even make people aware of the fact that there's something out there they might be interested in. Now, unfortunately, the music *business* is ahead of the music. Everything's ass-about-face. But it's cool. The little guys have to fight it, and that's what we're doing. We just have to keep going.

— MARK KNOPFLER —

BY DAN FORTE – SEPTEMBER 1984 & JUNE 1992

WHEN HE SAYS, "I'd love to have 60-hour days," he's not kidding. Mark Knopfler is certainly one of the *busiest* men in show biz. As a record producer he oversaw Aztec Camera's first LP; sessions with Roxy Music's Bryan Ferry; original soundtracks for such films as *Cal*, *Comfort and Joy*, and *Local Hero*; not to mention co-produced and appeared on Bob Dylan's rock and roll comeback, *Infidels*. As a sideman, the soft-spoken Scotsman has also managed to sit in on dates with Steely Dan, Van Morrison, Thin Lizzy's Phil Lynott, and Phil Everly, among others. But all that is spare-time stuff. As a singer, songwriter, guitarist, and bandleader of Dire Straits, Knopfler has had a plate already overflowing with the primary servings associated with his own band's sudden and continued superstardom — albums and tours in support of albums.

The band's self-titled debut LP, which included the hit "Sultans of Swing," was voted Best Guitar Album in *Guitar Player*'s Readers Poll that year [1978], and Knopfler won top honors in the New Talent category for his sinuous, melodic Stratocaster style. That year, he also appeared on Dylan's gospel milestone, *Slow Train Coming*, revealing a strong blues base reminiscent of Albert King. Although *Dire Straits* achieved gold or platinum status in virtually every country in which it was released, it was anything but an immediate success. In fact, the group was already recording its follow-up before the debut

LP began climbing the American charts. While *Communique* didn't fare as well in the States, it helped establish Dire Straits' reputation as a top international draw, becoming the first album ever to *enter* the charts at #1 in Germany (the previous LP was still at #3 at the time). The band went on to break attendance records at concerts all over the world, including the largest public gathering in the history of New Zealand: 62,000.

Mark Knopfler is more than just a frontman or a figurehead; in a very real sense, he *is* Dire Straits — virtually every song, melodic motif, bass line, and drum beat are a product of Knopfler's creativity. Mark and bassist John Illsley are the only original members on board today; brother David Knopfler (rhythm guitar) left the group just before *Making Movies*, their third LP, was recorded, and Pick Withers departed after recording the group's fourth album, *Love Over Gold*. Knopfler's distinctive guitar style — with its out-of-phase tone, eccentric melodicism, and extensive use of hammer-ons and pull-offs — relies on finesse and economy rather than brute force, and those plectrumless sounds have had a substantial impact on the guitar community.

Do you think there's an identifiable British sound to Dire Straits?

I don't really think of Dire Straits as a *sound*, you know. It just depends on the song, and the stuff we're doing is so varied. I don't think of sounds as being American or English or Japanese or German. That doesn't mean anything; it's all just music. It's either good music or bad music, and good music, to me, is the stuff that's got a bit of soul. The other stuff I'm not really interested in.

For Local Hero, *did you reach back for some Celtic influences you heard when you were growing up?*

Well, I was born in Scotland and spent the first six years of my life there. Then I went to Newcastle-on-Tyne in northeast England, close to Scotland. So I heard a lot of that music, and of course it's still very strong. In fact, what are the Everly Brothers but that Celtic thing? You can hear the Celtic influence in a lot of country music as well as in people like Gerry Rafferty [of "Baker Street" fame] — that Celtic drone. I had to get even closer still with *Cal*, which is set in Ireland. For that, I used a fair amount of uillean pipes played by Sean O'Flynn, who's maybe the best exponent of that. Lately, I've become friendly with an Irish singer called Paul Brady, who plays whistle on *Cal*.

Was rock and roll the first music you ever played?

Yes. I heard my uncle Kingsley playing boogie-woogie on the piano when I was about eight or nine, and I thought that those three chords were the most magnificent things in the world — still do. The first records I made my mom buy were Lonnie Donegan skiffle records. That was before I was 10 years old. I had to wait until I was 15 before I got a guitar, because my old man wanted me to appreciate it when I got it. It was a red Hofner V-2, I think they called it. Cost fifty quid. It was Strat-shaped, and it *had* to be red.

American-made guitars were pretty scarce in England in the early '60s.

Yeah. A Strat was a thing of wonder. When I was 14 or 15, the Shadows were a big influence, and they had the first Strats that came to England. Cliff Richard brought them back for me. Hank Marvin played lead on a Strat, and Bruce Welch played Tele rhythm.

Were you also influenced by American instrumental bands from the late '50s and early '60s?

Oh, yes. I went up the street to a little pal of mine and made him play me "Because They're Young" [by Duane Eddy] 49 times. I could spend the whole day listening to that: the twang. Do you remember the Fireballs? I have one Fireballs single with "Quite a Party" on one side and "Gunshot" on the other. I played that 4,900 times. Completely and utterly in love with it. Then you'd grow up into Radio

Luxembourg, and you'd sit up talking to your older sister. She talks about her boyfriends, and you listen to Ben E. King's "Spanish Harlem" or "Hey, Baby" by Bruce Channel — stuff like that.

Were you also into rockabilly?

Early Elvis, of course, and one of the biggest of all was the Everly Brothers — with Chet Atkins on guitar; but of course, I didn't know that, and they didn't put their names on records then. But he's probably the greatest of all. Then there was Ricky Nelson — a record called "Just a Little Too Much," which doesn't get a lot of exposure — and I didn't know then that that was James Burton on guitar. The sound on those records — just listen to the backing of "Hello, Mary Lou"— is astonishingly great. Jerry Lee Lewis was another complete genius.

A lot of English rock guitarists got their start playing "trad" jazz, dixieland. Were you involved in that at all?

No, the only thing young kids were really exposed to were the occasional novelty pop singles like "Midnight in Moscow" by [trumpeter] Kenny Ball or "Stranger on the Shore" by [clarinetist] Acker Bilk. Later on, I got into it some. Everything went in stages. After I'd gotten the solidbody Hofner, I didn't have the nerve to ask my dad for an amplifier — it cost so much — so I had to borrow a friend's acoustic guitar. All the time I wanted to play rock and roll, I got forced into playing sort of folk joints. Of course, that was very good, because I learned how to fingerpick. The first time I heard a 4/4 clawhammer picking pattern, I fell totally in love with that. So things were progressing on a number of fronts. Later, I got into National steel-body guitars from a guy in Leeds called Steve Phillips, who also builds beautiful guitars. I got involved in all kinds of slide playing and ragtime, country blues, jug band, and even western swing.

When you got into different styles, how studied was your approach?

Not studied at all. I was just trying to absorb the spirit of the thing, rather than take an academic approach. I've never had a guitar lesson. I'm not proud of it particularly, but it's just the way I seem to do it. It's not the best way. I don't recommend it to all your readers.

Considering the enormous impact the Beatles had on American groups, they must have been an even bigger influence on a young musician like yourself growing up in England.

Oh, huge! "Please, Please Me" was one of the first records that I bought. It's funny now, because while I've been working with Aztec Camera at Ayre Studio [in London], I've been playing Asteroids about every other day with Paul McCartney. It's slightly strange to think, "Oh, that's him" [laughs]. But I also liked the Rolling Stones, and I absolutely loved the Kinks. I got into trouble for writing *The Kinks* on notebooks and desks in school. I loved songs like "Where Have All the Good Times Gone," "Waterloo Sunset," and "You Really Got Me." I enjoyed that period, and then a few years later, when I was 18 or 19, I got into a lot of the American bands, like the Doors, and some of the English bands that didn't necessarily make it as big, such as Head, Hands & Feet [with Albert Lee]. I never really got into deep record collecting, because I was always moving around and was too impoverished.

When did you get into R&B guitar players?

When I was listening to Elvis and the Everlys, I suppose. Then shortly before Dire Straits, I was playing a Gibson Les Paul Special in a rockabilly/R&B band in London. When I heard B.B. King, at age 16, that was another big turning point, because I was really struck with the relationship between the guitar and the voice and the whole bending thing, the way it sounded. Later, when I was 20 or 21, I remember hearing Lonnie Johnson with Eddie Lang — the *Blue Guitars* album. Then I realized that there was a connection, and I read an interview with B.B. King saying that Lonnie Johnson had been a big influence on him. It's great to make these little connections and see how they do line up.

Bob Dylan is probably the most obvious influence on your singing and writing.

I was hugely influenced by him about the age of 14 or 15, going 'round to girls' houses, drinking 75 cups of coffee, smoking 90 cigarettes, and listening to *Blonde on Blonde* 120 times. I heard Bob Dylan from the very beginning, the "Hard Rain" days, and went with him all the way up, and I'm still with him. I still think he's great. *Blood on the Tracks* is one of my favorite records, with "Tangled Up in Blue." On *Infidels*, to hear the first lines of "I and I," that's enough to make anybody who writes songs want to retire. It's stunning. Bob's musical ability is limited, in terms of being able to play a guitar or a piano. It's rudimentary, but it doesn't affect his variety, his sense of melody, his singing. It's all there. In fact, some of the things he plays on piano while he's singing are lovely, even though they're rudimentary. That all demonstrates the fact that you don't have to be a great technician. It's the same old story: If something is played with soul, that's what's important. My favorite records, by and large, aren't wonderful technical achievements, with the exception perhaps of people like Chet Atkins. But generally speaking, all you've got to do is listen to a Howlin' Wolf album — that's just soul.

Were there any specific guitar influences that made your style take the form it did?

I don't know.

Some of your playing is reminiscent of J. J. Cale's.

Oh, of course, yeah. I listened to a lot of J.J. Cale around the time my style was developing. He's great. I'd love to meet him. He's very, very special to me.

On Slow Train Coming, *you didn't play the sorts of things you're known for with Dire Straits. It's very bluesy, à la Albert King.*

I was asked to do that. [Producer] Jerry Wexler said, "Try for a gutbucket style of thing." So I borrowed a Gibson ES-335 that somebody down there had, and off we went.

On Infidels, *whose idea was it to have Mick Taylor on guitar?*

Bob decided on the whole band, although I did suggest that Alan [Clarke] be there. And I suggested the engineer, Neil Dorfsman. We were like a three-man team at that point. Sly Dunbar and Robbie Shakespeare [reggae's top studio drummer and bassist, respectively] were Bob's ideas, as well as Mick Taylor. I suggested Billy Gibbons, but I don't think Bob had heard of ZZ Top. It would have been great to have done that with Billy. My roughs are different from the final record. Bob mixed it, because I had to go on tour in Germany with Dire Straits. I think he changed some things.

Was it difficult producing Dylan?

Yeah. You see people working in different ways, and it's good for you. You have to learn to adapt to the way different people work. Yes, it was strange at times with Bob. One of the great parts about production is that it demonstrates to you that you have to be flexible. Each song has its own secret that's different from another song, and each has its own life. Sometimes it has to be teased out, whereas other times it might come fast. There are no laws about songwriting or producing. It depends on what you're doing, not just who you're doing. You have to be sensitive and flexible, and it's fun. I'd say I was more disciplined. But I think Bob is much more disciplined as a writer of lyrics, as a poet. He's an absolute genius. As a singer— absolute genius. But musically, I think it's a lot more basic. The music just tends to be a vehicle for that poetry.

When you're playing on someone else's record, what sort of directions do you usually get from the artist or the producer?

In 99% of the cases, almost none. It's always very nice.

What do you want to know about the song you're playing on?

I want to know what the lyric is, what the song is about. I like to talk to the lyric to a certain extent. That's important to me. What was funny and kind of nice about doing Bryan Ferry's stuff is that Bryan works backwards from the way I work. He creates these very nice-sounding, very simple grooves, and they seem to instigate the lyric. The lyrics come last — which is great, just fine. But, you know, I would say to Bryan, "What do you think this is going to be about? A dragonfly. Oh." And that can create tension or whatever, too.

Do you usually get called to do a session because someone is after your specific sound?

It varies. It's usually all-around guitar playing. A lot of the things that I do on sessions don't relate to the Dire Straits sound, if there is such a thing. I might be just playing my Gibson Chet Atkins solidbody classical or a National, maybe just doing a part or something.

You don't feel as though you've been stereotyped for your identifiable sound and lead approach?

To me, that's never seemed to be limiting in terms of sessions. I like to play a lot of different styles of things on sessions. On Tina Turner's new album, she recorded a song I wrote called "Private Dancer," and she got the whole Dire Straits band to play on it, but I was busy doing the Bryan Ferry sessions. So she got Jeff Beck to play the second ugliest guitar solo you've ever heard on it.

What are the advantages and disadvantages to doing sessions or working on film scores as opposed to playing in a band?

Oh, it's all just advantages. It all makes you bigger. It's a challenge. I look at something like *Cal*, where I did all the music cues, and I didn't think I could do it at first. But I just started at the beginning and staggered through it from one piece to the next until it was finished. It's a finely tuned film, and the slightest thing you add or subtract really affects what's going on. It's very exacting. There are a lot of decisions to be made. It's part of a picture, but at the same time you want the music to stand up on its own. I don't like soundtrack albums that have one song and the rest is all filler.

On a film score, do you work along with the director?

Yes. For instance, with *Cal*, I made sure that Pat O'Connor, the director, was in the studio almost every day. I'd just drag him in there. That's another reason I like film work: You're trying to do something for somebody else, and you're cooperating. It's less selfish in a way than this egomaniac thing of Singer/Songwriter Does Own Record. It's nice to be a part of a bigger thing. To have musicians like [saxophonist] Mike Brecker and [vibist] Mike Mainieri or [bassist] Tony Levin play on your music is wonderful. Words can't express it. I love to play with other people. I think musicians should and, generally speaking, do intermingle a lot. I'm totally in favor of that. I'd love to have 60-hour days.

Has your composing for Dire Straits been influenced much by movie soundtracks? A lot of your songs have a feel somewhat like The Good, the Bad, and the Ugly.

Yes, that's Ennio Morricone. He's done *The Good, the Bad, and the Ugly; A Fistful of Dollars;* things like *1900*. Yes, he's a big influence.

Do you have any particularly strong literary influences in your songwriting?

Lots and lots. That was my subject at university, and I taught English for a while. There's too many to name: Shakespeare, a lot of American writers such as Raymond Chandler, metaphysical poets.

Do you find that certain keys or chord progressions give pieces a more majestic quality?

Yeah, I like certain keys more and more. I've been doing a lot of stuff in *F* and *D* minor. "Down to the Waterline" [*Dire Straits*] is *B* minor, which is a nice key as well.

Is that the Ennio Morricone influence coming through?

Probably, yes. That slightly comic, melodramatic thing. I call it "spaghetti music." Things like "Private Investigation" [*Love Over Gold*] are almost tongue-in-cheek — deliberately exaggerated.

Your guitar playing seems fairly delicate, yet there are a lot of dynamics, a lot of driving rhythms in your music.

Thank you. I like arranging other people's instruments, and working with the way verses go into choruses. I like dynamics and things to be a little bit dramatic. I work with every aspect of the whole thing: the bass, the piano, when a bass drum is hit, every hi-hat beat. Certain pieces just go, but with other pieces I like to get into everything that goes on.

On a studio album, how much overdubbing do you do?

We end up keeping quite a lot of the live takes,

actually. *Love Over Gold* was a heavily worked-on record. Too much attention was paid to that, I think, in a lot of respects. But it was interesting to have done it that way. I don't think I'd like to do another record that was so heavily produced, though.

Do you ever play rhythm guitar yourself?

Oh, I love to. I like to have two rhythm guitars on most pieces anyway.

Do you also instruct or direct the other rhythm guitarist's part?

Pretty much, usually. The bass and drums as well.

So you write the arrangement as well as the song itself?

Pretty much, but people always bring their own little bits and pieces to it. Sometimes they bring the entire thing, and that's even greater. Every musician will come up with things that only he could come up with, and I like to use those things. Hal [Lindes] often comes up with different voicings than I would have had in mind.

You have a very vocal-like guitar style, but it's not at all like the B.B. King style you mentioned earlier.

Part of the difference, I suppose, would be chucking away the pick when I was evolving my own style. Style, I find, is always impossible to define, but it's easy to recognize.

What made you start playing lead with your bare fingers?

It just started to happen. I remember sitting in a house in London — starvin' to death at the time — playing a cheap Japanese acoustic with really light electric guitar strings on it. I knew then that it was on a turn, it was developing. I was doing things with my fingers that I couldn't do with a pick — really fast things and what have you. I still love to play with a pick, and sometimes you have to record certain parts or songs with a pick — for instance, "Expresso Love" [*Making Movies*]. But it's interesting that now I'm not nearly as comfortable with a pick as I am with my fingers.

Did you go through different stages of developing techniques and experimenting with fingerpicks?

Yes. I went through thumbpicks and even steel fingerpicks with the Nationals, and I dispensed with them. It's a bit of a disadvantage without them sometimes, because a thumbpick is just great for that *chunk* thing that Chet Atkins can do so brilliantly.

What does your picking technique consist of now?

It's the thumb and first two fingers, and I tend to anchor with the back of my hand and my other two

fingers, so it's a solid base.

Do you pick with your fingernails or with the meat of your fingertips?

It's really from skin, but sometimes the nail will catch. You can use the nail to snap it. A lot of times, I hit a note with the thumb and second finger together, so it might seem as though I'm pinching the string, squeezing it. The second finger hits it first, I think, behind the thumb, so you can get a real physicality with a note.

Is your tone a product of the type of guitar you play, or is it a result of your picking technique?

I think it's a combination. I like to play all kinds of guitars, not just Strats, but I wasn't getting the sound I really wanted until I got a Stratocaster. It was about a '61 with a rosewood neck. I like rosewood necks a lot, even though I end up playing a lot of maple necks. I very rarely use a Fender Strat these days; it's usually a Schecter instead, which is a more powerful guitar.

Your old Fender Strat used to have the 3-way toggle switch taped so that it would stop in the position between the middle and rear pickups. Why didn't you just get a 5-position switch to achieve the same pickup combination?

I liked the 3-way switch better than the 5-position; it had a better sound. But I kept knocking it out. I have a 5-position switch on the Strat now. The roadies are always pulling bits out and sticking things in.

Why did you switch from your Fender to a Strat-style Schecter?

I didn't want to keep flogging a Strat around the world, getting it smashed to pieces. Same thing with my beautiful Telecaster that David [Knopfler] used to play rhythm on in the band. It's a double-bound sunburst Custom Tele, about a '67 or '68, and I'm not inclined to have it smashed to bits. The Schecter is beautifully made and very strong. Schecters do tend to weigh a lot more. Probably the best electric I ever had was a Schecter that I used on *Making Movies*, but it was stolen.

Have you amassed a very sizable instrument collection?

No, I haven't. For instance, I still haven't got a flat-top wooden acoustic, because I've never found one that was as good as the two best flat-tops I ever played. One was a David Russell Young guitar that Steve Khan lent me, which was absolutely stunning. The other was a hand-built Greco that Rudy [Pensa, of Rudy's Music Stop] lent me. I used the David Russell Young on *Love Over Gold*, and the Greco on *Infidels*. When I got my Ovation Adamases, I started using them straightaway on *Slow Train Coming* and *Local Hero.* For the Aztec Camera thing, I borrowed a couple of old Martins from Eric Clapton, because they'd been using Ovations, and you just can't get the personality out of them.

So on Dire Straits albums you played borrowed acoustics?

I have some Ovations, but no wooden flat-tops. Hal has a Martin, and my Adamas guitars — a 6- and a 12-string — have seen quite a bit of recording. One of my favorite guitars is the Gibson Chet Atkins solidbody classical, which has been on a lot of sessions since I got it. It's a beautifully made thing. I use it onstage, too, because you can get really loud with the thing. The action is low, so it tries to get the best of both worlds. By and large, I think it succeeds. It's a lot of fun to play. I used it on some sessions with Bryan Ferry, Phil Everly, and on the film scores.

When you record with an Ovation, do you play it through an amp?

It sounds great direct. I might have an amp out in the studio with a microphone on it, too. On *Local Hero,* we sent the Adamas direct quite a lot.

Do you ever work out solos ahead of time on a session?

No, not really. Sometimes it might break down in the middle, and then you figure out which way it should go, and punch it in. But generally speaking, it's pretty rough-and-ready. I'll often play three passes, record them all, and then make something by stitching them together.

Do you vary your amps and settings much in the studio?

We just take potluck and go.

What about effects? There's an interesting fast echo on "Waterline" [Dire Straits].

I have no idea what that was. Rhett Davies was the engineer on that record, and he's in love with Roland Chorus Ensembles, so it might well have been

that. I actually use a Roland onstage. Most of my effects are echoes. I have a DeltaLab that I like very much, too.

Do you prefer a certain brand and gauge of strings?

They're called Dean Markley Custom Lights. I'd have to check the gauges [high to low, .009, .011, .015, .026, .036, .046].

Is there a pattern to your creative process when you write a song?

No, there's no formula, no law. I'm lazy [*laughs*]. One song might come quickly, and another might take hundreds of hours over a long period of time with varying amounts of inebriation.

What's the most inebriated song you ever wrote?

"Once Upon a Time in the West" [*Communique*] was one of them. I was watching the film on TV in a slightly altered state.

Do you use a multitrack cassette recorder to keep track of ideas and come up with arrangements?

No, I should. I don't even use a tape recorder. I just write things down in a book. A lot of ideas come around, and I've forgotten them in the morning. Sometimes I figure, "Well, if I wake up and can still remember it, then it's worth remembering."

Do you just jam on guitar to come up with melodies and changes?

Yes, for hours and hours. And then for more hours. I can play by myself quite happily for days. Sometimes I sit down at the piano and hit the keys, make shapes, but I'm not what you'd call a player. I'm not even what I'd call a proper musician on the guitar. I feel as though I'm a student who's not going to school. I've been working from the Mickey Baker book [*Jazz and Hot Guitar, Book I*] to get some extra chords. I love to learn a new chord and find out what it means, and use it in what I write. I'm developing slowly that way.

— Yngwie Malmsteen —

By Jas Obrecht — May 1985 & January 1990

YNGWIE MANIA. Its rumblings started in Sweden, crossed to America in '83, and reached worldwide proportions with the release of Alcatrazz' *No Parole from Rock 'N' Roll* and Yngwie J. Malmsteen's *Rising Force* and *Marching Out*. Players stood with mouths agape at the exquisite, fire-breathing solos of "Kree Nakoorie," "Black Star," and "Icarus' Dream Suite Op. 4." While some pondered inevitable comparisons — "Who's faster, Eddie or Yngwie?" — others rushed to learn Malmsteen's trademark harmonic minor approach. ("Thank God," Joe Satriani reminisces, "that Yngwie came along and showed a new generation of players that it was okay to play arpeggios and learn scales.") With Malmsteen's imprimatur, Paganini, Bach, and Beethoven suddenly became hot items among big-hairs and metal heads.

Yngwie idolatry was especially prevalent at concerts, as *Guitar Player*'s May 1985 cover story described: "Pandemonium sweeps the audience as the curtain rises on Rising Force. In a mad rush, fans flood the front of the auditorium. Daring souls climb atop the mass of pressed flesh, only to dive headlong back into the crowd once they've stood onstage. Centering the maelstrom is Yngwie Malmsteen, the 21-year-old rock guitar wunderkind. Tossing his Strat high in the air and catching it one-handed, playing with his teeth, or offering his instrument up in symbolic sacrifice to the god of feedback, he pays homage to the T-Bone Walker/Jimi Hendrix school of

cool moves. But once the sweat evaporates and eardrums calm, one is left awestruck by the young Swede's musicianship. His overall technique is inspiring, his sheer speed and picking control paralleled by few others."

Yngwie had won a bout with tendonitis and was riding high with Rising Force's *Trilogy* and *Odyssey* when a 1987 car crash slammed his career to a halt. His right hand damaged, he began the painful task of regaining his style. Earlier this year, he was recovered enough to invade Russia, recording *Trial by Fire* during a single night in Leningrad. The concert LP recasts many of Yngwie's strongest tunes — *Rising Force*'s "Black Star" and "Far Beyond the Sun," *Trilogy*'s "Queen in Love" and "You Don't Remember, I'll Never Forget," and several from *Odyssey* — and climaxes with a ripping version of Jimi Hendrix' "Spanish Castle Magic." While Yngwie soars spectacularly, *Trial by Fire* somehow fails to incinerate the imagination in the manner of his earlier work. His Rising Force bandmates — vocalist Joe Lynn Turner, bassist Barry Dunaway, keyboardist Jens Johansson, and drummer Anders Johansson — have since been fired. The next album, Yngwie promises, will be an entirely different story.

At this stage, would you accept an offer to join a major metal band?

Absolutely not. I'm past the stage of having to play for someone else, so I don't need to do that. I might appear on somebody else's record as a guest.

What are the advantages of fronting your own band?

Everything. You are able to be totally satisfied with the end result. This is true not only with playing live, but with writing all the music, producing everything, and deciding how everything is going to be played on the albums. If I write something, I want it to be a certain way. The only disadvantage is that you never have any time off.

Do you consider yourself a heavy metal player?

To a certain extent, yes. The term is being widely used for all sorts of musical things now. I think heavy metal is when I'm standing in front of 5,000 people, banging my Strat into a Marshall stack. Heavy metal has been defined as just a music form. To me, it's more a way of performing. The form I'm using is much more sophisticated and progressive, especially the classical influence. But the way I'm performing it is like heavy metal.

Why does your music inspire such craziness in your audiences?

I wonder, too. It gives me kind of a kick, but I can't help wondering if they are hurting themselves — people just climbing onstage and jumping straight into the crowd. It's like in a punk rock show. Sometimes it's incredible.

Who are your peers?

I really don't know. I never look at myself that way. Musically, I don't think I have anything from anybody, because what I'm trying to do is not very common in any sort of way. As far as appreciation goes, I guess I get the same reaction as any guitar hero kind of thing.

Is your goal to be a hero?

No, not at all. That was never anything I wanted. From the beginning until now, my goal is just to achieve some sort of musical statement that actually has a meaning and depth to it. Rather than be a poser and just do bullshit, I want to make a statement for everybody, as well as satisfy my own musical desires and develop something that hasn't been done before.

Which recordings come closest to fulfilling that?

I like my guitar solo in "Kree Nakoorie" a lot. I like "Far Beyond the Sun" from the latest solo album very much. I really like some of my solos on *Marching Out*, because I recorded them in very much pain. I have tendonitis in my left hand, apparently from overplaying too much. There's nothing I can do about it. I've had some ridiculous, extreme problems: My little finger has been real swollen. When I do a

vibrato, the tendons in my whole wrist hurt. It's been hard to cope with. Normally, I would pick a guitar up three or four times a day, but since I have this pain in my hand, I never play. For the last four months, I haven't been playing at all except for shows and recordings.

How do you warm up?

I don't warm up. That's the problem: I've been doing it that way for so many years. I just start playing 180 miles an hour right away, and that's probably wrong. So now I've been having a lot of trouble working up to playing fast. The actual results are good, but whatever I have to do to reach them is not too good.

Do you ever play too fast?

Not too fast, but maybe too much. I don't see anything wrong with playing fast. I play a lot of slow notes, as well. That's something I'm going to start doing more because now I feel that I don't have to rush anything. In Alcatrazz, it always felt like I had to show off just in the small parts where I could do the solos.

What's involved with maintaining your level of skill?

I would compare it to a professional runner, ballet dancer, or someone else doing some extremely demanding thing. It's not like I'm trying to brag, but what I am doing is extremely demanding. I can't lay off: "Ah, well, I don't have to play." I need to be on top of myself. That's really hard to do when you're on the road and you tend to drink a little bit too much at night. But you wake up the next morning and still have to do it.

Is your playing constantly improving?

As a matter of fact, yes. It doesn't matter that five years ago I might have been able to play just as fast or faster. I think I'm improving as a musician. This is one thing I've always wanted to point out: I'm not at all looking at myself as a guitar player; I don't really care, you know. I'm a musician, and a composer, an arranger, and a producer — that's something that I'm really into lately. And those things are so demanding that the actual fact of being a guitar player is not so important anymore. You have to be concerned about everything. You start by writing the music and arranging it. You also finish the project by mixing it and producing it. There's so much involved from the first step to the last step. The guitar playing, you can always improve when you want. But the biggest improving I've done is in being a musician in general.

Are you a disciplined composer?

Not at all. It's a very uneven schedule I seem to have. I can be very uninspired, and then extremely inspired the next second. So, I don't have a certain way of doing it. Sometimes I compose without a guitar; I get very inspired just by reading a book or seeing a movie or something. Then, as soon as I pick the guitar up, I'll have that, like, presence. "Icarus' Dream" [*Rising Force*] was written that way. It just comes out of me. I don't go, "Okay, I have to write this song," or, "I'm gonna write that one."

Do you compose for the other instruments in your band?

I always do that — never anything else. The whole solo album was like that — the solos, keyboards, even the drum fills. Everything. That's the way I am. That's what I mean by improving — I have total control.

Is there any music that you find especially inspirational?

Classical music. Basically, anything Bach ever wrote, also Paganini. It's nothing I really try to do, like, "Yeah! I'm listening to Bach — I want to write something like that." I'm so into it now that whatever I write is going to sound like that, whether I want it to or not. I've been listening to other composers lately — Mussorgsky and Tchaikovsky, and stuff like that. I never used to listen to that before, but I really like it now. *Pictures at an Exhibition* by Mussorgsky is very good.

Would you consider any of your repertoire to be classical music of the 20th century?

I don't know. I took a heritage from classical music. It seems most rock musicians had the opportunity, but they didn't seem to appreciate the fact that we inherited this beautiful music and can utilize it in a more modern form. That's what I think I'm doing. When I do a live performance, it's a more powerful kind of thing. So that power side may show off more than my classical influence. I don't know, maybe it's a little bit of both. I don't play purely classical. I have other influences — Jimi Hendrix is my man. I love the guy. He's the greatest. Hendrix, Bach, and Paganini are my main influences.

Could you mimic a Jimi Hendrix piece?

I could do it. I know most of his stuff. Everybody knows that for his time, he was absolutely the ultimate, the superior. But now, 15 years later, what he did is not so hard to do on guitar. It's hard, but it's not extremely hard. People now progress quicker because they have more to refer to. Although, I must say, I don't like the fact that guitar playing is so much more than just music. It's like all

this hero-worshipping. You don't hear that about keyboard players. The guitar player is something that people look up to, it seems. That's wrong, because it takes away the value of the actual musicianship. It's becoming a sport — "Yeah, he can play much faster than anyone. He's much better than him, and da da da." Who cares? That's not what it's all about.

In the February 1985 issue of Guitar Player, Dio's guitarist, Vivian Campbell, expressed concern that he couldn't play as fast as you.

That's too bad. He shouldn't think of what I'm doing, and do what he wants to do. Why should that bother him? He's playing with who I consider to be the best singer in the world; Ronnie James Dio is a very inspiring guy.

In the early days of Alcatrazz, you were often compared to Ritchie Blackmore, who also played with Ronnie James Dio.

I really respect Ritchie a whole lot, and I think his new album with Deep Purple [*Perfect Strangers*] is great. But without trying to offend anybody, I really must say that anybody who says I play like Ritchie Blackmore must be totally tone deaf. It's ridiculous. And as far as my stage appearance, my influences are Jimi Hendrix and [Jethro Tull singer-flautist] Ian Anderson. If you ever checked out Ian onstage, you'll see quite a few things I've stolen. Jethro Tull is a great band.

How did you become aware of classical music?

That started when I was very young. My mother had a lot of classical records at home and my sister played classical flute and piano. When I started listening to music, it was Deep Purple, Jimi Hendrix, and stuff like that. Deep Purple was into classical. Then three or four years later, I started listening to progressive music — Emerson, Lake & Palmer; Genesis; Yes. I still loved the aggressive edge of Jimi Hendrix and Deep Purple, but I got more and more involved in actual music. From the bands like Emerson, Lake & Palmer, I went on to the purely classical thing. I later realized that the progressive bands' influences were apparently classical music. I got a C-disc [compact disc] digital player recently, and I listen to classical music all the time — classical or nothing. All of the albums I've done are out on C-disc, except for *Steeler*. Hard rock doesn't sound too good on C-disc, but classical music sounds incredible. It's the only way I can listen to it.

Have you ever thought of composing for electric guitar and orchestra?

Yes. I would very much like to do that, indeed. I can say this: I want to do it, and I probably will do it.

In terms of performing, do you prefer the studio to the stage?

Absolutely not. I prefer the stage.

What inspires you to play your best?

Everything. More than inspiration, I need to feel that I did something good. When the gig's done, I *have* to feel it was good. I criticize myself extremely hard.

What do you do if you hit the wrong note on-stage?

I usually do make mistakes, but there's nothing I can do about it. It just makes me realize that I have to do even better the next second.

Will you take chances during concerts — try things that you've never done before?

All the time. I get very inspired and do things right out of the blue. The other night I started playing "Hava Nagila" totally out of the blue, and the rest of the band just did it with me [*snaps fingers*] — it was great! I thought it was really cool. I don't even know how to play that thing, but I started playing it anyway, doing third harmonies and stuff. Especially with this group, I feel very free. It's not like I'm afraid that Graham Bonnet will go after the show, "What the hell did you do that for?" I can do whatever I want. This band is wonderful. I love it a lot.

Would you comment on why you left Alcatrazz?

I left Alcatrazz about a year too late, but that's okay. The advantage of being in that band was that I got a bigger name for myself. But I left simply because we couldn't agree musically and personally. I think it's due to the big age difference. They are like 15 years older than me, and their influences and inspirations are totally different from mine. We didn't seem to be able to agree upon almost anything. It was just a matter of time. I left a couple of times, and went back and forth. I was in the band a little bit longer than a year.

What was the strategy behind releasing Live Sentence *so soon after* No Parole from Rock 'N' Roll?

Don't ask me! I had absolutely nothing to do with it. I was very surprised when that thing [*Live Sentence*] came out, because I didn't like the production or anything on it. The way I played was really awful. Alcatrazz had a lot of off nights — almost all the time. My recent shows have been much better than anything I ever did with them.

Are you satisfied with the Rising Force LP?

It has its ups and downs. It was a very rushed operation, but I think it turned out really well, considering the circumstances. We recorded in a big

warehouse with a mobile truck. It sounded real nice. We only rehearsed for three days before the recording, and that's pretty intricate stuff. Barriemore [Barlow] laid down his drums first. He was very good; I'm really proud of him because he had a very tough gig. He was flown over from England, rehearsed for three days, and then we recorded the whole thing in two days.

When was most of that material written?

Some of it is from when I lived in Sweden — "Black Star," "Now Your Ships Are Burned," and "As Above, So Below." I wrote "Evil Eye" one New Year's Eve when Jens, Anders, and I had been playing for like 14 hours straight. It was 7:00 in the morning, and we were just messed up when I composed it. I really like the way it came out on the solo record; it was very awful on *Live Sentence*. "Little Savage" and "Icarus' Dream" were written just before they were recorded. "Icarus' Dream" is dedicated to my cat, Moje, who I grew up with for 13 years in Sweden. My mother called and said he was dead. I was really attached to that cat.

What guitars did you use for the project?

All acoustic work was done on Arias. The classical has a scalloped fingerboard and a cutaway. I played all the bass parts on an Aria with a tremolo bar. My main guitar was the one on the front cover, a cream-colored '69 Fender Strat.

How do you modify your electric guitars?

They are basically plain Strats with a scalloped fingerboard. I scallop them with files and sandpaper. When I press down, the string never touches the fingerboard, just the frets. Most people who play my guitars press too hard, and the strings go out of pitch. I can play any guitar, but I prefer scalloping because it gives you more control. It's much harder to play fast with a scalloped fingerboard, because the string action has to be much higher. I use DiMarzio pickups; they are really good. My guitar technician, Fergie, used to work for Ritchie Blackmore, and apparently my guitars feel similar to Ritchie's. He knows exactly how to keep them in tune.

What kind of tremolo system do you prefer?

I put Floyd Rose tailpieces on my two main stage guitars, but I don't have the clamped nut, so there's really no big difference. That tailpiece has a very smooth tremolo feel; I've been using it quite a lot. Sometimes I use four springs on my Strats, sometimes five. I put more springs on the bottom end because I'm using Ernie Ball strings with a pretty light top and extremely heavy bottom — it goes from .008 to .048. Sometimes I use a heavier bar, too.

Why do you have a left-hand neck on your stage guitar?

It's just a very good neck. I have a bunch of left-handed Strats. I probably have 40 Strats, all different ones. I've got one DiMarzio Strat-style guitar that is just amazing. It's got a red body, red neck, red pickguard, red pickup covers, red knobs. But it's not scalloped yet, so I cannot play it live. I'll get it scalloped.

Did you use many effects devices on Rising Force?

Absolutely nothing. It was just guitar and amp.

Does it take long to record a complex piece such as "Far Beyond the Sun"?

That was a very quick song, actually — second or third take for the drums. The guitar was almost right away, because I was very inspired when I recorded that. Even though that's a pretty demanding piece, it came down easily.

Did you double the harpsichord line in "Icarus' Dream"?

Yeah, I'm playing the part that goes in three beats.

Was the break in "Little Savage" spontaneous?

The guitar work on it, yeah [*laughs*]. I really couldn't reproduce that live too good. I don't remember it. It has a very weird chord progression; it's not like a regular minor key. It's hard to label music like that.

The fluidity of your electric solo in "Black Star" is reminiscent of Allan Holdsworth's style.

That solo has nothing to do with him. Of course, I know who he is, but I'm not trying to play like him at all. I got the tone using the same thing I always do — just my Marshalls and my Strat. I bypassed all of my effects. That part you're asking about sounds like a cleaner guitar; that's just the way I played. Later on in that song, I multi-tracked lines — one doubles another. That was first take.

What do you have to keep in mind when double-tracking?

Really, nothing. I could be drunk off my ass and play those things as easily as anything. If I've composed something, it doesn't matter how hard it is; I can always play it. What's demanding is to play something good and fast and really inspired, and do it just out of the blue [*snaps fingers*] — improvised, like on my solos. That's difficult. But to have something written and then do a third harmony to it, that's easy. I use the same guitar and amp settings and just go to another track. Often I do an improvised guitar solo, and then listen back and go, "That line there sounds really light. Maybe I should put a

harmony to that." I did that quite a lot on the new album.

Are any of the Rising Force *pieces particularly challenging to play onstage?*

They all are really demanding. They are not at all the same thing as playing the Alcatrazz tunes; you could just bang on the guitar and play those songs.

How do you route your onstage signal?

I just bought a Nady wireless system. It feels great to be freer, but some nights I can't use it because of the noise. From there, it goes through a Roland echo unit — a cheap, old version that's not sold anymore. I only use it for the solos; I don't overuse any pedals. I use a Boss Octaver octave divider during shows for the solo I do by myself; there's a part where I need it to be very heavy sounding. I also have [Moog] Taurus bass pedals. If they are out of tune when I hit the stage, I don't use them at all. But I normally use them quite a lot for intros and for my guitar solo, when I'm doing an echo thing and playing a part that's like a fugue. You can hear the bass pedals on *Rising Force* in the intro of "Icarus' Dream" and the end of "Little Savage." I also have an extremely nice Korg [SDD-1000] digital delay that has a setting like a stereo chorus or Harmonizer. I haven't been able to use it lately, though, because there's too much buzz. I'm thinking of having my Marshalls rebuilt; they tend to be too noisy. Normally I use three 50-watt Marshall heads and six cabinets, sometimes 10 heads and 10 cabinets. They are real old, stock British 50-watt tube models. I usually run them on full — everything except the bass, which is all the way off.

Are you comfortable playing acoustic guitar?

Yeah. I love playing acoustic guitar, but it's very difficult because of the way my sound is. My electric sound is actually extremely distorted and has a lot of sustain, but with the way I play, it sounds clean. But when I play the acoustic, I don't have any of that sustain or distortion. I do a lot of legatos — like sometimes onstage I do a whole solo with my left hand — but on acoustic, I can't do that. I have to rely on my right-hand technique, which I think is pretty dull. I want to develop that.

Do you always use a pick?

Not always, but most of the time. They have to be Fender extra-heavies; I couldn't play with anything else. I hold them the usual way — between my thumb and index finger, so the pointy end hits the string. When I play classical pieces on electric guitar, I don't use a pick.

Do you follow any standard picking patterns?

No, I never think about that. I just play.

As you move higher up the neck, do you change pickup selection?

Sometimes. It's not a pattern or anything. It's always different.

Which finger do you use to apply vibrato to a note?

I use any finger. The same for bending notes — whatever finger is there. I have strong hands, although now my hand is not what it used to be.

In the March '84 interview, you stressed the importance of recording practice sessions. Do you still do this?

Occasionally. Lately, I'm so involved in studio recording that I haven't been doing any 4-track recording at my house. But when I wrote all of the material for the latest album, I did a lot of recordings.

Are you developing any new techniques?

No. Musical improvement and technical improvement go hand-in-hand for me. It's not like, "Aw, I have to do this." Actually, I wrote a musical piece for the new album called "Disciples of Hell." It has an *extremely* difficult classical part in the middle, and that was a little bit demanding for me.

Have you been working on incorporating any new scales in your playing?

Sometimes, yeah. Like the melodic and the harmonic minor scales — I play both the harmonic and the melodic notes. For instance, for an *E* minor scale, I play *D* and *D#*, rather than just playing either one. It gives a very interesting effect. Do a broken chord and go to *D* and *D#*. But I still have my favorite scales. I love the Phrygian mode; I think it's great. I feel very good about expressing myself with a combination of the Phrygian and diminished modes. The harmonic minor scale is very good, too.

Can you offer any advice for guitarists wanting to break out of stock soloing patterns?

Stop listening to other guitar players. Stop listening to me. Don't do what I'm doing; do something else. Do what you want. That's my advice.

Does it bother you to hear somebody else play a line that's similar to something you've done?

There's nothing I can do about it, so it doesn't bother me. I don't find it flattering.

Can you discuss the next Rising Force album, Marching Out?

Yes. It's very commercial in many ways, and in many ways it's like the solo album [*Rising Force*]. Basically, we played real simple music — we had a lot more trouble doing that real clean and heavy, rather than playing very loosely and doing advanced stuff.

The album has a lot of short pieces. One is called "1383," where I play an acoustic guitar and a multi-tracked electric guitar and have an Emulator voice machine. It's a very interesting effect. There are four songs on there that could be radio hits. Every song has vocals. I sang backgrounds, and it turned out to sound pretty good. I wrote all the melody lines and music, as well as most of the words. This is all new, except for two songs that date back to Sweden.

Do you have quite a backlog of songs?

Oh, yeah. It's ridiculous. Whether they are good or not, I don't know. But I have millions of them. I don't feel good about using old songs; I always want to write new ones.

Do you ever write with video in mind?

No. I'd rather have music in mind. And then, after the song is written, do the video after whatever mood the song requires. I'm really disgusted with the way music tends to turn out nowadays. It becomes a film score! Music is not the main point anymore. Videos leave nothing to the imagination, and I really hate that. I watch MTV very rarely, but whenever I do, I find that most of the videos have really crap music. And they spend millions of dollars to sell the music by doing a minor movie around it. It's disgusting, because the music is the most important thing. But you should never get too worried about these kinds of things, because there's nothing you can do.

Is big-time rock what you imagined it would be when you were young?

No. It's much more hard work. It's worth it, but you really have to work a lot more than people seem to imagine.

Have you been treated fairly by the press?

I've never had any bad reviews, as far as I know, and I read almost all of that — except one publication. A guitar magazine really wrote me down, suggesting that I was "the god with the chip on his shoulder." I don't understand why they did that, because that's not the kind of person I am. I'm not at all like that, and I don't understand how they could do that. But things like that happen, I guess.

Is it hard to keep a perspective on yourself once fans come to regard you as a guitar hero?

It's no problem at all for me. I'm always looking at myself the same way, and I'm never going to change. Even though I was voted as Best New Talent in what I consider the major guitar magazine, it's not going to make me a big-headed guy — not at all. I appreciate it and think it's very nice that people think I'm good, but it doesn't make a difference to what I think about myself. This is contrary to a popular belief that I'm just a big-headed ego, but that's totally wrong. I must admit, though, that I have a pretty bad temper, but that has nothing to do with my personal outlook on myself. I can explode pretty easily, actually. It can be bad sometimes, but I can't help it.

What would you like to be doing in 10 years?

Basically the same thing, if I feel the same way I do now. Who knows? Maybe I'll be a race car driver or something.

Do you have any predictions for the future of rock guitar?

No. See, I'm not involved at all in rock guitar. I never listen to guitar players, and I really don't know what is going on. And I don't care. So, I can't really make any predictions. I hope people are aware that I'm trying to do something different.

But if you want to produce commercial music, doesn't it help to keep up with what's popular?

Yeah, but you don't have to listen to guitar players to do that. I really don't think you should have to be aware, because that's what makes everything so clinical. Everybody tries to be like everybody else. I refuse to do that.

After completing five albums in two years, are you satisfied with your accomplishments?

I must say that I am, yeah. I'm very happy with the way things are going, but I want to go a lot further than this.

— JOHN MCLAUGHLIN —

BY DON MENN & CHIP STERN — AUGUST 1978
AND BY JIM FERGUSON — SEPTEMBER 1985

JON SIEVERT

INNOVATOR, TECHNICAL avatar, eternal seeker — all of these terms apply to the extraordinary John McLaughlin, who helped pioneer jazz-rock in the early '70s. But what best describes the 50-year-old Englander is the less romantic label *musician*. While many guitarists seem trapped in a harmonically bleak, pentatonic prison, McLaughlin's depth enables him to freely explore the musical landscape, visiting points that have ranged from the Mahavishnu Orchestra to Indian-based Shakti to acoustic fusion with Paco de Lucia and Al Di Meola. Few musicians boast a resumé so rich in artistic triumph.

Born into a family of musicians in Yorkshire, England, on January 4, 1942, John listened to classical music as a child, studied piano and violin (his mother was a violinist), encountered the music of American blues artists such as Big Bill Broonzy and Lead Belly, and at age 11 learned a few guitar chords from one of his three brothers. At 13 he became involved in flamenco and Spanish classical music, and the next year he first heard Django Reinhardt and Stephane Grappelli (and started using a pick in an attempt to sound like Reinhardt.)

McLaughlin began to sit in with various jazz bands when he was 16, and he continued to seek new musical inspiration. Charlie Parker and Tal Farlow became heroes, as did Charles Mingus and Art Blakey. A turning point was his early discovery of the hard bop and soaring modal improvisations of Miles

Davis. In his early twenties, John "finally" grasped the complexity of John Coltrane.

In 1963, McLaughlin joined the Graham Bond Organization, which included bassist Jack Bruce and drummer Ginger Baker, later members of Cream. He also worked with Brian Auger's quintet. In a search for spiritual bearings after an introduction to the occult by Bond, McLaughlin joined London's Theosophical Society, which exposed him to the writings of various Eastern philosophical masters. He practiced yoga, discovered Ravi Shankar, and began to investigate the misty complexities of Indian music. Further probing led to his discovery of the Indian vina, a stringed instrument with movable frets and a gourd resonator at each end. John came to realize that the conventional 6-string guitar would probably never give him the fluidity of Coltrane's saxophone or Davis' trumpet; years later, as Mahavishnu, he would design his own instrument, an acoustic guitar with a scalloped fingerboard and extra strings.

A crucial discovery for John was *Miles Davis at Carnegie Hall*, an LP that featured an all-star lineup of avant-garde players; drummer Tony Williams had an especially numbing impact on McLaughlin. In the late 1960s McLaughlin shared a London apartment with Dave Holland, a jazz bassist, and one time the pair jammed with drummer Jack DeJohnette. Holland later joined Miles Davis in New York, and he told Tony Williams about his friend, the amazing guitarist back in London. DeJohnette, who had recorded the McLaughlin jam session, returned to the States and played the tape for Williams. In November of 1968 Tony called John and asked him to join his new group. McLaughlin came to America in early 1969 and was recording with Miles Davis — having met him through Williams — within 48 hours after his arrival. (Not long after that he found himself jamming with Jimi Hendrix.)

Williams and McLaughlin formed Lifetime with the late Larry Young, McLaughlin's favorite organist. The trio was so important to John that he turned down an invitation to become a member of Miles' group. After playing together as a threesome for about a year, Lifetime was augmented by Jack Bruce on bass. At about this time — mid-1970 — John associated himself with Sri Chinmoy and adopted the name Mahavishnu, from the Indian religious names Maha the Creator and Vishnu the Preserver. After months of playing to small, obscure houses, he left Lifetime because of various business disagreements.

McLaughlin cut *Devotion*, released in the summer of 1970, and then *My Goal's Beyond*, released in 1971. During these latter sessions he recorded with drummer Billy Cobham and violinist Jerry Goodman. The three soon got together in 1972 with keyboardist Jan Hammer and bassist Rick Laird. Calling themselves the Mahavishnu Orchestra, they played a long engagement at New York's Gaslight Club. Their first LP, *The Inner Mounting Flame*, was soon released on Columbia; guitar players and other listeners responded with much enthusiasm to the high-energy mystical jazz, and critics were left to ransack their dictionaries for new descriptive terms. Follow-up LPs included *Birds of Fire* and *Between Nothingness and Eternity*, a live album. In 1973 McLaughlin and fellow Chinmoy disciple Devadip Carlos Santana collaborated on *Love Devotion Surrender*.

The tensions of success and various conflicts over artistic and personal matters caused some bitter resentments and the eventual breakup of the Mahavishnu Orchestra. It reformed with violinist Jean-Luc Ponty and others. An expanded edition of the new group released *Apocalypse* in 1974 (with Beatles producer George Martin, conductor Michael Tilson Thomas, and the London Symphony), and *Visions of the Emerald Beyond*. John also recorded a number of albums with one of his heroes, Miles Davis, including the historic *In a Silent Way* and *Bitches Brew*.

McLaughlin had been studying Indian music for some time when, in 1973, he met violinist L. Shankar. The two struck up an immediate friendship and an intense interest in each other's musical experiences. Another friend, tabla player Zakir Hussain, joined McLaughlin and Shankar in forming an acoustic ensemble. Shankar's uncle, R. Raghavan, played the mridangam, an Indian drum, and T.H. Vinayakram played several Indian instruments. The group performed a few small concerts and did a little recording, but McLaughlin was still obligated to spend most of his energies on the Mahavishnu Orchestra's last LP, *Inner Worlds*. Shortly after that record's completion McLaughlin devoted himself to the group of Indian musicians. They took the name Shakti and recorded three albums from 1975 to 1977. In 1983, he reconstituted the Mahavishnu Orchestra, taking up the landmark Synclavier synthesizer guitar. After recording *Mahavishnu* and touring extensively, he turned his attention to the classically oriented score for his *Concerto for Guitar and Orchestra*, a collaboration with composer/orchestrator Michael Gibbs.

Like many true artists, McLaughlin has failed to receive full credit. "In terms of commercial success," John explains, "all artists are suffering. If you're not a pop or rock star, your music doesn't get propagated, but that doesn't mean I'm not excited about the future." Guitarists in particular too often let McLaughlin's advanced technique and vast musical vocabulary obscure his work's intelligence, passion, and wit. Known for his early, relentless intensity, his later work is more mature, with unprecedented subtlety.

McLaughlin defies categorization. Rooted in jazz, he was fascinated as well with classical composers from Beethoven to Bartók, and later Eastern philosophies, rhythmic theory, and instrumental technique. These factors, intermingled with elements of rock and blues, helped shape his approach to improvisation and composition, leading him to record with musicians as diverse as Jimi Hendrix, Miles Davis, bassist Jack Bruce, Indian violin virtuoso L. Shankar, Al Di Meola, and Paco de Lucia.

Unique custom instruments have often been necessary for John to realize his musical concepts. Through the years, he has played a Rex Bogue Double Rainbow double-neck and a series of drone-string-equipped instruments built by Gibson associate Abe Wechter, featuring scalloped fingerboards to facilitate microtonal bends. While he experimented with guitar synthesizers, McLaughlin soon abandoned them, finding the technology too cumbersome and slow. A decade later, he embraced the sophisticated Synclavier system made by New England

Digital (NED filed bankruptcy in 1992), employing a Roland G-303 guitar as controller, featured on *Mahavishnu* in early '84.

In the '70s, McLaughlin's progressive work was frequently referred to as ahead of its time. In the '80s and '90s, his endless experimentation and highly individual approach — oblivious to popular trends — suggest rather that he is in a *different* time altogether and still unendingly searching for new avenues of self-expression.

[August 1978]

Why do you think you're a guitarist instead of a pianist or a composer?

Oh, I don't know; I mean, why do I love the guitar? Why do I love jazz music? Why am I a musician? Why me? I don't know! Why is someone drawn to Buddhism? Why does someone make pornographic movies? I don't know the answers. That's something that I believe lies in past lives. All I know is that I love it — that's the self-evident proof. The very first time I ever played the guitar I fell in love with it. I loved the sound. I loved the feeling.

Do you feel the guitar is an unlimited instrument?

Unlimited! Absolutely! Are you kidding? I don't know any instrument that's limited. Music is unlimited, and human imagination and spirit are unlimited. I'm always dominated by musical mandates inside me, and that's the whole reason for whatever changes I've gone through. I have to obey them, and my whole life is to serve my perfect-as-possible idealization of music and my role in it, in this world. And my ideals of music belong to the highest I can possibly conceptualize artistically and musically.

How much do you think equipment or even specific guitars matter musically?

Well, your instrument is important. Every person has got a different tone inside — in their own minds, in their own hearts — and I'm no exception. And the same guitar would sound very different in two different people's hands.

An electric guitar with an amp gives rise to all sorts of things like strange, squeaky harmonics, feedback, and so forth. Do you work on these sorts of techniques?

Oh, sure. That's been a part of me for many years. I started to use feedback in 1962, before there were any big amps. I had this guy build me a big amp when I was playing with the Graham Bond Organization with Ginger Baker and Jack Bruce. And I discovered that feedback was nice.

Do you ever get harmonic effects by touching the string with the skin of your thumb after you pick?

Yes, sure, and one can get nice octave chords by using the outside edge of the palm. As far as left-hand technique goes — I think having big hands and long fingers helps. My hands are pretty big, so I can get some tough chords — partly because I use my thumb for some. On "My Foolish Heart" [*Johnny McLaughlin, Electric Guitarist*] I have to do some serious stretching. Tal Farlow, in fact, inspired me to do that. I worked on a lot of my own chords that you can only play with the thumb. If you're playing a chord that utilizes open strings, then the barre formula is inapplicable, and I use open strings. They have a beautiful resonance.

Do you pick hard enough to break strings?

No. I think if I break strings, it's from pulling or pushing too hard with my left hand.

How do you hold your pick?

The first finger of the right hand is crooked. The pick just sort of fits in there between the thumb and fingers very comfortably. It's quite a small pick. I make my own out of plastic pie boxes that I cut up with wire cutters. You know, when you want to keep a piece of apple pie in the refrigerator — those plastic boxes that are shaped like a piece of pie? They're the perfect size and material for me and perfect for pie. They make nonflexible picks, extremely stiff, which last about three weeks. When I play acoustic guitar, besides the regular flatpick I use, I have a fingerpick on the small finger of my right hand so I can easily accompany myself on the seven other strings.

When flatpicking, do you hit with the front, back, or edge of the pick? Or just flat on?

Just flat on — up and down.

Have you heard about "circle picking"? Many people insist you get your speed this way.

I've heard about it, but I don't know what it is. The pick is just flat in my hand, and my hand just floats — it doesn't touch the face of the guitar.

And you don't consciously attempt to follow any preconceived picking formula?

I just try to play phrasings the way I hear them. To a certain degree one adapts to one's own technique, but, on the other hand, one must adapt one's technique to the idea. This is the very fundamental crux of it: Technique should be a dynamically evolving state. To tend to play continuously beyond you will truly help achieve a dynamic state of evolving technique. But I think one can play anything if one has enough perseverance, enough devotion to it. Fingering is probably the big key to unlocking technique; it is crucial. For example, some of the things that I did with Shakti are very long, complex melodies, and some of them were extremely difficult. Sometimes I spent not just hours but days and weeks on different fingerings to discover the right one, because I believe there is a right fingering for everything if you just take time out to discover it. I can't just fall back on the usual fretboard patterns, since I'm not playing diatonically. For example, if you are involved in any of the synthetic modes, then you have to invent rules and fingering principles for yourself. I have one piece in which the scale goes up, then down, then back up — and you have to play it like that [*hums*]:

It calls for different technique and different perception for looking at the technique itself. It's not really essential to know the names of the various modes and scales that you play, but what is important is that you know their relationship to the chords. In effect, my whole view of chords is different now, having studied Indian music. I see chords as notes of the scale played simultaneously. And so my own view of music now is, in fact, much more linear. No matter how complex the harmonic progression, there's a linear movement through it which can suggest all harmonic possibilities.

What advice would you give guitar players who want to play modally on how to avoid sounding like they're merely running scales in keys other than the key they say they're in?

In every scale or in every mode there are king, queen, and prince notes — the notes of vivid strength and color. In the discreet and tasteful application of these, the possibilities and permutations are infinite. The most important thing is to think melodically. In fact, there's really nothing but melody, and so if you have C or D Dorian, the thing is to discover the relationship of each note to the fundamental chord, and *that* is the color of that chord.

Do you think there's an inherent mood to any mode or chord?

Absolutely. Every scale has a mood. You know "mode" and "mood" are very close to each other. They have a definite emotional content. This is another discovery I made in Indian music. Every raga has a specific quality, and those specific qualities can range from tragic to erotic to profound, in a devotional sense. You can have courageous moods, you can have passionate moods, and the whole gamut of idealized human emotions. The whole basis of the raga is to develop, amplify, and articulate — with as much profundity as possible — the various qualities of the human heart and mind and being. But to me, this applies to all music everywhere. In the West we have to kind of discover it on our own, because the systems are not taught. Over here, only harmony is taught, though our study of it is extremely highly developed — it is second to none. Ultimately, musicians have a vocabulary of modes, scales, ragas, or whatever, and must learn the color of each one in relation to their own hearts, their own selves; how you use it, of course, is indicative of the degree of development in artistic and aesthetic terms.

Do you believe the qualities and moods that you hear in certain intervals are universal, or do they simply become historically acceptable through time, change, and as other sounds become more acceptable?

You're talking about audiences and artists. Audiences are conditioned, and they've been conditioned since going back to the year "dot." Only the true artist and the enlightened listener are nonconditioned, although I can see changes, and I would not like to underestimate the capacity of the audience to appreciate something new. Especially in the last ten years, audiences have become much more educated and more open in a nonconditional way; but it's difficult to bring the two points together. For example, Anton Webern in my opinion is a celestial musician; he was writing stuff in 1902 and 1903 that is still ahead of its time, but it's absolutely dissonant nevertheless. I even think the word "dissonant" is a conditioned qualification, and that qualification is uttered from a lower point of view. How can you say "all that's dissonant"? It's like saying, if you're looking at a Rembrandt, "Oh, that's bright, isn't it?" It's silly. It comes from an invalid, completely conditioned viewpoint. It's unreasonable for the artist to even begin to think in those terms. It steals something from the music because you don't even give the music the first chance of being listened to the way it is — being listened to for what it is.

How much variety is really offered listeners?

Art and commerciality are diametrically opposed, and it's unfortunate because culturally, I think that the radio in America — and the whole media in America — is like starving for any type of innovative cultural impulse, only by virtue of its own stranglehold, from its own mercenary tendency. If radio would even begin to truly accept the jazz culture, the real art form of America — which it still hasn't done

— then you would have much greater education. People should be exposed to more music — horn players in Tibet, the music of Russia, China, Australia, everywhere — because music is such a fabulous, wonderful, unifying language understood by all. Listening would probably be different — the world would be different for that matter, if the media were to see programming as an enlightening process for the listening public. That would be the first big, big step in terms of mass deconditioning. But the media in America is extremely repressive culturally. It's disgusting, and I hope it changes, because I believe in the beautiful and spiritual and unifying power of music. It's such a mysterious and wonderful thing, and people love it everywhere, and so why don't we use it to bring greater understanding to the people of the planet?

How much do you practice now at home?

Ideally about seven or eight hours a day; that's a nice figure. I have many different aspects of practice. One of them is playing and using bends, which is more an Indian technique, starting off on a note where the string is already bent. I'm also playing inside the bends, which of course is difficult. And then I'll perhaps work on a complicated chordal sequence. I'll just write one down that I can't do and work on it until I can. And then just to complicate matters, I'll play it in a compound time signature. It's just a successive imposition of greater and greater discipline, because this is the only way one can grow — continuous mastery over one's own inabilities.

Do you follow the rule that "slow is fast," that is, that practicing something very slowly is the way to develop speed?

Yes, sure. I mean, you can't just jump in there — especially if it's a complicated sequence.

Do you work with a tape recorder?

Sometimes. I also work with a special metronome that a friend of mine named Leo Hoarty built for me. It has just fabulous possibilities of synchronous compound time. It gives up to four clicks simultaneously. I have the base time — you know, a certain number of beats to the minute. Then I can have a derivative multiple, and then a second derivative multiple which is synchronized but completely independent. If you want, you can get 31 against 30, or 99 against 98. Furthermore, I have the possibility of extracting any pulse on any number of beats from one to 99, and from any of the A or B multiples. That whole thing arose from my dire frustration with my other tools. You know the old saying, "Necessity is the mother of invention." I had been using a "tri-

nome," but I gave it to a friend as a present, went out and bought a new one, and broke it on the same day. So I went back again and again and ended up going through five. And then just out of frustration I called up Leo, who built my present metronome. I have the only one in existence, and it's a fabulous tool. Leo and I have also been working on another project, which is a 4-track self-sync cassette tape recorder.

Do you write your music down on paper and hand it to your sidemen?

Oh, yes, sometimes there is the need to be structured. Sometimes it's easier just to play something for somebody: They get a picture much quicker. Writing might even be unnecessary for something like a little motif.

Do you find that you use any chord progressions more often than others?

No, I don't think so. I kind of go my own way. Any chord can follow any chord in my book.

When doing a chord melody section, do you try to keep a flowing, four-part harmony going?

There's no hard-and-fast rule. It depends on the situation and the context. With three notes — the ♭7th, 13th, and 3rd — you can say everything about a 13th chord. Same with modulations: There are no rules. I prefer to find new ways of going. The ways of going even from *C* to *A* minor are infinite. The composition makes the demand and the improvisation makes that structure, but I don't like the normal ways.

Do you work on the final mix?

Oh, yes, I always do.

Do you ever overdub?

Yep. You just can't do a solo in certain situations. On *Natural Elements,* for example, both Shankar and I had been deeply involved in the compositions. We had no time to even think about solos, and for a solo you really need to work, and think, and explore in your own self what it means to you, the possibilities, and how you're going to articulate them.

So, it's not like you go into a studio and run off 15 solos and splice in the best?

No. But of course, you always hope and pray for inspiration, that's the magical thing that gives you some sense of immortality.

Why were you attracted to flamenco?

It was its passion, I think, that really took me out. And technically, it's virtuosic and devastating. You hear a great flamenco player, and he can just knock you off your feet. That's what I liked about the blues, too — it has such emotional impact.

What was it that stood out for you in Miles Davis' playing?

Miles was just really soulful. His style — well, that's the wrong word, because he created his own style. One would normally think of style as something someone picks up and uses, but he is the originator of that style. To quote William Blake: "I must create my own system or be enslaved by another's." With Miles, for me, it was his simplicity, his directness, the authority of his music from a rhythmic, harmonic, and melodic point of view. His conceptualizations, from my point of view, were revolutionary. Everything I could see in Miles touched me. He was a good-looking fellow, a sharp dresser, you know. He epitomized elegance to me in every way. His music is really elegant, and eloquent, too. Miles has the capacity and the ability to draw out of people things that even surprise the musicians themselves.

So, he's a musical avatar of sorts.

Well, yes. He's been a guru of sorts to a lot of people. He was certainly a musical mentor to me. It's ironic. I dreamed of playing with Miles for years. To play with him, I thought, would be the ultimate achievement, but I came to America to play with Tony Williams. The fact that Miles asked me on a date the day after I got here was just an unbelievable plus. Tony hadn't left Miles at the time, so we went into the studio and did *In a Silent Way*. Meanwhile, Lifetime had been rehearsing and our first gig was at the Club Baron up in Harlem, which was another big thrill for me. For a European, to come to New York City and play up in Harlem is the biggest thrill of all. But I was very naive when I got here, and I figured, "Well, everybody up in Harlem's got to be hip to what's really happening." We pull up outside the club, and they've got something like "Now Appearing — The Tommy Willis Lifestory." I mean I was shocked beyond belief that the owner of a club didn't even know Tony Williams' real name, and he was booking him — which to me showed utter ignorance of the music. Anyway, Miles called again while we were at the club, and he asked me to go into the studio with him to make *Bitches Brew*.

Did you do any concerts with him then?

As a matter of fact I did, because at the time Lifetime wasn't working much. That band had Wayne Shorter, Chick Corea, Dave Holland, Jack DeJohnette, and Miles; later on I did some dates in the band that had Keith Jarrett, Gary Bartz, Michael Henderson, Airto, and Jack DeJohnette — and, of course, there were a lot more musicians in the studio. That's how I met Billy Cobham — at a Miles date. I was very lucky. When I came to America I got to play with all my favorite musicians. I recorded with

Wayne Shorter, Larry Coryell, and Miroslav Vitous — that was a lovely session [*Mountain in the Clouds*; it also features Joe Henderson on tenor sax and Herbie Hancock on electric piano].

What were you doing at the time Miles asked you to join his band?

I was very involved with Lifetime. I was writing a lot for the group, so it was as much my group as Tony's. I was much more involved in a composing sense than I would have been with Miles's group. So after years of idolizing Miles I was feeling strongly about my own musical directions, and I had to turn him down. I obviously would have made a lot more money with Miles, but musically Lifetime was extraordinary — especially after Jack Bruce joined us — and it was a vehicle for me to write, which of course Miles could understand. Jack and I go back a long way together, playing all types of music. In those days there was only one club to play in London, so everyone worked with each other.

What club was that?

The Flamingo All-Nighter [*laughs*]. That was the club where everybody played: Alexis Korner, the Rolling Stones, John Mayall, Eric Clapton. I was with Georgie Fame and the Blue Flames then. There was such a small possibility of work that everybody kept running into each other. The whole scene in London was very turbulent and eclectic for almost everybody.

Why did you leave Lifetime?

Eventually I left because it was too crazy a scene. The management didn't know how to handle us; they didn't know what they had. They were managing people like Flip Wilson. They could have been getting us good work; instead we ended up in like Henry County, Illinois, in a high school gym — dates in these obscure places. In New York we'd play a lot at Slugs, a club that used to exist on the Lower East Side. That was a great gig. That's where I met Duane Allman. He was coming by every night — Janis Joplin, too. But we were totally mishandled. Jack spent a lot of his own money on the group, but I was barely scratching by, so I had to leave. I went up to Boston to do a night with Miles, and he told me, "John, you know you have to get your own band together." Sometime after that Sri Chinmoy told me the same thing, and that solidified the idea in my mind. I went on to make an acoustic album, *My Goal's Beyond*, but I already had an idea for the Mahavishnu Orchestra. That album gave me an opportunity to bring in Jerry Goodman and Billy Cobham and play with them. I talked about my ideas with them, and we were in accord. So I began looking for bass players, and I talked to a lot of people. I'd asked Tony Levin, but he was with Gary Burton at the time. Then I remembered Rick Laird, who I'd known since I was 20.

Are there any recordings of you and Rick with Brian Auger?

No. You see, that was in the days before cassette recorders, and a tape recorder was a mighty investment — too mighty for me. Rick and I went back to the days when I had a trio with a baritone player, Glen Hughes — God rest his soul — when Glenn and I were both 18 years old; guitar, baritone, and bass. We had such an incredible relationship as friends, and as musicians we had fantastic rapport. We used to do Jimmy Giuffre/Jim Hall things, and Chico Hamilton; Miles; and Sonny Rollins tunes — Sonny Rollins is a *musician and a man* whose influence is not small in my life. Finally Glenn and I formed a trio with Rick Laird on upright bass, but there are no tapes, it's gone forever. Back then I also had another drummerless trip with Danny Thompson, who was in Pentangle. He was a fantastic bass player; also in the group was Tony Roberts, a reedman who was just way ahead of his time. You've never heard of him; he lives in Canterbury, England. I do have a BBC broadcast recording of that trio, but we didn't leave any records. But to get back to Mahavishnu, Rick was in England, and he'd just finished doing a tour with Buddy Rich. So I called him and asked him to come over. In the process of putting the personnel together I got a call from Miroslav, who asked me to join Weather Report. I said no — I'm putting my own band together. So Miroslav said that if I were looking for a keyboard player I should call up Jan Hammer, who was with Sarah Vaughan at the time. I got the best musicians available at the time, I think. It was important to me that the musicians have their roots in jazz, although Jerry's roots are in classical music and rock. Billy Cobham is known as a great rock drummer, but his roots are in jazz. He made his big impact playing with people like Billy Taylor and Horace Silver. Anyway, we got together, rehearsed two weeks, and played our first club; within a month we went into the studio and recorded *The Inner Mounting Flame.* You know the rest.

What do you see as the impact of the original Mahavishnu Orchestra?

That question asks me to make an objectification of a subjective experience, which is difficult to do. Oh, it was a great band while it lasted, but it didn't embody what it should have embodied.

What should it have embodied?
Oh, more brotherly love, I'd say.
You feel there was too much competitiveness?

No, not competitiveness. Competition, in a sense, is very good because it makes you work. It's like sports. I love to play pingpong, and I play hard. There's nothing I like better than to have a great player on the other side, because that makes me transcend my own limitations, and it's the same in music. I constantly want to transcend my own limitations. So it wasn't competition on that point. It was the lack of mutual spiritual consciousness. That's the only way I can put it. I don't know if that sounds pompous or anything; it's just that at the time I was a disciple of Sri Chinmoy. I don't care what path anybody takes. It's just that I feel music needs the content of a consciousness that is in an ascendant attitude. This is all so difficult to put in words, because as soon as I say something it's not that. It's not what I just said because what I just said implies that you have to be religious, which is not true. I'm talking about consciousness and a mutual acknowledgment of God, the creator of us, the creator of music, and the One who's given us the capacity to realize these gifts in a physical sense. What happened to the Mahavishnu Orchestra was a misunderstanding. Tension in a group can be positive in a musical sense, sometimes, but not on a continual basis. Unfortunately it resolved itself into a kind of continuous tension, and you get to the point where that manifests itself on the physical plane. Too bad, but it's not too bad. It's part of the divine plan, of which we are all part, and whatever it has in store for me, I'm ready. I hate to sound holier-than-thou, because religious judgment is absolute nonsense. But I see causes which lie behind the effects, the effects of which are the dissolution of a group to the dismay of a lot of people. The causes go back to a very fundamental level, in a human sense, and that is the inability to make mutual acknowledgments of a higher order.

How did Miles organize rehearsals?

He's amazing to work with, because he'd never say, "I don't really want that"; he'd just say, "play long," or "play short." Once he told me, "Play like you don't know how to play guitar." That's Miles, and you just go along with it.

In gaining an understanding of Coltrane's lines, was it a matter of writing them out, or was it all just absorbed with the heart?

What I couldn't understand was the level he was operating on, the level that he lived on. In fact, *A*

Love Supreme was the first record that went over my head. I just couldn't grasp it until a couple of years after I'd first heard it. It was just astounding.

Spiritually as well as musically?

Yeah, but spiritual and artistic levels are the same — there's no difference.

How does one go about creating long lines like Coltrane's that are original, nonrepetitive, and still ongoing?

Oh, I don't know. Music is my voice to God. I mean, I pray, and God listens to me, and I try to listen to God. Music is my strongest voice, or rather, it's my public voice. And I'm very acutely aware of my need of God's loving kindness and His grace. My need of Him — just my utter longing for His presence — is part of my own being that just pushes me forward. I have to give everything to that. What I'm doing is basically a kind of musical prayer. And so I don't think of it as playing this or that line; of course that happens, but basically the only thing I live for is this presence of God. When I walk out onstage, I want inspiration to take everything that I have, everything that is me. I want it to be at His own disposal. Because then, if I can get out of the way, if I can be pure enough, if I can be selfless enough, and if I can be generous and loving and caring enough to just abandon what I have and abandon my own preconceived, silly notions of what I think I am — and become truly who in fact I am, which is really just another child of God — then the music can really use me. And therein is my true fulfillment. That's when the music starts to happen. And that's part of my process in my own spiritual life — to become more selfless, because it's selfish to impose myself on the music. I get that from Coltrane; I get that from other musicians, too — that giving, you know.

But before you can teach that sort of consciousness, don't you need technique that's virtually autonomic?

I don't mean that purely technical considerations are irrelevant. I have to practice; I have to do my best. If I didn't, then how is it going to happen? There's no point in kidding myself. I've got to work, and that's what my life is all about. I'll be working till I die, because every day I'm given strength and power to work, and to be in harmony with the evolution that has been taking place inside me. But at the same time, it's like everything that I have is at the disposal of the divine grace, which is manifested internally in the form of just real true inspiration, which gives the possibility of complete artistic and spiritual liberation — in musical form. And that's really all my goal is about. If onstage I can manifest or experience artistic and spiritual liberation, then the music will be full of it, and I believe whoever can identify with the music will enjoy the same experience.

Do you ever find yourself falling back into old habits or a run or two bars that are similar to those you used another night?

You have to keep that in perspective. You have to use what you have, but continuously hope for inspiration. I mean, sometimes I perform, and I just feel inspired before I even hit the stage. I feel a presence of love in me, and I feel just the wonder and awe of life. One plays the composition, but it's me — it's the spontaneity onstage which is of paramount importance, because how I feel now, I never felt before, and I'll never feel again.

You've said that music is about love, and that you've got to have humor everywhere, including music. What devices do you use to inject humor into your music?

That can only really happen spontaneously — otherwise it's just contrived. You can't really preplan true playing. It's dependent completely on the individual musician and the surrender of all his or her experience and knowledge and technique to the mood of inspiration, because every day it's so different. One night you go onstage and feel nothing but tragedy. Like the other night, I really felt the sorrow of life very heavily, and so I walked onstage feeling that, and so the music was just all about that. But then like the night before it may have been the opposite. It's just like suddenly you feel a certain mood and you just give vent to it. I don't know any techniques for injecting any human quality, because for me they are only valid at the moment they arrive.

Does a tragic sense of life make you have a less than inspired performance?

No. Tragedy is part of everybody's life. Just having a separate existence is, in a sense, conducive to tragedy and to pain. But still it's more or less inspiring, because it's such a natural part of life. I think if you took the pain of life away, you'd take away more or less everything.

What do you see as your legacy?

You're asking me to objectify something that is utterly subjective, so I can't really say. I think I've done very little, quite frankly, in this life. There's a lot more for me to do. I've attempted to make some contribution to world peace, minuscule though it might be. This world is really paradise, but we've forgotten, that's all. So if the music can remind people where they truly belong in the consciousness of love and kindness — which is really God-consciousness — then it might be a small contribution, but at least it's a positive one. Obviously the world cannot change — it is people who have to change. There's so much unhappiness and sickness in the world. I mean, there are still wars going on. People have not yet accepted the divine spark in man, the inviolability of human beings. If I can bring some comfort into someone's life, then I won't have lived in vain. All we can do is help each other, to remind ourselves that in the midst of all this anguish there is a sanctuary, that everything is all right. Music can do that. It is a healing force in the world.

[September 1985]

Do contemporary pop and jazz reflect the degree of creativity that they have in the past?

On the whole, no. There seems to be a kind of hiatus going on. Today, rock and jazz are rhythmically, harmonically, and experimentally inferior to what was happening even as far back as the '60s. But this kind of backlash against intellectuality of any kind is more of a sociological problem than it is a musical one. It's cyclical, and a more receptive mood will return. However, you can't deny that a lot of pop music — including easy-listening funk by so-called jazz musicians — is terribly banal. It's superficial, and it is not even covertly commercial; it's unashamedly blatant. Jazz is vital, living music that should be about life. Don't misunderstand me, because I don't knock any kind of music. I like Billy Idol, you know what I mean? There's room for everybody, and I like to think that if it's music, then it's good. It's the most profound spiritual power on earth. It sure beats the hell out of killing people.

You have a reputation as a great technician. Can the intellectual and technical aspects of music get in the way of speaking from the heart?

Not when the artist is wholly integrated in himself, which is something we're all working for. I'm alive. I have an intellect, a heart, and a physical side, and I want to integrate all three to be whole. In the process of evolution, you may emphasize one more than the other, but that is perfectly normal because you have to live life in order to integrate yourself. It's a lifelong work because it presupposes evolution as a human being.

You are also known for exploring different musical areas. Does that result from curiosity and the urge to experiment, or is it due to frustration and restlessness?

It's not due to frustration and restlessness. I get

that from myself because my greatest competitor is my own inability and incapacity. It's from my love of music. If I hear something great, I want to know more about it. When I hear a great musician, I can feel his life and his elegance and his eloquence inside the music, and that makes me want to know more about him. Whether it comes from east, west, north, or south, music is my language. When I first heard some of the great Indian musicians, I had an enormous desire to know them better. To be able to play with them is satisfaction you cannot imagine, although I don't really play their way. I'm able to communicate with them because I know the rules governing their approach.

Is communication generally improving between musicians of diverse backgrounds and cultures?

The barriers amongst instrumental musicians don't exist like they did in the past, which is wonderful. We all need enriching, and if we are to make any kind of progress, we need inspiration. This is especially true in the exchange that's happening between jazz and classical players. There is a great deal of mutual respect, and both genres are looking for new blood. It's terrific that musicians such as [trumpeter] Wynton Marsalis, who plays both styles, is very much appreciated by classical *and* jazz audiences. [Pianists] Chick Corea and Keith Jarrett are very involved with classical music. On the classical side, you have musicians like violinist Gidon Kremer, who has recorded with Keith. Gidon has asked me to write a piece for him. [Cellist] Yo Yo Ma has also expressed interest. Of course, if it weren't for the encouragement of Ernest Fleischmann, who is the executive director of the Los Angeles Philharmonic, I don't think I would have taken on a project of such gigantic proportions as my concerto.

How did you and Michael Gibbs come to collaborate on your concerto?

I asked Michael because orchestration is an art that I don't pretend to be a master of. He is very gifted in that area, and the textural tableau from an orchestral point of view is so important. The challenge that I've had in writing the piece has been in establishing dramatic development and in evolving a structure that doesn't also use a small group. Although I'm taking the privilege of not being a "classical musician," I feel I have to observe classical music rules. My appetite is most surely whetted now, and I think I'm going to write another orchestral piece soon.

Technically, is your concerto very challenging? How large a role does improvisation play?

Improvisation is included because that's very important to me, but it's featured to a lesser degree. For that reason, I would be delighted if classical players would attempt it; the repertoire for classical guitar and orchestra is very small. There are sections of the concerto that are very difficult for me, but difficulty is hard to assess in terms of another player's technique. If a fingerstyle player does eventually attempt it, he'll have to be very flexible and open to adaptation. There are things you can do with a pick that are difficult to play with the fingers. Being a jazz musician, you develop the ability to modify your technique. But in many respects, fingerstyle technique is superior to pick technique.

On Mahavishnu *the Synclavier seemed to change the way you phrase. Did you feel that yourself?*

Your impression is very close to home. The Synclavier allows me to play in a way that is very difficult to do on a guitar. Conventional electric and acoustic guitars don't lend themselves to the hornlike flow of improvisation that's very dear to me. Guitarists — pianists, too, for that matter — play in a different way than do horn players. The work of Miles Davis, John Coltrane, Sonny Rollins, and Clifford Brown made an indelible mark upon me, and I had to try to adapt my technique in order to accommodate the parameters that they use in their improvisation. I suffered because it was so difficult. I still suffer [*laughs*]. When I first began to experiment with the synthesizer guitar at the end of 1975, I realized that the potential was tremendous. The problem was that the technology was elephantine. The Synclavier helps break down the barriers that obstruct a guitarist from playing at his optimum. I owe a lot to the digital guitar. It's a revolution. Although it requires that you modify your technique a certain amount, it allows you to enter the world of creative synthesis. For guitarists who are looking for new ways to create sound, it's tremendous. It's very exciting to be able to apply that musically. I've tried the other synthesizer guitars, and they're toys in comparison to the Synclavier.

Do you feel the digital guitar eventually will replace more conventional instruments?

For me, no. I fell in love with the acoustic guitar when I was 11, and for the rest of my life it will be my first love. But I feel that guitarists' involvement with synthesizers will be like what has happened to keyboard: First there was the acoustic piano, then the Rhodes crept in, and finally there were synthesizers. It's not a question of whether I have to make a choice. You can have your feet in both worlds, although I foresee in the not-too-distant future a real-time instrument. By that, I mean a synthesizer so sophisticated that it responds exactly like an acoustic guitar.

Specifically, how does the digital guitar change your technique and approach to phrasing?

Part of it depends on the kind of timbre [tone color] you're using. When you get involved in the creation of timbres with the synthesizer, you're creating a new world of sound. Once you've got a particular timbre, its characteristics will directly influence you as soon as you start to play. It's as if you're suddenly playing another instrument. For example, if a timbre has a long sustain, you are able to articulate phrases that are impossible on a conventional guitar, so you must change your technique and your concept. If you have a given number of timbres, you have to approach them individually. Many timbres are impossible to play in a guitar type of way, and you almost have to caress the strings in order to coax the sound out.

One of the main criticisms of synthesizer guitars is that they don't track accurately or quite fast enough for guitarists' taste.

Perhaps players are asking too much and aren't willing to modify their technique. The nature of translating a guitar envelope — the characteristics of a sound — into digital information is very complex and sensitive. You have to be very precise because you're directing information, and if you miss something, the computer has a confused input and will act accordingly. Once you get used to the Synclavier, the tracking is phenomenal — even with bends and dynamic nuances — but if you don't tell it what to do correctly, it'll fight you. As far as speed of tracking is concerned, if you compare it to the responsiveness of an acoustic guitar, which involves nanoseconds, then in some sense there's a very, very slight delay. But I've played quickly with the digital guitar, and if I'm playing right, it's there.

Which cuts on Mahavishnu *best demonstrate the digital guitar's capabilities; why did you use the particular timbres on it?*

"Nostalgia" has a melancholy aspect that works well with the particular flute patch I used. The song has a classical Indian raga influence, where harmony is suggested by a drone. That timbre enabled me to play in a slow, melancholy manner, which can be difficult to evoke without being sugary. On "Clarendon Hills," there's a direct guitar in unison with the Synclavier. You can't really hear the direct guitar, but you can feel it. And "East Side West Side" has a funky kind of Wurlitzer organ sound on the opening.

Part of the problem was that I went into the studio about six weeks after I got the digital guitar. I went with timbres that I could identify with and felt comfortable with. Many players will think that the factory sounds are great and use just those because people are indolent — we all are. But I think it's very important to create the timbres yourself. The tendency to want to work less is just human nature.

How can you suggest you're indolent, in light of your busy schedule and your dedication to the guitar?

It's all relative. When I think about the discipline of some people, I'm very indolent in comparison. But if you love something enough, you automatically concentrate on it. That's the best kind of discipline you could ever have. However, in developing certain areas — technique, for example — it helps to know how to work. I would like to make a contribution to helping young musicians. Knowing how to work and how to attack a problem both in a technical and in a personal sense is an area that could use a little overhaul. Sometimes, if you get the right clue, you can unravel a great mystery. Many of my feelings about teaching and helping players have grown out of my relationship with a young friend I've been coaching.

What have you been helping him with?

Primarily, I was fairly concerned with his theoretical background, which was very weak. He was a very good rock and roll player, but he was dissatisfied and wanted to make progress, so we started on jazz harmony and its application to the guitar. We also talked about classical harmony.

How did you approach jazz harmony theory?

I began with chord structure, which is essential information for any occidental musician — oriental musicians don't approach music from a harmonic perspective. We took standards and looked for ways to extend the basic chords, using the rules governing chord extensions and related scales. In effect, we broke everything down into its scalar components and reassembled it using a scalar approach, which gives you a more linear view rather than a vertical one. And we thoroughly covered triads, which are such powerful units, especially when you begin to superimpose them in improvisation.

Can you recommend some books about chords and scales?

Vincent Perfichetti's *20th Century Harmony: Creative Aspects and Practice* is a very important book. And I also highly recommend Nicholas Slonimsky's *Thesaurus of Scales and Melodic Patterns*. Those two will take you a long way.

What do you do to improve your technique?

It varies. The other day, I invented an interesting right-hand exercise that is extremely difficult. I took a highly convoluted melodic line — it can be any series of notes, really — with strange intervals and string changes. I practiced playing it at various tempos and rhythms. That kind of thing does wonders for your articulation, speed, and phrasing — the usual, boring stuff that's very important.

What are the critical aspects of right-hand technique?

It depends on your style. There are so many styles that work; it's so individual. For example, Allan Holdsworth, who has such an original style and plays very fast, relies primarily on his left hand. I articulate everything, picking almost all of the notes, which calls for strong discipline on the part of the right hand and necessitates a lot of fluidity in the wrist. It takes a lot of work to develop speed while staying relaxed.

How do you stabilize your right hand?

I rest the heel of my hand on the bridge, regardless of the type of instrument. From that anchor, my hand is resting and relaxed and I'm able to move my wrist with no problems. Again, what works for me might not work for someone else. You find your position through trial and error. Larry Coryell, for instance, plays with much more arm movement than I do. If you suffer from tension in the arm or shoulder, perhaps there's something wrong with the position of your hand.

If your right hand is resting on the bridge, how do you move closer to the fingerboard?

For very difficult passages, I can't play close to the fingerboard. However, for chordal accompaniment or playing that moves back and forth between linear and chordal elements, my hand floats in the air.

Can you recommend some rudimentary right-hand exercises?

I have developed a series that is tremendous for articulation and rhythm. Start with the first string and slowly play four quarter-notes to the measure, all with downstrokes. Then, while maintaining the same tempo — preferably keeping time with your foot, although you can use a metronome — subdivide the measure into six quarter-notes or two quarter-note triplets. Next, switch to alternate strokes and start progressing from eighths to triplets to sixteenths to sextuplets to thirty-seconds to forty-eighths to sixty-fourths. Finally, go back down again. This involves simple mathematics, but to execute it without losing tempo is quite a challenge for the right hand. Of course, you can approach it a little at a time. Now, that's just the beginning. Instead of progressing through multiples of two and three, you can work with odd-numbered figures, moving from one to two to three to four to five to six to seven and so on.

If you were to play two triplets in a row, would the first one start with a downstroke and the second one start with an upstroke?

Yes. You strictly alternate. When you get to five and seven, things become more unusual. The figure of five should be subdivided into a group of two followed by a group of three. It's very important that you accent each group, which is demanding from the standpoint of articulation because one group of five starts with a downstroke, while the next one starts with an up. A figure of seven is two groups of two followed by a group of three. This exercise forces you to be very precise because you have to go from figure to figure without losing the flow. If your tempo is suspect, use a metronome. Otherwise, just keep time with your foot. The next step with these exercises is to do them while changing strings. At some point, you'll be confronted with the necessity of changing strings on either an upstroke or a downstroke without losing tempo and articulation. In a roundabout way, these exercises are related to the work I did with Indian rhythmical theory.

That's a vocal discipline, isn't it?

Yes. The whole Indian classical system is essentially vocal. The way they develop rhythm is extremely refined; the mathematics are of the highest order. There is a word for each rhythmic group, and each work is made up of syllables corresponding to the number of beats in a particular figure. Once you know the system, you can easily work out rhythmic compositions. I began using this method with Shakti, and I will continue to use it for the rest of my life because it's superior to any other approach. The greatest work that has gone on in rhythmic development has been by Indian percussionists. Zakir Hussain, the tabla player with Shakti, who also plays on "When

Blue Turns Gold" [*Mahavishnu*], has an astonishing mastery of rhythm.

Do you ever find it frustrating to work with musicians who are unaware of these concepts?

We each grow in our own way, you know. There are some people who don't need them. Tony Williams, who is one of the great jazz drummers, or Billy Cobham or Danny Gottlieb, in his own way, don't need to study Indian musical theory. If it interests you, fine. I introduced Danny to this system, and he is now really excited about it.

Have you ever wished you had gotten into fingerstyle more?

When I first picked up the guitar, I didn't know what a pick was. I still play fingerstyle a bit, but there's room for improvement. As far as jazz is concerned, there is phrasing and articulation that is possible only with a pick. There are advantages and disadvantages to both styles, but after playing with Paco de Lucia, I'd have to say that flamenco technique is the most superior approach to the guitar. Many classical players will consider that to be a heretical statement, and I hope I'm not being myopic. Flamencos have an incredibly smooth five-note tremolo, while classical players use a four-note one. They also have an advanced thumb technique that allows them to play very quickly. Don't misunderstand me, because I think classical technique is phenomenal. I'm one of Julian Bream's greatest admirers, and John Williams is amazing, but Paco is absolutely inspired.

Speaking of inspiration, how do you place yourself in the kind of mood that enables you to play at your best?

I've been involved in yoga and meditation and everything like that — I still am. But a state of receptivity is nothing more than a state of awareness. I want the music to come from the deepest possible point in me so that I speak from my soul. It's a magical dream when that happens. When you're inspired, you can do anything.

– PAT METHENY –

BY DAN FORTE – DECEMBER 1981

JON SIEVERT

MOST PEOPLE who like us don't know anything about the guitar," admits Pat Metheny. "They like the spirit of the music. We don't draw that many musicians; they're more into players who are expanding the vocabulary on a technical level. We're dealing with more of a 'life' approach, as opposed to just more notes, yet another chorus."

Though his approach to jazz guitar is unorthodox and often subdued in terms of technique, Pat Metheny has become a guitar hero — perhaps even a guitar anti-hero — forging a new aesthetic in jazz guitar, with the "Metheny sound" more closely tied to the jazz tradition than it is to anything known as "fusion." While he has not compromised his style and is still revered by the jazz community, Metheny has struck a chord with countless listeners who have never seen the inside of a jazz nightclub. Since the release of the *Pat Metheny Group* album in 1978, Metheny's records have consistently sold in the 200,000 range and have placed high (sometimes at the top) of the jazz charts.

Born in the small town of Lee's Summit, Missouri, Metheny took up the guitar at age 12, playing rock and roll with friends. "I was never attracted to the guitar per se," he states. "I got braces on my teeth when I was about 14, so I couldn't play trumpet anymore." The recordings of the late Wes Montgomery eventually led to Metheny's eight-hour-a-day obsession with the instrument, which in turn

earned him a scholarship to attend *Down Beat* magazine's summer music camps.

Upon graduating from high school, Pat entered the University of Miami's music program, where he earned a D in his first and only semester as a guitar major because, he admits, "I went to one lesson and never went again." Nevertheless, after one semester, Metheny was promoted to the faculty as a guitar instructor.

On hearing Metheny play backstage at a jazz festival, vibraphonist Gary Burton invited the then 19-year-old to come to Berklee College of Music in Boston. There Pat taught jazz improvisation and joined Burton's quintet, where he stayed for three years and as many albums before launching a solo career interrupted occasionally with side gigs with Joni Mitchell on her *Shadows and Light* tour and with bassist Charlie Haden and saxophonist Dewey Redman. On his most recent excursions Metheny has moved from showcase clubs to halls that seat 3,000 to 5,000 people.

Do you think contemporary guitarists overstress the importance of playing fast?

A guitar is easy for some people to learn how to play quickly — lots of notes and stuff — but that can be deceiving because you can tell there are players who don't really *hear* everything they're playing. They're just letting their fingers do the work without really letting their head or their feelings get involved. On a horn you can never really do that, because the notes come from inside you. You have to actually breathe the note out, so that tends to give horn players a certain kind of focus that other musicians sometimes don't have. This is a little bit true in the bass department, too, where now on both electric and acoustic bass you have musicians playing more notes per second than could possibly be digested. On the other hand there are people like Charlie Haden, who can play in a very simple way, but he says so much. And there are examples of that on guitar, too. Jim Hall is a very economical player, yet he's *extremely* expressive.

Both you and Haden are among the few jazz players to use influences other than just the blues foundation in a jazz context. You each take elements from folk and country. Is that the influence of growing up in the Midwest?

Well, I think that might have something to do with it. When Charlie was a little kid he was touring with his family band, performing on radio shows and playing shows with Mother Maybelle Carter. He's got that background in a much deeper way than me. I've always felt very close to the music that comes from out there, but I left when I was relatively young, so my experiences have been more world experiences. I'm very glad that I grew up there, not only for the Midwest groove, but for the Kansas City playing experiences that I was fortunate enough to be involved in when I was young.

You usually say that you fooled around with the guitar for a couple of years before you took it up seriously. What did the fooling-around stage consist of?

You know, playing "Louie Louie," "Little Latin Lupe Lu," and all those kinds of tunes with various friends in junior high.

Was this before you were exposed to jazz?

No. I already knew about it through my older brother [trumpeter Mike Metheny]. Around that time he had found a few friends who were very much into jazz. One important character in all this was a piano player named John McKee, who lived right up the street from us. He specialized in Thelonious Monk tunes. This guy knew every Monk tune ever written. He was about five years older than my brother, ten years older than me. But he would have jam sessions all the time, and I used to go up there and listen. My brother would sit in — it was kind of a little community of people who were aspiring to be jazz musicians. I was into rock and roll, but every now and then they'd let me play with them. I'd kind of fumble my way through some tune. I really liked doing it, plus I got to hang out with the older guys, which

made me feel special when I was 13. So through my brother I was exposed to jazz as early as ten or eleven.

When you started taking up jazz more seriously did you go to a teacher?

Not really, but only because the only guy who was kind of a jazz guitar teacher lived miles away in the next town, and I didn't have a way of getting over there to see him when I was 14 or so. As it turned out, within a few months after that, I started playing all the time with really good players around Kansas City, and those people became my teachers in a more direct way. It wasn't like I'd go to some music store for one day a week; I was playing jazz tunes four or five nights a week on the bandstand with excellent musicians. I had to sort of scuffle my way through those tunes, trying to make sense out of the whole thing. As I look back on it now, that's the best possible kind of experience I could have had.

Did you learn jazz harmony and phrasing by osmosis or did those guys actually tell you about such things as theory and modes?

No, they were very intuitive kinds of players. The main guy I worked for was a trumpet player named Gary Sivils, who even now is really inspiring for me to hear. But he's not a knowledgeable improviser in the sense that he can explain modes and all that kind of stuff; he just instinctively knows what to do. He can play on hard tunes and make all the changes; it's more an ear kind of thing. So I learned from them in an intuitive sense. They never sat down and said, "Play these notes on this chord." To tell you the truth, I didn't learn the actual names until I was about 18 and moved to Florida. I mean, I *knew* all the stuff, but I had my own names for things. For instance, I called a diminished scale a "half-step, whole-step scale." I'd heard it used on records by my favorite players. I knew that there was a chord progression called a II-V-I, but I didn't know exactly what it meant, even though I was playing tunes all the time that had II-V-Is going on all over the place. So I kind of learned what to do before I knew what you call it.

Besides jamming and playing in a band context did you sit down alone and practice guitar much?

Oh, yeah. About eight hours a day. I was a complete fanatic; I used to cut out of study hall and gym and go in the bathroom and practice during high school. I'd take something like [trumpeter Miles Davis'] "Solar" and play it all different tempos with a metronome beating on 2 and 4. I'd play in all keys, all over the guitar. I'd force myself just to play on one string, or on four strings, or just the lower two strings, or the upper strings — anything I could do to make myself feel comfortable with that tune. I've never been able to just sit around and play scales up and down. I get bored doing that. It never seemed to make sense to me why you'd be playing a scale up and down when you could be playing a tune. I wish that I had had somebody to guide me. Anything I practiced was more or less just an effort to sort of sound like my idols on records.

Who were some of those idols?

Wes Montgomery was definitely my favorite, although I was into all kinds of people. I loved Kenny Burrell and still do. Jim Hall and Jimmy Raney were very important figures. Those four were my biggest favorites, and I also really liked people like Grant Green because at that time I was playing with organ players a lot, and he functioned in those kinds of situations fantastically. I was playing mostly bebop then.

Was the Gibson ES-175 you now play your main guitar back then?

Yep, from the very beginning. Well, I actually had an ES-140T for a little while, but it got smashed up in an airplane; I was devastated. But the airlines bought me a guitar, so I got a Fender Mustang for a couple of months, and I remember playing that in the garage band scene. By that time I was into jazz pretty heavily, listening away, and I got my 175 for $120 or something.

How did you get the Down Beat *scholarship?*

I subscribed to *Down Beat* when I was young, and that was a great education just in terms of learning the names of everybody and who did what. I happened to see that they had a scholarship program where you send in a tape, and if you were good enough they sent you to the band camp. So I got together with John McKee and a flute player. That was when I was studying octaves, and I remember we played "Bumpin' on Sunset." I played Wes Montgomery's part pretty much note-for-note, and they comped along. I sent it in and figured nothing would ever happen. Then an issue of *Down Beat* listed the winners, and my name was in there. The camp was really a turning point for me. Attila Zoller was the guitar teacher there, and he was incredibly inspiring. He encouraged me more than anyone had encouraged me at that point. I got to do a lot of playing with kids my age who were into the same thing, which was also a new experience. There were a lot of kids from all over. That's where I realized I wasn't crazy, and that there were other people who were interested in the same music I was.

Back then were you primarily playing bebop?

All during my time in Kansas City — until I was 18 — I sounded awful. I don't want to give the impression that, "Yeah, I was playing bebop and burning, gigging," because I sounded horrible. I hear tapes of me from that period and I was scuffling, just like anybody who'd only been playing for a year or two. I had a certain amount of chops, and every now and then — like every 48 bars — you'll hear a little glimmer of an idea [*laughs*]. But for the most part it didn't sound too good at all. I wasn't writing my own music, other than just a few little tunes, until I was 16 or 17. I was just trying to learn to play bebop.

When you started writing and playing more melodic tunes, did you find you had a natural sense of melody?

I couldn't tell. Again, it was difficult because there was really no one to compare myself to, other than the records that I heard. And next to the records, I was awful. All I really knew was that I wanted to do it, and I was doing the best I could. After I'd been in Miami for about six months, all of a sudden something happened. I went through a period of trying out all kinds of guitars — a Gibson L-5, a Les Paul — everything I could, and it was frustrating because I couldn't get the sound I wanted. My 175 had been sitting under my bed for about six months while I flirted around with all these other instruments, and then one day I got it out again. All of a sudden it felt right, like that was the instrument I should be playing. When I hear old tapes from around then, stylistically I can tell it's me. This was about the beginning of 1973. It was still kind of raw, but the sort of quirks that have become my style were apparent then.

Despite your opinion of your playing at that stage, you must have been fairly advanced, because didn't the University of Miami put you on the faculty during those first six months?

Yes. That's one of those things that seems much more dramatic on paper than it actually was. A friend of mine named Stan Samole was a guitar teacher there, and all of a sudden all kinds of guitar players started going to the University of Miami. They'd just opened up the electric guitar program there, so kids saw it as an alternative to Berklee, I guess, which at that time was the only other place you could really go if you wanted to study electric guitar. Instead of two or three electric guitar majors, there were suddenly 50 or 60, so they needed more teachers. I was, like, one of the better players. Also, maybe I had a little bit of a knack for being a teacher.

It just kind of happened; I don't see that as being that significant. People who write press releases tend to build it up a little bit.

By this time you'd learned the formal names and theoretical concepts?

Yeah. I learned that in the first month or so at Miami, simply because I had to. Being a jazz major and all that, here's everybody talking about Dorian modes. Learning the labels was very easy, as you can imagine. It's like learning to count in another language.

When did you actually learn to read music — from trumpet?

Yes. My older brother taught me to read music. I'd read music in the high school band, and there was always trumpet music around. I knew how to read when I was quite young, like eight or nine years old. I feel very fortunate to be able to read and write music; as a time-saving device it's invaluable.

Was the University of Miami your first teaching experience?

No, when I was in high school I taught little kids C chords and all that every day after school, just as a way to make money. It was fun. By the time I finished teaching at Berklee I was tired of it. I'd given the same raps over and over again, so I was ready to cool it for a while. But I still enjoy doing it, especially with real promising players. There are some subtle things that I've learned I can tell them about; it's fun to turn people on to these things.

Do you have an overall philosophy you try to impress on students?

No. In fact, my only philosophy has been to make people aware of what their weaknesses are. But that's not really true, either, because with each person it's different. Some people really need to be encouraged that it's possible for them to become good players, and other people need to be made aware that there are things that they should work on other than what they've already got together. Players get to that intermediate level where they can already play pretty good, and that's kind of a dangerous period because they tend to start playing only the things that they can play well instead of things that they can't. This is especially true for people who are interested in improvisation. It's one thing if somebody's a really good modal player, but to actually be able to play on chord changes is a difficult thing that sometimes gets ignored. Learning that can help your modal playing, too.

How important do you think chops are — execution, facility on the neck, dexterity?

I think it depends on what kind of music you

want to play. Everybody finds their own path. It gets me when the technique becomes the featured item. It's like somebody spending hours polishing the water faucet thinking that's going to make the water purer or tastier. It doesn't really work like that. I've never really sat down and worked on technique — it just kind of takes care of itself as you become a better musician.

Were there any specific things you learned from being in Burton's band?

Oh, I learned so much from *everybody* in that band. Not only did I learn music from Gary, but he gave me a business sense that made it practical for me to start my own group later on. He was like a big brother to me because at that point I was just a green kid from Missouri. I didn't know anything about booking agents, tours, or how much money I was supposed to get for gigs. I didn't know anything other than I liked music and wanted to be a musician, and that I liked Gary's music in particular. Over the three years I was with him he taught me the realities of the music business, in addition to always being inspiring as a player. He also kind of kept on my case. If I was playing solos that didn't seem to have any direction or that didn't end well — or even had wrong notes on certain chords — he wasn't the kind of leader that would just let it slide. He'd say, "Hey, on such-and-such tune you've got to watch it during this section, because it's not working."

Were you able to take that as advice or constructive criticism from a more experienced player, or did you resent it?

Coming from him it meant a lot, and I was grateful for the advice. But being the restless youth that I was, towards the end I was tired of being the student. I wanted to be the one telling other people what they were doing wrong [*laughs*].

Did you adopt that attitude as leader of any of your subsequent groups?

Unfortunately for me and the other members of the group, the first year that I had my own band I was really trying to almost be the Gary Burton type. As time went by, I realized that that wasn't really my personality. I'm much more inclined to just let everybody do what they want to do and make the best of it. We still talk about things together, but it's in a friendlier sort of way. With Gary it was more like, "Okay, on such-and-such a tune you messed up." As I get older, it's harder and harder for people to do things that I think are wrong. Almost everything sounds right to me, if it's done with the right spirit. It was important for me to go through that phase of being a strict leader, especially at the time we started, because there was a danger of it becoming just another group and I wanted it to have its own sound. I'm sure that all the effort I put into molding and pushing it into certain directions had an influence on the way it came out. Now that the group is more established, I'm more into people taking chances.

Going back to the Burton Quintet, what did you gain from Mick Goodrick?

Mick Goodrick was the first guitarist I ever played with who made me feel really ridiculous [*laughs*]— because he was so good. I'd play my little solo and then he'd play this masterpiece afterwards, and I'd go back to the hotel thinking, "Aw, man, what's happening?" That would happen every night for pretty much the whole time he was in the band. It was a combination of him being great and me still getting my feet wet as a player. We always had, and still do have, a really good relationship. We played a lot of duet gigs during those years, and he was a big inspiration and influence for me.

Did you enjoy the work that you did with Steve Swallow?

Swallow, first of all, was and still is one of my favorite bass players, and playing with him was like a dream come true. In addition to being a great bassist, he's also one of my favorite composers, having written tunes like "Falling Grace" and "Hullo Bolinas" — just classic jazz tunes. He was very encouraging to me as a composer. I'd bring my new tunes in, and he'd look them over and offer suggestions. He encouraged me to write away from the guitar at the piano, and eventually I started doing that, which really helped. He also has this incredible spirit; I think I learned as much from him in nonmusical ways as in musical ways.

What are you thinking about during the course of a guitar solo?

I don't think about anything when I play. I think about how lucky I am to be playing music; I think about anything but what I'm playing.

You don't think about the solo you're in the process of constructing?

Subconsciously that's all happening. Yeah, I do think about that sort of thing, I guess, but it's not an analytical sort of process. If I make an attempt to construct a great solo, the craftsman in me can do that, but that's the last thing I want to do as an improviser. I just want it to be. I want it to happen.

The solo more or less constructs itself?

Exactly. And I spend almost all of my energy now as a player getting to the point where I can let go of my thoughts, and that's absolutely the most difficult part of being an improviser. I think that's much more relevant than saying, "I put my little finger here," and this and that.

Can you look back on a solo and analyze what you're doing theoretically?

I always feel funny when somebody comes up to me and says, "What kind of modes do you use?" or, "What scales do you use?" To me, that's the equivalent of someone asking, "What kind of verbs do you use?" The idea is to play music, and assuming you're a good musician, you've spent a lot of time learning the grammar of music which includes the knowledge of all those things. You can't know just a few modes or a few scales; you have to know all of them, and you have to get from one to the next without even thinking about it, without even blinking an eye. I understand all the technical details of improvising quite thoroughly. I don't see that as miraculous or anything special, other than I've spent the time to learn the grammar of improvising — just like a writer has spent the time to learn the grammar of English.

Some of your technique is fairly unorthodox — the way you hammer really hard with your left hand and sort of swish around with your picking hand.

[*Laughs*] That's a good way to put it.

Do you use a thin pick and fairly heavy-gauge strings?

Right. I don't think you'd want to use a thin pick with light-gauge strings. I've gone through unbelievable changes trying to get picks. I would buy a box of picks and only be able to use maybe ten out of a gross — all different brands. I prefer the Fender shape and pick with a rounded corner, so I hold it upside down. Also, the heavier the strings you use, almost without exception, the better the sound you'll get.

Did your picking technique come about through trial and error, or were you actually looking for a different sound?

I wasn't looking for a different type of sound, but a sound that had a vocal quality. To me, the very best players — like Wes Montgomery, George Benson, Pat Martino, Santana, Jimi Hendrix, Jim Hall — all have a sound that makes me think of someone singing. When I hear horns or people singing, I hear a legato sound. It's very rare that I hear a staccato sound. Since I couldn't pick very fast when I first started, I had to simulate the tempos that these guys in Kansas City were calling every night. That's where that sort of loose right hand started. But as it turned out that has evolved into a technique where I can get a lot of different kinds of phrasing without having to change my right arm. Playing with [drummer] Jack DeJohnette I noticed that he's totally relaxed as he plays, as loose as he can be. That's happened with me, too. You could come up behind me and just knock my arms off the instrument because I'm totally loose and relaxed.

Do you ever write things out purely from a theoretical standpoint without necessarily hearing a melody in your head, and then test them out to see how they sound?

Yeah, I do that for fun. Sometimes, just for an exercise, I'll write 12-tone rows and exercises based on those. They sound nice and everything, but I couldn't say that I've written tunes like that.

Do you have fairly big or small hands?

I have very small hands.

Does that have an influence on your choice of guitars?

None whatsoever. I think that's one of the biggest myths of all time. [Pianist] Keith Jarrett's hands are definitely not big, yet he can play more than almost anybody. I think there are some cases where big hands have helped a lot, like Tal Farlow or Jaco, who's got gigantic hands. I think it can help, but it's possible to play well with small hands.

What nonstandard tunings do you use?

One of my Guild acoustics is strung up in the high-strung Nashville tuning: The high *E* and *B* strings are the same as normal, then the bottom four strings are tuned up an octave. The *G* string is an .008, and the only wound string is the low *E*, which is a .021. I use that tuning for everything but the solo on "Phase Dance" on the *Pat Metheny Group*, as well as for "Sueño con Mexico," "Country Poem," and the title track of *New Chautauqua*. And I use it for an extra color a lot like on "Everyday (I Thank You)" on *80/81* way off in the distance.

What about the 12-string tunings?

Well, two of the 12-string tunings are more or less in the same family. They're based on keeping all the strings unwound, except for the lowest one. They range from an .008 down to an .018 unwound, and then I usually stick a .021 on the lowest string. They're tuned up in all kinds of strange ways. On "San Lorenzo" the top pair are two unison *F*'s, which is the *F* on the top line of the staff. The second pair is a *G* higher than the *F* and a fifth, a *C*. In other words, the first string is in unison, all the rest are fifths. The third pair is the same *F* as the first string but with a *B♭* a fifth below it. Fourth pair: an *E♭* a

whole step lower than the *F* and an *A♭* below it. Fifth: a *C* with an *F* a fifth below. And the sixth is *B♭* just below the *C* and an *E♭* under that. So the lowest *E♭* on the guitar would be written as the first line of the staff and the highest would be the *F* at the top of the staff. So the whole tuning is within one octave.

Do you have other 12-string tunings?

All the other tunings, like the one used on "Ice Fire" [*Watercolors*], are slight modifications of that tuning. I use the same gauge strings, but tune it to a different chord. Then I have a few weird 6-string tunings that usually involve something like a *D* tuning, but with the low string tuned weird. But I want to emphasize that my single-string electric playing is always in standard tuning.

What strings do you find hold up the best for these tunings?

I prefer D'Addario strings. Jimmy D'Addario has made me some special "Pat Metheny Deadwound" model strings [*laughs*]. This is weird to most people, but I prefer flatwound strings that are real old, to get that sort of thump sound. Then I brighten it up with the amp instead of using a real bright sound to start with. I don't like to hear my fingers squeaking on the strings, except on acoustic guitar, and then I love it.

Did you go after your present sound because that's what you heard in your head or did you want to sound unlike *other players?*

There was a time when I was anxious to establish my own sound, but I was never naive enough to think that it could come from a piece of equipment. That stuff always comes from inside. If I had to play through a Sears amp, you could still tell it was me. I think that's true of every good player. If you've gone to all the trouble of trying to establish your own kind of thing, it doesn't matter what you're playing on.

Can you foresee ever leaving music?

I suppose if I had a family and stuff I *might*, but even then I don't think so. I don't expect to be on the road 300 days a year when I'm 50 years old—I don't think if I kept this pace up I'd live to be 50. It's very taxing, difficult work. I just made a commitment to be a musician a long time ago, which still holds. And the process of becoming a musician is not an easy one, but I'm not going to break that commitment. If it requires that I spend the time I spend doing it, then that's what the requirement is. I'm spending the minimum amount of time I possibly can and still keep that commitment. And it just so happens that that minimum for me is 24 hours a day [*laughs*].

— WES MONTGOMERY —

BY RALPH J. GLEASON — JULY 1973

FRANK DRIGGS COLLECTION

THE FIRST TIME I heard Wes Montgomery play, it was like being hit by a bolt of lightning. Once he hit the guitar strings with his thumb, you could feel it in your gut anywhere within the reach of sound.

I heard a lot about Wes Montgomery before I ever saw him. His two brothers, Buddy and Monk, were in a group in San Francisco called the Mastersounds, and they kept saying, "Wait, wait until you hear Wes!" and they sure were right!

Wes came out to San Francisco and played with them on Sunday afternoon at the Jazz Workshop, and that was it. The club couldn't wait to have him back.

Eventually Wes moved to the Bay Area and played with his brothers. He also worked a long engagement with John Coltrane and Eric Dolphy at the Jazz Workshop, plus an appearance with them at the Monterey Jazz Festival, and then formed his own group.

For a while before he went out on his own, Wes lived up the street from me in Berkeley. It was a bizarre kind of feeling to look out the window in the middle of the day and see the world's greatest guitar player wandering down the street, but there he was. I got to know Wes a little (who ever knows anybody?) in those days, as he and I and his brothers put our heads together day after day trying to get the Montgomery Brothers, as a group, off and running. Despite Wes' genius that never did happen. He had to go out on his own to do that.

The interview which follows was done when he began to record under his own name, and it disclosed something to me of which I had not been aware: Wes was actually very insecure about his own playing and very worried that when it came his turn to solo night after night, he wouldn't be able to consistently maintain the standard he wanted. He really didn't think he was good enough to play with John Coltrane when he was offered a job by Trane (What a group that would have been!). It wasn't just the money, it was the fact that he couldn't think of himself as the leader in his field. He was always saying that he had played much better fifteen years before.

And of course, he never got the sound he wanted out of any amplifier, and spent thousands of dollars hassling with electronics. I don't believe that in his whole professional life he ever really got the kind of sound onstage that would have made him happy. The Fender people and everybody else must have been driven crazy.

It was easy to talk to Wes, but not when he saw a microphone. I deeply regret not succumbing to my original idea, which was to bug my living room so I could tape him without him knowing that his words were being recorded. I never got around to doing it; just one of those things.

There was one time when he was playing in a club on Broadway in San Francisco, Barney Kessel was playing in another, and Bola Sete was playing in a third. Each one of them had the other two guitar players in the audience for every show! I think they scheduled the sets to allow for it. And every guitar player in Northern California who wasn't working was busy running from one to another of those clubs all night long.

I took a young guitar player who was also a journalist with me one night to hear all three of them; his name was Jann Wenner [Rolling Stone's editor]. I don't think he's picked up a guitar since. In any case, he has never mentioned it to me!

Wes never took a lesson in his life. He thought all kinds of guitar players were better than he was, but the truth of the matter is that he will be remembered long, long after the other names are lost in the mists of history.

How long have you been playing the guitar?
I started in '43 when I was 19, right after I got married. I bought me an amplifier and guitar two or three months later. I used to play tenor [guitar], but it wasn't really playing. I've really gone into business since I got the 6-string, which was like starting all over.

How did you get interested in playing guitar?
Charlie Christian, like all other guitar players. There was no way out. That cat tore everybody's head up. I never saw him in my life, but he said so much on records. I don't care what instrument a cat played, if he didn't understand and feel the things Charlie Christian was doing, he was a pretty poor musician.

Did you hear any guitar players before him?
Reinhardt and Les Paul, those cats, but it wasn't anything you could call new, just guitar.

What was the first Charlie Christian record you heard?
"Solo Flight." Boy, that was too much! I still hear it. He was *it* for me. I didn't hear nobody else after that for about a year.

You taught yourself guitar?
Yeah. Charlie Christian's records. I listened to them real good, and I knew that everything done on his guitar could be done on mine, because I had a 6-string, so I just determined that I would do it. About six or eight months after I started playing I had taken all the solos off the record and got a job in a club just playing them. I'd play Charlie Christian's solos, then lay out. Then a cat heard me and hired me for the Club 440 (Indianapolis). I went on the stand and played the solos. The guys in the band helped me a lot about different tunes, intros, endings, and things that they had. They wired me up on all those, but after that, that was it.

You worked around Indianapolis from then on?
Well, I got pretty good and went on the road with a group. We starved. At that time I didn't realize that you'd work one gig in Kansas City, the next in Florida, and the next gig will be in Louisville. You know, a thousand miles a night. That was really tough, man.

Did you go out with other bands?
Hamp [Lionel Hampton] was the only big band I went with, '48–'50.

While you were running around the country with Hamp, did you hear any other guitarists you were interested in?
To me, all guitar players can play, because I know they're getting to where they're at. But, like one guy will come up like Tal Farlow. Tal came on the scene poppin' and burnin'. Well, instead of other guys getting their thing closed, they'd jump on Tal Farlow. Now, he can carry them for a long time, but when they get through they haven't done a thing by themselves. It's such a hard instrument that somebody has got to get things out for them to go by, evidently, because it's hard to get something on your own. It's a very hard instrument to accept, because it takes years to start working with it, that's first, and it looks like everybody else is moving on the instrument but you. Then when you find a cat that's really playing, you always find that he's been playing a long time, you can't get around it.

What do you want to do with the guitar, where do you want to go with it?
I've thought about it, but I'm so limited. Like playing octaves was just a coincidence. And it's still such a challenge, like chord versions, block chords like cats play on piano. There are a lot of things that can be done with it, but each is a field of its own, and like I said, it takes so much time to develop all your technique. Say if you wanted to play a chord like you would a melodic phrase, there's no telling how long it would take you to do it. I used to have headaches every time I played octaves, because it was extra strain, but the minute I'd quit I'd be all right. I don't know why, but it was my way, and my way just backfired on me. But now I don't have headaches when I play octaves. I'm just showing you how a strain can capture a cat and almost choke him, but after a while it starts to ease up because you get used to it.

You don't use a pick, do you?
No. That's one of my downfalls, too. In order to get a certain amount of speed you should use a pick, I think. A lot of cats say you don't have to play fast, but being able to play fast can cause you to phrase

better. But I just didn't like the sound. I tried it for about two months. Didn't use the thumb at all. But after two months I still couldn't use the pick, so I said I'd go ahead and use the thumb. But then I couldn't use the thumb either, so I asked myself which are you going to use? I liked the tone better with the thumb, but the technique better with the pick, but I couldn't have them both.

Did you ever run into any of the classical guitar players, like Segovia?

No, and I don't want to, because these cats will scare you. It doesn't make any difference that they're playing classic, but there's so much *guitar.* Like if you hear a classical guitar player, he'll make you feel like, "What're you playing the thing you're playing for? *This* is what you should be playing." He might make you want to back up, and I don't think anyone should try to get to you. But I imagine I'd be the same way with a classical guitar player. But if a jazz player is really playing, the classical player will have to respect him.

Is playing the guitar still kicks for you?

Yes, it is. But now I don't have the drive I used to. Like the time I was with Hamp, that was the time I had the best feeling of "getting in," of bringing it right out, because it was right under my hand, but I didn't pay it any mind. You could be fooling with the thing, and nobody is doing it, but you're not either, and you've got it right under your hand. That's the way I was. Later on, a thousand people said, "Why don't you try finishing it?" Well, I said, "I'll be darned." Like I'm 38 now.

If you had to name a half-dozen of your favorite guitarists, who would they be?

Barney Kessel is one. He's got a lot of feeling, he's got a good conception of chords in a jazz manner. And he's trying to play a little flamenco. He's trying to do a lot of things, not just standing still at one particular level. He's trying to get away from the guitar phrase, to get into the horn phrase. Tal Farlow strikes me as a different cat altogether. To me, he doesn't have as much feeling as Barney Kessel, but he's got more drive in his playing, and his technique along with his drive is pretty exciting. And he's got a better conception of modern chords than the average guitar player. Sometimes he gets kind of sloppy like a lot of guitar players, that's why a lot of cats have put him down. But I guess nobody has it all, but he's got a lot of *drive,* though, and he's so fast. Now, Jimmy Raney is just the opposite of Tal Farlow. It seems like they have the same ideas, the same changes, the same type runs, the same kind of feeling, but Jimmy Raney

is so smooth he does it without a mistake, a real soft touch, it's the touch he's got. Django Reinhardt, naturally, he's in a different thing altogether. To me, a lot of guitar players don't go to a particular place, they just sit down and play a whole lot of guitar, and Reinhardt is one of those cats. And I think Charlie Byrd is also a new cat on the scene that is trying to make the switch, trying to get into both bags at the same time, and he's got a lot of recognition from it, but it's a hard thing to do. I think that's why he came in like he did, because of a little flamenco and jazz vein along with unamplified guitar.

Would it suit your temperament to sit there like Freddie Green [with Count Basie] and not take solos?

It would be all right, but I don't know that many chords. I'd be loaded if I knew that many. I'd probably go join a band and just play rhythm, man, 'cause he's not just playing chords, he's playing a *lot* of chords. But, that's not my aim. My aim is to move from one vein to the other without any trouble. Like, if you're going to take a melody line or a counterpoint or unison line with another instrument, do that, then maybe drop out at a certain point, then maybe next time you'll play phrases and chords, or maybe you'll take an octave or something. That way you'll have a lot of variations there. The only difference is if you can control each one of them. Still, the biggest thing to me is keeping a feeling, regardless what you play. So many cats lose their feeling at various times, not through the whole tune, but at various times, and it causes them to have to build up and drop down, and you can feel it.

Why are there so few guitar players today?

I think it's like, the average person thinks he wants to play guitar, then he goes as far as, "I think I'll buy me a ten- or twelve-dollar guitar and mess around to see if I like it." Then they find out, after maybe the first week or two, their fingers feel like pins are sticking into them, but they can't stop, because once they stop it'll heal up. I think a lot of people don't realize that it's just crises you've got to go through. I think another reason is when they think about playing guitar they pick it up and feel they should automatically play what they are thinking. Then a guy thinks he'll go get himself a teacher, and the teacher has to do everything, and they won't try to do anything for themselves. But they are the one who has to learn guitar, because a teacher can only show you so much. You have melodic lines and chords, and you have the neck before you can do either one. It takes a long time, and you have to think ahead to your limits before you can do anything. Then you've got to figure if you want to slur up a note, then you've got to come back, so you've got to know where you're going. These things play so big of a part that you get discouraged when nothing happens.

It's like playing pool, isn't it?

Well of course I'm a pretty sharp pool player, but the guitar is just a hard instrument. A cat will listen to a guy that *is* playing and think he can do that, but he won't study on how long that cat's been playing. Then he gets discouraged because he can't even get two notes out. Then he says he'll struggle with it himself, and maybe he'll find out in six months that he still can't make a line, then he feels like he's a dumb cat. But when you find guitar players that are playing, you'll find out that at one time they never cared if they never played, they were going to keep on until they did. After a period of time the beginning player will hear a little difference in his playing, and that little inspiration is enough to go further, and the first thing you know you won't back out. The biggest problem is getting started. Then later every time you hear guitar players everybody plays more than you. And those things are not very inspirational, they're pretty discomforting. And then somebody says, "Why don't you put that thing down, you're not doing anything with it." Well, that's no help. And you'll find more people against you than for you, until you get started. Then you'll find more with you than against you.

— STEVE MORSE —

BY JAS OBRECHT – AUGUST 1982 & OCTOBER 1989

S TEVE MORSE MAKES every note count. One moment he soars across the fingerboard with amazing speed, and in the next lulls listeners with slow, poignant phrases. On record and in concert with the Dregs, Steve proves himself a master of tones and a stunning technician, with an emphasis on enunciation. Stylistically he creates lush crossbreeds of diverse elements, delivering heavy metal, Baroque/classical, free-form jazz/rock, bluegrass, chicken pickin' country, Irish jigs, and breakdowns with equal energy and finesse.

The main writer for the Dregs (critically acclaimed as one of the finest fusion bands), Morse composes instrumentals that, he says, are "electronic chamber music." Carefully worked out and orchestrated, the tunes become fast-paced, seamless dialogues in the hands of the five Dregs, who play together as a band rather than an aggregation of soloists. In fact, all of the Dregs — bassist Andy West, drummer Rod Morgenstein, keyboardist T Lavitz, violinist/guitarist Mark O'Connor, and Morse — are sufficiently virtuosic to record as soloists on their own.

Born in Hamilton, Ohio, on July 28, 1954, Steve Morse grew up in Michigan and moved to Georgia during his early teens. He had already played guitar for five years when he met Andy West at Augusta's Richmond Academy. The two high school sophomores gathered a keyboardist and singer to form a rock group called Dixie Grits. One day Steve chanced

to see classical guitarist Juan Mercadel perform, an event that changed his life: "I said, 'God, this is too much — I can't believe it.' I found out he was teaching at the University of Miami (UM), so I started concocting my scheme to get into college." Expelled from the Academy for refusing to cut his hair, Steve signed up for classes at a local college, which enabled him to transfer to UM. "After the Dixie Grits broke up," he adds, "all that was left was Andy and me, so we were the *dregs*."

The University of Miami had one of the most innovative jazz departments in the country, with a faculty that included guitarist Pat Metheny, bassist Jaco Pastorius, and drummer Narada Michael Walden. Steve became a jazz guitar major whose principal instrument was classical guitar. He formed the school's first rock ensemble for credit, enlisting classmates Andy West, Rod Morgenstein, and violinist Allen Sloan. Naming themselves the Dixie Dregs, the musicians worked at local venues playing Allman Brothers and Mahavishnu Orchestra material mixed with original tunes. As part of a class project, the Dixie Dregs recorded *The Great Spectacular* (currently out of print, this album has become a collector's item). Steve Davidowski was added on keyboards, and following graduation the band moved to Augusta.

During the mid-'70s the Dixie Dregs took their fusion of jazz, rock, classical, country, and bluegrass to clubs, gathering a devoted following. While playing in Nashville, they impressed Sea Level keyboardist

Chuck Leavell and former Allman Brothers road manager Twiggs Lyndon, Jr., who called Capricorn president Phil Walden on their behalf. Walden signed the Dixie Dregs to his label in late 1976.

Free Fall, issued the following spring, was the band's powerful debut album. Asked why the album featured all instrumental music, Morse would respond, "In my compositions I try to be real conscious of not boring people and keeping them interested. This music is more challenging to write and play, which is why it's more rare." In late 1977 Davidowski was replaced by Mark Parrish, an original member of Dixie Grits. With this lineup the group recorded *What If,* which was again characterized by precise, rapid changes and instrumental virtuosity. The group's last album for Capricorn, *Night of the Living Dregs,* was released in 1979. The live tracks on side two, recorded at the 1978 Montreux Jazz Festival, prompted the band's first Grammy nomination. According to press accolades at the time, the Dixie Dregs were giving new meaning to the term "southern music."

In 1980 the group switched to the Arista label and soon changed their name to the Dregs. T Lavitz took over keyboards, and their next two albums — *Dregs of the Earth* and *Unsung Heroes,* both produced by Morse, did well in the charts and earned Grammy nominations for Best Instrumental Performance. Meanwhile, Steve began placing high in various music polls, including the *Guitar Player* Readers Poll in which he became the five-time winner of the heaviest category of all — Best Overall Guitarist.

In addition to Dregs LPs, Steve has appeared on record or stage with Steve Walsh, Triumph, Lynyrd Skynyrd, and Kansas. "Somewhere I also played a part on a Liza Minnelli album," he says, "and I was on a Christian-label album for a nice guy named Rob Cassels. I played a lot on that." In addition to being a first-rate player, Steve is also a fine teacher, as well as a professional airline pilot, a career he actually took on fulltime in 1987 until his love of music got him out of the cockpit and back in the spotlight.

[August 1982]
You play very fast, yet you don't use hammer-ons and pull-offs.

I consciously stopped playing that way. I believe it was during the Jimmy Page era. The Alvin Lee and Jimi Hendrix licks could be played fast without picking, by just hammering. I was working on some Jimmy Page lick that I may have misunderstood, but for some reason I could not play it with hammer-ons. I had to pick across strings. I realized then that my picking technique was almost zero. It was at a time when we would play a gig every two months when the garage band could get a dance to play for free, so it didn't hurt me to stop playing for a few months to get it together. I started a new approach to playing the guitar: I said, "All right, I'm going to pick every note." Also, I wanted to play some classical sounding things, and they didn't work with the hammer-ons. It became clear to me that to do other than blues licks, you have to pick every note.

Being left-handed and holding the guitar like a right-handed player, you use your weaker hand to pick.

True. But I play left-handed: My left hand is fingering the guitar. I think that's the best way to play. The first thing I learned was to finger chords. My right hand held a triangular, shingle-type pick that I would just brush across the strings, so the coordination problem instantly was with the left hand. I knew that Paul McCartney played the way he did because he was left-handed, but to me it seemed best to be using my left fingers on the fretboard. I saw no reason to complicate my life by playing backwards. When you're just learning, what does it matter which hand does which?

How did you redevelop your picking dexterity?

I started from zero. I bought a metronome, set it on the lowest setting, and went dunt, dunt, dunt — one stroke up and one down. I kept speeding it up until finally I was about at three-quarters of the speed I could play at before, but I had more ability. I've never been able to play as fast as when I did hammer-ons, which is sort of disappointing. But I can do more things quicker.

Do you have exercises for increasing speed?

Nothing spectacular, although I do have exercises. I pick two-note patterns and triplet patterns across strings. A triplet pattern is a group of three notes per beat, all three notes on one string. You go down, up, down, and then cross the string to an up, down, up pattern. You get the feeling of picking up or down on the downbeat. Say if you do four notes on a string — down, up, down, up, and then down on the next string — it's real predictable. If you do triplet patterns, your pick will always have to be jumping the gap in an odd way since it reverses each time. It automatically gives you something weird there. You also get the same kind of thing when you pick scales across the strings.

How do you practice scales?

I do all the major scale modes in three different

positions, starting with my index, second, third, or foutth finger on the tonic. For any scale or mode, there's at least three different ways you can finger it starting on the same note and still stretch no more than one fret between your fingers. Say the *A* major scale on the 5th fret. If you start with your first finger, the first finger plays every note that falls on the 5th fret. The second finger plays every note on the 6th fret, the third finger every note on the 7th fret, and your pinkie plays every note on the 9th fret. There isn't any on the 8th, so the pinkie plays a one-fret stretch. Then do the same thing, only start with your second finger on the tonic. In this case there are no stretches at all because your first finger goes down to the 4th fret. You go across and it all fits. When you start with your pinkie, you stretch on one fret. Those little stretches shouldn't affect you because you do them all the time when you play, anyway. I do scales up and down the neck, starting picking up, starting picking down. I got this routine from Stan Samole, an instructor at the University of Miami.

Do you do anything else to warm up before shows?

Especially before a show I want to warm up my left hand, too. So I do vibrato exercises on every finger by itself — including the pinkie — pulling down on the string, holding each finger in vibrato for four beats. Then I do the same thing pulling up on, say, the third or second string. If my right hand is tired, I stop picking and do these vibrato and pulling exercises. The important part about warming up is not to do it too hard right at the beginning — do it slow and easy, then work up. You want to get your muscles warmed up, and then let them relax and loosen up. Then go and do it some more. In three to five minutes you can get warmed up enough to break for about 30 seconds or a minute. Then you can practice for as long as you want, as long as you mix it up. Don't do too much of one thing.

Is it best to practice new lines or techniques slowly before trying them full-speed?

I do something more like practice it slow 80% of the time, and then 20% of the time try to do it for speed. It's important to try to do it at speed, but keep going back to slow where you can play it perfectly. If you just play it all slowly, then you won't have the experience of doing it fast. If you do it all fast, you'll make too many mistakes and be sloppy.

Can you offer ideas on how to avoid repetitious soloing patterns?

Sure. The easiest way for me to describe it would be the key tone theory: Any progression has key notes that are going to have to change. Let's use a primitive example: Going from a rock and roll *C5* [a *C* chord without a 3rd] to *A* major. Your first and only key tone change is *C* to *C#*. Almost any note you hit in the *C* scale — except for the *B♭* — will work over the *A*. One of your main concerns will be to change all the *C*s to *C#*s in your mind. Right away this means that you don't have to use any scales or anything; you can just play melodic lines in *C*, and then continue right from where you left off using the same notes as you were. Just avoid the *B♭* and change the *C* to *C#*.

How could you avoid patterns while soloing over a blues progression in, say, *G*?

I think most people would play in *G* over the IV and V chords — *C* and *D*. That works mainly because they are used to hearing it. If it was a country-type blues progression, you would want to hit all the notes that are in the chords, rather than sitting on the *G* over the *D* chord. A key problem people have is when they think of a different chord, they think of a different position instead of realizing that right in their hand are the notes that will fit every single chord on the guitar — *without moving their hand.* Within four or five frets — anywhere, in any position — you can play lines that will fit all the chords. So when it goes to *C* from the *G* chord, don't slide up to *C* and play blues in *C*. Keep playing your position in *G*, but use an *E♭* to *E♮* a *B♭* to *C*, and things like that that are right there in the third position. When it goes to *D*, do the same thing: Follow the chord without doing a parallel of what you did in *G*. Practice this when you are jamming on any progression. By not moving your hand, you will be forced to realize what kind of hand positions are required to cover different chords. This is oversimplified, but it would be a start for a lot of people.

Is there an inherent mood in every key and mode?

More in every mode than every key. Chords suggest moods, but I'm not one of those people who thinks an *F* is a whole lot different than an *E*, pitch-wise. A mode, to me, is just a convenient way of describing a group of key tones. Once I understood what a Dorian mode was, I would never think of it as part of the major scale. I would just think of it as a *minor flat 7 regular 6th* scale. That's it. Never another thought about it. Of course that has a certain mood. I think of the Mixolydian as a *major flat 7* scale. I never worry about which major scale it's related to. With modes it's best to just think about what they sound like rather than what major scale they came from, although it is good to know where they come from so you can conceptualize what notes they are in case you forget. But the easiest way is just to know what they contain — that this is a dominant 7th with a major 3rd or minor 3rd — that kind of thing.

What aspects of music theory should guitarists learn?

I would place a lot of weight on where you want to take your music. A lot of people freak out at that attitude that says, "Wait a minute, I'm just into music. I don't want to think about it." But in reality it does matter. If you want to be a professional musician, you have to prepare yourself for a lot of different things. Start from the general and go to the specific. Decide what you would *love* to do most of all, because loving to do it is going to sustain you through some of those moments, days, or weeks [*laughs*]. If you want to play in a band that does progressive stuff or be a studio player, learn as much as possible. A studio musician would want a little different direction — an emphasis on ear training and sightreading on the spot — whereas in a band you don't have to emphasize the reading, although it is a learning tool and you should know how to do it. If you want to write, then learn a lot about composition and theory. That's the route I took: Learning about music and how to write it. Maybe all musicians should learn some more about business!

Is the music business what people commonly expect it to be?

I doubt anything is. When you first have a conception, it's bound to be a lot more optimistic, which is fine! Everyone's high expectations for the future are what make people tick. For me, there have been a lot of unexpected good things about playing, and some unexpected bad things.

What are some of the drawbacks?

People are going find that it's hard to get work, and there's an incredible amount of people trying to get it. And when you do get work, a lot of time it's repetitive and unenjoyable. I always had a different idea of what it's going to be like traveling, seeing new things. When I learned to drive a car, I couldn't wait to. Then after you've been driving a while, you want to hand the wheel to somebody else. It's the same way being on the road: I like to do it and it's a necessary part of my existence, but it's easy to get too much of it. When you're in a band, you'll find that people try and make you work longer than you want to because their income depends on it — promoters, managers, agents, even some band members. Bands are usually in two categories: They can't get enough

work, or they can't get enough days off. I've never seen anybody totally happy!

What is the most difficult part of your repertoire?

The rock stuff is the easiest because it's definitely the most natural for me as a guitar player. The solos are always real easy to play, partly because the sound of the amp is full and the beat is prevalent. The sort of in-between, complex, jazz-rocky kind of stuff is harder to play, something like "Chips Ahoy" [*Industry Standard*] which is in a nebulous category of music. Some of the newer country-type things I've written are the hardest because the amplifier setting is completely clear. If I hit a note sloppy, it will just go *pttt* and it's gone, whereas when you have distortion and hit a note sloppy, you hear a little weirdness, but you've still got a note. The picking patterns I'm making up for lines are also getting more and more ridiculous in terms of playing; they are not comfortable at all! I write lines on the guitar for the sake of the line, and then I see if they're playable.

Do you put them on paper?

No, I do them slow. I'll be playing a solo and say, "Wow, that would be great if I could make this line go down while this one went up." Eventually I get to where I can do it, and then the next thing I know we're learning the song. Then *always* it goes up two notches in tempo by the time we record it and play it live. It becomes faster than I ever thought I would play it when I wrote it, so those turn out to be some of the hardest things. "Pride O' the Farm" [*Dregs of the Earth*] and "Where's Dixie?" are two of the really hard ones.

Can you play everything you can hear?

Oh, God, no! I don't know anybody who really can.

Of all the styles you play, which is the most challenging?

Classical guitar, because there's absolutely no room for error. I definitely use the traditional approach. I learned from Juan Mercadel. It was pretty standard technically, but he showed me that the guitar could do powerful things as well as beautiful things. He was a very powerful player. Classical guitar is pretty conducive to doing things in standard technique — especially the left-hand position, although I wouldn't think twice about assuming a very awkward-looking position to make a certain chord that couldn't be done otherwise or to continue the melody and hit a bass note at the same time. Who cares if you have to do something weird to make it sound right? I use this approach because I think it works. The hard part is remembering all the unusual configurations your hand goes into, and if you do make one little mistake, you blow it.

Are you self-critical?

[*Laughs*] Extremely!

Have you ever lost your confidence onstage?

That's a good question. I think in order to be fair, I'd have to say yes. When that happens, I keep playing. If I make a mistake, I usually wait a few seconds and then ignore it if I can. But if I have to freak out about it, I try to put it on about a five-second delay, so that a good portion of the people won't know and I won't call attention to it. If I really have to turn around and curse out loud, I'll do it about ten seconds after I make the mistake or at the end of the tune.

Do you have to be in a certain state to play your best?

Georgia's my best state [*laughs*]. Everybody's needs and standards are different. I have to be totally straight, completely confident, and perfectly warmed up. In other words, it's a real rare circumstance in which I'm pleased with my playing. But at all the gigs I play at, I am straight and at least warmed up somewhat. My confidence will depend on how well my playing is at that moment. If the set's been going good, I'll keep playing better. If it's bad, I'll be trying a bit too hard to make up for it and I might keep making mistakes. This is on an introspective level, though. I have to emphasize that while this is happening, I still have a good time onstage. I don't make faces or throw down my guitar. I just keep on smiling because people have come to hear the band. Our first responsibility is to them, and I try to keep my own hypercritical attitude away from the audience because I don't think they want to see that.

Do you work out solos before recording them?

No, because every time I've tried to come up with some kind of musical concept, it turns out that there's something that would fit a little bit better that comes naturally. My approach to soloing is just play naturally and take takes. When you get one that sounds good, keep it. Go ahead and get another one that sounds good, and keep that. Sort of figure out what it is about it that sounds good — why does it feel good? If there's a way to make it better by changing a little bit more, do it. Otherwise, just keep one of the good ones. As most people will probably agree, your best solos generally come out of your first five to ten takes. A lot of times the very first ones will be some of the best.

Of all your recorded solos, which are your favorites?

A lot of my solos are real short, because we don't want to bore people. I like the solos in "Chips Ahoy" and "Bloodsucking Leeches" off of *Industry Standard*. "Hand Jig" from *Freefall*, the "Hereafter" solo on *Dregs of the Earth*. I also liked "Day 444" on *Unsung Heroes*. Some of my favorite solos are on the long, slow tunes where there's room to take a few choruses.

What is your philosophy of soloing?

A solo should divert attention away from the repetition of the melodies. That is, it's got to be a new section, but I like to use familiar underlying chord changes. In other words, it gives you something to focus on. We keep a lot of our solos short for the same reason you keep your eyes moving on the road: It keeps you from falling asleep. In your mind's eye, when you're listening to a record, it's good to keep it moving, too. As a listener, I appreciate it when I don't hear too much of one thing.

Is there much improvisation in your show?

Well, all the tunes are written with specific parts. There are little fills — three or four beats — that can be played one way or just like the record. A lot of times those are done in sync, but solos are improvisation. Basically, most of the improvisation with this band comes in the soloing and talking between tunes.

How do you compose songs?

I write them on guitar or piano late at night when there are no distractions. I start with some germ of an idea that I like a lot and believe in because I'm going to have to work with it for a couple of months, on and off. The main thing is getting an idea that will stand up to the test of repeated playing and listening. It could be a chord progression, a bass line, a guitar lick, or a complete piano section. On piano you generally come up with melody and bass line all at once. The hard part is continuing after that start, because you can't just get another idea that you love and smash into it. You have to get one that fits. You have to keep getting ideas and throwing them out.

When you present a new tune to the band, do you know what everyone's parts are?

Yes. If I don't have the ending for a tune, it doesn't mean I won't bring it into rehearsal. We just won't go past that point. I'll say, "We'll work on it up to this section, then we'll finish that tomorrow. Now let's go on to another tune."

So up to that point, the only place those parts have come together has been in your imagination.

Yeah, but when you don't use a tape recorder, you have to be ready for instantaneous editing. I'll show T [Lavitz] a keyboard part, and once he gets it good enough to play by himself while I'm playing something different, I can realize whether it's going to work or not. Then I'll say, "You know that note I just showed you? Well, change it to a C#." I do that a lot — little changes. The key is being able to quickly make changes while you are in rehearsal. Every once in a while I'll run into a problem where I'll say, "Wow, I've got to work this out," and everybody will leave the room or start making phone calls. It really slows down rehearsal, so I try to have it pretty much together before I go in.

How adamant are you about having parts the way you hear them?

I'm pretty bad about that. The reason I do hear it in my head a certain way is because I like it that way. I don't keep playing something over and over again in my head that I don't like. I wouldn't ask the guys in the band to play something I didn't like, so unless somebody proposes a change that sounds better, I'll keep saying, "That's fine, but let's try it the way I had in mind. "There are no big scenes or anything like that. Rod will do the most experimenting because he does what he feels and naturally comes up with the right thing. He knows what to do by instinct.

How can bands make optimum use of rehearsal time?

Let me paint an example. Here's a band where three of the guys work day jobs. They want to get together for three hours twice a week. It would be a good experience for whoever has got the tunes in mind to write out the parts. It would help them and make the rehearsal go fast — you can hear right away what it's going to sound like. The drawback to that is that the musicians who read music will keep on wanting to read, and they won't learn it. Either write out charts or prepare tapes with individual parts, so that most of your rehearsal time is spent trying variations or different arrangements rather than learning the licks themselves. Avoid distractions! Take out the phone. If you have business to discuss, take care of it first thing and as quickly as possible. Get it out of the way at a scheduled time, and then go to it.

During a decade when vocals have ruled the charts, why have you stayed so long with instrumental music?

Just because I like to play guitar. I started off just wanting to play, and obviously if you do instrumentals, you're going to *play*. But if you're in a band with vocals, you're going to have to do a lot of background, background, background, solo, and then background. Usually the words change, but not the music so much, so you get a lot of repetition. It's fun, but it's not as much fun as doing what we do. That's why we try to have a variety of styles, too. I like to work hard when I'm onstage, stay busy. I owe it to the audience — especially lately, when I look at some of the ticket prices. They are the ones who paid for it.

Is the guitar an unlimited instrument?

It will be once they develop a good interface to synthesizers, once the guitar can be translated into digital electricity. I'm sure that day is just around the corner.

Do you feel the days of the standard guitar's popularity are numbered?

No. There's always a place for something that's simple and does a good job — that's the electric guitar, the electric bass. They are cheap instruments that will provide a lot of music. There's no way they're going to be outmoded. You'll see bands playing synthesizer guitar and bass forever, I'm sure. But still, it's going to come down to the raw instrument — it's the touch. It's obviously the player that makes the difference. You see articles asking Van Halen how he gets his sound. Well, it's him who gets the sound, not the guitar.

Do you first imagine a tone and then try to find it, or does the equipment suggest the tone?

I pretty much try to get it in my mind. Like for a country thing, I know I want no distortion. I want more high end and less midrange. For rock and roll I want more midrange if I'm playing low, more bass if I'm playing high, or total screech if I want that effect. I'd say it's both. You get ideas from your equipment. But you also know if you're doing something complex or if you're playing more than one note at a time, you can't have too much distortion.

Let's discuss a few of your techniques. How do you chicken pick?

Some of my country stuff is an imitation Western swing style, and some of it is that chicken pickin'. I try to get the chicken pickin' sound by muting the strings slightly with my right hand. Most all the time I keep the heel of my right hand on the strings that I'm not playing. That keeps them from ringing, which is real important in high-volume situations. For chicken pickin', I bring that hand down even farther to slightly mute the strings that I am playing. I also choke the string with the pick, similar to the way you would to get a harmonic out — you simultaneously hit the string with a pick *and* the finger that's next to it. I do a little of that and a little muting, combined with excessively chromatic blues country licks.

How are your controls set?

I have the amp with minimum distortion and a little bit more high end. To get that chicken pickin' sound, I use a midrange-sounding pickup; there are several combinations on my guitar that will do that. On a typical guitar like a Les Paul, that would be the lead pickup turned down to about half. On a Tele you might try the middle pickup switch. Then as you get higher up the neck, you want to switch to the lead pickup on the Tele to get more highs. For the kind of Western swing style I use, which is liberally diluted with my own excessively chromatic approach [laughs], I go to more of a clear, high-end, piercing sound with a little bit of reverb. On most any guitar, that would be a combination of the lead and bass pickups turned down, with some reverb and a little bit of extra high end. That gives it that ringing sound.

In concert and at the end of the recording of "Conversation Piece" you double-pick sixteenth-notes.

There I use a bass pickup and a lot of distortion. I pick every note up and down, which is what my hand automatically does. It gives it percussion and helps it come out clearly. I use my standard picking approach, which is to keep dead all the strings that I'm not using. By muting the strings you aren't using, picking every note, and selecting the proper pickup for the part of the guitar you're playing on, you can still get a pretty clear sound while having a lot of distortion. I like distortion because it fattens the sound, but I also like to hear what I'm doing.

In a live solo, you play three different parts simultaneously.

It's sort of like a little illusion of three parts. I'll play a bass note — say, once every bar — with my right-hand thumb while fingering the note with my left-hand thumb, so the thumbs are playing bass. The fingers of my left hand are trilling between two notes, creating sort of a constant rhythm and suggesting a chord between those two notes and the bass notes. Then I play some melody notes by fingering up high on the guitar with my right-hand index finger and plucking with my thumb or third finger of my right hand. It sounds a lot more weird than it is. There's another thing I do where once every beat I play chords with my left hand by hammering down real hard and then holding them with a little bit of vibrato — this sustains them better than if you hit them straight on. I keep these chords moving back and forth, and then play a melody on the bass strings up near the very top of the fingerboard, once again picking with my thumb or third finger while fretting with

my index finger. I sometimes do this in "Cruise Control."

Do you have any formulas for vibrato?

It depends on what position I'm in. Down low I can use just my fourth finger alone. But generally I back up whatever finger is doing the vibrato with another finger if it's no problem to do so. Playing night after night, you want to save as much of your skin as possible. The only reason I get sore is from doing a lot of big bends. Two shows a night will get my fingers real sore. I wear my guitar low because the natural hand position for doing vibrato is clamped with your thumb over the top, whereas for classical guitar you want your thumb behind the neck. There you would want a high position.

How do you hold a pick?

I play with the side, which is a little bit more predictable than the point. I use two fingers and a thumb on the pick, so I have a lot of gripping surface. There's no way I can drop my pick unless I'm asleep.

Do you ever use just fingers or a combination of fingers and flatpick for country leads?

On the fast stuff I use just a pick. On something like the intro to "Ice Cakes" I am picking with my fingers and thumb, actually pulling the strings up like funk bass players do. The intro to "Ridin' High" on the new album starts without a pick. I'm pulling the strings up and letting them slap against the fingerboard — that's pretty radical technique. The solo in "Where's Dixie?" is a good example of the difference between plucking and picking: The first half of the solo is plucked with my thumb and middle finger. When I recorded that, I held my pick out of the way in my index finger so that I wouldn't develop a technique in the studio that I couldn't use live. Then in the middle of the solo I go to using a pick and different pickup settings, so it almost sounds like two different guitar players. Plucking actually sounds the best, but I can't do it fast or for too long because it tears my skin off.

Do you have advice as to how musicians can survive the road with health and chops intact?

Oh, yeah, I got plenty of that! Keep your lifestyle matched to your income. When you take away the worry of money, you have a lot less worries. Don't overdo it! If people are paying to see you, or if for any reason you are passing yourself off as a professional, then stay straight so you can practice and stay on top of it. Don't let people down who have come to see you, or else they won't come back. I have to practice a lot to stay loose — if I miss a day, it shows.

In the process of traveling and waiting to play, it's easy to not find the time to practice, especially if you party after the gig. It's fun to be on the road, but whatever you do, you have to practice. I practice two hours a day on technique and mix up some playing with it, either working on writing or going over lines I may have messed up the night before. If you have personal relationships, you've got to be straight with yourself and the person you're involved with. Realize that being apart is going to put a big strain on your relationship. For me, the only cure is to stay in contact by phone every day. That takes money, which requires that you be even tighter with yourself. That means you've got to pick the right place to eat at the right time and don't order too much — and you've got to say no to just about every party offer that comes up. But the reward is that when you get up onstage, you know that you've got it together.

Can success endanger artistic skills?

Yeah, you run the risk of getting shitty. When you get enough money where you don't have to work, it has got to take away some of the incentive, no matter how dedicated you are. When somebody becomes a *rich man* from doing something and then he plays something more simple and it makes him even bigger, he is rewarded for doing less as a guitarist. It's the 13-year-old girls who buy the records in mass quantities, so the guitarists who make huge amounts of money are in vocal bands. Think about the psychological conditioning that starts to happen: I do less, I make more. It doesn't matter. Nobody notices. The more poppy the band becomes, the less musicians there are. Certain days I'm real bitter about our lack of success, but other times I know this is the right way. My big gripe is with the way the radio stations program the listeners: It's all aimed at the pre-adolescent, everything. I'm proud to be in an underground band. If we ever do make it, I wish that people wouldn't hate us for it. We'd like to make it without being a letdown to the people.

What would you like to accomplish in the future?

I would really like to see the band be recognized as a success by those people in the business who don't know anything about music. I would like to show people that we did it as the Dregs. Personally, I would like to be remembered as somebody who writes and plays electric chamber music that moves and appeals to everyone. The guitar was just one of the instruments involved in that.

[October 1989]

What would you have a would-be Morse clone take from you?

Let me answer by example. I'm influenced by all these guitarists, but I'm more influenced by their accomplishments than their note selections. Pat Metheny was a big influence on me. I never strive to get his tone exactly or his sense of composition, but I admire his individuality. Same with John McLaughlin: I very much admire his personality and individuality. I admire Jeff Watson's drive and energy level. Eric Johnson is incredible, too. Vinnie Moore is another great guy who has that same kind of Eric Johnson attitude — you know, really mellow but very, very able, which I like. It's like those Ninja guys: They're real polite and everything, but you know they could break your neck in a second. The things that motivate you should be your influences, rather than the end product. I would like people to be influenced by my attitude more than my note selection. My note selections are the result of everything.

Do you know of many guitarists who are terrifyingly good?

Yes, a huge number of them. Guitar has attracted some very able personalities. They're starting young and getting serious young. As far as the guitar technique, it's a great, great step forward to have so many varieties. And of course with that come fads that seem kind of limited to me.

What fads are you referring to?

Well, for instance, the guitar being used as a single-note instrument for doing very fast runs, as opposed to being used in a very well-rounded, capable-of-anything kind of approach. I would prefer to see the next generation of guitarists be equal to keyboard players in terms of musical understanding and composition and polyphony. Obviously, it's impossible for a guitarist to be as polyphonic as a keyboardist, because at any given time you're dealing with six strings versus a possibility of ten notes on a keyboard. But I think it's healthy to have such a large number of guitarists eager to learn new techniques and to play proficiently at something — anything.

Are guitar schools a good thing?

Definitely. In fact, even if there were just a tree out in the middle of the field where people went every Thursday night just to get together and play and exchange licks, that would be beneficial. The fact that there are meeting places for musicians to have cultural exchange is significant, and it just accelerates the process.

What are the advantages of doing guitar clinics?

It keeps me in touch with the people who pay for my breakfast, and that's very important for me. Instead of approaching my career as looking for that one big break, I'm totally the other way around. I don't even care what the album sells. At one time I did, maybe in the first week it was coming out, and then I said, "Wait a second! What are you doing, Steve? Is there something you could do to change that, besides what you're already doing?" I said, "no," I forgot about it, and I started thinking about the music and the tour. And it's been a happy moment ever since I realized that. My business is in repeat business. I do my very best every time I tackle a project, and the people who are exposed to it reward me by coming back and buying the next one, if they like it. That's why these clinics are very special. It gives me a chance to give something back, because I can reach a lot more people than if I gave lessons.

There are some definite messages that I want to pass on. Things like, a guy shouldn't expect to be in one band and make it big and have enough money to live for the rest of his life. That happens to one out of literally ten-million people in the world. The fact is, you've got to be broad-based, very well educated, and you've got to be good with people just to get by in the business. I'm not discouraging people from getting into the business, but I'm trying to make it a realistic evaluation. Because reading *Guitar Player,* these guys are saying, "Wow, man, if I could just get this, I'd be happy." Then they get it, and they realize it's not what they meant. The business is just different than anyone could possibly imagine it. And you have to experience it to know what I'm talking about.

More ruthless?

Business in general is ruthless, yes [*laughs*].

How do you convey intense passages to your other soloists?

I believe musicians should be able to read and write music, and I have written it out, but it's like six hours of work for me to save 20 minutes for them, just to have them lose the paper later. So I started giving them tapes. I'd work on five tunes at once, and just give them tapes of difficult licks. They wouldn't know what it meant or why they were learning it, but they learned it. And then in rehearsal I'd say, "Here we go. We've got this chord progression, and all of a sudden there's this lick in there." And then they say, "Oh, that's where it goes. Huh. I wouldn't have thought of it." One of the important things about working with a band is to keep the rehearsals moving. If you don't have something challenging for

everybody every time there's a rehearsal, you're inviting things like, "Yeah, I'll be right there. I'm just going to drive through and get something to eat," or "Yeah, I'll be over, but there's this movie on." That starts to creep in, and pretty soon the whole thing is just kind of bogging down, and you're back to digging ditches. I've seen it happen to so many bands I was in.

I didn't really get smart until I was putting together the University of Miami rock ensemble that later became the Dregs. There were only two nights a week when we could rehearse, and we got more done in those two nights because we knew that's all the time we had. By having everybody do a little bit of homework, we could meet a lot more of our goals. Somebody's got to stand up and keep it moving. And by handing out the hard parts, you don't end up with a situation of everybody sitting around while you show the bass player this lick and then show the chords of the chorus to the keyboard player. I figure there's a time limit of about 15 minutes if you've got to show somebody something. If you can't show it in 15 minutes, then give them a tape. And in 15 minutes, I mean show it and have it ready to play. That's why I take it in sections. Take a little section, show it to everybody, and then everybody plays it together a bunch of different ways. It's new — except to you, of course — so they're real into it. It keeps the thing alive. And then go to a new section. Always keep it moving and challenging for the musicians; otherwise, you're going to end up with a bunch of reasons why you shouldn't practice.

How does self-producing an album at home compare with past projects?

It feels about the same. I just did this album more in the middle of the night. I'd come back while I was doing the flying thing and go into the studio. It was eerie creating stuff by myself in the middle of the night, but I've been doing it for a long time, and I really enjoy the idea of just getting kind of lost. When you're by yourself late at night with absolutely nothing to remind you of the passage of time — like the phone ringing or people coming over or anything like that — you can really get a very creative mood. Sometimes I'll spend four or five hours straight without talking to a single person or without thinking about anything but the problem at hand. It's very creative, but it's really lonely. If you're not sure what you want and you like to ask "Well, what do you think about that?" you're not going to get any help. But it's really neat to go in there and just get *out* in the ozone, so to speak — and I don't mean with drugs or anything, but just in terms of thinking of all the possibilities and just going way out on a limb. By the way, I unplug all my equipment when I'm not using it, because lightning has wrecked a lot of my equipment. Even with surge suppressors, you can't stop the lightning. Because the ground wire is connected to ground, if you get enough jolt in the ground, it comes through the ground wire, arcs across, and fries stuff. That's why I literally *unplug* everything and not just turn it off. I've had no problems since then.

What advantages do computers offer the average guitarist?

Well, it's very easy to manipulate the sequences. There are small, very inexpensive sequencers available that are just standalone boxes, and there are inexpensive sequencers built into keyboards. And the computer is graphic — you have a screen and can point at things and move them around. It makes it easy to change the form of a song and transpose. The Macintosh is set up to be intuitive anyway, which is great for musicians, because you use it creatively, rather than having to read the manual. I never read the manual. It's easy to use, and it gives you something to play if you want to practice.

Why do you turn your slant-front cabinet on its side?

Instead of having the slant-front focused at your head — with the result of totally ruining your hearing, which is already done in my case, and I didn't need that — I turn it sideways so the speakers are pointed out two different ways for a little bit more dispersement. This is one of my beefs about life in the music business: Why can't they make a cabinet with speakers pointed in four different directions? Why just kill three people in the front row, while nobody else can hear? And what makes it worse is taking a cabinet that kills three people in the front row, and then adding four more exactly in line with that on top. You might as well just have a death ray.

Your guitar parts sometimes sound very unguitaristic. Do you compose on other instruments?

I write a lot of stuff on piano. If you have a

melody you want to accompany, you can sit there and just figure it out. You can find something. Guitar-wise, creating something that doesn't sound like guitar usually involves something polyphonic. A lot of times, by taking the limitation of the guitar, you can come up with a more interesting part. Like, you can say, "Well, I want to play a *C#m* here, but how am I going to do it?" Well, break it up. Figure out what's more important: the bass notes, the melody, or just the chord. If it's just the chord, then play the chord. But if you want to fill it in, the notes are there somewhere. I don't care what you're playing, there are notes somewhere near that you can grab to enhance what you're doing.

Can you offer suggestions for enhancing the act of composing?

Ideas just kind of come from messing around with instruments, and they're almost a dime a dozen. Putting them together into a composition is the hard part. That's where the frustration comes in. You sit there and mess around with it, and you just can't come up with anything else. That's when you pull out your education. Whether your education is self-taught or from studying in a music school like GIT or just from listening, use what you know to give you other plans of attack: "Okay, I can go up a minor third; I can go to the relative minor. How about if I transpose to the fifth? I can use a diminished chord to go up to this key, or I could repeat it with a variation." Just give yourself ideas, and one of those ideas might spring into an inspiration. You might apply a simple theoretical idea to the music that you already have, and come up with the way you need to bridge the gap.

Another approach is to just sit there and play what you've got — do it on the piano, the guitar, whatever — and when you get to the part where there's nothing left, just stop and let your mind go. Ask yourself, "What was that I just heard in my mind?" and then go look for it on the instrument. As silly as it sounds, that's the only way I can come up with parts that don't want to be come up with, the ones that are hiding.

— JIMMY PAGE —

BY STEVE ROSEN — JULY 1977

ONDUCTING AN interview with Jimmy Page, lead guitarist and producer/arranger for England's notorious hard-rock band Led Zeppelin, amounts very nearly to constructing a mini-history of British rock and roll. Perhaps one of Zeppelin's more outstanding characteristics is its endurance, intact (no personnel changes since its inception), through an extremely tumultuous decade involving not only rock, but popular music in general. Since 1969 the group's four members — Page, bass player John Paul Jones, vocalist Robert Plant, and drummer John Bonham — have produced eight albums (two are doubles) of original and often revolutionary compositions with a heavy metal sound. For as long as the band has been an entity, their records, coupled with several well-planned and highly publicized European and American tours, have exerted a profound and acutely recognizable influence on rock groups and guitar players on both sides of the Atlantic. Page's carefully calculated guitar frenzy, engineered through the use of distortion, surrounds Plant's expressive vocals to create a tension and excitement rarely matched by Zeppelin's numerous emulators.

But the prodigious contributions of James Patrick Page, born in 1945 in Middlesex, England, date back to well before the formation of his present band. His work as a session guitarist earned him so lengthy a credit list (some sources cite Jimmy as having been on 50–90% of the records released in England during 1963–65) that he himself is no longer sure of each and every cut on which he played. Even without the exact number of his vinyl encounters known, the range of his interaction as musician and sometime producer with the landmark groups and individuals of soft and hard rock is impressive and diverse: the Who, Them, various members of the Rolling Stones, Donovan, and Jackie DeShannon to name a few. In the mid-Sixties, Page joined one of the best-known British rock bands, the Yardbirds, leading to a legendary collaboration with rock/jazz guitarist Jeff Beck. When the Yardbirds disbanded in 1968, Page was ready to start his own group. According to Jimmy, at the initial meeting of Led Zeppelin, the sound of success was already bellowing through the amps, and the musicians' four-week introductory period resulted in *Led Zeppelin*, their first of many gold-record–winning LPs.

Let's try to begin at the beginning. When you first started playing, what was going on musically?

I got really stimulated by hearing early rock and roll; knowing that something was going on that was being suppressed by the media. Which it really was at the time. You had to stick by the radio and listen to overseas radio to even hear good rock records — Little Richard and things like that. The record that made me want to play guitar was "Baby, Let's Play House" by Elvis Presley. I just sort of heard two guitars and bass and thought, "Yeah, I want to be part of this." There was just so much vitality and energy coming out of it.

When did you get your first guitar?

When I was about 14. It was all a matter of trying to pick up tips and stuff. There weren't many method books, really, apart from jazz which had no bearing on rock and roll whatsoever at that time. But that first guitar was a Grazzioso which was like a copy of Stratocaster; then I got a real Strato-caster; then one of those Gibson "Black Beauties" which stayed with me for a long time until some thieving magpie took it to his nest. That's the guitar I did all the Sixties sessions on.

Were your parents musical?

No, not at all. But they didn't mind me getting into it; I think they were quite relieved to see something being done instead of art work, which they thought was a loser's game.

What music did you play when you first started?

I wasn't really playing anything properly. I just knew a few bits of solos and things, not much. I just kept getting records and learning that way. It was the obvious influences at the beginning: Scotty Moore, James Burton, Cliff Gallup — he was Gene Vincent's guitarist — Johnny Weeks, later, and those seemed to be the most sustaining influences until I began to hear blues guitarists Elmore James, B.B. King, and people like that. Basically, that was the start: a mixture between rock and blues. Then I stretched out a lot more, and I started doing studio work. I had to branch out, and I did. I might do three sessions a day: a film session in the morning, and then there'd be something like a rock band, and then maybe a folk one in the evening. I didn't know *what* was coming! But it was a really good disciplinary area to work in, the studio. And it also gave me a chance to develop on all of the different styles.

Do you remember the first band you were in?

Just friends and things. I played in a lot of different small bands around, but nothing you could ever get any records of.

What kind of music were you playing with [early English rock band] Neil Christian and the Crusaders?

This was before the Stones happened, so we were doing Chuck Berry, Gene Vincent, and Bo Diddley things mainly. At the time, public taste was more engineered towards Top 10 records, so it was a bit of a struggle. But there'd always be a small section of the audience into what we were doing.

Wasn't there a break in your music career at this point?

Yes, I stopped playing and went to art college for about two years, while concentrating more on blues playing on my own. And then from art college to the [early British rock mecca] Marquee Club in London. I used to go up and jam on a Thursday night with the interlude band. One night somebody came up and said, "Would you like to play on a record?" and I said, "Yeah, why not?" It did quite well, and that was it after that. I can't remember the title of it now. From that point I started suddenly getting all this studio work. There was a crossroads: is it an art career or is it going to be music? Well anyway, I had to stop going to the art college because I was really getting into music. Big Jim Sullivan — who was really brilliant — and I were the only guitarists doing those sessions. Then a point came where Stax Records [Memphis-based rhythm and blues label] started influencing music to have more brass and orchestral stuff. The guitar started to take a back trend with just the occasional riff. I didn't realize how rusty I was going to get until a rock and roll session turned up from France, and I could hardly play. I thought it was time to get out, and I did.

You just stopped playing?

For a while I just worked on my stuff alone, and then I went to a Yardbirds concert at Oxford, and they were all walking around in their penguin suits. [Lead singer] Keith Relf got really drunk and was saying "Fuck you" right into the mike and falling into the drums. I thought it was a great anarchistic night, and I went back into the dressing room and said, "What a brilliant show!" There was this great argument going on; [bass player] Paul Samwell-Smith saying, "Well, I'm leaving the group, and if I was you, Keith, I'd do the very same thing." So he left the group, and Keith didn't. But they were stuck, you see, because they had commitments and dates, so I said, "I'll play the bass if you like." And then it worked out that we did the dual lead guitar thing as soon as [previously on rhythm guitar] Chris Dreja could get it together with the bass, which happened, though not for long. But then came the question of discipline. If you're going to do dual lead guitar riffs and patterns, then you've got to be playing the same things. Jeff Beck had discipline occasionally, but he was an inconsistent player in that when he's on, he's probably the best there is, but at that time, and for a period afterwards, he had no respect whatsoever for audiences.

You were playing acoustic guitar during your session period?

Yes, I had to do it on studio work. And you come to grips with it very quickly too, very quickly, because it's what is expected. There was a lot of busking [singing on street corners] in the earlier days, but as I say, I had to come to grips with it, and it was a good schooling.

You were using the Les Paul for those sessions?

The Gibson "Black Beauty" Les Paul Custom. I was one of the first people in England to have one, but I didn't know that then. I just saw it on the wall, had a go with it, and it was good. I traded a Gretsch Chet Atkins I'd had before for the Les Paul.

What kinds of amplifiers were you using for session work?

A small Supro, which I used until someone, I don't know who, smashed it up for me. I'm going to try to get another one. It's like a Harmony amp, I think, and all of the first album [*Led Zeppelin*] was done on that.

What do you remember most about your early days with the Yardbirds?

One thing is it was chaotic in recording. I mean we did one tune and didn't really know what it was. We had Ian Stewart from the Stones on piano, and we'd just finished the take, and without even hearing it [producer] Mickie Most said, "Next." I said, "I've never worked like this in my life," and he said, "Don't worry about it." It was all done very quickly, as it sounds. It was things like that that really led to the general state of mind and depression of Relf and [drummer] Jim McCarty that broke the group up. I tried to keep it together, but there was no chance; they just wouldn't have it. In fact Relf said the magic of the band disappeared when Clapton left [British rock/blues guitarist Eric Clapton played with the Yardbirds prior to Beck's joining]. I was really keen on doing anything, though, probably because of having had all that studio work and variety beforehand. So it didn't matter what way they wanted to go; they were definitely talented people, but they couldn't really see the woods for the trees at that time.

You thought the best period of the Yardbirds was when Beck was with them?

I did. Giorgio Gomelsky [the Yardbirds' manager and producer] was good for him because he got him thinking and attempting new things. That's when they started all sorts of departures. Apparently [co-producer] Simon Napier-Bell sang the guitar riff of "Over Under Sideways Down" [on LP of the same name] to Jeff to demonstrate what he wanted, but I don't know whether that's true or not. I never spoke to him about it. I know the idea of the record was to sort of emulate the sound of the old "Rock Around the Clock" type record; that bass and backbeat thing.

But it wouldn't be evident at all; every now and again he'd say, "Let's make a record around such and such," and no one would ever know what the example was at the end of the song.

Can you describe some of your musical interaction with Beck during the Yardbirds period?

Sometimes it worked really great, and sometimes it didn't. There were a lot of harmonies that I don't think anyone else had really done, not like we did. The Stones were the only ones who got into two guitars going at the same time from old Muddy Waters records. But we were more into solos rather than a rhythm thing. The point is, you've got to have the parts worked out, and I'd find that I was doing what I was supposed to, while something totally different would be coming from Jeff. That was all right for the areas of improvisation, but there were other parts where it just *did not work*. You've got to understand that Beck and I came from the same sort of roots. If you've got things you enjoy, then you want to do them — to the horrifying point where we'd done our first LP [*Led Zeppelin*] with "You Shook Me," and then I heard *he'd* done "You Shook Me" [*Truth*]. I was terrified because I thought they'd be the same. But I hadn't even known he'd done it, and he hadn't known that we had.

Did Beck play bass on "Over Under Sideways Down"?

No; in fact for that LP they just got him in to do the solos because they'd had a lot of trouble with him. But then when I joined the band, he supposedly wasn't going to walk off anymore. Well, he did a couple of times. It's strange: If he'd had a bad day, he'd take it out on the audience. I don't know whether he's the same now; his playing sounds far more consistent on records. You see, on the "Beck's Bolero" [*Truth*] thing I was working with that, the track was done, and then the producer just disappeared. He was never seen again; he simply didn't come back. Napier-Bell, he just sort of left me and Jeff to it. Jeff was playing, and I was in the box [recording booth]. And even though he says he wrote it, I wrote it. I'm playing the electric 12-string on it. Beck's doing the slide bits, and I'm basically playing around the chords. The idea was built around [classical composer] Maurice Ravel's "Bolero." It's got a lot of drama to it; it came off right. It was a good lineup too, with [the Who's drummer] Keith Moon and everything.

Wasn't that band going to be Led Zeppelin?

It was, yeah. Not Led Zeppelin as a name; the name came afterwards. But it was said afterwards that that's what it could have been called. Because Moony wanted to get out of the Who and so did [Who bass player] John Entwistle, but when it came down to getting hold of a singer, it was either going to be [guitarist/organist/singer with English pop group Traffic] Steve Winwood or [guitarist/vocalist with Small Faces] Steve Marriott. Finally it came down to Marriott. He was contacted, and the reply came back from his manager's office: "How would you like to have a group with no fingers, boys?" Or words to that effect. So the group was dropped because of Marriott's other commitment, to Small Faces. But I think it would have been the first of all those bands sort of like the Cream and everything. Instead, it didn't happen — apart from the "Bolero." That's the closest it got. John Paul [Jones] is on that too; so is Nicky Hopkins [studio keyboard player with various British rock groups].

You only recorded a few songs with Beck on record?

Yeah. "Happenings Ten Years Time Ago" [*The Yardbirds' Greatest Hits*], "Stroll On" [*Blow Up*], "The Train Kept a-Rollin'" [*Having a Rave-Up with the Yardbirds*], and "Psycho Daisies" [available only on the B side of the English single release of "Happenings Ten Years Time Ago" and an obscure bootleg titled *More Golden Eggs*, "Bolero"], and a few other things. None of them were with the Yardbirds but earlier on — just some studio things, unreleased songs, "Louie Louie" and things like that; really good though, really great.

Were you using any boosters with the Yardbirds to get all those sounds?

Fuzztone, which I'd virtually regurgitated from what I heard on "2000 Pound Bee" by the Ventures. They had a Fuzztone. It was nothing like the one this guy, Roger Mayer, made for me; he worked for the Admiralty [British Navy] in the electronics division. He did all the fuzz pedals for Jimi Hendrix later; all those octave doublers and things like that. He made this one for me, but that was all during the studio period, you see. I think Jeff had one too then, but I was the one who got the effect going again. That accounted for quite a lot of the boost and that sort of sustain in the music.

You were also doing all sorts of things with feedback?

You know "I Need You" [*Kinkdom*] by the Kinks? I think I did that bit there in the beginning. I don't know who really did feedback first; it just sort of happened. I don't think anybody consciously nicked it from anybody else; it was just going on. But

Pete Townshend [lead guitarist with the Who] obviously was the one, through the music of his group, who made the use of feedback more his style, and so it's related to him. Whereas the other players like Jeff and myself were playing more single notes and things than chords.

You used a Danelectro with the Yardbirds?

Yes, but not with Beck. I did use it in the latter days. I used it onstage for "White Summer" [*Little Games*]. I used a special tuning for that; the low string down to B, then A, D, G, A, and D. It's like a modal tuning; a sitar tuning, in fact.

Was "Black Mountain Side" [done on Led Zeppelin] an extension of that?

I wasn't totally original on that. It had been done in the folk clubs a lot; Annie Briggs was the first one that I heard do that riff. I was playing it as well, and then there was [English folk guitarist] Bert Jansch's version. He's the one who crystallized all the acoustic playing as far as I'm concerned. Those first few albums of his were absolutely brilliant. And the tuning on "Black Mountain Side" is the same as "White Summer." It's taken a bit of battering, that Danelectro guitar, I'm afraid.

Do those songs work well now on the Danelectro?

I played them on that guitar before, so I'd thought I'd do it again. But I might change it around to something else, since my whole amp situation is different now from what it used to be; now it's Marshall, then it was Vox tops and different cabinets — kind of a hodgepodge, but it worked.

You used a Vox 12-string with the Yardbirds?

That's right. I can't remember the titles now; the Mickie Most things, some of the B sides. I remember there was one with an electric 12-string solo on the end of it which was all right. I don't have copies of them now, and I don't know what they're called. I've got *Little Games*, but that's about it.

You were using Vox amps with the Yardbirds?

AC 30s. They've held up consistently well. Even the new ones are pretty good. I tried some; I got four in and tried them out, and they were all reasonably good. I was going to build up a big bank of four of them, but Bonzo's kit is so loud that they just don't come over the top of it properly.

Were the AC 30s that you used with the Yardbirds modified in any way?

Only by Vox; you could get these ones with special treble boosters on the back which is what I had. No, I didn't do that much customizing apart from making sure all of the points, soldering contacts, and things were solid. The Telecasters changed rapidly; you could tell because you could split the pickups — you know that split sound you can get — and again you could get an out-of-phase sound, and then suddenly they didn't do it anymore. So they obviously changed the electronics. And there didn't seem to be any way of getting it back. I tried to fiddle around with the wiring, but it didn't work so I just went back to the old one again.

What kind of guitar were you using on the first Led Zeppelin album?

A Telecaster. I used the Les Paul with the Yardbirds on about two numbers and a Fender for the rest. You see, the Les Paul Custom had a central setting, a kind of out-of-phase pickup sound which Jeff couldn't get on his Les Paul, so I used mine for that.

Was the Telecaster the one Beck gave to you?

Yes. There was work done on it but only afterwards. I painted it; everyone painted their guitars in those days. And I had reflective plastic sheeting underneath the pickguard that gives rainbow colors.

It sounds exactly like a Les Paul.

Yeah, well that's the amp and everything. You see, I could get a lot of tones out of the guitar which you normally couldn't. This confusion goes back to those early sessions again with the Les Paul. Those might not sound like a Les Paul, but that's what I used. It's just different amps, mike placings, and all different things. Also, if you just crank it up to distortion point so you can sustain notes, it's bound to sound like a Les Paul. I was using the Supro amp for the first album and still do. The "Stairway to Heaven" [fourth untitled album] solo was done when I pulled out the Telecaster, which I hadn't used for a long time, plugged it into the Supro, and away it went again. That's a different sound entirely from any of the rest of the first album. It was a good versatile setup. I'm using a Leslie on the solo on "Good Times Bad Times" [fourth LP]. It was wired up for an organ thing then.

What kind of acoustic guitar are you using on "Black Mountain Side" and "Babe I'm Gonna Leave You" [both on Led Zeppelin]?

That was a Gibson J-200 which wasn't mine; I borrowed it. It was a beautiful guitar, really great. I've never found a guitar of that quality anywhere since. I could play so easily on it, get a really thick sound; it had heavy-gauge strings on it, but it just didn't seem to feel like it.

Do you just use your fingers when playing acoustic?

Yes. I used fingerpicks once, but I find them too spiky; they're too sharp. You can't get the tone or response that you would get, say, the way classical players approach gut-string instruments. The way they pick, the whole thing is the tonal response of the string. It seems important.

Can you describe your picking style?

I don't know, really; it's a cross between finger-style and flatpicking. There's a guy in England called Davey Graham, and he never used any fingerpicks or anything. He used a thumbpick every now and again, but I prefer just a flatpick and fingers because then it's easier to get around from guitar to guitar. Well, it is for me anyway. But apparently he's got callouses on the left hand and all over the right as well; he can get so much attack on his strings, and he's really good.

The guitar on "Communication Breakdown" [on Led Zeppelin] sounds as if it's coming out of a little shoebox.

Yeah. I put it in a small room, a little tiny vocal booth-type thing and miked it from a distance. You see, there's a very old recording maxim which goes, "Distance makes depth." I've used that a hell of a lot on recording techniques with the band generally, not just me. You're always used to them close-miking amps, just putting the microphone in front, but I'd have a mike right out the back as well, and then balance the two, and get rid of all the phasing problems, because really, you shouldn't have to use an EQ in the studio if the instruments sound right. It should all be done with the microphones. But see, everyone has gotten so carried away with EQ pots that they have forgotten the whole science of microphone placement. There aren't too many guys who know it. I'm sure Les Paul knows a lot; obviously, he must have been well into that, well into it, as were all those who produced the early rock records where there were only one or two mikes in the studio.

The solo on "I Can't Quit You Baby" [Led Zeppelin] is interesting — many pull-offs in a sort of sloppy but amazingly inventive style.

There are mistakes in it, but it doesn't make any difference. I'll always leave the mistakes in. I can't help it. The timing bits on the A and B♭ parts are right, though it might sound wrong. The timing just *sounds* off. But there are some wrong notes. You've got to be reasonably honest about it. It's like the film-track album [*The Song Remains the Same*]; there's no editing really on that. It wasn't the best concert playing-wise at all, but it was the only one with celluloid footage, so there it was. It was all right; it was just one "as-it-is" performance. It wasn't one of those real magic nights, but then again it wasn't a terrible night. So, for all its mistakes and everything else, it's a very honest filmtrack. Rather than just trailing around through a tour with a recording mobile truck waiting for the magic night, it was just, "There you are — take it or leave it." I've got a lot of live recorded stuff going back to '69.

Jumping ahead to the second album [Led Zeppelin II], the riff in the middle of "Whole Lotta Love" was a very composed and structured phrase.

I had it worked out already, that one, before entering the studio. I had rehearsed it. And then all that other stuff, sonic wave sound and all that, I built it up in the studio, and put effects on it and things; treatments.

How is that descending riff done?

With a metal slide and backwards echo. I think I came up with that first before anybody. I know it's been used a lot now but not at the time. I thought of it on this Mickie Most thing. In fact some of the things that might sound a bit odd have, in fact, backwards echo involved in them as well.

What kind of effect are you using on the beginning of "Ramble On" [Led Zeppelin II]?

If I can remember correctly, it's like harmony feedback and then it changes. To be more specific, most of the tracks just start off bass, drums, and guitar, and once you've done the drums and bass, you just build everything up afterwards. It's like a starting point, and you start constructing from square one.

Is the rest of the band in the studio when you put down the solos?

No, never. I don't like anybody else in the studio when I'm putting on the guitar parts. I usually just limber up for a while and then maybe do three solos and take the best of the three.

Is there an electric 12-string on "Thank You" [Led Zeppelin]?

Yes; I think it's a Fender or Rickenbacker.

What is the effect on "Out On the Tiles" [Led Zeppelin III]?

Now that is exactly what I was talking about: close-miking and distance-miking. That's ambient sound. Getting the distance of the time lag from one end of the room to the other and putting that in as well. The whole idea, the way I see recording, is to try and capture the sound of the room live and the emotion of the whole moment and try to convey that across. That's the very essence of it. And so, consequently, you've got to capture as much of the room sound as possible.

On "Tangerine" [Led Zeppelin III] it sounds as if you're playing a pedal steel.

I am. And on the first LP [Led Zeppelin] there's a pedal steel. I had never played steel before, but I just picked it up. There's a lot of things I do first time around that I haven't done before. In fact, I hadn't touched a pedal steel from the first album to the third. It's a bit of a pinch really from the things that Chuck Berry did. But nevertheless it fits. I use pedal steel on "Your Time Is Gonna Come" [Led Zeppelin]. It sounds more like a slide or something. It's more out of tune on the first album because I hadn't got a kit to put it together.

You've also played other stringed instruments on records?

"Gallows Pole" [on Led Zeppelin III] was the first time for banjo, and on "The Battle of Evermore" [fourth album] a mandolin was lying around. It wasn't mine, it was Jonesy's. I just picked it up, got the chords, and it sort of started happening. I did it more or less straight off. But you see that's fingerpicking again, going on back to the studio days and developing a certain amount of technique. At least enough to be adapted and used. My fingerpicking is a sort of cross between Pete Seeger, Earl Scruggs, and total incompetence.

The fourth album was the first time you used a double-neck?

I didn't use a double-neck on that, but I had to get one afterwards to play "Stairway to Heaven." I did all those guitars on it; I just built them up. That was the beginning of my building up harmonized guitars properly. "Ten Years Gone" [Physical Graffiti] was an extension of that, and then "Achilles' Last Stand" [Presence] is like the essential flow of it really, because there was no time to think the things out; I just had to more or less lay it down on the first track and harmonize on the second track. It was really fast working on Presence. And I did all the guitar overdubs on that LP in one night. There were only two sequences. The rest of the band, not Robert, but the rest of them I don't think really could see it to begin with. They didn't know what the hell I was going to do with it. But I wanted to give each section its own identity, and I think it came off really good. I didn't think I'd be able to do it in one night; I thought I'd have to do it in the course of three different nights to get the individual sections. But I was so into it that my mind was working properly for a change. It sort of crystallized and everything was just pouring out. I was very happy with the guitar on that whole album as far as the maturity of the playing goes.

When you started playing the double-neck did it require a new approach on your part?

Yes. The main thing is, there's an effect you can get where you leave the 12-string neck open as far as the sound goes and play on the 6-string neck, and you get the 12-strings vibrating in sympathy. It's like an Indian sitar, and I've worked on that a little bit. I use it on "Stairway" like that; not on the album but on the soundtrack and film. It's surprising; it doesn't vibrate as heavily as a sitar would, but nonetheless it does add to the overall tonal quality.

You think your playing on the fourth LP is the best you've ever done?

Without a doubt. As far as consistency goes and as far as the quality of playing on a whole album, I would say yes. But I don't know what the best solo I've ever done is — I have no idea. My vocation is more in composition really than in anything else. Building up harmonies. Using the guitar, orchestrating the guitar like an army — a guitar army. I think that's where it's at, really, for me. I'm talking about actual orchestration in the same way you'd orchestrate a classical piece of music. Instead of using brass and violins you treat the guitars with synthesizers or other devices, give them different treatments, so that they have enough frequency range and scope and everything to keep the listener as totally committed to it as the player is. It's a difficult project, but it's one that I've got to do.

Have you done anything towards this end already?

Only on these three tunes: "Stairway to Heaven," "Ten Years Gone," and "Achilles' Last Stand," the way the guitar is building. I can see certain milestones along the way like "Four Sticks" [fourth LP], in the middle section of that. The sound of those guitars; that's where I'm going. I've got long pieces written; I've got one really long one written that's harder to play than anything. It's sort of classical, but then it goes through changes from that mood to really laid-back rock, and then to really intensified stuff. With a few laser notes thrown in, we might be all right.

When was the first time you used the violin bow?

The first time I recorded with it was with the Yardbirds. But the idea was put to me by a classical string player when I was doing studio work. One of us tried to bow the guitar, then we tried it between us, and it worked. At that point I was just bowing it, but the other effects I've obviously come up with on my own — using wah-wah, and echo. You have to put rosin on the bow, and the rosin sticks to the string and makes it vibrate.

Do you use special tunings on the electric guitar?

All the time; they're my own that I've worked out, so I'd rather keep those to myself, really. But they're never open tunings; I have used those, but most of the things I've written have not been open tunings, so you can get more chords into them.

Did you ever meet any of those folk players you admire — Bert Jansch, John Renbourn or any of them?

No, and the most terrifying thing of all happened about a few months ago. Jansch's playing appeared as if it was going down or something, and it turns out he's got arthritis. I really think he's one of the best. He was, without any doubt, the one who crystallized so many things. As much as Hendrix had done on electric, I think he's done on the acoustic. He was really way, way ahead. And for something like that to happen is such a tragedy, with a mind as brilliant as that. There you go. Another player whose physical handicap didn't stop him is Django Reinhardt. For his last LP they pulled him out of retirement to do it; it's on Barclay Records in France. He'd been retired for years, and it's fantastic. You know the story about him in the caravan and losing fingers and such. But the record is just fantastic. He must have been playing all the time to be that good — it's horrifyingly good. Horrifying. But it's always good to hear perennial players like that, like Les Paul and people like that.

You listen to Les Paul?

Oh, yeah. You can tell Jeff [Beck] did too, can't you? Have you ever heard "It's Been a Long, Long Time" [mid-Forties single by the Les Paul Trio with Bing Crosby]? You ought to hear that. He does everything on that, everything in one go. And it's just one guitar; it's basically one guitar even though they've tracked on rhythms and stuff. But my goodness, his introductory chords and everything are fantastic. He sets the whole tone, and then he goes into this solo which is fantastic. Now that's where I heard feedback first — from Les Paul. Also vibratos and things. Even before B.B. King, you know, I've traced a hell of a lot of rock and roll, little riffs and things, back to Les Paul, Chuck Berry, Cliff Gallup and all those — it's all there. But then Les Paul was influenced by Reinhardt, wasn't he? Very much so. I can't get my hands on the records of Les Paul, the Les Paul Trio, and all that stuff. But I've got all the Capitol LPs and things. I mean he's the father of it all: multi-tracking and everything else. If it hadn't been for him, there wouldn't have been anything really.

You said that Eric Clapton was the person who synthesized the Les Paul sound?

Yeah, without a doubt. When he was with the Bluesbreakers [British blues band with John Mayall], it was just a magic combination; he got one of the Marshall amps, and away he went. It just happened. I thought he played brilliantly then, really brilliantly. That was very stirring stuff.

Do you think you were responsible for any specific guitar sounds?

The guitar parts in "Trampled Under Foot" [*Physical Graffiti*], this guy Nick Kent [British rock journalist], he came out with this idea about how he thought that was a really revolutionary sound. And I hadn't realized that anyone would think it was, but I can explain exactly how it's done. Again it's sort of backwards echo and wah-wah. I don't know how responsible I was for new sounds because there were so many good things happening around that point, around the release of the first Zeppelin album, like Hendrix and Clapton.

Were you focusing on anything in particular on the first Led Zeppelin LP with regards to certain guitar sounds?

The trouble is keeping a separation between sounds, so you don't have the same guitar effect all the time. And that's where that orchestration thing comes in; it's so easy, I've already planned it, it's already there; all the groundwork has been done now. And the dream has been accomplished by the computerized mixing console. The sort of struggle to achieve so many things is over. As I said, I've got two things written, but I'll be working on more. You can hear what I mean on *Lucifer Rising* [soundtrack for the unreleased Kenneth Anger film]. You see, I didn't play any guitar on that, apart from one point. That was all other instruments, all synthesizers. Every instrument was given a process so it didn't sound like what it really was — the voices, drones, mantras, and even tabla drums. When you've got a collage of, say, four of these sounds together, people will be drawn right in because there will be sounds they hadn't heard before. That's basically what I'm into: collages and tissues of sound with emotional intensity and melody and all that. But you know there are so many good people around like John McLaughlin and people like that. It's a totally different thing than what I'm doing.

Do you think he has a sustaining quality as a guitarist?

He's always had that technique right from when I first knew him when he was working in a guitar shop. I would say he was the best jazz guitarist in England then, in the traditional mode of [jazz stylist] Johnny Smith and Tal Farlow; a combination of those two is exactly what he sounded like. He was easily the best guitarist in England, and he was working in a guitar shop. And that's what I say — you hear so many good people around under those conditions. I'll tell you one thing, I don't know one musician who's stuck to his guns, who was good in the early days, that hasn't come through now with recognition from everybody.

— LES PAUL —

BY JON SIEVERT – DECEMBER 1977

JON SIEVERT

WHEN LES PAUL appeared on the 1977 Grammy Awards show, more than a few people in the viewing audience were undoubtedly surprised to discover that he was neither (1) dead, nor (2) a guitar. Les, then 61, was not there for one of those tributes accorded creaking pioneers of the recording industry. He was there to receive a Grammy that he shared with Chet Atkins for the Best Country Instrumental Performance: *Chester & Lester*. The album was the first he had recorded in more than ten years, and the award represented just another notch in one of the most remarkable careers in show business history — one that now spans more than half a century.

Ralph J. Gleason, the late dean of music critics, suggested some years ago that "no one in the history of pop music has had a greater effect on the ultimate pop sound than Les Paul." Guitarists as diverse as Wes Montgomery, Michael Bloomfield, Ray Benson, Pat Martino, Jerry Hahn, James Burton, Steve Howe, Peter Frampton, Steve Miller, June Millington, and Link Wray have all cited his influence and publicly proclaimed their love for his music; there are literally thousands more in the same debt.

The reasons for Les Paul's importance are not hard to trace: Even before Charlie Christian gained fame for his playing in Benny Goodman's band (1939–41), Les's work with Fred Waring on network radio helped introduce the controversial electric guitar to a skeptical public. His designs of electric Spanish solidbodies were years ahead of the major manufacturers and his experiments with, and inventions of, presently routine recording techniques such as echo delay, phase shifting, sound-on-sound, overdubbing, and multiple-track recording, revolutionized the recording industry, catapulting himself and Mary Ford into national stardom in the early '50s. Additionally, he is responsible for the idea and design of the first eight-track recorder, and the world's most prestigious guitar bears his name.

Les Paul's story begins on June 9, 1916, in Waukesha, Wisconsin. Born Lester William Polsfuss, he had taken up the harmonica and built his first crystal set by age nine. The first thing he heard on that radio was someone playing the guitar, and he soon decided that he also wanted to play one, because it left him free to speak and sing.

His first guitar was from Sears Roebuck, and it wasn't long before he had learned enough chords — three — and songs to start performing at lunch hours for local Optimists and Lions Clubs and PTA meetings. The harmonica stayed in the act, as Rhubarb Red (Les' stage name at the time) fashioned his first harmonica rack from a coat hanger and began to develop the jokes and patter that remain a part of his performances today.

By the time he was 13, he had already built his first broadcasting station and recording machine and had amplified his guitar with a phonograph needle through the family radio. About that time, a western band featuring Joe Wolverton on guitar came through town, and Les discovered for the first time that it was possible to make music above the third fret. Wolverton, impressed with the precocious guitarist and harboring a grudge against the band's vocalist, convinced the leader to fire the vocalist and hire Les in his place.

Following a summer of touring, during which he acquired his first Gibson, an L-5, Les returned to Waukesha to resume his schooling and experimenting. Within a year he received a call from Wolverton, now doing a single act, who invited Les to join him in Springfield, Missouri, to form a duet. Thus was born Sunny Joe & Rhubarb Red, with Les playing guitar, jug, harmonica, and piano, while Joe played guitar, banjo, and fiddle; both sang.

The combination was a hit as the two toured the Midwest, playing radio stations, clubs, fairs, theaters, and dance halls. One of Les's first projects was to build a PA system for the band's truck so that they could announce their arrivals. The two hit Chicago in the early '30s just as the town was beginning to break wide open as a jazz haven. Following the 1933 Chicago World's Fair, the pair ended their musical association. Les wanted to play jazz and electric, and Joe wanted to remain country and acoustic. Joe left for California, but Les stayed in Chicago and became two persons: his mornings were spent hosting a radio show for WJJD as Rhubarb Red, playing country music and receiving thousands of cards and letters a day, while at night he fronted a jazz group under his real name on station WIND. The dual identity extended to his recording projects. As Red, he recorded for Sears Roebuck and Montgomery Ward and had several modest hits. As Les Paul, he turned up on a number of "race" records with blues singer Georgia White, playing piano and guitar. Through it all he kept up his interest in inventing and electronics. In 1934, Les retained Chicago's Larson Brothers to build a guitar that he had designed in order to test his theories concerning solidbody instruments.

In 1936, Les tired of his double life and dropped his Rhubarb Red persona. His reputation as a jazz guitarist had grown swiftly as a result of countless late-night jam sessions with artists such as Art Tatum, Roy Eldridge, Louis Armstrong, and Eddie South. Les decided to form his own trio. Jim Atkins — Chet's older half-brother — handled vocal chores and rhythm guitar, while Ernie Newton held down the bass and performed some comedy routines. Shortly thereafter, the trio left for New York. Les hustled a gig with Fred Waring and His Pennsylvanians, the large vocal ensemble with whom the trio worked five nights a week, coast to coast, on NBC. Audience response was immediate, and soon Les was receiving more mail than Waring because of the sound of his electric guitar. The Waring job lasted nearly three years, during which time Les began to experiment on a noncommercial basis with the concept of multiple recording. In 1940, he left Waring to become the musical director of radio stations WJJD and WIND in Chicago and to play with Ben Bernie's big band.

In 1941, Les built his first solidbody guitar, which he dubbed "the Log." It was actually a 4"x 4" board with a pickup and an Epiphone neck. An Epiphone body split in half was added to make it look like a guitar. Five years later he went to Gibson with his idea. Gibson turned him down.

Les' career took a significant turn in 1943, when he and Bernie left Chicago bound for Los Angeles. Bernie soon died, and Les formed another trio. Almost immediately they began to work with established stars such as Bing Crosby, Burns & Allen, and Rudy Vallee. With the war under way, Les was drafted into the Armed Forces Radio Service (AFRS) to provide entertainment for GIs. His commanding officer was composer Meredith Willson (*The Music Man,* etc.), and Les was stationed in Hollywood, where his trio became the house band behind major entertainers such as Jack Benny, the Andrews Sisters, Dinah Shore, and Bing Crosby. During this period he also recorded a classic album called *Jazz at the Philharmonic* under the pseudonym Paul Leslie. The piano player on that album was Shorty Nadine, better known as Nat King Cole.

In 1946, Les recorded "It's Been a Long, Long Time" with Crosby [*Best of Bing Crosby*], and the distinctive guitar work on that hit proved to be another big break. The superstar crooner was intrigued by Paul's recording experiments and urged him to build his own studio. Dissatisfied with existing equipment, Les decided he could build a system better than anything then available. His recording lathe was fashioned from a Cadillac flywheel, and he began to develop techniques such as close miking, echo delay, and multiple tracking. The studio was built in his garage, and its quality attracted many artists who soon recorded there, including the Andrews Sisters, Pee Wee Hunt, Kay Starr, Jo Stafford, and W.C. Fields (his only recordings). In 1948, Les released his first multiple recordings, "Lover" and "Brazil." Playing all the parts on both tunes, he achieved some very unusual effects, and the Les Paul sound — still one of the most distinctive and easily recognizable — was born.

The records were hits, but the bright promise of Les Paul's career was dimmed by the intervention of fate. On the way to a concert one winter evening, Les' car skidded off an icy bridge and dropped 50 feet into a snow bank. Eight hours later he was discovered with a broken nose, a broken collarbone, six broken ribs, a split pelvis, cracked vertebrae, and his right arm and elbow shattered. One doctor, a Les Paul fan, dissuaded a colleague from amputating the arm (perhaps preventing one of legal history's hugest verdicts for compensatory damages). When Les was informed that, at best, his right arm would be partially functional but immobile, he requested that it be pieced back together and positioned in a manner that would allow him to play the guitar. Les spent almost a year and a half in a hospital with a cast on his arm. While recovering, he released a number of follow-up tunes previously recorded with everything but the lead parts. Undaunted by his inability to properly hold the guitar or the fact that he had no right-hand movement except in his thumb, he laid his guitar flat and recorded the solo lines with a thumbpick. His biggest successes were yet to come.

In December, 1949, he married an attractive young vocalist working with Gene Autry named Colleen Summers and promptly changed her name to Mary Ford. That same year, he conceived and perfected the technique of sound-on-sound recording. With Les utilizing this revolutionary method to multitrack Mary's vocals and his many-layered instrumental parts, the couple was quickly elevated to international fame by a long string of hits that peaked in August, 1953, when "Vaya con Dios" reached the number one position on the national charts and stayed there for nine weeks.

The couple toured extensively and performed on nationwide television as guest stars several times a week. They were among the first name stars to endorse a commercial product — Rheingold Beer — and they soon agreed to host a TV show of their own, *Les Paul and Mary Ford at Home*, a hit for seven years.

In 1950, the instrument manufacturing industry was immersed in controversy over the solidbody guitar. Some traditionalists reacted to it with vehement resistance, but the pragmatists and money men could not discount the success of Leo Fender. When Gibson developed its own entry, they naturally went to Les Paul for support, since they had long desired an official endorsement from him anyway and especially because of his pioneering work in building solidbodies. In 1952 — the year in which Ampex marketed the world's first eight-track tape recorder, designed by Les Paul — Gibson introduced the gold-top Les Paul Model guitar. An immediate success, the line was soon expanded with a deluxe version (the Les Paul Custom) and economy models (the Junior, TV, and Special). The Les Paul Model became the Les Paul Standard in 1960. In the latter part of the following year, Gibson replaced the design with a thinner guitar, a double-cutaway. Les and the company soon terminated their endorsement agreement, and the name of the new series was changed to SG. In 1968, a second generation of single-cutaway Gibson Les Pauls was unveiled, including the Deluxe, reissues of earlier models, and, later, the low-impedance Les Pauls: Personal (1969), Professional (1969), Recording (1971), and the semi-acoustic Signature (1973).

Les and Mary were divorced in 1964, legally and professionally. Disappointed with the general state of the music industry, Les retired to his Mahwah, New Jersey, home to pursue his great love of inventing on a full-time basis. However, he did not isolate himself from the music business in his retirement, and he took great pains to keep abreast of industry developments and to stay in touch with musicians.

In 1970, Les was again the victim of a serious accident. A visiting friend playfully cuffed his ear and broke an eardrum. Three years of operations followed, involving serious difficulty with the inner ear. In early 1974, as he started to get around again, he got itchy to start playing. He cautiously allowed himself to be booked for a college concert in Elgin, Illinois, took one of his latest inventions — the Les Paulverizer — and knocked out the crowd. Since then he has appeared in a stream of concerts, club dates, and TV shows all over the country, and he took a brief tour of Europe. Les Paul was a hit all over again.

How did you begin making music?
At nine years old, something started to grow in me that became noticeable. I knew that there was something happening. I was walking down the street, and I saw this sewer digger on his lunch hour open up his lunch pail, dig out a harmonica, knock out the cracker crumbs, and play a bunch of tunes on it. I was fascinated by that harmonica, so I stared the guy out of it. I just stared at him. He said, "Here, kid, take it. Get out of here." So now I'm playing the harmonica, and I go over to my friend's house, and he's winding this piece of wire around a cardboard toilet

paper roll. He's making a crystal set. So he draws me out a plan to make one, and I go home and make one. The first thing I hear on it is a guitar. And then I'm hearing the *Grand Ole Opry*, and a guy named DeFord Bailey is blowing blues harmonica, and I figure it out; it's not blow, it's draw. That guy's got a C harmonica, and he's playing in G. I figure it out, and all of a sudden, I'm the king of Waukesha, and I'm playing in little places all over town for tips. So I'm coming home making $30–35 a week, and my brother's working 50 hours a week driving a truck and making $18.

When did you begin playing the guitar?

I didn't get my own guitar until I was 11 or 12, but I'd already learned a couple of chords on my friend's father's guitar. When I got my first guitar from Sears Roebuck, it came with a capo and a book called the *E-Z Method for Guitar*. The nut was adjustable so that you could make it Spanish or lap steel. The problem was that it was too big — I couldn't get my hands around the fingerboard.

How did you handle that?

I took the sixth string off. I just decided to leave it off until I grew enough to reach it. So I started out on five strings, and that's when I discovered that moving the bridge changed the intonation. I asked, "This is not in tune — why not?" So I marked it with a pencil and moved it, and the intonation changed. That led to other discoveries like height and action, and it progressed from then on. I was into customizing right away.

When did you start investigating electronics?

It was just sort of a thing with me that the electronics and the music grew at the same time. I started taking microphones and phonograph pickups apart to see how they worked right away. I had to know what everything was.

Did anyone help you? Any teachers?

Just the library. I'm a real book man. If it's in a book, I can get it. I used to spend hours in the library. Still do.

How did you get the guitar and the electronics together?

Well, when you play outdoors, where at least half of my jobs were, you can't be heard unless it's amplified. So immediately I go for a microphone, amplifier, and electric guitar.

How did you do that?

First with a phonograph needle. I took my mother's record player apart and jabbed the needle into the guitar, and it came out the speaker. I didn't realize it then, but I was also doing stereo back in the '20s.

The reason for that was my own ignorance. The only way I could figure out how to get amplified was to use my mother's radio, and I could plug a mike into that, and it was fine for my voice and harmonica, but I couldn't figure out how to put another mike in there so that I could also amplify the guitar. Then I took my dad's radio and hooked it all together and put one radio on one side of the stage and one on the other. Instant stereo. I just kept studying electricity and eventually figured out how to make a magnet, how to wind a coil, and what induction and capacitance are. It was fun. I built my own recording machine when I was 12.

How was that accomplished?

My dad owned a garage and had a lathe, so we could make a lot of the parts. It worked on a gravity-feed principle: You'd wind up a weight with a crank, and the weight comes down like a grandfather clock. When it hits the bottom, that's the end, and you'd better be done singing and playing before it hits, because that's all you get. That was before they had a motor. It was the only way to get consistent speed.

Were you getting any kind of guitar instruction at that time?

No, it was all on my own or what I could cop from someone else. When I was about 11, Gene Autry played my hometown. This was before they had a theater there, so when Gene came to town to promote one of his movies, they just picked a parking lot and showed the movie on the outside wall of a building. So I went down to see him, and he was singing his songs, like "Silver-Haired Daddy of Mine," and he was playing in the key of F. At that time I only knew about three chords, and F was not one of them, so I had written out a fingerboard diagram and had it with me so that I could put down what he was playing. I had a flashlight, and I sat in the front row. Every time he'd play an F, the light would come on, and I'd put a dot down on the diagram and then turn off the light. If he wasn't playing F, the light wasn't on. So finally, after an evening of this, he said, "You know, ladies and gentlemen, I've got to stop here for a second, because there's something that's really bugging me." And he went and hit F, and the light lit. And he says, "Why in the world does that light come on just when I hit an F chord?" So I confessed, and he called me up on the stage and asked me to play my guitar and sing. I was the hit of the town.

What guitars did you acquire after that?

I got the Sears guitar in 1927 and went almost immediately to a Gibson L-5. I went to the

Kalamazoo, Michigan, factory to pick out the one I wanted. I had the 1927 model for a little while and then went to a 1928 model; I still have the 1928 one. Gibson had a pretty good lock on the market then. I didn't even hear a D'Angelico until I came to New York in 1936. I had heard of Epiphone, of course, with George Van Eps and the others. I still have the real great-sounding Epiphone that I used in the late '30s. I've built a bunch of guitars and rebuilt other ones until you wouldn't know what they were, but the L-5 was the leader of the band until the Les Paul.

Were you playing electric guitar in your early act with Joe Wolverton?

No, he'd have none of that. Strictly acoustic.

What was the progression of development of your solidbody guitars?

Early on, I figured out that when you've got the top vibrating and a string vibrating, you've got a conflict. One of them has got to stop, and it can't be the string, because that's making the sound. So in 1934, I asked the Larson Brothers — the instrument makers in Chicago — to build me a guitar with a 1/2" maple top and no f-holes. They thought I was crazy. They told me it wouldn't vibrate. I told them I didn't *want* it to vibrate, because I was going to put two pickups on it. As far as I know, I was the first guy to put two pickups on a guitar. Before that, they always had just one. A guy picked a spot and put it there not because of how it sounded but just where it looked best or where it was convenient to install. Anyway, the next step was in the late '30s, when I took an Epiphone and bolted a 3/8" steel bar across the top of the body on the inside. The pickup was completely immune to vibrations from the bridge and from the neck. It was suspended, so it didn't touch the bar or the guitar and was shock-mounted so that it would not move. It gave me the equivalent of a solidbody guitar. The sides of the body were for cosmetic purposes only.

When did the Log come about?

That was 1941. Epiphone gave me the use of their factory on Sundays. I could go down there and use their tools and work all day. That's where I built it. It was the next logical step. The Epiphone people would come in and shake their heads when they looked at it.

Did you use it a lot?

Oh yeah. I used it to put down the bass guitar lines on my records. I used it a lot when I was in California in the '40s. I was living in Hollywood, and everybody — Leo Fender, Bigsby, all of them — were in my backyard looking at that Log and the Epiphone with the steel bar. When I took it to Gibson

around 1945 or 1946, they politely ushered me out the door. They called it the broomstick with the pickup on it.

What guitars did you use before the Gibson Les Pauls?

I was using the one with the steel bar and the Log most of the time. I made my first multiple recording, "Lover," with an aluminum guitar that I built.

A guitar made out of aluminum?

Yeah, I made three or four of them. I've got one here. I had a few hits on that guitar — "Caravan," "Brazil." I also did the recording session with W.C. Fields on that one. The problem with it didn't show up until I went out on the stage. I was working with the Andrews Sisters at the Paramount on Broadway, and the guy got up there with two hot spotlights and hit that aluminum guitar, and it started to do all kinds of crazy things. The first thing I know, I'm saying, "Holy God, what's wrong with my ear?" So I tune it again, and I get it right, and then the guy pulls the spot over to one of the Andrews Sisters, and I start sinking into another key again. I says, "There goes my invention." Many of my hiding places around here are full of inventions I've tried that were stupid. But they weren't so stupid that I wouldn't try them. I thought at the time that they were good.

Who were some players who influenced your style?

Eddie Lang. And there was a guy I used to hear on the radio who used a capo and a thumbpick; I don't know his name. He was one of the Three Keys. Django Reinhardt really knocked me out, of course. But that was later on. Back when I was starting to learn to play the guitar, there wasn't really anybody for me to look at. I'd hear some guys at the *Opry*, but they weren't doing a whole lot. I found a Chicago musicians' union book from 1929 not too long ago, and I think there were maybe six guitar players listed. There weren't any electric players to speak of. I'm the one who went to the union and insisted that they make a separate category for electric guitar in the union book.

Were you playing electric guitar as Rhubarb Red on Chicago radio?

Oh yeah. I had my L-5 with a pickup on it and then that guitar with the 1/2" maple top, the one that the Larsons had built for me.

How were you meeting all of the jazz players?

That was easy, because Chicago was the fireball in the early '30s. All the great music was in Chicago. They either came to town, or they were already there.

You never took a streetcar or bus to get to clubs. They were too close. You'd just take your guitar in your hand and walk from one club to another. Every theater in the neighborhood had vaudeville. We loved jamming. It was wonderful. I was playing jazz all night, so I would sleep in the lobby of the studio where we did the Rhubarb Red radio show. I needed every minute of sleep I could get. I worked out the concept that every minute of my life was valuable. So if I got the chance to play with Art Tatum and Roy Eldridge, I made the time, even if I didn't get much sleep.

When did you decide to go to New York?

In 1936. I thought — it's time to move, it's time to take this and go into the big time of tomorrow, which at that time was either New York or Los Angeles. So we packed the car — the Les Paul Trio — and flipped a coin. Heads, New York; tails, LA. It was heads. The guys said, "Well, what are we going to do when we get there?" I say, "Don't worry, because [bandleader] Paul Whiteman is a very good friend of mine." Now, I've never met the man, but here we are, on our way, driving like three fools. When we get to New York, we hit a cheap hotel with the bathroom down the hall, and Jim says, "Don't you think we ought to call up your dear buddy, Paul Whiteman?" So I look up his number and call the office, and the secretary wants to know who I am. I tell her Paul and I are old friends. She says, "Mr. Whiteman doesn't seem to remember you; what's it in regard to?" I told her that we had a trio, but she said, "Mr. Whiteman is very busy and doesn't have time to see you." I hung up.

Where did that leave you?

Well, the guys say, "What'd he say?" I tell them that he says to come right over. We went to 53rd and Broadway and pressed the button and went up there. It says "Paul Whiteman" on the door, and it's a hot day, and I can see him in the back. There's a girl at the reception desk. I tell her I called a few minutes ago and that I'm Les Paul, and I've got my trio here, and I'm sure Mr. Whiteman is anxious to hear us. Whiteman gets up and slams the door. The guys are not too happy with me, and we're standing in the hallway when Fred Waring starts to go into Whiteman's office. So I said, "Aren't you Fred Waring? We'd sure like to play something for you." He says, "Well, I've got 62 Pennsylvanians now, and I can't feed *them*." So I says, "You've got nothing to lose. The elevators are all down on the ground floor — can we play until the elevator gets here?" So we whipped out our guitars and started playing, and the faster the elevator came up, the faster we played. He

cracked up and said, "Put that stuff in the elevator." We did and went one floor down to his office, and we went into the rehearsal hall where all the Pennsylvanians were. And he says, "Men, I just had the damnedest thing happen to me, and if you like this trio as much as I do, I'm going to hire them." We went to work that day.

How did that affect your career?

That put us on the air coast to coast, and I received more letters than Waring, telling me to stop playing that electric guitar. We used to do two shows a night, one at seven, one at eleven. One for each coast because of the time difference. So one time, I did the show using the acoustic for one show and the electric for the other. We recorded them and listened to them, and took a vote among the trio and Fred, and it was unanimous to stay with the electric. So I says, "That's it."

Was Gibson building pickups for you at that time?

No, they never built them for me, and I wouldn't tell them what I was doing. They were on their knees begging me to tell them how I could run all this cable and how I could do this and that. I finally told them in 1967 after I had retired. I always built my own pickups or altered the ones they gave me.

And what was the secret?

Something that should have been pretty obvious: low-impedance pickups. Unfortunately, we started in the music industry with high impedance and locked ourselves in and for some reason haven't turned ourselves around. I figured out very early through my study of electronics that low impedance was the way to go. I figured that if the telephone company used it, that's the way to go. If you walked into a professional recording studio and someone handed you a high-impedance mike, you'd think he was nuts.

Why are low-impedance pickups superior?

Well, if you're in the club, you don't pick up the sound of the cash register or the neon lights, and you can run as much cord as you want. With high impedance, every foot of cord adds capacitance and knocks down the high frequencies, the treble.

So how did high-impedance pickups become the industry standard?

They're cheaper. With high impedance you wind the coil and go directly into the tube or transistor. With low impedance you need a transformer to transform the energy from low to high at the amplifier.

When did you first start getting interested in multiple recordings?

That actually goes all the way back to 1927,

which was the year my mother got her player piano. She didn't like to pump the thing, so she made me do it. As I pumped the piano and watched the keys go down, I could tell what was happening. Then it was a question of what *wasn't* being played. There was a lot of paper left over, so I started punching holes in it. If it was a wrong note, I'd just cover the hole with a piece of flypaper. My mother comes home to listen to her piano, and all hell breaks loose. There was always a long leader, so I cooked up some hot intros. So the first time I started adding parts to songs was on a piano roll.

When did you start doing disc-to-disc multiples?

That was around 1946, when I built the studio in my garage in Hollywood. I built the two recording lathes out of Cadillac flywheels — cost a lot less that way, and they worked better than anything else that was around then. I had seven number one hits with disc multiples: "Lover," "Nola," "Goofus," "Little Rock Getaway," and some others — they were all recorded on disc — no tape. You'd get two machines going, record on one, play that back, then play and sing along with it, recording on the other. And you just keep doing that, back and forth. "Lover" had some 24 parts on it. And you'd better not make a mistake, because if you do, it's back to number one.

What were disc recording's advantages over tape?

Tape has what you call modulation distortion, which is inherent in the tape, and this is one of the things they're still fighting with tape. You didn't have that kind of distortion with disc. But every dog has its day; the disc had its drawbacks. As you go to the inside of the record, you would lose highs. I got around that by recording at 78 rpm on the outside of a 17" disc. That gave me a lot of room, and I was burnin' up those discs. That's why the quality was so great. I was going at 78, with the EQ of 33 1/3, so when my records came out, they were hotter than a skunk.

When did you start doing sound-on-sound with tape?

That was about 1949. I never told Ampex what I was doing. I just asked them for a fourth head, and they just drilled a hole and put it there. They had no idea about what I was doing, and I didn't tell them until five years later. "How High the Moon" was our first big hit on tape. Eight-track came in 1952. I just went to Ampex with the idea and handed it to them. I never did patent it. They built it for me, but it took them four years to get it right. I've still got it here, and it's the best machine in the place. My modern

machines have one tough time trying to keep up with the old one. The original board is here too, and it also surpasses anything around.

In what way?

It's because everybody wants things small. They want them transistorized — everything on a little chip. Don't get me wrong — we work with the chip. We're heavily into research work, and I don't want to sound like a stubborn old-timer, but the tube will outperform the transistor or chip. The chip might cost 29¢ or whatever, and it draws very little current, and it doesn't dissipate nearly as much heat, and it's lightweight and compact, etc., etc., but the old-timer is still the most consistent. The change to solid-state is inevitable, though, because price forces you to compete, and maybe they'll come up with something better in the end.

How do you record your guitar?

I've gone directly into my amp and into my mixer since 1934.

How do you feel about modern recording techniques?

Much more complicated than they need be. One of the first things I learned in the multiple-track business is that this machine can run away from you — it can run *you*, instead of you running the machine. I learned that the machine can be a bitter enemy, because it will do anything you tell him to, and you better be careful. Another thing — just because there's a track open doesn't mean you have to put something on there. When I made "My Baby's Coming Home," the guy at Capitol called me up and said, "We didn't get the complete record — there's only one voice and one guitar on it." And I say, "That's it. That's the whole thing." And he said, "How can you do that, when the last one had about 28 voices and a million guitars on it?" I says, "Well, that's all it needs. If it only needs one, what do you want to put down 28 for?" What you have now is guys going into the studio and laying the parts down and searching for something. They use the studio like an arranger. They really don't know what it's going to sound like when it's done. Some may have an idea, but damn few.

How did you do it?

The way I do it and have always done it is like this: I don't touch that machine until I'm sure of the whole arrangement. Then I go to the machine, and in 15 minutes I'm done. I learned to do it like that working with sound-on-sound. You better know what the end is before you start, because you can screw yourself up in a hurry.

What is the Les Paulverizer?

It's a remote control box for a tape recorder, and it's mounted right in the guitar. Let me back up and tell you where the idea started. Making the multiple recordings — first on disc and then on tape — and doing the echo delay and sped-up sounds, it rapidly dawned on me that people would want to hear a sound like the records when we performed live. You walk out there with just one voice and one guitar, and you've got a problem. If they yell out, "'How High the Moon,'" you've got to give them something as close as possible. So I came up with the bright idea of taking Mary's sister and hiding her offstage in a john or up in an attic — whatever — with a long microphone. Whatever Mary did *onstage*, she did *off*stage. If Mary sniffled, she sniffled. It just stopped everyone dead. People couldn't believe it or figure it out. There was no tape then, so when this came around, it was highly different and shocking. One night I hear the mayor of Buffalo sitting in the front row tell his wife, "Oh, it's simple. It's radar." So a couple years after playing with the extra voice and an orchestra and everything, they began to think that they heard more than one guitar. They began to think they heard all kinds of things. They put things in there that weren't there. But I felt the real solution was to make it sound just like the record, as close as possible, and eventually I came up with the idea of the remote tape control unit, and I built the first box. I used it for the very first time in a performance for President Eisenhower.

Did you modify the equipment after that?

Yes, as time went on it got more sophisticated, more condensed. When I came out of retirement, I looked around and found that all that equipment weighed 1,100 lbs. So I told my engineers that I wanted it down to 120 lbs, and they said it couldn't be done. I said it could be done, and it *would* be done, and it was. And it does much more than it ever did before. Now when we go out on a job, we throw it in the back seat of the car or under the seat of a plane, and we're gone. It takes us maybe 15 minutes to set up. And you look at the other guys — five 18-wheelers pulling up with all their gear.

And all signals come out of one line?

All out of one line. I have my microphone mounted right on the guitar, and it comes out of the same line as the Paulverizer. Some of the stuff is so simple. I believe simplicity is the greatest, but it's the toughest thing to get sometimes. They'll make it complicated, the public will. The mayor says, "It's radar." You know who figured out the trick with Mary's sis-

ter? Nobody could figure it out. *Life* magazine couldn't. We wouldn't tell anybody; it was a secret for years. Then one night, a man came backstage with his little girl and says, "If I tell you how you're getting that sound, will you give me a yes or a no?" I said, "Sure." And the little girl says, "Where's the other lady?" It took a little kid who didn't have a complicated mind. Everybody saw machines, turntables, radar — everything but the simplest thing.

When you came out of retirement, was it difficult for you to get your chops back?

I was desperate, but still I didn't scramble. I guess I just leaned more on what was in my mind than what was in my chops. I learned a long time ago that one note can go a long way if it's the right one, and it will probably whip the guy with 20 notes. With 20 notes — he's got a lot of problems. My chops were not as fast as when I was a kid; things that were done a certain way before were harder to do when I came out of retirement. But then the speed came back. Chops come back, and you don't worry about them. I think the most important thing about playing is to walk out with confidence and look the people right in the eye and say, "Here I am," and go and do your thing. As soon as they know you're confident, they're confident. As long as you adjust to them, you're not in trouble. You should eyeball them and find out what they want and give it to them. They didn't pay to come and look at the tapestries.

Do you like any of the currently popular guitarists?

Oh, sure. There are a lot of them I like for certain things. It seems to me that there's a number of guys that got a lot of things going for them, and I can understand what they're doing. And I can't say that any one of them seems to have a corner on the market. I think everyone would agree: There is no one guy shining, no one guy who is king above it all. But one of the problems with the new crop on the horizon is they've got their razor-clean playing, but it's like a clock. It's about as musical as a metronome. It's easy to play like a machine, and when a guy gets to playing like a machine, it's frightening. You've lost all the feeling in it. We can appreciate how hard he practiced and studied and probably skipped playing basketball and going with girls, but I still feel that in many cases, what is lacking is that the guy is not *saying* anything. And that's what music is all about. He can pick clean, but the music is expressionless.

— CARL PERKINS —

BY JON SIEVERT – JUNE 1989

JON SIEVERT

FOR A MAN WHO'S had only one Top-40 hit in a recording career stretching nearly 35 years, Carl Perkins has had an inordinate impact on the history of rock guitar. His 1956 recording of "Blue Suede Shoes," with its hip lyrics, unrelenting groove, and stuttering, driving solos, introduced the world at large to rockabilly by becoming the first record to ever top the Pop, Country, and R&B charts simultaneously. And though none of his subsequent Sun Records releases had anywhere near that kind of chart success, they *did* serve to build a devoted following of young, impressionable guitarists riveted by his bluesy two-string bends, off-the-wall trebly licks, and rocking rhythm feel. Among the enthusiastic listeners admittedly captivated by his sound — and in whose work his influence is nakedly apparent — were George Harrison, Eric Clapton, Ricky Nelson, James Burton, John Fogerty, Dave Edmunds, Mark Knopfler, Phil and Dave Alvin, and Brian Setzer, to name a few. And now, with a rash of reissues of his early Sun recordings and a new album, *Born to Rock,* Perkins stands ready to directly influence a whole new generation of guitarists.

Carl Perkins' career presents a picture of wonderful songs, great guitar, missed timing, and terrible misfortune. Born dirt-poor on April 9, 1932, in Lake County, Tennessee, his early years were spent on a welfare-aided tenant farm, where he and his family were the only white sharecroppers. His love for the guitar began at age four, when his father built his first one from a cigar box, a broomstick, and baling wire. By the time Carl started school the following year, he'd graduated to a Sears Gene Autry model. A natural performer, Carl began entertaining his classmates in grade school and was playing for tips at a recreation area near a local army base by age nine. His musical influences came from the radio (in particular, the *Grand Ole Opry* and Memphis blues stations), the church, and an old black sharecropper named John Westbrook. At 14, the family moved southeast to Bemis, Tennessee, where Carl acquired his first electric guitar, a Harmony solidbody. That same year he won a local talent contest, which netted him $25 and the opportunity to perform his first composition, "Movie Magg," on a Jackson radio station.

Tired of playing by himself, Perkins taught his brother Jay a few chords so he could cover rhythm. Before long, his other brother, Clayton, had taken up the bass and the Perkins Brothers Band was formed. By early 1954, Carl had married, moved to Jackson (where he still lives), and acquired his first good guitar, a new Gibson Les Paul. With neighbor W.S. Holland joining them on drums, the band became a fixture in local juke joints, playing a hybrid mixture of country, honky-tonk, and blues. During that period, Carl's style came into sharp focus as he incorporated the influences of John Lee Hooker, Bill Monroe, B. B. King, Arthur "Guitar Boogie" Smith, Merle Travis, and Muddy Waters into a unique amalgam.

Convinced of his band's talent, Carl began sending tapes to record companies, but to no avail. Then, one summer afternoon in 1954, he heard Elvis Presley's first single on the radio, a jumped-up version of Bill Monroe's "Blue Moon of Kentucky." Because his band was playing a nearly identical version of the song, Carl set his sights on Memphis and Sun Records. An audition with owner Sam Phillips in December 1954 resulted in a two-year contract. Perkins' first single, "Turn Around" backed with "Movie Magg," was issued on the Flip label and was aimed at the country market, because Phillips feared that the record-buying public wouldn't support another artist doing the same kind of thing as Elvis. But when Sam put Carl on the road with Presley and another new Sun artist, Johnny Cash, the crowds responded with enthusiasm. According to reports, Perkins had developed such a volatile, unfollowable stage act that he sometimes closed the show, though Elvis was the label's star. When Phillips sold Presley's contract to RCA in November 1955, Carl was finally turned loose in the studio to rock. He responded with "Blue Suede Shoes" backed with "Honey Don't." By April 1956, "Shoes" stood at the top of *Cashbox'* pop, country, and R&B charts, and Carl was a star. The only problem was that, by then, he was broken up and lying in a hospital.

On March 22, with the song heading up the charts, Carl and the band were en route to New York for appearances on the Ed Sullivan and Perry Como shows when their car smashed into a truck, killing its driver and badly injuring them all. From his hospital bed, Carl watched Elvis perform his song on the *Ed Sullivan Show* several weeks later. Six months of recovery followed as Presley ascended to superstardom. Carl never regained his momentum, but his recording career was far from finished. Over the next three years, he wrote and waxed nearly three dozen songs for Sun. Among his classics are "Boppin' the Blues," "Everybody's Trying to Be My Baby," "Matchbox" (with Jerry Lee Lewis on piano), "Your True Love," "Dixie Fried," and "All Mama's Children." Several dented the charts, but nothing came close to matching the impact of "Blue Suede Shoes." During his four years at Sun, Carl recorded 39 sides, but only eight were released as singles. Seventeen cuts were never released at all. Fortunately, everything he recorded for Sun is now available.

Perkins left Sun for Columbia in 1958, where he scored a couple of minor country hits. In general, however, his career withered, and when Jay died of cancer that year, Carl fell into the bottle. In the fall of 1962 tragedy struck again. Playing a small club in Dyersburg, Tennessee, Carl accidentally stuck his left hand into a fan and nearly severed three fingers. A long period of recovery and depression followed. By spring of 1964, he was ready to quit the business for good when his wife persuaded him to tour England with Chuck Berry. There he was greeted by rabid audiences, treated as a star, and found that he was an idol of the Beatles. On June 1, he sat in the studio as they recorded "Matchbox," which they turned into a far bigger hit than it had been for him. A few months later they recorded several other Perkins tunes, including "Honey Don't" and "Everybody's Trying to Be My Baby."

He had not been back in the States for long when trouble found him again. A lifelong hunter, he nearly blew his left foot away with a shotgun in an accident. During recovery, Johnny Cash stopped by and asked Carl to play a couple of gigs with him. When the shows went well, Cash invited Perkins to become a regular member of his band and show. For the next 10 years, Carl opened the show, played in John's band, and appeared on every Cash record. He also wrote "Daddy Sang Bass," which was a #1 hit for Cash in the late '60s. During his tenure with Cash he continued to make his own albums, appearing on several labels and scoring a significant hit, "Restless," on Columbia in 1968. A 1969 collaboration with NRBQ, *Boppin' the Blues,* was an artistic, if not commercial, success. And in 1971, he and Cash scored the soundtrack for the film *Little Fauss and Big Halsey.*

Carl left Cash's show in 1976 to form a band with his sons Greg (on bass) and Stan (on drums), and they're still together and playing about 150 club dates and oldies revivals each year. And even if he hasn't been in the spotlight, it's clear that his old friends and admirers haven't forgotten him. In 1986, Dave Edmunds produced and directed a lively Cinemax tribute to Carl featuring George Harrison, Eric Clapton, Ringo Starr, Roseanne Cash, and Earl Slick, among others. Predictably titled *Blue Suede Shoes,* the one-hour special (available at many video rental outlets) demonstrates that Carl hasn't lost an iota of vitality or enthusiasm for his music.

Since re-forming his band there have been a few albums, including 1978's *Old Blue Suede's Back.* Perkins is a warm, gracious man without a trace of bitterness about what might have been.

Did you always record your guitar and vocals at the same time at Sun?

Yes, that's the way I love to do it, and I think it's time to really go after nailing the simplicity of the rhythm and that old, raw, unrehearsed guitar sound. I enjoy listening to a dude play himself into a hole. Sometimes working your way out of unknown areas on the guitar will produce some interesting things.

Can you recall some instances when that happened to you?

Everything I cut at Sun Records, I started digging myself a hole in the kick-off and stayed pretty well in that hole all the way through. Really. It was not a rehearsed thing. It was, for the most part, a spontaneous thing happening among a four-piece band. Things like "Matchbox," with Jerry Lee Lewis on piano. I didn't have an opening or anything. I started with that rhythm riff, and Jerry Lee said, "Yeah, I like that, man." So, Jerry started hitting the piano along with the guitar, and it just set up a little thing. I knew a line or two from an old blues song I'd heard in the cotton fields when I was a youngster, and the song "Matchbox" just happened. We never went in there with that sound or with that way of recording. I think that if there's anything good to be remembered about most of the old Sun records — and I include Elvis' — it was the fact that it wasn't rehearsed. There weren't any outstanding musicians. It was everybody playing a feel and just getting in the groove and really enjoying it. It was music that was born at the time right there. Those days are long gone. It's now a three-hour session and you'd better be ready. Back then it could go three days, or as long as the jug stayed about half full. For that reason, there were some licks that came out of there simply because a guy got up on the neck and he knew in his soul, "Whew, I gotta work my way back to where I usually play. I'm way down in here." And on the way back out, sometimes there'd be a hoss of a little lick. For Scotty Moore, Roland Janes and most of the guys at Sun, that type of thing would happen.

Do you think it's time for a rockabilly revival?

I feel like there's a place out there for what was first called rockabilly music. At Sun, that name soon left, and rock and roll became the name. But there's a difference. Rockabilly is a more ragged-edged country sound. I always thought it was a white man's lyric to a black man's rhythm. Rock and roll took over, and you didn't hear the name rockabilly anymore. The songs and production got better. We'd spent more attention to the beat and the guitar playing than we did to the words. It didn't matter what it said too much, because the kids were rockin' and dancin'. We were going after the overall feel of the record more than anything else. That changed pretty quick.

Photos of you over your career show you playing a lot of different guitars, including Gibsons, Fenders, Guilds, and Peaveys. What are you using now?

I'm using a little guitar that Leo Fender made called a G&L Broadcaster. He built some as his farewell to the industry, and they're all black. The old gentleman had a stroke, but he supposedly soldered all the wires in these. He wanted to do this for people that he felt through the years had helped his guitar's popularity along. I was very honored when he handed me mine out in California about two years ago. It's really a Telecaster design, with twin pickups. Prior to that, I'd been playing Peaveys. As a matter of fact, Peavey just made a Carl Perkins model. It's a fine little guitar, but that Broadcaster means so much to me that I have not played anything else onstage since. I actually wound up with two of them. Leo personally gave me the last one of the 50, and I may never play that one. I may put it with the first good one I ever owned — a 1954 Gibson Les Paul. That's the one I cut "Blue Suede Shoes," "Boppin' the Blues," and a lot of other Sun things with. I've got it here at the house, but it's not in playing condition.

Why did you quit using it?

I made my first trip to California in the summer of 1956 to do a TV show called *Town Hall Party*, which was emceed by Tex Ritter. We'd just finished a Saturday afternoon rehearsal when this fellow in khaki clothes with a big set of keys hanging on his belt loop walked up and asked me what kind of guitar I played. I said, "I play the only kind there is — a Gibson Les Paul." He said, "You're sure about that, ain't ya? If you don't have anything to do for the next few hours, would you take a little ride down the street with me? I promise you, you won't go wrong." So, I got in his car, still not knowing who he was, and he pulled up to the Fender factory and into a parking place that said "Leo." He popped that big key ring off that loop and socked it in that front door and that baby swung open. Sure, I'd heard of Leo Fender, but I'd never owned one of his guitars. He handed me a Jazzmaster and said, "See how that feels." He gave me that *and* a bass for my brother Clayton, who was playing upright, and said, "Now this is the coming thing. They're going to put that big one out of business." Well, I retired that Les Paul and started playing Fenders. I did, however, order a big blonde Gibson Switchmaster from a music store in Jackson. I saw it in a catalog and had to have it. The last songs I cut at Sun Records were "Glad All Over" and "Lend Me Your Comb," and I played that big

Switchmaster on the session. But I didn't play it for very long. I stayed with Fender through most of the years. Oh, once in a while a guitar company will give me one and I'll play it a while, but I always go back to my Fender. I would never leave on a tour without my Fenders. I've played some shows with other guitars, but when I felt the pressure, I knew they'd stay in tune and be there. I always trusted them and still do.

What do you look for in a guitar?

The feel. You can go down a line in a factory and there's no two that feel the same, even though they've been built the same. If you're lucky, there's one that will feel like an extension of your own arms — it's just magic. It feels like your baby in your arms and makes you confident. I'd tell any youngster looking for a guitar that beauty is secondary. You want that thing to speak back to you in such a way that it says, "We can accomplish together." The guitar talks to you, it really does. To somebody who doesn't play, this would sound odd or crazy, but it's not. There's something that sets up between the picker and the instrument. Many a time behind super stages — Vegas or the White House, whatever — I'll squeeze the neck on my little old box and say, "Okay, pal, me and you. Let's go." That's why I say I might use a new guitar sometimes, but that old Strat has always been close enough that if I was scared enough, I'd go get it.

How about amps?

I've used Fender Bassmans and Twins over the years, but I've got a Dean Markley right now. It's got a tone that I like. I don't know the model, but it has one 12" JBL speaker. I've been using it maybe three or four years. I'm not one for gimmicks. I've got nothing against them, but I just kind of like to watch a dude walk out and plug in and play. I like to see him bring it out pretty clean with his fingers and picks. A little echo doesn't bother me, but some of the flangers and things — a lot of these dudes work as hard with their feet as their hands. I could probably figure out a way to do it quicker than I could teach my feet which buttons to push. I'm not putting it down, but I'm from the old school. Just a simple amp is good enough for me.

Could you talk a bit about how you learned to play?

I was about four or five. On the Sunday before I started school, I cried all day. I remember hearing my mother telling my daddy, "Buck, I believe he doesn't want to leave his guitar at home." The first time I climbed on the school bus, I stepped up in there with an old beat-up guitar, and every kid was looking and wondering. I didn't want to spend the day without it.

I loved guitars, and that's never gone away. I can spend a day in anybody's music store. I love the feel of them. It's always been a part of my life.

Do you remember what kind of guitar you took to school?

It was a Gene Autry model with a picture of him and his horse painted on there. The strings were about an inch over the fretboard. Mama had one big comb that we all combed our hair with, and the big teeth in that comb made a nice little old pick. Most of the combs my poor mama had back in those days just had the little teeth in them. I'd break me out a couple of the big ones and put 'em in my shirt pocket for spares.

Was there anybody around to teach you the basics of the guitar?

My daddy knew G, C, and D, and that was about it. Oh, he had what he called an off-chord — an A — that he would throw into a few songs. And there was an old black man named John Westbrook who sharecropped on the same land we did. Uncle John had a little guitar that looked a little better than mine — the neck wasn't warped as bad. But he just really knocked me out because he had a chord called E. It had such a beautiful tone; you know, the bass string open and the bottom two open. It was a pretty easy chord to make down there on that 1st fret, and he could slide down and go [*sings sliding sound*]. Whoa, me. Quickly, the simple country got put on the back burner in my little old soul. I thought that little blues lick was the greatest sound I ever heard in my life. I thought he was the greatest guitar player who ever lived. As I got older, I realized he wasn't an accomplished player, but he just moved me to the bone.

That's the most important thing.

That's exactly right. It's like today, boys like Eric Clapton and George Harrison say, "If it hadn't been for you, I wouldn't have gotten into this business." And I say, "Man, I don't want to hear about none of my old simple licks in what you all do." They're great guitar players and play so much more than I ever dreamed of playing. But maybe, just maybe, it was that little old basic string-pushing thing that came off the fingers of that old black man and into my simple country soul that got them. I twisted them around and got them working as up-tempo country songs, but that's what some of these boys heard, and in some little way, he affected them as he affected me. Clapton told me, "Man, that lick on 'Matchbox' just hooked me. I decided then that's what I wanted to play." It's a humbling thing when these people say that, and yet it takes me back to how Uncle John affected me. He was old and tired, but he took the time with that little white boy. He said, "That guitar can take you miles away from these cotton fields, boy, if you work on it. There's somethin' about you, chile. I have that feeling that you will progress if you will practice." He died just a few years after I started playing, but his memory will be strong forever in my life. The black man loved the little white boy and shared his little blues with him. There's something awesome in that.

When did you actually start performing?

In the second grade. I got up in front of the class with my little guitar and sang "Jesus Loves Me," a little fast. I just always want to get on with it. I didn't mind going to church. I don't know nothin' the preacher said, and I didn't care too much about "The Old Rugged Cross" — it dragged. But when they would hit "I'll Fly Away," my foot would start poundin' that old plank floor, and my mama would reach and get hold of my ear and pull it over and say, "You're singing too loud and you're getting too fast." I liked to think it was the spirit of the thing.

When did you get your first electric guitar?

When I was 14. It was a little solidbody Harmony. And I got what I call a little one-lung amplifier. It was just a little bitty thing but that was enough, because it put me louder than Jay. I was trying to pick lead with him ringin' that rhythm and I couldn't hear. I'd lay my head against the guitar so I could hear over his rhythm playing. I think the guitar and amp cost $50.00, but it did what I wanted. I slept with it. It was a night-and-day thing, and pretty soon our younger brother Clayton got an old home-made upright bass fiddle, and we had the Perkins Brothers Band.

How did you develop your guitar style?

It was just something that came from inside, from the kind of music I liked. I liked country, but I also felt that it needed some of Uncle John in it. So I grew a mixture. I did a lot of string pushing because I couldn't always afford to buy new strings when they broke. I'd slide to where I'd had to tie a knot and push up on the string to get a note, because I couldn't jump over the knot.

It seems like you and Chuck Berry had a lot in common, because only a few guys on that early rock scene sang, played guitar, and wrote songs.

That's true. When I first heard "Maybellene," I could hear some three-chord country in it. We talked about that in the early days. I remember him saying, "I thought you were one of us when I heard them 'Shoes.'" I said, "Well, I sure heard some Bill Monroe

in 'Maybellene,'" and he said, "You'd better know it." I worked with Chuck on the first big tour I ever did. It was called the Top Stars of '56 and had people like Frankie Lymon & The Teenagers and Al Hibbler. Everybody rode in two big buses except Chuck and me. I had a brand new Cadillac, and he always wanted to ride in that. He knew a lot of old country songs.

Did you ever think that you were sort of two sides of the same coin? You're white and he's black, but you were both doing the same kind of thing that mixed elements of both.

That's true. Black was born from white and white was born from black. I remember Fats Domino telling me one night, "Carl, you know music might have done more to do away with segregation than Washington, D.C., did." People in all-white honky-tonks in the South didn't walk up to that Wurlitzer and drop a nickel in there and read, "Blueberry Hill," Fats Domino — black; "Blue Suede Shoes," Carl Perkins — white. It was music, and it mixed before people did. Something eased barriers, and pretty soon white teenyboppers were dancing to Chuck Berry, Little Richard, and Fats Domino, and it didn't make any difference. It really boils down to a period in time when music did a ring around the world from a little bitty studio in Memphis, Tennessee, with a cat named Elvis. He opened the door for so many. If he hadn't walked into Sun Records, music might be different today. As John Lennon once said, "Before Sun, there was none." That little old studio echoed around the world.

The Beatles had several hits with your songs. Isn't there at least one they recorded but never released?

Yes. They did another old Sun thing called "Your True Love." George *loves* that song. He told me he wanted it to come out when they were Beatles. When I went over to England to play for the 10th anniversary of his film company last year, he told me about the Traveling Wilburys album. He said, "I'm sorry you're not on this thing. If I'd had time to plan it, you would have been. If this thing sells, there'll be another one, and you and I are going to do "Your True Love." I said, "You got my phone number. Call when you're ready." I was so proud for Roy Orbison that the record did so well. Things were comin' his way in leaps and bounds, and they were way overdue. I loved him so dearly. Roy was a much better guitar player than most people knew. He could really get down and pick it.

How did you happen to stick your hand in a fan, and how has it affected your playing?

I was campaigning for the governor of

Tennessee, who was running for re-election. I'd do a number or two, and then he'd speak to the voters. I'd heard about a little band that was playing in a club just outside of Dyersburg, so I stopped by to hear them. Ironically, I was sitting at the table and noticed this big old window fan behind them without a cover on it. I thought that it looked dangerous. They called me up to do a song and somebody plugged the fan in while I was playing. I did three or four songs and was taking the guitar off to bow and stuck my hand in that thing. It almost destroyed it. I have no feeling in the little finger. The ring finger is half-dead — I've got a little feeling on the inside of it. The forefinger doesn't have much feeling — it cut the end of it off. They just threw a towel around it and got me to a local hospital that sent me on to Jackson because of bone damage. I did not look at the hand. I went into shock on the back seat and almost bled to death in the hour ride. They were going to amputate two of the fingers, but my wife begged them not to. I woke up the next day, and the doctor was sitting by my bed. He'd worked on it for six hours, hooking back all the nerves he could. He told me I'd never be able to straighten my little finger again and that I'd never use the one next to it. But after six weeks, when I got out of the cast, I started squeezing a rubber ball night and day. I was determined to get three fingers back so I could chord. There was a year there that I'd play and cry, because I couldn't stretch 'em or move 'em. And if I did, I had to look to see I'd put it in the right place. But I learned to just turn it up a bit and make do. It was like starting over, only worse. I'd had a taste of being able to really work at something and make it happen on the guitar. Now I was handicapped to where I just couldn't do what I wanted. The little finger played a big part in my playing, making the 7th notes and all that. Since '62, everything I've played is with three fingers. You make do with what you've got left. It makes you dig a little deeper and find ways. Maybe instead of moving up a fret, you just push up the string and stay in the same place.

Do you still like to practice?

I love it. That hasn't diminished at all. I have the guitar in my hands at least two hours just about every day. Once you stop learning, you're in trouble. The guitar is still the instrument that ain't been conquered. There's a cat out there right now who's ready to whop your brain. It ain't all been done on a guitar.

– VERNON REID –

BY JOE GORE – OCTOBER 1988

PAUL NATKIN

EVERY ASPECT OF the man and his music defies easy categorization. He's a rock and roller who came of age musically as a member of a free-form jazz group. He's a high-wattage screamer whose secret ambition is to master fingerstyle ragtime guitar. Soloing, he can move convincingly from pentatonic riffing to post-Ornette Coleman chromaticism and back again in just a measure or two. His playing is polished and subtle but never without a go-for-the-throat intensity. Although he's a literate, educated musician (his prose has appeared in the *Village Voice,* and he's composed a large-scale multimedia theater piece), he views music-making as a largely non-conscious, intuitive activity. His list of influences reads like an encyclopedia of 20th-century music; the names of everyone from jazz saxophonist Eric Dolphy to sonic experimentalist Edgar Varèse to blues great Lonnie Johnson are liable to pop up when Vernon Reid talks music. In short, he undermines a lot of commonly held assumptions about what "rock," "jazz," "funk," "popular," "classical," "blues," "black," and "white" guitar playing are *supposed* to sound like.

As a sideman, Vernon has been a fixture of the New York music scene throughout the '80s, but he finally received international attention as the leader of Living Colour, a full-throttle rock and roll quartet. Their debut album, *Vivid,* showcased the band's tough-as-nails sound. Corey Glover is an iron-throated belter who can shift effortlessly from a throaty

R&B growl to a metallic castrato shriek. Bassist Muzz Skillings and drummer William Calhoun are a thunderous, yet precise, rhythm section — imagine a cross between Led Zeppelin and Chic. At the heart of Living Colour's sound, however, is Vernon's over-the-edge guitar playing.

The 33-year-old musician was born in London of West Indian parents and raised in New York City. He took up the guitar at age 15 and was playing professionally within a couple of years. After a brief stint with R&B singer Kashif, he joined the Decoding Society, the highly acclaimed jazz ensemble led by Ronald Shannon Jackson [saxophonist/composer Ornette Coleman's onetime drummer.] After touring extensively and recording six albums with Jackson, Reid set out to form his own band. Living Colour's current lineup is the end product of years of personnel changes. Along the way, he's played with the art/dance band Defunkt, jazz guitarist Bill Frisell, militant rappers Public Enemy, avant-garde composer John Zorn, experimental guitarist Arto Lindsay, and others. Through it all, Vernon has blurred the boundaries between jazz, funk, rock, and art music without ever compromising his basic approach.

Unfortunately, the music industry doesn't usually *like* to have its boundaries blurred, and one of its most cherished boundaries is the one that stands between "black" and "white" music. Apart from a few rare exceptions such as Jimi Hendrix and Prince, rock and roll has become white turf. To a large extent, the music business can't accept the idea of a black hard rock band, despite the music's undeniably Afro-American origins. Of course, there's no law prohibiting black musicians from playing rock and roll, but those who do are not likely to be embraced by the industry. The career prospects are grim for a black musician who falls outside the rigid stylistic confines of the "urban contemporary" sound. ("Urban contemporary" is the industry's code name for music aimed at a predominantly black audience.) Black musicians who don't rap, croon romantic ballads, or make good-timey party records usually find themselves locked out of both black and white markets.

Vernon has attacked such stylistic stereotyping with his actions as well as his music. In September 1985, he and *Village Voice* writer Greg Tate formed the Black Rock Coalition, a "united front of musically and politically progressive black artists and supporters." They declared their intentions in a founding manifesto:

"The Black Rock Coalition opposes the racist and reactionary forces in the American music industry which deny black artists the expressive freedom and economic rewards that our Caucasian counterparts enjoy as a matter of course. We too claim the right of creative freedom and total access to American and international markets. Like our forebears — Chuck Berry, Jimi Hendrix, Sly Stone, Funkadelic, and Labelle, to name but a few — the members of the Black Rock Coalition are neither novelty acts nor carbon copies of white bands who work America's Apartheid-Oriented Rock Circuit."

The Coalition's founders argue that the very existence of "black charts," "black radio," "black concert promotion," and so forth perpetuates a separate-but-unequal economic system that excludes black artists from many avenues of musical expression. Vernon places the blame on both white and black elements within the music business; as he told Geoffrey Himes of the *Washington Post:* "The white side of the industry claims that it can't put a black band on an album cover and sell them in suburban malls. The black side of the industry claims that black audiences don't want to hear rock and roll."

If it's as bad as all that, how did Living Colour score a major-label deal? It wasn't easy — the band wasn't picked up by Epic until Mick Jagger caught one of their shows, became a fan, and produced two songs for the band. Despite having talent to burn and a stack of rave reviews the size of a small phone book, it took the direct intercession of one of the most powerful men in rock to bring Living Colour to the marketplace.

You've said that you don't consider yourself a "natural."

I'm not. I had an inclination towards music, because I loved it, but I wasn't a prodigy. I wish I was — I've met really young players who had it all together. Martin Aubert, who was the guitar player in the first Defunkt band, was *killing* when he was 13 or 14 years old. I came to playing late, when I was 15. Playing the guitar is something I really had to work at. Things had to happen to really push me; I had to be embarrassed. When I was with the Decoding Society, I sometimes found myself sitting in a hotel room, thinking, "Maybe I have no talent." Ronald Shannon Jackson was very demanding. You had to throw yourself into the music and not be distanced from it. A lot of people approach music in that way — "Yeah, I can *kind of* play it" — but don't immerse themselves headlong in the feeling of it. I *had* to because he demanded that. At the same time, I never left any of the other things that I loved behind. I never left my love for Santana or Hendrix or whoever.

Your playing over the years has a lot of continuity. Even though Living Colour sounds very different from the Decoding Society, you don't seem to have compromised your approach in an attempt to "go rock."

It's funny — rock was the music I felt I had the clearest voice in. I was always struggling with jazz, even though I loved it. I loved Dolphy, Coltrane, and Ornette so much that I tried to integrate the two things. The Decoding Society was a school for solidifying what I really wanted to do; it was my chance to integrate the blues with the harmolodic concept, to pick and choose and make it really coherent.

Could you explain harmolodic concept?

The harmolodic approach was developed by Ornette Coleman. It's a theory of music that frees melody from its subservience to harmony. Traditionally, certain chords dictate certain melodic lines, but in Ornette's theory, melody, harmony, and rhythm are free from each other; they can interact on different levels. You can play things in different keys and make it work because the combination of keys creates another, freer tonal center. Everyone has had the experience of being somewhere, listening to music, and then hearing a radio outside playing different music. For a brief moment, you hear the two songs together and you perceive the consonances between them. Harmolodic theory tries to synthesize that moment.

Like the story of how Charles Ives, the 20th-century American composer, was inspired by hearing two marching bands as they moved in different directions?

Exactly. It's an idea that's been around.

What is your response to people who accuse you of "going commercial"?

In all seriousness, look at the statistical averages of black rock and roll bands that are killing on the charts and really making it. You'll see that there's a definite amount of risk. It's not something that's happening in a mass, across-the-board sort of way — not since Hendrix. This is just as challenging as being in the Decoding Society, but it's challenging on another level because you're dealing with a whole social milieu, a whole way of thinking about rock and roll that's been locked in place since the middle '70s.

You're very outspoken on the issue of the black guitarist's position in rock and roll music.

It's a curious thing. We constantly ask ourselves, "Where do we fit in?" I remember how, years ago, the rock guitar poll in *Guitar Player* never included Ernie Isley, who was in the Isley Brothers, one of the few successful black rock bands after Hendrix. That always bothered me. It was like there was an alternate history; there was the history of everything you knew about, and there was this other thing happening off to the side. At least half the guitarists who really influenced me are not known. There are horrendously underrecorded players, like Ray Muton, from New Orleans — he played with [drummer] Billy Cobham's band for a couple of tours and one record. Charlie Singleton was also in that band; he went on to play with Cameo. He was an astounding, well-rounded player. I thought, "This guy is going to be a star," but since then, never heard from him. Arthur Rhames, from Brooklyn, had a fusion band called Eternity, a trio based around the Mahavishnu Orchestra. I've never heard a better guitar player. He also played piano and saxophone — he was frightening. Blackbird McKnight — he played with Parliament, the Brides of Funkenstein, and Herbie Hancock. Kelvyn Bell, from the original Defunkt band, and Ronnie Drayton, who plays on the latest Defunkt album. There are so many.

You have to hold on to the past. It's important to see things in perspective and see how one thing influences another. Eddie Van Halen says, "I never listened to Hendrix; I listened to Clapton," but Clapton — well, Robert Johnson was the one who influenced *him*. If you make a family tree or a timeline, you'll see that we're all influencing each other. To say Led

Zeppelin influenced me is to say that Led Zeppelin got me into Muddy Waters and made me say, "Ah! *That's* where it was coming from!" Michael Hill, another guitarist from the Black Rock Coalition, is a fantastic slide player, and he heard it first from Duane Allman. Being disconnected from the roots and dealing only with the branches is odd.

You told the New York Times: *"The existence of a 'black' music chart requires black artists to conform to what the industry considers rhythm and blues. That means you're not going to be able to sing about the illiteracy rate; you're going to have to sing about sex."*

There are certain expectations of black people: that they're into escapist entertainment, or that black people should provide escapist entertainment all the time. That's not cool because you start to do what's expected of you; if that's your only option, that's what you do. After a while, you say, "Why bother practicing all this stuff if I'll never get a chance to play like that?" That's the kind of thing I'm afraid of. It's a human issue.

In general, isn't it taboo for pop artists to deal with real life?

That's true; there's a conservatism all across the board. There are unique problems for black artists, but not all problems are unique to us. A lot of people are chafing under the strain of, "You gotta move those numbers, you gotta do silly love songs all the time." That can really frustrate and trap an artist. I hope we're entering into a time where there's going to be more creative music.

There's a great statement that you made to the Village Voice *a few years ago: "I don't separate Dolphy from Sly from Monk from Trane because the common thing that links all these people together is the blues. The blues is what links Ornette to the Temptations or Hendrix to Trane."*

It's true. The blues is really more than a structure; it's a real feeling. Once, I heard John Gilmore play a solo with [jazz composer and bandleader] Sun Ra, and he played just total *sound*. There was nothing linear, but the feeling of blues came across so strongly. Or I think of the first time I heard Dionne Warwick — such a clear, clean, but still human voice. It's interesting that Carlos Santana also credits her as an influence, since he was the first rock and roll guitarist who really grabbed me.

Blues is a thread that links all these different experiences. It's a matter of expressing the blues in one's life. Even getting past the point of, say, listening to Muddy Waters or Lonnie Johnson all the time, because when you do, you're listening to *their* lives. The only things you can draw from them are things that resonate in your own life. Other than that, everything will fall away, unless you're a total chameleon and you're trying to submerge your life. People either try to find resonances in their lives, or they try to obscure what their life is and take on another persona. It's like that Steely Dan song that says, "Any world that I'm welcome to is better than the one I come from." Some people will take on the persona of another player and say, "I want to be that, because I don't like my life." Is the music an expression of your state of being, or is it something you're just taking on?

So you consider yourself a blues player?

Yeah, I do. The blues is at the bottom of my playing. It's something that I constantly try to work with. I try to get to my center, to what I'm really feeling. Guitar playing is a sort of feeling analysis that tries to strip away all the crap.

Sometimes you play from a predominantly pentatonic vocabulary, and at other times you use more open, chromatic sounds. Do you shift gears conceptually when you move from a pentatonic idiom to a chromatic one?

Part of it is a matter of separating myself from the tonal center. Partly, it's trying to connect with the rhythm. Sometimes I concentrate purely on what's happening with the drums and free it up that way. I also find myself working with dominant figures along with the pentatonic and chromatic things. I do find myself shifting gears, but I'm not sure whether it's a conscious thing. When I'm practicing, I try to think of that stuff, but when I'm performing, I try to just be in the moment.

Were you in the moment when you recorded the "Cult of Personality" solo?

It's funny how that came about. That's a first take. I'd done the tracking for the song — doubled the guitar parts, and so on — when our producer, Ed Stasium, said, "Okay, we've got the stuff laid down, let's come in and do a solo tomorrow." But I said, "I've got to do it *now*." It was the funniest thing — I was really beat until he said, "The track is coming now," and then I plugged into a musical stream of consciousness. After it was done, I thought, "Did *I* do that?" I think I really plugged into what that song was about on that solo, and I really felt good about it.

It's not a stereotypically structured solo. You come out ripping away at maximum speed, then move into longer, more sustained sounds towards the end.

On the ending section, I feel like I got into a really "singing" thing over the chords. I did some other takes after that one, but . . . [*shrugs*].

It's cool how you develop the song's opening riff. You expand it into a longer phrase that sets a three-beat rhythmic grouping against a straight 4/4 backbeat. It creates the sort of metric clash that you find in both a Led Zeppelin song such as "Black Dog" [from Led Zeppelin IV*] and a Thelonious Monk tune such as "Straight, No Chaser."*

Yeah, like Monk's "I Mean You." "Cult of Personality" was a band composition; Corey was singing this phrase over and over, and I kept trying to work it into something. It made me think of the main phrase. Muzzy and I were working with it, and Calhoun laid this heavy backbeat against it. It was weird how it would turn around. Afterwards, I thought, "Hmm, this reminds me of something." People have called it a Zep-type approach. I guess if you listen to something enough, it becomes part of your consciousness and comes back out. Years ago, I was listening to Bill Connors on "Captain Senor Mouse," from Return to Forever's *Hymn of the Seventh Galaxy*, which is a great, great guitar record. Then while playing with Defunkt one night, I found myself playing this solo which seemed oddly familiar. When I listened back to the tape, I recognized some things from Bill Connors.

You get a larger-than-life tone on "Cult of Personality." What was your setup?

For the album, we used the old analog dinosaur setup. I used a Pro-Co Rat distortion, a Korg multi-effects box with compression, chorus, flanging, and overdrive, and an ADA Digitizer for additional chorusing. I also used a Boss Digital Delay/Sampler and an Alesis Microverb. We miked close, in the middle, and in the corners of a real big room. We had the "great wall of amps": a Carvin, a Dean Markley, a Vox, a Marshall head, and a Fender Showman head. It varied from cut to cut.

Did you record all the amps at once?

It averaged two or three amps per song, pretty much. On "Desperate People," we had everything on. It was so loud that the engineer would literally run into the room when he had to adjust something. That was really funny. [*Ed. Note: Dennis Diamond, Living Colour's guitar technician, said, "The volume was so loud it was killing rats as they walked past — and Vernon plays with no earplugs!"*] There were times when I thought I should be in the control room with them, but I wanted to get that wind. It fatigues you, though; if you're doing that stuff, you've got to watch out. I'm very careful with my hearing. You've got to take a break. Don't do it for three or four hours. It's like getting hit in your body.

Did you double many parts?

Yeah. "Cult of Personality" was done three different times with three different guitars. I used two ESPs — a Strat-style and a Tele-style — and a Fender. On "Broken Hearts," I used a Dobro and a lap steel. Mostly, though, it's the ESP on that song; I used the tremolo and a volume pedal to create slide-type effects.

You and Muzz voice the main riff on "I Want to Know" in fourths, instead of the fifths you'd probably expect. You also follow up on the fourths idea in your solo.

I try to do little things to change it up. I tried to get that particular solo to be more of a blues thing, even though there are the fourths. There's also some backwards guitar at the end.

There is a little Charlie Christian touch on the "Middle Man" solo; you play a phrase that's reminiscent of that little chromatic riff he always used.

That's a kind of Charlie Christian or Django Reinhardt thing. But I don't try to make a conscious nod to this or that; I just try to be open. Different things will just manifest themselves. I did listen a lot to Charlie and Django. The two of them, their stories! How Charlie died so young, but changed the course of everything. When I was 23, I was depressed, because I thought, "Wow! Charlie Christian died at this age, and what have I done?" And Django! He overcame a crippling disability, and a lot of people say he actually played better because he was driven.

The accents on the intro to "Funny Vibe" are so syncopated that it's difficult to determine the actual meter. In general, how do you reconcile "out" time with rock and roll?

Odd meters can backfire on you if they become too self-conscious. "Black Dog" is in odd time, but it feels so unconscious. When you say, "Hey! I'm going to do this phrase in 11/8," it might not be naturalistic. I wasn't thinking of that phrase as odd when I put the music together.

There's also an unusual 3+3+2 rhythmic grouping near the end of the tune. Where did you pick up these unusual metric ideas? Are you a Bartók fan?

I listen to a bit of Béla Bartók. I actually listen to Phillip Glass quite a bit. The jazz people turned me on to Stravinsky. Charles Ives is unbelievable, and I've got this Edgar Varèse record from the '50s that I listen to quite a bit.

There's a Varèse-like phrase in your "Funny Vibe" solo; you set up half-step motion in two isolat-

ed registers, and then you "hiccup" between them.

That's a little thing I learned from Rodney Jones when I studied with him. He showed it to me as a picking exercise, but I turned it into a linear thing. I'm working on developing that.

Why did you decide to do a cover of Talking Heads' "Memories Can't Wait"?

Because I liked the idea in the lyric of a party in your mind that you hope will never stop. I think of people in a situation where they have to be straight, but in their heads they're losing it completely. That duality really appealed to me.

Your solo on that song has a strong Band of Gypsys vibe.

Yeah, that's the one. If there's any sort of nod to Hendrix, that's where it comes in. I've talked about the issue of Hendrix and black guitar players, and that legacy is something that I have had to personally reconcile. The whole Hendrix thing looms over black guitar players in a way that I sometimes feel is unfair. But I love the man and his music, and there's definitely some acknowledgment of that in my playing, but I'm very careful to note that there are a lot of other acknowledgments, as well — to Coltrane, Dolphy, Ornette, and many others.

"Glamour Boys" is a sort of Caribbean-rock number. You and Muzz play fairly traditional soca parts against the drummer's straight backbeat.

The music is a tribute to my parents and to where they come from. I was really wanting to work with a calypso structure, and the music went really well with the words. Arrow is actually a second cousin of mine. [Ed. Note: Soca is modern, up-tempo, calypso-derived music from the West Indies. The word "soca" is a contraction of "soul-calypso." Arrow is a popular soca singer from Montserrat.]

Are you going to do any more music with an Afro-Caribbean flavor?

We've got another Caribbean thing that didn't make it onto the album, a song called "One Way Ticket." African music also fascinates me. I listen to some of the great African guitarists, like Francis Bebey, Ray Phiri — he was the musical director of Paul Simon's *Graceland* project — and Bob Ohiri from Sunny Ade's band. I also listen to kora players like Foday Musa Suso, who played with Herbie Hancock. [Ed. Note: The kora is a 21-string harp played by traditional West African minstrels.]

You and your drummer seem fond of the six-against-four polyrhythm. You often play 12/8 fills against a prevailing 4/4 meter. Is that spontaneous?

It's a little thing that we'll break into. It's something we do in rehearsal. I really try to connect with Calhoun, and we'll go into that together.

It looks as if you have two different right-hand positions. When you start to play a really speedy passage, you curl your right wrist more sharply.

When I started playing, I had very thin arms, and I had to find a comfortable position to pick from. Some people pick straight up and down with their wrists locked, but my picking comes more from my wrist than my forearm. I used to hold my pick between my thumb, index, and forefingers, with my fingers extended. I could play very quickly, but my playing had no articulation, so I began to hold the pick between my thumb and the side of my curled index finger. I used to glue three heavy Gibson teardrop picks together and sharpen them to a point, but I gave that up when I discovered Jim Dunlop Jazz IIIs. They're a lot thinner, but they've got about the same density. When I first started playing, I used only downstrokes; I really had to work at alternate picking. I don't do much sweep picking.

Do you play that way for rhythmic reasons? Do you associate the downstrokes with the strong beats of the measure?

Definitely. I got a lot from rhythm players like Jimmy Nolen [from James Brown's classic band] and Teenie Hodges, who played with Al Green.

It sounds as if you play hard, but your motions are actually quite delicate.

I work with my musculature. I do a lot of pushups, and I work with a small weight for my wrist. I try to make it so playing is easy and not a complete strain; it *is* a muscular activity, as well as a spiritual one. The weight of the ESP doesn't bother me, because it's not as heavy as the Les Paul, which was my main guitar in the Decoding Society. I use D'Addario jazz-rock strings, gauges .011 through .049. I used to use super-extra-slinky strings. I remember I was auditioning for an R&B singing group and my guitar was always going out of tune when I played rhythm. They said, "If you want this job, you've got to get it together." A friend of mine suggested a heavier gauge, so I tried .010s, and then .011s when I got the Les Paul.

You make very musical use of feedback. Do you have any special techniques for generating and controlling feedback?

Every guitar has its sweet spots. My main ESP, for example, is really good on the third string between the 5th and 9th frets. I usually try to find a good spot to stand onstage. I'll turn only part of the way towards the amp, and I'll hear it catch. I definitely got that from Santana. People say it's the neck,

or the nut, or the body, or the pickups, or the bridge, or the amp, or the speakers, or the tubes, but everything is so interdependent that you've got to take a holistic view. I usually keep my volume and tone controls up all the way and use a volume pedal, although I sometimes pull back on the volume knob to reduce the feedback.

You used guitar synthesizers with the Decoding Society and on your duet album with Bill Frisell. Can you see yourself using them with Living Colour?

I'm really thinking about it. I love synthesis and always have. I just recently got a Casio PG-300, the one with the onboard synthesizer. You can set it so that each string is on a different MIDI channel.

Do you practice much these days?

It's tough on the road; I have to sneak in an hour here and there. I used to get up every morning and play whatever — it didn't matter what — just to have the guitar in my hands. I worked a lot on chords from Ted Greene's *Chord Chemistry* book [Dale Zdenek]. I try to do a little reading; I consider myself a struggling sight reader. When I was with the Decoding Society, we had to sight-read everything.

You've composed a theater piece.

Afrerica is a multimedia theater piece that I'm writing with a writer named Sekou Sundiata. It's based on the idea of the Africa that black Americans have in their heads. There's the physical Africa, and then there's the African construct that we've put together to help us survive. Black nationalists have seized on Africa as this golden Valhalla or Asgard, this incredibly magical and good place. It's like an amalgam of what they would like to see happen here and the bit of African history that they know. There are so many Africas, and so many societies in Africa, each with its own morals. We've taken what we like about all these things. *Afrerica* is about this fantastical concept. It's one of my life projects; it will change as my compositional abilities improve [*laughs*]. An earlier version was about an hour-and-a-half long. I hope to mount another version within a couple of years.

You're very knowledgeable about a wide range of musical styles. You must have a hell of a record collection.

A *hellish* record collection is more like it! I do try to listen to a lot of music to keep a perspective. If you don't, what you bring to your own playing will start to become real shallow.

If you could go back in time to meet and play with any musicians who have ever lived, whom would you choose?

There's so many! I would love to sit in a room

with Eric Dolphy. I wouldn't even say anything, just sit. He wouldn't even have to have a saxophone. To sit in a club and hear Charlie Christian when he was 19. To see the band that had Wes Montgomery, Coltrane, and Dolphy that toured once and was never recorded. To meet Hendrix would have been fantastic. Charles Mingus. Tommy Bolin — if I could have said to Tommy, "Stop fucking with that shit!" Tommy was one of our great losses. If I could have just sat with Jimmy Nolen and said to him, "You're one of the greatest guitar players — you changed the music." Sonny Boy Williamson, just to have him curse me out — "Boy, what you doin' there? Get out of here!" Lonnie Johnson. Robert Johnson! Wait, I've got it — Reverend Gary Davis. A lesson with Reverend Gary Davis!

How about contemporary players?

I would love to sit with Carlos Santana. His attitude and the way he approaches music have been such an influence on me. I'd like to meet Frank Zappa; he's a 20th-century composer masquerading as a rock musician. Allan Holdsworth is fantastic because he's really searching. I never get a feeling from his playing that there's a heavy ego thing going on; it's just him trying to dig down. B. B. is truly great. People talk about "playing B. B. King-style," but I don't know what they mean, because nobody plays like him. I really admire Steve Vai, because he's so knowledgeable. And Van Halen — he's so popular, but he's actually great. His playing is like breathing.

One of the pleasures of working with Ronald Shannon Jackson was being able to play on stages with people like "Blood" Ulmer and Sonny Sharrock. I was able to meet Fred Frith and Hans Reichel. The first time I heard Reichel, it took the top of my head off! It sounded like his guitar was made of rubber. I had the real fortune of actually seeing Muddy Waters in Holland. Out of all the concerts I've seen, that was the greatest. I have a cheap tape of the concert that's one of my prized possessions. It was my first time out of the country, and I actually got to go backstage and shake Muddy Waters' hand.

Do you feel that you owe something to your audience, that you have a responsibility where they're concerned?

I have the responsibility to be honest and to do what it is in my power to do. That isn't to say that I should play a million notes every solo; it denotes a deeper responsibility than that. If you've got a lot of chops, you can play by rote. You've got to really work to connect.

What would you like to be able to do that you can't do now?

I've always been fascinated by ragtime guitar playing. I really want to do that — it's *killing* me. I want to have a richer chord vocabulary. I want to go back into jazz and really learn standards. I'd like to get to the point where I can smoothly integrate more intervallic skips in my playing. To keep learning stuff, to keep being fascinated, to keep loving it, to keep in touch with what makes guitar playing cool. That's how you keep yourself fresh.

Vernon's Advice for Young Musicians

1. Keep your mind open.
2. Learn the basics.
3. Acquaint yourself with written music — it's really important. Keep that as part of your regimen if you can.
4. Don't be hard on yourself because you're not Yngwie Malmsteen or Eddie Van Halen. You have to become yourself. The only things you should be learning from these players are the things that are going to resonate in your own life. It's cool to play an Allan Holdsworth phrase, but it's harder to play one of your own.
5. Don't listen only to guitar music. Listen to saxophonists or piano players.
6. If you have a lot of technique and can play really quickly, try to articulate your phrases. Sometimes you should play slowly.
7. Listen to blues — there's a lot there. It's the root of rock and roll guitar playing.
8. Be careful before you say somebody sucks, because somebody's going to listen to your playing and say *you* suck. There will always be somebody who is technically better than you.
9. Learn to work with yourself, not against yourself.
10. Have friends. Don't be totally competitive — it's crap.
11. Live your life. Don't lock yourself in your room eight hours a day and think of nothing but playing the guitar. Learn how to live well, to appreciate flowers. You have to have a human side. It sounds like silly hippie shit, but it's true.

That's about it.

— KEITH RICHARDS —

BY TOM WHEELER — APRIL 1983 & DECEMBER 1989

PAUL NATKIN

BACK IN 1964 WHEN Lennon and McCartney wanted to hold your hand, Jagger and Richards were walkin' the dog. Constantly compared to the Beatles and often to the Who, the Rolling Stones staked out their original turf with gritty music and a don't-mess-with-me stance. The Beatles disintegrated two decades ago, and the Who say they've unpacked their road cases for the last time.

The Stones are not about to bid farewell to anyone. They continue to vanish, then reunite to face competition not only from a new generation of rockers, but also from fellow veterans of the rock and roll wars of decades gone by. Some of the latter have aged well, while others have been exhumed, resuscitated with electroshock and chest-thumping, and then wheeled out into the spotlight to give it yet another go. As "classic rock" formats crowd the airwaves, critics and fans alike assail wheezing geezers in their celebration of glories past. How have the Stones, relics by pop music standards, avoided the dinosaur syndrome? They manage to use high-tech equipment to produce an album that has all the high-tech gloss of a rusty switchblade.

Of course, their magic runs deeper than their patented apocalyptic garage production techniques. Certain other strengths are obvious — the consistently fine Jagger/Richards compositions, the dynamic arrangements, the meticulous recording. Just as important is the way Keith Richards changes chords from G to C.

The band's real vitality derives from raw human elements — Keith's confederates could hardly be more impressive: A rhythm section of drummer Charlie Watts and bassist Bill Wyman that pumps and pulses like the heart of a great beast, a millionaire jetsetter frontman who still sings like a street punk, the able musicianship of Ron Wood, and a guitar sound like nothing else on earth.

Keith Richards stands in the eye of the hurricane. Around him swirls a rock and roll empire with 30 years of history and mystery, success and excess, acclaim and controversy. He and his mates have been called many things by discerning critics and impassioned fans. One description recurs: The World's Greatest Rock and Roll Band.

In most respects the Stones have few peers, and in terms of sheer durability they have none, having somehow survived at or near the top of the rockpile for the last three-fourths of rock and roll's entire history. They've gone the distance and still pack a heavyweight punch. The band is built around a two-guitar sound, itself an extension of Richards' own uniqueness. He helped blur forever the line between lead and rhythm guitar, substituting a riffing technique in which melodic embellishments are grafted onto a vigorous rhythmic treatment of chords, partial chords, and low-register lines. He often employs a 5-string open tuning (with or without capo) that facilitates adding the melodic notes to a major chord — particularly the 4th, the 6th, and the 9th. Among many examples, "Brown Sugar" is a classic killer.

Keith's most obvious influence is Chuck Berry. The original "Carol" is a textbook of Berry's double-string licks and was covered on *The Rolling Stones,* the debut album. Keith has had a taste for Berry flavoring ever since. Chuck Berry adapted boogie woogie piano techniques for the guitar's lower register, and this distinctive two-string rhythm pattern became another Stones staple. Richards made his mark on its development by sometimes slowing it down, piledriving the downbeat, and stoking up the tone to a grand raunch: a-*ronk* a-*ronk* a-*ronk*.

Richards' role in the group has been analyzed countless times. The consensus: Without Keith Richards there wouldn't *be* a Rolling Stones. Ron Wood explains, "In other bands they follow the drummer; the Stones follow Keith, and they always have." The guitarist himself is the first to stress that any band member's indispensability is a two-way street: "The musicians are there to serve the band. All that matters is whether something furthers the overall sound."

As co-producer (credited or uncredited) on virtually every record, Keith Richards has proved to be both a master of the bold stroke and a subtle colorist, evoking not only the thunder and the lightning but also a sky to put it in. For the Rolling Stones, atmosphere is everything. Reflecting Richards' image as a menacing bad hombre, several of the band's classic tracks begin with the hint of danger of the clang of alarm — the drums of doom heralding the "Street Fighting Man," the haunted stirrings of "Gimme Shelter," or in "Sympathy for the Devil" voodoo percussion that charges the opening line with a dark intrigue: "Please allow me to introduce myself."

Anyone who has heard these songs may not be surprised to learn that on December 18, 1943, when Keith Richards was born, the night sky over the hospital was filled with sirens and anti-aircraft gunfire. At about the age of five, Keith had a conversation with another tyke who lived on the same block in Dartford, 15 miles outside of London. He told Mick Jagger that he wanted to be like Roy Rogers and play guitar.

An only child, Keith hated the discipline of school, had frequent troubles with authorities, and considered a formal education generally irrelevant. In 1956, he heard his first Elvis Presley record and received his first guitar. He preferred to let his talents develop on their own, unencumbered by a teacher's interference. Shortly after enrolling in art school, he met up again with Mick Jagger. Sharing an affection

for American bluesmen such as Jimmy Reed and Howlin' Wolf, the two teenagers began jamming.

Keith and Mick met blues fanatic and multi-instrumentalist Brian Jones, and together they formed the band that Brian named the Rolling Stones, after the title of a Muddy Waters song. Wyman had joined by the winter of 1962; Watts in early '63. Needing a manager, the group hired Andrew Oldham; like Jagger and Richards he was 19. Decca records signed the band and a couple of months before the Beatles scored their first #1 hit, "She Loves You," the Rolling Stones released their first single, Chuck Berry's "Come On," which promptly disappeared.

After gradually building a British following over the next year, the band recorded "Not Fade Away," a Buddy Holly hit that Keith had reworked from the ground up. While the original was a jerky hillbilly bopper, the Stones' version was dark and frantic, an early mark of the mannish boy. "Time Is on My Side," which made it to the American charts, was spiked with something rarely heard in the Top 10: Electric blues guitar. Early evidence of the Stones' panoramic sound appeared in "It's All Over Now" (particularly in the fade-out), and again in the first Jagger/Richards composition with which Keith was fully satisfied, "The Last Time."

The Stones continued to break new guitar ground. Their first #1 single, 1965's "Satisfaction," featured one of the catchiest guitar hooks of the decade (and helped popularize the fuzztone), while the following year's "19th Nervous Breakdown" kicked off with an early example of the melodic riffing technique. Hits followed in rapid succession.

For Keith, 1968's "Jumpin' Jack Flash" marked a creative surge of still greater intensity. When Brian Jones' role diminished due to a long list of problems with drugs, the law, and fellow band members, Keith began to take over more and more of the musical duties. He was introduced to Gram Parsons, a member of the Byrds and later founder of the seminal country-rock group the Flying Burrito Brothers. Gram became a close friend and profoundly influenced the Stones by teaching Keith many country songs and a variety of guitar tunings.

Brian Jones had still another liability, a drug conviction that prevented him from touring. His contributions decreased steadily, and in the summer of 1969 he was fired. The replacement was 20-year-old Mick Taylor, a veteran of John Mayall's bands and a highly skilled blues-rock soloist who brought a new dimension to the Stones. Taylor quit the band on friendly terms after recording on over half a dozen albums, and on December 19, 1975 he was replaced by Ron Wood, a veteran of Jeff Beck's group and the Small Faces. The Stones' lineup has remained intact since then.

Watching Keith Richards strap on his Telecaster is like watching Thor pick up his hammer. He ambles onstage into a maelstrom of applause, oddly resplendent in his gauzy scarf and kick-your-ass boots, a mix of just-fell-out-of-bed dishevelment and continental flair, a Marlboro poked into his pirate's grin, red slits for eyes, hungry for action. He exhales a cloud of smoke, savages the opening chords of "Start Me Up," and the sold-out stadium threatens to come apart. The hammer has struck with an electrifying clang. The Rolling Stones are back to work.

As for the rock guitar scene of the late 1980s and early '90s, it's crowded with poseurs trying to look as menacing as possible; next to Keith Richards they seem as menacing as Richard Simmons. It's not so much a question of who's outposing whom, but of who's paid the dues, who's delivered the goods. As Chet Flippo writes in *It's Only Rock 'N' Roll*, "There is no man on earth who knows more or cares more about rock and roll." Keith Richards' face is the face of a rock guitar lifer, weathered and creased by a fabled, tease-the-Reaper lifestyle of scarcely imaginable excess. And yet, more than a quarter century after the Stones' first U.S. hit single, "Not Fade Away," his eyes still gleam with the spark of a teenage guitar wiseguy.

It's the sweetest of ironies: Elected by acclamation the band least likely to survive the '70s, the Rolling Stones enter the '90s in fighting trim, at the top of the heap, the competition nowhere in sight. Keith Richards gets the last cackle. Time is on his side, after all.

People have been predicting the end of the Stones...

...from the beginning [*laughs*]!

With the kind of life you seem to lead, longevity might appear to be the last thing you'd be able to gain. What's the secret?

The secret is, there *is* no secret. It's finding people that not only play well with you, but that you can get along with. There's no constant battle about who's Mister Big, none of those problems. When I see Charlie and Bill — I ain't seen 'em for a few weeks — it's like a pleasure. Ron says we're his closest friends. I guess that's the only secret.

Is that what it means to play in a band?

Most people don't know what a band is. People have heroes, and they copy them — I mean, we copied things very carefully when we started. But you don't get this picture and then do everything to fit it. You do what you do. The musicians are there to contribute to the band sound. The band isn't there for showing off solos or egos. A lick on a record — it doesn't matter who played it. All that matters is how it fits. The chemistry to work together like that has to be there. You have to work on it, always — figure out what to do with it. But basically it's not an intellectual thing you can think up and just put there. It has to *be* there. You have to find it.

Chuck Berry was a major influence on your guitar style.

That's quite a left hand he's got there [*laughs*].

Are the reports true that he punched you in the face?

Yeah, a little while back he did. I came up behind him to say hello. He didn't know it was me and didn't want to be bothered, but I got a nice note from him a little later, actually.

The "Bitch" solo is in a Chuck Berry style...

Which I do every night.

...and the beat turns around several times. Was that completely spontaneous, or semi-planned?

Maybe listeners knew a year or six months later that the beat turned around, but at the moment I wasn't conscious of that. It comes so naturally, as it's always happened, and it's always given that extra kick when the right moment comes back down again. That's what rock and roll records are all about. I mean, nowadays it's "rock" music. But rock and roll records should be two minutes, 35 seconds long, and it doesn't matter if you ramble on longer after that. It should be, you know — *wang*, concise, right there. Rambling on and on, blah blah blah, repeating things for no point — I mean, rock and roll is in one way a highly structured music played in a very unstructured way, and it's those things like turning the beat around that we'd get hung up on when we were starting out: "Did you hear what we just did? We just totally turned the beat around [*laughs*]!" If it's done with conviction, if nothing is forced, if it just flows in, then it gives quite an extra kick to it.

Can you judge the sound of an electric guitar before you plug it in?

To a certain extent. If the neck and the action feel right, you're more than halfway home, even before hearing the electronics. Things like weight and the density of the wood indicate certain things, but you simply need to play it to really tell. And it doesn't take long.

On record you've used several very different

types of guitars — *Gibson Les Pauls and ES-335s, Fender Telecasters, and others. And yet a listener can tell right away that it's you, from stylistic clues, but also from the sound alone.*

I use a whole load of different guitars, that's true, but they're not all that dissimilar in type. I mean, ninety percent are probably Telecasters, old ones, but more than that, you can't really separate style and sound, you see. People do separate them when they're talking about music, but all of that often misses the whole point.

You're suggesting that the style is the sound?

Yes, part of it, more than any particular tone setting or pickup or anything like that. I'll just adjust to the sound of the track as we go — the sound of the bass drum and especially Ronnie's guitar. The style is adjusting along with the sound. There's never a conscious effort to get that "Honky Tonk Woman" tone or a thing like that. You may get it or you may not. But that's not what you're thinking about. You're thinking about the track.

Some people were amazed to read in your first **Guitar Player** *cover story that on "Street Fighting Man" there are no electric guitars.*

Two acoustics, one of them put through the first Philips cassette player they made. It was overloaded, recorded on that, and then hooked up through a little extension speaker, and then onto the studio tape through a microphone.

You've paid quite a bit of attention to acoustic guitars in rock music.

Well, I started on acoustic guitar, and you have to recognize what it's got to offer. But also you can't say it's an acoustic guitar sound, actually, because with the cassette player and then a microphone and then the tape, really it's just a different process of electrifying it. You see, I couldn't have done that song or that record in that way with a straight electric, or the sustain would have been too much. The reason I did that one like that was because I already had the sound right there on the guitar before we recorded. I just loved it, and when I wrote the thing I thought, "I'm not going to get a better sound than this." And "Jumpin' Jack Flash" is the same, too. That's acoustic guitar.

Early Everly Brothers records have huge acoustic guitar sounds. Were any of them influential?

Yeah, *all* of their records, and also there's the fact that the first major tour we ever did was supporting the Everly Brothers, Little Richard, and Bo Diddley. Plenty to learn [*laughs*] in a real short time, following those guys around. The Everlys came on

with just their trio and themselves, and it was great. On their recordings there is a certain power in the steel-string. It's a different instrument from electric — not that different in the way you play it, but in terms of the sound. There are times when an acoustic guitar will *make* a track. You'll be despairing, nothing working, hashing away. Take 43 on electric guitar; and somebody will say, "Why don't you try it on acoustic?" And you try it one time and you've got it.

What kind of acoustics do you like to use?

Old Martins — several types of them — and certain Gibsons, particularly old Hummingbirds.

How important is the sound of the room itself?

The room is as important as the band and the producer and the song and the engineer. The room is *at least* as important as all that to the total sound. You can't separate rock and roll music instrument by instrument. You destroy the whole structure of it. Rock and roll music can only be recorded by jamming the sound all together.

Once you've got something to work right in the studio, do you try to use all the same equipment onstage?

Yeah, pretty much, just a larger version. I've never found the Stones or anybody else made great records by using huge stacks in the studio and blasting away. You can get very powerful sounding records playing very quietly, and with relatively small amps. Small amps turned way up have the tension you're trying to get anyway, and it sounds big. It also gets back to that recognition of the acoustic guitar and what it can do, and what you can get if you're thinking of the mix right from the beginning and all the way through the recording.

Have many of the songs that you've written for the Stones been composed on the piano?

Sometimes, yeah. I'm such an amateur on piano, and that can help. You play guitar every night and get to know it so well, and a lot of great songs are really accidents. On the piano I may come across something I wouldn't have done on guitar.

Let's talk about rhythm.

A hard subject to put into words.

In Chuck Berry songs such as "Sweet Little Rock and Roller," the hybrid rhythm mixes straight 4/4 and the shuffle; you also explore that in-between-the-beats territory.

It's always fascinated me, man, yeah. Mainly because I realized after quite a few years that the thing that really intrigued me, that turned me on to playing, was precisely that — *suggested* rhythms going on, or a certain tension. Especially in early rock and roll, there's a tension between the 4/4 beat and the eighths going on with the guitars. That was probably because the rhythm section was still playing pretty much like a swing band. There was still a regular *jazz* beat, 4/4 to the bar, a swing/shuffle, which is a lovely light rhythm, very African, with a lovely bounce to it.

It suddenly changed in '58, '59, '60, until it was all over by the early '60s. The drummers were starting to play eight to the bar, and I thought at first maybe they were just going for more power. Then I realized that, no, it was because of the *bass*, the advent of reliable electric bass guitar. The traditional double bass went bye-bye, this thing that's taller than most guys that play the goddamn thing [*laughs*]. The guitar players were being relegated to bass. If you didn't even have a bass, you could tune down a guitar and play four strings; once you had an actual bass, it was much louder than an acoustic pumping eight to the bar. And the natural inclination of the drummer is then to pick up on what the new bass is doing, because that's what you've got to follow.

Listening to what it was that turned me on in the first place, I see this pattern evolve that you wouldn't see in the beginning when you're so close up. One minute you're listening to, as you say, "Sweet Little Rock and Roller," and in a year or two you're listening to "Something Else" by Eddie Cochran, which is all *eighths*, and [Little] Richard's piano playing eighths and *sixteenths* against the fours: da-da-da-da. So really, figuring it out was just me doing my bit of research.

Rock seems to have turned its back on that kind of rhythmic ambiguity.

Well, *most* music has, in actual fact, because there's not many people who can do it, so there's not that much of an opportunity to actually hear it these days. You don't get a lot of shuffles or swings, but I think it's something that's innate in me. I grew up on that beat, even before they added the eighths. That swing/shuffle gives it quite a little lift. To me, the eighths are the rock, and that lift is the roll. But again, there's very few drummers that can really play eight to the bar and also make it take off with that *lift*. It's like flying, the Wright Brothers' theory of velocity. Your lift is very appealing but so hard to do properly, especially these days, when most records are made on a typewriter anyway.

Your music is similarly ambiguous in the way it scrambles conventional roles of rhythm and lead guitar, sometimes mixing them at the same volume, as in the first eight bars of the solo in "Rock and a Hard Place." Most people don't make records like that.

They have a fixed idea that rhythm is supposed to just do *this*, and the lead is supposed to be really loud, but I've been very fortunate. The guys that I've always worked with, they've all gotten off in the same way as I have. Rather than going for the *separation* of the guitars, we get them to start to sound to the point where it doesn't *matter* which guitar is doing what. They leap and weave through each other, so it becomes unimportant whether you're listening to rhythm or lead, because in actual effect, as a guitar player, you're in the other player's head and he's in yours, and you two are on this little mental plane where no one else is, trying to predict and guide and follow, all at the same time. You're in the front and you're at the back, and this is a fascinating thing, and on a larger scale that's what a good band is. See, a lot of guys are scared to do that. They don't *want* you to know what they're thinking [*laughs*], or they're out for personal glory, so with a lot of players, you can't do that. Or you have to sort of put them through a *rigorous re-education* [*laughs*], which is a lot of hard work.

Your music has a ragged edge. With high-tech studios, is it getting harder to make your kind of record?

Up until a year or so ago, yes, but maybe guys now are getting more familiar with the barrage of high-tech that's come along. There's always been evolution in recording. We started with 2-track and then went to 4 — "Wow!" — and then you've got stereo — "Golly!" So we're used to this constant unrolling of technology, but it did come fast in the last 10 years, and a lot of the '80s has been that kind of toy-town music, and everybody is trying to figure out what to do with all these toys. They know what they can do, but how to actually integrate them together kind of reduced everybody to the toy department for a bit. But we're using the highest-tech equipment — you have to, if you want to use a good studio these days, because a studio has to have that stuff to have business, whether you like it or not. But it is possible to use it as a tool and an aid without losing sight of what you're doing. You can still record in a *room*, as well as do it digital, and still get what you're going for. It's been like a kid let loose in a candy factory, but making good records has very little to do with all the possibilities you've got. It's, can you make the *decision*? That's the focus of the energy.

Your adopting the open tuning seems to have been a watershed.

That's what I did. A year off's a long time. You start to get bored eventually. I mean first off you go 'round and visit all the fleshpots, and then when you get slightly debauched and jaded, you remember, ah yes, the *music!* So I went back to blues, back to the beginning. I started to research and found out a lot more about the stuff, which I hadn't had a chance to do since we started working like maniacs. I caught up on *listening* to music, which to me is maybe the greatest art. Playing is not — maybe sometimes it is — but listening to the music is an art; it can keep your sanity.

Open tuning was something that had intrigued me for quite a while before I took it up, but I'd never had the opportunity or time to get to it, and it takes time — it's almost like picking up a brand new instrument. Brian Jones used to use certain forms of open tuning — tuning the third string down, or sometimes an open-*D*. I thought, I can't go any further in concert tuning, so I sat down with open tuning and it stretched out. Again, it wasn't really a conscious thing, but a necessary one, maybe. Sometimes the subconscious bits come up front and say, "In order to save you, we're taking over for a bit." [*Laughs.*] And so that sort of shoots the idea forward. I listened to some of the old-time blues, and read about it, especially on the back of album jackets. I got more and more intrigued about reading charts of different tunings — or *suspected* tunings, you know, the one that we *think* he's using. And then working with Ry Cooder, that was also a great spur to it.

That was around the time of Let It Bleed?

Right. Because I had already been working a lot with open-*E* and open-*D* tuning for *Beggars Banquet*, working from what I'd learned during that year off the year before.

But you weren't using the open-G at that time?

No, not at that time, except I played around with it for slide, but I very rarely play slide on records. There's always a better slide player in the band than me. I did use slide on things, mostly on acoustic stuff like "You've Got to Move" and "Prodigal Son," stuff like that, open-*D* or open-*E*. I only found out recently that the open-*G* tuning is also known as Russian tuning, because the Russian 7-string guitar is tuned to D, G, B, D, G, B, D, same notes.

When did you eliminate the sixth string?

When I started to use the open tuning electrically. It's not the root note of the tuning; the fifth string is your root note, and the sixth would start rumble, and also because you have to tune it down two notches it doesn't stay in tune very well, it's too slack, and it would just get in the way, kind of an unnecessary appendage. If a guy's only got one guitar and wants to use open-*G* tuning, then he's got to put up

with that, but I've got two [*laughs*].

Was "Honky-Tonk Women" [July '69] your first hit record in open-G?

Yeah.

Your open-string parts are always in tune, but in standard tuning the pitches are often kind of ragged — appealingly funky, out of tune a bit.

That's usually the way I finger, usually my thumb. I push the bass string just off of key a little. I don't know if it's because I'm sloppy or because I like the sound of it going slightly out of whack. Or maybe just because in a lot of the blues stuff, they would deliberately pull it off of key, especially on the bass notes. It's not so much on the top notes, usually, but when you hit the thing, you kind of compress the bass string. Sometimes I do it too much, though not as much as I used to. It depends on synthesizers and other instruments you're playing with. You can't go out of tune against any other instrument. But if it's just a guitar thing, I would do that. But I've often thought I do it just because to me it's natural now [*laughs*].

On the intro to "All Down the Line," for example, the guitar is out of tune, but it seems that if you tuned it up, you'd depersonalize the part. Does anyone ever try to tell you: Your guitar is out of tune, let me tune it for you?

Many times, but tell that to a Japanese, tell that to an Arab. I mean, there's plenty of times when maybe it's not "supposed" to have been out of tune when I cut it, but then when I hear it back I say it'd be *lost* without it. Just as we were talking about rhythm a bit earlier, with the eighths and sixteenths against the fours, here we're talking about a certain *tension* that's created by jarring the nerve just a little. If it's too obviously out of tune, then it's too much, but sometimes I'll say, "Yeah, I didn't mean to, I can easily go back and cut it again," and they'll say, "Nah, there's something about it." You realize that it's one of those psychological things that comes into the ear. As a professional musician, you cringe, and it's not perfect, and there is always that tendency to go for the perfect tuning, but that's kind of an illusion anyway. If you're a musician, it's very hard to stay a dispassionate listener, but try to preserve a bit of the *enjoyment* of listening without *dissecting*, without confusing it with work. I know drummers that don't actually hear anything on a track except the drums. It's a natural thing, but you're cutting yourself off from the reason that you're playing music. Once you are a musician it's easy to turn it into an exercise, and listen to it with a professional ear instead of what I call the real art of music: Just listening to it and what it does. Otherwise we wouldn't be sitting here talking.

Your sound has a lot of distortion, and yet you can still pick out the individual notes of a chord. Any tips on how to do that?

I don't know. I always wish that somebody could've told me that years and years ago, and I'm actually still working on that. It's really finding the right guitar with the right amp.

More than the boxes?

More than the boxes, yeah. If you've got a good sound, you can always add a bit of this or that and fiddle around with it, but it's got to be *there*. The main ingredients are the right amp with the right guitar, and it could be the weirdest mixture — I've had some Australian guitar or a Japanese, you know, and it might be only right for one particular track, with absolutely no relevance to everyday playing. The guitar I used for "Gimme Shelter" on *Let It Bleed* — as if by design, it fell apart on the last take.

When the Stones got their earliest gigs filling in for Alexis Korner's band, you thought that it might last six months; when did you realize that this might actually be your life's work?

Gosh, that's hard. In a way, when we started the band, there was not much prospect of even making the band pay for itself. It might have lasted six *days* — we never knew from one week to another. If we couldn't have come up with the rent for the joint once in a while, we would have been forced to dissipate or sell off the equipment, and that might have been the end of the band. After a few gigs and a year in the clubs, you suddenly get to make a record. And even if you managed to get a hit, the average lifetime of anybody except for Elvis was like two years. So although you were elated by the fact that you could get into the studio and actually get your little piece of immortality — if you're ever going to have any — at the same time you're filled with the dread of this imminent doom. Even if it's fortunate enough to be a hit record, that means it's the beginning of the end, because nobody gets longer than two years and then you're dead as a dodo. Maybe it was that desperation that made us think, if we get a chance to make a record, then every track will be treated with the same respect and not just tossed off.

Because it might be your last?

Yeah, so you wanted to get as much down as possible, and you really worked on it. But by the time we reached the allotted two years, or so we thought, actually we just started getting into our stride, and by making albums at least as important as singles, people simply started to buy albums, and if you're lucky you stood a pretty good chance of airing a record.

But when did you realize, this could go on — this is what I am?

I guess by around "Satisfaction" time, yeah, we started to realize that you could develop this thing, and if you did right, there's no reason why you shouldn't be able to do it as long as you wanted. But you don't even think about those things at the time. There was no way of foreseeing it going to like 1989, or foreseeing all this [the current tour]. It's actually reached a point where probably a good 80% of the people there at the concerts don't even know a world without the Rolling Stones. And so you become a fixture — like the moon.

— HOWARD ROBERTS —

By Don Menn – June 1979

JON SIEVERT

OWARD ROBERTS has played on so many records, over 5,000 sides, that he couldn't begin to remember them all. Not only did he work in the studio for over three decades for scores of TV and film soundtracks, but somehow he had also managed to record more than 20 albums as a featured artist, to teach seminars and write books of guitar instruction, and to take an active part in designing musical equipment — including the revolutionary Benson amplifier and, more currently, the Howard Roberts model jazz guitars for Epiphone and Gibson.

Versatility and innovation are two words that describe Howard's approach to music, and his influence has spread far beyond the LA studio scene. He, along with guitarist Barney Kessel, was one of the first recognized jazz musicians to go into studio work during the '50s, when it was considered anathema for such musicians to do so. And when it became fashionable during the early '70s for jazzers to enter the studio scene, he drastically curtailed his work there to devote a tremendous amount of time and energy, often without realizing any monetary gain, in offering seminars on guitar playing to the general public.

Howard Mancel Roberts was born in Phoenix, Arizona, on October 2, 1929. He spent the first 20 years of his life as a self-proclaimed "desert rat," wandering the sandy hills around Phoenix, taking odd jobs as a warehouseman and grease monkey while always keeping in touch with the guitar. He was sitting in at black jazz clubs around town when only 11, and by the time he was 15 he was playing gigs.

Roberts moved to LA in 1950 and remained active as a studio sideman until the early '70s when, needing a new outlet for his creative energies, he became increasingly active in making personal appearances at guitar seminars held throughout the U.S. "Eventually, I reached a point when I thought that seminars were no way for me to handle the guitar education thing," he said, "But I still had the feeling that there was something that must be done to promote the guitar: Many players were still going around kicking the can, picking up a lick or two every few years, and struggling through so-called 'easy' guitar methods that weren't easy at all. So along with Pat Hicks, who had been handling a lot of my personal seminar activities, we decided to form a school for guitarists." And the result was the founding of the Guitar Institute of Technology (GIT).

In addition to his work with GIT, Howard also formed the Playback Publishing Company in order to "develop and publish material that would upgrade guitar education. The reason I decided to publish books myself," he once said, "was very simple: I didn't feel that other publishers of music instruction texts put out really top-of-the-line material. Many of them just wanted to market the easy-to-learn stuff: They were paper merchants, basically, not information givers. So I decided to form my own publishing company so I could control the quality of materials."

In addition to being a regular columnist for *Guitar Player* magazine for a decade and a half, Howard also published several instructional books: *Howard Roberts Chord Melody, Howard Roberts Guitar Book,* and *Sight-reading by Howard Roberts*. He was one of the few electric guitarists for whom an extended musical score was written: the *Dialogue for Electric Guitar and Chamber Orchestra,* by Duane L. Tatro.

Many people might consider Roberts' approach to teaching as radical. For instance, he believed that beginning students can sometimes forgo basic instructional texts and instead plunge immediately into more complicated pieces of music. He also advocated speed learning and maintained that many popular methods of guitar instruction were inefficient. And he was adamant in his feelings that long-range goals can be destructive — in adopting them, the student often condemns himself or herself to a period of mediocrity.

Few musicians who accomplished as much as Howard are as selfless, or as concerned about artistic excellence. And although it might seem that there are no more mountains to climb for this Renaissance man of the electric guitar, Howard Roberts continues to shine as an inspirational beacon for present and future generations of musicians. He died June 28, 1992.

Did you have any teachers?

A lady gave me lessons for a few months. I learned the usual open-string stuff, chords like *C, E,* and *G,* and songs like "Swanee River." But soon after I began the lessons, she died. Then a new guitar teacher, Horse Hatchett, came to town. He had just gotten out of the service. That guy gave me a real straight career approach and he opened many doors for me. But I also learned a lot on my own. I used to wander around in those desert hills in a kind of daydreaming state, imagining myself playing tunes I had heard on the radio — not a visual image of myself sitting and playing, but a definite picture of a fingerboard. I didn't realize it at the time, but what I was doing then — practicing in my head — is a technique I now use as a teacher and something that maybe made all the difference in the world as to whether I'd be a professional guitarist or not.

How did this visualization help your learning?

Without realizing it, I grew to the point where I could hear the notes and the tones of a song in my head and then figure out where they went on the guitar. Although I didn't know the names of any chords or scales at that time, when I was 11 I could just sit down and play the tunes. Getting back to Horse Hatchett, all this stuff I had figured out in the desert on my own he really nailed down for me. He introduced me to other players and told me about many of the hot guitarists like Django Reinhardt, George Van Eps, and Barney Kessel. Hatchett himself wasn't a hot guitar player. He just had an approach to teaching that was particularly clear-headed, direct, and useful.

Did you have much trouble learning any technique?

When I was 14, I was introduced to bebop. There were several jazz clubs in Phoenix at the time that were really good. There were some hot players around, too, playing this really hard-ass bebop — real fast, you know. I'd go sit in at these places and stay all night. They were black clubs on the other side of the tracks, you might say, and I was just about the only white guy around. But everyone was very friendly to me. They went out of their way to help me with my music. But playing with those guys, who were mostly horn players, at those tempos, I found technique to be quite a problem.

Did you have any gigs when you were younger?

Yes. Besides going to the black clubs, I got a gig in one of the hottest high school dance bands in Phoenix when I was 13. And by the time I was 15, I was playing clubs. One time I played at a colored Elks Club, and Ezzard Charles, who was the heavyweight boxing champion of the world, was on bass.

Were you taking music lessons at this time?

In a manner of speaking. When I was 17, Fabian André, one of [composer] Joseph Schillinger's [1895–1943] students, moved to Phoenix. He started holding workshops in the Schillinger system — which is a mathematical approach to music — and I got to go to them by promising to sweep up after they were finished for the night. Shortly thereafter, another interesting thing happened to me. I was walking down the street one day, and I saw this guy about halfway down the block carrying a great big guitar. I knew that he had to be special, since there was nobody else in town that I knew of who played. So I caught up with him, and he introduced himself: Howard Haitmeyer was his name. It turned out that he lived out on the desert near me and had grown up out there. He was 23 and had just gotten out of the service.

Did you learn from Haitmeyer?

Yes. I talked with him, and discovered that he had already gone through just about every guitar book there was. He was a voracious learner: I would see progress from him on a weekly basis that I would expect from myself on a semi-annual basis. Eventually we started rooming together, and I learned how to learn from him. I discovered what it meant to keep going. He'd go to bed with an arranging book in his hand, and he'd wake up with it there. We'd go to breakfast, and he'd read it. We'd go to a movie, and on the way to and from the theater he'd read it. It was an around-the-clock activity for Howard, and it became so for me, too. One day he said, "I think I'll start composing." Next thing you knew, he was writing pieces for string and woodwind quartets, literally overnight. Then we would pick one and play it, and that's how I learned to read music.

At the time, did you ever make the distinction between yourself as a sight reader, improviser, etc.?

I can recall an incident when I was 18. One day I was sitting in a coffee shop, just staring out the window, and the jukebox was playing some popular tune of the day. After the song was over, a peculiar light went on in my head, and I had the feeling that I had played that tune. Intrigued by the awareness, I went home and got my guitar out and really did play it. That's when one category formed. There was a guitar in my head; I could see it and associate it with the sound I heard.

What was the specific mental image?

I visualized it in two ways. I saw the guitar as though I were playing it and also as if I were watching someone else playing. As a matter of fact, I had a dream when I was 17 that I was watching Barney Kessel doing a studio session. I was watching him through the glass: He was playing, but I couldn't hear. But I could see his hands move, and I heard the sound in my head of what those movements on the fingerboard would make. And, by golly, when I woke up I remembered those things — the sound and the shapes — and I played them myself on the guitar.

Why did you leave Phoenix?

I felt completely out of it there. The "other side of the tracks" jazz community I had known had dispersed — they all moved to LA, or New York, or somewhere. There was nothing left for me except playing at country clubs, and I wasn't that kind of person. So when I was 20, I moved to LA. I ran into [guitarist/composer] Jack Marshall, and he inspired me to take up classical guitar. I went out and bought a bunch of beginner's books and practiced exercises for about a year. After I'd been at it for a few months, Howard Haitmeyer came to visit. He stayed for a few weeks, then returned to Phoenix. Three months later, I visited him. I walked into his apartment, and there he was with a classical guitar. He

didn't even tell me he'd bought one. Anyway, he was playing a piece by Villa-Lobos. I, on the other hand, was still working in my exercise books.

How were you affected by this?

It was just another flagrant example of a guy having his stuff together while I was goofing off and not having my head put on right. So I took a hard look at the way I went about doing things. Ultimately, it turned out that I really didn't enjoy classical guitar very much. After studying it for a few years, I gave it up . . . . Something I neglected to mention is that while I lived in Phoenix, every now and then I'd split for LA. I'd go to this certain place — I don't recall the name — where they had jam sessions on weekends. Sometimes a famous jazz player like [trumpeter] Miles Davis or [pianist] Bud Powell would come in, and the sessions would last all night. Anyway, sometimes I'd walk in and they'd let me sit in. Nobody knew who I was, but they didn't seem to care. So when I finally moved to LA, I gravitated to that part of town. I didn't know about Hollywood because I didn't know anyone there.

So LA was just a big town to you then?

Yes, but it seemed that that was where things were happening. I spent my first year just wandering around town. I didn't have any place to live, or a car, or money, or a watch, or even a change of clothes. I had a blue suit, and I wore it constantly.

Is that how someone later came up with that album title, H.R. Is a Dirty Guitar Player?

[*Laughs*] I think I really *was* dirty. Actually, I would sometimes go for a week without a bath. And all I had with me, besides my blue suit, was a guitar and amp I bought in Phoenix. The guitar was a Gibson L-5 cutaway with a DeArmond pickup on it, and the amplifier was a Gibson GA-50 with one 12" and one 10" speaker. So my first year there I'd play jam sessions and somebody would say, "Hey, you can sleep in the back of my car tonight."

Were you lonely?

Sometimes. But I always found a way to get along. I knew I didn't want a car; I knew I didn't want a watch, because I didn't want to worry about time. I liked the idea of not being burdened with possessions, of being mobile. I didn't owe anyone anything, and vice versa. Even though it was a little lonely and uncomfortable from time to time, the trade-off was worth it.

Were you working steadily?

I would get a job every now and then, some kind of a left-field gig. I did different things, not all of which were musical, to pick up a few bucks. But I was still mostly into guitar, and cookies.

Cookies?

Yes, a bag of cookies, chocolate chip cookies, which I'd buy at the market to feed my guitar. I was the first guy in town that I know of to put a guitar in a bag instead of a case. Anyway, I'd carry it along, and when I'd get a sandwich or cookies, I'd carry them either in the back of my amp or in my guitar bag. Camping out in Hollywood, man, was weird [*laughter*].

Did you ever take a lesson from Barney Kessel?

Yes. He taught me that I didn't need to take lessons from him, and all I really needed to do was travel in faster company. It encouraged me, and he and I have remained friends ever since.

When did you get your first studio gig?

Well, I was playing in Bobby Walter's band, and I got a lot of exposure because of that. One day, I got a call from [pianist] Walter Gross, who said something about a TV show that he wanted me for. I asked him how he got my name, and he said I was recommended by some top studio players in town.

How did that come about?

At that time, the union imposed quotas where a guy was only allowed to do a certain amount of work. So this TV show came up and nobody was free to do it; and at that time, finding guys around town who could cut the gig was a hard thing to do. There just weren't that many. So I got my chance, and it was the good guitar players in town who gave it to me. That's a word of wisdom I'd like to pass along to other guitar players who wonder how you get a break: Hang around with the good guys, because they're the ones who are going to *help* you. The ones that aren't so good are often defensive, and they'll sometimes try to cut you down behind your back. But the good guys have got nothing to lose and wouldn't send an inferior player on a job in a million years.

At this time were you influenced by people in any real sense of the word?

Yes, it was a during that period that I got hung up on Béla Bartók [1881–1945], for example. I'd already known about and listened to his music from way back in Phoenix, but Buddy DeFranco was the guy that got me to bury my head into the string quartets and really get into it.

When did you finally give up road work?

After being on the road there with Buddy, I realized that I didn't want to live in hotels and just run around; I could see it was a dead-end street. And also, my lack of formal musical education, lack of

knowledge about what I was doing, contributed to it. So I decided to get off the road, settle down in LA, and start efficiently studying and upgrading myself.

What were your hopes as a guitar player when you first walked into a new situation?

Well, I always looked for something that would be artistically satisfying; I was always struggling to get some of that in all my work, just to preserve my sanity. I remember times when we were real busy and we'd go to work and get through with a record date and say, "Well, there's a Mixmaster." In other words, we made just enough money to buy a Mixmaster. And we'd go to another record date and, well, we made enough money for a car payment. It just all got translated that way until it reached the point where it was so commercial that it was absolutely ludicrous.

How long did it take for you to feel this way?

I'd say it took about three years after I first started working in the studio. I can't tell you how many times I got called on gigs for some producer who would decide that he was going to create a band; he'd make up a name, like "Little Joey and the Flashers," and they'd write this crap, which was just like V-IV-I major triads, only no dominant and minor 7ths allowed.

What happens when one of those groups makes it big?

Sometimes it can be very sad. If a group soars to the top and all of a sudden they run into a lean period, nobody in the business wants to talk to them. I've tended to shy away from the overnight success thing. I enjoy being a guitar player and I enjoy music — that's why it's my profession. Thank goodness I had the wisdom to know early on that I was no charmer, that I wasn't going to be able to charm anyone with my personality so I'd get work. If I was going to make a living playing, it would have to be based on my abilities as a player, nothing more. I would like to be doing what I'm doing right now when I'm 80 years old. And I truly believe that a good musician can do more to change the temperament and attitude of society than 30 of your average city mayors.

What's the average playing life expectancy of a studio guitarist?

I think it depends on what you're doing. You take a guy like Al Hendrickson, a marvelous guitar player. Well, Al was doing studio work in LA before I even got to town, and he's still doing it. That guy can sit down and play just anything that you put in front of him. So if you use him as a model, the life expectancy in studios is still unknown. Of course, if you're a specialist, like maybe you're a hot acid rock player and that's all you do, your life expectancy is going to be influenced directly by the life of that particular kind of music.

A lot of people always ask, "How do Howard Roberts and John McLaughlin pick so fast?" Does it have anything to do with circle picking?

Circle picking is a thing that came as a result of my playing bebop when I was a kid. There was no conscious effort on my part to want to develop it; it just happened to accommodate the music that I was doing. It was the only way I could get the notes out.

Exactly what is circle picking?

Remember how you'd draw ovals and circles with a pencil on paper, and how they'd tell you in school to just use your wrist and not your fingers? Well, I use the fingers and the wrist when I pick. You know how most people write, by moving their thumb and their forefinger, and so forth? It's that kind of a technique — just like writing your name across the strings.

But can that be up and down?

Yes, it is up and down.

But yours is also circular, so it's more like drawing curlicues.

That's exactly right. I was very self-conscious about that for many years, because it was considered to be wrong in classic plectrum technique. But here's the thing about picking, as I view it. I see the arm as a cantilever, a leverage device, if you want to look at it mechanically. And if you're going to be making great big movements, like drawing great big circles on the wall, your entire body may be involved. So the anchor point would be the floor. If you're going to make a smaller circle, you may have to move only the shoulder. In other words, you shorten the lever to make a smaller circle. If you make an even smaller move, say, with the wrist, you'll see that the wrist, if arched, rotates very nicely. And not only that, but it moves just about the distance that is a practical working distance across the strings. So as levers go, the wrist is mechanically better set up for handling the area of strings that one deals with than any other part of the lever system.

Do you vary this technique?

Yes, there are some small things, like playing one string at a time, in which you want to move the anchor on that lever, shorten the lever even more; and you may end up where the anchor is all the way up to the tip of the finger and the thumb where the pick is, and you're treating the thing like a little scalpel. There's no wrist action at all. But in the end, when performing, you don't think about any of that stuff:

Anything goes to get the sound to come out right. And the movements will range all the way from funny little anchors and things down at the tip of the pick to big sweeping movements originating at the shoulder.

How do you hold the pick?

Between the thumb and the first finger. It rests on the first joint of the first finger and is held lightly with the first joint of the thumb.

With the tip?

Yes. And I grip it moderately, just in the middle.

Do you ever do any strengthening or stretching exercises?

There's no better exercise in the world than just reaching for the chord. Guys work out things with rubber bands and stuff like that, but the guitar — you can't ask for a better exercise instrument. Just pick it up and do it!

When you're picking, do you do pull-offs and hammer-ons, or do you try to pick every note?

Oh no, I use pull-offs and hammer-ons. Once again, these are all part of the overall technique of playing the instrument.

Do you still have trouble with technique?

Sure, constantly. I don't just dream something up and then it automatically pours out of the instrument. The athletic aspect of guitar playing is ever-present, and any discussion of the aesthetics of musical expression is nonsense without the presence of those athletic, motor skills. I think that it takes from 20 to 100 repetitions to establish the nerve richness necessary to carry out a given move as a reflex. And it also takes about 21 days of maintaining that level of performance for that reflex to become permanent; that is to say, a player could conceivably lay off for a long period of time after 21 days of maintenance and, with practice, retrieve the technique he originally had.

What's a good way to improve your playing?

Players can improve their learning by putting what they study into immediate and practical use. If they don't, that knowledge will erode and eventually vanish. Another important point: Contrary to what you might think, long-range goals often can be very destructive to your development as a guitarist. If you say, "Two years from now I'm going to be a so-and-so," or "so-and-so good," what you've done is to sentence yourself to two years of intermediacy. How many people do you find walking around calling themselves "intermediate" guitar players? There's really no such thing; it's just a concept, a personal view of oneself. To me, you're either doing it, or you aren't. Yet we still see books that say, "Beginner," "Intermediate," and "Advanced" on them.

Some people would say that it's too hard for a student to learn a complicated piece of music right off.

That's what they say, but not I. If a player is going to have to know how to tremolo, use a rest stroke, and things like that, why have them encounter that in some dull, lifeless exercise like "Mary Had a Little Lamb"? Why don't they learn technique as it occurs in, say, a Rodrigo *Concierto*? It's no harder. And besides, a piece of music like that is just what it is: It will never get more or less difficult. So there's no point in fooling around with preliminaries, or wasting your time with a bunch of beginner's books. People can learn to read music, you know, before they learn how to play it well. And it should be music they enjoy.

How do most students learn?

More often than not, students will learn what they want to learn, when they want to learn it. You can give them a study, a scale, or an arpeggio and send them home; they'll work on it using the old by-rote method and then come back and pass a test, or win a gold star, and then promptly forget the whole deal. Whereas, if they were taught the scales as they would apply to something, like improvising, for example, then a good learning experience will result. There are few pieces of music that don't involve rhythm, melody, and harmony; those are the basics. And it doesn't matter if students play classical, rock, jazz, or country music — those three elements will be present. And students can build up their motor skills very nicely by playing any of that stuff; they don't have to play scales out of context.

Should the student look at the whole piece of music, or a measure at a time?

He or she should learn in very small, specific sections, and then hook them together. If you have a hundred notes to learn, the mistake factor is high. If, on the other hand, you have only one note to learn, you virtually eliminate any possibility of mistakes. Then you, not the material, are in control over the learning process.

At what point should the student pick up the guitar?

After he or she knows where to put their fingers. Remember, learning how to play the guitar is a combination of mental and motor skill acquisition. And to develop motor skills, repetition is essential. I've found that having the instrument in hand can be quite a distraction when learning. Whenever musicians have trouble executing a passage, they generally tend to blame their hands for what's wrong, or they blame themselves for not having enough talent. Actually, all that's wrong is they don't know where their fingers are supposed to go.

Are books useful instructional tools?

Yes, to a certain extent. There are books and educational programs that tell the student, either directly or indirectly, that there are literally hundreds of tunes to learn. What they don't tell him or her is that those hundreds of tunes are put together with the same doggone chords, sequences, scale passages, and interval skips. It's constantly being suggested to the beginning student that there are a thousand things to learn — but there aren't. For instance, if you have a complicated scale you want to play, it's just a compound of simple moves — a hammer, a board, a nail — that's it. So instead of learning, say, all 28 notes, you only learn three. That's one step in speed learning. And you practice for a short period of time, so that there is no possibility of exceeding your attention span. Also, you should learn the piece in your head before you play it. And when you do play it, play so slow that there's no possibility of making a mistake. So, slow is fast, and what I just laid out is the basic model of speed learning.

In preparing for performances, do you have any specific things that you do before beginning to play?

Yes, there is one thing that I do. I discovered this accidentally, a long time ago: I play notes very slowly all over the fingerboard, using upstrokes and down strokes. And then I make a quick jump to another note, maybe a long distance from the previous one — the idea being to close the gap so that you can't notice any silence or space between the two notes. Another reason for doing that is to get the right hand to sound the string at exactly the same moment that the left hand sounds it.

What happens when they're out of synch?

When you strike the string a little bit too early, you get kind of a thud with your pick; and then the string, when the finger depresses it, creates another sound, and you have two sounds. When this condition prevails, it destroys your technique. I'm sure the readers have heard guitar players play real fast, but they also sound nervous and a little bit disjointed — not quite right, not clean. They're actually hearing a discoordination between the two hands. And the only way to get that fixed is by not playing fast.

What's the problem with excessive speed?

If you play fast, you can't hear where the problem is; you don't know if it was the left hand that's hitting first or the right. You have to do it real slow, and if you press down a string down near the nut, the string doesn't travel very far in the picking area. But if you depress that string up high on the fingerboard, the string may move an eighth of an inch or so, and that can really throw your synchronization off with the right hand. So that's the reason for doing it all over the fingerboard. To me, playing slowly is a warm-up. And speed comes from accuracy, you see; I wouldn't warm up by playing fast. I would warm up by playing slow, going for accuracy.

How do you avoid clichés in playing?

I think you avoid clichés with a lot of courage. Jerry Hahn, for instance, is one of my favorite guitar players, and here's the reason why: He makes a deliberate effort to avoid certain things, like impressing the audience with technique, which usually involves playing passages and licks that we've acquired at some other time and stringing them together in some way. Granted, that's a fundamental technique and we all use it. But ideally, I would prefer not to play those — just literally avoid them at all costs — and play something brand-new that I've never played before, taking the risk of maybe not being able to execute it.

What kind of strings do you use?

Because of the acid in my hands, a set of strings goes completely dead after about 20 minutes of playing. So it doesn't make any difference to me what brand I use; I kill a set of strings before I ever have a chance to evaluate them! But I do have a handy hint for guys who have the same problem: Put a piece of cardboard under the strings, and spray them with WD-40, a silicon lubricant. The cardboard keeps it from getting on the fingerboard — you don't want that. And then wipe it all off with a cloth. And after playing every set, rub the strings down with a cloth with WD-40 on it. I've found that that increases the lifetime of the strings quite a lot for me.

How do you avoid feedback in a hollowbody guitar?

One good way is to put a soundpost in there under the bridge; it deadens the sound much more effectively than anything else that I've found — a lot better than stuffing it full of foam rubber or something like that. Oh, by the way, a flank steak in the *f*-holes also works very well [*laughter*].

What about your string action: Do you set it high or low?

I may change that during an actual performance. If I find I'm pressing, being real aggressive and playing real hard, the strings might choke up on me, so I would raise them.

Do you think teaching helps you as a guitar player?

Absolutely. Teaching and learning are essentially the same process. As a matter of fact, my point of view about it is that in the end there is no teacher other than oneself: One person cannot really teach another. A person can learn, but he or she cannot be taught.

So what is the role of the teacher?

The role of the teacher is to motivate and inspire students, and select materials that are pertinent and useful to them. In other words, the teacher can control the quality of the materials. He or she can also control the *quantity* of material that is studied so as to avoid any overload, which is a very real hazard in learning. And the teacher should be attentive to the way the student applies his or her time to learning. This is very important in order to avoid exceeding the individual's attention span, which is another form of overload.

And just who is Howard Roberts? Is he a composer, a studio player, a teacher, a jazzer?

That's hard to say. Let's face it, music doesn't exist in words. Can you, for instance, imagine anything falling shorter of the mark than to describe a form of music as "jazz"? Jazz doesn't say a doggone thing! You ask people on the street what is jazz, and one might say [pianist/composer] Stan Kenton, and another might say [saxophonist] John Coltrane. But their music is vastly different, totally unique. So for me, on a clear day, if all things were wonderful, I'd be an explorer: an astronomer looking for a new star. Or I'd be a hobbyist who fools around with putting combinations of pitch and notes together. The guitar to me is like what a typewriter is to a novelist — a tool for expression.

— CARLOS SANTANA —

BY DAN FORTE — JUNE 1978 AND BY JAS OBRECHT — JANUARY 1988

JON SIEVERT

TENOR SAX-ophonist John Coltrane, one of modern jazz's true innovators, once said, "We are always searching; I think that now we are at the point of finding." Carlos Santana, like Coltrane, is a searcher — or, as he puts it, a seeker. The similarities between the two artists don't stop there. As with Coltrane's music, Santana's music has reflected the spiritual lifestyle he has chosen. Like Coltrane, he is an innovator and above all an individual voice on his instrument, the guitar.

John Coltrane was a major inspiration for Carlos, so the parallels are no doubt more than coincidence. The title tune of the Santana band's seventh album, *Welcome,* was a Coltrane composition. The guitarist collaborated with the saxophonist's widow, pianist/harpist Turiya Alice Coltrane, on the album *Illuminations.* At one stage, Devadip would even sleep with a tape of Coltrane music playing all night long.

But Santana was wise enough to know that there could only be one John Coltrane, and he listened to the music for inspiration — not to cop lines or even stylistic modes. Carlos Santana is such an individualist that it's difficult to hear direct traces of the musicians he cites as influences, except on rare occasions. He will talk for hours about his deep love for the blues, rattling off an endless list of favorite performers of the genre; yet in all his albums with the Santana band and his various solo projects, he has never recorded a blues tune — at least not in stan-

dard blues form. The blues, like the other factors that make up Santana's sound, is reflected as a feeling — not as notes or rhythms.

To this day, the name Santana brings to mind a picture of a battery of Latin percussionists behind their leader, who leans backwards, eyes clenched shut in concentration, as he *squeezes* the notes from his guitar. The Santana band was the first group to successfully blend Latin and Afro rhythms with rock music. Originally known as the Santana Blues Band — later shortened to its leader's surname — the group built a strong following at Bill Graham's Fillmore Auditorium in San Francisco, eventually headlining shows with the likes of Taj Mahal, the Youngbloods, and Melanie before they had even recorded. The young band received national acclaim, thanks to the Woodstock festival in 1969, the same year their first LP, *Santana,* debuted. *Santana* produced two hit singles in "Jingo" and "Evil Ways" and turned platinum within a year — an achievement few groups of that period could claim.

More hit albums and singles followed — "Oye Como Va," "Black Magic Woman/Gypsy Queen," "No One to Depend On" — despite numerous personnel changes in the group. The Santana band's direction changed, as did its guitarist/leader's ideals. Artists such as Coltrane, Charles Lloyd, McCoy Tyner, Thelonious Monk, Miles Davis (whom Santana calls "the Muhammad Ali of music"), Weather Report, and John McLaughlin provided the inspiration that had previously come from B.B. King, Jimmy Reed, and others. Along with the continued reputation of the band, Carlos Santana's position in the elite of rock guitarists is secure to say the least.

[June 1978]

Did the Latin influences creep into the Santana band because of the things you'd heard as a kid, or did an outside musician bring that element to the band?

We were exclusively a blues band at first. I think the reason the change took place was that we'd go around "hippie hill" and Aquatic Park [in San Francisco], and they used to have congas and wine — they probably still do — and that's where we got the congas in the band. And then I heard Gabor Szabo, and his album *Spellbinder* has congas on it. Somebody brought this conga player to jam with us, and he threw us into a whole different thing. Actually, we never play "Latin music" — you know, it's a crossover. I just play whatever I hear.

Did you originally plan to add a conga player, yet continue playing blues?

Yeah. Even when we had a conga player, it was still the Santana Blues Band. Actually, Harvey Mandel was probably the first guy to put congas on a rock and roll album [*Cristo Redentor*]. I saw him and Charlie Musselwhite one time, and I was knocked out. I learned a lot from them. I really admire guys, like Harvey Mandel, whose sound I can identify, because it takes a lot of work. Nobody can say that you are born with it; you work for it and carve your own individuality. In fact, if people want to find out how to develop this: A good way is to get a tape recorder and for half an hour turn out the lights in your house and get into a room that's kind of dark, where you don't have interruptions. Then just play with a rhythm machine. After a while it's like a deck of cards on the table, and you can begin to see the riffs that came from this guy, the riffs that came from that guy, and then the two or three riffs that are yours. Then you start concentrating on yours, and, to me, that's how you develop your own individual sound. You play a couple of notes and say, "Gee, that sounds like Eric Clapton," or "That sounds like George Benson." But then you play two or three notes and say, "Man, that's me." Not until a couple of years ago did I consciously start doing it that way. I'd just sit down and turn everything off and get a rhythm machine and just play and play.

Do you find much time to practice guitar these days?

Yeah, I still do it a lot — as much as I can. Mainly with the rhythm machine. I practice so that my fingers will respond to what I feel. Sometimes I have this incredible craving just to get a music teacher to teach me chords and fancy scales that you'd find in *The Thesaurus of Scales and Melodic Patterns*. I pick up that book once in a while and play two or three lines. Sometimes it scares me, because I start playing something really significant. Then sometimes I start sounding like everybody else, and I don't want to sound like that. I prefer simplicity. It's like eating: If you don't discriminate what you eat, you get sick — you know, indigestion. It's the same thing — you have to know what's good for you. You are digesting it by learning it. It is stored up in your memory cells. One way I practice: I put on a record when there's nobody home, and if it hits me, my face contorts and I start crying. I feel that if I can't cry to something that is moving, I'm not going to cry onstage. I think a lot of musicians become very callous, and after a while they can't feel pain. That's not what music is about.

Do you prefer to do concept albums rather than just collections of songs?

Yes, that's the only thing that I always deal with. Mostly, it's like a vision. Each song is a vision, rather than a musical approach. It's like painting: I don't think of what kind of stroke I'm going to give it; I just picture it, and then I know instantly what instrument, what color, to use. It's just easier for me, because I can't read music. I don't know nothing about music. I should get into music, and I probably will this year — chords and harmony. It would make it easier. I used to think it would get in the way, because I've seen musicians who are so technical with music that they always get caught on a technique of approaching a song the same way. They're bound to a technique, whereas a child who never practiced music — he can get the song any variety of ways, because he's not bound to a certain approach to music. Of course, I've heard a lot of pros and cons about music. I was always put off by a lot of snobbish musicians who can read music, but, fortunately, I met a lot of good musicians who had an open attitude about it. I once heard someone putting someone else down because he couldn't read music, and it was almost like in the movie *Never on Sunday*, where the mandolin player was feeling so down — they told him he wasn't a musician, because he couldn't read music. Then somebody told him, "Birds don't read music." So, in a way, it's an excuse, and I know that I should learn it and really make an effort to understand more about music, so I don't have to stutter as much. But I always feel I have enough spontaneity and enough vision not to be bound by, "Gee, I have to start with a C#."

Have you ever felt hindered by your lack of formal training when you're playing with someone like Stanley Clarke or Chick Corea?

We can play together easily. As soon as I close my eyes, it's like where you're sitting right now — you can just take for granted that you're sitting. But when you close your eyes and feel the chair holding you, and you start feeling your surroundings, then it makes it easier, because you remove your mind out of the way. To me, the heart is always in tune with the time and the melody. But if you start to think about, "I wonder what key he is playing in," then you can't even tune your guitar, because you spend so much time calculating and fabricating and criticizing that by the time you get to the song, they've finished already. But if you just feel, it's the most natural thing to do — if you just feel, you can create. I think music training would help me from the point of writing my own songs a little bit faster. Sometimes it does take me longer, because what I hear I have to search for in different positions until I find it — instead of saying, "I think what I hear is a D-something."

When you hear an idea for a song in your head, is it usually a melody or a set of changes or a rhythmic motif or what?

It's a cry. It's a crying melody. That's mostly what I hear, and then I have to find the chords. Sometimes it's the other way around, and one chord could almost make up for three melodies. But sometimes the melody is so clear, you want to find three passing chords for that melody.

Your guitar solos seem to stay pretty close to the melody of the song itself. Are you thinking of the song's basic theme throughout your solo?

Yes. To me, the heart of the song is the melody. And I approach the melody from a singer's point of view — a simple singer, not a singer who scats a lot like George Benson. If you'll notice, a lot of guitar players riff like horn players. And I don't really like guitar players like that. Not that I dislike them with a passion, but it doesn't appeal to me; it's boring to me. I think more like the layman kind of person singing [*sings*] "Lovely Rita meter maid . . . ." You don't care what chords are underneath; it's the basic feeling of the song that gets you immediately. I listen to the radio a lot, so I don't think like *deedleedoodah* and that sort of thing. And I figure, why do it like that when there are so many thousands of cats who can do it a zillion times better? That's what they are, and

I just get into what I am now. It's like your signature. This is a very valid point for me now — some people may think it's negative, but I think it's positive — because I am aware that out of thousands and thousands of guitar players, there are only, like, thirty who you can listen to and know who they are. The rest all sound the same — at least that's what I think. And it took me a while to realize that that's a very beautiful gift, your own individuality — even if you only know three notes, man, if you are able to play those well and know who you are. I don't think I was aware of my sound until three or four years ago. Even when I did that album with Mahavishnu [*Love Devotion Surrender*] — after a while: "Gee, who's playing what?" It even took *me* a while to figure out who was doing what; because we were playing so many notes, after a while the sound was all the same. Then I started hearing a certain amount of chops, and I said, "That's Mahavishnu;" and then I'd hear three notes and say, "Well, that's me." I think it goes back to when I was listening to Johnny Mathis and Dionne Warwick and playing behind the melody, rather than doing what the trumpets and horns or somebody else was playing. I really didn't listen that much to bebop; I missed that era. I was into all these blues people like Jimmy Reed who only play three notes — but they grab you. As far as I'm concerned, the point of music is to tell stories with a melody. All that stuff about playing notes, to me, is just like watching some cat pick up weights. After a while, who wants to see somebody flex their muscles?

Your guitar playing is extremely vocal-like in tone and phrasing, yet you've never been the lead singer of the Santana band. Do you try to compensate for that in your playing?

Right; I think that's exactly it. I sing through the guitar. The main theme is always haunting melodies.

Your sets in concerts are almost like concept albums in that there are very few breaks between songs, and the transitions from mood to mood are very subtle.

Yes, it's the mood. I learned that from Miles — to put everything so that it's constantly transcending itself. You try to make it peak and resolve. Sometimes we feel like we do have to pause and let the people, like, gulp it in and digest it for a while. But I like to go from song to song to song. It's more fun.

Have you ever seen or gotten into any "guitar battles" onstage?

I don't like that kind of pressure. I used to hang around the Fillmore and see a bunch of guitar players come up to B.B. King like they were gunslingers —

you could see in their eyes that they wanted to burn him. And B.B. would just come out with some Django Reinhardt or Charlie Christian licks, and then after that play some B.B. King. I'd just laugh at the looks on those other guys' faces. When I went on tour with Mahavishnu we did about twelve concerts together, and for about the first six I think I was really intimidated by him. After that I started seeing how people were waiting for me; like, they'd had enough of him. And I said, "Well, maybe I do have a position where I'll say something and they'll listen." I was intimidated until I saw people being moved by what I was playing. After a while we gave some concerts together with acoustic guitars, and it's like anything: If you remove your mind, you can give someone a good run for their money, and you can even scare yourself. You just have to go inside yourself. If you spend your whole time thinking about what you're going to say, it's gone.

Did the collaboration with John McLaughlin come about because you were both involved with Sri Chinmoy?

I was a seeker, and I still am a seeker. Even music is secondary to me — as much as I love it. Mahavishnu called me and said they wanted to know if we could do this album together, and he also wanted to know if I was interested in coming to see Sri Chinmoy. He felt that I was aspiring or crying for another kind of awareness — because at that time I had already made a commitment to close the book on drugs and booze and that kind of stuff. Then I started reading books about India and about spiritual masters, and it inspired me to work harder. Some people call it ambition, but I call it inspiration. When you have that, it's like having a different kind of energy — pure energy — a different kind of fuel. Sometimes it's totally in this center of creativity, and it just flows through you, and all of a sudden you don't have to worry about who's going to like or dislike it. When it's over, you feel just like a bee: You don't know why you did it, but all of a sudden you've accumulated all this honey. So that's what brought us together. We had the same cry for the same purpose. But I did learn so much from him; he's an incredible musician. Of course, you always find the number one guitar player that you never heard before — someone who's probably never been recorded — but since I don't know him yet, Mahavishnu, George Benson, and Pat Martino are probably my favorite guitar players.

The people that I'm really close to, I don't even consider them to be guitarists; I consider them to be more like painters. B.B. [King] doesn't seem like a guitarist to me; he seems to cry and play the blues and that kind of stuff. So when I hear him play, I don't even hear a guitar; I just hear this cry. If I was really into guitar players, I would say Django Reinhardt was really a "guitar player." He had both — he could cry with the melody, and then scare you to death with a couple of runs. He had everything. He could play runs like a horn player, a piano player, or a guitar player, and then play some sweet melodies. And then when they told me he only had two good fingers, I really flipped.

It's still a struggle to get into my own sound and own individuality that God gave me; you always transcend yourself, no matter what you play. But at that time, I was struggling a little more, because it took me hours and hours. I would even sleep with a tape recorder on. I bought a tape recorder that would play both sides continuously, and I'd listen to John Coltrane all the time — because I couldn't understand the later albums; they were so hectic. Then all of a sudden it wasn't hectic at all; it was so sweet. It's like everything: You have to condition your mind to see that there's crying children in it, the love and compassion of a mother in the notes. The most significant thing that I learned in my whole life about music is the consciousness of it. It's like if you go to a bar where Elvin Bishop is playing, there's a certain consciousness he puts out. It's almost like being in a barn where there are chickens and pigs, and it's a very beautiful, happy atmosphere — very down-to-earth. Whereas if you go to a church or, say, to India, every music has its own consciousness. Music becomes like an empty glass, and whatever you put inside is the consciousness. If you play country and western or Brazilian samba music or whatever, that's just the shell. It's how you feel, what you put inside the music, that's really significant.

With a song like "Europa," which is very emotional, is it hard to play that night after night and still feel it as deeply as you did when you wrote it?

It's not as hard as it used to be, because I learned a trick to it, a way to condition the mind. I used to listen to B.B. King and say, "Wow, it took me forever to learn that riff, and I still don't have it down pat the way B.B. hits it." Then after I saw him play, I could see that he'd make a certain face and then hit the note. Every time he made the face like that, he'd hit the note. And I figured that he would go back somewhere in time to a certain place or somewhere inside himself and then hit the note. So that's what I do now. I forget that I'm maybe a significant figure in the world of music, and I become like a child who doesn't know anything except that I'm crying for spiritual values. I don't have to fabricate any grandeur trip or anything; it's like I'm very, very natural.

You've mentioned several artists as being crossovers, which is somewhat controversial, since some jazz purists no doubt resent a rocker like Jeff Beck winning this year's Playboy *poll as Best Jazz Guitarist. In fact, the term "jazz" has been used by some to describe your playing.*

And I'm not, right. I don't know why they classify certain artists like they do, but I'm not bothered by it, because I know that first and foremost I'm an instrument myself trying to play something back to you. I don't consider myself a guitar player as much as I am a seeker who wants to manifest his vision through that particular instrument. I consider a guitar player somebody who *sounds* like a guitar player. In this day and age, it's hard to tell who's *not* a crossover. I don't consider "crossover" to be a negative term. Some players have used it just to make more bread, and their heart isn't in it, and that's prostitution. But somebody who is making an honest attempt to master another kind of music his own way is a positive crossover. I think the only one, to my ears, who day or night doesn't sound like a crossover is Keith Jarrett. But to me it's a challenge to learn everything on earth. One time I felt like it was my duty to be a pioneer, but that kind of stuff I leave to someone else now. I don't care to be a pioneer, except for my own heart. But consciously I wouldn't make it a commitment to put that kind of pressure on myself. I just play whatever is comfortable without offending or belittling my instrument or my own integrity.

[January 1988]
You're one of the few guitarists who is instantly recognizable. Why is that?

It's an accumulation of a lot of things, man. My love for [saxophonist] John Coltrane and his tone. My love for B.B. [King] and his tone, or Aretha [Franklin]. All the things that my father passed on to me. My father is a musician; he taught me everything I know on the guitar, as far as the technical chords and stuff like that goes. His father before him was a musician, and my grand-grandfather was a musician. The main thing is the *cry.* It's not whining. You know, sometimes you go to a funeral, and maybe the guy wasn't such a good guy, but people still want to say something nice about him. Well, the tone in the music that I'm trying to write now is for people to learn to let go gently and quietly. It's to enhance the

beauty that, let's say, Jaco Pastorius had. I immediately erase all the *National Enquirer* stuff out of my mind, so all I remember is the great times that I had with Jaco Pastorius when we did get to jam and spend some time together. That's what I'm trying to do with the tone. It's the cry of "exalt the elegance in humanity."

Maybe that's what Jimi Hendrix meant by calling an album The Cry of Love.

Yeah. Sometimes you can laugh so much that you start to cry. Sometimes you can cry so much that you start to laugh. That's *pure emotion.* That's the foundation for my music, first of all. Some people learn all about the great composers and base their stuff on that, and that's fine. As long as we all get to the ocean and get wet together, it's cool. The approach is not as important as getting to a place where, like, Aretha or Patti LaBelle go when they sing a certain note and their eyes roll back to their ears, and they take you with them wherever they go. That's the goal for me in writing songs now. Whether it's fast, slow, reggae, African, or whatever, what can I do to get the listener intoxicated with it?

What advice would you give young, technical gunslingers for getting more emotion into their playing?

The only advice that I can give is that all that stuff is toys in their approaches. Nothing hits the listener in his heart of hearts faster than sincerity. I'll take sincerity over soulfulness *anytime.* Whether you play fast or slow, if you're sincere, the people will pick it up. If you are just running the changes, chord scales, and all that kind of stuff, it's like Sugar Ray [Leonard, champion boxer]. Sugar Ray can get you with 50 blows really fast, but if [singer] Marvin Gaye just hits you once, you're going to go down. It's the same thing when certain fast musicians jam with, let's say, Otis Rush. These cats can run the length and breadth of the guitar, playing all the notes at blinding speed. But if Otis Rush puts his finger on that guitar and hits you with one note and milks totally the cow, nobody stands a chance. I've seen him put away just about everybody in a nightclub in Chicago because of the *tone.* The tone is more important to me than anything else, because it will disarm the listener to let go of whatever is in your mind, and you embrace what's happening. Your soul identifies with it, and then you either laugh or cry. It's opening people's ears to their purest emotions. That's what people try to do when they go to church.

How much of your tone is in your hands?

I would say about 25%. The other 75% comes

from my legs, my guts. After I play a solo, my throat and my calves hurt. This is *projecting;* it's not volume. People don't know that there's a difference between being loud and learning how to project. A lot of musicians play from their fingers on out, so they ain't gonna reach you. But when a person hits from his calves — check out Jimi sometimes — and here [*slaps thighs, crotch, and stomach*] and puts it on that note, man, your hair stands up, your spine tingles. This is not a fantasy thing; this is for real. If you put your whole being into that note — your vitals, your body, your mind, your heart, and your soul — people will react to it.

What commonly gets in the way of that total connection?

Your mind. Self-doubt, insecurity. Deception, ego. Those are the things that block pure creativity. Ego, to me, is like a dog or a horse. Make him work for you. Don't you work for him.

Is your spirit more present in your music at certain times than others?

Yeah. That's when I feel like I took an inner shower. I'll give you an example: When I came back from this last tour, I heard about Jaco. I went to the Pacific Ocean near Bolinas [in northern California], and I jumped in. It was really cold. And then I cast, as they say, my troubles in the deep blue sea. Meditation helps you let go of everything — exaltation and when somebody puts you down. It's like emptying your pockets. Once you feel forgiven for whatever things we do as monkeys, imagination comes back. Einstein said that imagination is infinitely more important than knowledge. When you are clean, then you are not blocking the flow of creativity and spirit. Within two or three days of staying in that rhythm, you're playing becomes like a telephone. You're just monitoring what wants to come out through you. You become a pure channel. The most beautiful music goes beyond the musicians who played it. Certain people, like Jimi Hendrix or John Coltrane, don't play for just themselves and their immediate families. They play for a whole generation. That means that those people took a lot of time to become a cleaner vessel.

Don't you feel that you've sometimes achieved that?

Sometimes you tap into it. It's an everyday struggle. It's putting a leash on your mind and all the things that it brings, and making them work for you. Sometimes we forget that everything is run by grace — the Golden Gate hanging, the planes flying, the note sustaining. You know, when people sustain with

[effects] pedals, they are not using God's grace. They are using a company's electronics. There are good parts of it, but the bad part of it is that you are already going to sound like somebody else. The tone, first of all, is your face. So why do you want to look like somebody else? Your tone is how people know you; if you play one note, they know who you are. The most important thing people have to work on a lot of times is getting their own individual tone. I used to fight for this, but now not as much because [engineer] Jim Gaines knows how to capture my sound.

How do you make a note sustain?

First of all, you find a spot between you and the amplifier where you both feel that umbilical cord. When you hit the note, you immediately feel a laser between yourself and the speakers. You hear it catch like two train cars coupling together. It is like driving a real, real high-performance car. If you don't know what you're doing, man, you're going to be off the road [*laughs*]. So you have to be prepared for that. You have to practice with that intensity of playing. As Jimi Hendrix said before he left, he played loud, but his sound was never shrill. Even with all the knowledge they have, some people today sound shrill, which blocks a lot of the good that you're doing. But if you roll a lot of the highs down and put on a lot more bass, then you still sustain, but you don't have that piercing sound that kills dogs.

Do you have any special recording techniques for guitar?

For some reason, they always take the natural sound of the guitar to the board. It's hard for anything to sound the way we hear it. That's why they haven't invented microphones to capture [drummer] Tony Williams' sound or my sound or T-Bone Walker's sound. I don't use batteries on my guitars. Some people use preamps and a lot of pedals to sustain and stuff, and that's like having an automatic car. I like to stick-shift. Automatic means that you gain all these great sounds, but you sound like everybody else immediately. The only way you can tell who they are is by their chops — not by their tone anymore. The people whose tone I like still are B.B. King and Otis Rush, because they are back to playing with [Fender] Twin Reverbs, just naked. The emotion creates all the things that you are supposed to create, not the gadgets. The gadgets sound too generic.

What's the most important element to capture on tape?

For me, it's the ghost tones. I'll give you an example: If you blow into a balloon three times, the third time it will explode. And when it pops, you hear ghost overtones. That's what stimulates us to create. Unless you have a good engineer, when they run you straight into the board, the first thing they take from you is the ghost sound, the spirit sound — so they leave you really dry. The way to put it back is to open up things to give it that room sound. Sometimes we do that with a Lexicon [224X digital reverb], and sometimes with an extra microphone away from the amplifier. Without the ghost tones, I may as well be doing gardening or something else.

The ghost tones, then, are the harmonic overtones that help create sustain?

Yeah. The ear picks up a lot of things. To me, when the sound is right, everything rejoices in life. Whether it's blues, up-tempo, Brazilian, shuffle, whatever — when the groove is right and the tone is perfect, it all fits.

Can you get your tone from most guitars?

I can just about get it from any guitar. But I really go out and jam with a lot of people, and a lot of times as soon as I put my finger on a guitar, the guitar will say to me, "Who are you, and why are you playing me this way?" [*Laughs.*] So you know you are going to have to approach it differently. With my guitar, it's like, "Where do you want to go?" Amplifiers — unless they are old Twins or just straight Marshalls or old Boogies, I can't use them. The new stuff all sounds like Saran Wrap around your ears. It sounds very, very harsh. Even the new amplifiers that a lot of people make today sound edgy like transistors, like something on your teeth. It's weird. With anything that's tube and old, you already have an elegant tone to begin with. This is true for anything that's pre-'75; in '75 they started getting weird. Old amps make you hear the song completely.

How many left-hand fingers do you use to add vibrato while sustaining a note?

Sometimes the first three. Mostly I use my 1st and 3rd. I call these the emotion expression fingers. You can tickle it with the index finger [*demonstrates a trill*], and you can get total emotion with the ring finger. The middle finger is to help you for horn-like or piano-player-type chops.

Your choice of a large triangular pick is unusual for a linear player.

I just got in the habit of playing with big ones like that when I was in Tijuana. I can turn them any way I want to, and even if I make a mistake, it just keeps rotating. With the little ones, you've only got one way to pick the strings; I would be stuck. This way, if the pick is weird, I've still got two other

edges. Once in a while I don't play with the pick, but if I want to play fast, I have to use the pick. I'm not like Jeff Beck, who's fast without any pick at all.

What do you listen for in pickups?

I go through a lot of them now. The ones that I'm married to, I'm married to, because under any weather, any condition, any hall or bar, those suckers are going to sustain and sing the song. The pickups that work best for me are the old humbuckers — like the Gibson Patent Applied Fors — especially when they are dipped in wax. And even those are hard to find now. Pickups are your voice. The worst pickup setup for me gives you that out-of-phase sound — unless it's a Stratocaster. I like Stratocasters that are in the second or fourth positions; their single-coil pickups sound good. But I just can't use a double-coil pickup that's out-of-phase. It's immediately like playing with half a man, half a tone. I need the whole tone on the treble and on the bass to be able to sustain. Out-of-phase means half, and I can't use half. I have to have it all the way.

Are you hard on strings?

Yeah, but I don't break them as much as I used to. Sometimes I can go for a month or two without breaking a string. We change strings every two weeks. I use a heavier-gauge string at home to get my chops up, and on the road I mainly use .008s on the Strats and .009s on the regular ones. So it goes .009, .011, .014, .024, .036, .042 [high to low].

Do you do anything special to help the guitar stay in tune?

Yeah. When I change strings, I pull all the strings four or five times, count to seven, really stretch them almost to the point of breaking, and then let them go. By the third time, it'll stay in tune. They behave. They really give, even if you give them the whammy. Of course, it also helps to put pencil lead along the [nut's] string slots. But if you don't have the time, just pull the strings as much as you can. By the third time, they know who the boss is [*laughs*].

What's your all-time favorite guitar and amp setup?

If I want to just play at home and get the sweetest, most beautiful tone, it's still the old Strats or Les Pauls through anything old that's Fender. The amps they had with the separate reverbs — that stuff is the best. In fact, the best sound that I've heard lately from a guitar player was Eric Johnson.

What appealed to you about Eric's tone?

He had the most beautiful tone all the way around. It was very, very masculine, and round and warm and dark. And his playing is great, man. I'd like to record with him someday, because he is very pure. You can tell what people have in their eyes — malice, expectations, the beauty of things, this or that. With Eric, it's "Okay, I got my tone and my vision, and that's enough. The Lord will provide the rest." He has a beautiful soul. Even though he is from Texas, he doesn't have the gunslinger mentality: "I'm going to kick your butt with my gun." When we jam, we both complement each other, which is what musicians are supposed to do. Eric is somebody who should be playing with [keyboardist] Joe Zawinul, Miles Davis, and people like that, along with other musicians like Bill Connors. Those guys should be given a shot sometime at playing with the great musicians, because they have a lot of diverse techniques. Eric knows a lot of musical expressions; he understands that language a lot.

You've jammed with a who's who of post-'50s rock, jazz, and blues. Are there any musicians you would like to have jammed with?

My deepest regret until I die is going to be not playing with Bola Sete. I didn't find out until not too long ago that he really liked my music and wanted to play with me. And like an idiot, I never made it a point to give him the time. When I was a kid, his music or Joe Pass' music used to sound too restricted. That was something my father would play, not what I wanted to play. I wanted to play more raunchy. Now, that music is not so subdued anymore. It's just as powerful as Van Halen when you see Joe Pass doing his thing. Bola's record *Live at Monterey*, man, is just pure brilliance. He could play behind his back and between his legs like T-Bone Walker, and at the same time go right into Segovia. I see in Bola the same elegance as Duke Ellington and the fire of Hendrix, but he's sustaining this overtone on a natural acoustic guitar. And most of all, like John Coltrane, he had that tone and that way of putting notes together that made it more than mortal music. Mortal music deals with my baby left me, I can't pay the rent, or whatever. Bola's music tells you that inside we have roaring cosmic lions and that we're elegant and beautiful. His music enhanced the beautiful side of humanity to a supreme extent.

I'm looking for sincerity. I have gone through accommodating a lot of producers and record companies, and finally all of us have come to an agreement that the only thing we need to accommodate from now on is the *moment,* the sincerity of the song. I have the experience now not to accommodate plastic producers with their plastic attachés and their plastic ideas, so it's easy for me to concentrate. If I was

going to a Santana concert, what would I want? I want joy and a lot of vitality. I want the spirit of when a pastor tells you something really precious at church that applies to your life — something that's not condemning you or making you feel like you should apologize for being a human being. Whether in a cry or in a party atmosphere, the music should exalt humanity and the spirit of humanity, which is the Lord. That's enough, because anything else will be the crust. This is the real pure water.

Have you noticed growth in your style?

Yeah. I can tell when I played with John McLaughlin for about three years; you tend to sound like that. You don't want to, but we are all products of our environment. It's like Jeff Beck says — a lot of times I can't stand my playing. I need to take a break from my tone and everything. Other times, I can't believe that it's coming out of my fingers. To this day, I still pick up the guitar late at night, and it feels like it's the first time I'm putting my fingers on the fret. I read this [pianist] Keith Jarrett interview where he said that he was learning to play trumpet for a while, and for the first week or two he sounded like Miles. Then he started sounding really polished, and he didn't like it anymore. So in other words, there is a certain beauty in playing like Miles Davis or John McLaughlin — play like you don't know how to play. Take chances and make new mistakes. Go for what you don't know, and make it brutally honest. That appeals to me a lot, because then when you do get to the goodies, you rejoice. If you get to the goodies really quick, it means that you're playing something that you've already conceived. There's joy in rediscovering.

What path would you suggest for a young child who wants to play guitar?

My son is four-and-a half years old, and he's already asking me, "Is Jimi Hendrix badder than Michael Jackson?" First of all, I would just give him heavy doses of John Lee Hooker, Muddy Waters, Jimmy Reed, and Lightnin' Hopkins for two or three years. Once I feel that he's got that combination, then I'll say that Muddy Waters is the Miles Davis of Chicago, and Little Walter is the John Coltrane. By the time my son is listening to something like "A Love Supreme" by John Coltrane, he would have understood the order all the way from Django Reinhardt to Charlie Christian to Wes Montgomery. I want him to understand that order, because I don't want my son to be fooled by fool's gold. And there is a lot of it out there for kids, a lot of flash and guys who have the right poses for the right strokes on the guitar. But that stuff doesn't cut it when you really know how to play, and you put the note where it's supposed to be. I want to teach my son not to fake anything, but to earn it.

Is it important that he learn music theory?

Yeah. I'm going to have to make sure that he learns the old way of learning music on the piano — do, re, mi, fa, sol, la, ti, do. It's going to be hard, because there's not that many teachers who teach that nowadays. They still teach C, F, G, and all that kind of stuff. But I still think in terms of do, re, me; I still think in Spanish. When I record with, let's say, [pianists] Herbie Hancock or McCoy Tyner, that's how I have to write the melody for chord changes that are given me — a do, re, la, sol, mi kind of thing. That's how I hear my line, whether it's blues or whatever. It gives you a point of reference for where the melody falls. You know, if you teach your child the right vocabulary, he's on his way to really speaking the universal language, not just cowboy music or some other kind of music. Universal language is deeper than the surface. That way, when you play cowboy music, even the Japanese will be doing a hillbilly dance.

Do you always know what key you're in or what chords you're playing over?

No. A lot of times I force myself just to go for what I feel, rather than landing at the root note. If you approach everything from the root note, there is no mystery for what you are going to play, because intuitively you are going to go to the same thing. Even when I'm playing "Black Magic Woman," I force myself to feel like I don't know how to play.

Does this mean starting the solo from a different part of the fingerboard?

Sometimes. Most of the time it's a matter of where you are going to hit the note from — the stomach, the heart, the legs. Where are you going to tighten up? What muscle are you going to use? The main thing is to approach things in a new way. If you have a swimming pool, don't always jump in the same way. Surprise yourself.

Earlier on, you mentioned seeing something in Eric Johnson's eyes. Did you ever notice anything in Jimi Hendrix' eyes?

I saw Jimi Hendrix two or three times in person. The first time I really was with him was in the studio. He was overdubbing "Roomful of Mirrors" [*Rainbow Bridge,* Reprise MS 2040], and this was a real shocker to me. He said, "Okay, roll it," and started recording, and it was incredible. But within 15 or 20 seconds into the song, he just went out. All of a sudden the music that was coming out of the speakers was way beyond the song, like he was freaking out having a gigantic battle in the sky with somebody. It just didn't make sense with the song anymore, so the roadies looked at each other, the producer looked at him, and they said, "Go get him." I'm not making this up. They separated him from the amplifier and the guitar, and it was like he was having an epileptic attack. I said, "Do I have to go through these changes just to play my guitar? I'm just a kid!" When they separated him, his eyes were red and he was almost foaming from the mouth. He was gone.

What do you think caused it?

To me, it was a combination of the lifestyle — staying up all night, chicks, too much drugs, all kinds of stuff. It was a combination of all the intensities that he felt, along with a lack of discipline. In the rock style of life at that time, there was no discipline. You took *everything* all the time. I know one thing, man — it drained me. It made me realize that, like John McLaughlin, I needed to know about discipline. Now I know that out of discipline comes freedom. When you've got discipline in your pocket, you've got punctuality, regularity, meditation. When things get too crazy with the record, the companies, or the world, you can click a switch and go into your own sanctuary and play music that is stronger than the news.

Can you offer any parting advice for guitarists?

Whether you are doing it in the bar, the church, the strip joint, or the Himalayas, the first duty of music is to complement and enhance life. And once you approach it like that, then there is order. You have to have businessmen to help take care of you, so you have to develop that trust. You also have to not be naive. You have to know that there are a lot of people out there who are like leeches. They live out of musicians. They work you to get a contract, and then 10 years from now you realize that they stole you blind. You have to know when to trust and when to say, "Hey, man, I can't work with you, because I don't trust you. You are dishonest." All of that stuff is part of music, because whatever happens between the 23 hours that you're not onstage is going to affect you when you come onstage. So all that is important.

What's the greatest reward in your line of work?

It's like that movie *Round Midnight.* There's a part where this guy tells [saxophonist] Dexter Gordon, "When I was in the Army, the way you played these three notes changed my life." People come up to me and tell me that I did that. Someone said to me, "Man, I was ready to check out, put the gun to my head, and I heard this song. It made me cry, and it made me want to try it again. Now I feel better." That's not *me,* though; it's a spirit through me that wants to exalt itself. It says, "Don't take that out. Don't treasure frustration. Don't treasure depression. This is an imposter — don't make friends with him. You're more than that. Don't focus on the negative things in life. Accentuate the positive; otherwise you become darkened. Light up a candle." That's the tone; that's the story that I want to do through my music as much as possible. That's the best reward, because platinum albums and all that kind of stuff collect dust, and after a while you don't even know where you stored them. When you have children, all that stuff doesn't mean that much anymore. What means something is to be able to tell a story and put wings in people's hearts.

— JOE SATRIANI —

BY JAS OBRECHT — FEBRUARY 1988 & JANUARY 1989

CHUCK PULIN

"MY LIFETIME mission?" ponders Joe. "To boldly go where no man has gone before. To seek peace and harmony. In my own way, that's what I'm trying to accomplish."

Poignant, lyrical, and provocative, Joe Satriani's instrumental solo albums explore the outer limits of rock guitar. As Joe himself describes in language as imaginative as his music, the discs span "full-tilt boogie to ambient bliss, tongue-in-cheek psycho-Western to dire metallic adagio, cerebral cool to visceral hot, two-handed fantasies to foot-stomping wanged and wah-wahed surf and roll, and possibly the only heavy metal instrumental about an insect!" His work more than lives up to the name of his publishing company — Strange Beautiful Music.

What makes Satriani's playing special? He has amazing chops, unorthodox approaches to whammy and one- and two-handed techniques, and a talent for melodies that venture beyond the common. Thoroughly grounded in music theory, he's taught guitar almost as long as he's played, with Steve Vai and Metallica's Kirk Hammett being his most famous pupils. At the heart of it all, though, are Joe's imagination, ongoing quest for perfection, and uncanny ability to translate his emotions into groundbreaking guitar playing.

The Long Island native was raised in a musical household, with his mom and three sisters studying piano. While Joe and his brother were spared lessons,

they did enjoy pounding the 88s: "We invented this ridiculous little game called 'Constradi and Orchestra,'" Joe laughs. "Constradi was this ridiculous pompous conductor that we made up. We would sit down and say, 'Ladies and gentlemen, Constradi!' and then just *bang away* together on the piano. That's as far as it went. My brother went on to play blues harp and flute. I stuck with the piano, but my technique was just awful, instant tendinitis with the left hand. Now I can only play bass and chords on piano; I can't play like real players, but I know the keyboard. Guitar was quite natural."

Joe cites his older sister Marion, an amateur '60s folksinger, as being his first guitar influence. His decision to play guitar, though, came when he was 14 and heard Jimi Hendrix: "I was just completely floored. The first time I ever heard him on the radio, it was like a psychedelic event. I was just a little kid, but it seemed like the whole room was spinning. Before that there were all these really smoking jazz guys, but very few of them touched me. Wes Montgomery, to me, was perfect. First time I ever heard him, I needed no convincing, no introduction. And Hendrix sounded the exact same way — so natural and off the wall and anti-technique that I loved it." Satriani quit the football team and gave up his drums for guitar on September 18, 1970, the day Jimi Hendrix died.

A thorough grounding in music theory enabled Joe to begin teaching guitar almost immediately. He played with local Long Island bands, and in 1975 studied with jazz pianist Lennie Tristano for a couple of months. Struck by wanderlust, he then explored Los Angeles and Japan before settling in Berkeley, California, in 1977. From 1979 through '84, he played with a much-heralded but ultimately unsigned power-pop trio, the Squares.

Satriani surfaced on his own in 1984 with the generically packaged, self-produced *Joe Satriani*. For the few people who heard the EP, the much-needed clarification "every sound on this record was made on an electric guitar" was hard to believe, especially after hearing the sound effects of "Talk to Me" and the popping bass in "Dreaming Number Eleven." Satriani stepped out on guitar, bass, keyboards, and percussion for *Not of This Earth*, cut in '85 and released a year later by Relativity Records. His writing, arranging, and production kept the guitar center-stage, with tones ranging from dentist drills and record-scratch rubs to crunch metal and the squeaky clean. Best of all, he took lots of chances — musically and financially (he financed the album with a credit card) — pulling them all off with finesse.

While awaiting the release of *Not of This Earth*, Joe joined the Greg Kihn Band for its 1985 *Love & Rock & Roll* LP and tour. In other studio projects, he collaborated with drummer Tony Williams, worked on commissioned pieces for PBS, Dole Pineapple, and Otari, and sang backup vocals for Crowded House. He co-produced Possessed's EP *Eyes of Horror* and sightread a solo for drummer Danny Gottlieb's *Aquamarine*.

With 1987's *Surfing with the Alien*, Satriani became a bona fide guitar hero, garnering numerous guitaristic awards and securing the lead guitar position for Mick Jagger's 1988–89 solo tour. Since then, solo tours and CDs have continued to increase the superlatives.

What's important to you?

The songs, the music. What I'm feeling. I know that I'm not good if I'm not into what I'm playing. I don't believe in it if I'm not excited about it. I couldn't come here to the studio for 12 hours a day and not be inspired. I try to do what people say they won't do. Whatever is considered standard operating procedure, I generally try to go the other way, just to see what happens — usually with good results. I take chances a lot. A year or two goes by, and I look back at what we've worked on, and I like it because it's so outrageous and strange.

Some of your music has a disturbing, almost sinister quality.

Really? We did something right, then. I can definitely say "The Enigmatic" [*Not of This Earth*] is sinister. "Ice 9" [*Surfing with the Alien*] certainly has an edge to it. That title is a reference to Kurt Vonnegut; I'm a great fan of his.

When you first began on guitar, were you inspired to find your own way?

Yes. My parents encouraged all of my brothers and sisters to be individuals as much as possible, to seek out what it is we wanted to do and not give up no matter what.

Who helped you along the way?

Bill Wescott had a tremendous effect. I met him before I started playing, when I was a snotty little kid at Carle Place High on Long Island. Bill is an amazing teacher, because he transferred his feeling about music to me, and at the same time he taught me hands down all the theory that there is — how to read, what's music theory, what modes sound like. He brought to my attention Harry Partch, the best of Bartók, Erik Satie, Chopin, Handel, and everybody. I'd sit next to him and see him get into it. To me, it was like, *that's* how you play. Early on he said, "You know, Joe, it may turn out that you're not really gifted on the guitar, but don't let it stop you from writing and imagining whatever it is you want." He was just Mr. Inspiration, plus he taught how to get 90s in advanced theory and pass the Regents Exam in New York. When I got to Five Towns College to study music, there was absolutely no point in my being there.

What did your lessons with Lennie Tristano give you?

Discipline. He was another guy who was great just to be next to because he was so intense. Lennie showed me that technique was not music, that when you're practicing technique, don't fool around. You just do it right, and don't play things until you're ready. And if you play them and make a mistake, it's because you weren't ready and shouldn't have played them in the first place. With Lennie you had an enormous lesson, but you had to play technical things *perfectly*.

Does your knowledge of keyboards affect the way you play guitar?

That sort of technique wouldn't help me at all, because I'm a terrible keyboard player. Maybe at some point the piano's range allowed me to experiment with consonants and dissonants and how that changes when it's spread out over many octaves. For instance, a D chord on top of a C chord sounds awful when they are right next to each other, but when those chords are spread over two, three, or four octaves, it becomes more and more consonant — at least to my ear. When I realized that, it helped me think about things, about how I could actually play chords way up the neck while I had a basis.

Have you listened to much non-Western music?

Yes. I listen to what was originally called Oriental music — anything from Arabian music to Chinese and Japanese. I was exposed to a lot of things as I was growing up, and it just seemed very natural for me to like it and, as a result, to reflect it in my style.

Did timing come naturally, or did you have to teach yourself?

I taught myself. Timing is natural, but you have to practice it and work at it to convince yourself that it's there. When I was a young kid listening to the Beatles and the Stones, I didn't say, "Boy, he could have played groups of five there!" I wasn't thinking of that. But once you get exposed to that, you can feel things like groups of five. You'll like them, and you may use them with discretion and taste. I think I learned a lot from the timing of other people — Hendrix, Stevie Wonder, or Larry Graham. I listen back and say, "Yeah, they're late here, and they're early here, and that creates a sound." Some people push the beat when they are creating a certain kind of a song, some people drag, some people go right in the pocket. As your sense of time gets better, the idea of the beat becomes this huge circle, and you see that you can play with it and use it as a tool to get a song to come off a certain way and evoke a certain emotion, especially with bass.

Is there an inherent mood in every key and scale?

Not just one. In the hands of an artist, what you can do is almost limitless. I definitely operate on that assumption. I've heard so much beautiful music done in major keys, and yet very little of it is in heavy rock, exploratory jazz fusion, or whatever you want to call what we're doing. Most of the stuff is Dorian minor key, or else it's more ethnic-oriented; that's not the best word, but that's how it's printed up in most books. For instance, they'll call the Phrygian dominant mode the Jewish or Spanish scale. One scale can sound a lot of different ways, and I've really tried to work with that on the last two records. With "Always with Me, Always with You" [*Surfing with the Alien*] and "Rubina" [*Not of This Earth*], I tried to use those major scales to be tender and sharp and haunting and a whole bunch of things.

Does the same hold true for chords?

Yes, most definitely. The fewer notes in the chords, the easier it gets. In my mind I see the melodies, solos, and rhythms as being the chords. Maybe other people think simply of the rhythm guitar part as the chord, and they write from that way. "Ice 9" is in sort of a Dorian mode, but at the end of that solo I just flip it around and use a major third, because there is no third being played. I've just tricked you into assuming that I wasn't going to put it in, and that way you can play the note. Playing with small amounts of harmonic information, you get more mileage. You get more freedom, as far as writing the melody or the solo goes.

Do you imagine a melody before finding it on guitar?

Yes. It's like it comes to me; I hear it being laid out. But I do spend quite a lot of time editing. I edited the hell out of "Always with Me," because I was intrigued with how beautiful it was. I wanted the song to start with a melody, go into a slight improvisation, give a countermelody, go back to the original melody, do another little improvisation, and return to the melody. I wanted to be as cool as the sax player you see in a nice jazz club where there is a bassist, a piano player, and a drummer with brushes. And this guy just stands up with his sax, plays the melody, does the solo, plays the melody, and the song is over. No big rush, no ego solo, no exploding things. So it took me a while to get all the little subtleties down to where I felt that this was natural. I had to find that sort of player in me, those sensibilities, and then figure out the technique.

Was the second album recorded differently than the first?

Yes. *Surfing with the Alien* was recorded with Dolby SR noise reduction. The first record didn't use any noise reduction at all. In fact, we didn't even know we were making a record when we made it. Joe's credit card project [*laughs*]. I didn't even actually consider going through the humiliating process of sending it to record companies, so I sent it to Steve Vai, and Steve sent it to Cliff Cultreri [at Relativity]. Cliff called me back and said, "I do love it. It's really wild." We got together and worked it out.

You must have had a lot of self-assurance to finance your own album with a credit card.

It was a sign from God. I wanted to do a project, and the company mailed the card to me. It was completely at random: "Mister Satriani, you have been selected because of your . . . ." So this little light bulb went off in my head.

Do you have any suggestions for guitarists who

want to explore different styles?

Yes. Let's say you're a heavy rock player who is wondering about blues or soul. Get a 4-track tape recorder, because we are in the age of recording, and people's sound is built around their records. Put down a mock soul piece and retain your personality, but try to go with the track and pick out lots of different things. A bebop player who wants to get involved with stuff that he hears Ralph Towner or some thrash band play could do the same thing. Set up a little parameter, a little fake song, and just work on it until you find your own voice in that particular form of music. At first it will be a little unusual, but once you make an association with it, that's your approach to it. It's not like — what was the old phrase? — copping a feel. It's more of finding out how you can apply your personal voice through all styles. You have to think of it simply as just music.

What advice can you offer guitarists who spend their practice time trying to sound like Yngwie Malmsteen or some other favorite player?

You know, on one hand I really admire anybody who puts a lot of time into practicing and comes out with such a good result. It's amazing that there are guitarists like Yngwie Malmsteen. That's really good guitar playing. It's hard to say anything negative about it, because it's just so incredible. I've always tried to go the other way. Sometimes I think it comes down to personality. Yngwie is Yngwie. He's a person, and his personality drives him to sound the way he does and to write that kind of music; that's what's so great about him. So it's pointless. It's almost as if upon hearing Hendrix, I decided I'm just going to play like Hendrix. It's a dead end.

What are your practice sessions like?

Most recently I've been doing specific things. When you start doing records, you wind up with deadlines. You say, "I've got to practice this because I want it to be killer so I can put this on this record by such and such a date." So sometimes I'll play one one-minute piece for eight hours a day every day, and I won't play anything else. Other times I'll only play rhythm and bass and fool around with synthesizers and drum machines, just because I'm thinking about music. Sometimes I'll put down my guitar and just won't play it, because I'm being too repetitive and I'm angry with myself for being so stubborn, for not moving on. Then I'll pick it up and hear something that I didn't hear before. Other times it's just non-stop, and my wife, Rubina, will have to say, "You better stop. You're playing too much."

Do melodies ever come to you at odd times?

Most definitely. I've had songs come to me in the middle of guitar lessons, in the shower, in dreams. I write them down. There is a song called "Saying Goodbye" that I knew I wanted to write, but I didn't know what it was. I just said, "I'm going to dream this. I'm going to wake up and play it." Sure enough, I woke up the next day and there it was. I got right up out of bed, went to the guitar, and wrote this song down. But it's rare when I'm able to do that.

Do you tend to work on just one composition at a time?

Oh, I've got hundreds of songs going all the time. Some of them I can finish in an hour, some songs could take me a year, and some I'm still working on that I started writing 15 years ago, but I can't seem to please myself.

Are you aware of the mathematical relationships of notes as you're composing?

I wouldn't really call it mathematical. Although I am thinking in numbers, I'm not purely coming up with a numerical phrase and playing like that. If I play root, 3rd, 5th, I instantly know what that is, because I was trained to tag that information onto the sound. It's very possible that some of the things that I'm writing or playing are starting out mathematically, but it's quite automatic now.

Do you have to do anything special to protect or engender your creativity? Do you have to make sacrifices?

Yeah. I probably seem like a recluse or an eccentric to some people at times, and then they wonder why at other times I'm suddenly not. When I put my mind to something, that's the only thing that I'm going to do. If it's a song, I will stay in and do nothing but play the song over and over again for hours and hours a day. I disregard time frames of night and day; I just operate on my own schedule. When you do that, of course, you can't go out with people, you can't do things. So when you say, "No, I'm staying home and listening to a tape," they say, "Well, listen to it when you get back or when you're in the car." They don't realize that I play things in multiple speeds and change parts. I'll watch TV and during every commercial go back and listen to the song. Sometimes I just listen to it once; other times I sit there for three hours. I just need the freedom not to be bothered. Other times I have to go food-shopping; I enjoy that. I like being around fresh food. I get energized, and that helps my playing.

Does touring improve your playing?

It definitely has improved my playing. I could literally wake up in the middle of the night and do a solo from any number of my songs. I remember thinking 10 years ago, "How are people able to play consistently well?" I think it's a psychology that surrounds elements of success — personal and professional. Having a constant outlet for your ideas just increases your ability to play better, and finding acceptance in the musical community gives you more confidence. I remember when there was so much music I wanted people to hear, and they didn't hear it. They only heard me at my musical job, doing these other things, and this had a negative effect on my playing. That's why I dropped out of playing in traditional-type bands and decided to go into doing instrumentals.

Can you get everything you want from one guitar?

Just about, yeah. I've tried to get the ultimate Strat sound and the ultimate Gibson Les Paul sound from one guitar, but it's like a jinx. As soon as a guitar has too many wires in it, it starts to act funny. It *knows* that there's a capacitor, even if it's out of the circuit. It's spooky. Any technician will tell you that if it's out of the circuit, it won't affect the sound, but the guitar just doesn't play the same way as a gut-level SG-type or Strat. So I stopped trying to do that. I just make a sound around the guitar I've got.

We have guitar synths, locking whammies, digital effects. What's missing? What should be invented?

A new way to project sound. Something that replaces the setup of an audience filing into a room and facing paper-cone speakers blaring at their faces. Having an amp line and a PA line and microphones is an almost hilariously archaic setup. We're gonna look like cavemen in a couple of years, when they finally figure out that speakers are a very crude thing. The difference will be like going from the earliest Victrola to a CD or DAT machine — and just look at the technological leap there. But as far as the speakers go, not much has really been done. It seems to me that there should be a way to create sound in a space around your head. This sounds like *Star Trek*, but let's say I had the coordinates for where your head is right now — X for depth and Y for width — and I could tell a computer to project *Surfing with the Alien* at these coordinates. This sound particle beam dispenser or whatever it is would excite soundwaves only at those coordinates. Suddenly you'd be enveloped in sound that wouldn't be subject to the room's acoustics, because it's not being filtered through the atmosphere and broken up by the potted plants, the fan on the ceiling, the chairs and tables, and everyone with their jackets and hairdos. We'd be in full control of what you hear. Then if you moved your head out of coordinates X and Y, you'd be out of the sound.

What's your most productive method of composing?

It comes in all different ways. Songs like "Always with Me, Always with You" and "Circles" came when I was just sitting by myself with a guitar. I didn't really have any thoughts to begin with, and as I played I found something interesting. Then I exerted as much inspiration as I could to carry it through. Sometimes you get a burst of inspiration right at the beginning, and then the idea stops coming through you in that divine way. It's like, "Okay, now it's your turn to finish it," so you've got to keep it going. After I came up with those songs on guitar, I put them on tape and started working out the arrangements.

On tour, I bring along a little suitcase that's got my regular-speed Tascam Porta-One 4-track cassette machine and an Alesis HR-16 drum machine. I use the rack-mountable Rockman products, along with a Yamaha SPX90, and that gets set up in my hotel room. It really helps a lot, especially with a gig like Jagger's where we spend four or five days in one city. It makes a lot of difference to be able to go back to the hotel room and actually work on stuff.

As you compose, are you conscious of how the piece will sound on record?

No. Those are two different sets of approaches. I don't like to think of recording while I'm writing, because I'm afraid it might grossly affect composition. I might get excited about a sound in November that by March I'm bored with, and if I made that the pivotal theme of a piece, then it's sort of a vacuous finale. You wind up with a sound you don't like and the song loses its meaning, so I try to write the pieces with only bland working sounds. If I'm using a drum machine, I don't program changing parts. I just get a simple pattern to get the feeling of the rhythm going. Bass is almost the same way, except for one piece that's probably going to be on the next record; it's got a very unusual bass part that's the signature of the song. So certain instruments are designated the holders of the original direction and inspiration of the song, and I work the other things out later. Because those things are important, I usually keep all my first recordings. Although they have mistakes and melodies that don't quite come out, they have the original excitement and intensity. When you're working on up to 60 songs and doing different gigs, it's good to have a little reminder to bring you back into the world of that particular song.

Have any songs remained unchanged since the moment they came to you?

"Satch Boogie" has remained identical to how I envisioned it.

You seem to be much more sensitive to register — where you play on the neck — than most players.

I've always been impressed when I've heard guitarists play up and down — really low and really high — and that's affected the way I play. The whole thing of going way up high and wailing may have more to do with attitude than with actual music. I saw one of my students with a thrash band, and he played all the solos above the 12th fret. I said, "The band's great, but I bet if you played some solos below the 12th fret, it would actually sound more interesting. Why don't you pick one song and really hit somebody in the pelvis with some low notes?" He said, "I'd love to do that, but it sounds muddy and I can never hear it." That's a sad reason to discount an instrument's ability to have a wonderful quality, especially when the audience is just waiting to hear something interesting. It's your job to make it clear enough so they can hear it.

Maybe it's a physical predisposition. If you and I had our hearing tested right now, it might reveal that we're biased in a different way. It could be genetic or it could be our experience. If you like to go to the rifle range, then you may have some hearing loss in a particular notch. If you work around loud machinery a lot, you may lose it lower. I've seen very tired recording engineers cranking up too much high end. I've said, "Hey, I won't be at this session unless you turn it down." They'll answer, "You're crazy. It sounds great," and I'll say, "No. You're deaf. Take a break." [*Laughs.*] I've sat down with students who just don't hear things quite the same. I just had my hearing tested a few days ago, so I know that I don't have any unusual hearing loss.

Even with playing at loud volumes?

The trio doesn't play loud at all, and I have always limited my exposure to really loud volumes. I wear earplugs when I go to shows and during sound checks, although I've never worn them during a performance. But if it gets too loud, pride does not stand in the way of maintaining my sense of hearing. In fact, volume is one of the grossest problems of today's technology. It's clearly out of hand, and it's only because we're trapped with speakers. It's insane, like cars without seatbelts.

Where is rock guitar heading?

In a collection of fits and starts, it's going to continue progressing as it has. There will be wild bursts of intensity, like with Jeff Beck and Jimi Hendrix, then a cooling out, and then John McLaughlin and Al Di Meola, a cooling out, and then Allan Holdsworth and Van Halen, a cooling out, and then Yngwie, and then cooling out. These outrageous forms come along and push the envelope of acceptability. And people will always say, "Too many notes," or, "It doesn't have feeling in it," when in fact it does. It's just that it's new. It's just like people saying that drum machines don't have feeling, but they do because there are people controlling them and artistically using them.

There will always be a return to roots going on, because the sound that a beginner makes has a lot of validity. There will always be room for a very simple approach to songs. The instrumentalists and technicians will try to bring the technique further, and then there will be this great in-between. Some people will create music that simply is an example of the technique, while others go the opposite way. And then there will be people like myself who don't discriminate at all and just use whatever. I'm not afraid to play simple. I'm not afraid to play overwhelmingly at the risk of playing too many notes or being too outrageous and dumb. For some of us, that's what makes it interesting. I'm really fortunate that success came to me when I'm this old.

Why is that to your advantage?

Because I had so much time to read up on everything, and then I was lucky enough to attract good-quality management, an above-board record company, a good accountant, and a good counsel — all at the right time. Because I was self-managed for so many years, I read all the books and knew exactly what a manager and a record company did, so I went in without any misconceptions. You know, a lot of artists think that managers take care of everything beyond what you're instructing them to do, but in fact it's the other way around. You pay them to serve you, and they act on your instructions. If you don't give them instructions, then you're asking for some interesting decisions that they're going to make on their own. Management should guide you any way you want. It's sort of like the way we'd like to envision the President and his council and cabinet working. The President knows the course and has the vision, but eventually he's got to ask his economist or his military strategist, "Does this work?" or, "How do we do this?" Then, when these people say, "I think you should do this instead," you keep your ears open. You attract them to guide you in certain areas, since there's no way, for instance, that a musician could be 100%

on top of the publishing world. It's a really strange world, and if you can find counsel who can really explain it to you, then hang onto that person.

At what point should you get a lawyer?

Any time anything has to be signed. *Anything.* I'm a big believer in getting a great lawyer and paying lots of money to keep yourself protected. I know a lot of people who said, "Well, it's only a short contract; it's only two pages," or, "The people explained it to me, and I fully understand." With several contracts, I've spent more money on legal fees than I've actually gained from the initial singing of the contract. But, of course, years down the road you make a lot of money properly and honestly, and you're protected fully. You may have to spend $2,000 to set up a contract that maybe is only going to give you $1,000 up front, but 10 years from now that contract may be worth a million dollars. And what if you screwed up and gave too much of it away, just be-cause you were worried about $1,000? I probably spend more money than I have to, but I insist that my main counsel sees everything. Even though the management says, "Well, he really doesn't have to see this," I'll send it to him anyway.

It's also important to retain your publishing rights.

Absolutely. I went into it the same way: I knew all about it, and I retain 100% of all my publishing. My company Strange Beautiful Music is the sole publisher for North America. All along the line, people have said, "You should let me administer your publishing; I'll only take 12%." And I could honestly say, "You're wrong. I shouldn't." There are always people around me saying that I better do this or that. "You better let me help you collect" — that's the famous phrase. But they've never been able to pull that on me, because I knew about it very early on.

– JOHN SCOFIELD –

BY JIM FERGUSON – JUNE 1987

WHEN JOHN Scofield is at his best, his solos are like the chase scene in *The French Connection* — incredibly exciting and intense, constantly flirting with disaster and the unexpected, but rarely out of control. Even at slow tempos, his playing smolders with a rare combination of sophisticated angular lines and crying blues inflections. Sco's distinctive sound and approach, coupled with his expert talents as a composer, place him in the vanguard of contemporary jazz guitarists. After three years with Miles Davis in the mid-'80s and two uncommonly strong follow-up solo albums — *Still Warm* and *Blue Matter,* his most recent — John Scofield has come of age.

1986 was a banner year for the 41-year-old guitarist. Not only did he take top honors in *Down Beat*'s prestigious International Critics Poll and third place in its Readers Poll, he also performed with the French National Orchestra, master pianist McCoy Tyner, and Bass Desires, which features string bassist Marc Johnson, drummer Peter Erskine, and co-guitarist Bill Frisell. In Feb. '87 he released *Blue Matter,* a strong funk-blues effort with ample jazz-based blowing, supported by bassist Gary Grainger, keyboardist Mitch Forman (formerly with John McLaughlin and saxophonist Wayne Shorter), and drummer Dennis Chambers, a veteran of Parliament / Funkadelic. He also has produced *John Scofield on Improvisation,* an instructional video offered by DCI.

Not every musician who has played with Miles Davis has become a household word; however, the legendary trumpeter's eye for talent is unquestionable — the names of former band members reads like a jazz who's who and includes John McLaughlin, bassist Ron Carter, and keyboardists Keith Jarrett, Herbie Hancock, and Chick Corea, to name a few. While Scofield's recent work has been uncommonly strong, his abilities as a guitarist and composer promise even greater things to come.

Musically, what do you get from bebop that you don't get from material that's more electric?

For instance, with music that uses a 4/4 walking bass thrust, you can get incredible dynamics and shading, along with a certain sort of circular rhythmic propulsion. But when I play that kind of music all the time, I start thinking, "God, I'd love to do some funky-poppin', backbeat, get-down stuff." My new band has been working on dynamics and having things rise and fall, but if you listen to a lot of fusion records, things always seem to start and end in a frenzy; the inner dynamics aren't there. That's something I really miss. Miles and Weather Report had it, and I'd like my band to do that.

Do you miss the challenge of playing through standard jazz changes?

Not so much, because a lot of my tunes have harmonies that are very complicated. I love to play on things such as "Stella by Starlight," "All the

Things You Are," and 12-bar blues with jazz changes. There is something about standard changes that leads to a certain kind of expression that is great. But what I want to stay away from is the "Wynton Marsalis syndrome," where the result sounds like something from another era, even though the playing is brilliant. One of my frustrations with playing with a pick-up band is that things usually turn into jam-session jazz.

So you're looking for something that falls in between composed music and a more open situation?

Right. Having strong material and knowing who you're playing with is critical.

Tal Farlow doesn't have to write a set of new tunes every time he records an album. What's it like to be continually under pressure to compose high-quality material?

Tal comes from a different era; I'm sure he knows a lot more standards than I do. I like having to write; it adds to the pressure, but it also adds to the creativity. Playing standards with a rhythm section all the time would be rough. Even though I love that, it's not me. I love to hear Jim Hall play in that way, but it doesn't allow me to express myself completely.

In the January 1987 issue of Down Beat *you stated that you don't think of music in terms of separate categories, yet just now you've been speaking in terms of genres.*

Music can't accurately be described with words, but categories do exist, because people play out of certain idioms. When you categorize music, there's a danger of placing one form over the other. For instance, you can't say that jazz is better than rock, because there's always going to be some jazz that you don't like and some rock that you don't like. But don't get me wrong; I'm not trying to compare the Kingsmen with John Coltrane. For decades, people have gone around and put down jazz on the basis that classical music is a higher art form. Musicians speak in terms of categories just as much as writers do, but I try to be open to all kinds of stuff, although just because I like one thing doesn't mean I like all of it. For instance, I like Billy Idol, but I hate a lot of other groups. I've seen Billy Idol a couple of times and when I close my eyes and listen to what he's singing, I think that his phrasing is pretty good. I also sort of like his guitar player [Steve Stevens]. On the other hand, Twisted Sister has never moved me in any kind of musical way.

When you say that the Kingsmen can't be compared to John Coltrane, aren't you implying that

only the best rock is better than the worst jazz?

I'm not even going to get into it, because beautiful, poignant music — regardless of type — is all the same thing. There have been periods when I've listened to a lot of Ray Charles and [saxophonist] Ornette Coleman, but I never thought, "This is good, but it's not as serious as Bach." I love Duke Ellington, and his music has infinite mysteries to me, but I can't say that it's better than Howlin' Wolf, because I love both things in different ways. When you compare music, you lose the joy of listening to it.

As a jazz musician, do you feel any kind of responsibility?

I don't know what a musician's responsibility is; I suppose it's to make the gig if you've got a contract. People talk a lot about how if you're a jazz musician, you have a responsibility to do this or that, although it's usually said with good intention. I was the same way when I was in high school. I really wanted to show people how that other stuff is garbage and that jazz is an incredible art form that is being ignored by our country. I still have those feelings, too. I always get excited when I go to Europe and see a free-jazz group being accepted by an audience that honestly likes the music. But I have a hard time with the current jazz establishment because once you label art, you automatically limit everything else. This reminds me of a concert that Steve Swallow and I played in Italy. At the end of the night, the producer came up and asked us to play a standard and stated that she wished that we would have performed more of them. That's equivalent to somebody requesting "Melancholy Baby" or a tune by the Beach Boys. It represents a mentality that is stifling to creativity. I agree pretty much with Miles, whose philosophy is, "Fuck 'em; I'm gonna do what I want."

In the March '87 issue of Guitar Player, *Mike Stern talked about how Davis told him to not play any bebop.*

First of all, you have to remember that Miles *is* bebop; he exudes it and probably didn't want Mike to play any bebop clichés — stock licks, such as the opening phrase in "Donna Lee." Miles wasn't putting down bebop, although when I was in his band he'd say one thing one day and then contradict himself the next. There's a lot of wisdom in what he says, but you have to take it with a grain of salt. But he was always talking about how great [saxophonist] Charlie Parker, [drummer] Max Roach, and [pianist] Bud Powell were, so I figured he liked bebop.

Most players are continually trying to get the clichés out of their playing.

Right; that's what I think he was getting at. He puts down his past work, but he is a great jazz player and couldn't get it out of his playing. He swings all the time, too. He really lives and talks jazz.

Did you feel obliged to become a bandleader after working with him?

Yeah, but I've always had my own group, in one way or another. After playing with Miles, I found that I could get gigs because a lot more people in rock and jazz knew who I was. My public persona expanded 100%. When I left Miles, I felt that it was now or never, because I was afraid that if I had waited a year, people wouldn't have remembered me from *Decoy*. You have to seize the moment, but on the other hand, there are a lot of people who have played in Miles' band who aren't famous. Where's [saxophonist] Carlos Garnett today? He's probably playing his ass off somewhere, but he's not a household word. Gary Bartz, a wonderful sax player, was with Miles, but you don't see him on the cover of *Down Beat* every month. But so many greats have been in his bands — John McLaughlin, Wayne Shorter, Herbie Hancock — that you feel some responsibility to start your own.

Were you ever concerned that concentrating on your own band prematurely could have a negative impact on your personal musical growth?

Not really. It would have been negative if I had showboated and played anything to get over, but that hasn't happened. However, I did find myself acting a bit like Miles in that I'd try to tell the band members how to play, which made them resent me a bit. But I soon learned that I can't do that. The first band I put together right after Miles didn't work out as well as this one for that reason. So you learn some good things from Miles, and you learn some bad.

As a player, what are your weaknesses?

My klutziness. You know how some people are well coordinated? I'm not. My friend [pianist] Mark Cohen went to high school with [saxophonist] Mike Brecker, and he says that Mike always played beautifully — in tune, fast, and together. I had a couple of friends who played guitar like that, although they didn't end up being great. Sometimes I think that I hear the rhythm right, but it comes out at a different time, so I've really had to compensate for it. You have to evaluate what you can do and use it to make music. [Pianist] Paul Bley said something to the effect that you should hang on to your weird virtues and eccentricities, because they will give you a style, so I'm not scared to do that. Also, in the past I didn't know many chords. I was never a huge fan of Joe

Pass, although I was really knocked out by his early records, such as *Catch Me*. When he began to play solo in the mid-'70s, I was in a different place; I liked him better when he had a rhythm section. But then I heard him do a duet with Ella Fitzgerald on TV, and I was completely blown away. I thought, "This guy can really play the guitar." He was improvising on a standard, playing beautiful bass lines and chords at the same time, and his feel was incredible. I thought, "Man, why don't I know this?" Since that time I've tried to do that a little bit, and I've gotten better at it.

What do you mean that you didn't know very many chords?

I used to think, "I don't want to play that Barney Kessel-type jazz; I want to play like Wayne Shorter." Over the last seven years or so I've learned a lot more about chords through playing by myself and writing tunes instead of practicing single-note lines. To understand harmony better, I figure out the changes to songs such as "Auld Lang Syne," "Happy Birthday," or "America the Beautiful" — just real straight-ahead, $B\flat$ harmony. A lot of people think that you learn music by starting with Gregorian chants and going up through [avant-garde composer] John Cage, but it doesn't work like that. You can be very good at a vocabulary — in my case, the treble-register part of music — and not know how to put the bottom part together as well as you like. Another one of my weaknesses has been my sound. John Abercrombie and Pat Metheny have beautiful sounds — I don't mean just because of the equipment they play; it comes from their fingers, too. I've improved a bit in that regard over the last couple of years.

A lot of these elements enable you to have one of the most distinctive sounds going.

But there are some hard edges that came from being out of control. For instance, I learned that if I pick softer, the sound is better. One day I actually played through an oscilloscope, and I discovered that if I overpick — play too hard — notes are softer than if I lightened up a bit. Also, my rhythm has been weak, and it didn't come natural to me, but it's gotten better with study. It's hard to play music; it's not like falling off a log.

Do you work with a metronome?

I used to. It really helped me, because I tended to drag on difficult phrases. Now I notice myself rushing more than anything. I hate that. For instance, I just recorded with [Swiss trumpeter] Franco Ambrosetti, and the first tune he wanted to record was "Summertime." He did it real fast, and at first I wondered if my chops were up to it. But when I listened back to the session, everything was fine except for "Summertime," where I rushed like crazy because I was worried that I couldn't play the tempo. Lately most of my practice time at home centers around writing tunes. Other than that, I work on improvising in tempo, and if I come up with something interesting, I stop to work on it.

Do you ever take licks off of records?

I haven't done that in a while, although a few months ago I was listening to a tape of Mike Brecker at a New Year's Eve concert jam session. The band was doing "Invitation" in C minor, and he played a great intervallic lick that I've heard him do before, so I stopped and figured it out. It's an augmented-based sequence:

Soon after that I heard him use it with Chick Corea, but in a completely different way. He always seems to play it over a minor or a dominant chord. It's one of those ideas that you eventually just learn to hear where it fits. A lot of patterns like this are great, but they have to come out naturally or else they'll sound very contrived and give the impression that you ran out of ideas.

Your instructional video gets into some interesting theoretical areas, such as harmonizing the melodic minor scale.

Right. You can get some great melodic ideas by playing the modes of the melodic minor. The altered Lydian ♭7 scale is the mode starting on its fourth degree. I use those kinds of arpeggios and scales all of the time.

Have you analyzed pentatonic scales extensively, or do you just hear where they fit?

I've actually figured out how a C blues scale [C, E♭, F, G, B♭] works over D♭maj7, say. But you can hear it, too. Pentatonics can be rough, because they can be used in so many ways. For example, if you're in G minor, you can play a G minor pentatonic [G, B♭, C, D, B], a C dominant pentatonic [C, D, E, G, B♭], a D minor pentatonic [D, F, G, A, C], an F major pentatonic [F, G, A, C, D], or C major pentatonic [C, D, E, G, A]. Some lines that sound like pentatonics are really just arpeggios or a root, 2, 3, 5 thing, which is an old Coltrane lick. So you play by ear, but you also think about what you're doing. The greats of jazz use pentatonics with a lot of control. As chords progress, an experienced musician will sometimes play three of the four notes of the original scale, altering only one to fit the new harmony. For instance, play C major pentatonic for C, and if the sequence goes to A7, raise the C to C#. That's showing real mastery over chords.

It seems as if more jazz-rock guitarists are recording now than ever before. Has the interest in electric jazz dramatically increased recently?

They've been saying that since I've been making electric jazz records. When I first started playing with [drummer] Billy Cobham — electric jazz' peak, more or less — there was a whole lot of interest. My trio with Swallow — which was not particularly fusionish, although it was not particularly bebopish, either, compared to Barney Kessel — couldn't get any gigs for some reason. Playing with Miles got me a lot of exposure, and my records have done well since then. My music uses elements of rock, jazz, and pop, so now I can work more. Maybe there is some sort of interest because rock fans can understand it more than they understand bebop. I say that almost with a heavy heart, not because I want to play bebop. It's sad that the average young guitarist who somehow likes AC/DC and also maybe likes my band completely misses [saxophonist] Coleman Hawkins, or might not like Bass Desires or some of my trio stuff. It's scary, but luckily I'm not such an amazing success that I stand to lose millions [laughs].

– ANDRÉS SEGOVIA –

BY LARRY SNITZLER – OCTOBER THROUGH DECEMBER 1983

THE BETTMANN ARCHIVE

ANDRÉS SEGOVIA *is* classical guitar. Since the early 1900s his influence touched every facet of the instrument and its music. More than any other individual he was responsible for taking the guitar out of the parlors of Europe and onto the concert stages of the world. And while this one achievement is more than most players hope to accomplish in a lifetime, Segovia's other contributions made him a veritable legend in his own time. Remarkably, until his death late in his 90s, he continued to tour regularly, displaying his unmistakable rich tone and depth of interpretation.

Segovia reigned as patriarch of the classical guitar, but his ascension to that position was not without struggle. Surprisingly, early in his career he was received with disdain from many concertgoers and guitar aficionados. But that criticism was soon shouted down by those who recognized his virtuosity and musicianship. In addition, his romantic interpretation of certain pieces — primarily Baroque works — was sometimes taken to task. But whether or not Segovia's use of expressive devices such as the portamento (a slide with a vocal quality) are considered to be liberal for some music, they were always employed with artistic taste.

One of Andrés Segovia's most profound gifts to music was to increase the amount of literature for the classical guitar. His transcriptions and revisions of existing arrangements of works by Bach, Weiss, Handel, Tárrega, and many others have become mainstays of the repertoire. And while Segovia pro-

duced only a few short original works, he performed a more important task by commissioning material by some of the 20th century's greatest composers, including Heitor Villa-Lobos, Manuel Ponce, Federico Moreno Torroba, Mario Castelnuovo-Tedesco, and Alexander Tansman.

Segovia also had a significant effect on classical guitar pedagogy. His *Daily Exercises* and *Diatonic Major and Minor Scales* as well as his *Studies for the Guitar by Fernando Sor* are required texts for the development of technique. And the ultimate honor a student of classical guitar could experience was to be a pupil of the Maestro's. Many of the world's top players benefited from Segovia's tutoring, including Julian Bream, John Williams, George Sakellariou, Alexandre Lagoya, and Christopher Parkening.

Although Segovia toured consistently over the years, many guitarists were introduced to his music through a half-century-long legacy of recordings, which are a monument to his consummate artistry. (The Maestro made 78 RPM discs as early as 1927, and his last LP was recorded in 1977.) One of the most exciting recent additions to the Segovia discography is *The EMI Recordings 1927–39*, which features material by Tárrega, Sor, Bach, and Torroba. The earliest examples available of the Maestro's playing, this collection is a priceless musical document of his technical and interpretive abilities. *The Genius of Andrés Segovia/A Bach Recital* demonstrates his expressive versions of such standards as *Gavotte I and II*, *Prelude in D Minor*, and the *Chaconne*. A fine example of a typical Segovia concert was captured on *An Evening with Andrés Segovia*, while *My Favorite Spanish Encores* features Torroba's *Sonatina* and Albéniz' *Sevilla*.

Starting in April 1983, National Public Radio aired an ambitious 13-part series titled *Segovia!*, which was produced by classical guitarist Larry Snitzler and hosted by folk guitarist/musicologist Oscar Brand. A unique retrospective on the life and music of one of the great musicians of the 20th century, *Segovia!* features an in-depth, on-location interview interwoven with tributes from such luminaries of the guitar as José Tomas, Juan Martin, Alexandre Lagoya, Manuel Cano, and Oscar Ghiglia.

The following article is an edited version of *Segovia!* and was exclusive to *Guitar Player*.
— *Jim Ferguson*

Maestro, do you still feel to be an Andalusian?

Of course. I have Andalusia inside in all the respects. I was born there. I have my friends from childhood — maybe two or three; the others passed away. And the place where I was playing and beginning my career, the beginning of my illusions and my dreams for music and for everything. And then, it is beautiful, also. There is very little to say about Linares, because it is not monumental — no splendid and beautiful panoramas. Everything that I could say about Linares is that I was born there. Linares is not very interesting from the artistic point of view. What I well remember is the painful day my mother left me in the home of my childless aunt and uncle, Maria and Eduardo. When I was separated from the living cradle of my mother's arms, I cried with deep sorrow. My uncle, completely bald, toothless, and heavily built, but always with an expression of generosity in his countenance, sat in front of me, pretending to strum an imaginary guitar, humming this folk tune [*starts humming*]:

> El tocar la guitarra
> jum!
> no tiena cencia
> jum!
> sino juera en el brazo
> jum!
> Permanencencia
> jum!

That means to play the guitar does not require any science, but strength in the arms and perseverance. Time and again he repeated this tune and I calmed down and smiled. Taking then my little right arm, he rhythmed with it the downbeat of "jum." I felt such an intense and mysterious pleasure that still I remember it. This was the first seed that fell into the musical soil of my soul, which was later to become the most enduring tree of my life. I think that the gift of music, or for other things, comes from very far back. It is the seed coming through generation to generation to an individual.

When I was six years old, I heard the band of the place where I was growing up — Villacarillo. And they were playing and marching [*sings a tune*]. I remember that time. But underneath this figure there was [*sings another melody*] — I was listening to that melody underneath the other and I was happy. There was my uncle, who saw my vocation for music.

You have often used this word "vocation." What does it mean for you?

Vocation is what the very religious man says is the inspiration from heaven. It is the same. The music was calling to me. That is the vocation. He put me under the iron fingers of a violinist, who would pinch me every time I had an error of intonation or measures. And I was on the verge of hating the music because I hated him and what he was teaching me. My uncle, with very good sense, took me out. And then I did not do anything musically until I was in Granada. My uncle, with whom I was growing up, moved to Granada in order to give me a normal and decent career. But I distrusted them. I went to another — to music, following, obeying my vocation.

Do you remember the first impression that Granada made upon you when you arrived?

Well, when I arrived I was too small, too young to have an idea. But later on I opened my eyes to the beauty in Granada and to the art. One of the greatest Zarzuela [a form of opera] composers at that time was Tomas Breton, who made the *La Verbena de la Paloma*, which is really magnificent. He came with the orchestra to give a concert in the Charles the Fifth Palace, in the Alhambra [historic Moorish palace] close to the Arabian Palace. I had no money, but as it is without a roof, the music was flying out and to me came these marvelous harmonies and different timbres of the orchestral instruments. It was my discovery of musical emotion.

When you first began to play, the only guitar you had seen was the flamenco guitar.

Yes. The flamenco in the little town. I did not have a taste for the flamenco. My friends began to look in private houses and in music shops for something written for the guitar. And they found something by Sor, Giuliani, Aguado, and little things published by Tárrega. As I had a certain knowledge of the solfeggio — of the do-re-mi — it was not difficult for me to read, to decipher the music. It inaugurated my double function of professor and pupil in the same body.

Did you have to change the way of playing?

That was absolutely the work of the vocation. I don't know if you have seen the diatonic scale for fingers. I saw a friend of mine playing piano scales, and I devised the fingering simply like that. I never changed it. I asked my friends to bring to me a method for violin. And when they brought it I saw the different positions. The other way was not correct because this was not perpendicular — the finger to the strings. This way was much better because the whole top of the finger touched the string.

So in the old way people played from the side of the hand, and you knew that was wrong.

Yes. And they began to play in my way and they said, "This is even better."

How old were you when you made these decisions?

About 12 years old. When you have a strong vocation, everything is easy. Even if it is too hard to learn, it is easy because you have patience.

Patience is a word that I have often heard you use. Do you feel that is the most important quality?

May I restate a sentence by [German philosopher] Nietzsche? "Patience is bitter, but its products are sweet." The man without patience is like a lamp without oil.

The "Capricho Arabe" is such a lovely piece of music. Did you use to play this for young ladies at that time?

Oh, yes. And always when I finished the passage, the lady would sigh, "Aaah." It's true [*laughs*]. I was always waiting for that.

You never met Tárrega?

Tárrega? No, no, no. He died in 1908. There was a gentleman in Granada named Carmen, and he invited Tárrega to come there in order to teach me — to be there in his home for one month or so — and Tárrega accepted. But then he died. I could not know him.

You must have been very sad.

Oh, yes, because I had known little preludes composed by him. Tárrega was a kind of god for me.

I'm thinking about you when you were 12 years old. You already had the fundamentals of your technique, but you were without a repertoire.

Yes, it was my sorrow. About three or four years later I studied and built my technique, but afterwards

I found that I had no repertoire. A few pieces by Sor — a study in B♭, a study in B major, and one minuet. That was when I thought to ask a composer to write for the guitar. Even if he doesn't know the technique, I can do the transcription from the pieces to the guitar.

You had this idea when you were very young.

Yes, yes, I was. The first concert I gave was in Granada. Then I had to give it in Seville about two months later. I gave about 40 concerts, all the same program [*laughs*]. It was impossible to renew it.

What was in this program?

There was a very charming translation by Tárrega of "Aursoir" by Schumann — very, very good. Then I played my transcription of the Second Arabesque by Debussy.

You made that transcription when you were 15 or 16 years old?

Fifteen years old. And then I played the transcription everywhere, because it was already brilliant, you know? The day after [this first concert], I read a very nice and polite review in the most important paper in Granada. I thought I was going to be famous in the whole world [*laughs*]. Then I realized that the public that was there to listen to me was a public of friends, or friends of my friends. Then I was not satisfied. I went to Cordoba, and from Cordoba to Seville, and then my real concert life began. I gave about 13 or 14 concerts, always repeating my repertoire. One year later I made a mistake. The artist, when he has a great success, should leave immediately. But the beautiful eyes of a girl retained me there for one year.

What were you feelings about Francisco Tárrega?

He gave the guitar his soul. By that I mean that he has given all his life, all his thought, all his poetic temperament as a musician. But he lacked the power of impulse to play in front of a big public, and also, in vast places — in vast concert halls.

One of the reasons for this, at least, would be because he did not play with the fingernails.

Of course, he played very soft. And deprived the guitar of its richness and polyphonic merit. And from the difference of color in the voice of the guitar.

So for you, the use of the nails is not only a question of more volume?

No, no, no, no. The volume is necessary, but the most important thing was for giving to the guitar different colors in its voices. And that is the reason why I say that the guitar is a little orchestra. He deprived the guitar of one of its great merits — the illusion of different instruments.

And yet, this was a very important point of discussion during the 19th century, wasn't it? There was a great deal of argument between guitarists about this matter.

There arrived a real battle. There is even a drawing of a terrible battle — between the people with the guitar and destroying the guitar upon the heads of the people.

The quality of the nails. I have a strong nail, but at the same time, a soft nail. Look at everything I have for my nails.

How did your gala performance in Barcelona at the large concert hall come?

Before, I had already given about 13 concerts in and around Barcelona. But I wanted to give a concert in the Palau de Musica de Catalana. All the pupils of Tárrega thought me to be crazy, because they thought the guitar would not be heard there. I asked the manager of the Palau de Musica de Catalana to go everywhere in the hall, or in every corner and every little place, and tell me if he could hear these [*snaps fingers*]. At every point he said, "Yes, I can hear. But are you sure you want to do this? I remember that I asked Llobet to give a concert here in the Palau and he refused because he didn't think the guitar could be heard." I told the manager that it was the current thought of all the Tárregaists, but I am going to do the concert. The only thing that I had to ask of the manager of the Palau de Musica de Catalana was that he have the police prevent the klaxon of the automobiles and the boys from shouting the paper they wanted to sell. From that moment for all concerts, they asked the police to intervene.

And how big was the Palau de Musica?

I don't remember. But I think it held about 2,000.

So this must have been like a miracle to the people.

Oh yes, because the friends of Tárrega and Llobet thought it would be a flop.

What was Federico Torroba's first composition for you?

The first thing Torroba did was a kind of serenade, but it was impossible to play. And then he wrote the last pieces that are in the *Suite Castellana*. And then he composed the *Arada* and the *Fandanguillo*. I remember that when I played the *Fandanguillo* at home, when I was adapting it and learning it, my son, who is now 58 years old but only three or four months then, always laughed when I arrived at a certain spot. The best thing, and one of the most beautiful things written ever for the guitar, has been the *Sonatina*. When I played the *Sonatina* in

Paris in the house of the Director of the Revue Musical, Ravel told me that the *Sonatina* was exactly like the *Barber of Seville* [a famous opera by Rossini] — that it would be necessary not only to have talent, but to be young to compose such a thing. [From other composers] I selected pieces that were not too delicate in sound — the Sor variations and so forth. I played the *Homage to Debussy* by Manuel de Falla and *Segovia* by Ravel for the first time. But unfortunately the public made me repeat the *Homage* but not *Segovia*.

And what about Manuel Ponce?

Ponce was extraordinarily sensitive and pure. Everything was magnificently written — in harmonies and the line of the voices. He had a knowledge of the profundity of the counterpoint, the fugue, and the harmony. No Spaniard has been in such a position of mastering the form for the guitar. The variations upon the *Folies D'Espagne* is for the guitar almost what Bach's *Chaconne* is for the violin. He was so full of music. When his wife asked him why he didn't write more commercial compositions like the popular "Estrellita," he replied, "I cannot waste my time making money."

You stayed away from Spain for many years before returning.

Oh, yes. I was out of Spain 16 years, living first in the city of Montevideo in Uruguay, and then in New York.

Why did you stay so long from Spain?

Well, you know, it was the war in the whole world. It was very risky to take a boat and to go to Europe. I could not play in Europe because everything was on fire. It was very, very hard, the life in Barcelona at that time. Because it was taken by the communists and by anarchists. And they were here and there killing people. There were boys of 13 or 14 years with machine guns, amusing themselves by killing the people that were coming. I left Spain in 1936, the 28th of July. The 18th of July began the revolution. There were many bad people — not on account of their political feelings or ideas, but because they were bandits, they were thieves. And they took over my home. And they burned magnificent art books that I had to make a fire in the house because they were cold. According to neighbors, they were selling magnificent books for two or three pesetas. Materially, it is over; I have my house in my memory.

Why did you go first to Montevideo, and not the United States?

Because Uruguay was a more homogeneous country. There were not so many different races as in

Argentina. And also it is a very calm, very nice, very small country; it was very nice to be there. We settled there for six years.

But it was very difficult to maintain a career in South America at this time.

Well, yes but no. I was already well known in Europe and even in Hispano-America.

Should young guitarists follow your example and not study with other guitarists?

Sometimes I listen to one of the pupils, even those with good technique, and I see that he has imitated me through my records. But his way always is very cold. It is impossible to imitate. If you do a little ritardando, a little accelerando, a little forte, piano, pianissimo, all the tools of expression in music, that is your personality. To John Williams and to Ghiglia and to others, I never said that they do exactly like myself, because it's stupid. I develop their interest for music and their temperament, but not for the imitation.

For you, there are many interpretations of a piece of music.

Of course, but always respecting the author and the music.

So you're saying that musicality cannot be taught.

No absolutely. The art, it is impossible to teach. You teach the way to do things, but the other, no. If it would be possible to teach, imagine: Everybody would be an artist, like an engineer, a doctor, or so forth. It is impossible to teach, to transmit the feeling of art. Impossible.

What would you like young people to learn from your example?

The strongest advice I give to my pupils is to study music properly from the beginning to the end — like the career of a sergeant or a physician, it is the same. It is a shame that most guitarists are absolutely clean of this knowledge. My advice is to study music properly and not to omit any knowledge of music and not to be very impatient about giving concerts. He who is impatient mostly arrives at his goals late. Step by step is the only way.

Have you accomplished everything you set out to do when you were young?

I think so. I think that I have accomplished three parts of my tasks, and I am now contemplating the last one. The first was to redeem the guitar from the flamenco amusements. The second was to create a real musical repertoire for the guitar. The third was to play everywhere in the world in order to show the beauty of the instrument. And now I am trying to in-

fluence all the authorities in conservatories and academies of music that they may teach the guitar at the same level of dignity as the piano, violin, cello, and so forth. I am succeeding in that also.

You have played the music of Bach for so many years. Through Bach's music, do you have a feeling for what he could have been like?

Well, everybody who reads the life of Bach has the impression of a good man given to his art and to his family entirely. Bach seems to me the Himalaya of music. That does not mean that there are not other altitudes. Mozart, Haydn, Beethoven, Schumann, Brahms are altitudes also, but never the Himalaya. Enesco once said to a pupil: "My dear, work on the *Chaconne* [by Bach] every day possible through all your life. But do not play the *Chaconne* in public until you are about 50 years old, because it is very, very deep." It is not because I am a guitarist, but in the guitar, the *Chaconne* has found the right instrument. And another reason, the fact that it is written in D minor — the central key for the guitar! It was in the middle key of the guitar.

What was the reaction of the public, of violinists, of critics, to hearing you play such a work?

The violinists were the only musicians that didn't like the *Chaconne* on the guitar, but not for artistic reasons [*laughs*]. The composers, the conductors, the instrumentalists, all like the *Chaconne* very much. Imagine, polyphony secure, the different kinds of colors in the strings, in the notes, and in the phrases. All that enriched the *Chaconne* very much. On the guitar it is a kind of small orchestration.

You have often said the guitar is like a woman.

Feminine lines, you know? The spirit of the guitar forms the lines. All the sounds of the guitar are feminine because it's soft and very, very delicate. They arrive with such subtlety that it is almost impossible to hear it. It is as if you thought of that sound rather than heard it.

How did you meet Hauser, who was a German guitar maker?

I was giving concerts on my Ramirez in Munich, and I told him, "Come tomorrow, examine my instrument carefully, and make a guitar for me." He asked if I would use it and I said that I would if it was good. One year later he sent me a guitar that was exactly like mine, but without a soul. The sound was not the same. After a while I sent it back and asked him to keep working. Every year for 12 years he was sending me one guitar that was better than the previous. In the twelfth year, he sent me a magnificent guitar. And when I was in Berlin I wanted to play the *Chaconne* by Bach on this guitar, which was quite different in the fingerboard from mine. I was practicing the *Chaconne* the whole day, and I played it on that guitar. Then I played always on that guitar, but it developed a kind of sickness in the first string and in the high pitch it didn't sound well. All the stringed instruments have always a note — in the violin, in the cello, in the guitar — that doesn't sound like the others. And they call that note the "wolf." The guitar has many wolves. Since Hauser was already dead, I sent it to his son in order that he might find a remedy for that. Impossible. I sent it to the best luthier in Europe. Nothing. Then I had to let her rest.

This must have been a tragedy for you.

Yes, of course. I have not yet replaced it.

When you first thought of playing the guitar with an orchestra, were you afraid that it would not be heard? What gave you the idea that the guitar could be played with the orchestra?

With a small instrument — the little orchestra — I had this idea in order to lift up to the last level the prestige of the guitar. But as soon as I had achieved the prestige of the guitar, I didn't play anymore with an orchestra. Of course, you understand that the guitar, as I've always said, is a little orchestra. This means that the guitar has many different colors. It is alluding to the oboe, to the flute, to the cello, and to the brass. When you put the guitar at the side of the orchestra, the allusion is not necessary because the instrument is not there. The allusion becomes a very little thing. I have to force the sonority of the guitar in order not to be covered by the orchestra. I always tell the conductor before beginning, "More *piano* — take the pianissimo as if it were from below sea level, and then build to the forte as if it were fortissimo." In that way, we do not sacrifice the will of the author, and the orchestra doesn't cover the guitar. The volume of the orchestra has to be reduced. The recordings are the only things that may last from an artist, but their recording is not good for the guitar. Now we have suppressed all the little things that the nail used to do. [*Imitates surface noise of a 78 rpm recording.*] It accompanied the music. It was terrible in the first recordings. Now this is suppressed.

Have you grown to feel more comfortable in recording?

Oh yes, absolutely. I remember when I did my first record for His Master's Voice, it was done in wax. If I made a mistake, everything was to begin again from the beginning. It was terrible just to touch the guitar because of the tension with which I had to play to not have to begin again. I hate microphones.

You play differently now, the ritardandos are different.

It is natural, you know? No necessity of convincing the public or the critics of it. It makes the artist play with more tranquility — with more seriousness for the interpretation and more respect for the work they are doing.

In the beginning your interpretations were . . .

Very vehement. I tried to convince the people from the first note. It was impossible to do so. I tried to draw from the guitar its poetry and the expression. No more, no less. When you are already mature, you use first the spur and then the brake.

In spite of all the technological progress, are recordings still not satisfactory for you?

No. The needle that makes the noise in the record has been suppressed, but still the electricity falsifies real purity of the sound. And the guitar is an instrument of nuances; not the force, not the strength, but the nuance. It is the worst to be recorded. I don't hear my recordings — never. Very seldom. Downstairs I have all the records I have made. I never put on a record of mine because I don't like to hear the sound. It is very far away from the real sound of the guitar. This is the reason why I do not allow the microphone in my concert. Many others do. For instance, Bream plays with the microphone. He is very good. He plays very well. But I cannot. All the poetry of the sound goes away.

Do you play a piece in concert many times before you record or do you record first?

I record when I have played many times the piece. Because when I am recording, it seems that I am crippled. For avoiding the little [*imitates the squeaking sound of a wound string*] in the string. It is terrible. If God will pardon me all my sins, it is on account of the torture I had for making the records [*laughs*].

If you had not become a musician, what occupation would you have preferred?

First, a painter. Second, a man of letters. Two alternatives [*chuckles*].

Would you say you love practice as much as life?

First of all, my art, and at the same level, my family. That is all. I know all the aristocracy of Spain and many in France and Italy. In my studio, many people are coming, many friends of mine: Writers, painters, so forth. Then it's very important for me, my family, and my art. Once my family forced me to go to a clairvoyant. I never believed in such things. But in order to comply with their request, I went. And I knocked at the door and I heard the clairvoyant say, "Who is it?" I heard that and I left [*laughs*].

Do you think of yourself as a virtuoso?

I think that I am not, in any meaning of the word. I have seen the musician who is the slave of his instrument. [Violinist Jascha] Heifetz is the virtuoso. Less than the virtuoso is [violinist] Isaac Stern, because he is also a person that you can speak to. For his time he was not at all a virtuoso, because he loves life more than his instrument. Not more than music, more than his instrument.

You were not afraid of the public. You have a sympathy toward the public.

But I have stage fright like any other artist. And this is for many reasons. Not only for the insecurity that we have always if we are going to play well or not, but on account of the instrument. The guitar has very long strings, and the strings have the influence for good or for bad. If the hall is too warm or too cold or too damp or too noisy, it is impossible to predict how the guitar will behave when we begin. My feeling is when I am going to give a concert, to cancel it. And when I have ended the concert, to begin it again. Because already the instrument and myself are adapted to the hall.

Do you feel that the guitar is an international instrument now?

Completely. Absolutely. Most of the advanced pupils of mine are not Spanish. And the people who write for the guitar — Tansman, Castelnuovo-Tedesco, etc. — aren't Spanish.

The piano doesn't please you too much as an instrument?

My definition of the piano was my joke: It is a monster that screams when you touch its keys.

But I notice you have a piano in your studio.

Yes, for holding the pictures [*laughs*].

What about the violin? Do you like the violin?

The violin is the king of the stringed instruments, because it's powerful in sound; it sings, it's melodic. And then the prolongation of the sound. But it lacks the beauty of the guitar, because of the poetry of the instrument. And you can make it pianissimo — so ethereal that it is like a dream of music.

You are much more than a guitarist.

Because I am a man. Before everything I feel that I am a man. And possibly, a good man. Then reciprocating all the attention I've received, and apart from that, an artist. I always say that my life has been a line without interruption, ascending always. I gave my life to the guitar.

— MY FOUR GOALS —
BY ANDRÉS SEGOVIA

THERE EXISTS A LEGEND REGARDING THE origin of the guitar that is more beautifully suggestive than historic fact: Apollo was running in pursuit of a beautiful nymph, gallantly repeating to her all the while: "Don't tire yourself, don't tire yourself. I promise not to catch up with you." When, finally, he did succeed in taking her into his arms, she called out to her semidivine father, who instantly changed her into a laurel tree. Apollo made the first guitar from the wood of this tree and gave it as form the graceful, curved contours that forever reveal its feminine origin. That is why the guitar is of a reserved and changeable nature, even hysterical at times; but that is also why it is sweet and smooth, harmonious and delicate. When it is played with love and skill, there issues from its melancholy sounds a rapture that holds us fast to it forever.

From my youthful years I dreamed of raising the guitar from the sad artistic level in which it lay. At first my ideas were vague and imprecise, but as I grew in years and my love for it became intense and vehement, my will to do so became more assertive, and my intentions clearer.

Since then, I have dedicated my life to four essential tasks. The first: To separate the guitar from mindless folklore-type entertainment. It was born for something more and something better. Can you imagine Pegasus drawing a cart laden with vegetable greens?

My second item of labor: To endow it with a repertoire of high quality, made up of works possessing intrinsic musical value, from the pens of composers accustomed to writing for orchestra, piano, violin, etc. The masters, in accordance with usage, had written for it with passion, but with incompetence, allowing it to sink even lower than when Flamenco *tocaores* — some of whom were wonderful within their field — strummed it. Three names stand out in the modern history of the guitar: They are Sor, Giuliani, and Tárrega, although the little works of this last are not of transcendental import. The first symphonic composer to heed my request, offering to collaborate with me, was Federico Moreno Torroba; then, Falla and Turina; later, Manuel Ponce, Villa-Lobos, Castelnuovo-Tedesco, Tansman, Roussel, Cyril Scott, Rodrigo, Jolivet, Duarte, and others. Assisted by professional musicologists, I also dedicated myself to capturing delightful works written for the vihuela and the lute, and among the latter is a magnificent collection composed by Johann Sebastian Bach. Today, new works for the guitar number more than 300.

My third purpose: To make the beauty of the guitar known to the philharmonic public of the entire world. I began by giving concerts in Spain, disproving the truth of the saying "No one is a prophet in his own country." Theaters and music halls were filled and the public's interest and respect for the "classical" guitar grew. In 1919 I made my first tour of Latin America, and five years later the doors of the Paris Conservatory's hall opened to me. The French critics praised the guitar as an expressive medium for serious music, and mentioned the works of Bach in their words of praise. Concert societies and impresarios began to call me from London, Berlin, Vienna, Zurich, Amsterdam, Rome, Stockholm, etc. My first appearance in the United States took place in 1928, and during the summer and early autumn of that same year I undertook a tour of the Far East for the first time. Today, at 77, I continue my artistic activities throughout the civilized world. Like the poet, I can say: "I have felt the roundness of the world beneath my feet."

I am still working on my fourth and perhaps last task: That of influencing the authorities at conservatories, academies, and universities to include the guitar in their instruction programs on the same basis as the violin, cello, piano, etc. I have placed pupils of mine as teachers in four conservatories in Switzerland, as well as five in Italy, two in Spain, one in England, two in Australia, two in Argentina, three in the United States, and others in Germany, Holland, France, and the Scandinavian countries.

The future of the guitar is, therefore, assured. I have broken the vicious circle in which adverse fate had held it enclosed. Guitarists of worth did not appear because great composers did not write for the guitar, and the latter did not write for the guitar because it lacked virtuosos of talent. My disciples — many of whom are already famous teachers and artists — will continue my work, fervently adding their own artistic contributions to the history of this most beautiful instrument.

This article was written in 1970 and is taken from the liner notes to Segovia's LP The Guitar and I; *permission for its use courtesy MCA.*

— ON MEETING MANUEL RAMIREZ —
BY ANDRÉS SEGOVIA

I WAS NOT SATISFIED WITH MY GUITAR — the one made in Granada. I wanted to hire a guitar, like a pianist hires a piano for playing. Ramirez had never had such a request. And he showed me the guitar he had there; it was magnificent. I played everything I had learned up to then. Then I asked Ramirez, "Mr. Ramirez, will you rent me the guitar?" And he replied, "The guitar is yours, my dear. Pay me without money." Then I rose, and I was happy. I embraced him with tears in my eyes, and I told him, "This is something that has value, and no price."

Oh, Madrid was like a little village. Two or three automobiles in the street going here or there, and many fiacres — horse-drawn carriages — and it was very nice. Madrid at that time was very attractive. Now it is impossible. With the millions of automobiles circulating, it is impossible. The way of walking in Madrid has disappeared.

My first concert I gave with the guitar was at the Ateneo. I was very happy with the Ramirez guitar, and I played, according to my judgment, rather well. But later on — the day after — I did not see in the paper any mention of my recital. Neither the day after that. And when I was absolutely down — all my spirits were going down and I did not know what to do because I had put great hope in that concert. And I received a call from Ramirez telling me to come there. And I supposed that since no newspaper mentioned the success I had the other day in the Ateneo, maybe Ramirez wants to recover his guitar. And I went immediately there, ready to give back the guitar to him. But he asked why I didn't come to him after the concert. And I said, "Well, did you see that my concert has been a flop? Did you hear your guitar?" And he said, "I heard my guitar, and I'm very happy. The success was very good; no matter the critics.

There are no critics in Madrid for music. Do you know why I called you? Because there is a banker that heard you. He's very fond of music, and he would like to hear you in his home." Then I went to play and he gave me 200 pesetas — a great deal of money.

———————

I think it is the same in all artists. At the beginning they want to show their talents to convince the public and the greatest musicians. With me, I had to struggle for two things: Not only for me as an artist, but for the guitar as a musical instrument. The guitar had no reputation as a musical instrument. I had to struggle to convince the people that the guitar was a magnificent instrument on account of its philharmonic capacity. My stage fright was less than my wish to do well.

I have to tell you this: Before the age of 45, I liked neither the prodigy child nor the prodigy old man. I cannot say that anymore [*laughs*]. But really, before the public retires from me, I am going to retire from them.

When I am asked, "How long have you played the guitar?" I often say, "Since before I was born." And when I am asked, "Who has taught you?" I usually answer, "I have been my own teacher and pupil." And through the many years of this relationship, both have come to be satisfied.

———————

Once in Buenos Aires there came a group of men who were interested in the guitar. And one of them asked me why I played the second part of the *Canzonetta* so quickly. And I thought, "Why give him an aesthetic reason for that?" So I told him, "Because I can." They turned and they went [*laughs*].

— ANDY SUMMERS —

BY JAS OBRECHT — SEPTEMBER 1982

PAUL NATKIN

SURELY ONE OF rock's premier guitar texturalists, Andy Summers often eschews long, drawn-out solos and other forms of 6-string flash for subtle rhythms, rich tones, and short fills. A master of understatement and effects, as guitarist with the Police, he made innovative use of space, sending a rainbow swath of sound through Stewart Copeland's drumming and Sting's bass parts. Andy's uncommon command of rhythm guitar allows him to instantly segue from pounding new wave to idyllic reggae rhythms. When he solos, he never overplays his hand, emphasizing the unusual and making every nuance count. Summers' meteoric rise to international fame with the Police belied his many years spent as a journeyman guitarist for seminal British R&B and rock bands such as Zoot Money's Big Roll Band, the Soft Machine, and the Animals.

He was born Andrew James Somers in the English seaside resort town of Blackpool 49 years ago (he later changed his last name to Summers to avoid having to continually spell it for people). The Somers family soon moved to Bournemouth, another resort town on the south coast. This move proved fortuitous for Andy, since the town had many groups and venues. By the time he was 15, Summers was regularly appearing with a hotel band.

Before long Andy caught the ear of another Bournemouth resident, keyboardist/vocalist Zoot Money. Zoot invited Andy to join his Big Roll Band, which mainly covered black American R&B and jazz tunes. On May 31, 1966, the group recorded a live album, *The All Happening Zoot Money's Big Roll Band at Klook's Kleek*. Prominently featured in the lineup, Andy added fairly straight jazz solos to "Chauffeur" and "Florence of Arabia," and proved himself to be a competent R&B player in a medley of James Brown tunes. When the mid-'60s psychedelic movement hit London, Andy joined a lineup called Dantalion's Chariot.

From May to July 1968 Summers gigged with the Soft Machine. He then replaced Vic Briggs in the final '60s incarnation of Eric Burdon and the Animals, appearing on their December 1968 release, *Love Is*, which yielded hit versions of "River Deep, Mountain High" and "To Love Somebody." When the Animals later broke up in LA, Andy enrolled as a music and classical guitar major at the University of California. Completing his studies in the early '70s, he returned to England, where he became a sideman for vocalist Kevin Coyne. He played on three Coyne albums: *Matching Head and Feet, Heartburn,* and *In Living Black and White.* After his stint with Coyne, Andy went on retainer as a sideman for Kevin Ayers.

In January 1977, Stewart Copeland, formerly the drummer for Curved Air, organized the Police with Henri Padovani on guitar and Sting (born Gordon Mathews Sumner), a bassist he had seen playing with a Newcastle jazz combo. Copeland's initial idea was to have a bare-bones punk band. New Wave was sweeping England at the time, and although the Police saw themselves as part of a much broader hard rock tradition, it perfectly suited their purposes. Later that year the group toured on its own, backing Cherry Vanilla in England and supporting Wayne County's Electric Chairs across Europe. Sting and Stewart then journeyed to France for a musical project called Strontium 90, where they first played with Andy Summers. Impressed with the group, Andy went to see them at the Marquee Club the next time he was in London. They invited him to play a few gigs with them as a four-piece, and then to join the band. Soon Sting's extraordinary songwriting and singing talents led the Police in a new direction, and Padovani left the group.

Again a trio, the Police played their first gig with the now-familiar lineup of Sting, Stewart, and Andy at Birmingham's Rebecca Club on August 18, 1977. Afterwards they spent two months in Germany working with synthesizer wizard Eberhard Schoener's Laserium spectacular in Munich and playing club dates. To create a new three-piece style, the Police decided to move away from indulgent guitar solos. "Instead of the guitar wailing all the time and being supported by drums and bass," Andy says, "we found we had three soloists. The guitar became very harmonic and orchestral."

Things got so lean during the Police's first months together that they resorted to dying their hair blonde to appear as a mischievous punk rock group in a Wrigley's gum commercial. Things changed for the better in 1978, though, when Stewart's brother, Miles Copeland, formed Illegal Records and released the Police's first single, a punk rock screamer called "Fall Out" backed by "Nothing Achieved." The 45 sold out its initial pressing of 2,000 copies (eventually selling 10,000), but the break the band was hoping for didn't come until their next single, the reggae-influenced "Roxanne." The song shot to #42 on the English charts before the BBC banned in from radio. Included on No Wave, and A&M sampler album released in America, "Roxanne" quickly became a top U.S. radio add-on.

Still virtually unknown and without an LP, the group on their own initiative flew to the U.S. and began touring in a Chevy van with one roadie. (On one snowy night in Poughkeepsie, only two people showed up.) A score of other appearances in larger cities on the East Coast raised the pitch of excitement surrounding the band to an unheard-of level for an act available only on import 45s, and A&M rushed to release their debut album, Outlandos D'Amour.

Recorded on budget of $6,000, the album featured impressive musicianship, innovative arrangements, and — unusual to American ears — rhythmic sensibilities borrowed from Jamaican reggae. Generally following the philosophy that less is more, the Police gave their material room to breathe, causing their rhythms and hooks to be all the more hypnotic. On their initial effort, they had succeeded in recontextualizing the diverse elements of reggae, new wave, English pop, and hard rock into a sound that was recognizably their own.

Regatta De Blanc followed nine months later. Another powerful performance, this showed the band's increasing musical adhesion and polish. Andy provided rich, innovative rhythms, and as usual, his solo emphasis was on the unexpected. The album jumped to the #1 slot on the English charts, and by the end of the year its biggest single — "Message in a Bottle" — had become a #1 hit in 11 countries. "Walking on the Moon," the LP's second single, also became a #1 hit in England.

The Police were on the road for 20 months during the next two years. On April 4, 1979, they recorded at New York's Bottom Line; two of these cuts — "Landlord" and "Next to You" — were released on the new wave sampler album called Propaganda. In October 1980, the Police released Zenyatta Mondatta, which contained the hit "Don't Stand So Close to Me." Again Andy held back his solos until dramatic moments, most notably in the powerful statement in "Driven to Tears." He also turned in a searing instrumental composition — "Behind My Camel" — and made one of his more unusual displays of eccentric guitarmanship in "Shadows in the Rain." In 1981 the Police appeared on Eberhard Schoener's Video Magic LP. Andy shared guitar duties with Hansi Ströer, and between the two of them poignant solos were added to "Signs of Emotion" and "Octagon." Andy also provided nylon-string parts in "Code Word Elvis."

The Police achieved international stardom, globe-hopping to concerts in Hong Kong, Cairo, Nairobi, Bombay, Bangkok, Athens, and Mexico City. They have been the subject of books, and entire issues of pop magazines have been devoted to them.

Even after the group disbanded in the late 1980s, Andy Summers has continued to delight audiences and amaze guitarists through individual appearances with his penchant for off-the-wall solos, his command of sonic effects, and his innovative and experimental approaches to lead guitar.

Have you always been a texturalist in your approach to playing?

I've always been fascinated by that side of it, yeah. As a guitar player working in the modern world, one tends to cover most of it. I've played a long time, so I've played most styles. But obviously there are certain things that turn you on most, things that you want to hear. You hear it in other music, and you want to hear it in your own playing. To me it's more like a feeling or an emotion that you want to emulate or have come back through your own music. I think that's what I'm always looking for: A certain spirit or feeling rather than a string of notes or chords that make you feel that way.

When you started on guitar, did you lean more towards innovation or imitation?

Imitation. Actually, the first instrument I ever studied was piano. I was given a guitar when I was 14, and it was like an obsession immediately. I never put it down. I was trying to play like the guys on TV, and after a few months I sort of learned how to play D7 and G7 — wow! I got into listening to Django Reinhardt and people like that very quickly because my older brother was a real jazz fan.

Did you learn chords and leads at the same time?

Yeah, I was trying to figure it all out. Of course, I was listening to some pretty heavy, difficult stuff, so I eventually started playing easy stuff like Shadows tunes. I never put the guitar down; I was always playing. After a couple of years, I got quite good at it. I was listening to all kinds of American jazz guitarists, like Barney Kessel, Kenny Burrell, Wes Montgomery, and people like that.

What were the first solos that moved you?

One that I just played over and over and over again was the recording of "Nuages" by Django Rheinhardt [on *Quintet of the Hot Club of France*], the one with the clarinet on it. I remember listening to the runs he was playing in there, and it was amazing.

Did you participate in the British blues boom of the '60s?

I was in London, but I steered right away from that because everyone was doing it. Everybody was trying to be Jeff Beck. I was so into black American jazz players like Wes Montgomery and Kenny Burrell, I didn't want to swing over to that. At that time I was playing in a real rhythm and blues group. We had a Hammond organ and two saxophones, and we'd play lots of James Brown, Jimmy Smith, and all this sort of American black R&B jazz. That kind of funky music was happening in the mid- and late-'60s. It's organ-based music.

Did you participate in psychedelic music?

Well, I was in London doing what everyone else was doing. We became a psychedelic group. I was young and foolhardy at the time. We had a light show and went right through the whole thing, playing acid rock. I studied sitar for three or four years; I can still get along with that pretty good.

Did seeing any other players influence a change in your style?

Probably not as much as having listened to people on records. I don't listen to people on records that much anymore. I can't really think of one person about whom I'd say, "Well, that's it; I'm gonna play like that." I actually saw Wes Montgomery play in London once. I was moved by Jimi Hendrix quite a lot. It was great to see him. I remember when he first came to London, and he hadn't even started to make a record. At the time it was just mindblowing. I went down to this club, and there he was playing with Brian Auger. Chas Chandler, who was his manager and a friend of mine, said, "Come see this guy. You won't believe it." He was up onstage with this huge afro, this wild jacket, and a white Strat, which he had in his teeth. That was it!

When did you decide to pursue the experimental rock course you're on now?

I always was a serious musician because it was very natural. I loved music and wanted to play, and I wanted the knowledge of music. I eventually went to college in America and studied harmony totally and 20th century composition. I played classical guitar for a long time. Then I went back to England and got back into playing rock music because my personal life was confused and a lot of things happened to me. In the end I went back to what I knew, which was playing the electric guitar. It was the only thing I felt secure with. Suddenly I became conscious after being unconscious for many years, and decided that I was going to have a career with the guitar. So I was like looking for the opportunity, and eventually it came with the Police.

Is your music with the Police different from what you play on your own?

Yeah. I probably play much farther out on my own. Certainly as far as solo playing goes, when I'm on my own I play much more in a jazz vein. I'm just not interested in practicing like rock lead guitar anymore. I can do it — and I do it a bit with the Police — but it just grew really old for me. And there's so many guys who are so good at it. It's not an area I'm interested in competing in, because my ears go for other things, styles of guitar playing that are much more interesting to me. So my solo playing is much more jazzy and linear, but I don't really do it in the Police.

Do you view the guitar as an unlimited instrument?

I think so. Really, it depends upon the player. I don't think you ever master the instrument; I don't think that's possible.

Can you play most of the parts you imagine?

Yeah, if I work at it. Not always — depends on how much sleep I've had the night before [*laughs*].

Do you first imagine tones and textures and then find them on the instrument, or does the instrument suggest them to you?

A lot of it I hear first. It's like writing music on paper without an instrument. I think I can hear it and then go to the guitar and find it, which I think in a way is a much better discipline. It's like the old thing about composing on an instrument that you can't really play: You're more likely to come up with something original. You can play the guitar and you're so fast on it, you go into all the clichés. But you go to the piano, which you don't play, you're more likely to come up with something. It's the same thing about trying to hear sounds in your head. They're really hard to find. But if you can hear them, they're probably there somewhere.

What should a solo do?

Ideally, it should carry a person. It should have peaks and valleys, and highs and lows, and it should have a real climax. It should be organic, and it should be like a song. In its most ideal form, it should really be like someone singing. When I make a statement like that, it sounds like it's a really flowing kind of thing, which it doesn't have to be. One chord held ten bars could be a solo statement. I'm certainly into doing that. That's a lot of what I do with the Police: When we get into the free areas where we improvise, it's like we're all soloing totally all the time.

When do you play your best?

When I feel really good physically. In any performance there are certain mystical things that you can't pin down. The situation's right. The acoustics of the hall are right. Everybody feels good at the same time and sort of forms a proximity to one another onstage. Some nights are great and magical, and other nights it should be but isn't. It's competent, but it doesn't have that quality where everything opens up and it's wonderful. For me, it's usually when I feel rested, physically good, and in the mood for playing. Those are the nights when it really happens. If I'm feeling really happy, I'm gonna play better. Playing is a real mirror of the way you feel.

Some claim that they play best when angry or depressed.

Yeah, I can see that. To me, that's a slightly romantic view of it.

Can you play yourself in and out of moods?

Yeah, especially if I was feeling bad and went onstage and ripped off an amazing solo. I feel like my whole psyche is totally bound up in the guitar. I've played all my life. As you get older and play longer, you probably ought to be more objective and live with things a little more. But when I was younger and first playing, I lived from gig to gig. If it was a bad gig, then I was bummed out all week. If it was a great gig, I felt on top of the whole world for a whole week. It's still that way to some extent. Despite all the success and everything that goes on, it really all comes down to how well you're playing.

Would you say you're self-critical?

Highly.

Do you ever go through slumps?

Yeah. I think all players who play all the time — all their life is playing — do. Who can possibly go on year in and year out just going up, up, up. There's bound to be times when you go up a bit, and then you go along, and then you go up. I'm very aware of what you're asking. I'm continually trying to improve, to get my playing better and take it up a bit more, or open a new area. Being in a band like this where the pressure is so great and we're touring all the time, it's like I can never play the guitar because I'm always playing the guitar. I really would like to have a lot more time to sit down and just practice, to forget about all the bullshit and just play around, because I love to do it. So for me now to move up the scale musically, I need time off to practice. When I go home and I'm on my own — I've got a studio and a tape recorder — I get down there and play all day long. I haven't gotten fat with being in this band and being successful. I just want to go on and on, getting better and pushing it.

What is your philosophy of using effects?

I think they should be used. You have to be judicious and musical in your use of them. If you play everything with flanger, it's going to get really old fast. You have to continually change it and use the straight guitar sound as well — which I do — so that when you use the effect, it is an effect. And then it goes off. There's a danger in playing with that sound all the time because you turn it off, it sounds really dull. Straight guitar ought to sound as good as the effects. You have to try to keep it in perspective.

How much does equipment matter musically?

I like to think that it's still the same old thing: A song is a song. It's got to stand up on its own anyway, and then what goes on record is something else. People want to hear sort of what's on the record. I think that with some of the Police material, the effects and the way the sounds have been modified are an integral part of the music. They really belong in the music.

How much can you take from the studio and duplicate onstage?

We can reproduce virtually everything we do. We try to think about it. I use my pedalboard and the same gear in the studio and onstage.

Is it easier for you to play onstage or in the studio?

I much prefer to play live. Onstage we always have areas where chances are available. We're having fun playing around with it at the moment in a song called "One World." It's a very reggae type of thing on the album [*Ghost in the Machine*], and it's going well onstage. We stop in the middle and play beats that seem in the wrong places. Then we stop and they think the song has stopped, and then it starts again and we get the whole thing going. It's great fun. I like being in the studio as well; it's a different kind of work. It has more stress attached to it, and sometimes it happens really spontaneously. On this last album we had some really good spontaneous moments happen. But if you have to start working at it in the studio, it starts to show. It starts sounding labored. If possible, I like to get my parts really quick.

Do you plan parts out in advance?

No. I sort of work with the song. The way we work is to get the basic track down first: the guitar, bass, and drums. The most important thing is always the drums, to get a really good drum track. If the right feel is there on the drums, then it doesn't matter after that what you do. In a way it's like painting a picture. You put this color in, you pull this one out, until you've surrounded the song with the right kind of accompaniment, so that the song comes off best.

Do you often surprise yourself in the studio?

Yeah. I'm amazed that I have to still play the guitar [*laughs*]. I think we try to pull those elements out of ourselves and push it all the time. We take turns producing each other. We are very harsh with one another in terms of severely editing one another's playing a lot of the times, pulling stuff off of tracks. You know: "You can't do that. Don't do that rhythm. Don't play that chord. Play this. No, that line's wrong." We do this until we get the best out of one another. We reach totally — compromise is too weak a word for it — an agreement that is better than what one of us would have gotten on his own. It's heavy going. But our interests eventually are all in the same place: To get the best record and treat the song the best way, so we live with it.

Your brief solo in "Driven to Tears" [Zenyatta Mondatta] is surely one of your most unusual statements. Was that off the cuff?

Actually, we went into the studio and said, "Right, there's a hole left for the guitar solo." The solo on the record was the first one I played. I thought it was good, but maybe I could do better. There were three or four tracks left, so I did a couple more, but that was the one. That song is about too many cameras, not enough food, etc., etc. It's about the state of the world, and the solo was supposed to reflect the angst that the lyrics are talking about. So that's why the solo is angular and angry. If I went in there and did a Larry Carlton-type solo, it'd have been terrible. We try to make it short but really to the point, to have power in a short space.

Would you sacrifice technique to get emotion?

Absolutely. Technique is only a means to a musical end. There's no point in it otherwise. Some of the worst music in the world comes out of LA. I think there's a horrible, awful syndrome of Hollywood guitar playing. There are great guitar players, but boy, the music they come out with is so dreary! To me, that music reflects a lifestyle of a lot of money and really losing sight of what it's all about. You can see it all go to the same thing: This fat, rich sound in this sort of fluid style. It's a certain thing that they've all got, like Hollywood on the guitar. It makes me queasy when I listen to it; I can't stomach it. They have secure, happy harmonies that they always put in the same places, or certain chord sequences that they all use. You have to go back and listen to [saxophonists] Ornette Coleman and John Coltrane. Even someone like [guitarist] James Blood Ulmer is so much more exciting to me.

Let's examine a few of your styles and techniques. From a guitarist's point of view, how do you play reggae?

A lot of it is just rhythm. What you really have to get into are the bass lines and the drum parts more. The guitar playing is just a certain feel. You have to just listen to a hell of a lot of records and soak it up by osmosis. That's the way you really learn anything: Just continually listening and playing along with the records. If you have rhythm in your body, you start to feel it and it will come out in your playing, depending on how much talent you've got. Reggae is a simple music with very simple, straight chords like *Am*. The musicians in it don't play sophisticated chords because then it would not be reggae. They are all fairly straightforward diatonic chord sequences. The Police don't really play straight reggae. All we did was take the rhythmic count and incorporated it into whiter pop songs and added a little bit of punk in there to get these sort of jazzy, strange harmonies. It became something else, really. It became, hopefully, what we call Police music rather than just pure reggae. There are other English groups that play much closer to ethnic reggae than we do.

How did you achieve the massive effect in the middle of "Secret Journey?"

I'm playing really peculiar chords on the Strat, feeding it back at the same time, and wanging the tremolo arm. Then I've also got a background of guitar synthesizers playing in the middle part. There's like an opening minute-and-a-half of guitar synthesizer with all these chords going on, and then there's a break in the middle which is the two guitars together. I like the way it stops: You suddenly drop into this hole and a sort of Himalayan sheet of sound comes towards you.

In one interview you likened that effect to a painting.

It's very much like a painting: Being able to pull people in by using space. They fall into the hole you've prepared for them. It's musical seduction, really. The same thing in painting: It's that space that pulls people in. Gestalt psychology has a thing called closure which talks about the same thing: You provide space and people close it with their minds. I think onstage the three of us are getting to the point where we can improvise and all stop in the wrong place at the same time. The audience is feeling the rhythm, and then they suddenly have a shock and sort of all wake up. You hear like this massive gasp from about 20,000 people, and then we're into it again. It really works quite well.

What scales did you use in "Bombs Away" [Zenyatta Mondatta]?

It's like a minor pentatonic, I suppose. It would be something like G, A♭, B♭, B, and C.

Is there a backwards guitar track in "Masoko Tanga" [Outlandos D'Amour]?

I played piano on that. It's just like my forearm on the piano and then playing the tape backwards while you record it. Great sound.

How did you get such sustain in "Bring on the Night" [Regatta De Blanc]?

That was just the amp cranked up in a room that worked.

In "Spirits in the Material World" [Ghost in the Machine] there is an Oriental-sounding instrument.

Actually, that is just a guitar played up very high and plucked dry — you know, the palm on the string. I blended this with the setting on the Prophet-5 keyboard synthesizer to get that kind of sound.

Did you use a slide for "Next to You" [Outlandos D'Amour] and "It's Alright for You" [Regatta De Blanc]?

Yeah, I did. Those are the only bits I've done it on. I had some very heavy brass slides made specially in England. You couldn't buy them. They're quite big. I like them because you get a lot more tone out of them. "Next to You" uses just the standard open *E* and *G* tunings. I was very into slide for a while. I also like open tunings, but I don't use them with the Police.

Did you compose "Behind My Camel" [Zenyatta Mondatta] on guitar?

No. I worked out the melody on an organ. It might have come out of my playing to a drum box: I got this machine that was set to bossa nova plus rock one and tango rhythms. I wrote that tune in Ireland about three months before we recorded the album. That was up for a Grammy, actually.

What technique did you use for the flurries of notes in "Peanuts" [Outlandos D'Amour]?

I really like that one — the bit where the bass breaks and it's just like *rahhhhhh*. I was going for sheets of sound. All that's like playing wrong or badly, not trying to play cleanly, but trying to get the effect of a sheet of sound almost like John Coltrane or Ornette Coleman. It's like a great sort of clusters and flurries of notes rather than cleanly picked single lines. It's because of the excitement factor.

How do you add vibrato to a note?

I only know one way: I bend the string with only my third finger. Instead of giving it vibrato right away, I like to hold the note and then just as it's dying give it the vibrato. So you just hear the vibrato right at the end. There's a subtle difference. It's more exciting this way.

Where do you hold a pick?

Between forefinger and thumb. Depending on what I play, I use two different picks. For the sort of jazzy or lead stuff, I like to use a small, fat pick — a Jim Dunlop Jazz Two. You get that thick sound that way; the physical feeling in my hand makes me play a certain way. And for most of the Police stuff where there's more rhythm going on, I use a slightly larger, thinner pick.

Do you follow any particular stroke patterns?

In the rock stuff I use a lot of downstrokes to get that kind of feeling into it. Reggae is nearly all downstrokes. I like to play funk rhythms. That's what we like to jam on at our sound checks; we play for hours. I get a really loose right-hand wrist for that. I really enjoy funk because you can play what seems like a straight rhythm, but there's so many nuances that you can put into it. The B side on the single of "Every Little Thing," "Flexible Strategies," is a funk tune that's basically built around one chord, like an *Am* or something. I'm playing a hard funk rhythm, and then there's a long guitar solo that goes virtually all the way through the song, which is like totally against the harmony that's being played. It's sort of atonal. The sound is searing, and the notes are somewhere else. It's all like *E♭s* and *Bs* against an *A* chord and an *F#*, it just works really well, which I found interesting. In a way it seems to be the area James Blood Ulmer is moving into.

Do you rest your hand on the guitar when you play?

No.

Are most of your harmonics done with a pick?

Yeah. I do like the Lenny Breau stuff. I played with him a couple of times and he showed me, so I do a lot of that in the Police. Then there are the standard harmonics which everybody knows. And then I hit the string with the pick and catch it with my fingernail at the same time, so I get a note and the harmonic at the same time. It's really effective in a bluesier kind of playing, that Albert King kind of sound.

What do you look for when trying out a guitar? Do you usually know right away if you like it?

You can almost tell right away, but you can't always be sure. Sometimes if you work with a guitar, you adjust to the sound and start getting into it. I think it's something to do with the overtone series in a guitar. It works better on some than on others. It's something you can't make happen; it sort of happens on its own. I really believe that there are certain mystical elements in the building of guitars. No matter how hard you try to make your blueprints, there are those other things that are gonna work. You hear stories about guys in the old days — in the late '50s and '60s — and the way they used to wind pickups. Some got more turns than others, so there would be more windings than on the previous ones. These kind of things make for a certain bunch of guitars. It's amazing. Why is it that some of them sound so good? Is it just the age, or is it something else? I don't know. The standard was sort of set 20 years ago, and it's very

hard to get away from that. I think everybody's conditioned by it. Everybody is still playing the old 335s and the old Telecasters. I feel sorry for a lot of the modern guitar manufacturers. Old instruments are an obstacle. It's a strange sort of phenomena, just nostalgia.

What sound would you like it to have?

I like that really broad, thick, middley sound. Sort of like the old sound Chuck Berry was using — a guitar with jazz pickups, but with an edge. You get that fat sound with the edge as well. A lot of modern pickups get too thin, which I find disturbing, maybe because I'm conditioned by wanting to hear something else.

Do you have any desire to experiment with scalloped or fretless fingerboard designs?

No. I like a fairly flat fingerboard. The odd thing about my Tele's neck is that it's almost got a flat fingerboard. It's maple, but I prefer rosewood. I don't like ebony at all; I can't get enough grip on it. I like the woodenness of rosewood.

How do you prefer your action?

Not unusually low. I'm in the middle, really; I like actions that aren't too stiff and hard, and I don't want them to be right on the neck, either. I like it to be enough where I can really work with it. It depends on the guitar. I've got a Martin D-28 that I find a little heavy going to play — unless I play it for weeks on end, then I start to get into it. But you've got to have a bit of tension in the strings to push them; otherwise it's not as exciting when you bend a string. It's too easy. I think this translates psychologically. When you know you're bending an .008 instead of a .010, it's not as good. I use strings gauged from .010 to .046.

Do you do anything special to warm up before a show?

Yeah, I'll go sit in the tuning room and play scales and exercises. I just play by myself.

Do you ever play through music books?

Yeah. At home, when there's more time. I'll get into that kind of thing. I like Bartok. I like the violin duets. I play a lot of classical guitar music. In the last couple of years I've been playing Charlie Parker tunes. They are very challenging and difficult to play on guitar. I don't often play that kind of phrasing, so I get a lot of ideas from them.

Do you do anything to protect your hands?

Around playing time I keep them out of water. I don't want to shake hands with all these radio people who come in.

When you were teaching guitar, did you have any special advice for students?

I always just tried to point out clichés to people, to show why things become mundane. I think people should try to develop a nice, iconoclastic attitude as early on as possible.

Is your main complaint against today's guitarists the clichés?

Yeah. You've got two different things: Some amazing and technically gifted players, and some very vacant minds. I think the most important thing, really, is to go beyond guitar playing in a way and get into real music. Listen to lots of composers and try to find out what music is really about. All the heavy metal on the radio — there's a lot more to it than that. There are all sorts of interesting things that seem to be happening, and there are some great guitar players around. The most important thing is to live a full, exciting, rounded-out life. If you get so into playing guitar and living that life, you become a very boring person eventually. There are so many people like that. Develop as a person and try to keep things in perspective.

How do you keep your sanity on the road?

Well, I beat my head against the wall at least two hours a day — you know, got to keep the size down [*laughs*]. I go off and do a lot of other things. I like photography. I'm really into that; it's a passion of mine.

— PETE TOWNSHEND —

BY MATT RESNICOFF — SEPTEMBER & OCTOBER 1989

PAUL NATKIN

THREE VOCALISTS, a percussionist, and a lone acoustic guitar player are jamming to a backing tape on the great stage at Radio City Music Hall. The performers hold diligently to their positions, putting forth their parts with an earnest, almost workmanlike precision — all except the guitarist, who's passionately singing a song about friendship and trust while he bounces himself around his microphone and splashes harmonics over the quirky synthesized rhythms. Midway through the song, he catches his breath and makes a rather pointed set-up for something that in rock traditionally requires little or no introduction: "I'm going to play an acoustic guitar solo for you." His wrist is already in motion to summon the first few phrases as he shuffles back and realizes he can't be heard over the tape. Two glaring eyes shoot towards the soundman.

This is a Who concert. You can tell because the guy with the guitar yells at someone, dances around, and then finds a few seconds to play a great solo that doesn't go on as long as it should. It's at this kind of concert where you're supposed to experience the delights of rock and roll spectacle — guitars flying into cymbal stands, drums rolling over singers' toes, old ladies fainting. This most recent road show is a universe apart from the band's former self, at whose hands a song like "My Generation" might melt into scat rhythms, meander into valleys of harmonics and graceful chord melodies, catwalk through chicken-

picked funk-metal, and ascend into a shower of improvised ensemble riffs before segueing into the next piece. On today's bill, the movements are judiciously choreographed; the experience is designed to kick you in the seat of the pants at just the right moments, but the footprint it leaves on your behind is that of an expensive Doctor Marten, not the typical Who workboot.

Wearing the boot, stoking the flame, and generally stuck in the middle of all of this is an acoustic guitarist named Pete Townshend, who doesn't have it in his heart to allow a good thing to dic off completely. It certainly should only have been expected that Pete's inspired drop-kicks and scissor-leaps should produce crowd responses that overwhelmed the general fervor accompanying the Who's just being there. When he strikes that graceful balance between the limitations of form and tapping music's instinctive sense of pure release, Townshend embodies the complex ideal of rocking and rolling. He's a prototype punk guitarist who may have crystallized in a single line one of the most lucid observations about both art and the life it imitates — that "true beauty is time's gift to perfect humility" — and he lives and dies by it every time he picks up his instrument.

Be he ever so humble, no musician meshes power with purpose quite as eloquently as Pete Townshend. Like Miles Davis, Townshend's best work comes at once from everywhere and from nowhere at all, where impulses are pressed into service by a set of specific musical conditions that are just as easily disregarded as they are a necessary springboard for ideas. Once the barriers are rejected, the field is cleared for noisemaking of a very high order: Writing music infused with meaning in a format centered almost purely in anarchy, producing characteristically transcendental acoustic guitar work over a Synclavier pulse on a moment's notice, or having a rock trio beat bloody hell out of a synthesizer track and be left with foundation-stone rock anthems, as the Who did nearly 18 years ago with the renegade experiments with the ARP 2600.

Beginning in the '60s, along with the Beatles, the Rolling Stones, and other lads from the British Isles, the Who brought back to America what America had exiled. Fusing blues with volume, adding lyrics reflective of an era of media birth and chaos, and exploding with the antics of Chuck Berry at the high hurdles, Pete Townshend — lead guitarist — rose to media preeminence as the ripper of nails from windmilling power chords, the leaper on impulse, the vulnerable voice behind the voice of *Tommy*, the angry persona of "My Generation." Many consider him the father of Punk.

Originally an art student, Townshend — an initially-reluctant leader by default — cannot have helped being influenced by the sometimes literally fiery "happenings" of avant-garde artists of the era — precursors of today's "performance artists" — who used to drop pianos from cranes or burn them in the middle of streets for their "audiences." By smashing guitars and stabbing amps, Townshend brought such concepts to the rock and roll stage and ended up influencing the likes of Jimi Hendrix then and performers now who never even saw the Who, who learned such things from imitators of his imitators. Townshend was also the first rock musician to achieve huge commercial success with something approaching opera: *Tommy*, his tale of a blind pinball prodigy, is still heard twenty years after he first wrote it — painstakingly, given his lack of schooling in music notation and his lack of the computer technology he now uses for his latest epic, *The Iron Man*, and the Who's 25th Anniversary reunion tour in 1989, the backdrop of the following interview.

In a story called "Fish Shop" in your book Horse's Neck, *you give an emotional literary treatment to your complex relationship with your guitar teacher, Jacob. Is he a [Meher] Baba figure?*

That's right, but other things as well, like my father and my uncle Jack, who was a guitar player who worked for Gibson, for Kalamazoo guitars. He helped them design guitar pickups, and then when the War came, he went into radar — brilliant, brilliant guy. So it was him, and other guitar players who I came across, the main one being John McLaughlin, who was always generous and particular in his recommendations to me when he was a guitar salesman at Selmer. His playing even then was inspirational, and his willingness to listen and appreciate my own basic rhythmic style in 1964 gave me a lot of confidence. But there's a whole number of figures wrapped up in that. That was the most real story that I had in that book. Most of the stuff was complete fiction. I was trying to write a [Charles] Bukowski kind of thing.

I actually bring a gate down on pre-'82 Who, because I think that sound and that theatrical dynamic was exhausted by the Who within its own turf, but it's been inherited by Springsteen and U2 and lots of other bands as well who in a sense do it better now — certainly, they've given it new life.

What I'm concerned with, when I consider what I really want to be doing and addressing now as a musician, is trying to find some kind of dignity. I keep reading books and hearing stories and analyses of the early years of the Who as being the most exciting, and yet such a lot of turmoil and work and study went into the latter years. And I think it's unfortunate in a sense that the years were so culturally vapid, the Woodstock years. And also, that it was very, very difficult to deal with the ultimate, triumphant commercial success of *Tommy,* and it tends to overshadow everything else.

Since Tommy, *the acoustic guitar has provided a sonic cushion for almost everything you've recorded. But I detect that this record is the first time you've ever recorded without your Gibson J-200 since 1969.*

[*Smiling.*] That's correct, yeah. This is a weird thing about guitars and musical instruments. You know, I've smashed so fucking many guitars, and always maintained that they're just planks of wood, and "Don't give me that shit about guitars with all that 'it knows when I'm away' stuff," but because I hardly used it on this record at all, it died! It was in the studio waiting in its case, and I went back to do some work there with Boltz, the other guitarist. I opened the case and picked it up, and it had just completely fallen to bits. The strings had corroded to an extraordinary extent, the frets had grown mold, the bridge had come off, the back had popped open, and all of the top had delaminated. And yet, while I was working on the demos before I went into the studio, it worked perfectly well. It's almost like once it knew it was not going to be on the record, it just went *bing!* I had it rebuilt, and I'm going to have to take it home and play it. It's like a different guitar now, like a new guitar.

I've been trying to reassure people that there is genuine, explosive excitement in acoustic rhythm guitar. I mean, you only have to think back to the great players like Richie Havens, who've founded careers on it. And I can make acoustic guitar *fly*. You know, there's no question about it. And I feel much more comfortable on the acoustic than on the electric. But there are things it can't do. It's very difficult to make the transition, for example, from single-string work to heavy-flourished work on acoustic guitar. These are things that I've always known, that I'm reconfronting now. But when I get to a comfortable thing like the "Pinball Wizard" bit, it just sounds so obviously *right* to me. But there are other places where the guitar plays a much more subtle role, and I think it's then that it's really important that I'm at the front, holding it, and I'm seen to be physically making a subtle contribution. When I did my shows on my own [*Pete Townshend's Deep End*], I played acoustic on most of that, and although I didn't even have the guitar plugged in, I could actually change the feel of the track. I thought at first that it was the way I played it, and then I found that of course it isn't.

Is your current demoing process similar to the one you've been using over the last 20 years or so?

No, it's gotten much more sophisticated because I'm using the Synclavier, so my original Portastudio four-track demos are now actually done on a four-track direct-to-disc system which costs more than my house, literally. It means that odd little moments on *Iron Man*, like the vocals and basic accompaniment on "A Fool Says," are the demo; the whole thing is just something I knocked out very, very loosely. I tried redoing it, and I just thought, "Well, why? It's all there." I engineered it myself, and this is a problem — I was taking stuff into the studio and saying [*as if to himself*], "Can't you hear that buzz?" [*Laughs.*]

But in that respect, as I said earlier, my upper-frequency hearing is actually returning, and that's become a great relief. I think one of the things about tinnitus and hearing damage is that you psychologically close yourself off. You don't fight for hearing. The reverse happens: You kind of say, "No, no, please, no more loud noises. Stop. Stop!" A jet might go over, or somebody might toot their horn. Or yesterday my alarm in my car went off [*whines loudly*],

and I lifted up the bonnet to switch it off, and I couldn't get *near* it. I thought, "If I get close to this fucking alarm, I'm going to blow my brain out." The modern world seems to be full of these terrifying sounds.

So my demo process has changed only in terms of the more modern equipment, but that's enabled me to work on a much more sophisticated level, more like a composer than a songwriter. Now, I don't need the structure of a song before I start to work on it. Working on a Synclavier or on MIDI software or whatever it is that I happen to be using, I can actually approach a shape with a phrase, a musical phrase, and start to develop that. And I can actually try other intellectual ways of approaching a piece of music. Jesus Christ, I mean, *Tommy* would have been so much better if I had had modern equipment. It would have been much, much, much easier. I can't tell you how hard that was for me. I'm not a great memory man, I'm not very good at music, I'm not very good at ordering my thoughts. I'm very, very flitty, and I found it so difficult to write that. It was just a nightmare, because I had to write stuff on paper and I had no training. That's my one great regret.

It's a fair assumption that the pen and paper may one day be swallowed up in the shadow of the technology that gave us the Synclavier.

I think that the assumption these days that you don't need musical training because there are machines is just another myth. The myth that was around when I was a kid was that music, as it used to be, was dead, and I remember my father always saying to me, "Learn to read, learn to read, learn to read [music]. Whatever music you want to play, it doesn't matter, just learn to read. This is the language." And you feel a bit like you're at school and somebody's saying to you, "You know, this school has never been the same since they dropped classical Greek." You think, "Oh, *God*." And then you decide one day that you want to read Homer or Plato, and you buy five books, and they're all *utterly* different — not only is it a different translation, but different *subject* matter, and then you realize, "Hey, it might be *fun* to learn classical Greek. It would be fun to learn what these great, original foundation-stone philosophers were actually saying, and to make my own interpretation of it." Anyway, he made his musical point, and I ignored him, and I wish I hadn't. I think the other thing I wish I'd done is to develop my virtuosity. Reading a magazine like *Guitar Player*, you understand that one thing that is not neglected there is the possibility for, and the value of, virtuosity. I'd say to anybody who's fucking around with music computers now, "Well, that's fine, but make sure that if you're on a boat in the middle of the ocean and all you've got are sails, that there's an instrument that you can play to raise your spirit, without any electrical power." Because although this is the modern world, we are closer now than we've ever been to having to live naturally. It could happen at any moment, just at any moment; somebody could come and steal all the energy.

Actually, the acoustic portions of your work are among the most exciting. That's an organic relationship that must feed the whole acoustic rebirth you're undergoing.

Yeah, definitely. I've kind of taken refuge in it because of hearing problems, and then rediscovered the instrument — certainly by exploring new tunings, and finding that there's a tremendous range of expressions available. Harmonic expressions, not just structural things, are available to you, which, when you work on a piano, get lost in the clichés you tend to gather behind you. What's interesting is that on a guitar, you can gather all those clichés and then arrange the strings in a completely different order, and all those clichés become something else. It's like learning a new language.

Have any of your more well-known riffs or sequences come out of accidents like that, through playing with a tuning possibility?

Well, if *Iron Man* does well, then yes, because one fundamental thing involved was a voicing which is very unguitarlike, where the 3rd is in the bass, and that came about through a sort of stumble on my guitar. The tuning I used for "Parvardigar" [*Who Came First*], which I call "Parvardigar," incidentally, is a 12-string tuning that goes *C, G, C, G, C, D*. On regular guitar it can be used a whole-step up: *D, A, D, A, D, E*. I believe I've heard this used by Joni Mitchell. The *Iron Man* version on 6-string in *D* simply has the lower *A* string tuned down to *G*; I'm sure I've heard this one used by Ry Cooder. There are other examples. "Praying the Game" [*Another Scoop*] developed from a discovery of this thing where you have an open tuning but you put a thin *D* and a thin *G* string on the top, and I got that as a development of the *G* banjo; I thought about how to get a *G*-banjo–type tuning on guitar, and of course there was a string spare, so I made that even higher. Things like that actually make you think slightly differently about what you've been doing.

"The Sea Refuses No River" [All the Best Cowboys Have Chinese Eyes] *and "Crashing by Design"* [White City], *are very similar in tone and at some points, even the intervals used.*

I think my musical vocabulary is unbelievably limited. It astonishes me. I'll sit at a piano or work on a guitar and think that I've hit on something new, and then a couple of weeks later I'll go back and analyze it and realize that I'm drawing on a very limited "goodie bag" of ideas. I'm probably like everybody else in the world at the moment; I'm poaching like mad from exploratory players like Keith Jarrett, who spends five or six hours at a piano at a concert trying to find those odd groups of notes that haven't yet ever been played, which are beautiful and not just nonsense — and every now and again hits it off. You can't resist but be influenced by them. When I'm working on my own, that really doesn't happen at all. If I work instinctively — if I just write from the hip, as it were — I don't find that I'm going over similar ground all the time. I suppose there are emotional pathways in songs that evoke similar musical responses.

Well, it's kind of a stretch, but you could almost call Iron Man *a sort of "My Generation Redux," because as with other things you've addressed — even in songs like "Sea Refuses" — it's really innocence that's crucial to a pure, undiverted sense of self-expression. It's certainly a more optimistic celebration of youth than "My Generation," but it has fundamentally the same foundation.*

Yeah. Well, in a way, there's a mission that you accept when you start in rock and roll. I know a lot of people felt that what I was doing was taking things that we've known about in rock right from the beginning and reselling them — what, to some extent, Bono and U2 get accused of doing now, of telling an audience that it's not so much his idea, but that he has recognized that it was our idea originally, and he is reminding us of how wonderful it is. It's almost like somebody coming from the outside, like the prodigal son returning and discovering that family life was pretty good all along. And then you realize that rock began in the early '50s, and that there I was 15 years later, telling America about their own music. That was part of our job, to allow young white Americans to accept what was essentially a black music of emancipation, and to overcome all of those ethnic barriers that appeared on the surface, and yet to unite us by the music. And they were uniting us in the most extraordinary way, because you were dealing with sometimes third- or fourth-generation émigrés, but that isn't very much. That means that you've got a grandfather who can still sing Polish songs, or one who still knows the Jewish gypsy songs, or maybe a grandfather who remembers *his* grandfather, who was perhaps part of one of the families that moved through Bulgaria, and took all *that* music with them. You might even have Baltic or Balkan roots of some sort, so you might have a feeling for that kind of universal thing of Bulgarian music. But certainly, the African heritage was the one which really counted. But go further than that and look back to what Europe brought to America: the Swedish folk music, the French music, the German, the Austrian, the English, the Scottish, and in particular the Irish music — very, very strong influences. The Irish and the Swedish probably most of all, and maybe a bit of Scottish music as well. But seeing those rhythms and those folk traditions woven into a whole new form of pop and then played to the only audience in the world in which *every single note* had its representative — and that was an American audience — and suddenly you play and you think, "I can't get it wrong! Whatever I do, there's somebody somewhere who likes it, a bit of it." That's the beauty of the American cosmopolitan, universally international audience, and that's really what made rock and roll grow.

And one other big missing thing was that the black emancipation came through the church, and that was a very difficult pill for a lot of white Americans to swallow. The function of the early-'60s rock bands, then, was to bring R&B to America, where it belonged, to allow the people who had made the music grow to wake up again, the way that [disc jockey] Alan Freed had in the '50s, the way that Elvis had tried, and Buddy Holly tried.

Hendrix certainly served, maybe even unwittingly, a similar purpose.

Yeah. That's right.

You shared bills with him . . .

A lot. We were on the same record label. He was discovered by [Animals bassist] Chas Chandler and brought over and went onto Track, which we co-owned at the time, so he was actually on our record label.

You had a very specific approach to the guitar at the time. Was it in any way intimidating to have something like that happen around you?

It *destroyed* me. Absolutely, completely destroyed me. [*Pauses.*] Just destroyed me. I mean, I was glad to be alive, but it was horrifying. Because he took back black music. He took R&B back. He came and stole it back. He made it very evident that that's what he was doing. He'd been out on the road with people like Little Richard, had done that hard work

and then he'd come over to the U.K. And when he took his music back, he took a lot of the trimmings back, too.

You were quoted as saying that the guitar was really all you had, and that you'd put it through ceilings and amplifier grilles because you were frustrated by what you could do with it and what you perceived you couldn't. I'd guess Hendrix might have shifted your emphasis.

It did shift my emphasis. I suppose like a lot of people, like Eric, for a while there I think we gave up, and then we started again and realized . . . it was very strange for Eric and me. We went and watched Jimi at about 10 London shows together, and he wasn't with a girl at the time, so it was just me, my wife-to-be Karen, and Eric, going to see this monstrous man. It got to the point where Eric would go up to pay his respects every night, and one day I got up to pay my respects, and he was hugging Eric, but not me — he was kind of giving me a limp handshake — just because Eric was capable of making the right kind of approach to him. It was a difficult time. You have to remember the other thing about him, that he was astonishingly sexual, and I was there with my *wife*, you know, the girl I loved. And you could just sense this whole thing in the room where every woman would just [*claps*] at a snap of a finger. I mean, there were situations sometimes where Jimi would *do* it. He wasn't particularly in control of his ego at the time. There was this slightly princelike quality about him, this kind of imp at work. I found him very charming, very easy, a very sweet guy. You know, I just kept hearing stories. I mean, one story I've heard — I think I might have been there — was the night that he went up to Marianne Faithfull when she was there with Mick [Jagger], and said to her in her ear, "What are you doing with this asshole?" There were moments like that when he would be very, very attracted to somebody and felt that he would actually be able to get them, and he just couldn't resist trying. There were no boundaries, and that really scared me. You know, I don't like that kind of megalomanical perspective . . .

Ah! Except now . . .

Well, I think it's very important to respect other people's relationships. I'm not saying property or territory or emotional space, but their relationships. You know, with relationships there are always opportunities. If you're a sophisticated person, you know when you see somebody that if there's a chance of you and them having a relationship together somewhere else at some other time, that a look is enough.

It doesn't need you to go up and say in somebody's ear, "What are you doing with this asshole?" And slowly but surely, Jimi became sure of himself. I'm talking about the first two weeks he was in London; you know, it was a new *band,* and they were just taking London by fucking storm! You can't believe it. You'd look around and the audience was just full of record-company people and music-business people. I suppose I went away and got very confused for a bit. I kind of groped around, I had a lot of spiritual problems, I asked my wife to marry me before it was too late [*laughs*], and started work on *Tommy* a bit later. I just sort of felt that I hadn't the emotional equipment, really, the physical equipment, the natural psychic genius of somebody like Jimi, and realized that what I had was a bunch of gimmicks which he had come and taken away from me, and attached to not only the black R&B from whence they came, but also added a whole new dimension. I did actually feel stripped, to some extent, and I took refuge in my writing. The weirdest thing of the lot is that although people really, really value those early years, the Who was not a particularly important band at the time. We were at the end of an era; under normal circumstances the band should have just disappeared. But because he came along and, kind of like in early punk, just swept everything aside, I had to learn to write, and it became like a new art, from a new angle. And what that actually did was provide me with records that sold in America, somehow. I don't know why that is.

Do you recall the revelation of first stumbling onto the suspended chord?

Yeah. [Who manager] Kit Lambert gave me an album by a 17th-century English composer called Henry Purcell. It was just full of Baroque suspensions, and I was deeply, *deeply* influenced by it. I remember I'd just written "I Can't Explain," which was just a straightforward copy of [The Kinks'] "You Really Got Me," but with a different rhythm. I was on my way, but I was just copying. Then I sat down and wrote all the demos for the Who's first album, and it's just *covered* in these suspensions: "The Kids Are Alright," "I'm a Boy," they're full of them. And it's still one of my favorite pieces of music. In that sense, it was another very, very important thing that I got from Kit, because he wasn't just a manager and he wasn't just a record producer; he was a fantastic, extraordinary friend. I remember I was staying at his flat in Belgravia once, and he put it on for the first time. I heard it and went into the room, and there were tears streaming down his face, because it was

his father's favorite piece of music, and it reminded him of his dad.

Do you have a favorite period in your career, where you feel you broke down what you regarded as guitaristic barriers?

I think the significant moments have actually had a lot to do with *guitars,* actual guitars. Like being given an orange Gretsch Country Gentleman and an Edwards [volume] pedal by Joe Walsh, and being told exactly how to set up the amp to produce that amazing Neil Young noise, and using that sound on "Won't Get Fooled Again" and "Bargain" [*Who's Next*]. Or being given another wonderful guitar by Joe, an original [Gibson] Flying V, and getting that incredible kind of Jimmy Page noise. I used that guitar on *The Who by Numbers,* and once or twice for some flourishes on *Empty Glass.* It's about *guitars;* I once found a wonderful Fender Stratocaster that quite obviously had been owned by Buddy Holly. You just played it and said, "Ahh!" It had a lot to do with just kind of responding to sounds.

But I find that the biggest gateway that I've been through lately has been into Synclavierland. Not the guitar side of it — that side of it is a bit antiquated. But working in a sophisticated, studio-quality format has definitely been a revelation. I mean, the machine is one of the most expensive pieces of hardware in human history, and it's worth every fucking cent. I feel like a kid starting to learn about music, and it's released me as a guitar player from the responsibility of actually trying to organize on the guitar. I can just *respond* on the guitar, and it's so much nicer. It's good to know that there's other, cheaper Apple Mac-type software. I felt really guilty because I kept thinking, "This is so powerful, in what it allows you to do, that it's wrong that it should be limited to Frank Zappa and me and Stevie Wonder and a few other people who can afford to buy one." That will always be wrong.

Given the spiritual essence of Who Came First and much of the other music you were writing for the Who at the time, it's odd that you didn't make use of Indian sounds at all. In fact, a lot of your work at the time had what seems to crop up a lot in your solo and demo repertoire: An American, folk-country feel.

Well, that's because Indian music is classical music. It's a high art, and I don't find it easy to incorporate any of those ideas into my own work. I also prefer country music because I can see the country it comes from, and the backgrounds evoke certain images in me that I feel happier with. You know, when I was first introduced to the teachings of Meher Baba, I didn't really think of him as an Indian mystic at all; I thought of him as a Sufi. It was the Persian stuff, the Sufi dervish, the idea of literally *flailing* your way to God, that attracted me. I felt that Christianity was a cumbersome, distorted route to God, and I was more interested in pure Judaism and Sufism and Zoroastrianism. I didn't even really like any of the new teacher/master figures. I've just never been able to meditate very successfully. When I've been able to, it's frightened me. I've got a very delicate spirit. I can actually project myself into a sea of emotions very, very easily. I can go physically green talking about seasickness.

That's psychosomatic neurosia.

That's right. But I never really listened to that much or became a student of Indian music, although I *love* it. I went to George Harrison's house last year to a concert by Ravi Shankar and a couple of new 6-string guitarists, these young Indian kids who play a regular acoustic steel-string guitar on their lap. *Astonishing*. Absolutely astonishing. They make Ry Cooder look like a beginner. And they actually use a lot of modal scales, one of which is very European-sounding, very optimistic-sounding, compared to most Indian things, with none of that kind of superi-or heart searching. And then Ravi came on and did his bit, and then you feel like, "God, why did Jimi Hendrix have to die?"

It's been said that Live at Leeds *and the Who's live performances during that period gave birth to heavy metal. Yet it's been reported that you despise the form. Is that true?*

I don't despise it. I think it's very light-hearted, isn't it? You know, I'm not into men in Spandex trousers with hair like that [*holds palm one foot from head*]. I'm kind of confused as to why these guys look like that, and why it is that they think they look so cool. Maybe they would just say that I was old-fashioned, I don't know. But there's always been a kind of glam-rock thing that came out of the late '60s with bands like Sweet, and it was very underestimat-ed. *I* underestimated it, anyway, although there was some good music there, and some good musicianship. But today, a lot of these guys in Spandex trousers and hair like that are playing some of the most *unbeliev-able* guitar [*laughs*], and you can't really argue with it. It's just that sometimes the vehicles seem to leave a little bit to be desired. I mean, that W.A.S.P. record-ing of "The Real Me" [*Quadrophenia*, covered on W.A.S.P.'s *Headless Children*] — you give them a good song, and they're fuckin' out there; it's frighten-

ing. But it's interesting that they picked that song; they picked a song which is a boast, a threat. It's just that the form is limiting, and I suppose part of that I actually respect, because I think that limitations are very, very valuable, but I just can't understand how so many musicians just want to be the same as so many others. But if you've grown up in a college or a university where (instead of the situation in my school) there were only three guitarists, so we got to-gether and formed a band — there were 60. Some kid I was talking to the other day said, "Do you realize that when I was in college we had 40 groups, and they were all pretty good? [*Laughs.*] And that three of the fathers were millionaires and they had more gear than you've fucking got up there now?" And kids have been playing guitar and having lessons from the age of eight, sometimes younger, so when they hit 14 or 15 or 16, they're sort of going past their peak. There's some wonderful stuff happening there. I just wish there was a better medium for it. I wish we had something that was more akin to jazz in its ability to take virtuoso performers and give them a stage, rather than just be hit with little tongue flashings and wagging fingers and legs astride and waggling very big kind of psychedelic cocks at the audience. So in that sense, I suppose I do despise it [*smiles*]. So who knows where it will go? But I'd trade 50 Def Leppards for — that's not enough — I'd trade *150* Def Leppards for one R.E.M. It's as simple as that. I heard R.E.M., and my heart just soared. To me, that's just divine music; I like the sound of it. I think the words are brilliant, I think it's just perfec-tion, and the fact that none of them can kinda go *blidibidineeeaoowr* just doesn't interest me at all, be-cause if they wanted to, they could go out and they could hire any one of those guys [*laughs*], you know what I mean? What's really important is the music, the content, the heart of it.

You recorded "Driftin' Blues" [Another Scoop] during a pretty dour time in your life. And looking to the blues as a salve and as the most elemental mu-sical ideal, it seems strangely appropriate having John Lee Hooker portray the enigmatic character of the Iron Man.

He has said to me — and I've heard a lot of other people echo this — that the blues is a *friend*. I don't know about the quality of the recording or the performance of "Driftin'," but I can remember doing it: I was in my house in the country, I had been living away from my wife for about nine months, had had a string of unsatisfactory relationships with young women, and was feeling like shit because I wasn't able to accept their love, either because I wasn't completely cut off from my wife or just because I wasn't man enough to do it. I was drinking a lot, I'd gone back to cocaine, which I despised in other people, and I wasn't in very good spirits. I just started to play that song, and suddenly I just felt happy with myself. You know, I felt I had a friend in *me*. And I suddenly realized what the blues was. What it *is*. And it was a great, great, great thrill for me to work with John Lee Hooker. You know, just to hear him saying my name on the [studio intercom] talkback. I mean, he was the first blues performer I really adored. His music, his early albums — well, all his great albums were unbelievably early. I mean, the first couple were made before I was *born*. He's a fantastic guitarist. And he doesn't read, so he carries all his stuff around in his mind, but when he wants to produce the blues, he just *does* it, and it's extraordinary. Absolutely extraordinary.

"To Barney Kessel," from Scoop, *is the only unaccompanied guitar piece you've ever released. Was he a big influence?*

Well, yeah, in a way he was. I mean, he's just one of the many guitarists who interested me during a period I went through before I got stuck into the Who properly and really got into R&B. I used to listen to him, to Wes Montgomery, and to Kenny Burrell, and that's it, really. Then I got distracted; in my art school, there was a guy who was mad about Chet Atkins, and I got very interested in and started to learn how to play Chet Atkins-style. Then I got even further diverted by another guy who was a James Burton freak and would make me listen to the B-sides of Ricky Nelson records. Then the Who, the band, started to pick up R&B. My friend Barney [Richard Barnes] and I moved into a flat owned by an American guy named Tom Wright, who was drummed out of England because of pot busts, and had to go in such a hurry that he had to leave his record collection in our custody. And it was an extraordinary record collection: Jimmy Reed, Muddy Waters, Bo Diddley, Chuck Berry, Joan Baez, Ray Charles, Jimmy Smith — a fantastic collection for the time, and I never looked back. I found in R&B a way to pull my jazz and my pop influences together.

It's often been reported that you were the first guy to use Marshall stacks. Is that accurate?

Well, not really. John was the first person to use a Marshall stack on its *side*. He used two 4x12 cabinets, and I bought a single 4x12 and used it on a waist-high stand so my Rickenbacker would feed back. Then it seemed a logical extension to stand a

top 4x12 on another 4x12 that was actually a dummy, and then eventually to do what John was doing and have two amplifiers. I never, ever used a stack with one amplifier until I got into Hiwatts, and I didn't use Marshalls very long. In fact, I never used Marshall in the beginning at all. I used to use Fenders; I had a Fender Pro and a Fender Vibrasonic and a Fender Bassman top, and I used to drive Marshall 4x12s with those amplifiers. I thought Marshalls were just awful, and I'm afraid I still do, although that's just a personal opinion. I don't mean it's bad stuff, I just mean I didn't like the sound. And when I heard Hiwatt I was over the moon, because they sounded to me much more like a really good, top-line mid-'60s Fender amp. I still think it's hard to beat Fender amps; they're astonishing.

You went through a period in the '70s when you were performing with Les Paul Deluxes almost exclusively, and your models were decorated with large numerals on their faces. What was the code, and what purpose did their two extra toggles serve?

I had various versions: There was a three-pickup one that had three toggles to switch the pickups on and off, but I think the toggle on the others — these were Deluxes, with those small humbuckers — was an extra switch to double-boost the Seymour Duncan in the middle for feedback. They were numbered because I had 10 of them and they seemed to go in and out of action. I used to need four in good shape: I'd have one main guitar, one with a capo on it for "Baba O'Riley," another one with a capo on it for "Drowned," one spare for the capo guitars and another spare. I was carrying five, so another three on the road seemed to be logical. Alan Rogan, my guitar man, put the numbers on. I don't have very much to do with my guitars — it's absurd [*laughs*].

What was the tuning that gave you that full, rich F-chord sound on "Baba O'Riley"?

It's just normal tuning. The capo's at F, first position. It's the shapes that I play. None of the shapes that I play with loud distortion have a 3rd, because you *hear* the 3rd in the distortion. You're getting the second- and third-harmonic distortion, so the first note you're hearing is the 3rd, the second note you're hearing is the 4th, and the last note you're hearing is the 5th, so if you *played* the 3rd, you're going to get a note which is a 4th up from *that*, so, oh [*grimaces*]! That sound I can't stand is people playing a complete C chord with fuzz. They're actually getting something like a C13.

But that approach seems to have spilled over into your acoustic work, as well. When you play an open-position A *chord, for instance, you seldom include the* C#.

That's just habit. I mean, I like to have a ringing tone, so sometimes, like, for example, in "You Better, You Bet" [*Face Dances*], when I play C, F, G, C, F, G, the high G is in all the time on the F and the C chords. So effectively, I'm playing C with G at the top, then F with G at the top, and then G with G at the top. And that's a very distinctive part of the way I voice chords: Having a drone, but at the top rather than at the bottom. I went through a period in the early days with stuff like "Substitute" and "I Can See for Miles" where I was running a drone in the bottom, and I got very bored with that, so I started to find other ways of approaching it.

When you do your flamenco-style strumming, how rigid do you keep your picking hand?

It's quite slack. I'm using quite a heavy pick — a Manny's heavy — but I'm not actually holding it. It's floating, just literally being held in space [*laughs*]. It's a trad banjo technique [*sings twangy strums*], a ukelele/banjo technique that lends itself to the guitar quite well, although I think it's one of the things that has inhibited me being able to play *faster*, because I'm using such a heavy pick and I'm holding it in such a strange way.

You've been photographed with your picking hand literally soaked in blood, and actually appeared onstage in a heavy cast that reached almost halfway to your elbow. That must have made "Pinball Wizard" quite a painful challenge.

That's another hazard of the way that I worked. A lot of people have said, you know, "If you can't go out there and be Pete Townshend, how are a lot of kids going to feel?" Well, the problem is that not only has it made me deaf, but, you know, as soon as we'd hit "Baba O'Riley," I'd go *djaaang, swing, swing*, all my fingernails would just get broken off across, and from then on I would be in absolute agony for the rest of the tour. I wouldn't be able to sleep, you know, at night my hand would be throbbing. I'm not allowed to use any kind of opiates at all, so I can't use strong painkillers, and aspirins don't do anything. And the other thing is, when you swing your arm and you've got a cut finger, blood pours out of it at a great rate, and it goes all over your strings. You see, I've seen a lot of people do arm-swings, and I've never seen anybody do it right.

What is the right method?

Well, the right method is to *bleed*, you know? Your hand and the pick have to connect with the fucking strings. You don't open your fingers up and

just sort of *slap*. And you have to be able to do it in a downward direction as well as an upward direction. Doing it from the top is right easy, but coming up from below . . . you know, you're going around, the string catches under your fingernail, carves it back, *pulls* it out and then goes *poing*, backwards. If you get it *wrong*. And I thought, "Well, fuck this. Nobody knows." I just don't want to do that anymore. It's another example of the way that I developed a way of working which is disabling.

You've been around since before many of your fans were even born. It might seem intimidating to younger people; by the time you were their age, you were already "conquering the world."

And a lot of people say, "Oh, you're ever so humble." It's not humility that makes me say this, but I really do think it's a team that makes it, and that the people who are kind of at the spearhead of the team, group, or peer group have no real *conception* of what they've achieved, of what the *group* has achieved. That's probably why it's so preposterous that people should actually take any interest in what I've got to say about the subject of rock and roll — I probably know less about it than they do. You do it because the audience *allows* you to do it. You're on a stage because the audience has chosen you to do a job, and you're elected from among your peers. So in a sense, a lot of people I meet who were there at the very, very beginning of the Who's career, do act as though they *own* me.

I've got a very fancy house in England. I used to live in quite a modest house, and I wanted a studio and a garden. So we bought a house on one of the poshest streets in town, and there's a park next door. There's a parkkeeper, and he's got thinning, gray hair like me — less hair than I have — and he comes up to me and says, [*heavy Cockney*] "You know Pete, I used to come and see you — why don't you blokes do something *fucking* decent, like in the old days? You're *fucking* useless now. What are you doing in that big *fucking* house you've got 'ere? I'll bet you just sit up there and just do *fucking* nothing all fucking day! Why don't you fucking *do* something?" You know, I don't get any *respect,* as Rodney Dangerfield says. Those moments are precious, because then you realize, "Hold it. It wasn't just me. It wasn't just Roger. It wasn't just the Who. It wasn't just the band and a few hundred selected faces that used to hang out at the Marquee club. It was a whole generation of people, and we were just one of the bands."

I think that's the way you have to think about your role in life and your contribution. You know [*sighs*], it's lucky to get the larger rewards, there's no question about it, but now, at the beginning, in the middle, and at the end, and tomorrow, I can honestly say that I would trade places with the parkkeeper at the drop of a hat. I really would. He's got a divorce behind him, and I'd still trade places with him, because I can just see that he's happier than I am, and that he's been through less hassle than I have. Now, that's not to say that that's true of everybody, and maybe that's an ungracious thing, in a sense. I am happy with my lot. It's just that with the rewards come terrible problems, which is the fact that when you're in my position, you chastise yourself for not having made better use of the opportunities and the advantages. It's very difficult to respond to criticism like, "There you are, with a hundred thousand quid in the bank, moaning about how unhappy you are," and that often gets heard. "Don't give me your miserable songs. Cheer me up." And as an artist you say, "Well, I can't. I'm unhappy." "Well, if you're unhappy, fuck off. Just get off the face of the planet." And you don't say that to unhappy people. That's what "Slit Skirts" [*Chinese Eyes*] was about. You know, you don't say to somebody who's sad, "Fuck off! Get out of my life!" But people say that to artists. Artists have been elected by the public to be the happy people, to be the entertainers, to be the constructive, positive force. And when they fail to do that, they're expected to disappear. And it's very difficult to disappear. And you know you *should* disappear, because you also know that you feel that way about other performers. You pick up the paper and you say, "Oh, poor fucking Rod Stewart. You've lost one blonde and got another blonde and my heart bleeds for you. And this one's 50 times as good-looking as the other one — oh, you've got a tax bill to pay, you poor sod. You only earned *60* million dollars last year?" So you know how people feel about you, but nonetheless, it's a clearer perspective from this position. Being on the stage and looking at the audience, one thing is clear: We know better who the audience is [*chuckles*]. You know, we really do. They don't really know who we are. They don't really know that we're just shit like them. And that's what was really interesting about Elvis being put into the Army; I don't know whether he got an easier ride, but you can imagine if there was a really serious war and they take Michael Jackson and draft him into a crack Marine troop, you just know they'd have that little fucker in shape in six weeks. You *know* they would! And the interesting thing about it is that the guy's *fit*. And he's dangerous! Do you know what I'm saying? I mean, here

he is, a little plastic man who likes to [cavort] with a llama or whatever — he's a heavy guy. And he's bigger than he looks, too. It's that whole feeling of what happens when you strip people and just put them alongside one another and you see how different everybody is. And then in difference, everybody gets lost. The thing about large stadium audiences, which raise up the star, is that the larger the mass, the lower the level of humanity you seem to end up with. In a large enough mass, you just kind of average everything out, and the individual gets pointed up. You've just got to stop thinking of yourself as having to be measured by the achievements of anybody else at all — that's the important thing.

How do you respond to that dilemma these days?

I'm responding to that *now*. Just last night I was trying to find an empty piece of videotape to copy something for a friend, and I found the concert Prince did with the Revolution, the one around the time of Christopher Tracy's *Parade* album. I started looking at it, and [*sighs*] it's demoralizing — absolutely demoralizing. It's about 20 songs into his set and he hasn't even sweated a fucking *bead!* I mean, not only is he running a studio and a band and writing songs and playing great guitar and dancing, but he's obviously lifting weights and doing aerobic training. Where does the guy fit in his extraordinary sex life that I keep reading about? And I don't want to compare myself to him. I don't even want to try to aspire to *anything* that he's done, and yet, part of his attraction is his extraordinary capability. But there again, he was around for a long time. He was around for three or four years before the public decided that they were going to have him on any level at all — you know, when they granted him permission to be a star, when he'd been in the wings long enough: "Okay, just stay there for a while. Keep the corset on. No, actually, take the corset off. Put the gown back on. That's right. A bit more oil on it. Now *wait*, just wait there." And he waited and waited and waited. "Okay, all right, *now* we're ready for you. Out you come. *On* the motorbike, please, and, uh, I think you really . . . hmm . . . because you're such a weird guy — could you bring a girl with enormous tits with you, please? Great, that's perfect! Now you're a star!"

That's the process. And it happens at every level of life. The most important thing is actually being able to play that game with yourself, to actually recognize what your own pacing is, and where it is that you've already decided to go.

Well, that's the problem, isn't it? Certainly for a

musician, every little decision closes off an entire world of possibilities. When you recognize that each seemingly insignificant little choice you make is actually so crucial in determining that ultimate direction, it can become quite overwhelming.

What you need is to do something like sailing or mountaineering, where the philosophy is that you learn to control every aspect of what you *can* control, and you learn to accept and respect the influences of things that you can't control. And that's what life is about. There are some decisions that you can control, and those you should consider very carefully. But most of them you have no control over; it's just that you think you might. When you get on a plane, for instance, you don't control whether it's going to get where you're going in one piece. And there's no point *worrying* about that. That's the moment where you put yourself in the hand of destiny, or God, if you're lucky enough to believe in God. That kind of process really helps, I think, especially in the world of guitar, for example, in wanting to aspire, wanting to prac-tice, wanting to become a particular kind of player. In the modern world, some people can achieve what they want to do with such apparent ease, and you think, "What they found so easy is so unbelievably hard for me." So what you should actually be doing is looking for the difficult things, looking for the things where there *are* no possibilities. If you really feel that you're presented with so many options that you just don't know what to pick next, then go some-where where you've *got* no options. Go stand in the middle of the Kalahari desert for a couple of weeks. And not so you suffer, but just so that there are no options, so you know that the most important thing — the only thing — that you've got to do next is to make sure that your supply of water is kept up, and that you get some clean food. And *live* like that for a couple of weeks. I get that from sailing: You're out on the ocean, and the only thing that you've got to do next is find out where the fuck you are [*laughs*]. And you know that if a storm hits you, that you've just got to strap everything down.

— STEVE VAI —

BY TOM MULHERN – FEBRUARY 1983
AND BY JAS OBRECHT – OCTOBER 1986

STEVE VAI IS THE most exciting hard-rock guitarist since, well, Eddie Van Halen. He is as unique in his own way as Van Halen or Adrian Belew — or Allan Holdsworth, for that matter — are in theirs. Flashy, funny, and unpredictable, he boldly goes forth where no man has gone before. After performing for the enormous audiences of David Lee Roth, Vai became known as a touchstone for new directions in rock guitar. Vai laced his fills and solos with amazing whammy feats and unexpected turns. At the heart of it all is his unique personality and sense of humor — his *attitude*, as he calls it. That attitude (and the chops to go along with it), was developed long before he stood on stages in coliseum-sized venues.

Born on June 6, 1960, in Carleplace, Long Island, New York, Steve started on accordion at the age of 11, but soon switched to a $5 Tempo electric guitar. Lessons with local instructors followed, and Vai progressed steadily, enrolling in a music theory class and performing in rock bands. After graduating high school, he moved to Boston and enrolled at Berklee College of Music. While there, he diligently transcribed and arranged some of Zappa's pieces, including a piece entitled "Black Napkins" [*Zoot Allures*]. Upon hearing the young guitarist's unsolicited transcription and an accompanying cassette of his band, Zappa offered Steve work as a transcriber. Eventually, Frank asked him to join his band and often described Vai fondly as "our little Italian virtu-

oso." All before he'd exited his teens. Since then, he has enjoyed a popularity and celebrity reserved for few musicians in history, having appeared as the devil in the film *Crossroads*, and played lead guitar for such groups as Alcatrazz, The David Lee Roth Band, Whitesnake, as well as his own band. The interviews that follow — one at the beginning of his career and one more recent — show how dramatically his career changed in three short years.

[February 1983]
Transcribing is a very difficult art. How did you first become involved with it?
While at Berklee, I had a roommate who transcribed a Larry Carlton solo, and I'd never heard of transcribing. He showed it to me and I said, "You figured this out from the record?" I thought it was a neat idea, so I started transcribing all kinds of stuff. One of the first things I transcribed was Allan Holdsworth's solo from "In the Dead of Night." Then I did "Europa (Earth's Cry Heaven's Smile)" by Santana. I really got into it. When I heard "The Black Page" by Zappa, I almost died. I couldn't believe it.
So you were taken aback by the complexity of Zappa's music.
I was just awed by it, and I tried to transcribe it. It took me months. I did a rough copy of it, and then every week I'd add something to it. That's when I was first exposed to artificial groupings — like when you take an odd number of notes, say, and put them over one or two beats. It's just out of your ordinary

type of rhythmic structure. Here's an example of this kind of proportional grouping: Start with a normal grouping of a dotted eighth-note with a sixteenth. This is a *normal* grouping; you take the beat and it is divided into one or two or four — but it's even. Now, when you take something like five and put it over an even beat, it's called an artificial grouping, or a polyrhythm. That is, you have two rhythms going at once. And that's what I discovered about "The Black Page": There are a lot of polyrhythmic things in it. And I remember saying, "If you can do this, you can do that." One thing led to another and I transcribed "The Black Page" [*Zappa in New York*]. I sent it to Frank and he wrote back, telling me that he liked it, and he offered me a job transcribing. I took it, of course; Frank was my favorite.

How old were you then?

I was 18 or 19 when I transcribed all the stuff that's in the book. I started transcribing then, and I just finished, right before the 1982 tour.

How do you go about transcribing Frank's songs?

Well, besides doing transcriptions of guitar solos and drum solos, I've also done other things for him: Lead sheets and orchestral stuff. Now, in order to accurately do a song that news special care, such as "Waka/Jawaka" [from *Waka/Jawaka*], which was really tough, you have to take the masters and make several tapes of as many different tracks as you can get, because with the real close horn section in that song, it's almost impossible — if not impossible — to hear the individual voices. The human ear won't hear more than four voices moving in a closed voice motion individually.

Are the harmonies just too dense?

Yeah. When your four horns hit a chord, it's really hard to hear. So you have to go in and really tweeze-up the mix. Now, for those of you who want to transcribe something that complex and don't have the 24-track machine or the masters to help you, I've come across a couple of things that are really helpful. If the album you're transcribing from is well produced, and if you have a stereo tape recorder, here's what to do: Record the song onto the 2-track machine, and when you play it back, bring one channel down all the way, and the other channel into the middle of the mix. And whatever was panned to one side in the original mix, you'll hear better. So if there were four voices mixed, say, hard left — a lot of recordings these days have parts panned either hard left, hard right, or in the center — you can get a good idea what's happening in that channel. Then listen to the other channel, too.

Any other tips?

If the music is going by very fast, you can bring it down to half speed. That's one of the techniques I used throughout some of the big band transcribing for Frank. He had me working on "Greggery Peccary" [*Studio Tan*]. About 98% of it was written out, but there are sections that weren't. A lot was just improvised or pieced together. I had to tweeze through the score and transcribe the vocal part. It's strange to see, because the human voice has notes to it, but they're in such an order that they don't sound like notes from an instrument; the overall tone of the voice is completely different. But if you analyze a voice — for instance, take what I'm saying right now and stop on every syllable — you'll hear a note. There are notes to it. The thing that makes it sound like a human voice is the articulation — the slurs and dynamics and so forth.

Has any of this vocal transcribing been translated to guitar lines?

On *The Man from Utopia*, there's a song called "The Jazz Discharge Party Hats." On it, Frank does a part that's half talk and half singing. And I transcribed that part and doubled it on guitar. And it sounds really weird — like George Benson from Venus. It sounds so bizarre. If you listen hard enough after you write down the notes in each syllable, and use the right articulation markings to phrase the notes so that they sound like they're in a sentence, you'll come out with some really strange effects.

Did you major in guitar at Berklee?

Overall, I was just trying to get a good grasp on modal harmony and arranging for big bands. I started to go into music scoring for movies, although I never quite got to it, because I started working for Frank.

What did you see as the school's strong points?

It was really good for musicians who weren't on such a competitive level. Anytime you wanted, you could knock on someone's door and jam your face off. There are a lot of really great musicians there. And for the person who wants to really learn something by playing with other people, that's the place to do it, because there are lots of musicians and a lot of opportunities to play.

How much of an education have you gained by working with Frank?

Well, I'll put it like this: The stuff I've learned from Frank you can't acquire for money. Besides learning how to deal with perfection in the studio, I've learned how to deal with the ropes on the road, which is a very tough place — especially the way

Frank tours. He doesn't tour like a normal rock group; he has to keep going and going and going. We went three solid months without breaks, five or six gigs a week. That in itself is a total learning experience. Just working with the man's genius inspires you to become as much of a perfectionist as he is. You strive for that.

Is he really rough with the musicians?

I think there're a lot of false rumors around about Frank as far as his being the guy with the big iron whip or something. It's weird because he's totally mellow. If you can't do something, it's fine: Don't do it and he'll experiment with your abilities, and he'll get you to do things that you didn't think you could do.

He just pushes you a little harder?

Well, he doesn't exactly push you; he gets you to push yourself.

So, in all, it's not a bad gig?

Look, as far as the money goes, I've saved up over the years, and now I've got my house to show for it.

So, you don't blow all your money on guitars and drugs.

Not at all. I don't take any drugs, and I have just a couple of guitars that I really enjoy. I'd like to do what Frank does: Spend all my money on music. But as you can see, even if the pay is nothing, you're still coming out way ahead when you work for Frank. And I wish that every serious musician could get a crack at it. It really is an incredible learning experience. It's like the school of Zappa.

It's kind of a music onto itself.

You sure can't find anything like him. Also, the guy has a great sense of humor, and is able to incorporate that in the music, too. Listen to something like "Valley Girl" [*Drowning Witch*] and then listen to something like "The Purple Lagoon" [*Zappa in New York*] or 'Greggery Peccary' [*Studio Tan*] or "Bogus Pomp" [*Orchestral Favorites*]. Where does someone come off being able to do that?

When you come into a band like Frank's, how are the older pieces learned?

Well, Frank rinses out his band a lot, and it can be very troublesome for him to teach a song and then have to go back and teach it again. So he hires someone who knows the songs and who was perhaps at the original learning of it, and Frank has him teach it to the band — then Frank will come in and give it the final tweeze. With a new band, a song's never quite the same, but Frank compensates for that by changing the song or adding something else. An example of that is "Peaches en Regalia." You listen to the three versions

[*Hot Rats, Fillmore East,* and *Tinsel Town Rebellion*], and each is different. You know what I mean?

Did you finish up at Berklee?

No. I was in my fourth semester — I went straight summers and all — and right at the very end of the fourth semester I got the call from Frank to start transcribing. I was living in a Boston apartment about the size of my kitchen, with mice that you had to wrestle with. It was incredible. Well, working for Frank is a full-time thing; you can't go to college and work for Zappa — it just doesn't work. So it was a choice, and of course I started working for Frank. Right away, I was transcribing anywhere between 13 and 15 hours a day. That's nerve-wracking. There's a huge stack of my transcriptions that I'm sure he'll eventually find use for. God, I really worked my ass off. At the beginning I was getting paid nothing — I was getting paid like $10 a page, which is what a lead sheet transcriber would get. And I used to cram this stuff on the page and cram all the staffs so that Frank would see that I wasn't trying to rip him off.

Were you earning enough money transcribing to make it worthwhile?

Well, $10 a page was still a lot of money for someone who was living on $10 a week! And I remember the first one I did that I was on salary for was "Outside Now" [*Joe's Garage, Acts II & III*]. Then I did "He Used to Cut the Grass" [*Joe's Garage, Acts II & III*]. And this stuff was transcribed using a cassette recorder that was so small and weak and lousy. It was really hard. I used to sit and listen to one bar of music maybe a hundred times — hours and hours and hours of music. But it was fun; I enjoyed it. I felt *useful*. I was learning. I think that transcribing is one of the biggest learning experiences for a musician, and it's really good for a person.

Did you ever transcribe classical pieces or any jazz?

I didn't see anything challenging about the jazz stuff because it was just straight up and down, arpeggiated, eighth-note, laidback, swing-type stuff. There's no way you'd see meters like 13 against 16. But then again, I've missed certain qualities that you can learn by transcribing stuff like that, such as learning how to hear chord changes go by at the speed of light, because I haven't done much of that. Most of Frank's solos are played over a pedal tone. So I suggest that if someone is going to take up transcribing for a learning experience, they should try to cover a lot of different realms, including classical, jazz, and rock. Take the gruntiest Hendrix solo and try to write it out as colorfully and accurately as possible. Also, do a Bird [saxophonist Charlie Parker] solo or something similar. If you can do that and distinguish the difference on paper, you're ahead of the game.

Has transcribing drums and other instruments besides guitar made you a better sightreader?

Oh, yeah. But I don't stress sight-reading in my playing, because I'm the kind of guy who's not satisfied with sight-reading. It's not *real*. As far as I'm concerned, I wouldn't want to have to sight-read any music to play on the spot, because in order to get a piece of music to groove really well, it has to be played quite a few times. Then you really become a part of it. Sight-reading doesn't give you that chance unless you're Tommy Tedesco or someone like that. I'm sure he might have trouble with some of Frank's stuff, too. But transcribing definitely helps your sight-reading. It'll help your ears; it'll help your sense of time. It's a miracle drug. It's really worth it. Just don't ever try to transcribe too much at one time.

You do a lot of sound effects with your Strat.

Like on "We're Turning Again" where I do Hendrix-style things — Adrian Belew rip-offs [*laughs*]. Well, some nights it works, some nights it doesn't — just like Hendrix, I guess. As some magazine said about me, it's my never-ending quest to be more like Adrian Belew [*laughs*]. No offense against Adrian — I love the way he plays.

How do you like being called an imitator?

I don't really care, because the crux of the biscuit is if somebody hears it and likes it, then that's all that matters. Who cares if somebody says it sounds like someone else? Let's face it: I'm not original. Neither is anybody else, except the Shaggs [a vocal group from the Northeast].

When you're doing a solo, what do you focus on in your mind?

I haven't had enough soloing experience in front of large quantities of people to really sit back and say, "Okay. I'm going to open up my mind and do what I like," because I think of quite a few different things. Back when I was in Morning Thunder, I had a really open field, and I could solo for as long as I wanted. Now, it's according to the context of what else is going on. Sometimes I have to solo around a synthetic mode — something like John McLaughlin might play — which isn't derived from the major scale like the typical modes. Lydian, for instance, starts on the fourth degree of the major scale. If you're in the key of G, and you start on the fourth note, you'll still be in the key of G, but it's called the C lydian. A synthetic mode, on the other hand, isn't derived from the basic diatonic major scale system.

You make up a scale from scratch, and then you can build triads on it and devise a whole system around it.

How do you work within such a nonstandard framework?

In a situation like that, I figure out a lick that starts at X and goes to Y. I know it will work because I already had to figure it out. That's one way of doing a solo. But in my eyes, a scale or lick is just a device to show you what fingerings or notes are capable of being played. A lot of people get tangled up in scales and licks, and the next thing you know, they're doing finger exercises, scales, and licks; and it sounds like it.

Do you have any other approaches?

Another thing I do is *not* think about playing. If you don't think about it, you'd be surprised at what you come out with. It's like asking a centipede how it walks. How do you put one leg over the other? And he'll start to trip all over. If you think about what you're doing, it's really hard. One of the most difficult things to get away from — and I'm sure most musicians will know what I'm talking about — is the egotistical playing. It's very hard to get away from the fact that you're onstage, and that people are looking at you and you're trying to impress them. Frank is one of the people who can surmount that. I think subconsciously you're trying to impress the people in the audience, rather than trying to make a musical statement. As far as I'm concerned, many players don't try to make a serious statement. Once they've been around for a while they may get totally fed up with that kind of shit.

The want to singe everyone's eyebrows with their lightning speed and tricks.

Right. Totally egotistical, but subconscious. And that's hard to get away from. I do it myself. You're up in front of people, and there's nothing you can do about it. It's a strange feeling. The people came to be entertained. Now, by egotistical, I mean you're going to play differently when you're in your room playing than when you're onstage in front of even 20 people. It's just something psychological, and that's going to put a clamp on your soloing. So if you can just clear your mind of everything, and let your fingers go, strange things will happen.

What do you think makes a good solo?

A good solo is like a good book. It'll start out in sentences, or a phrase. It will be in paragraphs, and have pauses, and then it will go and have a great ending — a climax. And it should make sense that way, whether it's a big solo or a little one. There's one solo I really like, which Eddie Van Halen does in "Push Comes to Shove" [*Fair Warning*]. You just have to remember not to throw in all your tricks in that short a time. A lot of people try to shoot their load in the first ten seconds of the solo, and it looks totally preposterous and sounds even more ridiculous.

How do you organize a solo into sentences or phrases?

I sometimes develop a solo by taking a story I have in my head and reciting it. And as you say the story, sing it. No one will hear you singing because the amp's too loud. Then play what you're singing. That way, you're going to get sentences. And you do it that way and listen to what you play, you'll be shocked. It's a totally different approach.

What sets the tone of your solos?

When I solo, my realm of thinking is totally derived from the mood, the vamp, the musicians, and the audience. It's a lot of different factors. I can't get onstage and say I'm going to do this every night, because it really doesn't work that way. I mean, a song based on an *E* lydian-based vamp in 3/4 gives a totally different soloing aura than something like [saxophonist John Coltrane's] "Giant Steps," which has a chord change every eighth of a second. You can't think of the same thing. A lot of people give the rap that they play from the heart. They don't read music, but they play from the heart. And you'd be surprised how hard that really is. A lot of people say it, but I believe that only a few can understand what that phrase really means. Everyone understands it to a degree — a lot of people may get uptight at that statement, but I think that to truly play from the heart, only a few can experience that.

Do you have any favorite guitarists?

Jimi Hendrix, Jimmy Page. I like Brian May very much, too. I also like Ed Van Halen — he's a good high-energy rocker—and Randy Rhoads, and of course, Frank.

Are any jazz players of interest to you?

Joe Pass, who is a standard jazz player. Oh, Ted Greene, of course. Did you ever hear his album, *Solo Guitar?* He's a maniac the way he makes the rhythm and melody go at the same time. When I was about 15, I bought his book, *Chord Chemistry*. It's amazing. I learned so much just by reading through that book and trying to utilize it. When I borrowed his album from my guitar teacher, I just flipped out. I couldn't believe the stuff he was doing. And it's so mellow and it's so cool. Really enjoyable. Some of the chord structures are ridiculous.

What are your favorite guitar tricks?

Before I put a Floyd Rose [tremolo system] on, I used to reach back behind the nut — between the nut and the tuners — and pull on the strings. With the combination of pulling the string here and using the vibrato bar, you can get some nice effects. There's also the familiar string tapping. One of the things I've been doing a lot of lately is walking hand over hand down one string. I also like to hit harmonics and bring them down with the vibrato bar. You can also hit notes and lower the vibrato bar until the strings are completely slack.

[October 1986]

Does much trial-and-error go into the parts you come up with, or do you work them out before playing them?

When I'm writing a song, my best stuff usually comes when I pick up the guitar and play. "Goin' Crazy!" was like that. I had been working with Ry Cooder on *Crossroads*, and he inspired me. I'd be playing all these notes, and Ry would sit down and start tapping his foot and playing these grooves — and I felt embarrassed. God, man, this guy knows where the beat is! This guy's got *serious soul*. You ask him to play thirty-second notes in 10/16 time, and forget it. But I was very moved. One day he was warming up, getting ready to lay down a track, and I couldn't have paid enough money to be able to watch what he did in a half-hour. Later on, I picked up my guitar, and said, "I wonder how he fingerpicks like that?" I started using three fingers to play this lick that I used to flatpick, and that's how the "Goin' Crazy!" lick came out. Writing, for me, is a reflection of my state of mind at the time. I wrote "Big Trouble" in a hotel room in Albuquerque, New Mexico. It was beautiful day out, I loved being on the road, and five minutes before we had to get onto the bus, I picked up my guitar and blam, the song came out verbatim. Then there are things like "Ladies' Nite in Buffalo?" which took a long time. I pieced it together a little bit each day. It's more of a construction.

Are you ever surprised when you listen to yourself on playback?

Yes. A lot of times I listen back, and it doesn't sound like something I was capable of doing. Your own music speaks to you in different ways than it speaks to other people. Everybody can pull things out, but certain things keep them from doing that — like thinking, "Oh my God, should I play fast now? Do I look good enough up here?" When you don't think about it, there's more of an open line to that infinite warehouse where all the songs come from. The music I create is a gift to me. I try not to let my ego think that it's me that's doing it, because that's where all the problems come in. People get carried away and think, "This is great — I'm capable of this," and they start resting on their laurels. Sometimes they put that energy into different areas. Taking drugs and getting wasted takes a lot of energy. So does trying to run a business and play an instrument. If kids really feel that they are serious musicians, then that's what they should do. I've had students who are great musicians, but they don't really have a chance to develop that talent because they say, "I can't," "I won't," "I wish," or "I want."

When did you make that commitment?

I never wanted to or even thought about being a musician. I just was, from the very beginning. People say, "When did you get involved in music?" I don't know; it must have been lifetimes ago. When I came out of the chute, I must have had a pair of dark glasses on and a Strat in one hand and a tattoo on the other. I could do anything and be happy, but I'd always be a musician. I have no choice.

Do you sense competition with other rock guitarists?

Consciously, I don't participate in competing with them. But subconsciously I can't tell you whether I do or not. I would suspect that somewhere in there, Steve Vai is a very competitive person. I would very much not mind being in the greatest rock band of the day. Everybody is striving for something out there. But I really don't feel like I'm competing with people, because everybody expresses themselves differently. There's enough success to go around.

More than most players, you've managed to push far past your roots.

My influences are the same as anybody's, in the sense that they are events. But when people play an instrument, it's very personal because they are creating a complete reflection of their personality. What you create is what you are, and what you are is a product of your experiences in life. I don't mean to say that if somebody is a sloppy player, they're a sloppy person. It goes far beyond probably what you or I can analyze, but it's there and it's naked. If you've got your head on straight enough, you can see right into it. There's no hiding who you are when you create music. I could sit here and say I love Jimi Hendrix and Jimmy Page. Sure, they inspired me, but what brought me to be turned on by that music? Attitude is a big part of the way you play. I practiced endlessly when I was young. I still do, but what I do *now* is the way I feel *now*. An event that happens tomorrow could completely change the way you approach everything. You could have the same equipment and know the same scales, exercises, and bends, but they're going to sound completely different. You're a different person.

So your personal relationships have more impact on your style than other musicians do.

Exactly. There was a point in my teens where I thought it was really cool to be miserable and hate things and think that people were assholes, because then people gave me my space. And then I realize that it was just an act of my ego and that I was becoming a miserable person. The world started to take on an ugly glow. I reached a point in life where, through the grace of God, I went into a dark night of the soul. I realized that many of the things I loved to do weren't good for me, and I said I don't need this. I can play you tapes that I made back then, and you wouldn't believe the same cat was doing it. "Chronic Insomnia" [*Leftovers*] came out of that period, as well as darker things that I can't even bring myself to listen to. And that stuff wasn't an accident — I could duplicate it for years. But I don't want to go there anymore; there are other places I can go now. I was very lucky to have supportive people around me. My parents were the greatest. God bless them. Going on the road with Frank Zappa at such a young age was a bit traumatic, but I started appreciating other people's efforts. I began to realize that you have to be compassionate to the way anybody expresses himself and try to hone in on the beautiful things that a person tries to do. I became a happier person, and I was able to relate to people better.

What are the drawbacks of being a rock guitar hero?

Well, I never really saw myself that way, so it's hard for me to comment. There are so many great players, I can't consider myself a hero. I'm a reckless player. I'm sloppy sometimes, but I *love* playing. It's very hard for me at times, and then sometimes it's so easy, I just lose my mind. The kids are going to listen to what I do, and if they like it, they'll try to cop some of it. And then they're going to realize that this is the starting point, and that they've got to take it a lot higher than this. So to stroke myself and say, "I'm a guitar hero" will be very embarrassing in the future when somebody comes along and does what I'm doing at a technically infinite level.

What do you think the future holds for rock guitar?

I can visualize what the next step could be, but I'm not sure I can explain it. It's an approach where there's no technical or physical limitations — except, of course, the impossible ones. This kid might be in kindergarten or whatever, but somebody's going to come along who thinks of something like speed with a completely different attitude than what everybody thinks of it now. Speed is just going to be a silly device to make a very serious point. I could even see myself doing it, but it would take *total* concentration for a long period of time to develop this new approach. This person will do things that nobody else is doing, whether it be with unequivocal speed, vibrato bar work, a new device that could be put on a guitar, or a new piece of outboard gear. It could be anything. But it will take *imagination* and a certain personality. And then, of course, everybody will jump on it.

What are your views on young players mimicking their favorite guitarists?

Jumping on something right away and copying it verbatim shows you where you're standing. It's an insecurity statement. I don't want to freak anybody out, but it's saying, "I can't come up with things on my own. I've got to grab this." This is not to say that it's not beneficial to cop somebody else's stuff. I've copped a lot of Hendrix; that's how I got the basic foundation of my whole way of approaching chords. But there's a fine line between inspiration and loss of identity. That's something kids should be really careful of. Ask yourself; you'll always know. When you're doing it, there's a little voice that's telling you whether it's the right thing to do, or whether you're doing too much of it. You've got to listen to that voice and believe it. It's always fun to do what somebody else is doing, and maybe even play it faster or with more vibrato, but still, you're better than that because you're your own person and you can be original.

What's your ultimate goal?

My goal in life is to be internally happy. I love music, but there's other things. To sit here and say, "Well, my goal is to have my own studio to make my own records" — that's petty. I can make my own music on a cassette player if I want. One match, and the whole studio is gone. One axe, and my hand is off. One car accident, and I might never see you again. I accept that these things are possible, but believe me, I have a great time in life. I very much appreciate being able to do what I like. You might laugh, but if I wasn't a musician, I probably wouldn't mind being a mailman. Look at it — you get to exercise. You get to walk in the rain and sun; you meet people. It's your attitude that's going to make you happy. It's awfully nice to know that you can make somebody else happy, too, but the only way that you can do that is to make yourself happy.

When all is said and done, your sense of humor seems to be at the very heart of your playing.

Good. I don't want people to think I'm too serious. All the musicians who are reading this have a sense of humor. Apply it to your music. That's where all the diversity comes from.

— EDDIE VAN HALEN —

BY JAS OBRECHT — APRIL 1980

JON SIEVERT

FEW GUITARISTS have had as intense an impact as Eddie Van Halen. The sparkplug of the band that bears his family name, he exploded into ears around the world in February 1978 with the release of *Van Halen*. On this debut album, Eddie wrestled devastating feedback, kamikaze vibrato moans, sustained harmonics, white-hot leads, and liquid screams out of a cranked-to-the-max homemade guitar that combined a Fender Strat-style body with the electronics of a Gibson Les Paul. Even on this first effort, underneath the raw intensity of Eddie's solos — many of which were spontaneous first takes — lies a strong melodic and rhythmic sensitivity.

Born in Holland where he was a serious classical piano student, Eddie immigrated with his family to the United States in 1967. Over the next decade he developed and refined a guitar style unheard of before and showcased it boldly in his band, appropriately called Van Halen, which included his brother Alex on percussion, Michael Anthony on bass, and David Lee Roth as vocalist. The immediate success of *Van Halen* catapulted the group on a 10-month world tour, during which Eddie stunned audiences with his seemingly off-hand ability to instantaneously convey to his fingers what he heard in his head. He toted a suitcase full of guitar parts with him, building and fixing instruments in his spare time.

By the end of 1978, companies had cloned his trademark guitar, players had begun borrowing his

licks, and Eddie had walked away with *Guitar Player's* Best New Talent poll award. Platinum albums and poll awards worldwide became the norm.

Accolades were not limited to record buyers and poll balloters in the U.S. and abroad, though; players, too, began acclaiming his guitar wizardry. Ted Nugent proclaimed him "a fantastic guitarist." Cheap Trick's Rick Nielsen discussed Van Halen's deft use of the vibrato bar. Pat Travers declared Van Halen the state-of-the-art rock guitarist, adding, "I don't think there's anybody better for saying more, getting a better sound, or just taking advantage of the straight Stratocaster-style sound." Frank Zappa thanked Eddie for "reinventing the electric guitar."

With the enthusiasm of a mad scientist ready to pull the switch, he continues his quest for weird sounds, using his guitar to duplicate a prop plane revving up, shaking his bass *E* string against the pickup to heighten the intensity of a passage, and banging away on an electric piano hooked up to his pedalboard and Marshall stacks.

When you started playing guitar, how much time did you spend with it?

All day, every day. I used to cut school to come home and play. I was so into it.

Were you self-taught?

Definitely for guitar. I never had a lesson in my life, except when a friend of mine a long time ago showed me how to do barre chords. I just learned from there.

How did you teach yourself leads?

[*Duplicates Eric Clapton's solo in "Crossroads" from Cream's* Wheels of Fire *LP*]. I know that song note-for-note, and also "I'm So Glad" [*Fresh Cream*] and the live version of "Sitting on Top of the World" [*Cream, Goodbye*]. I used to know all that stuff.

Did your brother Alex jam along on drums while you were learning?

Actually, I started playing drums first. I bought the Sufaris' "Wipe Out." I loved that song, and said, "I'm going to go out and buy myself a $125 St. George drum set." So I got a paper route to pay for it. I'm out throwing the paper — five in the morning, in the rain, with a bicycle with a flat tire — and my brother is practicing on my drums. He got better, so I said, "You take my drums."

Is this when you got your first guitar?

Yeah. It was a $70 Teisco Del Ray electric with four pickups. I used to think, man, the more pickups, the better. And look at what I've got now! One pickup and one knob.

How did you develop your speed?

Well, I'll tell you. They used to lock me in a little room and go, "Play fast!" [*laughs*]. I was actually trained to be a classical pianist. I had this Russian teacher who couldn't speak a word of English, and he would just sit there with a ruler ready to slap my face if I made a mistake. This started in Holland, and both my brother and I took lessons. Then when we got to the U.S. my dad found another good teacher. Basically, that's where I got my ears developed, learned my theory, and got my fingers moving. Then when the Dave Clark Five and those bands came out, I wanted to go [*plays the riff from "You Really Got Me"*]. I didn't want to go clink, clink, clink. I still play piano, and I also play violin.

Did your piano study influence your guitar playing?

Things like this are classical [*plays the continuous left-hand tremolo technique from "Spanish Fly"*]. I know that had something to do with piano. I'm sure some things psychologically come out, but I don't actually sit down at a piano and try to apply it to guitar.

What are your views on using a vibrato bar?

It's more of a feeling as opposed to an effect. I don't really use it for freak-out effects; I use it to enhance a little more feeling. I really don't have any special chops with it. I just grab it when I feel like it. It calls for a totally different technique. I have special

tricks for keeping it in tune, but it still goes out. You have to play with it. Like if you bring the bar down, the G and B strings always go sharp when you let it back, so before you hit a barre chord you have to stretch those strings back with a real quick little jerk. The vibrato is actually like another instrument. You can't just grab it and jerk the thing and expect it to stay in tune.

How do you keep tuned while using a standard vibrato?

It's a combination of a lot of things. For one, some manufacturers don't keep in mind that the distance from the bridge to the machine heads has got to be a straight line so that the string windings won't get caught anywhere. A lot of people drill the machine holes off center, and the strings get caught up. I have extra-wide notches in the nut, and string trees for only the high E and B strings. I also set the vibrato bar so I can only bring it down; you can't pull back on it. See, I rest the palm of my hand on the bridge, so if I use a standard vibrato, I sound like a warped record. Sometimes I'll bring the bar down before I hit a note and then let it up.

What's the advantage of playing with your hand on the bridge?

I like getting a muffled effect with the side of my hand. It gets more tone. It's a definite texture you can use in combination with straight picking.

How do you hold your pick?

Between my thumb and middle finger. Sometimes when I play fast I'll put the tip of my index finger on the corner of the pick.

Do you ever use your other fingers to pick?

No. I can't fingerpick for anything. I've never had the time.

Did you use a pick for "Spanish Fly"?

Yeah, except for the part near the end that sounds like Montoya or something.

Do you ever use the side of your pick to get high-pitched harmonics?

Sometimes. I do it in "I'm the One" [*Van Halen*]. I also get harmonics by hitting a note with my left-hand finger while I tap my right index finger on the fingerboard exactly one octave up. When it's an exact octave, you bring out the harmonic plus the lower note.

Do you tap right on top of the fret wire or behind it?

On the fret, I guess. Like in "Spanish Fly" I start out by tapping harmonics and then do hammer-ons and pull-offs with my left hand while I tap above with my right-hand index fingertip. Now this is my latest: I hammer-on and pull-off with my left hand

and reach behind my left hand with my right and use my right index finger below my left hand, so that it acts as a sixth finger. In other words, my right-hand finger changes the lowest note. See, the way I play is in my fingers. I could play a Strat or a Les Paul, and it's going to sound like me. People say, "Oh, how do you get that sound?" They could play my guitar and it wouldn't sound the same. I have a style of playing where no matter what amp or guitar I use, it sounds like me.

How far can you reach on the fingerboard?

On the high *E* string I can reach from the 5th fret to the 12th. From the 12th fret I can hit any note on the fingerboard above. That's how I get weird noises.

Are you learning new things on the guitar all the time?

Yeah. Like if I sit down and play by myself I play completely different than I would with the band. I just really go for feeling in my playing. All our albums have mistakes — big deal, we're human. But they reek of feeling, and that, to me, is what music is all about. It's not like Fleetwood Mac — you know, they spend so much time and money on their albums. I think that if something is too perfect, it won't faze you. It'll go in one ear and out the other because it's so perfect. Like our stuff, to me, keeps you on the edge of your seat. It builds tension whether you like it or not. It slaps you in the face.

Like in "Ice Cream Man" [Van Halen] where the band comes in?

Exactly. It's almost like you're just waiting for us to blow it — waiting for something to go wrong, but it doesn't. That's what creates the feel, the tension: Just like winding something up and waiting to see when it's going to break. It's just inner feeling coming out; it's not conscious. The way I play is the way I am.

When you're playing onstage, what do you think about?

Nothing. It's like having sex, actually. I swear to God. It's definitely my first love. Got in a fight with my girlfriend before. I used to go over to her house and play my guitar in her bedroom, and she'd go, "You love your guitar more than you do me!" And I'd go, "You're right!" Hey, I'm sorry — it's a part of me.

How many times a day do you pick up a guitar?

All the time. Sometimes I play it for a minute, sometimes half an hour, and sometimes all day. There's no schedule; I don't run by schedules at all. Usually I play before I go to sleep, when I wake up, when I come home, when I'm bored.

What do you look for in a solo?

Feeling. I don't care if it's melodic or spontaneous. If it's melodic and has no feeling, it's screwed.

What should a good rock and roll song do?

Move you in any way. Depress you, make you happy, make you horny, make you rowdy. Anything. If it doesn't, it's like Fleetwood Mac! Excuse me, I should point out that I love *Rumours* — that's a hot album. I don't consider myself a songwriter to begin with. I've written songs on the piano, but they're not Van Halen. It's very easy to write a song on the piano. You just pick some chords and squeeze a melody out of it; I learned that in school. So when I write on guitar I always come up with a theme riff — you know, some powerful opener — and then a verse, a chorus, a bridge, and solo, back to the bridge, chorus, and then the end.

How do you decide what to do with the solo?

Sometimes it's spontaneous, sometimes it's set. Like the solo in "Runnin' with the Devil" [*Van Halen*] was set. And the same with "Ain't Talkin' 'Bout Love" [*Van Halen*]. By "set" I mean that I figured out something melodic instead of just going for it. When I wrote "Ain't Talkin' 'Bout Love" I thought it was about the lamest song I ever wrote in my life. It took me six months before I even worked up the nerve to show the guys, but kids go nuts for it! I love the beginning — *Am* and *G*.

What were some of your spontaneous solos?

"Ice Cream Man" was one — that was a first take. The solo in "You Really Got Me" was totally spontaneous. Next time you listen to it, turn the balance to one side, because the way Ted [Templeman] produces, my guitar is always on one side. Listen to it — there's only one guitar, no overdubs. But it sounds full.

Do you repeat solos from night to night, or do you change them around?

I rarely repeat. Sometimes I remember the way I did it on the record and kind of follow it, unless they are melodic solos like in "Runnin' with the Devil" and "Ain't Talkin' 'Bout Love." You know, if I start noodling around, kids go, "Hey, that ain't the same song!"

Are there some songs you stretch out on in concert?

"Feel Your Love Tonight" [*Van Halen*]. My guitar solo without the band, definitely "Eruption," [*Van Halen*]. "You Really Got Me" ends with a long jam.

It sounds like a lot of your solos are built off of lines rather than chords.

Well, the thing is, in rock and roll you only have so many chords. If you start hitting chords like this [plays 7ths and 9ths] in rock and roll, forget it! They have emotion, but they don't fit power rock. They're so dissonant that the vibrations of the overtones with that much distortion sound like shit. That's why most rock and roll songs are simple — straight major or minor chords. You start dickin' with chords like the 7ths and 9ths through a blazing Marshall, and it will sound like crap. It's very tough to come up with an interesting solo when you're just in one key. But see, there are ways to get around it — you can be playing in E and you can solo in D. There are certain chords that are relative to the key you're playing in, like in the key of A you can play around an F#m.

You seem to end a lot of phrasings with a blues feeling.

Yeah, well. I started out playing blues — the *Blues Breakers* album where Eric Clapton's on the front reading the Beano comic book. I can play real good blues — that's the feeling I was after. But actually I've turned it into a much more aggressive thing. Blues is a real tasty, feel type of thing; so I copped that in the beginning. But then when I started to use a wang bar [vibrato], I still used that feeling, but rowdier, more aggressive, more attack. But still, I end a lot of phrasing with a bluesy feeling. I like phrasing; that's why I always liked Clapton. He would just play it with feeling. It's like someone talking, a question-and-answer trip.

How do you warm up before going on stage?

Just scales. Fast or slow, depending on how cold my fingers are.

Do you put new strings on every night?

Yeah. I stretch them to death. With that new Rose thing, I boil the strings so they stretch, because if you just put them on and clamp it down, the strings stretch out on the guitar. I just take a pack and let it boil for 20 minutes in the hot water. And then I dry them in the sun, because otherwise they rust. But I only use them one night anyway, so who cares if they rust?

Do you experiment with open tunings?

No, because that's kind of a rule, too, that's been done. I don't care that much about things that have been done, where most players have only done what's been done. They look at the guitar as if that's all it's for. They don't even go beyond to think. Like they don't know how I get some of the weird noises I make, but it's just the guitar. Just do anything to it! I could drop a guitar and get a noise out of it. The guitar is not designed for one purpose — you can do anything with it. I'll do my damnedest to squeeze every noise out of this thing I can.

What is your philosophy on using effects?

What I'm really into doing is squeezing anything out of the cheapest possible thing. Like whenever I get something made or built or designed I always say, "Make it as cheap as possible." I'll walk into this music store, and they go, "Oh, I got this new this; got the new digital delay or something or other," and I go, "Got anything cheaper?" Because I can get weirder noises out of them than the expensive state-of-the-art shit.

Do you feel the state-of-the-art ones have too much control in them?

They don't have enough. You pay so much, and they're so precious. You can't take them around, you can't kick them, you can't drop them. If you ever saw my pedalboard!

Let's discuss some of the parts you did on the Van Halen album. How did you do the descending growl at the end of "Eruption"?

That's a $50 Univox EC-80 echo box, a real cheap thing that works off a cartridge. It's like a miniaturized 8-track cartridge. One day some kid turned me on to it and all of a sudden I hit a note, turned it all the way up, and got that growl. I go, "Whoa!" So I mounted it in an old World War II practice bomb that I picked up in a junkyard. I've read reviews in papers that have said, "Eddie Van Halen with a synthesizer solo." Actually, all it is a $50 piece of junk.

Did you plan the solo in "I'm on Fire"?

No. It's so funny — I wanted to do a melodic solo and the guys go, "Pretend you're John McLaughlin!" So then that solo came out. I don't even know what key I'm playing in! I just started playing and it fit perfect. That's how a lot of it works — totally spontaneous. It's not like I decided "I'm going to start here and end up there."

How did you get that scratchy sound in "Atomic Punk"?

A phase shifter was on, and I rubbed the strings by the bridge with the heel of my hand — I've got calluses on it. I do the same thing on "Everybody Wants Some" [*Women and Children First*]. I just love doing weird things.

What's the sound at the opening of "Runnin' with the Devil?"

Car horns. We took the horns out of all our cars — my brother's Opel, my old Volvo, ripped a couple out of a Mercedes and a Volkswagen — and mounted them in a box and hooked two car batteries to it and added a footswitch. We just used them as noisemakers before we got signed. Ted put it on tape, slowed it down, and then we came in with the bass. It sounds like a jet landing.

How many tracks did you use for "Ain't Talkin' 'Bout Love"?

Two. I soloed on the basic track, and if you listen real closely on one channel, I overdubbed the solo with an electric sitar.

In the solo section of "You Really Got Me," there's a staccato part that sounds like a car lurching. It's right before Dave starts in with the "Ooohs" and "Ahhs."

Yeah. I hit the G string at the 7th fret and bent it up to [the note] G and flicked my toggle switch back and forth.

Was there much of a difference in how the first and second albums were recorded?

I don't think we spent as much time on *Van Halen II.* We toured from the second week in February until December 5, 1978, and then on December 10th we went into the studio. We didn't spend as much time getting the sound. I like the guitar, but I'm not particularly pleased with the drum sound. I like the drum sound on the first album much better.

On the songs "Somebody Get Me A Doctor" and "You're No Good" you have an effect that sounds like a volume pedal.

That's just the knob of the guitar.

Did you double-track that harmonic intro to "Women in Love?"

Yeah, I played it twice. It sounds like a harmonizer, and live I get the same effect using the harmonizer. I like that chime, clock-like sound.

How long did it take you to cut Women and Children First?

We finished the music in six days, and the whole album took eight. I don't understand how people can take any longer. I'd say we did it for between $30,000 and $40,000.

What is the strange effect at the beginning of "And the Cradle Will Rock"? It resembles the sound of a prop plane starting up.

I pinged my strings above the nut and asked Ted to play it backwards so the attack comes at the end of the note. In conjunction with this, I scraped the springs in the back of my guitar. I also took my vibrato bar all the way down so that the strings were limp and then with my left thumb I flapped the low E string around the 3rd fret. Sounds great; I love it.

Is there a piano later on in that song?

Yeah, it's a Wurlitzer electric piano that I ran through my MXR flanger and my Marshalls. I just

banged on the keys — broke two of them doing it. Who would ever think of doing anything that lame? But it sounds good. You could never tell I had classical training on piano. I bought that piano in Detroit and started pounding on it one night in the bus and wrote "And the Cradle Will Rock."

How did you do the clicking sound in the middle of "Romeo's Delight"?

I shook my low E string against the pickup.

What kind of a 12-string did you overdub in "Simple Rhyme"?

It's a Rickenbacker electric. At first it didn't sound right through my amp, and I asked Ted, "Can you doctor it up later in the mix?" Then I told him to forget it. I wanted to make it good out of the amp before it's recorded. My theory is if it doesn't sound good coming out of the speaker box, it ain't going to happen on tape.

How did you come to play acoustic slide on "Could This Be Magic"?

They just handed me a guitar and a slide and said, "Come on, you can do it." I said, "Okay, I'll do my best." And I never in my life ever even played slide before! I'm going, "No, let me practice," and the guys said, "Come on, man, just play." I pulled it off decent. I think I used an old Gibson acoustic, and it was in standard tuning.

Your part almost sounds Hawaiian.

Yeah, it does. It almost sounds like Andy Griffith on the front porch. We wanted to get a horse in there at the end, or a cow going "Moooo." That song is funny as hell! That's one thing — slide never interested me, because you're going like that [*moves little finger up and down fingerboard*]. Why? I like to use all my fingers.

You don't have an instrumental on this LP.

No. What for? Maybe later on I'll do one if I figure out some finger thing that's just totally different. "Eruption" was the first one, and then the second one I did was in a flamenco style ["Spanish Fly"], but it was still the same type of thing. And what could I do this time? I didn't want to do one just for the sake of doing another solo, so I'm going to wait until I have something really good. Something that sounds classical — electric or acoustic — like some Bach stuff. I've been listening to a lot of classical music, especially Debussy. God damn, that mother wrote some hot shit!

Has seeing other guitarists ever inspired a change in your playing?

Allan Holdsworth — that guy is bad! He's fantastic; I love him. He's got a rock *sound.* I love his solo in "In the Dead of the Night" on the *U.K.* album. I love the solo in "Hell's Bells" on *One of a Kind*. [Drummer] Bill Bruford plays hot on that album. Holdsworth is the best in my book. I can kind of play like him, but it doesn't fit our style of music. He's a real artist. He plays a guitar like mine, too. He wears it up high, like a jazz guitar. I could play all that stuff, too, if I played with my guitar up that high, but how would a rock and roll kid look with a guitar up like that? I do have to sacrifice the amount of movement I do onstage for the way I play. I like playing much better on a stool. I don't do it, though, not even in the studio, because then it would sound like I'm sitting on a stool.

So the movement of your body is really tied in with the way you play?

Definitely. 100%. I never do anything the same. I have no choreographed steps where I have to be in any part of a song. I'm wherever I want and do whatever I want whenever I feel it.

What do you think when you hear other players using your licks?

I guess they always say that imitation is the highest form of flattery. I think this is a crock of shit. I don't like people doing things exactly like me. Some of the things I do I know no one has done, like the harmonic runs and the clock chime-like sound. The "Eruption" solo — I never heard anything done like that before, but I know someone must have figured some of it out. What I don't like is when someone takes what I've done, and instead of innovating on what I came up with, they do my trip! They do my melody. Like I learned from Clapton, Page, Hendrix, Beck — but I don't play like them. I innovated; I learned from them and did my own thing out of it. Some of those guys out there are doing my thing, which I think is a lot different.

Do you feel that your playing is constantly progressing?

I don't think it's ever progressed — just gets weirder all the time. How much can you progress? I'm as fast as I can possibly get. I can't picture myself being too much faster. I mean, you can only hear so much. What I'm trying to do is be weirder and different.

Do you get in slumps?

Yes and no. You always reach a plateau, and then moving up from there is a bit tough. But for me it's not that hard.

How do you do it?

Just continue to play and play and try different chops. It's especially hard for me after touring for ten months and playing the same songs. Now, depending on the beat of the song, I play differently. I'm a very rhythmically oriented guitarist; I really work off of rhythm, so if the song's fast, I play a certain way. If it's blues, I play completely different. So if I do the same set for almost a whole year, I get into a rut of that style, and it takes me a month or two to change and come up with new things. That's my rut.

— STEVIE RAY VAUGHAN —

BY DAN FORTE – OCTOBER 1984

JON SIEVERT

HE DIDN'T JUST play his guitar, he *mauled* it — as evidenced by the nonexistent finish and 1/4"-deep scratches on the face of his battered '59 Fender Strat. By the end of a Stevie Ray Vaughan set, he would have played the guitar behind his head, off his shoulder like a violin, behind his back, and on the floor — standing over the cutaways with one hand firmly on the guitar's neck, the other pulling up on the vibrato bar. By the end of his life in 1990 — in a tragic helicopter accident following a concert while on tour with Eric Clapton and Robert Cray — Stevie Ray had won the adulation of a world of fans, but more importantly the respect of his very mentors — Hubert Sumlin, Albert Collins, Lonnie Mack, and Buddy Guy to name just a few.

While making vintage guitar collectors wince and teachers moan, Stevie Ray gave the biggest exposure in years to one of the most fundamental but unsung musical forms: The blues. And with every achievement and accolade he received after he burst onto the charts on David Bowie's critically acclaimed album *Let's Dance*, he shared his honors with the bluesmen who preceded him and with the genre itself. "Most of all, I'm glad to see the blues getting the recognition it deserves," he emphasized on more than one occasion.

After being lifted out of the Austin, Texas, blues scene to play on *Let's Dance*, Stevie Ray went back to his hometown group, Double Trouble, and teamed up with A&R legend John Hammond to produce *Texas Flood*, which took top honors in *Guitar Player's* 1983 Readers Poll as Best Guitar Album. In the same balloting, Vaughan racked up two more blue ribbons — completely dominating the New Talent category and edging out no less than Eric Clapton as Best Electric Blues player — to become the first triple-crown winner since Jeff Beck's 1976 hat trick. Over the next six years he ended up with a total of eight *Guitar Player* Readers poll awards.

With *Texas Flood* still selling strongly, Double Trouble released *Couldn't Stand the Weather*, which hit the *Billboard* pop chart on June 13, 1984 at #144, leaped up to #63 in its second week, and bulleted to 37 and 31 in the following two weeks. "What happened, I guess," he drawled, "is that we've come from playing clubs to where we can pretty much fill a 5,000-seat hall now. We just worked our butts off."

And play he did — too hard for a time with alcohol and drugs, problems which he kicked — but never too hard with the music he left in the ears of the world and the albums on which he can still be heard: Solo works with Double Trouble such as *Texas Flood*, *Couldn't Stand the Weather*, *Soul to Soul*, *Live Alive*, and *In Step*, but also as a guest on albums of his older brother Jimmie Vaughan with the Fabulous Thunderbirds, Bob Dylan, Jennifer Warnes, David Bowie, Lonnie Mack, and others.

Vaughan's popularity is as worthy of scrutiny as his phenomenal guitar playing. While numerous blues-based rockers have become guitar heroes after crossing over to the rock camp — including Clapton, Michael Bloomfield, and Jimi Hendrix — Stevie was the first since fellow Texan Johnny Winter (who also eventually drifted into out-and-out rock and roll) to make the major leagues by sticking with the blues. His videos of "Love Struck Baby" (from *Flood*), "Couldn't Stand the Weather," and "Cold Shot" (from *Weather*) were in steady rotation on MTV's playlist, and "Pride and Joy" (from his debut LP) received substantial airplay on FM stations. He teamed with George Thorogood for a tribute to Chuck Berry at the 1984 Grammy awards, and appeared on such unlikely TV shows as *Solid Gold*.

Most people's first exposure to Stevie Ray's searing solos, of course, was via Bowie's *Let's Dance*. But even though the material was not the type of R&B he had mined in Texas bars for more than a decade, Vaughan's razor-edged leads were pure blues, relying heavily on Albert King for tones and riffs. *Texas Flood* revealed a debt to blues masters such as Jimmy Reed, Magic Sam, Lonnie Mack, Buddy Guy, and Hubert Sumlin, and paid that debt with interest. On tour in support of the album — opening for coliseum acts such as Men at Work, the Moody Blues, Huey Lewis and The News, and the Police — Stevie riveted audiences with his passionate homages to Jimi Hendrix, including "Voodoo Chile," "Little Wing," and "Third Stone from the Sun."

While countless guitarist have been influenced by the creative genius of Hendrix, few have attempted to cover any of his songs. There are several obvious similarities between Vaughan and the late southpaw — each led a trio, had incredible control of feedback and volume with a minimum of effects devices, and could sing adequately but not well enough to make it strictly as a vocalist. But what set Stevie above other pretenders to the Hendrix throne was his ability to play lead and rhythm simultaneously — like Jimi, he fired a nonstop barrage of chords, licks, hammer-ons, pull-offs, and unorthodox tricks at the listener. Vaughan's guitar technique didn't just impress; it *overwhelmed*.

Instrumentals such as "Rude Mood" (*Texas Flood*), and "Scuttle Buttin'" (*Weather*) are textbook studies of the pedal-to-the-metal Vaughan style, while "Lenny" (*Flood*) is reminiscent of Hendrix' most sensitive ballads, and "Stang's Swang" (*Weather*) reveals a firm grounding in organ-trio guitarists such as Kenny Burrell, Grant Green, and early George Benson.

Unlike many other guitar-based trios, Double Trouble overdubbed next to nothing in the studio; the 12-inch pieces of vinyl are still accurate representations of the sort of thing Vaughan & Co. played onstage from the time the band formed in 1978 until the night Vaughan climbed in for his last flight home. Stevie was only 35 when he died, but his impact will be felt and heard for generations to come.

When you first took up guitar, was it blues that you were mainly attracted to?

A lot — because of my brother Jimmie. He'd bring home records by B.B. and Buddy Guy. And he was the one who hit me with Lonnie Mack, too; the first record I ever bought was *The Wham of That Memphis Man*. Jimmie brought home a Hendrix record, and I went, "Whoa! What is this?" I'll never forget that.

Did Jimmie show you things on guitar, or did you just pick up things from hearing him around the house?

At first, he taught me a couple of things, and then he taught me how to teach myself — and that's the right way.

Your brother was heavily influenced by another Texas bluesman, Freddie King. Did that style rub off on you as well?

Yeah, it did. I had that instrumental album of his, *Let's Hide Away and Dance Away*. Jimmie used to know him pretty well, but Freddie wouldn't talk to me in public. In private, but not in public. I guess I was a young white boy he didn't want to be seen with [*laughs*]. I played with him once, sitting around a table when no one else was around.

What specifics did you get from various players?

I got a lot of the fast things I do from Lonnie Mack — just the ideas and the phrasing. Like on "Scuttle Buttin": [*plays a barrage of chicken-picked pull-offs*]. That's really a Lonnie Mack thing — that's dedicated to him. I got a lot of turnarounds from Freddie King.

Who were the main blues players you heard on records?

Well, let's run 'em down. There was Buddy Guy, Muddy, of course, and all the various guitar players who were with him [including Jimmy Rogers and Pat Hare], Hubert Sumlin, Lonnie Mack, B.B., Albert King, Freddie, Albert Collins, Guitar Slim — he'd just turn it all the way up. I can just imagine people saying, "Slim, why do you always play so loud?" "Because it sounds like this" [*laughs*].

Johnny Winter was the first white Texas bluesman to make it on a big scale. Were you influenced much by him?

Yes, although I never heard him as much then. I listened more to people like Albert Collins, Albert and Freddie King, Johnny Guitar Watson. But around '71 or '72, I got to jam a lot with Johnny over at Tommy Shannon's house — that was a little bit after his initial big success.

Your playing on Let's Dance *isn't along the lines of* Texas Flood; *it's more like Albert King.*

I kind of wanted to see how many places Albert King's stuff would fit. It *always* does. I love that man. When that album first came out, Albert heard it. He said, "[*sneering*] Yeah, I heard you doin' all my shit on there. I'm gonna go up there and do some of yours" [*laughs*]. We were doing this TV show right outside of Toronto — Hamilton, I think — and during the lunch break, Albert went around to everybody in there looking for an emery board. I didn't think anything of it. We were jamming on the last song, "Outskirts of Town," and it comes to the solo, and he goes, "Get it, Stevie!" I started off and I look over and he's pulling out this damn emery board, filing his nails, sort of giving me this sidelong glance [*laughs*]. I loved it! Lookin' at me like, "Uh-huh, I got you swinging by your toes." He's a heavy cat.

Do you ever play with your thumb to get an Albert King sound?

I play with a pick and a finger. I use the round end of the pick, too. You break less of them and don't get tangled up in the strings. Sometimes I play with both together, or I'll palm the pick and use my fingers, or sometimes I'll just "Hubert" it [play with bare fingers à la Hubert Sumlin].

Is that to get a variety of tones?

Different tones, different moods. It depends on how the amps are working that night, how dead the strings are, how much I can hear, how crazy I'm feeling.

On "Cold Shot," did you play through a Leslie speaker to get that underwater sound?

It's a Fender Vibratone, which is basically like a Leslie. It's a 10" speaker with a Styrofoam rotor in front of it — so the speaker is stationary, but a drum with a slit in it revolves — and then you mike it from both sides.

On Couldn't Stand the Weather, *were there any tracks where you cut a rhythm part and overdubbed a lead, or vice versa?*

No, on some of the songs I just played and then did the vocal later — which sometimes is a mistake, because you play differently when you're not singing than you would if you were singing along. A lot of times the licks won't match the phrasing of the vocals. Most of the solos were cut live. I redid one line

in "Voodoo," because my amp went crazy on me. The punch-in didn't come off very well; it still doesn't sound right to me.

Texas Flood *sounds like there are hardly any overdubs.*

There aren't. Only if I broke a string or something.

So you played the lead and rhythm in the same take, rather than laying down a rhythm track and soloing over it later?

Right. We redid a few vocals, but some of them were live, too. That was mainly to go back if a word was left out or not real clear; plus, we got a better vocal sound by redoing them. I don't think that's cheating too much.

Was John Hammond in the studio for the first album?

No, he wasn't there at all, except for the mixdown and the mastering. This time he was there a lot for the recording.

Did that affect the recording environment much?

He wants you to sound exactly like yourself. He doesn't like you to overproduce. In other words, he does it the other way around in a way: He keeps you sounding like yourself, instead of trying to change you, like most producers do.

Do you play slide in open tuning?

I usually just tune up the G string to A♭ and leave everything else the same.

How did you go about recreating the sounds you heard on Hendrix' records?

You just keep listening and trying to find the sound, because it's in your hands as much as anything. It's the way you play. There are different techniques to playing everybody's styles, and it's not just necessarily the amp or the guitar. It's the way you pick, the way you hold the guitar. For instance, T-Bone [Walker] played like this more of the time [*holds guitar horizontally, away from his body*], and the tone is different when you play that way. Can you hear the difference? [*Holds guitar against his body and plays the same lick — gets a bassier tone.*] It's the way your fingers hit the strings, and you're more prone to pick closer to the neck when you hold the guitar like T-Bone.

Your '59 Strat has the vibrato bar anchored off the bass side of the bridge. Did you set it up that way because Jimi Hendrix' guitar bodies were upside down?

Well, I started listening to people and noticed that when Otis Rush used one, he had it on the top — he played upside-down. And Hendrix had the guitar upside-down, except he strung it regular. It seemed to me that the people who did that the best had it on top, so I moved mine. Sometimes it does get in the way. I've had it tear my sleeve halfway off.

So instead of working it with the little finger of your picking hand, it lays right in the middle of your palm.

Yeah, and I've got the springs set up so I couldn't move it with my little finger anyway. It's pretty tight, with four springs tightened all the way up. That's how I can do "Third Stone from the Sun" and still be in tune. See, I have my old Strat set up where it won't go up at all. On my newer Strats, the vibrato handles are on the bottom, in the regular place.

I have big hands and I always play barre chords with my thumb wrapped around. What happens a lot of times is my thumb will end up pushing the low E string accidentally. So the wider neck keeps me from doing that.

It's a lot easier to get under the strings when you use big strings like I do. You can work yourself to death with those little frets. Instead of the note fading out when you bend a string, it'll get bigger when you bend with the jumbo frets.

Do any of your Strats have maple necks?

Yeah, Lenny does. It's got a real clear tone, and the pickups are microphonic — you can hear it when you hit the pickguard. But when you play it soft, it sounds great. When I first got the guitar, it had a rosewood fingerboard, but it was thinner, and that bothered me. So I put a copy of a Fender maple neck on there that Billy Gibbons gave me. I like the rosewood necks usually, because for one thing, when you sweat, you don't get blisters. It seems like the finish on a maple neck gets hotter and there's more friction. As hard as I play and as much as I sweat, I get sore enough as it is. There's a fatter sound on the rosewood, as far as I can tell; it's not as bright. The ebony fretboard seems a little bit clearer, but it's fat, too.

Which guitars have you recorded with most?

Lenny on the song "Lenny," and everything else has been the '59. I'd like to record with the one with the Danelectro pickups; I like it a lot.

How do you do some of the tricks you do onstage — like getting the whole guitar behind your back so fast?

As I'm spinning around, I'm taking the strap loose and the guitar pivots behind my back, and then I rehook it behind my back. It's really playing the same way, except you've got to hold the guitar out a little bit, and you just can't see as well.

In "Third Stone from the Sun," you have the guitar laying on the stage while you straddle it, pulling up on the neck with one hand and on the wang bar with the other.

Yeah, I wouldn't recommend that anybody do that on their 335 [*laughs*]. A Stratocaster's a pretty tough thing, though. Then I figured out how to get the guitar to rumble. I put it on the middle pickup, turn the tone knob down, grab it by the wang bar, and just shake it on the floor.

With the amount of amplification you use, do you still pick fairly hard with your right hand?

Yeah, terribly. That's just how I play. Sometimes I literally pull the strings off. I can deaden a set of strings completely after one set, because I play 'em hard and do a lot of this — [*snaps bass string*] — to get bottom notes, like Albert Collins. Sometimes, though, I play really soft. That's probably the best Albert King tone I can get.

The tendency on the part of most white blues-rock artists has been to eventually drift more towards mainstream rock.

We try to keep it going in both directions. There's no reason for us to leave behind what we've got, you know, but there is a good reason to expand on it. I'd like to keep it as a trio, keep that identity, but I have nothing against playing with great horn players or keyboard players or other guitar players — or more than one drummer, even.

"Stang's Swang" is still blues, but it's a departure from the type of stuff you're known for.

I wrote that four or five years ago. I like guys like Kenny Burrell and Grant Green a lot. I like Django Rheinhardt a lot, too, and Wes [Montgomery], of course.

What's the turnaround on that song — II V's?

I don't know. I don't know what key I'm in sometimes. I just try to listen.

Are you completely self-taught when it comes to any theoretical vocabulary?

I don't know any of that stuff.

What about the chord voicings you use?

I just look for things that sound right.

So if you're playing something like, say, a diminished 7th . . .

I don't know it. I *almost* learned how to read chord charts doing some of those Bowie things. But as soon as I learned how to read the charts, they took the charts away. Most of the time, I'd listen to a couple of run-throughs while he was doing his vocals, to get an idea of where the song was going. Then I'd just figure out in my head where this Albert King lick or that Albert King lick would fit [*laughs*].

— FRANK ZAPPA —

BY TOM MULHERN – FEBRUARY 1983

WITHOUT Frank Zappa, where would popular music be? Most likely, right where it is — or very close. That is to say, his approach to music — complex, unpredictable, and often cynical — doesn't quite fit in with the pre-programmed mainstream of pop music. Elements of all types of music, including classical, jazz, disco, heavy metal, and practically every other recognizable form, are employed with equal stature in Zappa's work.

In just the last 26 years, the 51-year-old guitarist/composer/producer has completed five dozen LPs — among them double-albums — and there's a raft of material still awaiting mixdown and pressing. He has amused millions and become legendary for the finely honed (some say offensive) sense of humor in his songs. His fans are devout, although many other people simply don't like him — in many cases their opinions are formed solely upon the basis of what they've heard *about* him, rather than as a reaction to his music. (In a 1979 interview with *Record Review* magazine, he said. "Most of 'em don't know what I do, but they know my name.") On one occasion, the criticism went beyond mere displeasure: While performing in London in 1971, he was pushed from a stage by an irate member of the audience, receiving a compound leg fracture and many bruises.

While his reputation is worldwide (largely as a result of former onstage antics, biting social commentary, and his lampooning of music, musicians, and mu-sical consumers), his work has made hardly a ripple in the pop realm — which is just fine, as far as Frank is concerned. In fact, operating outside the slick, trendy format constraints of pop music — AM radio in particular — has afforded him the freedom to write and perform exactly what he wants to do, without having to drastically alter his direction every time the public's whims shift. Sure, he's had a few hits: "Don't Eat the Yellow Snow" [*Apostrophe*] "Dancin' Fool" [*Sheik Yerbouti*], "I Don't Wanna Get Drafted" [*You Are What You Is*], and of course "Valley Girl" [*Ship Arriving Too Late to Save a Drowning Witch*]. However, airplay for the overwhelming majority of his hundreds of songs has been sporadic.

As a result of his low visibility in the mainstream of Top 40 pop, one might be inclined to think that he's gone nowhere and that he's had no substantial impact on music. Wrong on both counts. With the exception of a scant few groups, Zappa has been putting out records for one of the longest stretches, and he has certainly been far more prolific than most of his contemporaries. A few of his LPs have even been certified for gold-record status. *Someone* is buying his material. He has also been responsible for some unheralded ground-breaking: In 1966, he simultaneously introduced the "concept" album and the double-album with the Mothers of Invention's debut LP, *Freak Out*. In 1968, he dared to parody the mighty Beatles' *Sgt. Pepper's Lonely Hearts Club Band* with his *We're Only in It for the Money*.

Early in his musical pursuits, Frank developed an avid interest in composers Edgard Varese, Igor Stravinsky, and Anton Webern, whose nontraditional uses of harmony and rhythmic orchestration had a profound effect on his approach to writing. In 1968, his *Lumpy Gravy* spotlighted his incorporation of various idioms, and featured 50 musicians (among them Tommy Tedesco, Al Viola,. Tony Rizzi, and Dennis Budimir), as well as a 16-piece string section. In recent years, his "serious" musical pursuits have become a prime focus of his output both on CDs and in live performances with such orchestras as the London Symphony, Pierre Boulez' Ensemble Intercontemporian, Frankfurt's Ensemble Modern, and the Los Angeles Philharmonic, and others. In September 1992, he was given the honor of a composer's lifetime when he was selected as one of four composers to have his works featured for an entire "Zappa" week in Germany during the esteemed Frankfurt Festival.

Frank also introduced elements of jazz into rock, long before it was fashionable, with his 1968 *Hot Rats* LP, and throughout his career he has brought together many well-known and soon-to-be-well-known high-caliber musicians such as Adrian Belew, bassist Jack Bruce, keyboardist George Duke, drummer Aynsley Dunbar, and violinist Jean-Luc Ponty. Frank has also made a few movies, including *200 Motels* and *Baby Snakes* (the soundtrack of the latter is due for release sometime this year), and is currently editing miles of videotape for future presentation.

What about Zappa's guitar playing? He's done a great deal, and provided the majority of the band's 6-string solos before he quit touring to devote his life to composing. Though he often downplayed his skills as a guitarist, most who have worked with him hold him in the highest esteem as an original and groundbreaking instrumentalist. He has always been a stickler for just the right tone, and thrives on a sound that laps against feedback — especially when an electric guitar was in his hands. However, he doesn't view himself as any kind of guitar hero and considers the notion almost laughable. Paradoxically, he assembled the multi-album series of instrumentals called *Shut Up 'N Play Yer Guitar* that spotlight his fingerboard excursions, and transcriptions of many of his solos have been prepared for publication under the title of *The Frank Zappa Guitar Book*. Zappa produced these as a result of thousands of requests from guitarists wanting huge doses of his playing recorded and in printed form.

Why are you such a prolific composer?

I'm different.

Do you have an inherent desire to put out a lot of records?

Well, the putting out of the material is not the desired end result. I mean, I really don't care whether it comes out; I like to hear it. I write because I am personally amused by what I do, and if other people are amused by it, then it's fine. If they're not, then that's also fine. But I do it for my own amusement. The fact that it comes out is just something that has to do with the business world, rather than the artistic world. Even if I wasn't releasing records I would still do it.

How do you budget your time between audio and video recording and composing?

The composing actually takes up the smallest amount of my time. I wish I could spend more time doing it, but for everything that you write down, that engenders 20 other mechanical procedures farther down the line that you have to go through in order to hear what you wrote. So, I've pretty much limited the amount that I write. I've already written so much that hasn't gone through all those in-between steps before it turns into music on tape, or music in the air, or whatever, that I could sit still for five years and have tons of stuff coming out.

Do you spend much time, then, working with your guitar?

Hardly ever touch it. The only time I play my guitar is when I know I'm going to tour. I practice a little bit before we go into rehearsal to get the calluses built up again. Then I play during rehearsals, and when we got out on the road, I usually practice an hour a day before each show. Once the tour is over, I don't touch it. I haven't touched my guitar for about six months.

Do you miss playing guitar at all?

In a way, yes; in a way, no. I really like the instrument and I really like to play, but when the responsibility for running the business rests on my shoulders, there isn't any time to practice. There's no time for the kind of guitar player enjoyment that the readers of your magazine might imagine a person would indulge in. If you really love the guitar, then you're going to spend every waking hour stroking the thing and playing through peculiar rituals.

Is your having to devote more of your energies to other projects besides playing guitar the reason why you have other guitarists in your band?

No. What usually happens is this: If I put another guitarist on my album, I hire that person because he plays things that I can't play. And if the music requires a certain type of performance, and the composition is the real crux of the biscuit, then you don't want to be unfair to the composition and play it yourself if you're going to play it wrong. So I get people who can do it. It's not a matter of being lazy: If there's something on a given song that I think is in my department, I'm going to play it. But if it's something that will be difficult or impossible for me to do, I'd just as soon get somebody who feels comfortable with that style and have them do it.

In concert, you often put down your guitar altogether.

Right. There's a good reason for that: I'm not a very good singer and I don't have very good breath control. And the weight of the guitar on your shoulder pushes down on your lungs. I find it easier to sing in tune with the other guys onstage if I don't have that weight on my body. It's easier to take it off, and it also allows me to give it to a roadie to tune it up, rather than be standing there with a prop like the Bruce Springsteen syndrome: Swinging your guitar around your back just so you look good with a guitar on. Why dirty-up the arrangement, which is planned to be concise and accurate, by randomly whacking a couple of chords or a couple of extra tweezy notes just because that's what everybody else would do? The music isn't designed that way. That's not the reason why I have the thing out there. It's something to make music on. And I really don't care what I look like out there as long as I can get my work done.

In generating your pieces, what comes first?

Every song is different. It could start off with just two or three words. Songs that are basically vocal-oriented, I usually start off with a story idea or just a phrase. "Baby Take Your Teeth Out" — just those words turned into a song. Other ways: You can start off with something from a sound check, where you're playing a few chords while warming up. You say, "Those chords sound good," and the next step is to decide what you're going to do with it. That's for the most basic type of material — the easy stuff where you can just hum it to the band and say, "Okay, I'm doing this, you do that, you play this beat, and you come in here." That's the easy way of putting rock and roll together. The compositions on paper are done a totally different way.

To put together the type of song where you can just hum the words, do you sit at the piano and arrange?

I very seldom touch a piano unless I'm writing stuff for orchestra. That's the only time I need it. I can just sit in an airport and write it down on paper,

too. Some of the pieces to be performed by the London Symphony were written in airports or hotel rooms, with no appliances whatsoever.

Once you get a piece composed — especially something on a grand scale such as an orchestral work — do you make a demo tape for yourself to see if you like the final composition?

No. What I usually do is come back from a tour with a briefcase full of sketches, and I'll test the parts of the harmony and the lines on the piano, refine it, and then generate a handwritten score in fairly messy condition, which I then give to the copyist I have on the payroll. He'll ink it and copy the parts, and it's done. Usually, something that complicated doesn't roll very fast, such as this orchestral stuff we've been trying to get played for about five years now.

Who will take on the expense?

Well, the entire orchestral thing is on my own budget. I've had requests from orchestras all over the world asking to play my music, but basically it comes down to one thing: They want *me* to pay for it. Because once it's recorded, they all want to get recording scale for doing it — 110 people. We're talking basically about several recording sessions for 110 people. If you were to do that in Hollywood, and say, "Okay, I'm going to do five or six sessions with 110 guys," and have them come in and sight-read it, I don't think you would get a good performance out of it.

How do you determine which guitarist in your band does what part, and do you record several solo tracks on a song and edit them together?

It depends on whether it's a studio song or a live song.

Some of your songs are mixtures of live and studio recordings.

Okay, then that's a third category. But we're talking about the solos now. In the case of a live take, I will find a solo that I like from a live performance and edit it. I wouldn't play any extra on it; I would just shorten it to fit the time frame that it's supposed to function in. And as far as the ones in the studio go, I very seldom play studio guitar solos. On the *Drowning Witch* album, the solo on "I Come from Nowhere" was a studio solo, and that was like two hours' worth of work to get a sound that I thought was suitable, and then about 20 minutes' worth of playing: Punching in or doing a take and not liking it and wiping the whole thing, or fixing part of it, or just tweezing it up.

Do you usually wait until after you've edited a part to add the effects?

Not necessarily. Sometimes I record with the effects, and sometimes they're added later. It just depends.

Steve Vai said that the "Peter Gunn" sounding guitar in "Teenage Prostitute" [Drowning Witch] sounded much different after it was mixed than when he recorded it.

We can change the sound of just about anything, because we have a lot of sound-modifying tools in the studio. When you arrange something, the arrangement is always modified by what comes before it or after it on a side. If you want the side to play smoothly, you may equalize all the different parts of a tune to sound one way, but when you start mixing a whole side — that's what we do: We start on song one and work through to the end to make the continuity work in terms of the tonal quality of the whole side, sometimes we have to change things around drastically.

Then you don't follow a brittle-sounding song with a mushy one.

Right. You want to smooth-out the whole spectrum so that when a person puts the needle down at the beginning of the record, they feel that there's a continuity through the whole side. It just makes it easier to listen to.

What prompted you to put out the book of solo transcriptions?

There were lots of requests for it. We've got over a thousand postcards from people interested in that type of music. It's really thick; it looks just like a little telephone book. And that's not even all the stuff that's on the guitar albums.

Your music embraces satire and complex rhythmic and harmonic concepts. Where do you derive your ideas from? Do you watch a lot of TV or hang out in unusual settings?

I do not hang out anywhere but my own house, and the TV I get to watch is usually the late-night stuff. And I like to watch the news.

Do you have any favorite contemporary musicians?

No.

Are there any that you severely dislike?

No. I think that if a person is making music — even if it's the most crass, commercial kind of crud — that person should be doing that because there are people who want to consume crass, commercial crud. And they're doing a necessary function for the audience that needs to be entertained. Just because I'm not the consumer of that stuff, it's no reason for me to go on some big campaign against it. I don't think

it's particularly aesthetic, but then again, if it's providing enjoyment for somebody, then fine.

So for you it's easier to ignore it.

Well, I'm not a consumer of pop music. I don't listen to the radio. I don't go to see groups; I don't buy albums. I've got too much other stuff to do; that world is not for me. I'm not interested.

How important do you think the video medium is becoming for music?

It's becoming more important for the people who own the cable companies because the artists who are doing the video things are being ripped off. And here's how the rip-off works: If you're a person who has a band, and you make a video, you do this because you think if you get your video on TV, everybody will go out and buy your album and think you're fantastic. And this myth is perpetuated by cable companies who show these things, but they don't pay you. And it costs lot of money to make these videos.

They don't have to pay ASCAP or BMI for performance rights?

Well, when you consider what it costs to make a video versus what they have to pay any performing rights society, you can see it's not even close. Look, a decent-looking video is going to cost you $40,000 or $50,000; some groups have spent $150,000 for just a few minutes' worth of video. So, the way it usually goes, some record companies will put up the money to begin with, to make the video. But that's only like going to the bank to get a loan, because the *real* cost of the video comes out of the artist's pocket. The record company deducts all that out of the artist's royalties, if there are any. Before the artist sees a nickel for his work, the record company makes sure they get their investment back for making the video. The artist is really the one who has to pay for that advertising, ultimately. And in most record contracts, any money that is spent promoting the product comes out of the artist's pocket — usually by some roundabout accounting method. They cover it up, but you're paying. No record company does you any favors. Then, to add insult to injury, the cable companies that show these things never give any money for this material. And what it does for them is fill up their air time with colorful pieces of videotape and they get to sell commercials; they get revenues from advertisers who want to have their spots included in the middle of all this colorful musical videotape menagerie, and the cable company gets a free ride.

And their production costs are zip.

That's right. All they do is sit there and wait for

the cassettes to roll in, because all these groups want to get their things on TV. They think, "Oh, boy, we're really going to be famous now." And they're getting hosed.

So the only one benefiting, then, is the guy sitting at home watching.

Well, no. Because he doesn't make any money from it. The cable company that sells commercials for the thing is really benefiting, and the guy sitting at home may or may not get any benefit from it because the cable company is only going to show those videos that are tame — within a certain framework. You know, the weirder stuff never gets on. It's the same as the control they have on AM radio. It's all formatted to look and feel a certain way.

How do you think the video medium will affect guitarists in general?

If you have to function in a visual medium, you're going to wind up doing things that *look* good instead of sound good. I mean, you can be playing the most beautiful music in the world, but if you're just sitting there like a lump, that really doesn't stimulate the video viewer, nor does it stimulate the guy who programs the videotapes. And it probably won't even get on the air.

So it's time to do cartwheels.

That's right. Make faces, jump up and down . . .

What do you think of the fire-breathing young guitar players who play in the Randy Rhoads vein?

Randy Rhoads was my son Dweezil's favorite guitar player. He really loved Randy. For the people who love that kind of music, there should be those types of guitar players doing that kind of stuff to entertain them.

Do you think young guitarists who start out learning every flashy technique are missing anything by not learning basics such a blues à la Elmore James?

Well, Elmore James is an acquired taste, and I happen to really like Elmore James, and I like all blues-type guitar players and all that sort of stuff. I happen to think that what they play really means something, as opposed to most of what happens on most rock and roll records — it's very calculated sound effects that fit the song. But to say that a person has to start with Elmore James before he graduates up to fire-breathing guitar playing status is stupid, because you really don't need to. If you don't have any feeling for that type of music, why involve yourself with it? I would rather see a guitar player totally ignore that realm of music in an honest way — saying, "That's just not my stuff" than get a cursory

glance of it and say, "Now I understand it," because they'll just do a parody of it. You've really got to love that stuff. I really hope that one of these days that sort of blues comes back. Everything else comes back. And I think that kind of music is great.

But the recording of the great bulk of original old blues material isn't that great.

Well, I'm not talking about re-releasing those old things. I'm talking about the idea that a person can stand up there with a guitar and just play blues on it. Not just play flash and trash, but play the fucking blues, because it's good to listen to.

What do you think would be a good guitar and amp complement for a beginning guitarist?

Depends on what kind of music they want to play. If they want to be a fire-breathing guitar player, they go out and get a Marshall 100-watt and turn it all the way up. And a Stratocaster — all the way up. What else do they need? Playing music is different, though. If you're just going to get started in that rock and roll world, that's the way it goes.

What kind of hours do you generally keep?

I work until I can't stand it, and then I go to sleep. It varies from day to day. I've been working a few 20-hour days recently, but it's settled down to a mild 12 hours in the last couple of days.

Do you foresee any way that musicians can avoid being burned by a record company?

No. Not unless that musician also happens to he a combination of expert lawyer and maybe a billionaire. Because the only way you can fight a record company is to be able to afford the legal battle that they'll whip on you. A company as big as Warner Bros. has lawyers from here to Pacoima. And all they do is smother you in paperwork, and then you have to wait five years before you go to court.

Of the many guitarists that you hired in recent years — Adrian Belew, Warren Cuccurullo, and Ray White — what did you like about each one that made you want them in your lineup?

Adrian Belew, I thought, had potential to add something to the band as it was constituted at that time [1977], which was kind of a funny band. We blew out a lot of comedy stuff like "Punky's Whips." That was the band that originated "Broken Hearts Are for Assholes" [*Sheik Yerbouti*], and that kind of material. And Adrian just fit in with that, and so that's why he got the job. And Warren Cuccurullo was and still is a talented guitar player who had a desire to play standard repertoire — songs he already knew from all the other albums. And he knew a lot of tunes; probably as many, if not more, than some of the other guys who were in the band at the time. And on the tour he did with us, we were doing a lot of the complicated songs off the records that people thought they would never hear on a stage. We were doing "Brown Shoes Don't Make It" [*Tinsel Town Rebellion*], "Inca Roads," and "Andy" [the latter two from *One Size Fits All*]. We were doing a lot of hard repertoire. And he was good for that. Ray has been in the band twice. The first time, he felt a little bit out of place because he is an extremely religious person, and our band is not. And I think that there was some religious/emotional conflict the first time that he was in the band. He was always great: He had a good attitude about working and he did a good job. But I sensed that there was a certain amount of discomfort about him being in there versus the type of material we were playing. So I let him go. And later on I said, well, why not try him again, because I had a band that I thought his personality would fit in with. So I called him up, he came down and tried out, and it clicked right away.

He's got a really good blues style.

He's wonderful; he just loves that kind of music.

What attracted you to Steve Vai?

Steve Vai got the job because he sent a cassette and a transcription of "The Black Page" [*Zappa in New York*], and from hearing that, I could tell that he had a superior musical intelligence and very great guitar chops. And this showed me that there was a possibility to write things that were even harder for that instrument than what had already been used in the band. That's why he got the job.

What do you look for in a guitar?

If you pick up a guitar and it says, "Take me, I'm yours," then that's the one for you. You don't go into a guitar store and say, "Hey, what a great paint job." You have to put it in your hand, because a real guitar that's going to be something you make music on — as opposed to a piece of machinery that makes you look good onstage — is going to have some relationship to your hand and body. It feels right when you pick it up. And that's the way I felt when I got the first SG that I had. It felt right in my hand, so I got it. Same thing with the Gibson Les Paul.

Will you overlook such things as lousy pickups?

Well, you can always change the pickups.

Do you collect guitars?

I don't go out and buy guitars all over the place. I'm not one of those kinds of guys. I do have a lot of guitars, but I don't know how I accumulated them. I've got about 25 guitars. They just keep piling up.

Do you have favorites?

I've got the Les Paul that I use. It was a brand new guitar when I bought it. It's not a vintage thing. It was a very well made production-line Gibson Les Paul right off the rack.

You didn't go to the Gibson factory and have them custom-build one to your specifications?

You know, considering how long I've been playing Gibson guitars, I've never spoken to or heard from anyone connected with that company. There's no factory connection with Gibson whatsoever. I also have a Stratocaster with a Floyd Rose [Tremolo System] installed on it. It was the guitar that I used the most on the last European tour. And the Hendrix Strat [a burned Stratocaster formerly owned by Jimi Hendrix], which has a special size neck on it. It's an SG-size neck. It does certain things that other guitars won't do. The width and depth of the neck is different from that of a Strat, so you can do all kinds of things that just don't feel right on another guitar.

What distinguishes one instrument from another?

Each guitar has its own character and its own sounds that it likes to make, that come naturally to that instrument. So, I'm going to choose an instrument that matches the character of the song. I also have a Telecaster, one of the copies of the originals that Fender put out about a year ago. It's a real good blues guitar. The fifth guitar would be the SG copy that I got from this guy in Phoenix, Arizona. It says "Gibson" on it, but it's handmade, and it's got an ebony fretboard with 23 frets on it; it goes one fret higher than a normal SG. I play that a lot.

Do you use the 23rd fret often?

Since the cutaways on that guitar are so deep, it's very easy to get up all the way to the top. So, I can play higher on that one than on any of the other ones that I have.

How do you synchronize parts from different performances for final mixing into one song?

First of all, you start off with a band that is highly rehearsed, that maintains their tempo. They learn it at a certain tempo, then they'll play it the same way night after night. Do you know how many edits there are in "Drowning Witch"? Fifteen! That song is a basic track from fifteen different cities. And some of the edits are like two bars long. And they're written parts — all that fast stuff. It was very difficult for all the guys to play that correctly. Every once in a while, somebody would hit the jackpot, but it's a very hard song to play. So there was no one perfect performance from any city. What I did was go through a whole tour's worth of tape and listen to every version of it and grab every section that was reasonably correct, put together a basic track, and then added the rest of the orchestration to it in the studio.

Besides synching-up the rhythm, how did you deal with variations in pitch?

Do you hear any? There were no VSO [variable-speed oscillator, which controls the speed of the tape recorder] changes of the sections at all, because when we go out on the road, everything is tuned to a tune-up box every day. We have a standard: Everybody tunes to the vibes, because their tuning doesn't drift. We calibrate all our Peterson Strobe Tuners to them. That gives you consistency.

Last year you were doing the Allman Brothers' "Whipping Post" [At Fillmore East]. Why?

It started about ten or twelve years ago when some guy in the audience at a concert in Helsinki, Finland, requested it.

In English?

Yes. He just yelled out "Whipping Post" in broken English. I have it on tape. And I said, "Excuse me?" I could just barely make it out. We didn't know it, and I felt kind of bad that we couldn't just play it and blow the guy's socks off. So when [pianist/vocalist/ saxophonist] Bobby Martin joined the band, and I found out that he knew how to sing that song, I said, "We are definitely going to be prepared for the next time somebody wants 'Whipping Post' — in fact we're going to play it before somebody even asks for it." I've got probably 30 different versions of it on tape from concerts all around the world, and one of them is going to be *the* "Whipping Post" — the *apex* "Whipping Post" of the century.

Maybe they mistook you for Duane Allman.

Oh sure they did. People do all the time.

When it comes to guitars, we wrote the book

Jaco • **The Extraordinary and Tragic Life of Jaco Pastorius, "The World's Greatest Bass Player"**
By Bill Milkowski

This is a fitting tribute to the talented but tormented genius who revolutionized the electric bass and single-handedly fused jazz, classical, R&B, rock, reggae, pop, and punk—all before the age of 35, when he met his tragic death.
Hardcover, 264pp, 6 x 9, ISBN 0-87930-361-1, $22.95

Blues Guitar
The Men Who Made the Music
Second Edition • Edited by Jas Obrecht

Readers get a look inside the lives and music of thirty great bluesmen, through interviews, articles, discographies, and rare photographs. Covers Buddy Guy, Robert Johnson, John Lee Hooker, Albert King, B.B. King, Muddy Waters, and more.
Softcover, 280pp, 8-1/2 x 11, ISBN 0-87930-292-5, $19.95

Bass Heroes
Styles, Stories & Secrets of 30 Great Bass Players
Edited by Tom Mulhern

Thirty of the world's greatest bass players in rock, jazz, studio/pop, and blues & funk share their musical influences, playing techniques, and opinions. Includes Jack Bruce, Stanley Clarke, James Jamerson, Paul McCartney, and more.
Softcover, 208pp, 8-1/2 x 11, ISBN 0-87930-274-7, $17.95

Picks! **The Colorful Saga of Vintage Celluloid**
Guitar Plectrums • By Will Hoover
An eye-catching look back at the vast variety and fascinating history of vintage celluloid guitar picks. "Will Hoover has taken what you might imagine to be a mundane subject and made it fascinating." —*Billboard*
Softcover, 107pp, 6-1/2 x 6-1/2, ISBN 0-87930-377-8, $12.95

Guitar Player Repair Guide
How to Set Up, Maintain, and Repair Electrics and Acoustics • By Dan Erlewine—Second Edition

Whether you're a player, collector, or repairperson, this hands-on guide provides all the essential information on caring for guitars and electric basses. Includes hundreds of photos and drawings detailing techniques for guitar care and repair.
Softcover, 309pp, 8-1/2 x 11, ISBN 0-87930-291-7, $22.95

Do-It-Yourself Projects for Guitarists
35 Useful, Inexpensive Electronic Projects to Help Unlock Your Instrument's Potential

By Craig Anderton
A step-by-step guide for electric guitarists who want to create maximum personalized sound with minimum electronic problems, and get the satisfaction of achieving all this themselves.
Softcover, 176pp, 7-3/8 x 10-7/8, ISBN 0-87930-359-X, $19.95

The Musician's Guide to Reading & Writing Music • By Dave Stewart
For the brand new rocker, the seasoned player or the pro who could use new problem-solving methods, this is a clear and practical guide to learning written music notation.
"Essential reading for hitherto lazy rock musicians!" —*Keyboard*
Softcover, 112pp, 6 x 9, ISBN 0-87930-273-9, $9.95

The Musician's Home Recording Handbook
Practical Techniques for Recording Great Music at Home • By Ted Greenwald

This easy-to-follow, practical guide to setting up a home recording studio will help any musician who wants to get the best results from the equipment already at hand.
Softcover, 176pp, 8-1/2 x 11, ISBN 0-87930-237-2, $19.95

Electric Guitars and Basses
A Photographic History
By George Gruhn and Walter Carter

This striking, full-color companion volume to Gruhn and Carter's acclaimed book on acoustics traces the technical and aesthetic development of American electric guitars and their manufacturers from 1935 to the present.
Hardcover, 256pp, 8-3/4 x 11-1/2, ISBN 0-87930-328-X, $39.95

Acoustic Guitars
And Other Fretted Instruments
By George Gruhn and Walter Carter

This lavishly illustrated book tells the complete story of American acoustic guitars, mandolins, and banjos—from the 1830s to the present. Hundreds of dazzling color photos showcase luthiers' exquisite and stunning craftsmanship.
Hardcover, 320pp, 8-3/4 x 11-1/2, ISBN 0-87930-240-2, $49.95

The Story of the Fender Stratocaster
"Curves, Contours and Body Horns" — A Celebration of the World's Greatest Guitar • By Ray Minhinnett and Bob Young
This loving profile of the American electric guitar that gave us rock 'n' roll and changed pop culture forever features exclusive interviews and color photos of the legendary Strat, its creators, and famous players.
Hardcover, 128pp, 9-1/6 x 11, ISBN 0-87930-349-2, $24.95

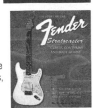

Gibson's Fabulous Flat-Top Guitars
By Eldon Whitford, David Vinopal, and Dan Erlewine
250 photos and detailed text illustrate the development of Gibson's flat-tops, showing why these guitars have been the choice of so many great musicians over the decades. Includes detailed specs on historic and modern Gibson flat-tops.
Softcover, 207pp, 8-1/2 x 11, ISBN 0-87930-297-6, $22.95

The Gibson Super 400
Art of the Fine Guitar • By Thomas A. Van Hoose

This book captures the beauty, design genius, and superior craftsmanship of the famous Gibson Super 400. In-depth text and 200-plus color and black-and-white photos depict this landmark guitar's evolution.
Softcover, 240pp, 8-1/2 x 11, ISBN 0-87930-344-1, $24.95

Gruhn's Guide to Vintage Guitars
An Identification Guide for American Fretted Instruments
By George Gruhn and Walter Carter

This portable reference for identifying American guitars, mandolins, and basses provides comprehensive dating information and model specifications for nearly 2,000 instruments made by all major U.S. manufacturers. For collectors, dealers, players, and fans.
Hardcover, 384pp, 4 x 7-1/2, ISBN 0-87930-195-3, $22.95

The Art of Inlay
Contemporary Design & Technique

By Larry Robinson

This is a dazzling, full-color celebration of both the magical art of inlay and a hands-on guide to its endless creative potential. Includes 70 photos of exquisitely inlaid guitars, banjos, mandolins and various objets d'art, plus how-to instructions.
Hardcover, 112pp, 7-1/2 x 9-1/2, ISBN 0-87930-332-8, $24.95

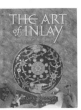

Fender: The Inside Story
By Forrest White

As Leo Fender always wanted, here's the story of the Fender Electric Instrument Co. "just the way it happened." His friend and only general manager traces the company's history, from Leo's start as a radio repairman through the sale to CBS, and beyond.
Softcover, 272pp, 7-3/8 x 9-1/4, ISBN 0-87930-309-3, $22.95

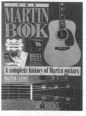